MODERN DRAMA

ALTERNATE EDITION

MODERN DRAMA

ALTERNATE EDITION

Edited by

OTTO REINERT

University of Washington, Seattle

Little, Brown and Company

BOSTON TORONTO

SECOND PRINTING

*Published simultaneously in Canada
by Little, Brown and Company (Canada) Limited*

PRINTED IN THE UNITED STATES OF AMERICA

PREFACE

EIGHT OF THE ELEVEN plays in this alternate edition of *Modern Drama* are new selections. It is difficult to represent adequately in any single anthology a vast and various body of plays; I have tried to include the main types of plays without sacrificing literary distinction to mere representativeness.

The general introduction offers a theory of drama as literature and briefly surveys some of the chief movements in drama since about 1880. In the comments on the individual plays, I have tried to be specific and inclusive but also tried *not* to be exhaustive or dogmatic. It is surely one of the marks of significant plays of any age, and perhaps particularly modern plays, that they admit more than one critical approach. The appendix includes brief biographies and bibliographies. I have made them as up-to-date as I could.

O. R.

Seattle, July, 1965

CONTENTS

INTRODUCTION

A Definition of Drama

Drama, like poetry and fiction, is an art of words. In drama, the words are mainly dialogue: people talking is the basic dramatic action. The talk may be interrupted by wordless activity — sword-play, love-making, silence — but such activity will derive its significance from its context of dialogue. If not, we are dealing with pantomime and not with drama.

In general theory, however, the line between drama and the related arts is not so easy to draw. Film is even less literary than theater, and yet film scripts have been published to be read (*e.g.*, some of Ingmar Bergman's). At what point of verbal artistry do they cease being scenario and production notes and become drama? Conversely, to what extent is the concept of drama covered by Pirandello's "three boards and a passion" as a formula for theater?

Such questions are posed by the double aspect of dramatic language. As written words, drama is literature; as spoken words in a spectacle, it is theater. A novel or a poem is read (or listened to in recital). A play can be either read or performed, but performance affects its status as literature. Dialogue can be performed directly, intact, but stage directions, however skillfully written, do not survive the transfer from script to stage. Their referents in performance — speech manner, movement, costume, set, etc. — are creations of the theater rather than of literature. The significance of the look in Hedda Gabler's eyes, described by Ibsen as "expressive of cold, clear calm," must on stage be conveyed by means of acting and make-up. This is only to say that a performance of drama is much more than just an art of words. It is the joint product of many arts, of which direction, acting, and stage design are the chief.

The fact that successful playwrights make more money in the box office than in the bookstores is evidence that for most people the theatrical medium of drama takes precedence over the literary one and that they find *reading* a play a pallid substitute for *seeing* it. As stage spectacle a play is intensely *there* — a three-dimensional and audible progress of coherent, absorbing, physical action. While words are consecutive and reading is an act in the time dimension, seeing a play is an experience of both time and space. At any one moment the spectator may be simultaneously aware of weather or time of day or of rich or shabby furniture, or of one character speaking, another listening, and a third crawling noiselessly toward the speaker with a knife between his teeth. The spatial concreteness and immediacy of staged drama enlist the attention of a larger set of the spectator's sensory responses, and do so more intensely, than the purely imaginative evocations of a printed play ever can.

Still, the popular assumption that the theatrical medium of drama is primary may be challenged. Performance is no more the play than the concert is the symphony. Most plays — like symphonies — have been written to be performed, but the artistic construct exists complete in the written words, just as the melody, harmony, rhythm, tempo, and orchestration of the symphony "are" in the printed score. The only difference between a printed play and a printed musical composition in this respect is that for most of us it is easier to "see" and "hear" a play in the imagination than it is to "hear" the music in the read score. A play is a potential but never-to-be-realized performance, an "ideal" performance in the philosophical sense, inherent in the configuration of the playwright's words and independent of the artists of the theater whom it keeps challenging to produce performed drama. Items may be cut or added in the performance of a play, just as an enterprising editor may alter a text or a conductor a score, but this does not prove that the original work was not an autonomous artistic entity.

Drama is distinguished from the other forms of literature not just by performability but also by the objectivity and externality that performability implies. The statement "She is a woman without hope" is, as stage direction, undramatic. It could become a speech by one of the characters, or it could inspire an actress to perform an electrifying gesture of fluttering futility, but as *stage direction* it is novelistic. Not only does it not denote anything actable, it also violates the objectivity that is the condition for the playwright's craft: the tacit agreement between him and us that for the duration of the make-believe he does not exist at all, that the characters can be known only by what they reveal of themselves in speech and action. The play shows and tells itself; the characters speak for themselves. The theatricalist devices which certain plays (both old and new) deliberately use to distance the speaker from what happens on stage, reminding him that what he experiences is "only" theater, are themselves part of the dramatic spectacle. The god Ra's Prologue in Shaw's *Cæsar and Cleopatra*, the rehearsal frame of

Pirandello's *Six Characters in Search of an Author*, and the narrative frame of Brecht's *Caucasian Chalk Circle* sophisticate the stage-audience relationship, but Shaw's god, Pirandello's Stage Manager, and Brecht's Singer are just as much "characters" within the playwright's imaginative artifact of drama as are Hjalmar Ekdal, Strindberg's Captain, and Albee's Jerry and Peter within their formally simpler worlds. Even the play that by design expresses the playwright's inmost self or features a "playwright" (acted, it may be, by the playwright himself) as mouthpiece or commentator, who speaks directly to the audience on the significance of the "inner" play he shows us — can reach us only as objective stage reality, a dynamic spectacle of speakers of parts. Either the framing figure is simply a prologue-epilogue, in which case he is no organic part of the play, or he *is* part of the play, in which case he has exactly the same formal status as Shaw's Egyptian god, Pirandello's Manager, and Brecht's Caucasian Singer. As a framing device he may make it necessary for us to distinguish between the play's "outer" and its "inner" action, but not to distinguish between drama and non-drama. The objectivity of drama is not only inviolate but inviolable. Whatever he may be in his private life, the dramatist is *ex officio* Keats's man of "negative capability," "capable of being in uncertainties, mysteries, doubts, without any irritable reaching after fact and reason." His vision is multiple. He "has as much delight in conceiving an Iago as an Imogen. What shocks the virtuous philosopher delights the chameleon poet." Drama is suspended tension, a dialectic in moving equilibrium.

Plays and movies based on novels prove that there is much that is performable in the other genres of literature as well. The art of poet and novelist, however, extends beyond dialogue and description of stageables. The lyric poet explores his own inner world of feeling and sensation, a world different in kind from the externalized world of drama. But even narrative, whether in prose or verse, is, despite an area of possible overlap, different from drama. A novelist or an epic poet can suspend action indefinitely, do without dialogue and physical setting and event altogether ("epics of the mind"), and discourse abstractly on any number of subjects in slow or quick sequence. He can judge and analyze his characters in authorial comment, by godlike ubiquity and omniscience enter at will into their hearts and souls, and just as easily exit back into straight narrative of external events. And if he never makes use of any of these novelistic freedoms, he is, in effect, a playwright, whether he calls his work a play or not.

Actually, this is a stricter definition of drama than many plays allow. Bernard Shaw, for example, often violates dramatic objectivity in stage directions that interpret his characters for us. The most flagrant example is perhaps the ending of *Candida*. When the heroine has sent her would-be lover, a young poet, "into the night" and turns to her husband, Shaw tells us, "They embrace. But they do not know the secret in the poet's heart." The former of these two sentences is stageable, a genuine stage direction. But no theatrical ingenuity can stage the latter — except as words flashed on a screen, like the subtitles of old silent movies. The point is not that Shaw's plays occasionally include bits of novels; we are concerned here with isolating a quality that all plays have in common, the quality that makes them, distinctly, *drama*. Performability is that quality. The spectator is in the theater to watch and listen. Shaw's comments do not exist for him, except insofar as they may have been translated into the language of the theater: sights and sounds the audience can perceive through the senses. A reader of *Candida* will, of course, make Shaw's last sentence part of his experience of the play, and an important part, too. But that does not make it a sentence of drama. The distinction is, if one likes, "academic," "purely theoretical." It certainly does not turn *Candida* into something other than a play. But to abandon it is to abandon an effort to make a general distinction between drama and other forms of literature. We *want* to be "theoretical" at this point; we are trying to suggest the outlines of a theory of drama.

This is not to exclude from the genre of drama works that cannot, for technical reasons, be staged (or staged in their entirety) in any existing theater or which, if staged, would overtax the patience and subtlety of an audience. Not only are such pragmatic criteria obviously relative; there is also a sense in which dramatic poems like *Samson Agonistes*, *Prometheus Unbound*, and *Peer Gynt*, though not intended for the stage and in some respects unperformable (if only by being bad box office), are completely dramatic. That is, their form is a system of speaking parts developing a coherent action. Whatever abstracts their total meaning includes are expressed in speech, and speech is performable by impersonators of the fictitious speakers.

The mode of drama is the objectivity of the performable. Movement, directness, concreteness are its characteristics. The dramatic experience, whether in the theater or over a printed page, is one of urgent immediacy, of watching and listening to human destinies in the making, here and now, which the novelist or the poet can evoke only by being, precisely, dramatic.

Drama and the Reader

From such a definition of drama it follows that in a skillful and successful reading of a play the mind is being filled with a sequence of vivid and relevant images, called up by speeches and stage directions. The reader translates everything performable into concretes that participate in the total, complex image of words, physical movement, and scene that makes up the drama being enacted in the infinitely resourceful and adaptable stage of his mind. Whatever is not performable, or whatever he cannot conceive of as being performable, he will also incorporate into his inclusive reading experience, though not, strictly speaking, as *drama*.

Basic to any kind of meaningful response to literature is understanding of the author's words in context and of the underlying conditions for action in the imagined world. "Understanding" depends on more than conscientious use of footnotes and dictionary; it entails a total response: intellectual, emotional, sensory. And though all readers cannot respond equally well, they can all make the effort to engage more than the top of their minds and the shallows of their souls. Generally, in the case of plays from ages and cultures different from our own, *some* awareness of cultural background will be imperative, and *more* desirable, but the line between some and more is hard to draw in given cases. For some readers, at least, certain plays will create their own climate of understanding.

Perhaps the ideal performance of the play, the standard by which both a theatrical production and a reading of it should be judged, will be thought of as the performance the playwright himself envisioned for his play. But this is neither a practicable nor even a really reasonable formula. There are playwrights who have left no record as to how they thought their plays should be produced, or whose ideas are too vague or incomplete to be of much help, or who refuse to answer when asked. And even if we assume that the original staging realized the playwright's ideal, for most older plays we can reconstruct it only by means of more or less inferential evidence, either within the play itself or supplied by research. Nor are the playwright's views, when available, necessarily more valid than someone else's — just as composers are not necessarily the best performers of their own works or even the best critics of the performance of their works by others. Intention is not accomplishment.

There is more force to the argument that a meaningful reading of a play requires knowledge of the kind of theater for which it was written. To read Sophocles or Shakespeare, the argument goes, we must know something about Greek and Elizabethan stagecraft, see productions that try to reproduce the contemporary performance, see models or pictures or diagrams of the playhouses, or at the very least read descriptions of them.

It is certainly true that the more knowledge the reader has of the culture — including the theatrical culture — reflected in what he reads, the more significant and enjoyable his reading will be. And the impossibility of ever knowing everything about a play and the fact that knowledge alone is insufficient for recreating the sense impressions, the beliefs, attitudes, and moods of a bygone audience cannot invalidate the efforts of historians of drama and theater to know as much as possible. Though each culture, each age, each reader, even the same reader at different times, reads a literary work differently, knowledge of what can be factually known about it and its times is a protection against an anarchic subjectivity of interpretation that could eventually destroy its continuum of identity. This is part of the justification of scholarship.

But though knowledge of theatrical conditions, past or present, can discipline and enrich one's experience of a play and make the play more intelligible, and though such knowledge is valuable for its own sake, it is still not a precondition for the dramatic imagination itself. The images that arise in the mind during the reading of drama can be translated into stage actualities, but they are not images of such actualities. The reader does not ordinarily imagine a staged scene but its real life counterpart — not a stage castle, crypt, or kitchen, but the real thing — Hjalmar Ekdal, not actor A or actor B impersonating Hjalmar Ekdal. The exceptions are the director, designer, or actor who read with a projected performance in mind and — and he is the one who concerns us — the reader who comes to his reading of the play fresh from an impressive performance of it. His reading experience will no doubt be more vivid than it otherwise would have been, but it will also be more limited. His imagination will be channeled by his memory of the hundreds of big and little details of voice and mimicry, movement and set, costume and light, that together make up any particular actualization of the ideal abstract the play is. Any one performance, however brilliant, is bound to be different from — both more and less than — the literary work that occasioned it, forever detached as the latter is from the impermanent particulars of the real. A good production may help a reader imagine what he found unimaginable as he read the play, or it may cool and contain an imagination that catches fire too easily, but a reader to whom a play is nothing but a blueprint for an evening in the theater has abdicated his rights as reader. It is only because most people *can* stage a play in their imagination, alive with the sights and sounds of reality, that drama is literature at all — that is, capable of being experienced through reading. The theater is the home of drama, and drama may be the occasion for theater, but all theater is not drama, nor is the drama lost without the theater.

Dramatic Conventions

Understanding the underlying condition for action in the imagined world involves understanding dramatic conventions. These are the conditions which playwright and audience between them have implicitly (whether they are conscious of it or not) agreed to accept as reality in the play. In the sense that what is called for is a willingness to take the world of imagination as reality for the time being, acceptance of conventions enters into any kind of successful experience of figurative (representational, non-abstract) art. But because the theater makes tangible the forms of the make-believe, conventions operate with particular force in the experience of drama — most insistently in the theater, but also in reading. There is a widespread, though tacit and largely uninspected, assumption that drama is the most referential of the literary genres (*i.e.*, that it corresponds most closely to some real world of sensory phenomena) and the least purely expressive (*i.e.*, lyrical). For this the sensory immediacy of the performable must be responsible. And when an audience hesitates to accept a play that flouts all pretense to mirror an objective world of things and facts, or which makes use of unfamiliar conventions, some form of the referential fallacy in the public concept of drama is likely to be involved. Among the playwrights represented in this collection, Ibsen, Strindberg, and Chekhov purport to record reality, while Pirandello, Brecht, and Williams exploit a convention by which a phase in the flux of phenomenal experience is transfixed and "seen" as pattern-with-meaning.

Chorus, soliloquy, and aside are examples of conventions, mainly of older drama. They were no more everyday realities then than they are now, but as artistic devices they were given status as reality because they satisfied needs for dramatic expression without going beyond what the contemporary public was willing to tolerate as make-believe. Some conventions may have been means to achieve certain kinds of communication under the technically limiting conditions of older theater. For example, such "facts" of the imagined world as location and time of day, which in the modern theater can be established by sets and electric lights, were on the Elizabethan stage communicated by the dialogue itself. Hence the rather remarkable number of Shakespearean characters who mention time and place in their speeches, particularly in the opening of scenes. To the extent that such information is for the benefit of the audience rather than for the listeners on stage, the device is conventional: a breach of reality for the sake of establishing, economically and often beautifully, "reality" within the play.

Conventions vary with time and place. Yesterday's conventions are today's absurdities and tomorrow's brilliant innovations. No play is without them. In the ceremonial tradition of drama (Greek, Elizabethan, neoclassical tragedy), ritualistic use of language in verse and imagery and of archetypal action of aristocratic agony raises life to a plane of greater dignity, significance, intensity, and eloquence than that of ordinary life lived on naturalistic terms (classical comedy). In the illusionistic tradition (some forms of older comedy, modern dramatic realism like Ibsen's and Chekhov's), convention ignores the theatrical situation and assumes the commonplace surface of stage life to be that of actuality. In the expressionistic tradition (allegorical and symbolic drama, some of Strindberg's and most of Pirandello's plays, aspects of the modern "theater of the absurd"), scenic abstractionism and stylization, dream sequences of realistic or distorted fragments of reality, montage techniques, and freedom of time and place are conventional means to the end of insinuating the reality of the single, subjective consciousness.

Because our popular theater of stage, film, and television is still very largely the heir of the realist tradition of the late nineteenth century, the modern reader or playgoer may at first find older drama and contemporary avant-garde experiments "odd," "unrealistic," "obscure." The distance between his own ordinary language and Elizabethan blank-verse rhetoric or the non-communication of absurdist dialogue may frustrate and alienate him, and he is not likely to be put at ease by the proposition that the spectacle has been put on not for its reality but for its art. Taking the conventions of realism for granted, he may fail to see that they *are* conventions. Or if he is sophisticated enough to recognize them for what they are, he may still feel they are the only "natural" conventions. But if he objects to the artificiality of the neoclassical convention of the three unities (which demanded that the action of the play be confined to a single plot, a single place, and a single day), he ought also to object to the convention of today's film and television that presents human beings as disembodied heads in facial close-ups and to the three-walled rooms of most post-Renaissance theater. And there is no reason to believe that playgoers of the past would have found a modern theater, with its artificially lighted box peeked into by a supposedly nonexistent audience, any less unnatural than we presume to find the choric rituals and public unburdenings of soul in soliloquy in their plays. If the naïve or stubbornly literal-minded is bothered by the hero's apparent deafness to the villain's stage whisper, by the scarcity of actors on stage during Shakespeare's battle scenes, or by the free and flexible treatment of time and place in a contemporary play like *The Caucasian Chalk Circle*, he simply fails to understand or accept dramatic convention.

Action, Plot, Conflict

Like most serious writing, drama represents man's use of words to make sense out of the myriad perplexities that befall him. The dramatist sees the world not primarily as shapes and colors and feelings, or as an object for religious or philosophical or scientific contemplation, or as a market, or as a reluctant machine that challenges his skill and ingenuity to make it run better. He sees it rather as an arena for human action manifested in speech. The arena may be expansive and crowded, as in such panoramic plays as *Antony and Cleopatra, Cæsar and Cleopatra,* and *The Caucasian Chalk Circle,* or it may be small, close, and sparsely populated, as in such focussed plays as *The Father* and *The Zoo Story.* The speech may be the heightened utterance of verse or everyday, colloquial prose. Or a single play may employ both media. In *The Hour-Glass,* speech itself becomes a dramatic image as the shifts from one to the other extend the antithesis between the materialist's Reason ("prose") and the visionary's Soul ("poetry") beyond characterization, action, and overt meaning.

The newcomer to the reading of drama may at first find confusing the conversations of unknowns, surprised in the embroilments with a life of which he knows nothing. He may miss preliminary explanations, the novelist's guiding hand. And if he has had experience with performed drama, he may also miss the aid to understanding provided by the presences and the voices of actors and by the physical spectacle in which they appear. That he can be guided by stage directions and ponder the dialogue at his leisure he may feel to be poor compensation for the absence of the sights and sounds of performance.

What the characters say and do begins to make sense only as we learn more about them, but we learn more about them only by what they say and do. Gradually they become more than a list of names. They reveal their antecedents and their present situations, their motives and purposes, they assume plot identity and "character." We learn to respond to the revealing remark or gesture, to listen to the eloquence of their silence, to sense their continuous pressure on the plot. Among them, they define and develop the dramatic action.

Dramatic action is neither physical activity nor simply the sum of everything that happens on stage: conversation, eating, people running up and down staircases, laughter, doors closing, lights going on. These are part of the action, but in the traditional (mainly Aristotelian) definition action itself is a more comprehensive concept. A set of definitions may be useful at this point.

A play is a patterning of language, character, event, and spectacle, each element a function of the other three. Its plot is the particular sequence of events that gives it the coherence and movement toward a given end that could not inhere in a random aggregate of happenings. Plot is the way the playwright has chosen to tell his story, the detailed arrangement of incidents for maximum meaning or beauty or suspense. The action of the play is both the summation of the plot and the abstraction of its meaning, the distillation of the play's totality, the answer, in a single phrase, to the question, "What happens?" For example, the violent despair of Jerry's zoo world dispossessing Peter's peaceful complacency defines the action of *The Zoo Story*. We call tragic the action that ends by exacting suffering or death from the protagonist as the price at which we (and perhaps he) are brought to new or heightened awareness of man's being and his relation to the ultimate moral or metaphysical issues in life. We call comic the action that concerns man in his mundane or social relationships, exposes vice and folly for contempt and laughter, and ends by vindicating reason, moderation, good will, love, virtue, or other sane and normal human values. Tragedy's domain is the infinite, its characteristic subject matter the mystery of evil and suffering. Comedy's domain is the finite, its characteristic subject matter man's triumphs and tribulations as gregarious animal.*

The nature and function of plot differ in different plays. It may be a strong, causal story line which we find suspenseful and convincing because of constant interaction between character and event. Gregers Werle's idealistic mission in *The Wild Duck*, so totally misapplied to Hjalmar's character and situation, is expiation for the guilt and compensation for the self-contempt that growing up in a disharmonious home has bred into him, but the evolving logic of his mission once he has launched it keeps revealing the characters of the reformer and his victim alike, until both seem defined by their entanglement in the events. Successful plot manipulation makes a character's behavior seem surprising and inevitable at the same time. Keeping a duck in the attic seems like a most unlikely detail in what purports to be a snapshot of daily life in a lower middle-class family. But as a wounded escapee that catalyzes speech and action, the duck's presence, as unseen "character,"

---

* "Tragedy" and "comedy" (and, on a cruder level, "melodrama" and "farce") are not inflexible absolutes and should not be taken to imply that every labeled play is all of one piece. There are elements of both melodrama and farce in serious moral fables like *Cæsar and Cleopatra* and *The Caucasian Chalk Circle*. Physical farce is a form of high comedy in *Playboy*, of a tragic, riotous nightmare in *Chronicles of Hell*. There are clowns in classical and Shakespearean tragedy. Hjalmar in *The Wild Duck* is a ridiculous phrasemaker in a context of serious realism. The contemporary social satire in *The Zoo Story* is partly expressed through an atavistic combat. And so on.

as plot ingredient, and as focusing symbol, among these particular people, ceases to seem extraordinary.

In other plays plot is less a matter of dramatized narrative than of conveying a vivid sense of human presence. Molière in *The Misanthrope* and Chekhov in *The Cherry Orchard* do not base their dramas on the convenient convention that life runs in plots. They seek rather to illuminate a certain kind of human response to experience by means of juxtaposed scenes that subtly modify one another by discordant or mutually ironic styles, tones, and content. Molière takes Alceste through his paces, by turns admirable, ridiculous, and ominous, in an exposure of misanthropy in its several facets. Here plot is the display of a master passion in the round. *The Cherry Orchard* poses moments of emotional stasis against a background of moving time. The apparently arbitrary intermittence of the static moments and our simultaneous awareness of the resistless flow of time — and the contrast between them — constitute Chekhov's plot, in the sense that they give shape and point to the string of individual happenings. In *Chronicles of Hell*, the spite, the terror, and the obscenity of much of the incessant and largely pointless physical action do not so much amount to plot in any ordinary sense as they serve as metaphors for the demonic values that determine action in Lapideopolis, "the city of the stone god." As a sequence of non-causal, but not quite incoherent, events, plot here is determined not by story as much as by the moral and mental climate of a place that is, the title tells us, Hell.

In traditional anatomies of drama plot is usually divided into four parts: (1) The *exposition*, which gives essential information about the pre-play background of the characters and sets the plot in motion. (2) The *complication*, usually the bulk of the play, interweaving the characters' shifting fortunes and including the climax, a point of tension and the critical juncture at which a decision or an event irretrievably determines the outcome. (3) The *reversal*, or peripety, the point at which the complication culminates in the resolution of the plot: the protagonist's fortune changing from good to bad (tragedy) or from bad to good (comedy). (4) The *denouement*, or unraveling, which presents the consequences of the reversal, ties up loose ends, and allows the audience time to regain emotional equilibrium. Exposition and complication are likely to be the longest phases of the dramatic progress, the denouement is normally shorter, and the reversal may be marked by a single speech or event that occurs, most often, quite late in the play.

The plays in which the four parts of the plot are neatly distinct and laid end to end are few and not likely to be of the highest order. Good plots are complex, organic structures, whose parts blend into one another, overlapping and alternating. In *The Father*, the story of the pre-play relationship between the Captain and Laura is not confined to the early scenes. There is, for example, the Captain's dying memory of how he and his young wife "used to walk in the birch woods. There were primroses and thrushes — lovely, lovely!" In *The Caucasian Chalk Circle* the rebellion scenes in the beginning of the play are expository relative to the story of Grusha and the child, but so are the flashback scenes of Azdak's judgeship, which follow the completion of the story of Grusha's journey. *The Wild Duck* and *Six Characters*, fragments of explanation of past events responsible for the present crisis keep appearing almost throughout. As a result, both plays seem retrospective in structure. On stage we see, not the past itself, but only the consequences of the presumably buried past rushing in to overwhelm the present. They are "fifth-act plays," dramas of ripe condition, and to separate exposition from complication in such plays is not only difficult but senseless: exposition *is* complication. In fact, the traditional paradigm of formal plot analysis often seems to apply only partly, or insignificantly, or not at all, to individual plays in the heterogeneity of modern drama, the story of which, to a very large extent (at least, from the viewpoint of a contemporary), is the story of revolt and experimentation superseding a sense of formal tradition. Where does the complication begin and end in *The Cherry Orchard?* What is the climax in *Six Characters* — the Father's visit to Madame Pace's? The Manager's decision to let the characters enact their destinies? We do not conclude that the traditional terms are useless but that to apply them mechanically is likely to end in critical disaster, particularly in analysis of modern plays. We may illustrate their use in an analysis of a play with a traditional plot structure.

The *story* of *The Wild Duck* is the entire chronicle of the interlocking fortunes of the Ekdal and Werle families, beginning with Hjalmar's and Gregers' boyhood and youth (only glimpsed and hinted at in the play), Werle's philandering, his wife's jealousy and drinking, and the shady forest deal that eventually ruined Old Ekdal. The *plot* is the causally connected sequence of events that gradually reveals the significance of the past. The *action* is the enlightenment of Hjalmar, for that enlightenment is what motivates Greger's moves, and the action is over when the enlightenment is complete — ironically so — the moment Hedvig's suicide proves to Hjalmar her love for him. The *exposition* begins in the very first speech in Act I, and it may be said to continue, intermittently, to the point near the end of Act IV when Hjalmar realizes (or *thinks* he realizes) that Hedvig is not his child. It follows that the exposition and the *complication* overlap — in fact, the complication may be defined as the conflict between Gregers' efforts to further the revelation of the past (*i.e.*, the exposition) and Relling's and Gina's efforts to prevent it. Act I is almost all exposition — the gossip between the two servants, conversations between Gregers and Hjalmar and between Gregers and Werle — but its conclusion, Gregers' announcement that he has a "mission" to fulfill, looks forward to the complication, which begins in Act II with Gregers' arrival at the Ekdals'. Henceforth, the Ekdal household is both troubled and divided, as the exposition-complication continues. The play's *climax* is the moment at the end of Act III when Hjalmar accepts Gregers's invitation to go for a walk and thus dooms himself to learn "the truth." The *reversal* is double. There is first the scene in which Gregers interprets the shot in the attic for Hjalmar and the latter as a result decides once again to give Hedvig his love. Then there is his discovery a few moments later that the proof of her deserving his love is her suicide. Within seconds Hjalmar moves from disillusionment and cynicism through joy to sorrow. The *denouement* is what follows Relling's pronouncement that Hedvig is dead: Molvik's drunken and fragmentary burial service, Hjalmar's and Gina's reactions, and Gregers's and Relling's final comments.

Plot generates and releases suspense — the feeling in the audience that keeps it wondering what happens next. One characteristic of great drama is that suspense survives knowledge of "how things come out," because our absorbed wait for what is going to happen concerns the outcome less than it concerns the happenings themselves and the patterns we see them forming. We may know exactly what happens in *The Wild Duck* and still attend, half moved, half amused, to every step in the developing tragicomedy. In fact, superior plays have a way of seeming better in later readings. What we lose in mere thrill we gain in understanding and enjoyment through our intimacy with the characters and our knowledge of events to come. Familiarity also increases our appreciation and enjoyment of dramaturgy: the exercise of the playwright's craft, the dexterous manipulation of plot and character in the integrated structure of successful dramatic action. As the football fan goes to the game not just to learn who wins and by what score but to enjoy the game being played and the skill of coach and players, so the lover of drama seeks vicarious experience of significant action in artistic form, and not just information about a result. The ideal spectator attends both kinds of play in a mood of disinterested fascination.

Conflict is the element in plot that creates suspense; it is what the plot is about. In *The Wild Duck* the conflict may be variously defined — perhaps most simply as idealism (Gregers) against realism (Relling) with Hjalmar as the bone of contention between them. Or we may sense the conflict chiefly as irony: the distance between what Gregers *thinks* his purpose — to re-establish the Ekdal marriage on a foundation of truth — will accomplish both for the Ekdals (true happiness) and for himself (a degree of atonement of his father's guilt) and what it actually *does* accomplish: bereavement for the Ekdals (ironically involving new lies for Hjalmar to live on) and complete futility for himself. Or the conflict may be felt to inhere in the bitter or cynical wisdom that contrasts the saving lie with the destructive truth.

Conflict may be multiple, a collection of variants of a many-sided subject, each presenting it in a new view, and all covered by a wider definition of the play's conflict. In Shakespeare's *King Lear* the main plot about Lear and his daughters and the subplot of Gloucester and his sons allow Shakespeare a fuller treatment of the theme of filial ingratitude than either plot alone would have allowed him, and the doubleness of the plot suggests the pervasiveness of the evil. In *Cæsar and Cleopatra* there is no subplot in this sense, but the conflicts of Rome against Egypt and of Cæsar against Pothinus are in the end seen to be, respectively, military and political variants of the moral conflict between Cæsar and Cleopatra and of the still more comprehensive conflict between saint and sinner, god and man, promoter and frustrater of the Life Force. In Chekhov, the situations of the several characters who fail in different ways to fulfil themselves, to achieve happiness, to establish human contact, to take decisive action, cohere in a single image of frustration, the clash of hope with reality. Plot unity is obviously not the same kind of thing in all plays. Contrasting the rambling diffuseness of events in *The Cherry Orchard* with the concentrated complexity of the interlocking patterns of parent-child, husband-wife relationships in *The Wild Duck* suggests the range in kinds of conflict.

Conflict is opposition of forces, one of which is likely to be a human will — heroically uncompromising and therefore doomed in tragedy, abortive or reformable in comedy. Man against god, man against nature (a mountain, the sea, hunger), man against society, man against man, and man against himself, represent (in rough terms) the five main kinds of conflict. Conflict may be as simple as it is in a fairy tale (bad queen against good princess, bad guy against good sheriff). It may be morally unequivocal as in *Cæsar and Cleopatra* and *The Caucasian Chalk Circle*, ambiguous as in *The Wild Duck* and *Playboy*, elementally amoral as the sexual battle in *The Father*, religious as in *The Hour-Glass* and *Chronicles of Hell*, philosophical as in *Six Characters*, psychological as in *The Wild Duck*, *The Father*, and *The Glass Menagerie*, historical as in *Cæsar and Cleopatra*, legendary as in *The Hour-Glass* and *The Caucasian Chalk Circle*, social as in *The Caucasian Chalk Circle*, of ultimate importance as in *The Hour-Glass*, banal as in *The Cherry Orchard*, supernatural as in *Six Characters* and *Chronicles of Hell*, plausible as in *The Wild Duck*, preposterous as in

The Zoo Story. Drama without conflict is unthinkable. For the essence of the dramatic experience is the fascination with the progress of clashing forces toward resolution: the hero's death or enlightenment, the villain's defeat; the re-integration of a threatened social order in a wedding, a settlement of a quarrel, an eviction, a verdict; the revelation of the transcendent nature that shapes our lives as order and meaning or as silence and darkness.

The spoken word is the medium of drama, the objectivity of the performable its mode or manner of being, the surrender of our imaginations to that of the playwright the condition for its existence for us, but the drama itself is the action of man in conflict. This action we witness partly as safe and superior deities, enjoying the pleasure of dramatic irony at the expense of people who do not know what is happening to them; partly as sympathetic observers, commiserating with the good, relishing the downfall of the bad; and partly as fellow fools and sufferers: there, but for the grace of God, *we* strut and fret.

Some Notes on the History of Modern Drama

The reasons why certain periods excel in certain forms of literature rather than in others involve too many incalculables of individual talent and experience and of collective temper of the times to be confidently set down. A brief account of modern drama can only record the fact that during most of the eighteenth and nineteenth centuries in the Western world literary imagination of high order tended to express itself in lyrics and novels rather than in actable plays. There were exceptions — the comedies of Holberg and Goldsmith and Sheridan, Goethe's and Schiller's romantic dramas of storm and stress — but the exceptions only set off the surrounding gloom. The period was one of great performers, from Garrick to Bernhardt; of smaller, more numerous theaters and growing audiences; and of the introduction of footlights, box sets, and historical accuracy in costume and setting. It is important in the history of the theater. But original, serious playmaking was largely limited to closet plays in verse (among them Goethe's *Faust*, Byron's *Manfred*, Shelley's *Prometheus Unbound*, perhaps Ibsen's *Brand* and *Peer Gynt*, and a series of turgid imitations of Shakespeare), Gothic melodrama of rant and spectacle, and craftsmanlike but empty intriguery.

Ibsen's European success (or notoriety) with naturalistic[1] plays about 1880 is usually taken to mark the beginning of modern drama.

---

[1]As few writers on modern drama fail to point out, "naturalism" and "realism" are troublesome terms. "Naturalism" commonly connotes philosophical determinism and, as a literary term, a program, based on determinism, of depicting human life, with as much scientific objectivity and accuracy as possible,

Like all such divisions this too involves a degree of arbitrariness, and its importance tends to diminish in our lengthening perspective on modern drama and its historical antecedents. For if naturalism is defined as the faithful representation in action, dialogue, and setting of the social, psychological, and moral conditions of ordinary life, then there were naturalistic plays before 1880: Büchner's *Woyzeck* (1836), Hebbel's *Maria Magdalena* (1844), Turgenev's *A Month in the Country* (1850) — and non-naturalistic plays not very long after: Rostand's *Cyrano de Bergerac* (1897), Yeats' *Cathleen ni Houlihan* (1902), Maeterlinck's *Pelléas and Mélisande* (1903). And if Ibsen can be said to have fathered modern drama by being the first to bring dramatic genius to bear upon realistic material and form at a time when the public was ready at least to go and see naturalism in the theater, if not yet to be very comfortable with it as art or ideology, another way of describing his achievement is to say that he transcribed old themes into terms relevant to the changing social and material conditions of a new age. His housewives and businessmen question absolutes and reject compromise and are restless with yearnings for freedom and self-fulfilment that the very conditions of human life forever frustrate. The vocabulary of the new social science is new, but it denotes the same concepts as the old metaphors of Nemesis, Providence, and Fortune. Ibsen's *Master Builder* is a version of the Faust legend, an essentially Romantic motif, in which the rebel against God appears as a building contractor in a small Norwegian town. There is ageless metaphysical dynamite as well as a symbol for the dilemma of an age of science in the demonstration in *The Wild Duck* of how truth destroys innocence. And Ibsen did not invent naturalism either in theory or in practice. He was not even a consistent practitioner of naturalism. Many of his plots are constructed on the model of Eugene Scribe's well-made carpentry of coincidence and intrigue, and not all his plays, even after the 1880's, can be called naturalistic except in externals. Nevertheless, the triumph of naturalism and the subsequent modifications of it, departures from it, and reactions against it, both literary and theatrical, tell in broad outline the story of drama during the last eighty years or so. And so

---

as conditioned by heredity and environment. "Realism" is usually a more general term, denoting representationalism in any art. As a literary term it is independent of genres and periods. Both terms have occasionally been appropriated for that branch of late nineteenth-century literature that dealt primarily with the sordid and the vicious in lower-class life. I use "naturalism" (lower case *n*) for the Ibsen-Chekhov tradition in modern drama. For my purposes, "naturalism" and "realism" are roughly synonymous terms, but except in a few cases where I think the usage justifies itself I have preferred the more specific term in order not to divorce my key term altogether from the idea of determinism that is implicit both in Zola — "Naturalism" capitalized — and, though less extremely and dogmatically, in Ibsen and Chekhov.

viewed an apparently chaotic development assumes at least a semblance of order.

For the commonplace of histories of modern drama is perfectly true: it is not any one thing. We feel we can make certain valid generalizations about different plays and playwrights within the major eras of earlier drama: if Marlowe, Shakespeare, and Webster (say) do not share all the same assumptions about life — one thinks of *Tamburlaine* and *Hamlet, The Tempest* and *The Duchess of Malfi* — their uses of the theater and of dramatic language all seem to belong to the same inclusive convention. But what formula, either philosophical or artistic, will link Ibsen and Yeats, Chekhov and Pirandello, Shaw and Albee, Williams and Ghelderode? The implication of such questions is not that positive answers cannot be given — that in itself would provide a measure of clarity and certainty — but that they are elusive, tentative, and not obvious. The old distinctions between tragedy and comedy, melodrama and farce, have largely lost their meaning in today's generic confusion. Their lapse seems like a symptom of our sense of flux and ambiguity, of our fear of commitment. A sense of revolt has superseded a sense of tradition, but even "a theater of revolt" is too narrow a generalization for our drama. It has affirmed faith as well as skepticism, used verse as well as prose, presented verisimilitude as well as fantastic fabulation, and developed conventions and stereotypes of its own. It may be that we are still too close to modern drama to see it in proper perspective, but it is difficult to imagine a future generation of literary historians to whom our variety of style and purpose will appear as sameness. Besides the general democratization of subject matter and a shift in emphasis from public to private life, from communal archetypes to archetypes of the individual self, in dramatic imagery of speech and action, just about the only safe generalization one can make about modern drama is an assertion of its heterogeneity. And the variety is evident not only in a chronological view but in cross-sections of modern drama at any time. This is hardly surprising. Wars, depressions, revolutions, social change, technological advance, new concepts in science and philosophy — in this welter of phenomena, drama, traditionally of all the arts the most sensitive to the cultural matrix, has naturally been various. So restless is our time, so doubt-ridden, so rapid and cosmopolitan the spread of our culture — Ionesco and Ibsen are both hits in Tokyo — that it would be strange if our drama did *not* appear protean in its quest for expressive form.

The success of stage realism — that is, approximation, usually within but sometimes deliberately outside artistic form, to photographic and stenographic replicas of actuality — about 1880 was only a belated manifestation of a revolution which had already taken place in poetry and fiction and which was itself the natural result of a series of industrial, political, and scientific revolutions that profoundly altered Western man's material life, institutions, and ideas from about 1750 on. Some one hundred years later the new society was, however imperfectly and disastrously, industrialized, urbanized, democratized, and probably also secularized to a degree beyond that of any earlier known society. When Nietzsche's Zarathustra in 1885 announced the death of God at the hand of man, the general absence of a shocked reaction was a measure of the depth and extent of the revolution in thought that had already taken place. The postulate underlies a considerable number of subsequent plays. It has, in fact, become commonplace enough to be vigorously challenged in turn.

The uneasy peace of the Victorian age was presided over by a prosperous and proper middle class. The representation of this new bourgeois culture on the stage was an obvious task for drama, but it rose to the challenge only decades after the contemporary novel had done so, partly because of official censorship in different forms (the almost-two-hundred-year monopoly of the two patented playhouses in London ended only in 1843, when London was a city of almost two millions), partly because of long-established middle-class attitudes to plays as sinful or at least frivolous, and partly because no playwright succeeded in creating an audience for a new kind of play. It was not that models were lacking or the need not felt. In English drama, for example, the tradition of the middle-class play goes back to the anonymous *Arden of Feversham* and to Thomas Heywood's *A Woman Killed with Kindness*, both Renaissance plays contemporary with a dominant aristocratic blank verse tragedy. The common man was again the hero of a serious play in George Lillo's *London Merchant* (1731), although Lillo's sententious moralizing and his occasional use of blank verse remove the play from consideration as a genuine precursor of nineteenth-century stage naturalism. In 1758 the French encyclopedist Diderot deplored the non-existence of middle-class drama. His sentiment was repeated, in different forms, by Friedrich Hebbel (himself the author of the pre-naturalistic *Maria Magdalena*), Otto Ludwig, and Hermann Hettner in Germany, by the brothers Goncourt in France, and by Georg Brandes in Denmark. By his call, in 1872, for a drama that would "submit problems to debate," Brandes influenced Ibsen, who in the early seventies had come to a crossroads in his dramatic career. Thus Brandes became the godfather of the problem play and, more indirectly, of its propagandistic cousin, the thesis play. In 1873 Émile Zola dramatized his naturalistic novel *Thérèse Raquin* in order to provide a specimen of Naturalistic drama in the narrow, philosophical sense of the term, *i.e.*, meticulous and artless slice-of-life writing on the deterministic premise that only a clinical description of man's conditioning circumstances will yield the objective truth about him. Thus was the ground prepared for a playwright who could shape the ideology of naturalism to the demands of art. Clearly, the new drama was not going to be of men and gods, of aristocratic scapegoats for cosmic ills, of titanic poetic utterance, but of common words and common lives, fit for democratic audiences. Existentially restive, the age could take pride and comfort in the unpretentiousness of a drama that modestly and honestly merely affirmed that things exist.

Ibsen pioneered in naturalism with plays that disclosed the death of the spirit behind the outward decencies of the bourgeois family. Despite their objective surface the liberal implications of *A Doll's House* (1879), *Ghosts* (1881), and *An Enemy of the People* (1882) are so obvious that Ibsen in the popular mind ever since has been identified with liberal iconoclasm. This was the Ibsen that was acted in the new theaters, all bearing names denoting "freedom," that opened in the great European capitals as fora for new ideas and new dramatic forms and battlegrounds for attacks on bigotry, prudery, and reaction: André Antoine's Théâtre Libre in Paris (1887), Otto Brahm's Freie Bühne in Berlin (1889), and J. T. Grein's Independent Theater in London (1891). These are the theaters of ideological Ibsenism, as Shaw explained it in his *Quintessence of Ibsenism* in 1891. There are good historical reasons why much subsequent naturalistic drama was written in the service of liberalism and radicalism, both political and nonpolitical.

But the crusading spirit of the champions of the naturalistic movement has to some extent obscured the nature of the achievement of the playwrights they championed. Irrelevant to the argument of the liberal exegetists were the symbolism and near-mysticism, akin almost to the contemporary neo-romanticism in France, of Ibsen's last phase and the delicate patterns of Chekhov's action. We see more than message and verisimilitude (if we see them at all) in Ibsen's multi-leveled interiors, Strindberg's cataclysmic sexual battles, Shaw's gay butchery of sacred and profane cows, and Chekhov's records of moral and psychological paralysis in the landed gentry in pre-revolutionary Russia. We no longer rank thesis playwrights such as Galsworthy and Brieux with the four classic writers of naturalistic theater. With all their sincere liberalism and all their technical competence the disciples lacked what their masters had: command of action, believable on its own terms, so patterned and so submitted to imaginative pressure as to glow and heat, the art of dialogue that vibrates with more than lifelikeness, psychological wisdom not subservient to thesis. Much of the liberalism in the name of Marx and Freud that went into the making of naturalistic plays in the twenties and thirties is forgotten today, not because it argued corrupt theses but because it failed to raise topical indictment and espousal to the level of universal art. The names likely to endure from among the second generation of naturalists are those of playwrights who did not allow their compassion or indignation or enthusiasm to make their vision of life simple — Gorky (*The Lower Depths*), Hauptmann (*The Weavers*), Schnitzler (*The Lonely Way*). More objective, more impassioned, and more talented than the thesis playwrights, Eugene O'Neill almost staggered under a burden of schematic Freudianism in his two most ambitious naturalistic plays, the neo-tragedies *Mourning Becomes Electra* and *Strange Interlude*. The less intellectualized and less theme-conscious *Desire Under the Elms* came closer to realizing his ambition: to elevate the destiny of the common man in his socio-economic setting to the dignity of classical tragedy. But dogmatism is risky when speaking of modern drama. There is, on the other hand, Bertolt Brecht's epic theater, which, though a more spacious and flexible scenic world than that of strict naturalism, is still not so far removed from it as not to be evidence in support of the argument that thesis — in this case social thesis of Marxist bias — can serve as the basis for excellent drama.

Besides major plays the naturalistic tradition has also engendered one of the main influences on modern acting (and, one assumes, though the case would be hard to prove, on modern playwriting): the Stanislavsky method. Deliberate emphasis on realistic ensemble acting rather than on brilliant elocution and posturing by individual star performers characterized the productions of the Duke of Meiningen's company that toured Europe between 1874 and 1890. But in his rehearsals at the Moscow Art Theater beginning in 1898 Konstantin Stanislavsky broadened and systematized the Meiningen manner. The main points of his method are: repertory system of production and long rehearsal periods in order to turn a company of individual actors into a true ensemble, the cultivation of the actor's "magical if" that enables him to believe in the reality of what he is doing, his use of his private memories and imagination to further that conscious and intense concentration of his whole being by which alone he can hope to achieve complete identification with his part (the actor should "be," not "act"), and his creation of "the fourth-wall illusion" in the audience by acting as if the audience were not there. Despite challenges from stylized acting and Brechtian theories of *Verfremdung* (esthetic distancing), the Stanislavsky method continues to dominate our popular theater — if not our important dramatists. Today the revolution it effected is so much an accomplished fact that we must make an effort to remember that Stanislavskyism has not always been axiomatic.

Non-naturalism in modern drama has (to make the complex simple) assumed four major forms. Needless to say, there are plays that defy such rigorous classification, just as there are some that straddle the whole fissure between naturalism and non-naturalism. Nevertheless, for the rather desperate purpose of a survey the distinctions are useful as long as they are not taken to represent a temporal sequence and as long as the existence of exceptions is kept in mind.

Two of the four forms are literary: neo-romanticism and verse drama. One is both literary and theatrical: expressionism. One is theatrical: the new stagecraft.[2] In various ways and to various degrees the impetus behind them all has been a reaction against what has been felt to be the inhibiting factuality, dogmatic thesis-mongering, and generally arid prosaism of much naturalistic staging and writing.

Of the four, neo-romanticism has been the least important. It culminated around the turn of the century in Rostand's exuberant poetic melodrama *Cyrano de Bergerac*, in the dreamily symbolic medievalism of Maeterlinck (in one of his phases), and in the poeticized Irish legends of the early Yeats. Today it survives mainly outside of serious drama altogether, as sweetmeats for Broadway sophisticates in the form of spectacular musicals of fantasy, pathos, whimsy, and sentimentality — *Peter Pans, Brigadoons, Camelots*. A Ghelderode's medievalism is not a matter of neo-romantic nostalgia but of raucous, ribald metaphors for a being whose immortal longings are lodged in a vessel of corruption.

Verse drama, on the other hand, has enjoyed a kind of intermittent renaissance so far in this century. In Yeats the two movements fuse. It was very largely thanks to his efforts to create a center for Irish poetic drama based on national romanticism that the Abbey Theater came into being — interestingly enough, at just about the same time as its naturalistic counterpart, the Moscow Art Theater. Though Yeats' own verse plays were produced there, the Abbey is better known as the theater of Synge and O'Casey, realists of Irish peasant life (Synge's *Riders to the Sea* and *Playboy of the Western World*) and urban slum life (O'Casey's *Juno and the Paycock* and *The Plough and the Star*), but both gifted with a lusty lyricism that transmutes the sordid and the drab into loveliness and which in Synge's case found expression also in plays in verse. Other major figures in twentieth-century poetic drama are T. S. Eliot and the Spanish peasant poet Garcia Lorca, while Max-

---

[2] I use "new stagecraft" for certain, largely non-illusionistic, styles of staging and design. The playwright's defiance of illusionism by way of deliberate acknowledgement and use of his theatrical medium in the written play — as in some of the plays by Pirandello, Wilder, and Brecht — I call "theatricalism." "New stagecraft" refers to the art of the theater; "theatricalism" denotes a quality of drama.

well Anderson in a series of blank verse tragedies and historical plays and Christopher Fry in image-studded comedies seem less original contributors to the genre. Eliot, like Yeats, has been a subtle and forceful champion-critic of verse drama, arguing that in committing himself to record the surface appearance of ordinary life the naturalistic playwright has cut himself off from the richest, most beautiful resources of language: rhythm, precision, intensity, grandeur. His own best play, *Murder in the Cathedral*, is an impressive piece of evidence for the viability of dramatic verse in other than the Elizabethan idiom, though, as Eliot himself has pointed out, technically it hardly solves the problems of writing plays of *modern* themes and settings in verse.

Expressionism is both an elusive and an inclusive term. It is used here for drama that does not pretend to be a record of objective reality (for what is "objective reality," anyway?) and which departs from the conventions of illusionistic staging and coherent action. Not communication of meaning but intimation of an experience is its end. The "stories" expressionistic drama tells — such as they are — happen in the soul and not in the external Nature that men used to believe God had ordained for His creatures' common habitat. World events, social facts, and a general feeling that nada philosophy is a dead end may be about to effect a turn in the trend, but today it is still true that the three main axioms of the dominant mode of modern drama are that to make the stage look and sound like real life is not an adequate or worthwhile expression of human reality, that an excess of realism corrupts the integrity of artistic detachment, and that to try to reform the actual is no true artistic end at all. (Even the neo-objectivists of pop-art betray philosophical pretensions beyond those of the naturalists in their very insistence that their flat, overblown images of comic strip fragments and of the empty containers of a consumer civilization mean nothing but that such things, and only such things, "are.")

Positivistic empiricism is as dead as the god it was supposed to supplant. Surrealism, abstractionism, and non-representationalism in all the arts are the products of a whole complex of supra-rational, relativistic concepts of reality. Psychology gives us man as an irrational creature chained to his subconscious. The bleak moral imperatives of Existentialism have erected no syncretic system of thought in which both artists and their audiences can share. Physical science threatens to reduce empirical reality to one vast illusion, a meaningless flux of lawless force. The emphasis on subjective, inner reality, fragmentary and inchoate, in some characteristic forms of both expressionism and the new stagecraft, reflects the philosophical nihilism and despair that appear to be modern man's birthright — but also his continuing quest for authentic visual and auditory correlatives for his anxieties. The absurdity within mirrors the absurdity "out there." If every soul is a prisoner in quarantine, the words it utters are of no consequence as communication, except, perhaps, as monologue. Dialogue in Ionesco's *Bald Soprano* is a ritual of noise, a circular recitative of small talk, accurate and meaningless, funny and frightening: the living room as still life. And already a classical passage in contemporary drama are the two identical act endings in Beckett's *Waiting for Godot*: "Well? Shall we go? — Yes, let's go. — *They do not move.*" When Ghelderode proclaims the world's need for fables to nurture its fact-glutted soul, and Brecht writes materialist parables on good and evil, and Beckett's tramps and cripples wait for release from pain in a dead landscape (the wait is hopeless, but not to wait is to abandon all hope), and Ionesco and Albee walk through the modern megalopolis and discover bestial features behind bland physiognomies (as did Ibsen's sculptor Rubek in his last play, *When We Dead Awaken*), they may all be dramatists in search of human "character." Meanwhile, their image for man is an incoherent sequence of states of consciousness and their theatrical record of his reality is kaleidoscopic, illusory, ambiguous, grotesque, pointless, "absurd." Their cult of excess is a form of protest against isolation and meaninglessness. "No Exit" could be the title of several other modern plays than one of Sartre's.

Expressionism, of course, takes in more than dramatic absurdism, just as not all absurd drama is expressionistic. Beckett, for example, in *Waiting for Godot* and *Endgame*, insinuates the existential revolt and despair directly in a frankly fantastic-allegorical form, while a non-expressionistic, pseudo-realist surface overlays similar attitudes in some of the plays by Albee (*The Zoo Story*, among them) and the British playwright Harold Pinter. At its best, as in Beckett's metaphysical and Ionesco's and Genet's basically satirical drama, expressionistic absurdism achieves quaintly moving images of surrealist futility.

Any play in which it is suggested that the stage represents the mind's interior is to that extent expressionistic. The definition loosely covers plays that used to be called "experimental" or "avant-garde." It follows that the category is a large and miscellaneous one. It includes Strindberg's chamber plays (such as *The Dream Play* and *The Ghost Sonata*) Alfred Jarry's proto-Dadaistic, Rabelaisian rendering of *Macbeth* in *Ubu Roi* (1897), and O'Neill's dramatizations of atavism (*Emperor Jones, The Hairy Ape*) and his plays for masks and chorus (*The Great God Brown, Lazarus Laughed*). It includes the left-wing allegories of mass scenes, abstract sets, and nameless (or rather generically named) heroes and heroines in Kaiser's and Toller's German expressionism of the twenties (*e.g.*, Kaiser's *Man and the Masses*), Andreyev's (*He Who Gets Slapped*) and Pirandello's somber-ironic probings of reality, Wilder's theatricalism (*Our Town, The Skin of Our Teeth*), Cocteau's and

Giraudoux's sardonic reworkings of old legend (*The Infernal Machine, Orpheus, Electra, Judith*), Dürrenmatt's only vaguely implausible story of the venality of decent people in *The Visit,* and Ghelderode's super-natural pantomime-fables. These plays are not all similar — most of them are quite dissimilar — but they are all part of a many-faceted re-volt against the naturalistic proposition that representationalism is the means to the end of discovering truth about man. It follows also that expressionism, though often based on psychoanalysis (the stage is the subconscious; action is by free association) and often radical in its moral or political fervor, is not the exclusive property of any one school of thought. Such filmic elements as brief scenes, varied setting, visual symbols, abrupt movement, and large casts tend to be among its formal characteristics.

The free and flexible staging called for by many expressionistic plays takes us, finally, to a consideration of the new stagecraft. What has just been said about expressionism explains why and in what manner these two forms of anti-naturalism so frequently are found together in script and production, why it could be argued, in fact, that the new stage-craft is simply an aspect of expressionism. Playwrights have always written with the physical conditions of their theater in mind, and the enormous technical resources available to the modern director and de-signer allow a range of experimentation and innovation that was hardly open to earlier playwrights. True, the unencumbered Elizabethan stage gave freedom to a Shakespeare's dramatic imagination, but it was the freedom offered by a void to be filled, not the freedom of a craftsman choosing among a multitude of tools.

Richard Wagner may be considered the father of the new stagecraft, because of his theory of the *Gesamtkunstwerk,* the work of all arts, in which poetry, musical composition, choreography, painting, acting, singing, lighting, directing all co-operated. Wagner's operas hardly be-long to the history of modern drama, but it is relevant here to note the important influence of his theory on modern workers in the theater. Not even Stanislavsky's ideal of ensemble acting has contributed as much as Wagner's grand synthesis of all the theatrical arts to the apotheosis of the director as the co-ordinator of them all at the expense of both playwright and actor, which is one of the most distinctive phenomena in what may be called the sociology of the modern theater.

Despite their differences the various theories and practices of the new stagecraft all share an ambition to free the theatrical medium from the written word, particularly from the convention that actors are real people engaged in real conversations in real rooms. The new stagecraft is, essentially, the use of non-verbal means to the end of a more adapt-able, comprehensive, and expressive medium of the theater. The ideal entails the obvious danger of dethroning the word for mere spectacle and mechanical ingenuity, but no one denies that it has enriched modern drama. Its development and diversification have been aided by innovations in the physical theater which at first seemed mainly to further the illusionism of naturalism. Chief among these were the revolving stage (brought to Europe from Japan in 1896 and used by Ibsen in *John Gabriel Borkman* that same year) and, above all, electric lighting. There are modern departures from conventional staging that appear to have been made for their own sake — because of the stager's understandable delight in his medium.

The Swiss Adolphe Appia and the Englishman Gordon Craig were influential theorists of the new stagecraft during the early decades of this century. Appia anatomized stage production into four plastic elements: vertical scenery, horizontal floor, moving actor, and lighted space. The playwright's words were to be subordinated to the total scenic spectacle of line, light, color, and movement, all focused on the actor's dramatic presence. Craig went even farther in visualizing a wordless theater of super-marionettes performing before vast and abstract designs. Neither Appia nor Craig gained enough of a hearing to be important practitioners of their own theories, but they were influential as writers and designers. Early Soviet theater (before the dreary triumph of social realism), represented by a "constructivist" like Meyerhold (later condemned and perhaps executed for "formalism"), was indebted to them. So was the productive and versatile German Max Reinhardt, perhaps the most eclectic worker in the modern theater, producing plays of all times and kinds in colossal and intimate theaters alike, re-introducing the Elizabethan apron stage, experimenting with theater-in-the-round. The fluid stylization of platform and staircase staging in Jacques Copeau's Vieux-Colombier (opened in 1913) and the use of transparencies and light to free stage realism from the solidities of the older naturalistic manner, as in some of Elia Kazan's recent productions of plays by Tennessee Williams and Arthur Miller, are other proofs of the versatility and adaptability of the new stagecraft.

These notes come to no conclusion — as perhaps it is impossible for notes on such a subject as modern drama to do. The diversity of that drama is obvious — in origin, content, literary and theatrical form and style, and present trends. To forecast its future seems foolish, to establish its rank among the great ages of drama premature. But the example of a single play may serve to support the belief that there is artistic vitality in the very heterogeneity of our drama. The dialogue of *The Glass Menagerie* is the naturalistic prose of ordinary people, but the many, short, and disjunctive scenes are a characteristic of new stagecraft, while the whole "memory play" apparatus is expressionistic. Like Ibsen's stage families, the Wingfields are trapped by their past: Amanda's image of herself as popular belle, the photograph of the absconded father, the return of Laura's high-school hero. The near-plotlessness and the repertory of modal counterpoint echo Chekhov. And in Tom's speeches and situation in the memory play (as distinct from the theatricalist present) there is a note of left-wing protest against constricting and degrading socioeconomic conditions. The wonder is that such a mixture of styles and motifs can be an artistic whole at all, but it is.

MODERN DRAMA

ALTERNATE EDITION

MODERN DRAMA

Henrik Ibsen

THE WILD DUCK

A New Translation by Otto Reinert

Characters

WERLE, *a manufacturer and merchant*
GREGERS WERLE, *his son*
OLD EKDAL
HJALMAR EKDAL, *his son, a photographer*
GINA EKDAL, *Hjalmar's wife*
HEDVIG, *their daughter, fourteen years old*
MRS. SØRBY, *Werle's housekeeper*
RELLING, *a physician*
MOLVIK, *a former student of theology*
GRÅBERG, *a bookkeeper in Werle's office*
PETTERSEN, *Werle's servant*
JENSEN, *a hired waiter*
A FLABBY GENTLEMAN
A THIN-HAIRED GENTLEMAN
A NEARSIGHTED GENTLEMAN
SIX OTHER GENTLEMEN, *Werle's dinner guests*
OTHER HIRED WAITERS

SCENE: *The first act takes place at* WERLE'S; *the other four,*
in HJALMAR EKDAL'S *studio.*

ACT I

An expensive-looking and comfortable study in WERLE'S *house;*
bookcases and upholstered furniture; in the middle of the room a
desk with papers and ledgers; lamps with green shades give the
room a soft, subdued light. In the rear, open double doors with

1

*portieres pulled apart reveal a large, elegant drawing room, brightly
illuminated by lamps and candles. Front right, a small door to the
office wing. Front left, a fireplace with glowing coals in it. Farther
back on the left wall, double doors to the dining room.*

PETTERSEN, WERLE'S *servant, in livery, and the hired waiter*
JENSEN, *in black, are setting the study in order for the guests. In
the drawing room, two or three other hired waiters are lighting
candles, moving chairs, etc. Sounds of conversation and laughter
of many people come from the dining room. Someone signals he
wishes to make a speech by touching his glass with his knife. Silence follows, a short speech is made, there are noises of approval,
then again conversation.*

PETTERSEN (*lights a lamp by the fireplace and puts a shade on it*): Just
listen to that, Jensen. There's the old man now, proposing a long
toast to Mrs. Sørby.

JENSEN (*moving an armchair*): Do you think it's true what people say,
that the two of 'em — y'know — ?

PETTERSEN: Couldn't say.

JENSEN: I bet he used to be quite a goat in the old days.

PETTERSEN: Maybe so.

JENSEN: They say this dinner is for his son.

PETTERSEN: That's right. He came home yesterday.

JENSEN: It's the first I've heard Werle has a son.

PETTERSEN: He has a son, all right. But he's up at the works at Høydal
all the time. He hasn't been home as long as I've been here.

A HIRED WAITER (*in the drawing room doorway*): Pst, Pettersen,
there's an old fellow here, says he —

PETTERSEN (*under his breath*): Dammit! Can't have anybody in here
now!

(OLD EKDAL *appears from the right in the drawing room. He is
dressed in a shabby old coat with a high collar. Wool mittens. He
carries a walking stick and a fur cap in his hand. Under his arm a
parcel in thick paper. Dirty, reddish brown wig. Small, gray mustache.*)

PETTERSEN (*going towards him*): Good Lord! What are *you* doing
here?

EKDAL (*in the doorway*): Got to get into the office, Pettersen.

PETTERSEN: The office closed an hour ago, and —

EKDAL: They told me that downstairs. But Gråberg is still in there. Be
a good boy, Pettersen; let me in this way. (*Points to the small office
door.*) Been through here before.

PETTERSEN: Oh well, all right. (*Opens the door.*) But see you go out the other way. We're having guests tonight.

EKDAL: I know, I know — h'm! Thanks a lot, Pettersen, old boy. Good old friend. Thanks. (*Mutters.*) Ass!

(*He enters the office.* PETTERSEN *closes the door behind him.*)

JENSEN: Is he one of them office people, too?

PETTERSEN: Oh no. He just does some extra copying for them, when they need it. But he's been a fine enough fellow in his day, old Ekdal has.

JENSEN: You know, he sort of looked like that.

PETTERSEN: Oh yes. He used to be a lieutenant.

JENSEN: I'll be damned! A lieutenant!

PETTERSEN: Yessir: Then he got mixed up in some forest deal or something. They say he pretty near ruined Werle once. The two of 'em were partners — owned the Høydal works together. Oh yes, Ekdal and I are good friends. We've had many a drink together at Madam Eriksen's place, we have.

JENSEN: Didn't look to me like he'd have much to buy people drinks with.

PETTERSEN: Good Lord, Jensen. It's my treat, of course. I always say one should be nice to people who've seen better days.

JENSEN: So he went bankrupt?

PETTERSEN: Worse than that. He went to prison.

JENSEN: Prison!

PETTERSEN: Or something. — (*Listens.*) Shhh. They are getting up from the table.

(*Servants open the doors to the dining room.* MRS. SØRBY *appears, in conversation with a couple of the dinner guests. The rest of the company follows in small groups.* WERLE *is among them. The last to appear are* HJALMAR EKDAL *and* GREGERS WERLE.)

MRS. SØRBY (*to the servant, in passing*): Pettersen, tell them to serve the coffee in the music room, will you?

PETTERSEN: Very well, Mrs. Sørby.

(*She and the two guests go into the drawing room and disappear, right.* PETTERSEN *and* JENSEN *follow them out.*)

A FLABBY GENTLEMAN (*to* A THIN-HAIRED *one*): Phew! That dinner — It was almost too much for me.

THE THIN-HAIRED GENTLEMAN: Oh, I don't know. With a little bit of good will, it's amazing what one can accomplish in three hours.

THE FLABBY GENTLEMAN: Yes, but afterwards, afterwards, my dear chamberlain!

A THIRD GENTLEMAN: I am told the coffee and liqueurs will be served in the music room.

THE FLABBY GENTLEMAN: Wonderful! Then maybe Mrs. Sørby will play something for us.

THE THIN-HAIRED GENTLEMAN (*in a low voice*): If only she doesn't play us a different tune one of these days.

THE FLABBY GENTLEMAN: Don't worry. Bertha isn't one to let old friends down.

(*They laugh and enter the drawing room.*)

WERLE (*in a low and troubled voice*): I don't think anybody noticed, Gregers.

GREGERS (*looks at him*): Noticed what?

WERLE: You didn't either?

GREGERS: What?

WERLE: We were thirteen at the table.

GREGERS: Really? Were we thirteen?

WERLE (*with a glance at* HJALMAR EKDAL): Usually we are only twelve. (*To the other guests:*) Gentlemen!

(*He and the remaining guests, except* HJALMAR *and* GREGERS, *leave through the drawing room, rear right.*)

HJALMAR (*who has overheard the conversation*): You shouldn't have invited me, Gregers.

GREGERS: Nonsense! This is supposed to be a party for *me.* Shouldn't I invite my one and only friend?

HJALMAR: But I don't think your father approves. I never come to this house.

GREGERS: So I hear. But I wanted to see you and talk to you. — Well, well, we two old school fellows have certainly drifted apart. It must be sixteen — seventeen years since we saw each other.

HJALMAR: Is it really that long?

GREGERS: It is indeed. And how are you? You look fine. You're almost stout.

HJALMAR: Stout is hardly the word, but I suppose I look a little more manly than I used to.

GREGERS: Yes, you do. Your appearance hasn't suffered any all these years.

HJALMAR (*gloomily*): But the inner man — ! Believe me, that's a different story. You know, of course, how utterly everything has collapsed for me and mine since we last met.

GREGERS (*in a lower voice*): How is your father these days?

HJALMAR: I'd just as soon not talk about him. My poor, unfortunate father lives with me, of course. He has no one else in the whole world to turn to. But it is so terribly difficult for me to talk about these things. Tell me rather how you have been — up there at the works.

GREGERS: Lonely — blissfully lonely. I've had all the time in the world to think over all sorts of things. — Here. Let's make ourselves comfortable.

(*He sits down in an armchair near the fireplace and gets* HJALMAR *to take another chair beside him.*)

HJALMAR (*softly*): All the same, I do want to thank you, Gregers, for inviting me to your father's table. It proves to me you no longer bear me a grudge.

GREGERS (*surprised*): Grudge? What makes you think I ever did?

HJALMAR: You did at first, you know.

GREGERS: When?

HJALMAR: Right after the tragedy. Of course, that was only natural. After all, your own father only escaped by the skin of his teeth. Oh, that terrible old business!

GREGERS: And so I bore you a grudge? Who told you that?

HJALMAR: I know you did, Gregers. Your father said so himself.

GREGERS (*startled*): Father! Really? H'm. So that's why you've never written — not a single word.

HJALMAR: Yes.

GREGERS: Not even when you decided to become a photographer?

HJALMAR: Your father thought it would be better if I didn't write about anything at all.

GREGERS (*looking straight ahead*): Oh well, maybe he was right, at that. — But tell me, Hjalmar — do you feel you have adjusted pretty well to your situation?

HJALMAR (*with a small sigh*): Oh yes, I think I have. Can't say I haven't, anyway. At first, of course, things seemed very strange. My circumstances were so completely different. But then, everything had changed. Father's great, ruinous tragedy — The shame — The disgrace —

GREGERS (*feelingly*): Yes, yes. I see.

HJALMAR: Of course there was no way in which I could pursue my studies. There wasn't a penny left. Rather the opposite; there was debt. Mainly to your father, I think.

GREGERS: H'm —

HJALMAR: Well — then I thought it best to take the bull by the horns and make a clean break with the past — you know, all at once. Your father thought so, too, and since he had been so helpful, and —

GREGERS: Father helped you?

HJALMAR: Yes, surely you know that? Where do you think I got the money to learn photography and to set up my own studio? Things like that are expensive, I can tell you.

GREGERS: And father paid for all that?

HJALMAR: Yes, didn't you know? I understood him to say he had written to you about it.

GREGERS: Not a word that it was *he*. He must have forgotten. We only write business letters. So it was father — !

HJALMAR: It certainly was. But he has never wanted people to know that. It was he who made it possible for me to get married, too. Or maybe — maybe you didn't know that, either?

GREGERS: No! How could I? (*Shakes* HJALMAR's *arm.*) My dear Hjalmar, I can't tell you how happy all this makes me — and pains me, too. Perhaps I have been unfair to father. In some respects, anyway. For this shows he has a heart, you know. A kind of conscience —

HJALMAR: Conscience?

GREGERS: Or whatever you want to call it. No, really, I can't tell you how glad I am to hear this about father. — So you are married, Hjalmar. That's more than I ever will be. I trust you find yourself happy as a married man?

HJALMAR: Yes, I certainly do. She is as good and competent a wife as any man could ask for. And she is by no means without culture.

GREGERS (*a little taken aback*): No, of course not.

HJALMAR: Life itself is an education, you see. Being with me every day — And then there are a couple of remarkable men we see quite a lot of. I assure you, you'd hardly recognize Gina.

GREGERS: Gina?

HJALMAR: Yes. Surely you remember her name was Gina?

GREGERS: Whose name? I haven't the slightest idea —

HJALMAR: But don't you remember she was here in the house for a while?

GREGERS (*looks at him*): Is it Gina Hansen — ?

HJALMAR: Of course it is Gina Hansen.

GREGERS: — who kept house for us the last year of mother's illness?

HJALMAR: That's it. But my dear friend, I know for a fact that your father wrote you about my marriage.

GREGERS (*who has risen*): Yes, so he did, that's true, but not that — (*paces the floor*). Wait a minute — Yes, he did — now when I think back. But father always writes such short letters. (*Sits down on the arm of the chair*.) Listen, Hjalmar — this interests me — how did you make Gina's acquaintance — your wife, I mean?

HJALMAR: Quite simply. You remember she didn't stay here very long. Everything was so unsettled during your mother's illness. Gina couldn't take that, so she gave notice and moved out. That was the year before your mother died. Or maybe it was the same year.

GREGERS: It was the same year. I was up at Høydal at the time. Then what happened?

HJALMAR: Well, Gina moved in with her mother, Madam Hansen, an excellent, hardworking woman, who ran a small eating place. And she had a room for rent, too. A nice, comfortable room.

GREGERS: Which you were lucky enough to get?

HJALMAR: Yes. Through your father, in fact. And it was there I really learned to know Gina.

GREGERS: And then you got engaged?

HJALMAR: Yes. It's easy for young people to fall in love, you know. H'm —

GREGERS (*gets up, walks up and down*): Tell me — after you'd become engaged, was that when father — I mean, was that when you took up photography?

HJALMAR: That's right. Naturally, I wanted to get married and have a place of my own, the sooner the better. And both your father and I agreed that photography was the best thing I could get into. Gina thought so, too. Oh yes, that was another reason. It so happened that Gina had learned how to retouch.

GREGERS: What a wonderful coincidence.

HJALMAR (*smiling contentedly*): Yes, wasn't it? Don't you think it worked out very well?

GREGERS: Remarkably well, I should say. So father has really been a kind of Providence for you, Hjalmar; hasn't he?

HJALMAR (*moved*): He did not abandon his old friend's son in his days of need. That's one thing about your father: he does have a heart.

MRS. SØRBY (*enters on* WERLE'S *arm*): I don't want to hear another word, my dear sir. You are not to stay in there staring at all those bright lights. It isn't good for you.

WERLE (*letting go of her arm and moving his hand across his eyes*): I almost think you are right.

(PETTERSEN *and* JENSEN *enter carrying trays with glasses of punch.*)

MRS. SØRBY (*to the guests in the drawing room*): Gentlemen, if you want a glass of punch, you'll have to take the trouble to come in here.

THE FLABBY GENTLEMAN (*to* MRS. SØRBY): Dear Mrs. Sørby, please tell me it isn't so. You have not withdrawn your cherished permission to smoke?

MRS. SØRBY: Yes, Chamberlain. No smoking here in Mr. Werle's own sanctum.

THE THIN-HAIRED GENTLEMAN: And when did you append these harsh paragraphs to the tobacco regulations, Mrs. Sørby?

MRS. SØRBY: After the last dinner, Chamberlain, when certain persons abused their liberties.

THE THIN-HAIRED GENTLEMAN: And will not even the smallest infraction be tolerated, Mrs. Sørby? Really none at all?

MRS. SØRBY: None whatsoever, Chamberlain.

(*Most of the guests are gathered in the study. The servants are serving punch.*)

WERLE (*to* HJALMAR, *over by a table*): Well, Ekdal, what is that you are looking at?

HJALMAR: Oh, just an album, sir.

THE THIN-HAIRED GENTLEMAN (*moving about*): Ah yes! Photographs! That's your line, of course.

THE FLABBY GENTLEMAN (*seated*): Haven't you brought some of your own along?

HJALMAR: No, I haven't.

THE FLABBY GENTLEMAN: Too bad. Looking at pictures is good for the digestion, you know.

THE THIN-HAIRED GENTLEMAN: And then it would have contributed a mite to the general entertainment.

A NEARSIGHTED GENTLEMAN: And all contributions are gratefully received.

MRS. SØRBY: The chamberlains think that when one has been invited to dinner, one ought to work for one's food, Mr. Ekdal.

THE FLABBY GENTLEMAN: With a cuisine like this that's only a pleasure.

THE THIN-HAIRED GENTLEMAN: Oh well, if it's a question of the struggle for existence —

MRS. SØRBY: You are so right!

(*They continue their conversation, laughing and joking.*)

GREGERS (*in a low voice*): You must join in, Hjalmar.

HJALMAR (*with a twist of his body*): What am I to say?

THE FLABBY GENTLEMAN: Don't you believe, sir, that Tokay may be considered relatively beneficial to the stomach?

WERLE (*by the fireplace*): I'll guarantee the Tokay you were served to-night, at any rate. It is one of the very best years. I am sure you noticed that yourself.

THE FLABBY GENTLEMAN: Yes, it really was unusually delicate-tasting.

HJALMAR (*hesitantly*): Do the years differ?

THE FLABBY GENTLEMAN (*laughs*): Ah, Mr. Ekdal! Splendid!

WERLE (*with a smile*): I see it is hardly worth while to serve you fine wine.

THE THIN-HAIRED GENTLEMAN: Tokay is like photographs, Mr. Ekdal. Both need sunshine. Or isn't that so?

HJALMAR: Yes, sunshine has something to do with it.

MRS. SØRBY: Just the same with chamberlains. They need sunshine, too — royal sunshine, as the saying goes.

THE THIN-HAIRED GENTLEMAN: Ouch! That's a tired old joke, Mrs. Sørby.

THE NEARSIGHTED GENTLEMAN: The lady will have her fun —

THE FLABBY GENTLEMAN: — and at our expense. (*Wagging his finger.*) Madam Bertha! Madam Bertha!

MRS. SØRBY: But it is true that vintages differ widely sometimes. The older the better.

THE NEARSIGHTED GENTLEMAN: Do you count me among the older vintages?

MRS. SØRBY: Far from it.

THE THIN-HAIRED GENTLEMAN: Well, well! But what about me, Mrs. Sørby?

THE FLABBY GENTLEMAN: And me? What vintages do we belong to?

MRS. SØRBY: I reckon you among the sweet vintages, gentlemen.

(*She sips a glass of punch. The chamberlains laugh and flirt with her.*)

WERLE: Mrs. Sørby always finds a way out — when she wants to. But gentlemen, you aren't drinking! Pettersen, please see to it that — ! Gregers, let's have a glass together.

(GREGERS *does not move.*)

Won't you join us, Ekdal? I had no opportunity at the table —

(GRÅBERG *comes in through the office door.*)

GRÅBERG: Beg your pardon, Mr. Werle, but I can't get out.

WERLE: They've locked you in again, eh?

GRÅBERG: Yes, they have, sir. And Flakstad has left with the keys.

WERLE: That's all right. You just come through here.

GRÅBERG: But there is somebody else —

WERLE: Doesn't matter. Come on, both of you.

(GRÅBERG *and* OLD EKDAL *enter from the office.*)

WERLE (*involuntarily*): Damn!

(*Laughter and talk among the guests cease.* HJALMAR *gives a start when he sees his father, puts down his glass, and turns away toward the fireplace.*)

EKDAL (*does not look up but makes quick little bows to both sides, as he mutters*): Beg pardon. Came the wrong way. Gate's locked. Gate's locked. Beg pardon. (*He and* GRÅBERG *go out, rear right.*)

WERLE (*between his teeth*): That idiot Gråberg!

GREGERS (*staring, his mouth hanging open, to* HJALMAR): Don't tell me that was — !

THE FLABBY GENTLEMAN: What is it? Who was that?

GREGERS: Nothing. Just the bookkeeper and somebody else.

THE NEARSIGHTED GENTLEMAN (*to* HJALMAR): Did *you* know that man?

HJALMAR: I don't know — I didn't notice —

THE FLABBY GENTLEMAN (*getting up*): What the devil has gotten into everybody? (*He walks over to some other guests, who are talking in low voices.*)

MRS. SØRBY (*whispers to the servant*): Give him something from the kitchen to take home. Something good.

PETTERSEN (*nods his head*): I'll do that, ma'am. (*Goes out.*)

GREGERS (*shocked, in a low voice to* HJALMAR): Then it really was he?

HJALMAR: Yes.

GREGERS: And you stood there and denied him!

HJALMAR (*in a fierce whisper*): But how could I — ?

GREGERS: — acknowledge your own father?

HJALMAR (*pained*): Oh, if you had been in my place, maybe —

(*The low conversation among the guests changes to forced gaiety.*)

THE THIN-HAIRED GENTLEMAN (*approaching* HJALMAR *and* GREGERS, *in a friendly mood*): Aha! Reminiscing about university days, gentlemen? — Don't you smoke, Mr. Ekdal? Can I give you a light? Oh that's right. We are not allowed —

HJALMAR: Thanks, I don't smoke.

THE FLABBY GENTLEMAN: Don't you have a nice little poem you could recite for us, Mr. Ekdal? You used to do that so beautifully.

HJALMAR: I am sorry. I don't remember any.

THE FLABBY GENTLEMAN: That's a shame. Well, in that case, Balle, what do we do?

(*They both walk into the drawing room.*)

HJALMAR (*gloomily*): Gregers — I am leaving! You see, when a man has felt Fate's crushing blow — Say goodbye to your father for me.

GREGERS: Yes, of course. Are you going straight home?

HJALMAR: Yes. Why?

GREGERS: I thought I might come up and see you a little later.

HJALMAR: No, don't do that. Not to my home. My home is a gloomy one, Gregers, particularly after a brilliant banquet such as this. We can meet somewhere in town.

MRS. SØRBY (*has come up to them; in a low voice*): Are you leaving, Ekdal?

HJALMAR: Yes.

MRS. SØRBY: Say hello to Gina.

HJALMAR: Thank you. I'll do that.

MRS. SØRBY: Tell her I'll be up to see her one of these days.

HJALMAR: Fine. (*To* GREGERS) You stay here. I'll slip out without anybody noticing. (*Drifts off. A little later he goes into the drawing room and out right.*)

MRS. SØRBY (*in a low voice to the servant who has returned*): Well, did you give the old man something?

PETTERSEN: Oh yes. A bottle of brandy.

MRS. SØRBY: Oh dear. Couldn't you have found something better?

PETTERSEN: But Mrs. Sørby, there's nothing he likes better than brandy.

THE FLABBY GENTLEMAN (*in the doorway to the drawing room, with a sheet of music in his hand*): Will you play a duet, Mrs. Sørby?

MRS. SØRBY: Yes, gladly.

THE GUESTS: Good! Good!

(*She and all the guests go out rear right.* GREGERS *remains standing by the fireplace.* WERLE *is looking for something on the desk and appears to wish to be left alone. Since* GREGERS *does not leave,* WERLE *walks towards the drawing room door.*)

GREGERS: Father, do you have a moment?

WERLE (*stops*): What is it?

GREGERS: I'd like a word with you.

WERLE: Couldn't it wait till we're alone?

GREGERS: No, it can't, for maybe we'll never be alone again.

WERLE (*coming closer*): What does that mean?

(*During the following scene, the sound of a piano is faintly heard from the music room.*)

GREGERS: How is it that that family has been allowed to go to ruin so miserably?

WERLE: I suppose you refer to the Ekdals?

GREGERS: Yes, I do mean the Ekdals. Lieutenant Ekdal was once your close friend.

WERLE: Yes, unfortunately. Too close. I have felt that keenly enough for many years. It was his fault that my good name and reputation, too, were — somewhat tarnished.

GREGERS (*in a low voice*): Was he the only one who was guilty?

WERLE: Who else, do you mean?

GREGERS: The two of you were together on that big purchase of forest land, weren't you?

WERLE: But it was Ekdal who surveyed the area — surveyed it fraudulently. It was he who felled all that timber on state property. He was responsible for everything that went on up there. I didn't know what he was doing.

GREGERS: I doubt that Lieutenant Ekdal himself knew what he was doing.

WERLE: That may well be. The fact remains that he was convicted and I was not.

GREGERS: Yes, I know there were no proofs.

WERLE: Acquittal is acquittal. Why do you want to bring back that miserable old business that gave me gray hairs before my time? Is that what has been on your mind all these years up there? I can assure you, Gregers, here in town that whole story has been forgotten long ago, as far as *I* am concerned.

GREGERS: But what about that unfortunate family?

WERLE: Well, now, exactly what do you want me to do for those people? When Ekdal got out, he was a broken man, beyond help altogether. Some people go to the bottom as soon as they've got some buckshot in them and never come up again. Believe me, Gregers, I've done all I possibly could do, if I didn't want to put myself in a false light and give people occasion for all sorts of talk and suspicion —

GREGERS: Suspicion? I see.

WERLE: I have given Ekdal copying work to do for the office, and I pay him far, far more than he is worth.

GREGERS (*without looking at him*): H'm. I don't doubt that.

WERLE: You are laughing? Don't you think I am telling you the truth?

Oh, to be sure, you won't find it in my books. I never enter expenses like that.

GREGERS (*with a cold smile*): No, I suppose there are certain expenses that are better not entered.

WERLE (*puzzled*): What do you mean?

GREGERS (*being brave*): Have you entered what it cost you to let Hjalmar Ekdal learn photography?

WERLE: I? What do you mean — entered?

GREGERS: I know now it was you who paid for it. And I also know it was you who set him up in business — quite comfortably, too.

WERLE: All right! And you still say I have done nothing for the Ekdals! I assure you, Gregers, those people have cost me a pretty penny!

GREGERS: Have you entered those expenses?

WERLE: Why do you ask?

GREGERS: I have my reasons. Listen — at the time you were providing so kindly for your old friend's son, wasn't that just when he was getting married?

WERLE: Damn it, Gregers! How can I remember — ! After so many years — !

GREGERS: You wrote me a letter at the time. A business letter, of course. And in a postscript you mentioned very briefly that Hjalmar Ekdal had married one Miss Hansen.

WERLE: That's right. That was her name.

GREGERS: But you did not say anything about Miss Hansen being Gina Hansen, our ex-housekeeper.

WERLE (*with scornful but forced laughter*): No, to tell the truth, it didn't occur to me that you were particularly interested in our ex-housekeeper.

GREGERS: I wasn't. But — (*Lowers his voice.*) somebody else in this house was.

WERLE: What do you mean? (*Flaring up.*) Don't tell me you're referring to me!

GREGERS (*in a low but firm voice*): Yes, I am referring to you.

WERLE: And you dare — ! You have the audacity — ! How can that ingrate, that — that photographer fellow — how dare he make accusations like that!

GREGERS: Hjalmar hasn't said a word. I don't think he has the faintest suspicion of anything like this.

WERLE: Then where do you get it from? Who could have said a thing like that?

GREGERS: My poor, unfortunate mother. The last time I saw her.

WERLE: Your mother! I might have thought so! You and she — you always stood together. It was she who first turned you against me.

GREGERS: No, it was all she had to go through, till things became too much for her and she died in sheer misery.

WERLE: Oh, nonsense! She didn't have to go through anything! No more than what others have had to, anyway. There's just no way of getting on with morbid, hysterical people — that's something *I* have had to learn! And here you are, with a suspicion like that — dabbling in old rumors and gossip against your own father. Listen here, Gregers. It really seems to me that at your age you might find something more useful to do.

GREGERS: Yes, it is about time.

WERLE: Then maybe your mind would be more at ease than it seems to be now. What is the point of working away, year in and year out, as just an ordinary clerk up there at Høydal, with not so much as a penny beyond regular wages? It's plain silly!

GREGERS: I wish I could believe that.

WERLE: Not that I don't understand, mind you. You want to be independent, don't want to be obliged to me for anything. But right now there is a chance for you to become independent, to be on your own in everything.

GREGERS: Oh? How so?

WERLE: When I wrote you that I needed you here in town right away — h'm —

GREGERS: Yes, what is it you want of me? I've been waiting to hear all day.

WERLE: I am offering you a partnership in the firm.

GREGERS: I! In your firm? As a partner?

WERLE: Yes. That doesn't mean we have to be together all the time. You could take over the business here in town and I could go up to Høydal.

GREGERS: You would want to do that?

WERLE: Well, you see, Gregers. I can't work as well as I used to. I'll have to save my eyes. They are getting weaker.

GREGERS: You have always had weak eyes.

WERLE: Not as bad as now. Besides — there are other things, too, that may make it advisable for me to live up there — for a while, anyway.

GREGERS: Nothing like this has ever even occurred to me.

WERLE: Look here, Gregers. I know there are many things that stand between us. But after all, we are father and son. It seems to me we ought to be able to come to some sort of understanding.

GREGERS: For appearance's sake, I suppose you mean.

WERLE: Well, that would be something, anyway. Think it over, Gregers. Wouldn't that be possible? What do you say?

GREGERS (*looks at him coldly*): There is something behind this.

WERLE: I don't understand.

GREGERS: You want to use me for something.

WERLE: In a relationship as close as ours I suppose one person can always be of use to the other.

GREGERS: Yes. So they say.

WERLE: I want to have you at home with me for a while. I am a lonely man, Gregers. I have always been lonely, but mostly now, when I am getting older. I need somebody around me.

GREGERS: You have Mrs. Sørby.

WERLE: So I do, and she has become almost indispensable to me. She is bright, she has an even temper, she brings life into the house — and I badly need that.

GREGERS: Well, then, everything is just as you want it.

WERLE: Yes, but I am afraid it won't last. A woman in her circumstances can easily have her position misconstrued in the eyes of the world. I'll almost go so far as to say it does a man no good either.

GREGERS: Oh, I don't know. When a man gives the kind of dinner parties you do he can take quite a few liberties.

WERLE: Yes, but what about *her*, Gregers? I am afraid she will not put up with it much longer. And even if she did, even if she ignored what people are saying and all that sort of thing, out of devotion to me — Do you really think, Gregers, you with your strong sense of justice, do you feel it would be —

GREGERS (*interrupting*): Just tell me this: are you going to marry her?

WERLE: What if I did? What then?

GREGERS: That's what I am asking. What then?

WERLE: Would it displease you very much?

GREGERS: No, not at all.

WERLE: Well, you see, I didn't know — I thought perhaps out of regard for your mother —

GREGERS: I am not given to melodramatics.

WERLE: Well, whether you are or not, you have lifted a stone from my heart. I can't tell you how pleased I am that I can count on your support in this matter.

GREGERS (*looks intently at him*): Now I see what you want to use me for.

WERLE: Use you for? What an expression!

GREGERS: Let's not be particular in our choice of words — not as long as we're by ourselves, at any rate. (*Laughs.*) So that's it. That's why I had to come to town at all costs. Because of Mrs. Sørby, there are arrangements being made for family life in this house. Touching scene between father and son! That would indeed be something new!

WERLE: I won't have you use that tone!

GREGERS: When were we ever a family here? Never in my memory. But now, of course, there is need for a display of domestic affection. It will look very well to have the son hastening home on wings of filial feeling to attend the aging father's marriage feast. What happens then to all the talk of what the poor, deceased mother had to suffer? It evaporates. Her son takes care of that.

WERLE: Gregers, I don't believe there is anyone you detest as much as me.

GREGERS (*in a low voice*): I have seen too much of you.

WERLE: You've seen me with your mother's eyes. (*Lowers his voice a little.*) But don't forget that those eyes were — clouded at times.

GREGERS (*his voice trembles*): I know what you have in mind. But who's to blame for mother's tragic weakness? You and all those — ! The last one was that female you palmed off on Hjalmar Ekdal, when you yourself no longer — !

WERLE (*shrugs his shoulders*): Word for word as if I were hearing your mother.

GREGERS (*paying no attention*): — and there he is now, with his great, trusting child's soul in the middle of all this deceit — sharing his roof with a woman like that, unaware that what he calls his home is based on a lie! (*Steps closer to* WERLE.) When I look back upon all you have done, I seem to see a battlefield strewn with mangled human destinies.

WERLE: I almost think the gap between us is too wide.

GREGERS (*with a formal bow*): So I have observed. That is why I take my hat and leave.

WERLE: You're leaving? The house?

GREGERS: Yes. For now at last I see a mission to live for.

WERLE: What mission is that?

GREGERS: You'd only laugh if I told you.

WERLE: A lonely man doesn't laugh so easily, Gregers.

GREGERS (*pointing to the rear*): Look, father. The chamberlains are playing blindman's buff with Mrs. Sørby. — Goodnight and goodbye.

(*He goes out rear right. The sound of people talking, laughing, and playing games can be heard from the drawing room, where the guests are now coming into view.*)

WERLE (*mutters scornfully*): Hah — ! The fool! And he says he is not melodramatic!

ACT II

(HJALMAR EKDAL's *studio, a large attic room. To the right, a slant-ing roof with skylights, half covered by blue cloth. The entrance door from the hallway is in the far right corner; the door to the living room farther forward on the same wall. There are two doors to the left, as well, with an iron stove between them. In the rear, wide, sliding, double doors. The studio is unpretentious but cozy. Between the two doors on the right and a little out from the wall is a sofa with a table and some chairs in front of it. On the table is a lighted lamp with a shade. Near the wall by the stove is an old armchair. Various pieces of photographic equipment here and there in the room. In the rear, to the left of the sliding doors, a shelf with a few books, bottles with chemical solutions, tools, and some other objects. Photographs, brushes, paper, etc., are lying on the table.*

GINA EKDAL *sits by the table, sewing.* HEDVIG *sits on the sofa, read-ing, her hands shading her eyes, her thumbs in her ears.*)

GINA (*glances at* HEDVIG *a few times, as if secretly anxious*): Hedvig!

HEDVIG (*does not hear.*)

GINA (*louder*): Hedvig!

HEDVIG (*takes away her hands and looks up*): Yes, mother?

GINA: Hedvig, be a good girl. Don't read any more tonight.

HEDVIG: Please, mother, just a little bit longer? Can't I?

GINA: No. I want you to put that book away. Your father doesn't like you to read so much. He never reads at night.

HEDVIG (*closing her book*): Well, father doesn't care much for reading, anyway.

GINA (*puts her sewing aside and picks up a pencil and a small notebook from the table*): Do you remember how much we spent for the butter today?

HEDVIG: One crown and sixty-five øre.

GINA: That's right. (*Writes it down.*) We're using an awful lot of butter in this family. Then there was the sausage and the cheese — let me see — (*writing*) — and the ham — (*mumbles figures while adding up*). Goodness! it does add up —

HEDVIG: And the beer.

GINA: Right. (*Writes.*) It gets terrible expensive, but it can't be helped.

HEDVIG: And you and I didn't need anything hot for supper since father was out.

GINA: No, that's right. That helps some. And I did get eight crowns and fifty øre for the pictures.

HEDVIG: Was it that much?

GINA: Eight-fifty, exactly.

(*Silence.* GINA *picks up her sewing.* HEDVIG *takes paper and pencil and starts drawing, her left hand shading her eyes.*)

HEDVIG: Isn't it nice to think that father is at that big dinner party at Mr. Werle's?

GINA: Can't rightly say he's *his* guest. It was the son who invited him. (*After a pause.*) We have nothing to do with the old man.

HEDVIG: I can't wait till father comes home. He promised to ask Mrs. Sørby if he could take home something good for me.

GINA: Why yes, you can be sure there are plenty of good things in *that* house.

HEDVIG (*still drawing*): Besides, I think I am a little bit hungry, too.

(OLD EKDAL *enters right rear, the brown paper parcel under his arm, another parcel in his coat pocket.*)

GINA: So late you are today, Grandpa.

EKDAL: They'd locked the office. Had to wait for Gråberg. And then I had to go through — h'm —

HEDVIG: Did they give you any more copying to do, Grandpa?

EKDAL: This whole parcel. Look.

GINA: That's nice.

HEDVIG: And you've got another one in your pocket.

EKDAL: What? Oh never mind. That's nothing. (*Puts his walking stick away in the corner.*) This will keep me busy a long time, Gina. (*Slides one of the double doors half open.*) Shhh! (*Peeks into the attic for a while, then he cautiously slides the door shut. Chuckling.*) They're sound asleep the whole lot of 'em. And she herself's in the basket.

HEDVIG: Are you sure she won't be cold in that basket, Grandpa?

EKDAL: Cold? With all that straw? Don't you worry about *that*. (*Goes towards the door left rear.*) There are matches, aren't there?

GINA: On the dresser.

(EKDAL *goes into his room.*)

HEDVIG: It's nice that he got all that new work to do.

GINA: Yes, poor old thing. It will give him a little spending money.

HEDVIG: And he won't be able to stay down at that awful Madam Eriksen's all morning.

GINA: No; there's that, too.

HEDVIG: Do you think they're still at the table?

GINA: Lord knows. Could be.

HEDVIG: Just think of all that delicious food. I'm sure he'll be in a good mood when he comes home. Don't you think so, mother?

GINA: Yes, but what if we could tell him we'd rented the room. Wouldn't that be nice?

HEDVIG: But we don't need that tonight.

GINA: Oh yes we do. We could always use the money. The room is no good to us as it is.

HEDVIG: No, I mean that father will be in a good mood tonight, anyway. It's better to have the room for some other time.

GINA (*looking at her*): You like it when you have something nice to tell father when he comes home nights, don't you?

HEDVIG: It makes things more pleasant.

GINA (*reflectively*): Yes, I guess you're right about that.

(OLD EKDAL *enters from his room, heads for the kitchen door, left front.*)

GINA (*turning half around in her chair*): Do you need anything in the kitchen, Grandpa?

EKDAL: Yes. But don't you get up. (*Goes out.*)

GINA: I hope he isn't fooling around with the fire out there. (*After a while.*) Hedvig, go out and see what he's doing.

(OLD EKDAL *enters with a pitcher of hot water.*)

HEDVIG: Getting hot water, Grandpa?

EKDAL: That's right. Got some writing to do, but the ink's as thick as gruel. H'm —

GINA: But hadn't you better have supper first? It's all ready for you in your room.

EKDAL: Never mind supper, Gina. I tell you I'm busy. I don't want anybody coming in to me. Not anybody. H'm.

(*He goes into his room.* GINA *and* HEDVIG *look at each other.*)

GINA (*in a low voice*): I can't think where he got the money from. Can you?

HEDVIG: From Gråberg, maybe.

GINA: No, it wouldn't be that. Gråberg always gives me the money.

HEDVIG: Maybe he got a bottle on credit.

GINA: Him! Who'd give him credit?

(HJALMAR EKDAL, *in overcoat and gray hat, enters right.*)

GINA (*throws down her sewing, gets up*): Heavens, Ekdal! Home already?

HEDVIG (*getting up at the same time*): Father? So soon!

HJALMAR (*lays down his hat*): Most of them seemed to be leaving now.

HEDVIG: Already?

HJALMAR: Well, it was a dinner party, you know. (*Takes his coat off.*)

GINA: Let me help you.

HEDVIG: Me too. (*They help him off with his coat.* GINA *hangs it up in the rear.*) Were there many there, father?

HJALMAR: Not too many. About twelve or fourteen at the table.

GINA: Did you get to talk to all of them?

HJALMAR: Oh yes, a little. Though Gregers kept me engaged most of the evening.

GINA: Is he as ugly as he used to be?

HJALMAR: Well — I suppose nobody would call him handsome. Is father back?

HEDVIG: Yes, he is in there writing.

HJALMAR: Did he say anything?

GINA: No. About what?

HJALMAR: He didn't mention — ? I thought I heard he'd been with Gråberg. I think I'll go in to him for a moment.

GINA: No, you'd better not.

HJALMAR: Why not? Did he say he didn't want to see me?

GINA: He doesn't want to see anybody.

HEDVIG (*making signs to her*): Ahem!

GINA (*doesn't notice*): He's gotten himself some hot water.

HJALMAR: Ah! So he is —

GINA: Looks that way.

HJALMAR: Ah yes — my poor old white-haired father. Let him enjoy his little pleasures as best he can.

(OLD EKDAL, *a lighted pipe in his mouth, enters in an old smoking jacket.*)

EKDAL: Home again? Thought it was you I heard talking.

HJALMAR: Yes. I just came back.

EKDAL: Guess you didn't see me, did you?

HJALMAR: No, but they told me you'd gone through, so I thought I'd catch up with you.

EKDAL: H'm. That's good of you, Hjalmar. Who were they — all those people?

HJALMAR: Oh — all sorts. Chamberlain Flor and Chamberlain Balle

and Chamberlain Kaspersen and chamberlain this and that. I don't
know —

EKDAL (*nodding his head*): Hear that, Gina? He's been with nothing
but chamberlains all evening.

GINA: Yes, I hear as they've become quite fancy in that house now.

HEDVIG: Did the chamberlains sing, father? Or recite poetry?

HJALMAR: No. They just talked nonsense. They wanted *me* to recite,
though, but I didn't want to.

EKDAL: They couldn't get you to, eh?

GINA: Seems to me you might have done that.

HJALMAR: No. I don't see any reason why one has to oblige every Tom,
Dick, and Harry all the time. (*Walks up and down.*) At any rate, I
won't.

EKDAL: No point in being too obliging, you know. That's Hjalmar for
you.

HJALMAR: I don't see why *I* always have to be the one who provides
entertainment on the rare occasions when I am out for dinner. Let
the others exert themselves for a change. Those fellows go from one
big meal to the next, stuffing themselves day in and day out. Let
them do something for all the food they are getting!

GINA: You didn't tell them that though, did you?

HJALMAR (*humming a little*): Well, I don't know about that. They
were told a thing or two.

EKDAL: The chamberlains?

HJALMAR: Mmm — (*Casually.*) Then we had a little controversy over
Tokay wine.

EKDAL: Tokay, no less! Say, that's a fine wine!

HJALMAR (*stops his walking*): It *may* be a fine wine. But let me tell
you: not all the vintages are equally fine. It depends on how much
sunshine the grapes get.

GINA: If you don't know everything — !

EKDAL: And they quarreled with that?

HJALMAR: They tried to, but then it was pointed out to them that it
was the same way with chamberlains. Not all vintages are equally
fine among chamberlains, either — so they were told.

GINA: Goodness! What you don't think of!

EKDAL: Heh-heh! So they got that to put in their pipe.

HJALMAR: Right to their face. That's how they got it.

EKDAL: Gina, d'ye hear that? He gave it to them right to their face!

GINA: Right to their face! Imagine!

HJALMAR: Yes, but I don't want you to talk about it. One doesn't talk
about such things. Of course, the whole thing was done in the

friendliest possible way. They are all of them pleasant, easy-going people. Why should I hurt them? No!

EKDAL: Right to their face, though —

HEDVIG (*ingratiatingly*): It's so nice to see you all dressed up, father. You look very well in tails.

HJALMAR: Yes, don't you think so? And it really fits me perfectly. As if it were tailor-made. Possibly a trifle tight in the armpits, that's all. Help me, Hedvig. (*Takes his dinner jacket off.*) I'd rather wear my own coat. Where is it, Gina?

GINA: Here it is. (*Helps him on with it.*)

HJALMAR: There now! Be sure to have Molvik get his suit back first thing in the morning.

GINA (*putting the clothes away*): I'll take care of it.

HJALMAR (*stretching*): Aaahh. This feels cozier after all. And this kind of loose-fitting, casual wear is really more in keeping with my whole appearance; don't you think so, Hedvig?

HEDVIG: Oh yes, father!

HJALMAR: Especially when I tie my neckcloth with loose, flying ends — like this? What do you think?

HEDVIG: Yes, it goes extremely well with your mustache. And with your curls, too.

HJALMAR: I'd hardly call my hair curly. Wavy, rather.

HEDVIG: Yes, for the curls are so large.

HJALMAR: Waves, really.

HEDVIG (*after a moment, pulling his sleeve*): Father?

HJALMAR: What is it?

HEDVIG: Oh, you know very well what it is!

HJALMAR: I certainly don't.

HEDVIG (*laughing and pleading*): Oh come on, father! Don't tease me!

HJALMAR: But what is it?

HEDVIG (*shaking him*): Father! Give it to me! You know, you promised me. Something good to eat.

HJALMAR: Oh, dear! I completely forgot!

HEDVIG: You are only teasing, father. Shame on you! Where is it?

HJALMAR: No, honest, I really did forget. But wait a moment. I have something else for you, Hedvig. (*Goes and searches his coat pockets.*)

HEDVIG (*jumps up and down, clapping her hands*): Oh mother, mother!

GINA: See what I mean? If you just give him time —

HJALMAR (*with a piece of paper*): Here it is.

HEDVIG: That? But that's just a piece of paper.

HJALMAR: It's the menu, Hedvig, the entire menu. Look here. It says "Menu." That means what you get to eat.

HEDVIG: Haven't you anything else for me?

HJALMAR: I tell you, I forgot all about it. But take my word for it: it's not such a great treat, all that rich food. You just sit down and read the menu, now, and I'll tell you later what the things taste like. Here you are, Hedvig.

HEDVIG (*swallowing her tears*): Thank you.

(*She sits down but doesn't read.* GINA *signals to her.* HJALMAR *notices.*)

HJALMAR (*pacing the floor*): It is really unbelievable all the things a father is supposed to keep in mind. And if he forgets the smallest item — ! Long faces right away. Oh well. One gets used to that, too. (*Stops by the stove where* OLD EKDAL *is sitting.*) Have you looked at them tonight, father?

EKDAL: I certainly have! She's in the basket!

HJALMAR: No! Really? In the basket? She is getting used to it then, I guess.

EKDAL: Didn't I tell you she would? But look, Hjalmar, there are still a few things —

HJALMAR: — improvements, yes, I know.

EKDAL: They've got to be done.

HJALMAR: Right. Let's talk about it now, father. Come over here to the sofa.

EKDAL: All right. H'm. Guess I want to fill my pipe first, though. Need to clean it, too — h'm — (*Goes into his room.*)

GINA (*with a smile, to* HJALMAR): Cleaning his pipe —

HJALMAR: Oh well, Gina — let him. The poor shipwrecked old man. — About those improvements — We'd better get to them tomorrow.

GINA: You won't have time tomorrow, Ekdal.

HEDVIG (*interrupting*): Oh, yes, mother.

GINA: For remember those prints you were going to retouch? They came for 'em again today.

HJALMAR: I see. It's those prints again, is it? Well, they'll get done. You can be sure of that. Perhaps there are some new orders come in, too?

GINA: Not a thing, worse luck. Tomorrow I've got only those two portraits I told you about.

HJALMAR: Is that all? Well, if one doesn't exert oneself, what can you expect?

GINA: But what can I do? I advertise in the papers all I can, seems to me.

HJALMAR: The papers, the papers — you see yourself how far that gets us. I suppose there hasn't been anyone to look at the room, either?

GINA: No, not yet.

HJALMAR: Just as I thought. Well, no — if one doesn't *do* anything — One has to make a real effort, Gina!

HEDVIG (*going to him*): Shall I get your flute, father?

HJALMAR: No, not the flute. *I* need no pleasures. (*Paces up and down.*) You'll see if I don't work tomorrow! You don't need to worry about *that!* You can be sure I shall work as long as my strength holds out —

GINA: But Ekdal, dear — I didn't mean it that way.

HEDVIG: How about a bottle of beer, father?

HJALMAR: Not at all. I don't need anything — (*Stops.*) Beer? Did you say beer?

HEDVIG (*brightly*): Yes, father; lovely, cool beer.

HJALMAR: Oh well — all right — since you insist, I suppose you may bring me a bottle.

GINA: Yes, do that. That'll be nice and cozy.

(HEDVIG *runs towards the kitchen door.*)

HJALMAR (*by the stove, stops her, looks at her, takes her by the head and presses her to him*): Hedvig! Hedvig!

HEDVIG (*happy, in tears*): Oh father! You are so sweet and good!

HJALMAR: No, no, don't say that. There I was — seated at the rich man's table — gorging myself on his ample fare — and I couldn't even remember —

GINA (*seated by the table*): Nonsense, Ekdal.

HJALMAR: It is not nonsense. But you must not reckon too strictly. You know I love you, regardless.

HEDVIG (*throwing her arms around him*): And we love you, father, so much, so much!

HJALMAR: And if I am unreasonable at times, remember — God forgive me — remember I am a man beset by a host of sorrows. Well, well! (*Drying his eyes.*) No beer at such a moment. Give me my flute.

(HEDVIG *runs to the shelf and fetches it.*)

HJALMAR: Thank you. There now. With my flute in my hand and you two around me — ah!

(HEDVIG *sits down by the table next to* GINA. HJALMAR *walks back and forth, playing a Bohemian folk dance. He plays loudly but in slow tempo and with pronounced sentiment.*)

HJALMAR (*interrupts his playing, gives his left hand to* GINA, *and says with strong emotion*): Our home may be mean and humble, Gina. But it is our home. And I say to you both: here dwells contentment!

(*He resumes his playing. Presently there is a knock on the door.*)

GINA (*getting up*): Shh, Ekdal. I think somebody's coming.

HJALMAR (*putting the flute back on the shelf*): Yes, yes of course. Somebody would —

(GINA *goes to open the door.*)

GREGERS WERLE (*out in the hall*): I beg your pardon —

GINA (*taking a step back*): Oh!

GREGERS: — isn't this where Mr. Ekdal lives, the photographer?

GINA: Yes, it is.

HJALMAR (*going to the door*): Gregers! So you did come, after all. Come in.

GREGERS (*entering*): I told you I wanted to see you.

HJALMAR: But tonight — ? Have you left the party?

GREGERS: Both party and home. Good evening, Mrs. Ekdal. I don't know if you recognize me.

GINA: Oh yes. Young Mr. Werle isn't hard to recognize.

GREGERS: No, for I look like my mother, and you remember her, I am sure.

HJALMAR: You have left your home?

GREGERS: Yes. I have taken a room at a hotel.

HJALMAR: Really? — Well, since you're here, take off your coat and sit down.

GREGERS: Thanks. (*Removes his overcoat. He has changed clothes and is now dressed in a plain, gray suit, of somewhat unfashionable cut.*)

HJALMAR: Here on the sofa. Make yourself comfortable.

(GREGERS *sits down on the sofa,* HJALMAR *on a chair by the table.*)

GREGERS (*looking around*): So this is your residence, Hjalmar. This is where you live.

HJALMAR: This is the studio, as you can see.

GINA: It's roomier in here, so this is where we mostly keep ourselves.

HJALMAR: The apartment we had before was really nicer than this, but there is one big advantage here: we have plenty of space.

GINA: And we have a room across the hallway that we're renting out.

GREGERS (*to* HJALMAR): You have lodgers, too?

HJALMAR: No, not yet. These things take time, you see. One has to be on the lookout. (*To* HEDVIG.) What about that beer?

(HEDVIG *nods her head and goes out into the kitchen.*)

GREGERS: So that's your daughter.

HJALMAR: Yes, that's Hedvig.

GREGERS: Your only child, isn't she?

HJALMAR: Our only one. Our greatest joy in the world, and (*lowers his voice*) our greatest sorrow, as well.

GREGERS: What are you saying!

HJALMAR: Yes, Gregers, for there is every probability that she'll lose her sight.

GREGERS: Becoming blind!

HJALMAR: Yes. So far, there are only early symptoms, and things may be well with her for some time yet. But the doctor has warned us. It is coming, irresistibly.

GREGERS: But this is nothing less than a tragedy! How do you account for it?

HJALMAR (*with a sigh*): Heredity, most likely.

GREGERS (*struck*): Heredity?

GINA: Ekdal's mother had weak eyes.

HJALMAR: That's what father says. I of course don't remember her.

GREGERS: Poor child. How does she take it?

HJALMAR: Oh, we can't bring ourselves to tell her — I'm sure you can understand that. She suspects nothing. Joyous and carefree, chirping like a little bird, she'll flutter into life's endless night. (*Overcome by emotion.*) Oh Gregers, this is such a terrible burden for me.

(HEDVIG *enters with a tray with beer and glasses. She puts it down on the table.*)

HJALMAR (*stroking her hair*): Thanks. Thank you, Hedvig.

HEDVIG (*puts her arms around his neck and whispers something in his ear.*)

HJALMAR: No. No sandwiches now. (*Looks off.*) That is — unless Gregers wants some?

GREGERS (*with a gesture of refusal*): No. No thanks.

HJALMAR (*still in a melancholic mood*): Oh well, you might as well bring in some, all the same. A crust, if you have one. And plenty of butter, please.

GREGERS (*who has followed her with his eyes*): Otherwise she seems healthy enough.

HJALMAR: Yes, thank God, there is nothing else wrong with her.

GREGERS: I think she is going to look like you, Mrs. Ekdal. How old is she?

GINA: Hedvig is just about fourteen. Her birthday is day after tomorrow.

GREGERS: Quite big for her age, isn't she?

GINA: Yes, she has grown a lot lately.

GREGERS: It's by the children we tell we're growing older ourselves. How long have you two been married now?

GINA: We've been married for — let's see — fifteen years, pretty near.

GREGERS: Just imagine! Has it really been that long?

GINA (*taking notice, looks at him*): It certainly has.

HJALMAR: That's right. Fifteen years, less a few months. (*Changing topic.*) Those must have been long years for you up there at the works, Gregers.

GREGERS: They were long while they lasted. Now afterwards I hardly know where they went.

(OLD EKDAL *enters from his room, without his pipe, but with his old-fashioned lieutenant's cap on his head. His walk is a trifle unsteady.*)

EKDAL: I'm ready for you now, Hjalmar. Let's talk about this — h'm — What was it again?

HJALMAR (*going towards him*): Father, there's someone here. Gregers Werle. I don't know if you remember him?

EKDAL (*looks at* GREGERS, *who has stood up*): Werle? That's the son, isn't it? What does he want from me?

HJALMAR: Nothing. He has come to see me.

EKDAL: Then there's nothing wrong?

HJALMAR: Of course not.

EKDAL (*swinging one arm back and forth*): Not that I am scared, mind you, but —

GREGERS (*goes up to him*): I just wanted to bring you greetings from your old hunting grounds, Lieutenant Ekdal.

EKDAL: Hunting grounds?

GREGERS: Yes, the woods up around the Høydal works.

EKDAL: Oh yes, up there. Yes, I used to know that country quite well in the old days.

GREGERS: You were quite a hunter then, weren't you?

EKDAL: Could be. Maybe I was. You're looking at my get-up. I don't ask anybody's permission to wear it in the house. Just as long as I don't go outside —

(HEDVIG *brings a plate with open-faced sandwiches, which she puts down on the table.*)

HJALMAR: You sit down, father, and have a glass of beer. Help yourself, Gregers.

(EKDAL *mutters something and shuffles over to the sofa.* GREGERS *sits down on a chair next to him;* HJALMAR *is on the other side of* GREGERS. GINA *sits some distance from the table, sewing.* HEDVIG *is standing by her father.*)

GREGERS: Do you remember, Lieutenant Ekdal, when Hjalmar and I used to come up and visit you summers and Christmas?

EKDAL: You did? No; can't say as I do. But it's true I used to be a good hunter, if I do say so myself. I've killed bears, too. Nine of 'em.

GREGERS (*looks at him with compassion*): And now your hunting days are over.

EKDAL: Oh — I wouldn't say that. I still go hunting once in a while. Well, yes, not in the old way, of course. For you see, the woods — the woods — the woods —! (*Drinks.*) Nice-looking woods up there now?

GREGERS: Not as in your time. They have cut a great deal.

EKDAL: Cut? (*In a lower voice and as if afraid.*) That's risky business, that is. It has consequences. The woods are vengeful.

HJALMAR (*filling his glass*): Here, father. Have some more.

GREGERS: How can a man like you — such an outdoors man as you used to be — how can you stand living here in the middle of a musty city, within four walls?

EKDAL (*chuckles, glancing at* HJALMAR): Oh, it's not so bad here. Not bad at all.

GREGERS: But surely — all the things your soul grew used to up there — ? The cool, invigorating breezes? The free life in woods and mountains, among beasts and birds — ?

EKDAL (*smiling*): Hjalmar, shall we show it to him?

HJALMAR (*quickly, a little embarrassed*): Oh no, father. Not tonight.

GREGERS: What is it he wants to show me?

HJALMAR: Oh, it's just — something. You can see it some other time.

GREGERS (*continues addressing* OLD EKDAL): You see, this is what I had in mind, Lieutenant. Why don't you come up to Høydal with me? I'll probably be going back shortly. I'm sure you could get some copying work to do up there as well. For down here you can't have a thing to cheer you up and keep you occupied.

EKDAL (*looks at him in astonishment*): Don't I have —!

GREGERS: Yes, of course, you have Hjalmar. But then he has his own family. And a man like you, who have always loved the outdoors —

EKDAL (*striking the table*): Hjalmar, he *shall* see it!

HJALMAR: But father, do you really think so? It's dark and —

EKDAL: Nonsense. There's a moon. (*Getting up.*) I say he's got to see it. Let me out. Come and help me, Hjalmar!

HEDVIG: Oh yes, father! Do!

HJALMAR (*getting up*): Oh well, all right.

GREGERS (*to* GINA): What is it?

GINA: Oh, don't expect anything much.

(EKDAL *and* HJALMAR *have gone to the rear of the room. Each of them slides one of the double doors back.* HEDVIG *is helping the old man.* GREGERS *remains standing by the sofa.* GINA *keeps on sewing, paying no attention. Through the opened doors can be seen a big, elongated, irregular-shaped attic, with nooks and corners and a couple of chimneys standing free from the wall. Moonlight falls through several skylights, illuminating some parts of the room, while others are in deep shadow.*)

EKDAL (*to* GREGERS): You are welcome to come closer, sir.

GREGERS (*goes up to them*): What is this really?

EKDAL: See for yourself. H'm.

HJALMAR (*somewhat embarrassed*): This is all father's, you understand.

GREGERS (*at the door, peering into the attic*): Do you keep chickens, Lieutenant?

EKDAL: Should say we do. They're roosting now. But you ought to see those chickens in daylight!

HEDVIG: And there is —

EKDAL: Hush, don't say anything yet.

GREGERS: And I see you've got pigeons, too.

EKDAL: Could be we have. We've got pigeons, all right! The roosts are up on the rafters, for pigeons like to be up high, you know.

HJALMAR: They aren't all of them just ordinary pigeons.

EKDAL: Ordinary! I should say not! We've got tumblers and even a couple of pouters. But come over here. Do you see that pen over by the wall?

GREGERS: Yes. What do you use that for?

EKDAL: That's where the rabbits are at night.

GREGERS: Oh? You have rabbits, too, do you?

EKDAL: Damn right we have rabbits! He asks if we have rabbits, Hjalmar! H'm. But now we're coming to the *real* thing. Here we are. Move, Hedvig. You stand here and look down — there; that's right. Now, do you see a basket with straw in it?

GREGERS: Yes, I do. And I see a bird.

EKDAL: H'm — A "bird."

GREGERS: Isn't it a duck?

EKDAL (*offended*): I'd say it's a duck!

HJALMAR: But what kind of duck, do you think?

HEDVIG: It's not just an ordinary duck.

EKDAL: Hush!

GREGERS: And it's not a muscovy duck, either.

EKDAL: No, Mr. — Werle; it's not a muscovy, for it's a wild duck!

GREGERS: Is it really? A wild duck?

EKDAL: That's what it is. The — "bird," as you called it. A wild duck.
It's our wild duck.

HEDVIG: *My* wild duck. For it belongs to me.

GREGERS: And it lives here in the attic? It's thriving?

EKDAL: What's so odd about that? She's got a big pail of water to
splash around in.

HJALMAR: Fresh water every other day.

GINA (*turning to* HJALMAR): Ekdal, please. I'm freezing.

EKDAL: H'm. All right; let's close up. Just as well not to disturb their
night's rest, anyway. Help me Hedvig.

(HJALMAR *and* HEDVIG *slide the double doors shut.*)

EKDAL: You can have a good look at her some other time. (*Sits down
in the armchair by the stove.*) I'm telling you, they are strange birds,
those wild ducks.

GREGERS: But how did you ever catch it, Lieutenant?

EKDAL: I didn't. There's a certain man in this town we can thank for
her.

GREGERS (*struck by a thought*): Would that man be my father?

EKDAL: Indeed it is. It's your father, sure enough. H'm.

HJALMAR: Funny you'd guess that, Gregers.

GREGERS: You told me before that you owed a great deal to my father,
so I thought that perhaps —

GINA: But we didn't get the duck from Werle himself.

EKDAL: It's Håkon Werle we have to thank for her all the same, Gina.
(*To* GREGERS.) He was out in a boat, see, and took a shot at her.
But he doesn't see so well, your father doesn't. H'm. Anyway, she
was only wounded.

GREGERS: I see. She got some buckshot in her.

HJALMAR: Yes. A little.

HEDVIG: Right under the wing, so she couldn't fly.

GREGERS: Then she went to the bottom, I suppose.

EKDAL (*sleepily, his voice muffled*): So it did. Always do that, wild
ducks. Dive straight to the bottom — far as they can, sir. Bite them-

selves fast in the grasses and roots and weeds and all the other damn stuff down there. And never come up again.

GREGERS: But, Lieutenant, *your* wild duck did.

EKDAL: He had such a wonderfully clever dog, your father. And that dog — it went down and got the duck up.

GREGERS (*to* HJALMAR): And so it came to you?

HJALMAR: Not right away. First your father took it home with him, but it didn't seem to get on too well there, and then he told Pettersen to get rid of it.

EKDAL (*half asleep*): H'm — Pettersen — Ass —

HJALMAR: That's how we got it, for father knows Pettersen a little, and when he heard about the wild duck, he asked Pettersen to give it to him.

GREGERS: And now it seems perfectly contented in there in the attic.

HJALMAR: Yes, you would hardly believe how well it gets on. It's becoming fat. I think perhaps it's been in there so long that it has forgotten what wild life is like. And that makes all the difference.

GREGERS: I am sure you are right, Hjalmar. The thing to do is never to let it look at sea and sky again. — But I don't think I should stay any longer. I believe your father is asleep.

HJALMAR: Oh, as far as that is concerned —

GREGERS: Oh yes, one thing more. You said you had a room for rent? A vacant room?

HJALMAR: We do. What of it? Do you know anyone who — ?

GREGERS: Could I get it?

HJALMAR: You?

GINA: Oh, Mr. Werle, I'm sure *you* don't want to —

GREGERS: Couldn't I have it? If I can, I'll move in first thing in the morning.

HJALMAR: Yes, indeed, with the greatest pleasure.

GINA: No, but Mr. Werle, that's not a room for you.

HJALMAR: Gina! How can you say that?

GINA: It's not large enough or light enough, and —

GREGERS: That doesn't matter, Mrs. Ekdal.

HJALMAR: I think it's quite a nice room myself, and decently furnished, too.

GINA: But remember those two downstairs.

GREGERS: Who are they?

GINA: There's one who used to be a private tutor.

HJALMAR: Molvik is his name. He studied to be a minister once.

GINA: And then there's a doctor, name of Relling.

GREGERS: Relling? I know him slightly. He used to practice up at Høydal.

GINA: They are a couple of real wild characters those two. Out all hours of the night, and when they come home they aren't always — y'know —

GREGERS: One gets used to that sort of thing. I hope I'll be like the wild duck.

GINA: H'm. Well, I think you ought to sleep on it first.

GREGERS: I take it you don't really want me in the house, Mrs. Ekdal.

GINA: Good Lord! How can you say a thing like that?

HJALMAR: Yes, Gina. It really does seem very odd of you. (*To* GREGERS.) Does this mean you'll be staying in town for a while?

GREGERS (*putting on his overcoat*): Yes, I think I'll stay.

HJALMAR: But not with your father? What do you intend to do?

GREGERS: If I knew that, Hjalmar, I'd be much better off. But when you're cursed with a name like "Gregers" — and then "Werle" after that — Did you ever hear of an uglier name?

HJALMAR: I don't think it's ugly at all.

GREGERS: Ugh! I feel like spitting in the face of anybody with a name like that. But since it's my cross in life to be Gregers Werle, such as I am —

HJALMAR: Ha-ha! If you weren't Gregers Werle, what would you like to be?

GREGERS: If I could choose, I'd like to be a really clever dog.

GINA: A dog!

HEDVIG (*involuntarily*): Oh no!

GREGERS: Yes, an exceptionally skillful dog — the kind that goes down to the bottom after wild ducks when they've dived down among the weeds and the grass down there in the mud.

HJALMAR: Honestly, Gregers. This makes no sense whatever.

GREGERS: I suppose it doesn't. But tomorrow morning, then, I'll be moving in. (*To* GINA.) You won't have any trouble with me; I'll do everything myself. (*To* HJALMAR.) The other things we can talk about tomorrow. — Goodnight, Mrs. Ekdal. (*Nods to* HEDVIG.) Goodnight!

GINA: Goodnight, Mr. Werle.

HEDVIG: Goodnight.

HJALMAR (*who has lighted a candle*): Wait a moment. I'll see you down. I'm sure it's all dark on the stairs.

(GREGERS *and* HJALMAR *go out through the entrance door, right rear.*)

GINA (*staring ahead, her sewing lowered in her lap*): Wasn't it funny all that talk about wanting to be a dog?

HEDVIG: Do you know, mother — I think he really meant something else.

GINA: What would that be?

HEDVIG: No, I couldn't say, but it was just like he had something else in mind all the time.

GINA: You think so? It sure was funny, though.

HJALMAR (*returning*): The lamp was still burning. (*Blows out the candle and sits down.*) Ah, at last it's possible to get a bite to eat. (*Starts on the sandwiches.*) Now do you see what I mean, Gina — about seizing the opportunity?

GINA: What opportunity?

HJALMAR: Well — it was lucky, wasn't it, that we got the room rented? And then to somebody like Gregers, a dear old friend.

GINA: Well, I don't know what to say to that.

HEDVIG: Oh mother, you'll see it will be fun.

HJALMAR: I must say you are strange. First you wanted nothing more than to get a lodger; then when we do, you don't like it.

GINA: I know, Ekdal. If only it had been somebody else. What do you think old Werle will say?

HJALMAR: He? It's none of his business.

GINA: But don't you see that something's bound to be wrong between the two of 'em, since the young one is moving out. Sure you know how those two are.

HJALMAR: That may be so, but —

GINA: And maybe Werle will think you are behind it!

HJALMAR: All right! Let him think that. Oh, by all means, Werle has done a great deal for me — I'm the first to admit it. But that doesn't mean I everlastingly have to let him run my life.

GINA: But Ekdal, dear, it could hurt Grandpa. Perhaps he'll lose what little he's making from working for Gråberg.

HJALMAR: I almost wish he would! Is it not humiliating for a man like me to see his gray-haired father treated like dirt? Ah, but soon now the time will be ripe. I feel it. (*Takes another sandwich.*) As sure as I have a mission in life, it shall be accomplished!

HEDVIG: Oh yes, father!

GINA: Shhh! Don't wake him up.

HJALMAR (*in a lower voice*): I say it again: I *will* accomplish it! The day will come, when — That's why it's such a good thing we got the room rented out, for that makes me more independent. And that's necessary for a man with a mission in life. (*Over by the armchair, with feeling.*) Poor old white-haired father. Trust your Hjalmar. He has broad enough shoulders — powerful shoulders, at any rate. Some day you'll wake up, and — (*to* GINA.) Or don't you believe that?

GINA (*getting up*): Sure I do, but let's first get him to bed.
HJALMAR: Yes, let us.

(*They tenderly lift the old man.*)

ACT III

(*The studio. It is morning. Daylight comes in through the sky-light, the blue cloth having been pulled aside.*

HJALMAR *sits at the table, retouching a photograph. Several other photographs are lying in front of him. After a while,* GINA, *in coat and hat, enters from outside. She is carrying a covered basket.*)

HJALMAR: Back already, Gina?
GINA: Yes. I'm in a hurry. (*Puts the basket down on a chair and takes off her coat and hat.*)
HJALMAR: Did you look in at Gregers's?
GINA: I did. It looks real nice in there. He fixed up the place real pretty, soon as he moved in.
HJALMAR: Oh?
GINA: Remember, he was to take care of everything himself? Well, he built a fire in the stove, but he hadn't opened the flue, so the whole room got filled with smoke. Phew! It smelled like —
HJALMAR: Oh dear —
GINA: Then do you know what he does? This really beats everything. He wanted to put out the fire, so he pours the water from the wash basin into the stove. The whole floor is sloppy with filth!
HJALMAR: I am sorry.
GINA: I've got the janitor's wife to clean up after him, pig as he is, but the room can't be lived in till this afternoon.
HJALMAR: Where is he now?
GINA: He said he was going out for a while.
HJALMAR: I went in there for a moment, too — right after you had left.
GINA: He told me. You've asked him for breakfast.
HJALMAR: Just a bit of a late morning meal. It's the first day and all. We can hardly do less. I am sure you have something.
GINA: I'll have to find something, at any rate.
HJALMAR: Be sure it's plenty, though. I think Relling and Molvik are coming, too. I ran into Relling on the stairs just now, and so of course I had to —

GINA: So we are to have those two as well.

HJALMAR: Good heavens, one or two more or less — can that make any difference?

EKDAL (*opens his door and looks in*): Listen, Hjalmar — (*Sees* GINA.) Well, never mind.

GINA: Do you want something, Grandpa?

EKDAL: No. It doesn't matter. H'm! (*Goes back inside his room.*)

GINA (*picking up her basket*): Make sure he doesn't go out.

HJALMAR: Yes, I will. — Say, Gina — how about some herring salad? I believe Relling and Molvik made a night of it again last night.

GINA: If only they don't get here too soon.

HJALMAR: I'm sure they won't. Just take your time.

GINA: Well, all right. Then you can work some in the meantime.

HJALMAR: I *am* working! I'm working as hard as I can!

GINA: All I mean is you'd have it out of the way for later. (*Goes into the kitchen.*)

(HJALMAR *picks up the photograph and the brush and works for a while — slowly and with evident distaste.*)

EKDAL (*peeks in, looks around, says in a low voice*): Pst! Are you busy?

HJALMAR: Yes. I am struggling with these everlasting pictures —

EKDAL: All right, all right. If you're busy, then you're busy. H'm! (*Goes back inside his room. The door remains open.*)

HJALMAR (*works in silence for a while, puts his brush down, walks over to* EKDAL's *door*): Are *you* busy, father?

EKDAL (*grumbling inside his room*): When *you* are busy, *I* am busy! H'm!

HJALMAR: Oh all right. (*Returns to his work.*)

EKDAL (*appears in his door again after a while*): H'm, Hjalmar, listen — I'm not so *terribly* busy, you know.

HJALMAR: I thought you were writing.

EKDAL: Dammit all! Can't that Gråberg wait a day or two? Didn't think it was a matter of life and death.

HJALMAR: Of course not. And you aren't a slave, after all.

EKDAL: And there is this other job in there —

HJALMAR: Just what I was thinking. Do you want to go in there now? Shall I open the door for you?

EKDAL: Good idea.

HJALMAR (*getting up*): Then we'd have that job out of the way.

EKDAL: Exactly. It has to be ready for tomorrow, anyway. It *is* tomorrow, isn't it?

HJALMAR: Sure it's tomorrow.

(They slide the double doors open. The morning sun is shining through the skylight. Some pigeons are flying around; others are cooing on their perches. From farther inside the room the chickens are heard clucking once in a while.)

HJALMAR: All right, father. Guess you can go ahead.

EKDAL *(entering the attic)*: Aren't you coming?

HJALMAR: Yes, do you know — I almost think I will. *(Notices GINA in the kitchen door.)* I? No, I don't have the time. I have to work. But then there is this thing —

(He pulls a cord. A curtain comes down from within the attic. Its lower part is made out of a strip of old sailcloth; its upper part is a piece of stretched-out fish net. The attic floor is now no longer visible.)

HJALMAR *(returns to the table)*: Now! Maybe I can have peace for a few minutes.

GINA: Is he fooling around in there again?

HJALMAR: Would you rather he went down to Madam Eriksen? *(Sitting down.)* Do you want anything? I thought you said —

GINA: I just wanted to ask you if you think we can set the table in here?

HJALMAR: Yes. There aren't any appointments this early, are there?

GINA: No — only those two sweethearts who want their picture taken.

HJALMAR: Damn! Couldn't they come some other time!

GINA: Goodness, Ekdal, they'll be here after dinner, when you're asleep.

HJALMAR: Oh, in that case it's all right. Yes, let's eat in here.

GINA: Fine. But there's no hurry with the table. You're welcome to use it some more.

HJALMAR: Can't you see I *am* using it?

GINA: Then you'll be all done for afterwards, you know. *(Goes into the kitchen.)*

(Brief silence.)

EKDAL *(in the door to the attic, inside the fish net)*: Hjalmar!

HJALMAR: What?

EKDAL: Afraid we'll have to move the pail, after all.

HJALMAR: What else have I been saying all along?

EKDAL: H'm — h'm — h'm! *(Disappears inside again.)*

HJALMAR *(keeps on working for a moment, glances over towards the attic, half rises, as HEDVIG enters from the kitchen. He quickly sits down again)*: What do you want?

HEDVIG: Just to be with you, father.

HJALMAR (*after a short while*): Seems to me like you're snooping around. Have you been told to watch me, perhaps?

HEDVIG: No, of course not.

HJALMAR: What is mother doing?

HEDVIG: Mother is in the middle of the herring salad. (*Comes over to the table.*) Isn't there any little thing I can help you with, father?

HJALMAR: Oh no. It is better I do it all alone — as long as my strength lasts. There is no need for you to worry about anything, Hedvig, as long as your father is allowed to keep his health.

HEDVIG: Oh father. I won't have you talk that horrid way. (*She walks around a bit, stops by the opening to the inner room and looks in.*)

HJALMAR: What is he doing in there?

HEDVIG: Looks like a new ladder up to the water pail.

HJALMAR: He'll never manage that by himself! And here I am condemned to sit — !

HEDVIG (*goes to him*): Give me the brush, father. I can do it.

HJALMAR: I won't hear of it. You'll just be ruining your eyes.

HEDVIG: No, I won't. Give me the brush.

HJALMAR (*getting up*): It would only be for a minute or two —

HEDVIG: What possible harm could that do? (*Takes the brush.*) There now. (*Sits down.*) And here is one I can use as model.

HJALMAR: But don't ruin your eyes! Do you hear me? I will not take the responsibility. It's all yours. I'm just telling you.

HEDVIG (*working*): Yes, of course.

HJALMAR: You are really very good at it, Hedvig. It will only be for a few minutes, you understand.

(*He slips into the attic by the edge of the curtain.* HEDVIG *keeps on working.* HJALMAR *and* EKDAL *can be heard talking behind the curtain.*)

HJALMAR (*appearing inside the net*): Hedvig, please give me the pliers on the shelf. And the chisel. (*Turns around.*) See here, father. Just let me show you what I have in mind first.

(HEDVIG *fetches the tools from the shelf and gives them to him.*)

HJALMAR: Thank you. It was a good thing I went in.

(*He leaves the doorway. Sounds of carpentering and conversation are heard from inside.* HEDVIG *remains watching them. After a while there is a knock on the entrance door. She does not notice.*)

GREGERS (*bareheaded and coatless, enters, stops near the door*): H'm!

HEDVIG (*turns around and walks towards him*): Good morning! Won't you please come in?

GREGERS: Thank you. (*Looks towards the attic.*) You seem to have workmen in the house.

HEDVIG: Oh no. It's just father and Grandpa. I'll tell them you're here.

GREGERS: Please don't. I'd rather wait a while. (*Sits down on the sofa.*)

HEDVIG: It's such a mess in here — (*Begins removing the photographs.*)

GREGERS: Never mind. Are they pictures you are retouching?

HEDVIG: Yes. It is something I help father with.

GREGERS: I hope you won't let me disturb you.

HEDVIG: I won't.

(*She moves the things more within her reach and resumes work.* GREGERS *watches her in silence.*)

GREGERS: Did the wild duck sleep well last night?

HEDVIG: Yes, thank you. I think so.

GREGERS (*turning towards the attic*): In daylight it looks quite different from last night when there was a moon.

HEDVIG: Yes, it varies so. In the morning it looks different than in the afternoon, and when it rains it looks different than when the sun is shining.

GREGERS: You have noticed that?

HEDVIG: Yes, of course.

GREGERS: Do you too spend much time with the wild duck?

HEDVIG: Yes, when I can.

GREGERS: I suppose you don't have much spare time, though. You are going to school, of course?

HEDVIG: Not any more. Father is afraid I'll ruin my eyes.

GREGERS: Then he reads with you himself?

HEDVIG: He has promised to, but he hasn't had the time yet.

GREGERS: But isn't there anyone else who can help you?

HEDVIG: Well, yes, there is Mr. Molvik, but he isn't always — you know — quite —

GREGERS: You mean he is drunk sometimes.

HEDVIG: I think so.

GREGERS: Well, in that case you have time for many things. And in there, I suppose, it's like a world all its own?

HEDVIG: Yes, quite. And there are so many strange things in there.

GREGERS: There are?

HEDVIG: Yes, there are big closets with books in them, and in many of the books there are pictures.

GREGERS: I see.

HEDVIG: And there is an old desk with drawers and drop-down leaves and a big clock with figures that come out. But the clock doesn't run any more.

GREGERS: So time has stopped in there where the wild duck lives?

HEDVIG: Yes. And there are old coloring sets and that sort of thing, and then all the books.

GREGERS: I expect you read the books.

HEDVIG: Yes, whenever I have a chance. But most of them are in English and I can't read that. But I look at the pictures. There is a great, big book that's called "Harrison's History of London." I think it is a hundred years old. There are ever so many pictures in it. In front it shows a picture of Death with an hourglass and a girl. I think that is horrible. But then there are all the pictures of churches and castles and streets and big ships that sail the seas.

GREGERS: Tell me — where do all those strange things come from?

HEDVIG: There was an old sea captain who used to live here. He brought them home. They called him The Flying Dutchman. And that's odd, I think, for he wasn't a Dutchman at all.

GREGERS: No?

HEDVIG: No. But finally he disappeared at sea, and all the things were left here.

GREGERS: Listen — when you sit in there looking at the pictures, don't you ever want to travel and see the real, big world for yourself?

HEDVIG: Oh no. I want to stay here at home always and help father and mother.

GREGERS: With the photographs?

HEDVIG: Not just with that. Best of all I'd like to learn how to engrave pictures like those in the English books.

GREGERS: H'm. And what does your father say to that?

HEDVIG: I don't think father likes the idea very much. He is funny about things like that. You know, he says I ought to learn basket-weaving and straw-plaiting. But I don't think that sounds like much of anything at all.

GREGERS: No, I don't think it does either.

HEDVIG: Though of course father is quite right in saying that if I had learned basket-weaving I could have made the new basket for the wild duck.

GREGERS: That's true. And that really ought to have been your job, you know.

HEDVIG: Yes. Because it is my wild duck.

GREGERS: So I hear.

HEDVIG: Oh yes. I own it. But father and Grandpa get to borrow it as often as they like.

GREGERS: So? And what do they do with it?

HEDVIG: Oh — they take care of it and build things for it and that sort of thing.

GREGERS: I see. For of course the wild duck is the noblest of all the animals in there.

HEDVIG: Yes, she is, for she is a real, wild bird. And then I feel sorrier for her than for any of the others, because she's all alone, poor thing.

GREGERS: No family, like the rabbits.

HEDVIG: No. And the chickens, they have so many they were little chicks together with. But she is all alone, with none of her own near by. And there is the strange thing about the wild duck. Nobody knows her and nobody knows where she is from.

GREGERS: And she has been down to the depths of the sea.

HEDVIG (*glances quickly at him, suppresses a smile, asks*): Why do you say "the depths of the sea"?

GREGERS: What should I say?

HEDVIG: You could say "the sea bottom" or "the bottom of the sea."

GREGERS: Can't I just as well say "the depths of the sea"?

HEDVIG: Yes, but I think it sounds so strange when other people say "the depths of the sea."

GREGERS: Why is that? Tell me.

HEDVIG: No, I won't, for it is so silly.

GREGERS: I don't think so. Please tell me why you smiled.

HEDVIG: It's because every time I think of what's in there — when it comes into my head all of a sudden, I mean — I always feel that the whole room and everything that's in it are the depths of the sea. But that's silly.

GREGERS: Don't say that.

HEDVIG: Yes, for it's just an old attic, you know.

GREGERS (*looking intently at her*): Are you sure?

HEDVIG (*surprised*): That it's an attic?

GREGERS: Yes. Are you sure it is?

(HEDVIG *stares at him in silence, her mouth open in astonishment.* GINA *enters from the kitchen with linen, silverware, etc., to set the table.*)

GREGERS (*getting up*): I am afraid I am too early for you.

GINA: Oh well. You have to be somewhere. Things are almost ready now, anyway. Clear the table, Hedvig.

(*During the next scene* HEDVIG *clears the table and* GINA *sets it.* GREGERS *seats himself in the armchair and starts leafing through an album of photographs.*)

GREGERS: I understand you know how to retouch, Mrs. Ekdal.

GINA (*looks at him out of the corner of her eye*): That's right.

GREGERS: That was fortunate.

GINA: How — fortunate?

GREGERS: I mean since Ekdal is a photographer.

HEDVIG: Mother knows how to take pictures, too.

GINA: Oh yes, I've had to learn *that* business, all right.

GREGERS: Perhaps it is you who are responsible for the daily routine?

GINA: Yes, when Ekdal himself doesn't have the time —

GREGERS: I suppose he busies himself a great deal with his old father?

GINA: Yes, and then it's not for a man like Ekdal to waste his time taking pictures of everybody and his grandmother.

GREGERS: I quite agree, but since he did choose this as his profession, shouldn't he — ?

GINA: You know just as well as I do, Mr. Werle, that Ekdal isn't just one of your common, ordinary photographers.

GREGERS: Of course not, but — nevertheless —

(A *shot is heard from the attic.*)

GREGERS (*jumps up*): What was that?

GINA: Ugh! There they go, firing away again!

GREGERS: They shoot, too?

HEDVIG: They go hunting.

GREGERS: What? (*Over by the door to the attic.*) Do you go hunting, Hjalmar?

HJALMAR (*inside the curtain*): Have you arrived? I didn't know — I've been so busy — (*To* HEDVIG.) And you — not letting us know — ! (*Comes into the studio.*)

GREGERS: Do you go shooting in the attic?

HJALMAR (*showing him a double-barreled pistol*): Oh, it's only this old thing.

GINA: You and Grandpa are going to have an accident with that pestol of yours one of these days.

HJALMAR (*irritated*): I believe I have told you that this kind of firearm is called a pistol.

GINA: I don't see that that makes it any better.

GREGERS: So you have taken up hunting, too, Hjalmar?

HJALMAR: Only a little rabbit hunting now and then. It's mostly for father's sake, you understand.

GINA: Menfolks are strange. They always need something to diverge themselves with.

HJALMAR (*grimly*): That's right. We always need something to divert ourselves with.

GINA: That's exactly what I'm saying.

HJALMAR: Oh well — ! H'm! (*To* GREGERS.) Well, you see, we're fortunate in that the attic is situated so that nobody can hear the shots.

(*Puts the pistol on the top shelf.*) Don't touch the pistol, Hedvig! Remember, one barrel is loaded!

GREGERS (*peering through the net*): You have a hunting rifle, too, I see.

HJALMAR: That's father's old gun. It doesn't work any more. There's something wrong with the lock. But it's rather fun to have it around all the same, for we take it apart and clean it once in a while and grease it and put it back together again. It's mostly father, of course, who amuses himself with things like that.

HEDVIG (*standing next to* GREGERS): Now you can get a good look at the wild duck.

GREGERS: I was just looking at it. One wing is drooping a bit, isn't it?

HJALMAR: Well that's not so strange. She was hit, you know.

GREGERS: And she drags her foot a little. Or doesn't she?

HJALMAR: Perhaps a little bit.

HEDVIG: Yes, for that is the foot the dog seized her by.

HJALMAR: But aside from that she has no other hurt or defect, and that's really quite remarkable when you consider that she has a charge of buckshot in her and has been between the teeth of a dog.

GREGERS (*with a glance at* HEDVIG): Yes, and been to the depths of the sea — for so long.

HEDVIG (*smiles*): Yes.

GINA (*busy at the table*): Oh yes, that precious wild duck. There sure is enough circumstance made over it.

HJALMAR: H'm. Will you be done setting the table soon?

GINA: In a minute. Hedvig, I need your help. (GINA *and* HEDVIG *go into the kitchen.*)

HJALMAR (*in a low voice*): You had better not watch father. He doesn't like it.

GREGERS (*leaves the attic door.*)

HJALMAR: And I ought to close this before the others arrive. (*Shoos the birds away with his hands.*) Shoo! Shoo — you! (*Raising the curtain and sliding the doors back.*) This arrangement is my own invention. It is really quite amusing to fool around with these things and to fix them when they get broken. And it's absolutely necessary to have something like it, for Gina won't stand for rabbits and chickens in the studio.

GREGERS: No, I suppose not. And perhaps the studio is your wife's department?

HJALMAR: I generally leave the daily run of the business to her. That gives me a chance to retire into the living room and give my thoughts to more important things.

GREGERS: What things, Hjalmar?

HJALMAR: I have been wondering why you haven't asked me that before. Or maybe you haven't heard about the invention?

GREGERS: Invention? No.

HJALMAR: Really? You haven't? Oh well — up there in the woods and wilderness —

GREGERS: So you have invented something!

HJALMAR: Not quite yet, but I am working on it. As you can well imagine, when I decided to devote myself to photography it was not my intent to do nothing but take portraits of all sorts of ordinary people.

GREGERS: I suppose not. Your wife just said the same thing.

HJALMAR: I made a pledge to myself that if I were to give my powers to this profession, I would raise it so high that it would become both an art and a science. That is how I decided to make some remarkable invention.

GREGERS: What is it? What does it do?

HJALMAR: Well, Gregers, you must not ask for details just yet. You see, it takes time. And don't think I am driven by vanity. I can truthfully say I am not working for my own sake. Far from it. It is my life's mission that is in my thoughts night and day.

GREGERS: What mission?

HJALMAR: The old man with the silver hair — can you forget him?

GREGERS: Yes, your poor father. But what exactly do you think you can do for him?

HJALMAR: I can resurrect his respect for himself by once again raising the name of Ekdal to fame and honor.

GREGERS: So that is your life's mission.

HJALMAR: Yes. I will rescue that shipwrecked man. For he was shipwrecked the moment the storm broke. During those terrible inquiries he was not himself. The pistol over yonder — the one we use to shoot rabbits with — it has played its part in the tragedy of the Ekdal family.

GREGERS: The pistol? Really?

HJALMAR: When sentence had been pronounced and he was to be confined — he had that pistol in his hand —

GREGERS: He tried to — !

HJALMAR: Yes, but didn't dare. He was a coward. So much of a wreck, so spiritually ruined was he already then. Can you understand it? He, an officer, the killer of nine bears, descended from two lieutenant colonels — I mean one after the other, of course — Can you understand it, Gregers?

GREGERS: I can indeed.

HJALMAR: Not I. — But the pistol came to figure in our family chronicle a second time. When he had begun to wear the garb of gray and sat there behind bolt and bar — oh, those were terrible days for me, believe me. I kept the shades down on both windows. When I looked out, I saw the sun shining as usual. I saw people in the street laughing and talking about nothing. I could not understand it. It seemed to me that all of existence ought to come to a standstill, as during an eclipse of the sun.

GREGERS: I felt that way when mother died.

HJALMAR: In such an hour Hjalmar Ekdal turned the pistol against himself —

GREGERS: You too were thinking of — ?

HJALMAR: Yes.

GREGERS: But you did not pull the trigger?

HJALMAR: No. In the decisive moment I won a victory over myself. I remained alive. Take my word for it: it requires courage to go on living in a situation like that.

GREGERS: That depends on how you look at it.

HJALMAR: No, it doesn't. At any rate, it all turned out to be for the best. For soon now I will finish my invention, and when I do, Doctor Relling thinks, as I do myself, that father will be allowed to wear his uniform again. I shall claim that as my only reward.

GREGERS: So it is this business with the uniform that mostly —

HJALMAR: Yes, to be able to wear it again is what he dreams of and longs for. You have no idea how it cuts me to the quick to see him. Whenever we have a little family celebration here, like Gina's and my wedding anniversary or whatever it may be, then the old man appears in his lieutenant's uniform from happier days. But no sooner is there a knock on the door than he scuttles back to his own little room as fast as his old legs will carry him. He doesn't dare to show himself to strangers, you know. A sight like that lacerates a son's heart, Gregers!

GREGERS: About when do you think the invention will be ready?

HJALMAR: Heavens, you must not ask for details like that. An invention, you see, is something you don't altogether control yourself. It is very largely a matter of inspiration — a sudden idea — and it is next to impossible to tell beforehand when that may come.

GREGERS: But it is progressing?

HJALMAR: Certainly, it is progressing. It occupies my thoughts every day. It fills me. Every afternoon, after dinner, I shut myself up in the living room to ponder in peace. I just can't be hurried; it won't do any good. That is what Relling says, too.

GREGERS: And you don't think that all this business in the attic interferes too much, distracts you from your work?

HJALMAR: No, no, no. Quite the contrary. You must not say a thing like that. After all, I cannot everlastingly be pursuing the same exhausting train of thought. I need something else, something to occupy me during the waiting period. The inspiration, the sudden flash of insight, don't you see? — when it comes, it comes.

GREGERS: My dear Hjalmar, I almost think there is something of the wild duck in you.

HJALMAR: The wild duck? How do you mean?

GREGERS: You have plunged down through the sea and got yourself entangled in the grasses on the bottom.

HJALMAR: Are you perhaps referring to the well-nigh fatal shot that lodged in father's wing and hit me, too?

GREGERS: Not to that so much. I won't say you are crippled. But you are in a poisonous marsh, Hjalmar. You have contracted an insidious disease and gone to the bottom to die in the dark.

HJALMAR: I? Die in the dark? Honestly, Gregers. You really shouldn't say such things.

GREGERS: Don't you worry. I'll get you up again. For I, too, have got a mission in life. I found it yesterday.

HJALMAR: That may well be, but I shall ask you kindly to leave me out of it. I assure you that — aside from my easily explainable melancholia, of course — I am as contented a man as anybody could wish to be.

GREGERS: The fact that you are — that is one of the symptoms of the poisoning.

HJALMAR: No, really, Gregers. Please don't talk to me any more about disease and poison. I am not used to that sort of talk. In my house we never discuss unpleasant topics.

GREGERS: That I can well believe.

HJALMAR: No, for it isn't good for me. And there is no marshy air here, as you call it. The roof may be low in the poor photographer's home — I know very well it is — and my lot is lowly. But I am an inventor, and a provider as well. That is what raises me above my humble circumstances. — Ah! Here's lunch!

(GINA *and* HEDVIG *enter with bottles of beer, a decanter of brandy, glasses, and other appurtenances. At the same moment,* RELLING *and* MOLVIK *come through the entrance door. Neither one wears hat or coat.* MOLVIK *is dressed in black.*)

GINA (*putting the things down on the table*): Well, you two arrive just in time.

RELLING: Molvik thought he could smell herring salad, and then there was no holding him. — Good morning again, Ekdal.

HJALMAR: Gregers, may I introduce you to Mr. Molvik — And Doctor — that's right, you two already know each other, don't you.

GREGERS: Slightly.

RELLING: Oh yes, young Mr. Werle. We used to do some skirmishing up at the Høydal works. I take it you have just moved in?

GREGERS: This morning.

RELLING: Well, Molvik and I live downstairs, so you don't have far to go for doctor and minister if you need them.

GREGERS: Thank you; maybe I shall. We were thirteen at the table yesterday.

HJALMAR: Come now! Please don't start any of that unpleasantness again!

RELLING: Calm down, Ekdal. You are immune.

HJALMAR: I hope so, for my family's sake. — Sit down. Let's eat, drink, and be merry.

GREGERS: Aren't we going to wait for your father?

HJALMAR: No, he'll eat later in his own room. Do sit down!

(*The men seat themselves and begin eating and drinking.* GINA *and* HEDVIG *wait on them.*)

RELLING: Molvik got pretty high last night, Mrs. Ekdal.

GINA: Again?

RELLING: Didn't you hear me bring him home?

GINA: Can't say I did.

RELLING: That's good, for Molvik was awful last night.

GINA: Is that true, Molvik?

MOLVIK: Let us consign last night's events to oblivion. They do not represent my better self.

RELLING (*to* GREGERS): It comes over him like an irresistible impulse. Then he has to go out and get drunk. You see, Molvik is demonic.

GREGERS: Demonic?

RELLING: That's right. Molvik is demonic.

GREGERS: H'm.

RELLING: And demonic natures aren't made to follow the straight and narrow path. They have to take off for the fields once in a while. — So you still stick it out up at that filthy old place?

GREGERS: So far.

RELLING: Did you ever collect on that claim you went around presenting?

GREGERS: Claim? (*Looks at him and understands.*) Oh I see.

HJALMAR: Have you been a bill collector, Gregers?

GREGERS: Oh nonsense.

RELLING: Oh yes, he has. He went around to all the cottages up there, trying to collect on something he called "the claim of the ideal."

GREGERS: I was young.

RELLING: You're right. You were very young. And the claim of the ideal — you never collected as long as I was up there.

GREGERS: Not since then, either.

RELLING: In that case, I suppose you have been wise enough to reduce the amount somewhat.

GREGERS: Never when I have to do with a real and genuine human being.

HJALMAR: I think that is reasonable enough. — Some butter, Gina.

RELLING: And a piece of bacon for Molvik.

MOLVIK: Ugh! Not bacon!

(*There is a knock from inside the door to the attic.*)

HJALMAR: Go and open, Hedvig. Father wants to get out.

(HEDVIG *opens the door a little.* OLD EKDAL *enters with the skin of a freshly flayed rabbit.* HEDVIG *closes the door after him.*)

EKDAL: Good morning, gentlemen! Good hunting today. Got me a big one.

HJALMAR: And you skinned it yourself, I see.

EKDAL: Salted it, too. It's nice, tender meat, rabbit is. It's sweet, y'know. Tastes like sugar. Good appetite, gentlemen! (*Goes into his room.*)

MOLVIK (*getting up*): Excuse me — I can't — Got to get downstairs —

RELLING: Drink soda water, you idiot!

MOLVIK: Uh — Uh — (*Hurries out, right rear.*)

RELLING (*to* HJALMAR): Let us drink to the old hunter.

HJALMAR (*touching* RELLING's *glass with his own*): For the sportsman on the brink of the grave — yes.

RELLING: For the gray-haired — (*Drinks.*) Tell me, is his hair gray or is it white?

HJALMAR: In between, I think. Though I don't think there are many hairs left on his head at all.

RELLING: Oh well. One can live happily with a wig, too. Ah, yes, Ekdal. You are really a very happy man. You have this beautiful ambition of yours to strive for —

HJALMAR: Believe me, I am striving.

RELLING: Then you have your excellent wife, shuffling about in slippered feet with that comfortable waddle of hers, making things nice and pleasant for you.

HJALMAR: Yes, Gina — (*Nods to her.*) — you are a good companion on life's journey.

GINA: Aw, you don't need to sit there and dissectate me!

RELLING: And your Hedvig, Ekdal.

HJALMAR (*moved*): Ah yes, the child! The child above all. Hedvig, come to me. (*Stroking her hair.*) What day is tomorrow?

HEDVIG (*playfully shaking him*): Oh, stop it, father!

HJALMAR: It's like a knife through my heart, when I consider how little we can do. Just a small celebration here in the attic.

HEDVIG: But that's just the way I like it!

RELLING: You wait till the invention is all done, Hedvig.

HJALMAR: Yes! Then you'll see, Hedvig. I have decided to secure your future. You shall be made comfortable for as long as you live. I will ask for something for you, something or other. That will be the impecunious inventor's sole reward.

HEDVIG (*whispers, her arms around his neck*): Oh you good, sweet father!

RELLING (*to* GREGERS): Well, now, don't you think it's nice for a change to sit down to a good table in a happy family circle?

HJALMAR: Yes, I really relish these hours at the table.

GREGERS: I, for one, don't like to breathe marsh air.

RELLING: Marsh air?

HJALMAR: Oh, don't start all that again!

GINA: I'll have you know there is no marsh air here, Mr. Werle. The place is aired every single day.

GREGERS (*leaving the table*): The stench I have in mind you don't get rid of by opening windows.

HJALMAR: Stench!

GINA: Yes, how do you like that, Ekdal!

RELLING: Begging your pardon — it wouldn't by any chance be you yourself who bring the stench with you from the Høydal mines?

GREGERS: It's just like you to call stench what I bring to this house.

RELLING (*walks over to* GREGERS): Listen here, Mr. Werle junior. I strongly suspect that you still carry the claim of the ideal around in your rear pocket.

GREGERS: I carry it in my heart.

RELLING: I don't care where the hell you carry it as long as you don't go bill collecting here while *I* am around.

GREGERS: And if I do so, nevertheless?

RELLING: Then you'll go head first down the stairs. Now you know!

HJALMAR: No, really, Relling — !

GREGERS: Go ahead! Throw me out!

GINA (*interposing*): No, we won't have any of that, Relling. But I will say this to you, Mr. Werle, that it seems like you are not the right person to come here and talk about stench after what you did to the stove in your room this morning.

(*There is a knock on the door.*)

HEDVIG: Mother, someone's knocking.

HJALMAR: Oh yes, let's have customers on top of everything else — !

GINA: I'll handle it. (*Opens the door, gives a start, steps back*): Oh dear!

(WERLE, *in a fur coat, steps inside.*)

WERLE: I beg your pardon, but I am told my son is here.

GINA (*swallowing hard*): Yes sir.

HJALMAR (*closer*): Sir, wouldn't you like to — ?

WERLE: Thanks. I just want a word with my son.

GREGERS: Well. Here I am.

WERLE: I want to talk with you in your room.

GREGERS: In my room — ? Oh, all right. (*Is about to leave.*)

GINA: Good Lord, no! That's not a fit place!

WERLE: All right; out here in the hall, then. I want to see you alone.

HJALMAR: You may do that right here, Mr. Werle. Relling, come into the living room with me.

(HJALMAR *and* RELLING *go out, right front.* GINA *takes* HEDVIG *with her into the kitchen, left front.*)

GREGERS (*after a brief silence*): Well. We are alone.

WERLE: You dropped some hints last night. And since you have moved in with the Ekdals, I can only assume that you are planning something or other against me.

GREGERS: I plan to open Hjalmar Ekdal's eyes. He is to see his position as it really is. That's all.

WERLE: Is that the life mission you mentioned yesterday?

GREGERS: Yes. You have left me no other.

WERLE: So you feel it is I who have twisted your mind, Gregers?

GREGERS: You have twisted my whole life. I am not thinking of all that with mother. But it is you I can thank for the fact that I am being haunted and driven by a guilty conscience.

WERLE: Ah, I see. So your conscience is ailing.

GREGERS: I should have opposed you the time you were laying traps for Lieutenant Ekdal. I should have warned him, for I suspected how things were going.

WERLE: Yes, in that case you certainly ought to have said something.

GREGERS: I didn't have the courage. I was a coward — frightened. I felt an unspeakable fear of you — both then and for a long, long time afterwards.

WERLE: That fear appears to have left you now.

GREGERS: Yes, fortunately. What has been done to Old Ekdal, both by me and by — others, for that there is no remedy. But Hjalmar I can rescue from the web of lies and deceit in which he is suffocating.

WERLE: Do you think that is a good thing to do?

GREGERS: I am sure it is.

WERLE: I take it you think Mr. Photographer Ekdal is the kind of man who will be grateful for your friendly services?

GREGERS: Yes! He is that kind of man.

WERLE: H'm. We'll see.

GREGERS: Besides, if I am to continue living, I have to find a way to heal my sick conscience.

WERLE: It will never get well. Your conscience has been sickly from the time you were a child. It's hereditary, Gregers. You have it from your mother. The only inheritance she left you.

GREGERS (*with a contemptuous half smile*): I see you still haven't forgotten your disappointment when you found out mother wasn't rich.

WERLE: Let's not change the subject. Am I to think, then, that you are firmly resolved to guide Hjalmar Ekdal into the path you consider the right one?

GREGERS: Yes. That is my firm intent.

WERLE: In that case I could have saved myself coming all the way up here. For then I suppose there is no point in my asking you to move back home again?

GREGERS: No.

WERLE: And you don't want to join the firm?

GREGERS: No.

WERLE: Very well. But since I am to marry again, your part of the estate will have to be paid you.

GREGERS (*quickly*): No, I don't want that.

WERLE: You don't want it?

GREGERS: I dare not, for my conscience's sake.

WERLE (*after a brief pause*): Are you going back up to Høydal?

GREGERS: No. I consider myself released from your service.

WERLE: But what do you want to do with yourself?

GREGERS: Accomplish my mission. Nothing else.

WERLE: But afterwards? What are you going to live on?

GREGERS: I have saved some of my salary.

WERLE: How long do you think that will last?

GREGERS: I think it will do for the time I have left.

WERLE: What is that supposed to mean?

GREGERS: I won't answer any more questions.

WERLE: Well, goodbye, Gregers.

GREGERS: Goodbye.

(WERLE *leaves.*)

HJALMAR (*looks in*): Did he leave?

GREGERS: Yes.

(HJALMAR *and* RELLING *enter from the living room,* GINA *and* HEDVIG *from the kitchen.*)

RELLING: Now that was a very successful breakfast.

GREGERS: Put on your coat, Hjalmar. I want you to take a long walk with me.

HJALMAR: Gladly. What did your father want? Did it have to do with me?

GREGERS: Just come. We'll talk. I'll go and get my coat. (*Goes out.*)

GINA: You shouldn't go with him, Ekdal.

RELLING: No, don't. Stay here.

HJALMAR (*taking his hat and coat*): What! When an old friend feels the need to open his heart for me in private — !

RELLING: But goddamit! Can't you see that the fellow is mad, cracked, insane!

GINA: Yes, listen to Relling. His mother used to have physicological fits, too.

HJALMAR: All the more reason why he needs a friend's alert eyes. (*To* GINA.) Be sure to have dinner ready at the usual time. Goodbye. (*Goes out.*)

RELLING: It's nothing less than a disaster that that man didn't go straight to hell down one of the shafts up at Høydal.

GINA: Heavens — ! Why do you say that?

RELLING (*mutters*): I have my reasons.

GINA: Do you really think young Werle is crazy?

RELLING: No, unfortunately. He is no madder than most people. He is sick, though.

GINA: What do you think is wrong with him?

RELLING: That I can tell you, Mrs. Ekdal. He suffers from an acute attack of moral integrity.

GINA: Moral integrity?

HEDVIG: Is that a disease?

RELLING: Yes, it is a national disease, but it occurs only sporadically. (*Nods to* GINA.) That was a good meal, thank you. (*Goes out.*)

GINA (*troubled, walks up and down*): Ugh! That Gregers Werle — he's always been a weird fish.

HEDVIG (*by the table, looks at her searchingly*): I think this is very strange.

ACT IV

(*The studio. Photographs have just been taken. A cloth-covered camera on a tripod, a couple of chairs, and a small table are standing about in the middle of the floor. Afternoon light. The sun is about to disappear. After a while darkness begins to fall.*

GINA *stands in the open entrance door with a small box and a wet glass plate in her hand. She is talking to someone not in sight.*)

GINA: Absolutely. When I promise something, I keep it. I'll have the first dozen ready for you on Monday. — Goodbye.

(*Sounds of someone descending the stairs.* GINA *closes the door, puts the plate inside the box and the box into the camera.*)

HEDVIG (*enters from the kitchen*): Did they leave?
GINA (*putting things in order*): Yes, thank goodness. I finally got rid of them.
HEDVIG: Can you understand why father isn't back yet?
GINA: You're sure he is not down at Relling's?
HEDVIG: No, he is not there. I just went down the kitchen stairs to ask.
GINA: His food is getting cold and everything.
HEDVIG: Yes. And father who is always so particular about having dinner on time.
GINA: Oh well. You'll see he'll be back soon.
HEDVIG: I wish he'd come. Everything seems so strange.

(HJALMAR *enters from outside.*)

HEDVIG (*towards him*): Father! If you knew how we've been waiting for you!
GINA (*glancing at him*): You've been gone quite some time.
HJALMAR (*without looking at her*): Yes, I suppose I have.

(*He starts taking his coat off.* GINA *and* HEDVIG *both go to help him. He turns them away.*)

GINA: Maybe you and Werle had something to eat some place?
HJALMAR (*hanging up his coat*): No.
GINA (*towards the kitchen door*): I'll get your dinner.
HJALMAR: Never mind. I don't feel like eating now.

HEDVIG (*coming closer*): Are you sick, father?

HJALMAR: Sick? No, I'm not sick — exactly. We had a strenuous walk, Gregers and I.

GINA: You shouldn't do that, Ekdal. You aren't used to it.

HJALMAR: H'm. There are many things in life a man has to get used to. (*Paces up and down.*) Anybody here while I've been gone?

GINA: Only that engaged couple.

HJALMAR: No new appointments?

GINA: No, not today.

HEDVIG: There will be some tomorrow, father, I am sure.

HJALMAR: I hope you are right, for tomorrow I plan to go to work in earnest.

HEDVIG: Tomorrow! But don't you remember what day is tomorrow?

HJALMAR: That's right. Well, then, the day after tomorrow. From now on I'll do everything myself. I want to assume the entire work load.

GINA: Whatever for, Ekdal? That's only making yourself miserable. I'll manage the pictures. You just go on with the invention.

HEDVIG: And the wild duck, father. And the chickens and the rabbits and —

HJALMAR: Don't ever mention all that junk to me again! Starting tomorrow, I'll never more set foot in the attic.

HEDVIG: But father, you promised that tomorrow we're having a celebration —

HJALMAR: H'm. That's right. Day after tomorrow then. That damn wild duck. I'd like to wring its neck!

HEDVIG (*with a cry*): The wild duck!

GINA: Now I've heard everything!

HEDVIG (*shaking him*): But father — it's *my* wild duck!

HJALMAR: That's why I won't do it. I don't have the heart — for your sake, Hedvig. But deep down I feel I ought to do it. I shouldn't harbor under my roof a creature that has been in those hands.

GINA: For heaven's sake! Even if Grandpa *did* get it from that awful Pettersen.

HJALMAR (*walking up and down*): There are certain demands — what shall I call them? Let me say ideal demands — certain claims, that a man disregards only at the peril of his soul.

HEDVIG (*following after him*): But think — the wild duck! That poor wild duck!

HJALMAR (*halts*): Didn't I tell you I'll spare it — for your sake? Not a hair on its head will be — h'm. Well, as I said, I'll spare it. After all, there are bigger tasks awaiting me. But you ought to go out for a little walk, Hedvig. The twilight is just right for you.

HEDVIG: I don't care to go out now.

HJALMAR: Yes, do. Seems to me you are squinting. The fumes in here aren't good for you. The air is close under this roof.

HEDVIG: All right. I'll run down the kitchen stairs and walk around a bit. My hat and coat? Oh yes, in my room. Father, please — don't do anything bad to the wild duck while I'm gone!

HJALMAR: Not a feather shall be plucked from its head. (*Clutches her to him.*) You and I, Hedvig — we two! Be on your way now.

(HEDVIG *nods goodbye to her parents and goes out through the kitchen door.*)

HJALMAR (*pacing back and forth*): Gina.

GINA: Yes?

HJALMAR: Starting tomorrow — or let's say the day after tomorrow — I'd like to keep account of the housekeeping expenses myself.

GINA: So you want to keep the accounts too, now?

HJALMAR: Keep track of what we take in, at any rate.

GINA: Lord knows, that's easily done!

HJALMAR: One wouldn't think so. It seems to me you make the money go incredibly far. (*Stops and looks at her.*) How do you do it?

GINA: It's because Hedvig and I need so little.

HJALMAR: Is it true that father is overpaid for the copying work he does for Werle?

GINA: I couldn't say about that. I don't know the rates.

HJALMAR: Well, what *does* he get? In round figures. — I want to know.

GINA: It differs. I guess it comes to about what he costs us, plus a little extra in spending money.

HJALMAR: What he costs us! And you haven't told me that!

GINA: No, I couldn't, for you were so happy because he got everything from you.

HJALMAR: And it has really been Werle all the time!

GINA: Oh well. He can afford it.

HJALMAR: Light the lamp!

GINA (*lighting the lamp*): And as far as that is concerned, how do we know it is Werle himself? It may be Gråberg —

HJALMAR: Really, Gina. You know that isn't so. Why do you say a thing like that?

GINA: I don't know. I just thought —

HJALMAR: H'm!

GINA: It wasn't me who got Grandpa all that copying to do. It was Bertha, when she took service there.

HJALMAR: It sounds to me like your voice is trembling.

GINA (*putting the shade on the lamp*): Does it?

HJALMAR: And your hands are shaking. Aren't they?

GINA (*firmly*): You might as well tell me straight, Ekdal. What has he been saying about me?

HJALMAR: Is it true — *can* it be true — that there was some kind of affair between you and Werle while you were in his house?

GINA: That's not so. Not then. He was after me, though. And Mrs. Werle thought there was something going on, and she made a fuss and a big hullaballoo about it, and she beat me and pulled me around — and so I quit.

HJALMAR: But afterwards — !

GINA: Well, then I went to live with mother. And you see — mother — she wasn't all the woman you thought she was, Ekdal. She talked to me about this, that, and the other. For Werle was a widower by that time —

HJALMAR: And then — ?

GINA: You might as well know it, I guess. He didn't give up till he had his way.

HJALMAR (*striking his hands together*): And this is the mother of my child! How could you keep a thing like this from me?

GINA: Yes, I know it was wrong. I should have told you long ago, I suppose.

HJALMAR: You should have told me right away; that's what you should have. Then I would have known what sort of woman you were.

GINA: But would you have married me, irregardless?

HJALMAR: Of course, I wouldn't!

GINA: I didn't think so, and that's why I didn't dare to tell you. I had come to care for you, you know — a whole lot I cared for you. And I just couldn't see making myself as unhappy as all that —

HJALMAR (*walking about*): And this is my Hedvig's mother! And to know that everything I lay my eyes on here (*Kicks a chair.*) — my whole home — I owe to a favored predecessor! Oh, that seducer, that damn Werle!

GINA: Do you regret the fourteen-fifteen years we've had together?

HJALMAR (*fronting her*): Tell me if you haven't felt every day and every hour to be one long agony of repentance for that web of deceitful silence you have woven around me, like a spider? Answer me! Haven't you lived here in perpetual torture of guilt and remorse?

GINA: Bless you, Ekdal! I've been plenty busy with the house and the pictures —

HJALMAR: So you never cast a probing glance at your past?

GINA: No, to tell the truth, I had almost forgotten all those old stories.

HJALMAR: Oh, this dull, apathetic calm! There is something shocking about it. Not even repentant — !

GINA: Just tell me this, Ekdal. What do you think would have become of you if you hadn't got yourself a wife like me?

HJALMAR: Like you — !

GINA: Yes, for you know I have always been more practical and able to cope with things than you. Of course, I am a couple of years older —

HJALMAR: What would have become of me!

GINA: For you've got to admit you weren't living exactly right when you first met me.

HJALMAR: So you call that living wrong! Oh, what do you know about a man's feelings when he sorrows and despairs — especially a man of my fiery temperament.

GINA: No, I guess I don't know. And I don't mean to execrete you for it, either, for you turned into as decent a man as they come as soon as you got a house and a family of your own to take care of. And now we were getting on so nicely here, and Hedvig and I were just thinking that pretty soon we might spend some money on clothes for ourselves.

HJALMAR: Yes, in the swamp of deceit!

GINA: That that fellow ever poked his nose inside here!

HJALMAR: I, too, thought our home a pleasant one. That was a mistake. Where now do I gather the necessary inner resilience to bring my invention into the world of reality? Perhaps it will die with me. If it does, it will be your past, Gina, that has killed it.

GINA (*on the verge of tears*): Please, Ekdal — don't be saying such things! I that have all my days only tried to make things nice and pleasant for you!

HJALMAR: I ask — what happens now to the breadwinner's dream? As I reclined in there on the sofa, pondering the invention, it came to me that it was going to drain me of my last drop of vitality. I knew that the day the patent was issued and in my hands — that day would be my — my day of farewell. And then it was my dream that you were to live on as the late inventor's well-to-do widow.

GINA (*wiping her tears*): I won't have you talk that way, Ekdal. May the good Lord never let me live the day when I'm your widow!

HJALMAR: Oh what difference does it all make! It is all over now, anyway. Everything!

(GREGERS *cautiously opens the entrance door and peers in.*)

GREGERS: May I come in?

HJALMAR: Yes, do.

GREGERS (*goes up to them with a beaming, happy face, reaches out his hands to them*): Now, then — you dear people — ! (*Looks from one to the other, whispers to* HJALMAR:) It hasn't happened yet?

HJALMAR (*loud*): It has happened.

GREGERS: It has?

HJALMAR: I have lived through the bitterest moment of my life.

GREGERS: But also, I trust, its most exalted one.

HJALMAR: Anyway, it's done and over with.

GINA: May God forgive you, Mr. Werle.

GREGERS (*greatly bewildered*): But I don't understand — !

HJALMAR: What don't you understand?

GREGERS: As crucial a conversation as this — a conversation that is to be the foundation for a whole new way of life — a life, a partnership, in truth and frankness —

HJALMAR: I know. I know it very well.

GREGERS: I was so sure that when I came in here now I would be met with a splendor of revelation shining from both husband and wife. But all I see is this dull, heavy gloom —

GINA: So that's it. (*Removes the lamp shade.*)

GREGERS: You refuse to understand me, Mrs. Ekdal. Well, I suppose you need time. But you, Hjalmar? Surely, you must have felt a higher consecration in this great crisis.

HJALMAR: Of course I did. That is, in a way.

GREGERS: For surely nothing in the world can be compared to finding forgiveness in one's heart for her who has erred and lovingly lifting her up to one's own heights.

HJALMAR: Do you think a man so easily forgets the draught of wormwood I just drained?

GREGERS: An ordinary man, maybe not. But a man like you — !

HJALMAR: Oh, I know. But you must not rush me, Gregers. It takes time.

GREGERS: There is much of the wild duck in you, Hjalmar.

(RELLING *has entered.*)

RELLING: Ah! Here we go with the wild duck again!

HJALMAR: Mr. Werle's crippled prey — yes.

RELLING: Werle? Is it him you're talking about?

HJALMAR: About him — and about ourselves.

RELLING (*in a low voice, to* GREGERS): Damn you to hell!

HJALMAR: What are you saying?

RELLING: I am just expressing an ardent wish that this quack here would betake himself home. If he stays around he is likely to ruin both of you.

GREGERS: Those two cannot be ruined, Mr. Relling. Of Hjalmar I need say nothing. Him we know. But she, too, has surely in the depths of her being something reliable, something of integrity —

GINA (*almost crying*): Why didn't you leave me alone then?

RELLING (*to* GREGERS): Is it impertinent to ask exactly what you want in this house?

GREGERS: I want to lay the foundation for a true marriage.

RELLING: So you don't think the Ekdals' marriage is good enough as it is?

GREGERS: I daresay it is as good a marriage as most, unfortunately. But a true marriage it has yet to become.

HJALMAR: You have never had an eye for the claim of the ideal, Relling!

RELLING: Nonsense, boy! — Begging your pardon, Mr. Werle — how many — roughly — how many true marriages have you observed in your life?

GREGERS: Hardly a single one.

RELLING: Nor have I.

GREGERS: But I have seen a number of the other kind. And I have had occasion to witness what havoc a marriage like that can work in a pair of human beings.

HJALMAR: A man's whole moral foundation may crumble under his feet; that's the terrible thing.

RELLING: Well, I can't say I've ever been exactly married, so I can't judge about that. But I do know this, that the child belongs to marriage too. And you had better leave the child alone.

HJALMAR: Oh, Hedvig! My poor Hedvig!

RELLING: Yes — keep Hedvig out of it, you two! You are grown-ups. In God's name, do whatever fool things you like to your marriage. But I am warning you: be careful what you do to Hedvig. If you're not, there is no telling what may happen to her.

HJALMAR: Happen to her!

RELLING: Yes, she may bring a disaster upon herself — and perhaps on others, too.

GINA: But how can you tell about that, Relling?

HJALMAR: Are you saying there is some immediate danger to her eyes?

RELLING: This has nothing whatever to do with her eyes. Hedvig is in a difficult age. She may do all sorts of crazy things.

GINA: I know — she does already. She's taken to fooling around with the woodstove in the kitchen. Playing fire, she calls it. Sometimes I'm scared she'll burn the whole house down.

RELLING: There you are. I knew it.

GREGERS (*to* RELLING): But how do you explain a thing like that?

RELLING (*sullenly*): Her voice is changing, sir.

HJALMAR: As long as the child has *me* — ! As long as *my* head is above the ground!

(*There is a knock on the door.*)

GINA: Shhh, Ekdal. There are people outside.

(MRS. SØRBY *enters, wearing hat and coat.*)

MRS. SØRBY: Good evening!

GINA (*going to her*): Goodness! Is it you, Bertha!

MRS. SØRBY: So it is. Maybe it's inconvenient — ?

HJALMAR: Oh by no means! A messenger from *that* house — !

MRS. SØRBY (*to* GINA): Frankly, I had hoped you'd be without your menfolks this time of day. I've just dropped in to have a word with you about something and say goodbye.

GINA: You're going away?

MRS. SØRBY: Tomorrow morning — to Høydal. Mr. Werle left this afternoon. (*Casually, to* GREGERS.) He asked me to say hello.

GINA: Imagine — !

HJALMAR: So Mr. Werle has left? And you are going after him?

MRS. SØRBY: Yes. What do you say to that, Ekdal?

HJALMAR: Look out, is all I say.

GREGERS: I can explain. Father and Mrs. Sørby are getting married.

GINA: Oh Bertha! At long last!

RELLING (*his voice trembling a little*): Surely, this cannot be true?

MRS. SØRBY: Yes, my dear Relling, true it is.

RELLING: You want to get married again?

MRS. SØRBY: That's what it amounts to. Werle has got the license. We'll have a quiet little party up at the works.

GREGERS: I suppose I should tender my felicitations like a good stepson.

MRS. SØRBY: Thank you, if you really mean it. I hope this will be for the best for both Werle and myself.

RELLING: I am sure you have every reason to think it will. Mr. Werle never gets drunk — at least not to my knowledge. Nor do I believe he is in the habit of beating up his wife, like the late lamented horse doctor.

MRS. SØRBY: Let Sørby rest quietly in his grave. He had his good sides, too.

RELLING: Mr. Industrialist Werle has better ones, I am sure.

MRS. SØRBY: At least he has not thrown away what is best in himself. The man who does that must take the consequences.

RELLING: Tonight I'll go out with Molvik.

MRS. SØRBY: Don't do that, Relling. Don't — for my sake.

RELLING: There's nothing else to do. (*To* HJALMAR.) Want to come along?

GINA: No, thank you. Ekdal doesn't go in for excapades like that.

HJALMAR (*angrily, in a half whisper*): For heaven's sake! Keep your mouth shut!

RELLING: Goodbye — Mrs. Werle! (*Goes out.*)

GREGERS (*to* MRS. SØRBY): It appears that you and Doctor Relling know each other quite well?

MRS. SØRBY: Yes, we've known each other for a good many years. At one time it looked as if we might have made a match of it.

GREGERS: I'm sure it was lucky for you that you didn't.

MRS. SØRBY: You may well say that. But I've always been wary of acting on impulse. A woman can't just throw herself away, you know.

GREGERS: Aren't you afraid I'll let my father know about this old acquaintanceship?

MRS. SØRBY: Do you really believe I haven't told him myself?

GREGERS: Oh?

MRS. SØRBY: Your father knows every little thing people might say about me with any show of truth at all. I have told him everything. That was the first thing I did when I realized what his intentions were.

GREGERS: It seems to me you are more than usually frank.

MRS. SØRBY: I have always been frank. For us women that's the best policy.

HJALMAR: What do you say to that, Gina?

GINA: Oh, women differ. Some do it one way, others do it different.

MRS. SØRBY: Well, Gina, in my opinion I have followed the wiser course. And Werle hasn't kept back anything either. You see, that's what mainly brought us together. Now he can sit and talk to me as openly as a child. He has never been able to do that before. A healthy, vigorous man like him — all through his youth and all the best years of his life he had his ears drummed full with angry sermons. And very often sermons about sins he hadn't even committed — according to what I have been told.

GINA: That's the truth.

GREGERS: If you ladies want to pursue that topic any further, I had better absent myself.

MRS. SØRBY: You may just as well stay as far as that's concerned. I won't say another word. I just wanted you to know I haven't kept anything back or played him false in any way. Maybe people will say I am a very fortunate woman, and in a way of course that's true. But I don't think I am getting any more than I am giving. I'll certainly never desert him. And I can be of more service and use to him than anybody else, now that he'll soon be helpless.

HJALMAR: Will he be helpless?

GREGERS (*to* MRS. SØRBY): Don't say anything about that here.

MRS. SØRBY: It can't be kept secret any longer, much as he'd like to. He is going blind.

HJALMAR (*struck*): Blind? That's strange. He, too?

GINA: Lots of people go blind.

MRS. SØRBY: And I'm sure you can tell yourself what that must mean to a businessman. Well, I'll try to be his eyes, the best I know how. — But I can't stay any longer. I have so much to do right now. — Oh yes, What I wanted to tell you, Ekdal, is that if Werle can be of any service to you, all you need to do is to get in touch with Gråberg.

GREGERS: That is an offer I am sure Hjalmar Ekdal will decline.

MRS. SØRBY: Really? It seems to me he hasn't always been so —

GINA: Yes, Bertha. Ekdal doesn't need to accept anything more from Mr. Werle.

HJALMAR (*slowly, with weight*): Tell your husband-to-be from me, that in the very near future I intend to go to Mr. Gråberg —

GREGERS: What! You want to do that!

HJALMAR: — I say, go to Mr. Gråberg, and demand an account of the sum I owe his employer. I desire to pay this debt of honor — ha-ha-ha! — let us call it a debt of honor! Enough! I shall pay it all, with five per cent interest.

GINA: But Ekdal — goodness! We don't have that kind of money!

HJALMAR: Be so good as to inform your fiancé that I am working incessantly on my invention. Please tell him that what sustains my mind during this exhausting enterprise is my ambition to free myself from a painful burden of debt. This is why I am an inventor. The entire proceeds from my invention are to be devoted to liberating myself from the obligation to remunerate your husband-to-be for his expenses on behalf of my family.

MRS. SØRBY: Something has happened here.

HJALMAR: Indeed, something has.

MRS. SØRBY: Well, goodbye. I had something else I wanted to talk to you about, Gina, but that will have to wait till some other time. Goodbye.

(HJALMAR *and* GREGERS *return her greeting silently.* GINA *sees her to the door.*)

HJALMAR: Not beyond the threshold, Gina!

(MRS. SØRBY *leaves.* GINA *closes the door.*)

HJALMAR: There, now, Gregers. I have that burdensome debt off my chest.

GREGERS: You soon will, at any rate.

HJALMAR: I believe my attitude must be deemed the proper one.

GREGERS: You are the man I have always taken you to be.

HJALMAR: In certain cases it is impossible to disregard the claims of the ideal. As provider for my family, I am bound, of course, to find my course of action difficult and painful. Believe me, it is no joke for a man situated as I am, without means, to assume a debt of many years' standing — a debt, you might say, covered by the sands of oblivion. But never mind. The man in me demands his rights.

GREGERS (*placing his hand on his shoulder*): Dear Hjalmar — wasn't it a good thing that I came?

HJALMAR: Yes.

GREGERS: That your whole situation was made clear to you — wasn't that a good thing?

HJALMAR (*a bit impatiently*): Of course it was. But there is one thing that shocks my sense of justice.

GREGERS: What is that?

HJALMAR: It is this that — But I don't know that I ought to speak so freely about your father —

GREGERS: Don't let that worry you. Say what you want.

HJALMAR: All right. Well, you see, there is something shocking in the notion that now it's he and not I who realizes the true marriage.

GREGERS: How can you say a thing like that!

HJALMAR: Well, it is. For your father and Mrs. Sørby are about to solemnify a union built on full mutual confidence, on complete, unconditional frankness on both sides. They conceal nothing from each other, there are no deceitful silences, there has been declared, if I may put it so, mutual absolution between them.

GREGERS: Well, what of it?

HJALMAR: Well, then — it's all there! All the difficult conditions you yourself said are prerequisites for the building of a true marriage.

GREGERS: But that's in quite a different way, Hjalmar. Surely, you won't compare either yourself or Gina with those two —? Oh I am sure you know what I mean.

HJALMAR: Yet I can't get away from the thought that in all this there is something that offends my sense of justice. It looks exactly as if there were no just order in the universe.

GINA: Ekdal, for God's sake, don't talk like that!

GREGERS: H'm. Let's not get involved in those issues.

HJALMAR: Though, on the other hand, I do in a way discern fate's ruling finger, too. He is going blind.

GINA: We don't know that yet.

HJALMAR: There is no doubt about it. At least, we ought not to doubt it, for in that very fact lies the proof of just retribution. He did once hoodwink a trusting fellow being.

GREGERS: I am afraid he has hoodwinked many.

HJALMAR: And here comes the inexorable, the inscrutable, claiming Werle's own eyes.

GINA: How you talk! I think it's scary.

HJALMAR: It is salutary at times to contemplate the night side of existence.

(HEDVIG, *dressed for the outside, enters. She is happy, breathless.*)

GINA: Back so soon?

HEDVIG: Yes. I didn't feel like walking any farther. It was a good thing, too, for I met somebody as I was coming in.

HJALMAR: Mrs. Sørby, I suppose.

HEDVIG: Yes.

HJALMAR (*pacing the floor*): I hope you have seen her for the last time.

(*Silence.* HEDVIG, *troubled, looks from one to the other in order to gauge their mood.*)

HEDVIG (*approaching* HJALMAR, *ingratiatingly*): Father?

HJALMAR: All right — what is it, Hedvig?

HEDVIG: Mrs. Sørby had something for me.

HJALMAR (*halts*): For you?

HEDVIG: Yes. Something for tomorrow.

GINA: Bertha always brings you a little something for your birthday.

HJALMAR: What is it?

HEDVIG: No, you're not to find out now. Mother is to give it to me in the morning, when she brings me breakfast in bed.

HJALMAR: What is all this mystification that I am to be kept in the dark about!

HEDVIG (*quickly*): I'll be glad to let you see it, father. It's a big letter. (*Takes the letter out of her coat pocket.*)

HJALMAR: A letter too?

HEDVIG: The letter is all there is. I suppose the other thing will come later. Just think — a letter! I never got a letter before. And it says "Miss" on the outside of it. (*Reads.*) "Miss Hedvig Ekdal." Just think — that's me!

HJALMAR: Let me see that letter.

HEDVIG: Here you are. (*Hands it to him.*)

HJALMAR: It's Werle's handwriting.

GINA: Are you sure, Ekdal?

HJALMAR: See for yourself.

GINA: How would I know?

HJALMAR: Hedvig? May I open the letter? Read it?

HEDVIG: If you like.

GINA: Not tonight, Ekdal. It's supposed to be for tomorrow.

HEDVIG (*in a low voice*): Please let him read it! It's bound to be something nice, and then father will be in a good mood, and everything will be pleasant again.

HJALMAR: You say I may open it?

HEDVIG: Yes, please, father. I'd like to know what it is about, too.

HJALMAR: Good. (*Opens the envelope, reads the letter inside. Appears confused.*) What *is* this — ?

GINA: What does it say?

HEDVIG: Please, father — tell us!

HJALMAR: Be quiet. (*Reads the letter again. He is pale, but his voice is controlled.*) It is a gift letter, Hedvig.

HEDVIG: Imagine! What is it I get?

HJALMAR: Read for yourself.

(HEDVIG *goes over to the lamp and reads.*)

HJALMAR (*in a low voice, clenches his fists*): The eyes, the eyes! And now that letter!

HEDVIG (*interrupting his reading*): Seems to me like it's Grandpa who gets it.

HJALMAR (*taking the letter away from her*): You, Gina — can you make any sense out of this?

GINA: I don't know a blessed thing about it. Why don't you just tell me?

HJALMAR: Werle writes to Hedvig that her old grandfather no longer needs to trouble himself with the copying work he has been doing, but that he may go to the office every month and draw one hundred crowns —

GREGERS: Aha!

HEDVIG: One hundred crowns, mother! I read that.

GINA: That will be nice for Grandpa.

HJALMAR: — one hundred crowns for as long as he needs it. That means, of course, till he closes his eyes.

GINA: So *he* is all taken care of, poor soul.

HJALMAR: Then it comes. You can't have read that far, Hedvig. After his death, that money will be yours.

HEDVIG: Mine? All of it?

HJALMAR: He writes that the same amount has been set aside for you for the rest of your life. Are you listening, Gina?

GINA: Yes, I hear.

HEDVIG: Just think — all the money I'll be getting! (*Shaking* HJAL-MAR's *arm.*) Father! Father! But aren't you glad?

HJALMAR (*going away from her*): Glad! (*Walking about.*) Oh what vistas, what perspectives, open up before me! It is Hedvig he is so generous to!

GINA: Well, she's the one with the birthday.

HEDVIG: And of course you will get it anyway, father! Don't you know I'll give it all to you and mother?

HJALMAR: To mother, yes! That's just it!

GREGERS: Hjalmar, this is a trap being prepared for you.

HJALMAR: You think this may be another trap?

GREGERS: When he was here this morning, he said, "Hjalmar Ekdal is not the man you think he is."

HJALMAR: Not the man — !

GREGERS: "You just wait and see," he said.

HJALMAR: You were to see me selling myself for money — !

HEDVIG: Mother, what *is* all this?

GINA: Go out and take your wraps off.

(HEDVIG, *about to cry, goes out into the kitchen.*)

GREGERS: Well, Hjalmar — now we shall see who is right — he or I.

HJALMAR (*slowly tearing the letter in two, putting the pieces down on the table*): Here is my answer.

GREGERS: Just as I thought.

HJALMAR (*to* GINA, *who is standing near the stove; in a low voice*): No more concealment now. If everything was over between you and him when you — came to care for me, as you call it, then why did he make it possible for us to get married?

GINA: I guess he thought he'd make free of the house.

HJALMAR: Just that? He wasn't worried about a certain possibility?

GINA: I don't know what you're talking about.

HJALMAR: I want to know — if your child has the right to live under my roof.

GINA (*drawing herself up, her eyes flashing*): You ask me that!

HJALMAR: Just tell me one thing. Is Hedvig mine or — ? — Well?

GINA (*looks at him with cold defiance*): I don't know.

HJALMAR (*with a slight tremble*): You don't know!

GINA: How can I? A woman like me!

HJALMAR (*quietly, turning away from her*): In that case I have nothing more to do in this house.

GREGERS: Think it over, Hjalmar!

HJALMAR (*putting his overcoat on*): For a man like me there is nothing to think over.

GREGERS: Yes, there is ever so much to think over. You three must stay together if you are to attain to the sacrificial spirit of sublime forgivingness.

HJALMAR: I don't want to attain it! Never! Never! My hat! (*Takes his hat.*) My house is in ruins about me. (*Bursts out crying.*) Gregers! I have no child!

HEDVIG (*who has opened the kitchen door*): Father! What are you saying!

GINA: Oh dear!

HJALMAR: Don't come near me, Hedvig! Go far away from me. I can't stand looking at you. Oh those eyes — ! Goodbye. (*Is about to go out.*)

HEDVIG (*clings to him, cries*): No! No! Don't leave me!

GINA: Look at the child, Ekdal! Look at the child!

HJALMAR: I will not! I cannot! I must get out — away from all this! (*He tears himself loose from* HEDVIG *and exits.*)

HEDVIG (*her eyes desperate*): He's leaving us, mother! He's leaving us! He'll never come back!

GINA: Just don't cry, Hedvig. Father will be back. You wait.

HEDVIG (*throws herself sobbing down on the sofa*): No! No! He'll never come back to us any more!

GREGERS: Do you believe I meant all for the best, Mrs. Ekdal?

GINA: Yes, I suppose you did, but God forgive you all the same.

HEDVIG (*on the sofa*): I want to die! What have I done to him, mother? You just have to get him back again!

GINA: Yes, yes, yes; only be quiet. I'll go out and look for him. (*Putting on her coat.*) Perhaps he's gone down to Relling's. But you're not to lie there, bawling like that. Promise?

HEDVIG (*sobbing convulsively*): All right, I'll stop, if only father comes home again.

GREGERS (*to* GINA, *who is leaving*): But would it not be better to let him fight his agony through by himself?

GINA: He can do that afterwards. First we've got to get the child quieted down. (*Goes out.*)

HEDVIG (*sitting up, drying her eyes*): Now you have to tell me what this is all about. Why doesn't father want me any more?

GREGERS: You must not ask that till you're big and grown-up.

HEDVIG (*sobbing*): But I just can't stay as miserable as this all the time till I'm grown up. — But I know what it is. Maybe I'm not really father's child.

GREGERS (*uneasily*): How could that be?

HEDVIG: Mother might have found me. And now perhaps father has found out about it. I have read about things like that.

GREGERS: Well, if it really were so —

HEDVIG: I think he could love me just as much, regardless. More, almost. The wild duck is a gift, too, and I love her very, very much.

GREGERS (*glad to turn the conversation*): Oh yes, the wild duck. Let's talk about the wild duck, Hedvig.

HEDVIG: That poor wild duck. He can't stand the sight of her, either. Just think, he wants to wring her neck!

GREGERS: Oh, I don't think he'll do that.

HEDVIG: No, but he said it. And I think that was horrid of father, for I pray for the wild duck every night, that she may be kept safe from death and all that's evil.

GREGERS (*looks at her*): Do you usually say prayers at night?

HEDVIG: Yes, I do.

GREGERS: Who taught you that?

HEDVIG: Myself, for father was terribly sick once and had leeches on his neck, and then he said that death was his dread companion.

GREGERS: And — ?

HEDVIG: So I prayed for him when I went to bed. And I have done so ever since.

GREGERS: And now you pray for the wild duck, too?

HEDVIG: I thought it was best to mention her as well, for she was so sickly when we first got her.

GREGERS: Do you say morning prayers, too?

HEDVIG: Of course not.

GREGERS: Why is that so of course?

HEDVIG: Because it's light in the morning. There's not so much to be afraid of then.

GREGERS: And the wild duck you love so much — your father said he'd like to wring her neck?

HEDVIG: No, he said it would be better for him if he did, but he was going to spare her for my sake. And that was good of him.

GREGERS (*closer to her*): How would it be if you decided to sacrifice the wild duck for *his* sake?

HEDVIG (*getting up*): The wild duck!

GREGERS: What if you willingly gave up the dearest thing in the whole world for him?

HEDVIG: Do you think that would help?

GREGERS: Try it, Hedvig.

HEDVIG (*softly, with shining eyes*): Yes. I want to.

GREGERS: Do you think you have the right kind of strength for doing it?

HEDVIG: I shall ask Grandpa to shoot the wild duck for me.

GREGERS: Yes, do that. But not a word to your mother about this!

HEDVIG: Why not?

GREGERS: She doesn't understand us.

HEDVIG: The wild duck? I'll try it in the morning!

(GINA *enters from the hall.*)

HEDVIG (*towards her*): Did you find him, mother?

GINA: No, but I found out he's got Relling with him.

GREGERS: Are you sure?

GINA: Yes, the janitor's wife said so. Molvik's with them also.

GREGERS: Just now, when his soul so sorely needs to struggle in solitude — !

GINA (*taking off her coat*): Yes, men are funny. God knows where Relling is taking him! I ran over to Madam Eriksen's, but they aren't there.

HEDVIG (*struggling with her tears*): What if he never comes back!

GREGERS: He'll come back. I'll get word to him tomorrow, and then you'll see *how* he comes back. You count on that, Hedvig, and get a good night's sleep. Goodnight. (*Goes out.*)

HEDVIG (*throws herself sobbing on* GINA's *neck*): Mother! Mother!

GINA (*patting her back, sighing*): Yes, Relling was right. This is what happens when crazy people come around pestering us with the claim of the ordeal.

ACT V

(*The studio. Cold, gray morning light. There is wet snow on the big panes of the skylight.*

GINA, *aproned, with broom and dust cloth in her hand, enters from the kitchen and goes towards the living room door.* HEDVIG *hurries in from the outside at the same moment.*)

GINA (*stops*): Well?

HEDVIG: Yes, mother, I almost think he's down at Relling's —

GINA: What did I tell you!

HEDVIG: — for the janitor's wife said she heard Relling bring two others home with him last night.

GINA: I knew it.

HEDVIG: But what good does it do, if he doesn't come up here to us?

GINA: I want to go down and have a talk with him, anyway.

(OLD EKDAL, *in dressing gown and slippers and with his lighted pipe, appears in the door to his room.*)

EKDAL: Eh — Hjalmar — ? Isn't Hjalmar here?

GINA: No, he is out, Grandpa.

EKDAL: So early? In this blizzard? Well, I can walk by myself in the morning, I can, if it comes to that.

(*He slides the attic door open.* HEDVIG *helps him. He enters. She closes the door behind him.*)

HEDVIG (*in a low voice*): Mother, what do you think will happen when poor Grandpa hears that father has left us?

GINA: Silly! Grandpa mustn't hear anything about it, of course. It was a good thing he wasn't home last night, during all that hullaballoo.

HEDVIG: Yes, but —

(GREGERS *enters.*)

GREGERS: Well? Have you traced him yet?

GINA: They say he's down at Relling's.

GREGERS: At Relling's! Has he really been out with those two?

GINA: It looks like it.

GREGERS: But he is so badly in need of solitude — to find himself in earnest —

GINA: Yes. I should think so, too.

(RELLING *enters.*)

HEDVIG (*goes towards him*): Is father with you?

GINA (*at the same time*): Is he down there?

RELLING: He certainly is.

HEDVIG: And you haven't told us!

RELLING: I know. I am a big, bad beast. But I had this other big, bad beast to take care of, too — I mean the demonic one. And after that, I just fell asleep — sound asleep —

GINA: What does Ekdal say today?

RELLING: Not a thing.

HEDVIG: Doesn't he say anything at all?

RELLING: Not a blessed word.

GREGERS: I think I understand that.

GINA: But what is he doing?

RELLING: He is on the sofa, snoring.

GINA: Oh. Yes, Ekdal does snore a lot.

HEDVIG: He's asleep? Can he sleep now?

RELLING: It certainly looks that way.

GREGERS: That's reasonable enough, after the spiritual turmoil he's just been through —

GINA: And he isn't used to be out revelling nights, either.

HEDVIG: It may be a good thing that he is sleeping, mother.

GINA: That's what I am thinking. Anyway, we'd better not wake him up too soon. Thank you, Relling. First of all I've got to clean things up a bit and make the place look nice. Come and help me, Hedvig. (*They go into the living room.*)

GREGERS (*turning to* RELLING): Can you account for the present spiritual unrest in Hjalmar Ekdal?

RELLING: To tell you the truth, I haven't noticed any spiritual unrest in him.

GREGERS: What? At such a turning point — When his whole life is acquiring a new basis? How can you think that a personality like Hjalmar Ekdal — ?

RELLING: Personality? He? If he ever had any tendency to sprout the kind of abnormal growth you call personality, I can assure you that all roots and tendrils were thoroughly extirpated in his boyhood.

GREGERS: That would indeed be strange, considering the loving up-bringing he enjoyed.

RELLING: By those two crackpot, hysterical spinster aunts of his, you mean?

GREGERS: Let me tell you that they were women who never forgot the claim of the ideal — though I suppose you'll just be making fun of me again.

RELLING: No, I'm not in the mood. I do know about them, though. He has often enough held forth about "his soul's two mothers." Personally, I don't think he has much to be grateful to them for. Ekdal's misfortune is that he has always been looked upon as a shining light in his own circle.

GREGERS: And you don't think he is that? I mean, when it comes to depth of soul?

RELLING: I have never noticed it. That his father thought so is one thing. The old lieutenant has been an idiot all his days.

GREGERS: He has all his days been a man with a childlike mind. That is what you don't understand.

RELLING: All right. But after dear, sweet Hjalmar had taken up studying — after a fashion — right away he was the light of the future among his friends, too. He was handsome enough, the rascal — red and white, just the way little shop-girls like the fellows. And he had this sentimental temperament and this warm-hearted voice, and he could give such pretty declamations of other people's poetry and other people's thoughts —

GREGERS (*indignantly*): Is this Hjalmar Ekdal you are describing?

RELLING: Yes, if you please. For this is what he looks like on the inside, the idol you are prostrating yourself for.

GREGERS: I didn't know I was as blind as all that.

RELLING: Well — not far from it. For you are sick, too, you see.

GREGERS: That is true.

RELLING: Yes it is. And yours is a complicated case. First, there is this pesky integrity fever you're suffering from, and then something worse — you are forever walking around in a delirium of adoration, always looking for something to admire outside of yourself.

GREGERS: Yes, there certainly wouldn't be much point in looking for it within myself.

RELLING: But you are always so hideously wrong about all those big, wonderful flies you see and hear buzzing around you. Once again you have entered a cottage with your claim of the ideal. People here just can't pay.

GREGERS: If this is the way you think of Hjalmar Ekdal, what sort of pleasure can you derive from your constant association with him?

RELLING: Oh well. I am supposed to be a kind of doctor, believe it or not, so the least I can do is to look after the poor patients I share quarters with.

GREGERS: Ah, I see. Hjalmar Ekdal is sick, too?

RELLING: Most people are, worse luck.

GREGERS: And what treatment do you apply in Hjalmar's case?

RELLING: My usual one. I see to it that his vital lie is kept up.

GREGERS: Vital — lie? I am not sure I heard what you said.

RELLING: That's right. I said the vital lie. You see, that's the stimulating principle.

GREGERS: May I ask with what vital lie you have infected Hjalmar?

RELLING: You may not. I never reveal professional secrets to quacks. You are capable of messing him up for me even more than you have. But the method is proven. I have used it with Molvik, too. I have made him demonic. That's the suppurative I have applied to *his* neck.

GREGERS: But *isn't* he demonic?

RELLING: What the hell does it mean — being demonic? It's just some nonsense I thought of to save his life. If I hadn't, the poor, pitiful swine would have succumbed to self-hatred and despair many a year ago. Not to mention the old lieutenant! Though he has found his own cure.

GREGERS: Lieutenant Ekdal? What about him?

RELLING: What do you think? There he is, the old slayer of bears, chasing rabbits in a dark attic. And yet, there isn't a happier hunter alive than that old man when he is playing with all that junk. The four or five dried-out Christmas trees he has saved are the whole big, wild Høydal forest to him. The rooster and the chickens are wild fowl in the tree tops, and the rabbits bouncing about on the floor are bears he's grappling with — the frisky old sportsman.

GREGERS: Ah, yes — that unfortunate old Lieutenant Ekdal. He has certainly had to compromise the ideals of his youth.

RELLING: While I think of it, Mr. Werle — don't use the foreign word "ideals." We have available a good native one: "lies."

GREGERS: You think the two things are related?

RELLING: About as closely as typhus and putrid fever.

GREGERS: Doctor Relling! I won't give up till I have rescued Hjalmar from your clutches!

RELLING: That might be his bad luck. Take his vital lie away from the average person, and you take his happiness, too. (*To* HEDVIG, *who enters from the living room.*) Well, now, little duck mother. I am going down to see if papa is still in bed pondering that wonderful invention of his. (*Goes out.*)

GREGERS (*approaching* HEDVIG): I can tell from looking at you that it has not yet been accomplished.

HEDVIG: What? Oh, that about the wild duck? No.

GREGERS: Your strength of purpose deserted you, I suppose, when the time for action had come.

HEDVIG: No, it wasn't that. But when I woke up this morning and remembered what we had talked about, it all seemed so strange.

GREGERS: Strange?

HEDVIG: Yes, I don't know — Last night, just at the time — I thought there was something very wonderful about it, but when I had slept and I thought about it again, it didn't seem like anything much.

GREGERS: I see. I could hardly expect you to grow up in this environment without injury to your soul.

HEDVIG: I don't care about that, if only father would come home again.

GREGERS: If only your eyes were opened to what gives life its worth — if only you possessed the true, joyful, brave, sacrificial spirit, then you'd see he'll return. But I still have faith in you, Hedvig. (*Goes out.*)

(HEDVIG *walks around aimlessly. She is about to enter the kitchen, when there is a knock on the inside of the door to the attic.* HEDVIG *opens the doors wide enough for* OLD EKDAL *to come out. She shuts them again.*)

EKDAL: H'm. Not much fun taking a walk by yourself, y'know.

HEDVIG: Wouldn't you like to go hunting, Grandpa?

EKDAL: It isn't hunting weather today. Too dark. Can hardly see a thing.

HEDVIG: Don't you ever want to shoot something beside rabbits?

EKDAL: Aren't the rabbits good enough, perhaps?

HEDVIG: Yes, but what about the wild duck?

EKDAL: Haw! So you're scared I'll shoot your wild duck? I'll never do that, Hedvig. Never.

HEDVIG: No, for I bet you don't know how. I've heard it's difficult to shoot wild ducks.

EKDAL: Don't know how! Should say I do!

HEDVIG: How would you do it, Grandpa? — I don't mean *my* wild duck, but another one.

EKDAL: Would try to get a shot in just below the breast; that's the best place. And try to shoot *against* the feathers, not *with*.

HEDVIG: Then they die?

EKDAL: Damn right they do — if you shoot right. — Well, better go in and dress up. H'm. Y'know. H'm — (*Goes into his own room.*)

(HEDVIG *waits a moment, glances towards the living room door, stands on tiptoe, takes the double-barreled pistol down from the shelf, looks at it.* GINA, *with broom and dust cloth, enters from the living room.* HEDVIG *quickly puts the pistol back, without* GINA'S *noticing.*)

GINA: Don't fool with father's things, Hedvig.

HEDVIG (*leaving the shelf*): I just wanted to straighten up some.

GINA: Why don't you go into the kitchen and see if the coffee is keeping hot? I am taking a tray with me when I go down.

(HEDVIG *goes into the kitchen.* GINA *starts putting the studio in order. After a short while, the door to the outside is hesitantly opened and* HJALMAR *looks in. He is wearing a coat but no hat. He looks unkempt and unwashed. His eyes are dull and luster-less.*)

GINA (*stands staring at him, still with the broom in her hand*): Bless you, Ekdal — so you did come back, after all!

HJALMAR (*enters, answers in a dull voice*): I return — only to leave.

GINA: Yes, yes, I suppose. But good Lord! how you look!

HJALMAR: Look?

GINA: And your nice winter coat? I'd say that's done for.

HEDVIG (*in the kitchen door*): Mother, don't you want me to — (*sees* HJALMAR, *gives a shout of joy and runs towards him.*) Father! Father!

HJALMAR (*turning away, with a gesture*): Go away! Go away! (*To* GINA.) Get her away from me, I say!

GINA (*in a low voice*): Go into the living room, Hedvig.

(HEDVIG *leaves silently.*)

HJALMAR (*busy, pulling out the table drawer*): I need my books with me. Where are my books?

GINA: Which books?

HJALMAR: My scientific works, of course — the technical journals I need for my invention.

GINA (*looking on the shelf*): Do you mean these over here, with no covers on them?

HJALMAR: Yes, yes, of course.

GINA (*puts a pile of journals down on the table*): Don't you want me to get Hedvig to cut them open for you?

HJALMAR: No. Nobody needs to cut any pages for me.

(*Brief silence.*)

GINA: So you *are* going to leave us, Ekdal?

HJALMAR (*rummaging among the books*): That goes without saying, I should think.

GINA: All right.

HJALMAR (*violently*): For you can hardly expect me to want to stay where my heart is pierced every single hour of the day!

GINA: God forgive you for thinking so bad of me!

HJALMAR: Proof — !

GINA: Seems to me, you're the one who should bring proof.

HJALMAR: After a past like yours? There are certain claims — I might call them the claims of the ideal —

GINA: What about Grandpa? What is *he* going to do, poor man?

HJALMAR: I know my duty. The helpless one goes with me. I'll go out and make arrangements— H'm (*Hesitantly.*) Has anybody found my hat on the stairs?

GINA: No. Have you lost your hat?

HJALMAR: I most certainly had it on when I came home last night; there isn't the slightest doubt about that. But now I can't find it.

GINA: Good Lord! Where did you go with those two drunks?

HJALMAR: Oh, don't ask about inessentials. Do you think I'm in a mood for remembering details?

GINA: I only hope you haven't got a cold, Ekdal (*Goes into the kitchen.*)

HJALMAR (*speaking to himself, in a low voice, angrily, as he empties the drawer*): You're a scoundrel, Relling! — A villain is what you are! — Miserable traitor! — I'd gladly see you assassinated — !

(*He puts aside some old letters, discovers the torn gift letter from the day before, picks it up and looks at the two pieces, puts them down quickly as* GINA *enters.*)

GINA (*putting a tray with food down on the table*): Here's a drop of coffee, if you want it. And some salt meat sandwiches.

HJALMAR (*glancing at the tray*): Salt meat? Never under this roof! True it is, I haven't taken solid nourishment for almost twenty-four hours, but that can't be helped. — My notes! My incipient memoirs! Where is my diary — all my important papers! (*Opens the door to the living room, but steps back.*) If she isn't there, too!

GINA: Heavens, Ekdal. She's got to be somewhere.

HJALMAR: Leave! (*He makes room.* HEDVIG, *scared, enters the studio. With his hand on the door knob; to* GINA.) During the last moments I spend in my former home I wish to be spared the sight of intruders — (*Enters the living room.*)

HEDVIG (*starts, asks her mother in a low and trembling voice*): Does that mean me?

GINA: Stay in the kitchen, Hedvig, or no — go to your own room. (*To* HJALMAR, *as she enters the living room.*) Wait a minute, Ekdal. Don't make such a mess in the dresser. I know where everything is.

HEDVIG (*remains motionless for a moment, in helpless fright, presses her lips together not to cry, clenches her hands, whispers*): The wild duck!

(*She tiptoes over to the shelf and takes the pistol down, opens the doors to the inner attic, goes inside, closes behind her.* HJALMAR *and* GINA *are heard talking in the living room.*)

HJALMAR (*appears with some notebooks and a pile of old papers, which he puts down on the table*): The bag obviously won't be enough. There are thousands of things I need to take with me!

GINA (*entering with the bag*): Can't you leave most of it behind for the time being and just pick up a clean shirt and some underwear?

HJALMAR: Phew — ! These exhausting preparations — ! (*Takes off his overcoat and throws it on the sofa.*)

GINA: And there's the coffee getting cold too.

HJALMAR: H'm. (*Without thinking, he takes a sip, and then another one.*)

GINA (*dusting off the back of chairs*): How are you ever going to find a large enough attic for the rabbits?

HJALMAR: You mean I have to drag all those rabbits along, too?

GINA: Grandpa can't do without his rabbits — you know that as well as I do.

HJALMAR: He'll have to get used to that. I shall have to give up higher values in life than a bunch of rabbits.

GINA (*dusting off the shelf*): Shall I put the flute in for you?

HJALMAR: No. No flute for me. But give me my pistol.

GINA: You want that old pestol?

HJALMAR: Yes. My loaded pistol.

GINA (*looking for it*): It's gone. He must have taken it inside with him.

HJALMAR: Is he in the attic?

GINA: Sure, he's in the attic.

HJALMAR: H'm. The lonely grayhead — (*He eats a sandwich, empties his cup of coffee.*)

GINA: If only we hadn't rented that room, you could have moved in there.

HJALMAR: And stay under the same roof as — ! Never! Never again!

GINA: But couldn't you stay in the living room for a day or two? There you'd have everything to yourself.

HJALMAR: Not within these walls!

GINA: How about down at Relling's and Molvik's, then?

HJALMAR: Don't mention their names to me! I get sick just thinking about them. Oh no — it's out into the wind and the snowdrifts for me — to walk from house to house seeking shelter for father and myself.

GINA: But you have no hat, Ekdal! You've lost your hat, remember?

HJALMAR: Oh, those two abominations! Rich in nothing but every vice! A hat must be procured. (*Takes another sandwich.*) Arrangements must be made. After all, I don't intend to catch my death. (*Looks for something on the tray.*)

GINA: What are you looking for?

HJALMAR: Butter.

GINA: Just a moment. (*Goes out into the kitchen.*)

HJALMAR (*shouting after her*): Oh never mind. Dry bread is good enough for me.

GINA (*bringing a plate with butter*): Here. This is supposed to be freshly churned.

(*She pours him another cup of coffee. He sits down on the sofa, puts more butter on his bread, eats and drinks in silence.*)

HJALMAR (*after a pause*): Could I, without being disturbed by anyone — and I mean *anyone* — stay in the living room for a day or two?

GINA: You certainly can, if you want to.

HJALMAR: You see, I don't know how to get all of father's things moved out on such short notice.

GINA: And there is this, too, that first you'd have to tell him that you don't want to live together with the rest of us any more.

HJALMAR (*pushing his cup away*): Yes, yes — that, too. I shall have to go into all those intricate relationships once again, to explain — I must think, I must have air to breathe, I can't bear all the burdens in one single day.

GINA: Of course not. And in such awful weather too —

HJALMAR (*moving* WERLE's *letter*): I notice this piece of paper still lying around.

GINA: Well, *I* haven't touched it.

HJALMAR: Not that it concerns *me* —

GINA: I'm sure *I* don't expect to make use of it —

HJALMAR: Nevertheless, I suppose we shouldn't let it get completely lost. In all the fuss of moving, something might easily —

GINA: I'll take care of it, Ekdal.

HJALMAR: For the gift letter belongs to father, first of all. It's his affair whether he wants to make use of it or not.

GINA (*with a sigh*): Yes, poor old Grandpa —

HJALMAR: Just to make sure — Is there any glue?

GINA (*walks over to the shelf*): Here's a bottle.

HJALMAR: And a brush?

GINA: Here. (*Brings him both.*)

HJALMAR (*picks up a pair of scissors*): Just a strip of paper on the back — (*Cuts and glues.*) Far be it from me to lay hands on somebody else's property — least of all the property of a poverty-stricken old man. — Well — not on — that other one's, either. — There, now! Leave it to dry for a while. And when it's dry, remove it. I don't want to see that document again — ever!

(GREGERS *enters.*)

GREGERS (*a little surprised*): What? So this is where you are, Hjalmar!

HJALMAR (*quickly gets up*): Sheer exhaustion drove me to sit down.

GREGERS: And I see you've had breakfast.

HJALMAR: The body, too, makes demands at times.

GREGERS: Well, what have you decided to do?

HJALMAR: For a man like me, there is only one way open. I am in the process of gathering up my most important possessions. Obviously, that takes time.

GINA (*a trifle impatient*): Do you want me to make the living room ready for you, or do you want me to pack the bag?

HJALMAR (*after an irritated glance at* GREGERS): Pack — and make the room ready.

GINA (*picking up the bag*): All right. I'll just put in the shirts and those other things. (*She goes into the living room, closing the door behind her.*)

GREGERS (*after a short silence*): I had no idea this would be the end of it. Is it really necessary for you to leave house and home?

HJALMAR (*paces restlessly up and down*): What do you want me to do? I am not made to be unhappy, Gregers. I require peace and security and comfort around me.

GREGERS: But you can have all that, Hjalmar. Just try. It seems to me there is a firm foundation to build upon now. Start all over again. And remember, you still have your invention to live for.

HJALMAR: Oh don't talk about that invention. It may take a long time yet.

GREGERS: So?

HJALMAR: Well, yes, for heaven's sake, what do you expect me to invent, anyway? The others have invented most of it already. It's getting more difficult every day.

GREGERS: But all the labor you have put into it — ?

HJALMAR: It was that dissipated Relling who got me started on it.

GREGERS: Relling?

HJALMAR: Yes, it was he who first called attention to my talent for making some fabulous invention or other in photography.

GREGERS: I see. It was Relling — !

HJALMAR: Ah — I have been so wonderfully happy about it. Not so much about the invention itself, but because Hedvig believed in it — believed with all the strength and power of a child's soul. — That is, I *thought* she did — fool as I was.

GREGERS: Can you really think that Hedvig would be false to you?

HJALMAR: I can believe anything now. It is Hedvig who is in the way. She it is who is shutting the sun out of my entire life.

GREGERS: Hedvig? You mean Hedvig? How in the world is she going to be an obstacle?

HJALMAR (*without answering*): I have loved that child more than I can ever say. You have no idea how happy I was whenever I came back to my humble dwelling and she rushed towards me with her sweet, squinting eyes. Ha, credulous fool that I was! She was so unspeakably dear to me — and so I lulled myself into the dream that I was equally dear to her.

GREGERS: You call that a dream?

HJALMAR: How can I tell? I can't get anything out of Gina. Besides, she completely lacks any sense of the ideal aspects of the issue. But to you I can open up, Gregers. It is this terrible doubt — perhaps Hedvig has never really loved me.

GREGERS: Maybe you'll receive proof — (*Listens.*) Shh! What's that? The wild duck?

HJALMAR: It's just quacking. Father's in the attic.

GREGERS: He is! (*Joy lights his face.*) I tell you again, Hjalmar — maybe you will find proof that your poor, misunderstood Hedvig has always loved you!

HJALMAR: Pah! What proof could she give? I dare not trust to mere asseverations.

GREGERS: Surely, Hedvig doesn't know what deceit is.

HJALMAR: Ah, Gregers — that is just what I cannot be certain of. Who knows what Gina and this Mrs. Sørby may have been whispering and scheming? And Hedvig's ears are big enough, believe you me. Maybe that gift letter didn't come as such a surprise to her. It seemed to me I noticed something like that.

GREGERS: Good heavens, Hjalmar! What kind of spirit is this that's taken possession of you!

HJALMAR: I have had my eyes opened. You just wait. It may turn out that the gift letter was just the beginning. Mrs. Sørby has always been very fond of Hedvig, and now, of course, it's in her power to do anything she likes for the child. They can take her away from me what day and hour they choose.

GREGERS: Hedvig will never leave you, Hjalmar. Never.

HJALMAR: Don't be too sure. If they beckon her with their arms full — ? And I who have loved her so infinitely much! I, whose greatest joy it was to take her tenderly by the hand and lead her, as one leads a frightened child through a dark and deserted room! Now I feel this painful certainty that the poor photographer in his attic has never really meant very much to her. She has only cleverly managed to keep on good terms with him while she bided her time.

GREGERS: You don't believe this, Hjalmar.

HJALMAR: That is just what is so terrible — I don't know what to believe — I'll never be able to find out! But do you really doubt that I am right? Ah, Gregers, you put too much trust in the claim of the ideal! If those others were to come now, with their ample offerings, and called to the child: Leave him; life awaits you here with us —

GREGERS (*quickly*): Yes, what then — ?

HJALMAR: If then I were to ask her: Hedvig, are you willing to give your life for me? (*Laughs scornfully.*) Oh yes — you'd find out soon enough what answer I'd get!

(*A pistol shot is heard from within the attic.*)

GREGERS (*with a shout of joy*): Hjalmar!

HJALMAR: Must he go shooting today — !

GINA (*enters*): Can't say I like this, Ekdal — Grandpa in there all by himself, banging away.

HJALMAR: I'll take a look —

GREGERS (*agitated, feelingly*): Wait! Do you know what that was?

HJALMAR: Yes, of course, I do.

GREGERS: No, you don't. But *I* know. It was the proof!

HJALMAR: What proof?

GREGERS: It was a child's sacrifice. She has got your father to shoot the wild duck.

HJALMAR: Shoot the wild duck!

GINA: Heavens — !

HJALMAR: Whatever for?

GREGERS: She wanted to sacrifice to you what she held dearest in the whole world. For then she thought you'd love her again.

HJALMAR (*softly, moved*): Oh that child!

GINA: What she thinks of!

GREGERS: All she wanted was your love, Hjalmar. Without it, life didn't seem possible to her.

GINA (*struggling with tears*): Now, do you see, Ekdal?

HJALMAR: Gina, where is she?

GINA (*sniffling*): Poor thing. She is sitting out in the kitchen, I guess.

HJALMAR (*walks to the kitchen door, flings it open, says*): Hedvig — come! Come to me! (*Looks around.*) No. She isn't here.

GINA: Then she must be in her own room.

HJALMAR (*offstage*): No, she isn't there, either. (*Re-entering the studio.*) She must have gone out.

GINA: Yes, for you know you didn't want to see hide nor hair of her in the house.

HJALMAR: If only she'd come back soon — so I can tell her — Now I feel that everything will be all right, Gregers. Now I think we can start life over again.

GREGERS (*quietly*): I knew it. Restitution would come through the child.

(*Old* EKDAL *appears in the door to his room. He is in full uniform and is buckling on his sabre.*)

HJALMAR (*surprised*): Father! You're in there!

GINA: Do you go shooting in your room, now, Grandpa?

EKDAL (*approaches indignantly*): So you're off hunting by yourself, are you Hjalmar?

HJALMAR (*tense, confused*): You mean it wasn't you who fired that shot in the attic just now?

EKDAL: I? Fired? H'm.

GREGERS (*shouts to* HJALMAR): She has shot the wild duck herself!

HJALMAR: What *is* this? (*He hurriedly slides the attic doors open, looks in, gives a loud cry.*) Hedvig!

GINA (*runs to the door*): Oh God! What is it?

HJALMAR (*going inside*): She is lying on the floor!

GREGERS: Lying — ! (*Follows* HJALMAR *inside.*)

GINA (*at the same time*): Hedvig! (*Enters the attic.*) No! No! No!

EKDAL: Ho-ho! So *she* has taken to hunting too, now!

(HJALMAR, GINA, *and* GREGERS *drag* HEDVIG *into the studio. Her trailing right hand clasps the pistol tightly.*)

HJALMAR (*beside himself*): The pistol went off! She's hit! Call for help! Help!

GINA (*running out into the hallway, shouts down*): Relling! Relling! Doctor Relling! Hurry up here, fast as you can!

(HJALMAR *and* GREGERS *put* HEDVIG *down on the sofa.*)

EKDAL (*quietly*): The woods avenge themselves.

HJALMAR (*on his knees beside* HEDVIG): She's coming to now. She is coming to. Oh yes, yes, yes —

GINA (*having returned*): Where's she hit? I can't see a thing.

(RELLING *enters hurriedly, followed by* MOLVIK. *The latter is without vest and tie, his tailcoat thrown open.*)

RELLING: What's the matter?

GINA: They say Hedvig has shot herself.

HJALMAR: Come and help us!

RELLING: Shot herself! (*He pulls the table back and begins to examine her.*)

HJALMAR (*still on his knees, looking anxiously at* RELLING): It can't be dangerous, can it, Relling? What, Relling? She hardly bleeds at all. It can't possibly be dangerous?

RELLING: How did this happen?

HJALMAR: Oh, I don't know —

GINA: She was going to shoot the wild duck.

RELLING: The wild duck?

HJALMAR: The pistol must have gone off.

RELLING: H'm. I see.

EKDAL: The woods avenge themselves. But I'm not afraid. (*Enters the attic and closes the doors behind him.*)

HJALMAR: Relling — why don't you say anything?

RELLING: The bullet has entered her chest.

HJALMAR: Yes, but she's coming to!

RELLING: Can't you see that Hedvig is dead?

GINA (*bursts into tears*): Oh, the child, the child — !

GREGERS (*hoarsely*): In the depths of the sea —

HJALMAR (*jumps to his feet*): She must live! I want her to live! For God's sake, Relling — just for a moment — just so I can tell her how unspeakably much I have loved her all the time!

RELLING: Her heart has been pierced. Internal hemorrhage. She died instantly.

HJALMAR: And I who chased her away from me like an animal! Frightened and lonely she crawled into the attic and died for love of me. (*Sobbing.*) Never to be able to make up for it! Never to tell her — ! (*Shakes his fists upwards.*) You! You above! If thou art at all — ! Why hast thou done this unto me?

GINA: Shhh, shhh. You mustn't make such a fuss. We had no right to keep her, I suppose.

MOLVIK: The child is not dead. It sleepeth.

RELLING: Rubbish!

HJALMAR (*quieting down, walks over to the sofa, looks at* HEDVIG, *his arms crossed*): There she lies, so stiff and still.

RELLING (*trying to release the pistol*): She holds on so tightly, I can't —

GINA: No, no, Relling. Don't break her fingers. Let the pestol be.

HJALMAR: Let her have it with her.

GINA: Yes, let her. But the child isn't going to lie out here for a show. She is going into her own little room, right now. Give me a hand, Ekdal.

(HJALMAR *and* GINA *carry* HEDVIG *between them.*)

HJALMAR (*carrying*): Gina, Gina — do you think you can bear this?

GINA: The one has to help the other. Seems to me like now we both have a share in her.

MOLVIK (*raising his arms, muttering*): Praise be the Lord, to dust thou returnest, to dust thou returnest —

RELLING (*whispers*): Shut up, man! You're drunk.

(HJALMAR *and* GINA *carry* HEDVIG *through the kitchen door.* RELLING *closes the door behind them.* MOLVIK *slinks quietly out into the hall.*)

RELLING (*goes up to* GREGERS): Nobody is going to tell me this was an accident.

GREGERS (*who has remained stunned, moving convulsively*): Who is to say how this terrible thing happened?

RELLING: There were powder burns on her dress. She must have placed the muzzle against her chest and pulled the trigger.

GREGERS: Hedvig has not died in vain. Did you notice how grief released what is great in him?

RELLING: There is a touch of greatness in most of us when we stand in sorrow by a corpse. How long do you think that will last with him?

GREGERS: As if it won't last and grow throughout the rest of his days!

RELLING: Within a year little Hedvig won't be anything to him but an occasion for spouting pretty sentiments.

GREGERS: And you dare say that about Hjalmar Ekdal!

RELLING: Let's talk about this again when the first grass has withered on her grave. You'll hear all about "the child so early taken from the father's heart." You'll see him wallow in sentimentality and self-admiration and self-pity. You just wait!

GREGERS: If you are right and I am wrong, life isn't worth living.

RELLING: Oh, life would be fairly tolerable if only we'd be spared these blasted bill collectors who come around pestering us paupers with the claim of the ideal.

GREGERS (*staring ahead*): In that case I am glad my destiny is what it is.

RELLING: Beg your pardon — what *is* your destiny?

GREGERS (*about to leave*): To be the thirteenth man at the table.

RELLING: The hell it is.

"TO BE AN AUTHOR," said Ibsen, "is to see." He meant an author of imaginative literature, *ein Dichter*. Yet in his later years he rarely went to the theater and always referred to his plays as "books" and to his audience as his "readers." If there is a contradiction here it disappears in the concept of drama as visualized dialogue. *The Wild Duck*, which, like all of Ibsen's later plays, appeared in book form before it was staged, *can* be successfully staged because it was first of all conceived and realized in a poet's imagination.

In a dramatic canon that Ibsen himself urged should be read as one continuous, unbroken whole, *The Wild Duck* marks a transition. The sequence is continuous in the sense that all Ibsen's plays deal with the individual's struggle for self-realization (though Ibsen denied being influenced by Kierkegaard). Still there is a shift. In the early plays within the phase of his development of the modern prose drama that began with *Pillars of Society* (1877) and ended with *Hedda Gabler* (1890), Ibsen emphasizes the pressures of social institutions that corrupt and inhibit the self. In the later plays the struggle is internalized, the issues are revealed rather than debated, and the realistic surface is charged with multiple symbolic meaning. The change is from implicitly engaged polemics on social problems to disinterested exhibits of the psychology of the subconscious. *The Wild Duck* (1884) deals with domestic morals in a carefully delineated milieu, but its inner movement is on submerged levels of the psyche.

Its earliest readers and audiences found it obscure and morbid ("a facetious genre picture with a meaningless and uninteresting splotch of blood away in one corner"), and even today, when it is generally considered one of Ibsen's greatest plays, there are critics who accept the judgment but insist that it does not say very much. They object to the Scribean machinery of the too-logical action, to the disingenuousness of the carefully casual disclosures of the past in innuendo, to the unrelieved mediocrity of language, to the inelegant and perfunctory opening expository scene between the two servants, to the shift in setting between Acts I and II that tends to reduce the former to mere prologue, to the note of pseudo-poetic profundity and melodrama in Old Ekdal's vengeful woods, to the way discussions issue in slogans of resounding platitude ("Take his vital lie away from the average man, and you take his happiness, too"), and to the stereotypes of naturalistic characterization: the old roué, the drunken lodger, the broken father, the drab but loyal wife, the innocent and suffering child. Hjalmar, they say, may be fine enough with beer and chamberlains, but the total figure is a caricature. This would not matter in some kinds of plays, but it matters here, for Ibsen writes in a convention that puts a premium on plausibility of character and incident. It is hard to accept as basic plot premise Gregers Werle's continuing faith in the greatness of a man who shows himself to be an obvious phony every time he opens his mouth. Gregers may be sick, but he is not supposed to be stupid.

For others, however, the play survives its imperfections, real or alleged, and it may illuminate the nature of the strength of naturalistic drama to try to answer why and how it does so.

It stays close to Ibsen's usual pattern. A member or a friend of a middle-class family returns after long absence and by his return triggers disastrous revelations. The action is nearly all exposition — the gradual discovery of the painful truth about the past concealed in the family's decorous and complacent present. We recognize the pattern from *Oedipus Rex*, and *The Wild Duck* does, in fact, share with Sophocles' play a tightness of structure, a concentration of events in small compass of time and space, that have been made possible by the playwrights' seizure of their stories near their climax. The plot is a looking-back on the past responsible for the present crisis. It is a "fifth act play" compared with the panoramic, expansive, chronologically developed Shakespearean drama.

But aside from its retrospective structure, *The Wild Duck* has little enough in common with classical tragedy. No kingdom trembles when Hjalmar Ekdal is in agony. His suffering is not ceremonial. He is too small a man to be the concern of gods, too meanly petty to be even wicked. His case is too random to appear archetypal. Beside the language of traditional tragedy, dialogue here is small talk indeed and Hjalmar's eloquence merely absurd. Hedvig innocently exposes him when she asks whether the chamberlains sang and recited poetry at Werle's party; that, in her experience, is what admirable men do when they function socially. Compared with the public settings of tragedy, focuses for the life of an entire society, the Ekdal studio is a small and shrunken world — banal, pathetic, ridiculous. But can it not be argued that the inapplicability of the yardstick of great tragedy to *The Wild Duck* is less a comment on the play than on modern man and his disoriented values? Every age gets the drama it deserves.

And if *The Wild Duck* is not in the tragic tradition, neither does it belong with those pat, once shocking, now commonplace, social messages that date such a large part of naturalistic drama of the last and this century: exposés of skeletons, today more dead than fearful, in Victorian closets. Ibsen has been unfairly blamed for the dreary successes of what Shaw with a misnomer called "Ibsenism." The battles won, their champions have become bores, holding forth apropos of nothing. People had resented what they took to be Ibsen's attack on the entrenched sanctities of religion, married life, and democracy in the plays immediately preceding *The Wild Duck* and been scandalized by his reference (in *Ghosts*) to incest and venereal disease. *The Wild Duck* records, with deceptive blandness, the meaning of the public's reaction to the playwright's anatomies of bourgeois values: most people not only do not want the truth about themselves, they are actually much better off with comfortable lies. Its mood is delicately balanced between two statements, opposite in tone, of the same single fact about man: Swift's virulent irony in *A Tale of a Tub* in defining "the sublime and refined point of felicity" as "the possession of being well deceived" and the compassionate excuse for the grieving women of Canterbury that T. S. Eliot puts into the mouth of Saint Thomas à Becket in *Murder in the Cathedral*: "Human kind cannot bear very much reality." In conjunction with *An Enemy of the People*, *The Wild Duck* demonstrates Ibsen's nearly compulsive habit — the genuine dramatist's — of seeing every issue from opposite sides. In the earlier play he had put much of himself into Dr. Stockmann, the hearty, indomitable fighter for truth. Here he seems to parody his own reforming self in the character of the gloomy Gregers Werle, whose officious mania for truth ends in a child's death.

But the play never surrenders the ambiguities of its poise between tragedy and farce, pathos and cynicism, pity and ridicule. It is skeptical and relativistic, not doctrinaire. If its whole point is to tell us that the ordinary person's happiness depends on a protective illusion against brutal fact, its spokesman appears oddly chosen. As in so many realistic plays of the late 19th century (including some of Ibsen's own), the voice of the common-sensical *raisonneur* in *The Wild Duck* is that of a man of science, but Dr. Relling is pretty much a human wreck. Mrs. Sørby, who should know and who is the play's most sensible character, calls him a man who has "thrown away what is best in himself." At the news of her marriage to Werle he promptly takes his own medicine and runs off to a saloon — just like Old Ekdal scuttling off to his room at the advent of reality. His much-quoted formula for happy adjustment can be regarded as the play's thesis only if we ignore his flawed personality and his inferior plot position as commentator rather than main actor and, for that matter, the shoddiness of his tolerant and cynical psychological wisdom. Nor is the principle of the "vital lie" a major plot issue, for only incidentally does Hedvig kill herself in order to restore Hjalmar's faith in his "invention."

The action of the play may be defined as the conflict between Relling and Gregers for control of Hjalmar. They are rival social workers, or amateur psychologists, on the Ekdal case. Hjalmar's character renders the *agon* ridiculous rather than heroic. He is a photographer who is blind even to his own reality and whose only professional activity, significantly, is retouching. Self-indulgent, confused, borrowing his image of himself from his worshiping friend, acted upon rather than acting, he seems like an early version of the contemporary anti-hero. Gregers initiates the action but is its antagonist rather than its protagonist. His mission of truth succeeds only ironically when it leads to the death of the one lovable and wholly innocent member of the entire household. There is no real recognition. Hedvig dies because her sight fails spiritually as well as physically: she never sees through Hjalmar. Gregers's belief in Hjalmar's greatness of soul remains unshaken at the end. And there is no reason to doubt the accuracy of Relling's prediction that Hedvig's death soon will be nothing to Hjalmar but an occasion for mawkish sentimentality. And as if to keep us from extracting any larger significance from these sordid events, Ibsen ends his play by having Relling's profanity explode the pretentious melodramatics of Gregers's belief — *his* vital lie — that he is "the thirteenth man at the table" — superfluous, tragically chosen by destiny to bring bad luck to others. Neither the cynic's realism nor the neurotic's idealism receives ultimate sanction. They balance inconclusively on Hjalmar's rhetoric of grief. We don't even know with absolute certainty that he is *not* Hedvig's real father. Gina herself says she doesn't know, and there is no proof she is lying. Certainty, the plays suggests, is a luxury that paupers cannot afford.

By convention, naturalism admits only symbols whose credentials as naturalism are in order — that is, they must first be facts or concretes in the surface life-likeness. The unseen wild duck is the symbolic center of the play, from which "meanings" radiate. But before it is anything else it is part of the Ekdal establishment, an object as real as the photographs and the flute and the herring salad. It presides in the attic world of fantasy and escape, a denizen of the depths of the sea, content among the shipwrecked skipper's assorted belongings. It is one of Ibsen's triumphs that the whole unlikely contrivance of the barnyard attic is both believable as solid fact and rich and beautiful in its symbolic suggestiveness. It convinces because it is comical and pitiful, haunting and bizarre, all at the same time.

Seeing the wild duck as a symbol is a part of the plot. The idea is Gregers's, not that of critics bent on "reading things into" the play. As the Messiah figure he aspires to be, Gregers, in fact, is addicted to symbol-mongering, insisting that things are not just what they seem to be but something else. Reality to him is a metaphor. The attic is not just an attic, Hjalmar and Gina live in a poisonous marsh, his father is a callous and wanton and inexpert hunter, Hjalmar a wounded wild duck, Gregers himself a clever retriever, his "mission" collecting outstanding bills on behalf of some moral or metaphysical absolute.

But the wild duck is a more versatile symbol than Gregers's monomania can recognize. It offers — and has offered — irresistible and endless game for interpretive ingenuity. What does it stand for? Escape from reality? Wounded innocence? The guilty past? Whom does it represent — and *for* whom? Gregers thinks Hjalmar is a wild duck, but aren't there ways in which the duck could be said to symbolize as well not only Molvik and Old Ekdal, but Hedvig and Relling and Old Werle and Gregers himself? May we ignore Relling's reference to Gina's "comfortable waddle" or the fact that she, like the duck, has passed from Werle's hands into Hjalmar's, somewhat the worse for wear? To make choices here seems wrong. Rather, by defining the attitudes of the different members of the household to the wild duck and to the attic where it lives one grasps the play's main unifying image and goes a long way toward understanding the characters and their relationships and their position vis à vis the general issue of reality versus illusion. Like all successful symbols, the wild duck is not elaboration but concentration, does not obscure but clarifies, is not a poetic device but what the poetry is about.

All this further suggests that "meaning" in *The Wild Duck* is not to be sought in a thesis or a concept but in such realities as Old Ekdal's reluctance to use the pronoun "I," in Hjalmar's uncut technical journals, in Gina's infinitely patient and competent housekeeping. The stage language — both scenic and verbal — of naturalism did not banish poetry from the theater. There is in *The Wild Duck* careful organization of words for esthetic purposes. In addition to its utilitarian value in establishing social milieu and setting off Hjalmar's excursions into oratory, the drab, colloquial dialogue also reveals deeper levels of imagery that bear upon theme and character. The allusions to sight and blindness, darkness and light, that weave in and out of Hjalmar's and Gregers's speeches, reinforce the blindness motif in the plot and achieve effects of telling irony with reference to "blindness" as a spiritual quality: Gregers rejecting Relling's estimate of Hjalmar's character with the words, "I didn't know I was as blind as all that"; Hjalmar being forced by circumstance to admit to weaker eyesight than "the Near-sighted Gentleman" and refusing to "look at the child" after "he has had his eyes opened." The subdued green light in Werle's study in Act I is a relevant scenic image in preparing us visually for "the depths of the sea" that are, figuratively, the setting for the four acts that follow.

What Ibsen "saw" in the world of *The Wild Duck* was something more than the trivialities of middle-class life, the pointless thrill of adultery and uncertain parentage, or the proof of a social tract. His vision takes in neither tragedy's sublime affirmation of man's significance in a dark world nor the scrupulous factuality of a documentary but, compassionately and unsentimentally, the lives of small people suffering under the high cost of truth.

August Strindberg

THE FATHER

Translated by Elizabeth Sprigge

Characters

THE CAPTAIN	THE PASTOR
LAURA, *his wife*	THE NURSE
BERTHA, *their daughter*	NÖJD
DOCTOR OSTERMARK	THE ORDERLY

The whole play takes place in the central living-room of the Captain's home. He is a cavalry officer in a remote country district of Sweden.

It is about 1886, shortly before Christmas.

At the back of the room, towards the right, a door leads to the hall. In the left wall there is a door to other rooms, and in the right-hand corner another, smaller door, covered in the same wall-paper as the walls, opens on to a staircase leading to the Captain's room above.

In the centre of the room stands a large round table on which are newspapers, magazines, a big photograph album and a lamp. On the right are a leather-covered sofa, arm chairs and a smaller table. On the left is a writing-bureau with a pendulum clock upon it. Arms, guns and gun-bags hang on the walls, and military coats on pegs by the door to the hall.

ACT ONE

(Early evening. The lamp on the table is lighted. The CAPTAIN *and the* PASTOR *are sitting on the sofa talking. The* CAPTAIN *is in*

Reprinted by permission of Willis Kingsley Wing. Copyright © 1955, by Elizabeth Sprigge. All rights whatsoever in this play are strictly reserved and applications for performances, etc. should be made to Willis Kingsley Wing, 24 E. 38th Street, New York, N.Y. 10016.

undress uniform with riding-boots and spurs; the PASTOR *wears black, with a white cravat in place of his clerical collar, and is smoking a pipe.*

The CAPTAIN *rises and rings a bell. The* ORDERLY *enters from the hall.*)

ORDERLY: Yes, sir?

CAPTAIN: Is Nöjd there?

ORDERLY: Nöjd's in the kitchen, sir, waiting for orders.

CAPTAIN: In the kitchen again, is he? Send him here at once.

ORDERLY: Yes, sir.

(*Exit.*)

PASTOR: Why, what's the trouble?

CAPTAIN: Oh, the ruffian's been at his tricks again with one of the servant girls! He's a damn nuisance, that fellow!

PASTOR: Was it Nöjd you said? Didn't he give some trouble back in the spring?

CAPTAIN: Ah, you remember that, do you? Look here, you give him a bit of a talking to, there's a good chap. That might have some effect. I've sworn at him and thrashed him, without making the least impression.

PASTOR: So now you want me to preach to him. How much impression do you think God's word is likely to make on a trooper?

CAPTAIN: Well, my dear brother-in-law, it makes none at all on me, as you know, but . . .

PASTOR: As I know only too well.

CAPTAIN: But on him? Worth trying anyhow.

(*Enter* NÖJD.)

What have you been up to now, Nöjd?

NÖJD: God bless you, sir, I can't talk about that — not with Pastor here.

PASTOR: Don't mind me, my lad.

NÖJD: Well you see, sir, it was like this. We was at a dance at Gabriel's, and then, well then Ludwig said as . . .

CAPTAIN: What's Ludwig got to do with it? Stick to the point.

NÖJD: Well then Emma said as we should go in the barn.

CAPTAIN: I see. I suppose it was Emma who led you astray.

NÖJD: Well, not far from it. What I mean is if the girl's not game, nothing don't happen.

CAPTAIN: Once and for all — are you the child's father or are you not?

NÖJD: How's one to know?

CAPTAIN: What on earth do you mean? Don't you know?

NÖJD: No, you see, sir, that's what you never can know.

CAPTAIN: You mean you weren't the only man?

NÖJD: That time I was. But you can't tell if you've always been the only one.

CAPTAIN: Are you trying to put the blame on Ludwig? Is that the idea?

NÖJD: It's not easy to know who to put the blame on.

CAPTAIN: But, look here, you told Emma you would marry her.

NÖJD: Oh well, you always have to say that, you know.

CAPTAIN (*to the* PASTOR): This is atrocious.

PASTOR: It's the old story. Come now, Nöjd, surely you are man enough to know if you are the father.

NÖJD: Well, sir, it's true, I did go with her, but you know yourself, Pastor, that don't always lead to nothing.

PASTOR: Look here, my lad, it's you we are talking about. And you are not going to leave that girl destitute with a child. You can't be forced to marry her, but you must make provision for the child. That you must do.

NÖJD: So must Ludwig then.

CAPTAIN: If that's how it is, the case will have to go before the Magistrate. I can't settle it, and it's really nothing to do with me. Dismiss!

PASTOR: One moment, Nöjd. Ahem. Don't you think it's rather a dirty trick to leave a girl destitute with a child like that? Don't you think so — eh?

NÖJD: Yes, if I knew I was the father, it would be, but I tell you, Pastor, you never can know that. And it wouldn't be much fun slaving all your life for another chap's brat. You and the Captain must see that for yourselves.

CAPTAIN: That will do, Nöjd.

NÖJD: Yes, sir, thank you, sir.

CAPTAIN: And keep out of the kitchen, you scoundrel!

(*Exit* NÖJD.)

Why didn't you haul him over the coals?

PASTOR: What do you mean? Didn't I?

CAPTAIN: No, you just sat there muttering to yourself.

PASTOR: As a matter of fact, I scarcely knew what to say to him. It's hard on the girl, of course, but it's hard on the boy too. Supposing he's not the father? The girl can nurse the baby for four months at the orphanage, and after that it will be taken care of for good. But the boy can't nurse the child, can he? Later on, the girl will get a good place in some respectable family, but if the boy is cashiered, his future may be ruined.

CAPTAIN: Upon my soul, I'd like to be the magistrate and judge this case! Maybe the boy is responsible — that's what you can't know. But one thing you *can* know — if anybody's guilty, the girl is.

PASTOR: Well, I never sit in judgment. Now what was it we were talking about when this blessed business interrupted us? Yes, Bertha and her confirmation, wasn't it?

CAPTAIN: It's not just a question of confirmation, but of her whole future. The house is full of women, all trying to mould this child of mine. My mother-in-law wants to turn her into a spiritualist; Laura wants her to be an artist; the governess would have her a Methodist, old Margaret a Baptist, and the servant girls a Salvation Army lass. You can't make a character out of patchwork. Meanwhile I . . . I, who have more right than all the rest to guide her, am opposed at every turn. So I must send her away.

PASTOR: You have too many women running your house.

CAPTAIN: You're right there. It's like going into a cage of tigers. They'd soon tear me to pieces, if I didn't hold a red-hot poker under their noses. It's all very well for you to laugh, you blackguard. It wasn't enough that I married your sister; you had to palm off your old stepmother on me too.

PASTOR: Well, good Lord, one can't have stepmothers in one's house!

CAPTAIN: No, you prefer mothers-in-law — in someone else's house, of course.

PASTOR: Well, well, we all have our burdens to bear.

CAPTAIN: I daresay, but I have more than my share. There's my old nurse too, who treats me as if I still wore a bib. She's a good old soul, to be sure, but she shouldn't be here.

PASTOR: You should keep your women-folk in order, Adolf. You give them too much rope.

CAPTAIN: My dear fellow, can you tell me how to keep women in order?

PASTOR: To tell the truth, although she's my sister, Laura was always a bit of a handful.

CAPTAIN: Laura has her faults, of course, but they are not very serious ones.

PASTOR: Oh come now, I know her!

CAPTAIN: She was brought up with romantic ideas and has always found it a little difficult to come to terms with life. But she is my wife and . . .

PASTOR: And because she is your wife she must be the best of women. No, brother-in-law, it's she not you who wears the trousers.

CAPTAIN: In any case, the whole household has gone mad. Laura's determined Bertha shan't leave her, and I won't let her stay in this lunatic asylum.

PASTOR: So Laura's determined, is she? Then there's bound to be trouble, I'm afraid. As a child she used to lie down and sham dead until they gave in to her. Then she would calmly hand back whatever she'd set her mind on, explaining it wasn't the thing she wanted, but simply to get her own way.

CAPTAIN: So she was like that even then, was she? Hm. As a matter of fact, she does sometimes get so overwrought I'm frightened for her and think she must be ill.

PASTOR: What is it you want Bertha to do that's such a bone of contention? Can't you come to some agreement?

CAPTAIN: Don't think I want to turn her into a prodigy — or into some image of myself. But I will not play pander and have my daughter fitted for nothing but the marriage market. For then, if she didn't marry after all, she'd have a wretched time of it. On the other hand, I don't want to start her off in some man's career with a long training that would be entirely wasted if she did marry.

PASTOR: Well, what do you want then?

CAPTAIN: I want her to be a teacher. Then, if she doesn't marry she'll be able to support herself, and at least be no worse off than those unfortunate schoolmasters who have to support families on their earnings. And if she does marry, she can educate her own children. Isn't that reasonable?

PASTOR: Reasonable, yes — but what about her artistic talent? Wouldn't it be against the grain to repress that?

CAPTAIN: No. I showed her attempts to a well-known painter who told me they were nothing but the usual sort of thing learnt at school. Then, during the summer, some young jackanapes came along who knew better and said she was a genius—whereupon the matter was settled in Laura's favour.

PASTOR: Was he in love with Bertha?

CAPTAIN: I take that for granted.

PASTOR: Well, God help you, old boy, I don't see any solution. But it's a tiresome business, and I suppose Laura has supporters . . . (*indicates other rooms*) in there.

CAPTAIN: You may be sure of that. The whole household is in an uproar, and between ourselves the method of attack from that quarter is not exactly chivalrous.

PASTOR (*rising*): Do you think I haven't been through it?

CAPTAIN: You too?

PASTOR: Yes, indeed.

CAPTAIN: But to me the worst thing about it is that Bertha's future should be decided in there from motives of sheer hate. They do nothing but talk about men being made to see that women can do this and do that. It's man versus woman the whole day long . . . Must you go? Won't you stay to supper? I don't know what there is, but do stay. I'm expecting the new doctor, you know. Have you seen him yet?

PASTOR: I caught a glimpse of him on my way here. He looks a decent, reliable sort of man.

CAPTAIN: That's good. Do you think he may be my ally?

PASTOR: Maybe. It depends how well he knows women.

CAPTAIN: But won't you stay?

PASTOR: Thank you, my dear fellow, but I promised to be home this evening, and my wife gets anxious if I'm late.

CAPTAIN: Anxious! Furious, you mean. Well, as you please. Let me help you on with your coat.

PASTOR: It's certainly very cold to-night. Thank you. You must look after yourself, Adolf. You seem a bit on edge.

CAPTAIN: On edge? Do I?

PASTOR: Yes. You aren't very well, are you?

CAPTAIN: Did Laura put this into your head? For the last twenty years she's been treating me as if I had one foot in the grave.

PASTOR: Laura? No, it's just that I'm . . . I'm worried about you. Take my advice and look after yourself. Goodbye, old man. By the way, didn't you want to talk about the confirmation?

CAPTAIN: By no means. But I give you my word this shall take its own course — and be chalked up to the official conscience. I am neither a witness to the truth, nor a martyr. We have got past that sort of thing. Goodbye. Remember me to your wife.

PASTOR: Goodbye, Adolf. Give my love to Laura.

(*Exit* PASTOR. *The* CAPTAIN *opens the bureau and settles down to his accounts.*)

CAPTAIN: Thirty-four — nine, forty-three — seven, eight, fifty-six.

LAURA (*entering from the next room*): Will you please . . .

CAPTAIN: One moment! — Sixty-six, seventy-one, eighty-four, eighty-nine, ninety-two, a hundred. What is it?

LAURA: Am I disturbing you?

CAPTAIN: Not in the least. Housekeeping money, I suppose?

LAURA: Yes, housekeeping money.

CAPTAIN: If you put the accounts down there, I will go through them.

LAURA: Accounts?

CAPTAIN: Yes.

LAURA: Do you expect me to keep accounts now?

CAPTAIN: Of course you must keep accounts. Our position's most precarious, and if we go bankrupt, we must have accounts to show. Otherwise we could be accused of negligence.

LAURA: It's not my fault if we're in debt.

CAPTAIN: That's what the accounts will show.

LAURA: It's not my fault the tenant farmer doesn't pay.

CAPTAIN: Who was it recommended him so strongly? You. Why did you recommend such a — shall we call him a scatterbrain?

LAURA: Why did you take on such a scatterbrain?

CAPTAIN: Because I wasn't allowed to eat in peace, sleep in peace or work in peace till you got him here. You wanted him because your brother wanted to get rid of him; my mother-in-law wanted him because I didn't; the governess wanted him because he was a Methodist, and old Margaret because she had known his grandmother as a child. That's why, and if I hadn't taken him I should be in a lunatic asylum by now, or else in the family vault. However, here's the housekeeping allowance and your pin money. You can give me the accounts later.

LAURA (*with an ironic bob*): Thank you so much. — By the way, do you keep accounts yourself — of what you spend outside the household?

CAPTAIN: That's none of your business.

LAURA: True. As little my business as the future of my own child. Did you gentlemen come to any decision at this evening's conference?

CAPTAIN: I had already made my decision, so I merely had to communicate it to the only friend I have in the family. Bertha is going to live in town. She will leave in a fortnight's time.

LAURA: Where, if I may ask, is she going to stay?

CAPTAIN: At Sävberg's — the solicitor's.

LAURA: That Freethinker!

CAPTAIN: According to the law as it now stands, children are brought up in their father's faith.

LAURA: And the mother has no say in the matter?

CAPTAIN: None whatever. She sells her birthright by legal contract and surrenders all her rights. In return the husband supports her and her children.

LAURA: So she has no rights over her own child?

CAPTAIN: None at all. When you have sold something, you don't expect to get it back and keep the money too.

LAURA: But supposing the father and mother were to decide things together . . . ?

CAPTAIN: How would that work out? I want her to live in town; you want her to live at home. The mathematical mean would be for her to stop at the railway station, midway between home and town. You see? It's a deadlock.

LAURA: Then the lock must be forced. . . . What was Nöjd doing here?

CAPTAIN: That's a professional secret.

LAURA: Which the whole kitchen knows.

CAPTAIN: Then doubtless you know it too.

LAURA: I do.

CAPTAIN: And are ready to sit in judgment?

LAURA: The law does that.

CAPTAIN: The law doesn't say who the child's father is.

LAURA: Well, people know that for themselves.

CAPTAIN: Discerning people say that's what one never can know.

LAURA: How extraordinary! Can't one tell who a child's father is?

CAPTAIN: Apparently not.

LAURA: How perfectly extraordinary! Then how can the father have those rights over the mother's child?

CAPTAIN: He only has them when he takes on the responsibility — or has it forced on him. But of course in marriage there is no doubt about the paternity.

LAURA: No doubt?

CAPTAIN: I should hope not.

LAURA: But supposing the wife has been unfaithful?

CAPTAIN: Well, such a supposition has no bearing on our problem. Is there anything else you want to ask me about?

LAURA: No, nothing.

CAPTAIN: Then I shall go up to my room. Please let me know when the doctor comes. (*Closes the bureau and rises.*)

LAURA: I will.

CAPTAIN (*going out by the wall-papered door*): As soon as he comes, mind. I don't want to be discourteous, you understand.

(*Exit.*)

LAURA: I understand. (*She looks at the bank-notes she is holding.*)

MOTHER-IN-LAW (*off*): Laura!

LAURA: Yes, Mother?

MOTHER-IN-LAW: Is my tea ready?

LAURA (*at the door to the next room*): It's coming in a moment.

(*The* ORDERLY *opens the hall door.*)

ORDERLY: Dr. Östermark.

(*Enter* DOCTOR. *Exit* ORDERLY, *closing the door.*)

LAURA (*shaking hands*): How do you do, Dr. Östermark. Let me welcome you to our home. The Captain is out, but he will be back directly.

DOCTOR: I must apologize for calling so late, but I have already had to pay some professional visits.

LAURA: Won't you sit down?

DOCTOR: Thank you.

LAURA: Yes, there is a lot of illness about just now, but I hope all the same that you will find this place suits you. It is so important for people in a lonely country district like this to have a doctor who takes a real interest in his patients. I have heard you so warmly spoken of, Dr. Östermark, I hope we shall be on the best of terms.

DOCTOR: You are too kind, dear lady. I hope, however, for your sake that my visits here will not often be of a professional nature. I take it that the health of your family is, on the whole, good, and that . . .

LAURA: Yes, we have been fortunate enough not to have any serious illnesses, but all the same things are not quite as they should be.

DOCTOR: Indeed?

LAURA: No, I'm afraid not really at all as one would wish.

DOCTOR: Dear, dear, you quite alarm me!

LAURA: In a family there are sometimes things which honour and duty compel one to keep hidden from the world.

DOCTOR: But not from one's doctor.

LAURA: No. That is why it is my painful duty to tell you the whole truth from the start.

DOCTOR: May we not postpone this conversation until I have had the honour of meeting the Captain?

LAURA: No. You must hear what I have to say before you see him.

DOCTOR: Does it concern him then?

LAURA: Yes, him. My poor, dear husband.

DOCTOR: You are making me most uneasy. Whatever your trouble, Madam, you can confide in me.

LAURA (*taking out her handkerchief*): My husband's mind is affected. Now you know, and later on you will be able to judge for yourself.

DOCTOR: You astound me. The Captain's learned treatise on mineralogy, for which I have the greatest admiration, shows a clear and powerful intellect.

LAURA: Does it? I shall be overjoyed if we — his relatives — are mistaken.

DOCTOR: It is possible, of course, that his mind is disturbed in other ways. Tell me . . .

LAURA: That is exactly what we fear. You see, at times he has the most peculiar ideas, which wouldn't matter much for a scientist, if they

weren't such a burden on his family. For instance, he has an absolute mania for buying things.

DOCTOR: That is significant. What kind of things?

LAURA: Books. Whole cases of them, which he never reads.

DOCTOR: Well, that a scholar should buy books isn't so alarming.

LAURA: You don't believe what I am telling you?

DOCTOR: I am convinced, Madam, that you believe what you are telling me.

LAURA: Well, then, is it possible for anyone to see in a microscope
what's happening on another planet?

DOCTOR: Does he say he can do that?

LAURA: Yes, that's what he says.

DOCTOR: In a microscope?

LAURA: In a microscope. Yes.

DOCTOR: That is significant, if it is so.

LAURA: If it is so! You don't believe me, Doctor. And here have I let
you in to the family secret.

DOCTOR: My dear lady, I am honoured by your confidence, but as a
physician I must observe and examine before giving an opinion.
Has the Captain shown any symptoms of instability, any lack of
will power?

LAURA: Has he, indeed! We have been married twenty years, and he
has never yet made a decision without going back on it.

DOCTOR: Is he dogmatic?

LAURA: He certainly lays down the law, but as soon as he gets his own
way, he loses interest and leaves everything to me.

DOCTOR: That is significant and requires careful consideration. The
will, you see, Madam, is the backbone of the mind. If it is injured,
the mind falls to pieces.

LAURA: God knows how I have schooled myself to meet his every wish
during these long hard years. Oh, if you knew what I have been
through with him, if you only knew!

DOCTOR: I am profoundly distressed to learn of your trouble, Madam,
and I promise I will do what I can. You have my deepest sympathy
and I beg you to rely on me implicitly. But now you have told me
this, I am going to ask one thing of you. Don't allow anything to
prey on the patient's mind. In a case of instability, ideas can sometimes take hold and grow into an obsession — or even monomania.
Do you follow me?

LAURA: . . . You mean don't let him get ideas into his head.

DOCTOR: Precisely. For a sick man can be made to believe anything.
He is highly susceptible to suggestion.

LAURA: I see . . . I understand. Yes, indeed. (*A bell rings within.*)

Excuse me. That's my mother ringing. I won't be a moment . . .
Oh, here's Adolf!

(As LAURA *goes out, the* CAPTAIN *enters by the wall-papered
door.*)

CAPTAIN: Ah, so you have arrived, Doctor! You are very welcome.

DOCTOR: How do you, Captain. It's a great honour to meet such a
distinguished scientist.

CAPTAIN: Oh please! Unfortunately, my military duties don't give me
much time for research . . . All the same, I do believe I am now
on the brink of a rather exciting discovery.

DOCTOR: Really?

CAPTAIN: You see, I have been subjecting meteoric stones to spectrum
analysis, and I have found carbon — an indication of organic life.
What do you say to that?

DOCTOR: Can you see that in a microscope?

CAPTAIN: No, in a spectroscope, for heaven's sake!

DOCTOR: Spectroscope! I beg your pardon. Then you will soon be
telling us what is happening on Jupiter.

CAPTAIN: Not what is happening, what *has* happened. If only that
blasted Paris bookseller would send my books. I really think the
whole book-trade must be in league against me. Think of it, for two
months I've not had one single answer to my orders, my letters or
my abusive telegrams! It's driving me mad. I can't make out what's
happened.

DOCTOR: Well, what could it be but ordinary carelessness? You
shouldn't let it upset you.

CAPTAIN: Yes, but the devil of it is I shan't be able to get my article
finished in time. — I know they're working on the same lines in
Berlin . . . However, that's not what we should be talking about
now, but about you. If you would care to live here, we can give you
a small suite of rooms in that wing. Or would you prefer your
predecessor's house?

DOCTOR: Whichever you please.

CAPTAIN: No, whichever *you* please. You have only to say.

DOCTOR: It's for you to decide, Captain.

CAPTAIN: Nothing of the kind. It's for you to say which you prefer. I
don't care one way or the other.

DOCTOR: But I really can't . . .

CAPTAIN: For Christ's sake, man, say what you want! I haven't any
opinion, any inclination, any choice, any preference at all. Are you
such a milksop that you don't know what you want? Make up your
mind, or I shall lose my temper.

DOCTOR: If I am to choose, I should like to live here.

CAPTAIN: Good! — Thank you. (*Rings.*) Oh dear me! — I apologise, Doctor, but nothing irritates me so much as to hear people say they don't care one way or the other.

(*The* NURSE *enters.*)

Ah, it's you, Margaret. Look here, my dear, do you know if the rooms in the wing are ready for the doctor?

NURSE: Yes, Captain, they're ready.

CAPTAIN: Good. Then I won't detain you, Doctor, for you must be tired. Goodnight, and once again — welcome. I look forward to seeing you in the morning.

DOCTOR: Thank you. Goodnight.

CAPTAIN: By the way, I wonder if my wife told you anything about us — if you know at all how the land lies?

DOCTOR: Your good lady did suggest one or two things it might be as well for a newcomer to know. Goodnight, Captain.

(*The* NURSE *shows the* DOCTOR *out and returns.*)

CAPTAIN: What is it, old girl? Anything the matter?

NURSE: Now listen, Mr. Adolf, dear.

CAPTAIN: Yes, go on, Margaret, talk. You're the only one whose talk doesn't get on my nerves.

NURSE: Then listen, Mr. Adolf. Couldn't you go halfway to meet the mistress in all this bother over the child? Think of a mother . . .

CAPTAIN: Think of a father, Margaret.

NURSE: Now, now, now! A father has many things besides his child, but a mother has nothing but her child.

CAPTAIN: Quite so, my friend. She has only one burden, while I have three and bear hers too. Do you think I'd have been stuck in the army all my life if I hadn't had her and her child to support?

NURSE: I know, but that wasn't what I wanted to talk about.

CAPTAIN: Quite. What you want is to make out I'm in the wrong.

NURSE: Don't you believe I want what's best for you, Mr. Adolf?

CAPTAIN: I'm sure you do, my dear, but you don't know what is best for me. You see, it's not enough to have given the child life. I want to give her my very soul.

NURSE: Oh, that's beyond me, but I do think you two ought to come to terms.

CAPTAIN: Margaret, you are not my friend.

NURSE: Not your friend! Ah God, what are you saying, Mr. Adolf? Do you think I ever forget you were my baby when you were little?

CAPTAIN: Well, my dear, am I likely to forget it? You have been like a mother to me, and stood by me against all the others. But now that things have come to a head, you're deserting — going over to the enemy.

NURSE: Enemy?

CAPTAIN: Yes, enemy. You know perfectly well how things are here. You've seen it all from beginning to end.

NURSE: Aye, I've seen plenty. But, dear God, why must two people torment the lives out of each other? Two people who are so good and kind to everyone else. The mistress never treats me wrong or . . .

CAPTAIN: Only me. I know. And I tell you, Margaret, if you desert me now, you'll be doing a wicked thing. For a net is closing round me, and that doctor is no friend of mine.

NURSE: Oh, goodness, Mr. Adolf, you believe the worst of everyone! But that's what comes of not having the true faith. That's your trouble.

CAPTAIN: While you and the Baptists have found the one true faith, eh? You're lucky.

NURSE: Aye, luckier than you, Mr. Adolf. Humble your heart and you will see how happy God will make you in your love for your neighbour.

CAPTAIN: Isn't it strange — as soon as you mention God and love, your voice grows hard and your eyes fill with hate. No, Margaret, I'm sure you haven't found the true faith.

NURSE: However proud you are and stuffed with booklearning, that won't get you anywhere when the pinch comes.

CAPTAIN: How arrogantly thou speakest, O humble heart! I'm well aware that learning means nothing to creatures like you.

NURSE: Shame on you! Still, old Margaret loves her great big boy best of all. And when the storm breaks, he'll come back to her, sure enough, like the good child he is.

CAPTAIN: Forgive me, Margaret. You see, you really are the only friend I have here. Help me, for something is going to happen. I don't know what, but I know it's evil, this thing that's on its way. (*A scream from within.*) What's that? Who's screaming?

(BERTHA *runs in.*)

BERTHA: Father, Father! Help me! Save me!

CAPTAIN: What is it? My darling, tell me.

BERTHA: Please protect me. I know she'll do something terrible to me.

CAPTAIN: Who? What do you mean? Tell me at once.

BERTHA: Grandmother. But it was my fault. I played a trick on her.

CAPTAIN: Go on.

BERTHA: Yes, but you mustn't tell anyone. Promise you won't.

CAPTAIN: Very well, but what happened?

(*Exit* NURSE.)

BERTHA: You see, sometimes in the evening she turns the lamp down and makes me sit at the table holding a pen over a piece of paper. And then she says the spirits write.

CAPTAIN: Well, I'll be damned! And you never told me.

BERTHA: I'm sorry, I didn't dare. Grandmother says spirits revenge themselves on people who talk about them. And then the pen writes, but I don't know if it's me doing it or not. Sometimes it goes well, but sometimes it doesn't work at all. And when I get tired nothing happens, but I have to make something happen all the same. This evening I thought I was doing rather well, but then Grandmother said it was all out of Stagnelius* and I had been playing a trick on her. And she was simply furious.

CAPTAIN: Do you believe there are spirits?

BERTHA: I don't know.

CAPTAIN: But I know there are not.

BERTHA: Grandmother says you don't understand, and that you have worse things that can see into other planets.

CAPTAIN: She says that, does she? And what else does she say?

BERTHA: That you can't work miracles.

CAPTAIN: I never said I could. You know what meteorites are, don't you? — stones that fall from other heavenly bodies. Well, I examine these and see if they contain the same elements as the earth. That's all I do.

BERTHA: Grandmother says there are things she can see and you can't.

CAPTAIN: My dear, she is lying.

BERTHA: Grandmother doesn't lie.

CAPTAIN: How do you know?

BERTHA: Then Mother does too.

CAPTAIN: Hm!

BERTHA: If you say Mother is a liar, I'll never believe a word you say again.

CAPTAIN: I didn't say that, so now you must believe me. Listen. Your happiness, your whole future depends on your leaving home. Will you do this? Will you go and live in town and learn something useful?

BERTHA: Oh yes, I'd love to live in town — anywhere away from here! It's always so miserable in there, as gloomy as a winter night. But

* Erik Johan Stagnelius, Swedish poet and dramatist. (1793-1823.)

when you come home, Father, it's like a spring morning when they take the double windows down.

CAPTAIN: My darling, my beloved child!

BERTHA: But, Father, listen, you must be kind to Mother. She often cries.

CAPTAIN: Hm! . . . So you would like to live in town?

BERTHA: Oh yes!

CAPTAIN: But supposing your mother doesn't agree?

BERTHA: She must.

CAPTAIN: But supposing she doesn't?

BERTHA: Then I don't know what will happen. But she must, she must.

CAPTAIN: Will you ask her?

BERTHA: No, you must ask her — very nicely. She wouldn't pay any attention to me.

CAPTAIN: Hm! . . . Well now, if you want this and I want it and she doesn't want it, what are we to do then?

BERTHA: Oh, then the fuss will begin all over again! Why can't you both . . .

(*Enter* LAURA.)

LAURA: Ah, so you're here, Bertha! Well now, Adolf, as the question of her future is still to be decided, let's hear what she has to say herself.

CAPTAIN: The child can hardly have anything constructive to say about the development of young girls, but you and I ought to be able to sum up the pros and cons. We've watched a good number grow up.

LAURA: But as we don't agree, Bertha can give the casting vote.

CAPTAIN: No. I won't allow anyone to interfere with my rights — neither woman nor child. Bertha, you had better leave us.

(*Exit* BERTHA.)

LAURA: You were afraid to hear her opinion because you knew she would agree with me.

CAPTAIN: I know she wants to leave home, but I also know you have the power to make her change her mind.

LAURA: Oh, have I much power?

CAPTAIN: Yes, you have a fiendish power of getting your own way, like all people who are unscrupulous about the means they employ. How, for instance, did you get rid of Dr. Norling? And how did you get hold of the new doctor?

LAURA: Yes, how did I?

CAPTAIN: You ran the old doctor down until he had to leave, and then you got your brother to canvass for this one.

LAURA: Well, that was quite simple and perfectly legal. Then is Bertha to leave home?

CAPTAIN: Yes, in a fortnight's time.

LAURA: I warn you I shall do my best to prevent it.

CAPTAIN: You can't.

LAURA: Can't I? Do you expect me to give up my child to be taught by wicked people that all she has learnt from her mother is nonsense? So that I would be despised by my own daughter for the rest of my life.

CAPTAIN: Do you expect me to allow ignorant and bumptious women to teach my daughter that her father is a charlatan?

LAURA: That shouldn't matter so much to you — now.

CAPTAIN: What on earth do you mean?

LAURA: Well, the mother's closer to the child, since the discovery that no one can tell who the father is.

CAPTAIN: What's that got to do with us?

LAURA: You don't know if you are Bertha's father.

CAPTAIN: Don't know?

LAURA: How can you know what nobody knows?

CAPTAIN: Are you joking?

LAURA: No, I'm simply applying your own theory. How do you know I haven't been unfaithful to you?

CAPTAIN: I can believe a good deal of you, but not that. And if it were so, you wouldn't talk about it.

LAURA: Supposing I were prepared for anything, for being turned out and ostracised, anything to keep my child under my own control. Supposing I am telling the truth now when I say: Bertha is my child but not yours. Supposing . . .

CAPTAIN: Stop it!

LAURA: Just supposing . . . then your power would be over.

CAPTAIN: Not till you had proved I wasn't the father.

LAURA: That wouldn't be difficult. Do you want me to?

CAPTAIN: Stop.

LAURA: I should only have to give the name of the real father — with particulars of place and time, of course. For that matter — when was Bertha born? In the third year of our marriage . . .

CAPTAIN: Will you stop it now, or . . .

LAURA: Or what? Very well, let's stop. All the same, I should think twice before you decide anything. And, above all, don't make yourself ridiculous.

CAPTAIN: I find the whole thing tragic.

LAURA: Which makes you still more ridiculous.

CAPTAIN: But not you?

LAURA: No, we're in such a strong position.

CAPTAIN: That's why we can't fight you.

LAURA: Why try to fight a superior enemy?

CAPTAIN: Superior?

LAURA: Yes. It's odd, but I have never been able to look at a man without feeling myself his superior.

CAPTAIN: One day you may meet your master — and you'll never forget it.

LAURA: That will be fascinating.

(*Enter* NURSE.)

NURSE: Supper's ready. Come along now, please.

LAURA: Yes, of course. (*The* CAPTAIN *lingers and sits down in an armchair near the sofa.*) Aren't you coming?

CAPTAIN: No, thank you, I don't want any supper.

LAURA: Why not? Has anything upset you?

CAPTAIN: No, but I'm not hungry.

LAURA: Do come, or they'll start asking questions, and that's not necessary. Do be sensible. You won't? Well, stay where you are then!

(*Exit.*)

NURSE: Mr. Adolf, whatever is it now?

CAPTAIN: I don't know yet. Tell me — why do you women treat a grown man as if he were a child?

NURSE: Well, goodness me, you're all some woman's child, aren't you? — All you men, big or small . . .

CAPTAIN: While no woman is born of man, you mean. True. But I must be Bertha's father. You believe that, Margaret, don't you? Don't you?

NURSE: Lord, what a silly boy you are! Of course you're your own child's father. Come along and eat now. Don't sit here sulking. There now, come along, do.

CAPTAIN (*rising*): Get out, woman! To hell with the hags! (*At the hall door.*) Svärd! Svärd!

ORDERLY (*entering*): Yes, sir?

CAPTAIN: Have the small sleigh got ready at once.

(*Exit* ORDERLY.)

NURSE: Now listen, Captain . . .

CAPTAIN: Get out, woman! Get out, I say!

NURSE: God preserve us, whatever's going to happen now?

CAPTAIN (*putting on his cap*): Don't expect me home before midnight.

(*Exit.*)

NURSE: Lord Jesus! What *is* going to happen?

ACT TWO

(*The same as before, late that night. The* DOCTOR *and* LAURA *are sitting talking.*)

DOCTOR: My conversation with him has led me to the conclusion that your suspicions are by no means proved. To begin with, you were mistaken in saying that he had made these important astronomical discoveries by using a microscope. Now I have learnt that it was a spectroscope. Not only is there no sign in this of mental derangement — on the contrary, he has rendered a great service to science.

LAURA: But I never said that.

DOCTOR: I made a memorandum of our conversation, Madam, and I remember questioning you on this vital point, because I thought I must have misheard. One must be scrupulously accurate when bringing charges which might lead to a man being certified.

LAURA: Certified?

DOCTOR: I presume you are aware that if a person is certified insane, he loses both his civil and his family rights.

LAURA: No, I didn't know that.

DOCTOR: There is one other point I should like to be clear about. He spoke of not getting any replies from his booksellers. May I ask whether — from the best of intentions, of course — you have been intercepting his correspondence?

LAURA: Yes, I have. It is my duty to protect the family. I couldn't let him ruin us all and do nothing about it.

DOCTOR: Excuse me, I do not think you understand the possible consequences of your action. If he realises you have been interfering with his affairs behind his back, his suspicions will be aroused and might even develop into a persecution mania. Particularly, as by thwarting his will, you have already driven him to the end of his tether. Surely you know how enraging it is to have your will opposed and your dearest wishes frustrated.

LAURA: Do I not!

DOCTOR: Then think what this means to him.

LAURA (*rising*): It's midnight and he's not back yet. Now we can expect the worst.

DOCTOR: Tell me what happened this evening after I saw him. I must know everything.

LAURA: He talked in the wildest way and said the most fantastic things. Can you believe it — he even suggested he wasn't the father of his own child!

DOCTOR: How extraordinary! What can have put that into his head?

LAURA: Goodness knows, unless it was an interview he had with one of his men about maintenance for a child. When I took the girl's part, he got very excited and said no one could ever tell who a child's father was. God knows I did everything I could to calm him, but I don't believe anything can help him now. (*Weeps.*)

DOCTOR: This can't go on. Something must be done — without rousing his suspicions. Tell me, has he had any such delusions before?

LAURA: As a matter of fact, he was much the same six years ago, and then he actually admitted — in a letter to his doctor — that he feared for his reason.

DOCTOR: I see, I see. A deep-seated trouble. But . . . er . . . the sanctity of family life . . . and so forth . . . I mustn't probe too far . . . must keep to the surface. Unfortunately what is done cannot be undone, yet the remedy should have been applied to what is done . . . Where do you think he is now?

LAURA: I can't imagine. He has such wild notions these days . . .

DOCTOR: Would you like me to stay until he comes in? I could explain my presence by saying — well, that your mother is ill and I came to see her.

LAURA: That's a very good idea. Please stand by us, Doctor. If you only knew how worried I am! . . . But wouldn't it be better to tell him straight out what you think of his condition?

DOCTOR: We never do that with mental patients, unless they bring the subject up themselves, and rarely even then. Everything depends on how the case develops. But we had better not stay here. May I go into some other room, to make it more convincing?

LAURA: Yes, that will be best, and Margaret can come in here. She always waits up for him. (*At the door.*) Margaret! Margaret! She is the only one who can manage him.

NURSE (*entering*): Did you call, Madam? Is Master back?

LAURA: No, but you are to wait here for him. And when he comes, tell him that my mother is unwell and the doctor is with her.

NURSE: Aye, aye. Leave all that to me.

LAURA (*opening the door*): If you will be so good as to come in here, Doctor . . .

DOCTOR: Thank you.

(*They go out. The* NURSE *sits at the table, puts on her glasses and picks up her hymn-book.*)

NURSE: Ah me! Ah me! (*Reads softly.*)

> *A sorrowful and grievous thing*
> *Is life, so swiftly passing by,*
> *Death shadows with his angel's wing*
> *The whole earth, and this his cry:*
> *'Tis Vanity, all Vanity!*

Ah me! Ah me!

> *All that on earth has life and breath,*
> *Falls low before his awful might,*
> *Sorrow alone is spared by Death,*
> *Upon the yawning grave to write:*
> *'Tis Vanity, all Vanity!*

Ah me! Ah me!

(*During the last lines,* BERTHA *enters, carrying a tray with a coffee-pot and a piece of embroidery.*)

BERTHA (*softly*): Margaret, may I sit in here with you? It's so dismal up there.

NURSE: Saints alive! Bertha, are you still up?

BERTHA: Well, you see, I simply must get on with Father's Christmas present. And here's something nice for you.

NURSE: But, sweetheart, this won't do. You have to be up bright and early, and it's past twelve now.

BERTHA: Oh, that doesn't matter! I daren't stay up there all alone. I'm sure there are ghosts.

NURSE: There now! What did I tell you? Mark my words, there's no good fairy in this house. What was it? Did you hear something, Bertha?

BERTHA: Oh Margaret, someone was singing in the attic!

NURSE: In the attic? At this time of night?

BERTHA: Yes. It was such a sad song; the saddest I ever heard. And it seemed to come from the attic — you know, the one on the left where the cradle is.

NURSE: Oh dear, dear, dear! And such a fearful night too. I'm sure the chimneys will blow down. "Alas, what is this earthly life? Sorrow, trouble, grief and strife. Even when it seems most fair, Nought but tribulation there." — Ah, dear child, God grant us a happy Christmas!

BERTHA: Margaret, is it true Father's ill?

NURSE: Aye, that's true enough.

BERTHA: Then I don't expect we shall have a Christmas party. But why isn't he in bed if he's ill?

NURSE: Well, dearie, staying in bed doesn't help his kind of illness. Hush! I hear someone in the porch. Go to bed now — take the tray with you, or the Master will be cross.

BERTHA (*going out with the tray*): Goodnight, Margaret.

NURSE: Goodnight, love. God bless you.

(*Enter the* CAPTAIN.)

CAPTAIN (*taking off his overcoat*): Are you still up? Go to bed.

NURSE: Oh, I was only biding till . . .

(*The* CAPTAIN *lights a candle, opens the bureau, sits down at it and takes letters and newspapers from his pocket.*)

Mr. Adolf . . .

CAPTAIN: What is it?

NURSE: The old mistress is ill. Doctor's here.

CAPTAIN: Anything serious?

NURSE: No, I don't think so. Just a chill.

CAPTAIN (*rising*): Who was the father of your child, Margaret?

NURSE: I've told you often enough, it was that heedless fellow Johansson.

CAPTAIN: Are you sure it was he?

NURSE: Don't talk so silly. Of course I'm sure, seeing he was the only one.

CAPTAIN: Yes, but was he sure he was the only one? No, he couldn't be sure, only you could be. See? That's the difference.

NURSE: I don't see any difference.

CAPTAIN: No, you don't see it, but it's there all the same. (*Turns the pages of the photograph album on the table.*) Do you think Bertha's like me?

NURSE: You're as like as two peas in a pod.

CAPTAIN: Did Johansson admit he was the father?

NURSE: Well, he was forced to.

CAPTAIN: How dreadful! — Here's the doctor.

(*Enter* DOCTOR.)

Good evening, Doctor. How is my mother-in-law?

DOCTOR: Oh, it's nothing much. Just a slight sprain of the left ankle.

CAPTAIN: I thought Margaret said it was a chill. There appear to be different diagnoses of the case. Margaret, go to bed.

(*Exit* NURSE. *Pause.*)

Won't you sit down, Dr. Östermark?

DOCTOR (*sitting*): Thank you.

CAPTAIN: Is it true that if you cross a mare with a zebra you get striped foals?

DOCTOR (*astonished*): Perfectly true.

CAPTAIN: And that if breeding is then continued with a stallion, the foals may still be striped?

DOCTOR: That is also true.

CAPTAIN: So, in certain circumstances, a stallion can sire striped foals, and vice versa.

DOCTOR: That would appear to be the case.

CAPTAIN: So the offspring's resemblance to the father proves nothing.

DOCTOR: Oh . . .

CAPTAIN: You're a widower, aren't you? Any children?

DOCTOR: Ye-es.

CAPTAIN: Didn't you sometimes feel rather ridiculous as a father? I myself don't know anything more ludicrous than the sight of a man holding his child's hand in the street, or hearing a father say: "My child." "My wife's child," he ought to say. Didn't you ever see what a false position you were in? Weren't you ever haunted by doubts — I won't say suspicions, as a gentleman I assume your wife was above suspicion?

DOCTOR: No, I certainly wasn't. There it is, Captain, a man — as I think Goethe says — must take his children on trust.

CAPTAIN: Trust, where a woman's concerned? A bit of a risk.

DOCTOR: Ah, but there are many kinds of women!

CAPTAIN: The latest research shows there is only one kind . . . when I was a young fellow and not, if I may say so, a bad specimen, I had two little experiences which afterwards gave me to think. The first was on a steamer. I was in the saloon with some friends, and the young stewardess told us — with tears running down her cheeks — how her sweetheart had been drowned at sea. We condoled with her and I ordered champagne. After the second glass I touched her foot, and after the fourth her knee, and before morning I had consoled her.

DOCTOR: One swallow doesn't make a summer.

CAPTAIN: My second experience was a summer swallow. I was staying at Lysekil and got to know a young married woman who was there with her children — her husband was in town. She was religious and high-minded, kept preaching at me and was — or so I thought — the soul of virtue. I lent her a book or two which, strange to relate, she returned. Three months later, I found her card in one of those books with a pretty outspoken declaration of love. It was innocent — as innocent, that's to say, as such a declaration from a married woman could be — to a stranger who had never made her any advances. Moral: don't believe in anyone too much.

DOCTOR: Don't believe too little either.

CAPTAIN: The happy mean, eh? But you see, Doctor, that woman was so unaware of her motives she actually told her husband of her infatuation for me. That's where the danger lies, in the fact that women are unconscious of their instinctive wickedness. An extenuating circumstance, perhaps, but that can only mitigate the judgment, not revoke it.

DOCTOR: You have a morbid turn of mind, Captain. You should be on your guard against this.

CAPTAIN: There's nothing morbid about it. Look here. All steam-boilers explode when the pressure-gauge reaches the limit, but the limit isn't the same for all boilers. Got that? After all, you're here to observe me. Now if I were not a man I could sniff and snivel and explain the case to you, with all its past history. But as unfortunately I am a man, like the ancient Roman I must cross my arms upon my breast and hold my breath until I die. Goodnight.

DOCTOR: If you are ill, Captain, there's no reflection on your manhood in telling me about it. Indeed, it is essential for me to hear both sides of the case.

CAPTAIN: I thought you were quite satisfied with one side.

DOCTOR: You're wrong. And I should like you to know, Captain, that when I heard that Mrs. Alving* blackening her late husband's memory, I thought what a damned shame it was that the fellow should be dead.

CAPTAIN: Do you think if he'd been alive he'd have said anything? Do you think if any husband rose from the dead he'd be believed? Goodnight, Doctor. Look how calm I am. It's quite safe for you to go to bed.

DOCTOR: Then I will bid you goodnight. I wash my hands of the whole business.

CAPTAIN: So we're enemies?

DOCTOR: By no means. It's just a pity we can't be friends. Goodnight.

(*The* CAPTAIN *shows the* DOCTOR *out by the hall door, then crosses to the other and slightly opens it.*)

* Reference to Mrs. Alving in Ibsen's GHOSTS.

CAPTAIN: Come in and let's talk. I knew you were eavesdropping.

(*Enter* LAURA, *embarrassed. The* CAPTAIN *sits at the bureau.*)

It's very late, but we'd better have things out now. Sit down. (*She sits. Pause.*) This evening it was I who went to the post office and fetched the mail, and from my letters it is clear to me that you have been intercepting my correspondence — both in and out. The result of this has been a loss of time which has pretty well shattered the expectations I had for my work.

LAURA: I acted from the best of intentions. You were neglecting your military duties for this other work.

CAPTAIN: Scarcely the best of intentions. You knew very well that one day I should win more distinction in this field than in the Army, but what you wanted was to stop me winning laurels of any kind, because this would stress your own inferiority. Now, for a change, I have intercepted letters addressed to you.

LAURA: How chivalrous!

CAPTAIN: In keeping with the high opinion you have of me. From these letters it appears that for a long time now you've been setting my old friends against me, by spreading rumours about my mental condition. So successful have your efforts been that now scarcely one person from Colonel to kitchen-maid believes I am sane. The actual facts about my condition are these. My reason is, as you know, unaffected, and I am able to discharge my duties both as soldier and father. My emotions are still pretty well under control, but only so long as my will-power remains intact. And you have so gnawed and gnawed at my will that at any moment it may slip its cogs, and then the whole bag of tricks will go to pieces. I won't appeal to your feelings, because you haven't any — that is your strength. I appeal to your own interests.

LAURA: Go on.

CAPTAIN: By behaving in this way you have made me so full of suspicion that my judgment is fogged and my mind is beginning to stray. This means that the insanity you have been waiting for is on its way and may come at any moment. The question you now have to decide is whether it is more to your advantage for me to be well or ill. Consider. If I go to pieces, I shall have to leave the Service, and where will you be then? If I die, you get my life-insurance. But if I take my own life, you get nothing. It is therefore to your advantage that I should live my life out.

LAURA: Is this a trap?

CAPTAIN: Certainly. You can avoid it or stick your head in it.

LAURA: You say you'd kill yourself, but you never would.

CAPTAIN: Are you so sure? Do you think a man can go on living when he has nothing and nobody to live for?

LAURA: Then you give in?

CAPTAIN: No, I offer peace.

LAURA: On what terms?

CAPTAIN: That I may keep my reason. Free me from doubt and I will give up the fight.

LAURA: Doubt about what?

CAPTAIN: Bertha's parentage.

LAURA: Are there doubts about that?

CAPTAIN: Yes, for me there are, and it was you who roused them.

LAURA: I?

CAPTAIN: Yes. You dropped them like henbane in my ear, and circumstances encouraged them to grow. Free me from uncertainty. Tell me straight out it is so, and I will forgive you in advance.

LAURA: I can scarcely admit to guilt that isn't mine.

CAPTAIN: What can it matter to you, when you know I won't reveal it? Do you think any man would proclaim his shame from the housetops?

LAURA: If I say it isn't so, you still won't be certain, but if I say it is, you will believe me. You must want it to be true.

CAPTAIN: Strangely enough I do. Perhaps because the first supposition can't be proved, while the second can.

LAURA: Have you any grounds for suspicion?

CAPTAIN: Yes and no.

LAURA: I believe you want to make out I'm guilty, so you can get rid of me and have absolute control of the child. But you won't catch me in any such trap.

CAPTAIN: Do you think, if I were convinced of your guilt, I should want to take on another man's child?

LAURA: No, I'm sure you wouldn't. So evidently you were lying when you said you'd forgive me in advance.

CAPTAIN (*rising*): Laura, save me and my reason! You can't have understood what I was saying. If the child's not mine, I have no rights over her, nor do I want any. And that's how you'd like it, isn't it? But that's not all. You want complete power over the child, don't you, with me still there to support you both?

LAURA: Power, that's it. What's this whole life and death struggle for if not power?

CAPTAIN: For me, as I don't believe in a life to come, this child was my life after death, my conception of immortality — the only one, perhaps, that's valid. If you take her away, you cut my life short.

LAURA: Why didn't we separate sooner?

CAPTAIN: Because the child bound us together, but the bond became a chain. How was that? I never thought of this before, but now memories return, accusing, perhaps condemning. After two years of marriage we were still childless — you know best why. Then I was ill and almost died. One day, between bouts of fever, I heard voices in the next room. You and the lawyer were discussing the property I still owned then. He was explaining that as there were no children, you could not inherit, and he asked if by any chance you were pregnant. I did not hear your reply. I recovered and we had a child. Who is the father?

LAURA: You are.

CAPTAIN: No, I am not. There's a crime buried here that's beginning to stink. And what a fiendish crime! You women, who were so tender-hearted about freeing black slaves, kept the white ones. I have slaved for you, your child, your mother, your servants. I have sacrificed career and promotion. Tortured, beaten, sleepless — my hair has gone grey through the agony of mind you have inflicted on me. All this I have suffered in order that you might enjoy a care-free life and, when you were old, relive it in your child. This is the lowest form of theft, the cruellest slavery. I have had seventeen years of penal servitude — and I was innocent. How can you make up to me for this?

LAURA: Now you really are mad.

CAPTAIN (*sitting*): So you hope. I have watched you trying to conceal your crime, but because I didn't understand I pitied you. I've soothed your conscience, thinking I was chasing away some nightmare. I've heard you crying out in your sleep without giving your words a second thought. But now . . . now! The other night — Bertha's birthday — comes back to me. I was still up in the early hours, reading, and you suddenly screamed as if someone were trying to strangle you. "Don't! Don't!" you cried. I knocked on the wall — I didn't want to hear any more. For a long time I have had vague suspicions. I did not want them confirmed. This is what I have suffered for you. What will you do for me?

LAURA: What can I do? Swear before God and all that I hold sacred that you are Bertha's father?

CAPTAIN: What good would that do? You have already said that a mother can and ought to commit any crime for her child. I implore you by the memory of the past, I implore you as a wounded man begs to be put out of his misery, tell me the truth. Can't you see I'm helpless as a child? Can't you hear me crying to my mother that I'm hurt? Forget I'm a man, a soldier whose word men — and even beasts — obey. I am nothing but a sick creature in need of pity. I renounce every vestige of power and only beg for mercy on my life.

LAURA (*laying her hand on his forehead*): What? You, a man, in tears?

CAPTAIN: Yes, a man in tears. Has not a man eyes? Has not a man hands, limbs, senses, opinions, passions? Is he not nourished by the same food as a woman, wounded by the same weapons, warmed and chilled by the same winter and summer? If you prick us, do we not bleed? If you tickle us, do we not laugh? If you poison us, do we not die? Why should a man suffer in silence or a soldier hide his tears? Because it's not manly? Why isn't it manly?

LAURA: Weep, then, my child, and you shall have your mother again. Remember, it was as your second mother that I came into your life. You were big and strong, yet not fully a man. You were a giant child who had come into the world too soon, or perhaps an unwanted child.

CAPTAIN: That's true. My father and mother had me against their will, and therefore I was born without a will. That is why, when you and I became one, I felt I was completing myself — and that is why you dominated. I — in the army the one to command — became at home the one to obey. I grew up at your side, looked up to you as a superior being and listened to you as if I were your foolish little boy.

LAURA: Yes, that's how it was, and I loved you as if you were my little boy. But didn't you see how, when your feelings changed and you came to me as a lover, I was ashamed? The joy I felt in your embraces was followed by such a sense of guilt my very blood seemed tainted. The mother became the mistress — horrible!

CAPTAIN: I saw, but I didn't understand. I thought you despised my lack of virility, so I tried to win you as a woman by proving myself as a man.

LAURA: That was your mistake. The mother was your friend, you see, but the woman was your enemy. Sexual love is conflict. And don't imagine I gave myself. I didn't give. I only took what I meant to take. Yet you did dominate me . . . I felt it and wanted you to feel it.

CAPTAIN: You always dominated me. You could hypnotise me when I was wide awake, so that I neither saw nor heard, but simply obeyed. You could give me a raw potato and make me think it was a peach; you could make me take your ridiculous ideas for flashes of genius. You could corrupt me — yes, make me do the shabbiest things. You never had any real intelligence, yet, instead of being guided by me, you would take the reins into your own hands. And when at last I woke to the realisation that I had lost my integrity, I wanted to blot out my humiliation by some heroic action — some feat, some discovery — even by committing *hara-kiri*. I wanted to go to war, but I couldn't. It was then that I gave all my energies to science. And now — now when I should be stretching out my hand to gather the fruit, you chop off my arm. I'm robbed of my laurels; I'm finished. A man cannot live without repute.

LAURA: Can a woman?

CAPTAIN: Yes — she has her children, but he has not . . . Yet you and I and everyone else went on living, unconscious as children, full of fancies and ideals and illusions, until we woke up. Right — but we woke topsy-turvy, and what's more, we'd been woken by someone who was talking in his own sleep. When women are old and stop being women, they grow beards on their chins. What do men grow, I wonder, when they are old and stop being men? In this false dawn, the birds that crowed weren't cocks, they were capons, and the hens that answered their call were sexless, too. So when the sun should have risen for us, we found ourselves back among the ruins in the full moonlight, just as in the good old times. Our light morning sleep had only been troubled by fantastic dreams — there had been no awakening.

LAURA: You should have been a writer, you know.

CAPTAIN: Perhaps.

LAURA: But I'm sleepy now, so if you have any more fantasies, keep them till to-morrow.

CAPTAIN: Just one thing more — a fact. Do you hate me?

LAURA: Sometimes — as a man.

CAPTAIN: It's like race-hatred. If it's true we are descended from the ape, it must have been from two different species. There's no likeness between us, is there?

LAURA: What are you getting at?

CAPTAIN: In this fight, one of us must go under.

LAURA: Which?

CAPTAIN: The weaker naturally.

LAURA: Then is the stronger in the right?

CAPTAIN: Bound to be as he has the power.

LAURA: Then I am in the right.

CAPTAIN: Why, what power have you?

LAURA: All I need. And it will be legal power to-morrow when I've put you under restraint.

CAPTAIN: Under restraint?

LAURA: Yes. Then I shall decide my child's future myself out of reach of your fantasies.

CAPTAIN: Who will pay for her if I'm not there?

LAURA: Your pension.

CAPTAIN (_moving towards her menacingly_): How can you have me put under restraint?

LAURA (_producing a letter_): By means of this letter, an attested copy which is already in the hands of the authorities.

CAPTAIN: What letter?

LAURA (_retreating_): Your own. The one in which you told the doctor you were mad. (_He stares at her in silence._) Now you have fulfilled the unfortunately necessary functions of father and bread-winner. You are no longer needed, and you must go. You must go, now that you realise my wits are as strong as my will — you won't want to stay and acknowledge my superiority.

(_The_ CAPTAIN _goes to the table, picks up the lighted lamp and throws it at_ LAURA, _who escapes backward through the door._)

ACT THREE

(_The same. The following evening. A new lamp, lighted, is on the table. The wall-papered door is barricaded with a chair. From the room above comes the sound of pacing footsteps. The_ NURSE _stands listening, troubled. Enter_ LAURA _from within._)

LAURA: Did he give you the keys?

NURSE: Give? No, God help us, I took them from the coat Nöjd had out to brush.

LAURA: Then it's Nöjd who's on duty?

NURSE: Aye, it's Nöjd.

LAURA: Give me the keys.

NURSE: Here you are, but it's no better than stealing. Hark at him up there! To and fro, to and fro.

LAURA: Are you sure the door's safely bolted?

NURSE: It's bolted safe enough. (_Weeps._)

LAURA (_opening the bureau and sitting down at it_): Pull yourself together, Margaret. The only way we can protect ourselves is by keeping calm. (_A knock at the hall door._) See who that is.

NURSE (_opening door_): It's Nöjd.

LAURA: Tell him to come in.

NÖJD (_entering_): Despatch from the Colonel.

LAURA: Give it to me. (_Reads._) I see . . . Nöjd, have you removed the cartridges from all the guns and pouches?

NÖJD: Yes, Ma'am, just as you said.

LAURA: Wait outside while I write to the Colonel.

(*Exit* NÖJD. LAURA *writes. Sound of sawing above.*)

NURSE: Listen, Madam. Whatever is he doing now?

LAURA: Do be quiet. I'm writing.

NURSE (*muttering*): Lord have mercy on us! What will be the end of all this?

LAURA (*holding out the note*): Here you are. Give it to Nöjd. And, remember, my mother's to know nothing of all this.

(*Exit* NURSE *with note.* LAURA *opens the bureau drawers and takes out papers. Enter* PASTOR.)

PASTOR: My dear Laura! As you probably gathered, I have been out all day and only just got back. I hear you've been having a terrible time.

LAURA: Yes, brother, I've never been through such a night and day in all my life!

PASTOR: Well, I see you're looking none the worse for it.

LAURA: No, thank heaven, I wasn't hurt. But just think what might have happened!

PASTOR: Tell me all about it. I've only heard rumours. How did it begin?

LAURA: It began by him raving about not being Bertha's father, and ended by him throwing the lighted lamp in my face.

PASTOR: But this is appalling. He must be quite out of his mind. What in heaven's name are we to do?

LAURA: We must try to prevent further violence. The doctor has sent to the hospital for a strait-jacket. I have just written a note to the Colonel, and now I'm trying to get some idea of the state of our affairs, which Adolf has so shockingly mismanaged. (*Opens another drawer.*)

PASTOR: It's a miserable business altogether, but I always feared something of the kind might happen. When fire and water meet, there's bound to be an explosion. (*Looks in drawer.*) Whatever's all this?

LAURA: Look! This is where he's kept everything hidden.

PASTOR: Good heavens! Here's your old doll! And there's your christening cap . . . and Bertha's rattle . . . and your letters . . . and that locket . . . (*Wipes his eyes.*) He must have loved you very dearly, Laura. I never kept this kind of thing.

LAURA: I believe he did love me once, but time changes everything.

PASTOR: What's this imposing document? (*Examines it.*) The purchase of a grave! Well, better a grave than the asylum! Laura, be frank with me. Aren't you at all to blame?

LAURA: How can I be to blame because someone goes out of his mind?

PASTOR: We — ell! I will say no more. After all, blood's thicker than water.

LAURA: Meaning what, if I may ask?

PASTOR (*gazing at her*): Oh come now!

LAURA: What?

PASTOR: Come, come! You can scarcely deny that it would suit you down to the ground to have complete control of your daughter.

LAURA: I don't understand.

PASTOR: I can't help admiring you.

LAURA: Really?

PASTOR: And as for me — I shall be appointed guardian to that Free-thinker whom, as you know, I always regarded as a tare among our wheat.

(LAURA *gives a quick laugh which she suppresses.*)

LAURA: You dare say that to me, his wife?

PASTOR: How strong-willed you are, Laura, how amazingly strong-willed! Like a fox in a trap that would gnaw off its own leg rather than be caught. Like a master-thief working alone, without even a conscience for accomplice. Look in the mirror! You daren't.

LAURA: I never use a mirror.

PASTOR: No. You daren't look at yourself. Let me see your hand. Not one tell-tale spot of blood, not a trace of that subtle poison. A little innocent murder that the law cannot touch. An unconscious crime. Unconscious? A stroke of genius that. Listen to him up there! Take care, Laura! If that man gets loose, he will saw you in pieces too.

LAURA: You must have a bad conscience to talk like that. Pin the guilt on me if you can.

PASTOR: I can't.

LAURA: You see? You can't, and so — I am innocent. And now, you look after your charge and I'll take care of mine.

(*Enter* DOCTOR.)

Ah, here is the Doctor! (*Rises.*) I'm so glad to see you, Doctor. I know I can count on you to help me, although I'm afraid not much can be done now. You hear him up there. Are you convinced at last?

DOCTOR: I am convinced there has been an act of violence. But the question is — should that act of violence be regarded as an out-break of temper or insanity?

PASTOR: But apart from this actual outbreak, you must admit that he suffers from fixed ideas.

DOCTOR: I have a notion, Pastor, that *your* ideas are even more fixed.

PASTOR: My firmly rooted convictions of spiritual . . .

DOCTOR: Convictions apart, it rests with you, Madam, to decide if your husband is to be fined or imprisoned or sent to the asylum. How do you regard his conduct?

LAURA: I can't answer that now.

DOCTOR: Oh? Have you no — er — firmly rooted convictions of what would be best for the family? And you, Pastor?

PASTOR: There's bound to be a scandal either way. It's not easy to give an opinion.

LAURA: But if he were only fined for violence he could be violent again.

DOCTOR: And if he were sent to prison he would soon be out again. So it seems best for all parties that he should be treated as insane. Where is the nurse?

LAURA: Why?

DOCTOR: She must put the strait-jacket on the patient. Not at once, but after I have had a talk with him — and not then until I give the order. I have the — er — garment outside. (*Goes out to hall and returns with a large parcel.*) Kindly call the nurse.

(LAURA *rings. The* DOCTOR *begins to unpack the strait-jacket.*)

PASTOR: Dreadful! Dreadful!

(*Enter* NURSE.)

DOCTOR: Ah, Nurse! Now please pay attention. You see this jacket. When I give you the word I want you to slip it on the Captain from behind. So as to prevent any further violence, you understand. Now it has, you see, unusually long sleeves. That is to restrict his movements. These sleeves must be tied together behind his back. And now here are two straps with buckles, which afterwards you must fasten to the arm of a chair — or to whatever's easiest. Can you do this, do you think?

NURSE: No, Doctor, I can't. No, not that.

LAURA: Why not do it yourself, Doctor?

DOCTOR: Because the patient distrusts me. You, Madam, are the proper person, but I'm afraid he doesn't trust you either. (LAURA *grimaces.*) Perhaps you, Pastor . . .

PASTOR: I must beg to decline.

(*Enter* NÖJD.)

LAURA: Did you deliver my note?

NÖJD: Yes, Madam.

DOCTOR: Oh, it's you, Nöjd! You know the state of things here, don't you? You know the Captain has had a mental breakdown. You must help us look after the patient.

NÖJD: If there's aught I can do for Captain, he knows I'll do it.

DOCTOR: You are to put this jacket on him.

NURSE: He's not to touch him. Nöjd shan't hurt him. I'd rather do it myself, gently, gently. But Nöjd can wait outside and help me if need be — yes, that's what he'd best do.

(*A pounding on the paper-covered door.*)

DOCTOR: Here he is! (*To* NURSE.) Put the jacket on that chair under your shawl. And now go away, all of you, while the Pastor and I talk to him. That door won't hold long. Hurry!

NURSE (*going out*): Lord Jesus, help us!

(LAURA *shuts the bureau and follows the* NURSE. NÖJD *goes out to the hall. The paper-covered door bursts open, the lock broken and the chair hurled to the floor. The* CAPTAIN *comes out, carrying a pile of books.*)

CAPTAIN (*putting the books on the table*): Here it all is. You can read it in every one of these volumes. So I wasn't mad after all. (*Picks one up.*) Here it is in the Odyssey, Book I, page 6, line 215 in the Uppsala translation. Telemachus speaking to Athene: "My mother says I am Odysseus' son; but for myself I cannot tell. It's a wise child that knows its own father."* And that's the suspicion Telemachus has about Penelope, the most virtuous of women. Fine state of affairs, eh? (*Takes up another book.*) And here we have the Prophet Ezekiel: "The fool saith, Lo, here is my father; but who can tell whose loins have engendered him?" That's clear enough. (*Picks up another.*) And what's this? A history of Russian literature by Merzlyakov. Alexander Pushkin, Russia's greatest poet, was mortally wounded — but more by the rumours of his wife's unfaithfulness than by the bullet he received in his breast at the duel. On his deathbed he swore she was innocent. Jackass! How could he swear any such thing? I *do* read my books, you see! Hullo, Jonas, are you here? And the Doctor, of course. Did I ever tell you what I said to the English lady who was deploring the habit Irishmen have of throwing lighted lamps in their wives' faces? "God, what women!" I said. "Women?" she stammered. "Of course," I replied. "When things get to such a pass that a man who has loved, has

---

* English translation E. V. Rieu. Penguin Classics.

worshipped a woman, picks up a lighted lamp and flings it in her face, then you may be sure . . ."

PASTOR: Sure of what?

CAPTAIN: Nothing. You can never be sure of anything — you can only believe. That's right, isn't it, Jonas? One believes and so one is saved. Saved, indeed! No. One can be damned through believing. That's what I've learnt.

DOCTOR: But, Captain . . .

CAPTAIN: Hold your tongue! I don't want any chat from you. I don't want to hear you relaying all the gossip from in there like a telephone. In there — you know what I mean. Listen to me, Jonas. Do you imagine you're the father of your children? I seem to remember you had a tutor in the house, a pretty boy about whom there was quite a bit of gossip.

PASTOR: Take care, Adolf!

CAPTAIN: Feel under your wig and see if you don't find two little nobs. Upon my soul, he's turning pale! Well, well! It was only talk, of course, but my God, how they talked! But we married men are all figures of fun, every man Jack of us. Isn't that right, Doctor? What about your own marriage bed? Didn't you have a certain lieutenant in your house, eh? Wait now, let me guess. He was called . . . (*Whispers in the* DOCTOR's *ear.*) By Jove, he's turned pale too! But don't worry. She's dead and buried, so what was done can't be done again. As a matter of fact, I knew him, and he's now — look at me, Doctor — no, straight in the eyes! He is now a major of Dragoons. Good Lord, I believe *he* has horns too!

DOCTOR (*angrily*): Be so good as to change the subject, Captain.

CAPTAIN: See! As soon as I mention horns he wants to change the subject.

PASTOR: I suppose you know, brother-in-law, that you're not in your right mind?

CAPTAIN: Yes, I do know. But if I had the handling of your decorated heads, I should soon have you shut up too. I am mad. But how did I become mad? Doesn't that interest you? No, it doesn't interest anyone. (*Takes the photograph album from the table.*) Christ Jesus, there is my daughter! Mine? That's what we can never know. Shall I tell you what we should have to do so as to know? First marry, in order to be accepted by society, then immediately divorce; after that become lovers and finally adopt the children. That way one could at least be sure they were one's own adopted children. Eh? But what good's that to me? What good's anything now you have robbed me of my immortality? What can science or philosophy do for me when I have nothing left to live for? How can I live

without honour? I grafted my right arm and half my brain and
spinal cord on to another stem. I believed they would unite and
grow into a single, more perfect tree. Then someone brought a
knife and cut below the graft, so now I'm only half a tree. The
other part, with my arm and half my brain, goes on growing. But
I wither — I am dying, for it was the best part of myself I gave
away. Let me die. Do what you like with me. I'm finished.

(*The* DOCTOR *and* PASTOR *whisper, then go out. The* CAPTAIN
sinks into a chair by the table. BERTHA *enters.*)

BERTHA (*going to him*): Are you ill, Father?
CAPTAIN (*looking up stupidly at word "Father"*): Me?
BERTHA: Do you know what you did? You threw a lamp at Mother.
CAPTAIN: Did I?
BERTHA: Yes. Supposing she'd been hurt!
CAPTAIN: Would that have mattered?
BERTHA: You're not my father if you talk like that.
CAPTAIN: What d'you say? Not your father? How d'you know? Who
told you? Who is your father, then? Who?
BERTHA: Not you, anyway.
CAPTAIN: Anyone but me! Who then? Who? You seem well informed.
Who told you? That I should live to hear my own child tell me to
my face I am not her father! Do you realise you're insulting your
mother by saying this? Don't you understand that, if it's true, *she* is
disgraced?
BERTHA: You're not to say anything against Mother, I tell you!
CAPTAIN: Yes, all in league against me, just as you've always been.
BERTHA: Father!
CAPTAIN: Don't call me that again!
BERTHA: Father, Father!
CAPTAIN (*drawing her to him*): Bertha, my beloved child, yes, you
are my child. Yes, yes, it must be so — it *is* so. All that was only
a sick fancy — it came on the wind like an infection or a fever.
Look at me! Let me see my soul in your eyes . . . But I see *her*
soul as well. You have two souls. You love me with one and hate
me with the other. You must love me and only me. You must have
only one soul or you'll have no peace — neither shall I. You must
have only one mind, fruit of my mind. You must have only one
will — mine!
BERTHA: No, no! I want to be myself.
CAPTAIN: Never! I am a cannibal, you see, and I'm going to eat you.
Your mother wanted to eat me, but she didn't succeed. I am Saturn

who devoured his children because it was foretold that otherwise they would devour him. To eat or to be eaten — that is the question. If I don't eat you, you will eat me — you've shown your teeth already. (*Goes to the rack.*) Don't be afraid, my darling child. I shan't hurt you. (*Takes down a revolver.*)

BERTHA (*dodging away from him*): Help! Mother, help! He wants to kill me!

NURSE (*hurrying in*): What in heaven's name are you doing, Mr. Adolf?

CAPTAIN (*examining the revolver*): Did you remove the cartridges?

NURSE: Well, I did just tidy them away, but sit down here and take it easy and I'll soon fetch them back.

(*She takes the* CAPTAIN *by the arm and leads him to a chair. He slumps down. She picks up the strait-jacket and goes behind the chair.* BERTHA *creeps out.*)

Mr. Adolf, do you remember when you were my dear little boy, and I used to tuck you up at night and say your prayers with you? And do you remember how I used to get up in the night to get you a drink when you were thirsty? And how, when you had bad dreams and couldn't go to sleep again, I'd light the candle and tell you pretty stories. Do you remember?

CAPTAIN: Go on talking, Margaret. It soothes my mind. Go on talking.

NURSE: Aye, that I will, but you listen carefully. D'you remember how once you took a great big kitchen knife to carve a boat with, and I came in and had to trick the knife away from you? You were such a silly little lad, one had to trick you, you never would believe what anyone did was for your own good . . . "Give me that snake," I said, "or else he'll bite you." And then, see, you let go of the knife. (*Takes the revolver from his hand.*) And then, too, when it was time for you to dress yourself, and you wouldn't. I had to coax you, and say you should have a golden coat and be dressed just like a prince. Then I took your little tunic, that was just made of green wool, and held it up in front of you and said: "In with your arms, now, both together." (*Gets the jacket on.*) And then I said: "Sit nice and still now, while I button it up behind." (*Ties the sleeves behind him.*) And then I said: "Up with you, and walk across the floor like a good boy, so Nurse can see how it fits." (*Leads him to the sofa.*) And then I said: "Now you must go to bed."

CAPTAIN: What's that? Go to bed, when I'd just been dressed? My God! What have you done to me? (*Tries to get free.*) Oh you fiendish woman, what devilish cunning! Who would have thought you had the brains for it? (*Lies down on the sofa.*) Bound, fleeced, outwitted and unable to die!

NURSE: Forgive me, Mr. Adolf, forgive me! I had to stop you killing the child.

CAPTAIN: Why didn't you let me kill her? If life's hell and death's heaven, and children belong to heaven?

NURSE: What do you know of the hereafter?

CAPTAIN: It's the only thing one does know. Of life one knows nothing. Oh, if one had known from the beginning!

NURSE: Humble your stubborn heart, Mr. Adolf, and cry to God for mercy! Even now it's not too late. It wasn't too late for the thief on the Cross, for Our Saviour said: "To-day shalt thou be with me in paradise."

CAPTAIN: Croaking for a corpse already, old crow? (*She takes her hymn-book from her pocket. He calls.*) Nöjd! Are you there, Nöjd?

(*Enter* NÖJD.)

Throw this woman out of the house or she'll choke me to death with her hymn-book. Throw her out of the window, stuff her up the chimney, do what you like only get rid of her!

NÖJD (*starring at the* NURSE): God save you, Captain — and that's from the bottom of my heart — but I can't do that, I just can't. If it were six men now, but a woman!

CAPTAIN: What? You can't manage one woman?

NÖJD: I could manage her all right, but there's something stops a man laying hands on a woman.

CAPTAIN: What is this something? Haven't they laid hands on me?

NÖJD: Yes, but I just can't do it, Sir. Same as if you was to tell me to hit Pastor. It's like religion, it's in your bones. I can't do it.

(*Enter* LAURA. *She signs to* NÖJD, *who goes out.*)

CAPTAIN: Omphale! Omphale! Playing with the club while Hercules spins your wool.

LAURA (*approaching the sofa*): Adolf, look at me! Do you believe I'm your enemy?

CAPTAIN: Yes, I do. I believe all you women are my enemies. My mother did not want me to come into the world because my birth would give her pain. She was my enemy. She robbed my embryo of nourishment, so I was born incomplete. My sister was my enemy when she made me knuckle under to her. The first woman I took in my arms was my enemy. She gave me ten years of sickness in return for the love I gave her. When my daughter had to choose between you and me, she became my enemy. And you, you, my wife, have been my mortal enemy, for you have not let go your hold until there is no life left in me.

LAURA: But I didn't mean this to happen. I never really thought it out. I may have had some vague desire to get rid of you — you were in my way — and perhaps, if you see some plan in my actions, there was one, but I was unconscious of it. I have never given a thought to my actions — they simply ran along the rails you laid down. My conscience is clear, and before God I feel innocent, even if I'm not. You weighed me down like a stone, pressing and pressing till my heart tried to shake off its intolerable burden. That's how it's been, and if without meaning to I have brought you to this, I ask your forgiveness.

CAPTAIN: Very plausible, but how does that help me? And whose fault is it? Perhaps our cerebral marriage is to blame. In the old days one married a wife. Now one goes into partnership with a business woman or sets up house with a friend. Then one rapes the partner or violates the friend. What becomes of love, the healthy love of the senses? It dies of neglect. And what happens to the dividends from those love shares, payable to holder, when there's no joint account? Who is the holder when the crash comes? Who is the bodily father of the cerebral child?

LAURA: Your suspicions about our daughter are entirely unfounded.

CAPTAIN: That's the horror of it. If they had some foundation, there would at least be something to catch hold of, to cling to. Now there are only shadows, lurking in the undergrowth, peering out with grinning faces. It's like fighting with air, a mock battle with blank cartridges. Reality, however deadly, puts one on one's mettle, nerves body and soul for action, but as it is . . . my thoughts dissolve in fog, my brain grinds a void till it catches fire . . . Put a pillow under my head. Lay something over me. I'm cold. I'm terribly cold.

(LAURA *takes off her shawl and spreads it over him. Exit* NURSE.)

LAURA: Give me your hand, my dear.

CAPTAIN: My hand! Which you have bound behind my back. Omphale, Omphale! But I can feel your shawl soft against my mouth. It's warm and gentle like your arms and smells of vanilla like your hair when you were young. When you were young, Laura, and we used to walk in the birch woods. There were primroses and thrushes — lovely, lovely! Think how beautiful life was then — and what it has become! You did not want it to become like this, neither did I. Yet it has. Who then rules our lives?

LAURA: God.

CAPTAIN: The God of strife then — or nowadays the Goddess!

(*Enter* NURSE *with a pillow.*)

Take away this cat that's lying on me. Take it away! (NURSE *removes the shawl and puts the pillow under his head.*) Bring my uniform. Put my tunic over me. (*The* NURSE *takes the tunic from a peg and spreads it over him. To* LAURA.) Ah, my tough lion's-skin that you would take from me! Omphale! Omphale! You cunning woman, lover of peace and contriver of disarmament. Wake, Hercules, before they take away your club! You would trick us out of our armour, calling it tinsel. It was iron, I tell you, before it became tinsel. In the old days the smith forged the soldier's coat, now it is made by the needlewoman. Omphale! Omphale! Rude strength has fallen before treacherous weakness. Shame on you, woman of Satan, and a curse on all your sex! (*He raises himself to spit at her, but sinks back again.*) What sort of a pillow have you given me, Margaret? How hard and cold it is! So cold! Come and sit beside me on this chair. (*She does so.*) Yes, like that. Let me put my head on your lap. Ah, that's warmer! Lean over me so I can feel your breast. Oh how sweet it is to sleep upon a woman's breast, be she mother or mistress! But sweetest of all a mother's.

LAURA: Adolf, tell me, do you want to see your child?

CAPTAIN: My child? A man has no children. Only women have children. So the future is theirs, while we die childless. O God, who holds all children dear!

NURSE: Listen! He's praying to God.

CAPTAIN: No, to you, to put me to sleep. I'm tired, so tired. Goodnight, Margaret. "Blessed art thou among women."

(*He raises himself, then with a cry falls back on the* NURSE's *knees.*)

LAURA (*at the door, calling*): Doctor!

(*Enter* DOCTOR *and* PASTOR.)

Help him, Doctor — if it's not too late! Look, he has stopped breathing!

DOCTOR (*feeling his pulse*): It is a stroke.

PASTOR: Is he dead?

DOCTOR: No, he might still wake — but to what, who can say?

PASTOR: ". . . once to die, but after this the judgment."*

DOCTOR: No judgment — and no recriminations. You who believe that a God rules over human destiny must lay this to his charge.

NURSE: Ah Pastor, with his last breath he prayed to God!

---

* HEBREWS: ix, 27.

PASTOR (*to* LAURA): Is this true?

LAURA: It is true.

DOCTOR: If this be so, of which I am as poor a judge as of the cause of his illness, in any case my skill is at an end. Try yours now, Pastor.

LAURA: Is that all you have to say at this deathbed, Doctor?

DOCTOR: That is all. I know no more. Let him who knows more, speak.

(BERTHA *comes in and runs to* LAURA.)

BERTHA: Mother! Mother!

LAURA: My child! My own child!

PASTOR: Amen.

END

⟨ STRINDBERG'S major writings are autobiographical to an extent far beyond the truism that imaginative literature always reflects the writer's inner life. Among the most compelling works in his vast and various production are those in which his neuroses appear least mediated and the dark powers that haunted and shaped his strange life most pressing and pervasive. The anxieties and obsessions that drove him to write were also his subject matter. We sense an anguished soul continually and compulsively trying to relieve itself of psychic pressure. Besides Kafka, Strindberg is perhaps the most striking example in modern literature of how serious psychic disturbance can issue, sometimes directly, in great art. Both expressed their private suffering in images of existential agony that are felt to have more than private validity.

The plays from both his major phases as a dramatist convey this impression. In the late 1880's he sought to adapt his personal vision of life as hellish doom to the naturalistic doctrine that literature should document and explain human behavior in a spirit of scientific inquiry and on the premises of materialistic determinism. From 1898 to 1909 (when he wrote his last play) he initiated modern expressionism by largely abandoning objective verisimilitude for lonely journeys through fantastically inhabited soulscapes. Between the two periods lay the crucial years of his paranoia, recorded in the autobiographical narrative *Inferno*. He emerged from the *Inferno* crisis with a precarious but — as it was to prove — lasting hold on his sanity. There is in this career something that looks like a paradox in terms of conventional literary history. An acknowledged master of the two main modes of modern drama, Strindberg appears, in his restless exploration of his own tortured self for an authentic image of human experience, to be possessed by a romantic temperament. His intense subjectivity transcends the conventional division of his plays into two categories.

Determining the exact relevance of an author's biography (in the widest sense) to criticism of his work is a particularly perplexing problem in dealing with a romantic writer. Can and should the art be abstracted from the man when it is obvious that the man's private experience has been the inspiration for the art? General esthetic theory answers that if the meaning of the work can only be unlocked by the life, the work must be adjudged something less or other than a fully realized and independent work of art — essentially diaristic, less an object of criticism than a document of biography or evidence of the ways of the creative process. But at any point beyond general theory such distinctions are hard to draw. The issue, however, forces itself upon any commentator on Strindberg and nowhere more insistently than in the case of *The Father*.

For Strindberg projected himself unreservedly into his title character. A few months after finishing the play he wrote a friend:

> I feel like a somnambulist. My life and my fictions are becoming one. I don't know whether *The Father* is a work of the imagination or whether my life is, but I have a feeling that soon now I shall find out, and then I shall collapse in guilt and insanity or commit suicide. Through an excess of imagination my reality has become shadowy. I no longer walk the ground but float in an atmosphere not of air but of darkness.

The Captain's wife taunts him with his poet's mind. Like Strindberg himself, he is an amateur scientist who worries over the household accounts. In 1872 Strindberg had asked to be admitted to a mental hospital. When he wrote the play (in January-February, 1887) he had recently learned that his wife had consulted a doctor about his sanity. Always pathologically jealous, Strindberg feared (as far as we know, without reason) that he was not the father of their two daughters and thought she was trying to have him declared insane in order to gain exclusive control over them. When he read Ibsen's *The Wild Duck* he took Hjalmar Ekdal's degrading marital situation to be modeled on what he thought was his own. He and his wife had quarreled over the children's christening, to which Strindberg, an atheist at the time, had objected. Now in 1887 — when the girls were five and six years old! — they differed just as sharply over their education and future profession. Siri Strindberg, an actress, wanted them to follow careers in the arts; Strindberg wanted them to become midwives.

His somewhat odd choice of vocation for his girls reflects the ambivalent attitude to women that made a shambles of all his marriages. The ambivalence appears in the play not only in the portrayal of Laura but also in the old Nurse, who as a non-erotic servant of fecundity performs the same kind of role that he wanted for his daughters. One hesitates to label as a misogynist a man who married three times and would have again if only the girl had accepted him. It seems rather that his domestic failures — like the Captain's — were rooted in a love-hate complex toward woman that was the result of childhood feelings of being unwanted. He worshipped the mother in woman but felt enslaved and degraded by the sexual partner. Intellectually, however, Strindberg often sounded like a fanatic misogynist. He called Ibsen "an old bluestocking" because of what he regarded as the arrant feminism of *A Doll's House*. Part of the impulse for *The Father*, he admitted, came from an article in a French periodical, arguing that Western civilization was threatened with resurgent matriarchy. The author of the article professed to find traces of an older matriarchal order in the Homeric poems and in Aeschylus's *Oresteia*. This is dubious both as anthropology and as literary criticism, but Strindberg eagerly made the argument his own. In Act III the Captain enters armed with classical authorities for his view of marriage as a deadly battle between two hostile species.

Clearly, references to Strindberg's personal circumstances, to his attitudes and opinions, and to his admitted near-identity with his father-protagonist belong in any inclusive discussion of *The Father*. A great writer's life is interesting both in itself and for the light it may throw on the ways in which the creative mind transmutes life experience into art. No biographer wants to ignore *The Father* as a documentation of Strindberg's feelings about his first marriage. But the student of literature can and must make a distinction between *accounting* for a literary work — that is, explaining how the work came to be what it uniquely is — and *describing* and *analyzing* it as an artifact and *assessing* its literary value. Criticism of *The Father*, in short, must decide whether the play is meaningful to an audience that is ignorant of the facts of Strindberg's married life, his paranoia, and his eccentric ideas about women. Criticism and literary biography are contiguous disciplines that may collaborate for mutual enrichment in establishing a truth — as complete as scholarship can establish — about the writer, but the possibility or even desirability of such collaboration does not impinge upon the sovereignty of either discipline.

The Father (I think it can be held) possesses artistic integrity apart from Strindberg's biography, but the integrity can be demonstrated only if its nature is carefully defined. Traditionally, the play is said to be naturalistic, and Strindberg himself apparently so regarded it. He sent a copy to Émile Zola, who in the '80's was the acknowledged leading theorist and one of the main practitioners of literary Naturalism. He hoped, we may guess, to be praised by Zola for the classically simple and concentrated structure of his play, for its dispensing with lengthy exposition and involved intrigue, for its emphasis on psychology, for its everyday setting and language, for the grandly elemental nature of its conflict, and for the ruthless causality by which the hero moves toward psychic collapse and physical death. If so, he must have found Zola's answer disappointing. His compliments were vague and perfunctory, his reservations polite but specific. He missed the fullness of conditioning background for the two principals that would have explained their behavior; Strindberg, he said, had taken "psychological shortcuts." He objected (if only obliquely) to the play's obvious failure to be a disengaged, clinically and scrupulously observed, representation of the posturings of the human animal. The Captain's invectives against the entire female sex amount to more than a dispassionate exhibit of a breaking mind; they are the play's thesis, and a thesis play by definition defies Naturalistic doctrine. And *as* thesis, the play seems to ignore its own evidence that its weak, imperious protagonist must be a very difficult man to live with. The ideal of scientific verifiability is at odds with the major ambiguity that we cannot be certain, or remain certain for long, that the Captain is a lunatic rather than a fine and sensitive intelligence intolerably provoked to violence. There is, on the other hand, too little balance for Naturalistic unbias in the depiction of the wife-antagonist. If her statement near the end that she never consciously planned the catastrophic outcome is felt to complicate her character, it is only because it is so obviously contradicted by her actions earlier. Zola might have added further objections. It does not seem very plausible that the idea that a man can never be sure of being the father of his child should be appalling news to an intelligent and educated person, or that a jealous husband should never before have questioned the fidelity of a wife whom he has long regarded as his enemy, or that he should be naïve enough to believe that a six-year old letter would suffice for having him declared legally insane, or that a doctor should consider scientific brilliance as disproof of insanity. And plausibility of character and action is very much part of naturalistic convention. A strict Naturalist might even feel — in paradoxical agreement with the 17th-century archclassicist Thomas Rymer — that the Captain's vulnerability of temperament and personality and his literary interests are out of keeping with his military profession. Really the only significant piece of Naturalistic doctrine in the play is its implication that both men and women are driven by forces serving some vast, impersonal biotic scheme.

What all this suggests is that Strindberg's conscious intent with his play was defeated by his unconscious need to use, once again, his writing as a means to achieve personal catharsis. Only with serious qualifications can *The Father* be called a naturalistic drama. It is subjective, it hardly carries conviction as psychology or sociology, and it does not with any care observe the surfaces of life. If it can be said to belong anywhere in a literary classification, it is not with Zola's *Thérèse Raquin* but with Shakespeare's tragedies of the fall of great but flawed individuals. Despite the generic implication of the title, the Captain seems like an extraordinary rather than a typical character. The rapidity of his fall is terrible but not really quite coherent by realistic decorum. The power of the play is in the raw hyperboles of a high-strung and delicately organized sensitivity tragically disintegrating. There is a note of Elizabethan extravagance, both emotional and verbal, in his passion and in the elliptical logic of his dialogues with his wife. Othello's jealous rages and Lear's "O, reason not the need!" come to mind; the paraphrase of Shylock ("Has not a man eyes? . . .") does not seem incongruous. One does not agree or disagree with such a man. One feels horror and pity at the spectacle of his self-consuming imagination. The Victorian drawing-room in a Swedish garrison town is too small a world for his downfall; for all his impotent pathos it makes sense to learn that Strindberg conceived of him as a kind of Nietzschean superman. Literary and mythological allusions give his destroyer dimensions larger than those of a small-minded and domineering housewife. Omphale, Clytemnestra, Dalilah, and Lady Macbeth loom as ominous tutelary presences behind Laura. The straitjacket takes on symbolic meaning reminiscent of the robe in which Clytemnestra traps her husband Agamemnon before killing him. The qualities that remove the play from consideration as a pure specimen of naturalism connect it, on one side, with the heightened life and inscrutable metaphysics of older tragedy, and, on the other, with Strindberg's own and subsequent dramatizations in expressionistic form of man's existential plight. Against the impassioned subjectivity what there is of overt naturalism works in dynamic tension: rationalism is subverted by passion, social life by eruptive psychic forces. The mode of the play is nightmare, not documentary.

The prologue scene with the trooper Nöjd introduces the notion of the uncertainty of fatherhood that becomes Laura's first weapon. Like a female Iago she systematically undermines her husband's will and reason, deliberately provoking the mental imbalance that the Doctor tells her to guard against. In apparent ingenuousness she plies her insinuations, never committing herself to either confess her adultery or protest her innocence. Instinctively she knows that rational uncertainty will break him. Once she succeeds in provoking him to violence she has won. When he throws the lighted lamp at her he surrenders simultaneously to the darkness of her malice and the darkness of his unreason.

What Laura really seeks is not so much control of the child as revenge on the husband who has outraged the mother in her with his lover's embrace. Like him, she is a victim of the built-in polarity in the nature of both sexes, the "two souls" at war within each: in man, son against lover; in woman, mother against mistress-wife. Sex is conflict within and without. "Human kind," as Strindberg was to put it later in *A Dream Play*, "is to be pitied."

Everything in the play centers on the battle between a will paralyzed by intellectual and moral scruple and one that triumphs because it is relentless in the healthy amorality of its sly instinct. The irony of the soldier succumbing to women involves the yet more bitter irony that the Captain succumbs because it is precisely his superiority in intellect and morality to his enemy that makes him the weaker of the two. The child over whom they fight is a cipher. The Pastor and the Doctor are more fully developed characters and for that very reason lose some of their believability when in the end the pattern of the sexual struggle pulls them to Laura's side even though both suspect that they have witnessed what Strindberg (with reference to the play) called "psychic murder." The Nurse is important mainly in her ambiguous symbolic function in the final tableau, where she is at the same time betrayer-mother and siren-comforter. But she is also, like the off-stage grand-mother, part of the formidable pressure of ubiquitous femininity and a representative of the piety which, however foolish, contrasts as a source of spiritual strength with the atheism that fails to sustain the Captain once his child, his concept of personal immortality, is taken from him. The universe in which he suffers is ruled neither by the Christian God nor just by the determinist's blind forces of heredity and environment but by a female deity "of strife." Shackled by sex, warrior man loses the battle with the Eternal Mother.

This is the master image of the action: Hercules disarmed among women, the prototypal *miles*, or soldier, clubless, emasculated. The first fact established by the dialogue is of man drawn by sex to woman's domain: the trooper's presense among the kitchen maids. At the end, the soldier-scientist-atheist has been reduced to a helpless child bab-bling his evening prayers on the treacherous maternal breast. When the Doctor challenges to speak whoever knows better than medical science how to account for the Captain's death, no man's voice is heard but a girl's and a mother's, and they speak not in conscious, rational answer but in invulnerable, self-absorbed emotion:

> BERTHA: Mother! Mother!
> LAURA: My child! My own child!

To which the man of the church adds his sanctifying "Amen."

Bernard Shaw

CAESAR AND CLEOPATRA

A History

PROLOGUE

(*In the doorway of the temple of Ra in Memphis. Deep gloom. An august personage with a hawk's head is mysteriously visible by his own light in the darkness within the temple. He surveys the modern audience with great contempt; and finally speaks the following words to them:*)

Peace! Be silent and hearken unto me, ye quaint little islanders. Give ear, ye men with white paper on your breasts and nothing written thereon (to signify the innocence of your minds). Hear me, ye women who adorn yourselves alluringly and conceal your thoughts from your men, leading them to believe that ye deem them wondrous strong and masterful whilst in truth ye hold them in your hearts as children without judgment. Look upon my hawk's head; and know that I am Ra, who was once in Egypt a mighty god. Ye cannot kneel nor prostrate yourselves; for ye are packed in rows without freedom to move, obstructing one another's vision; neither do any of ye regard it as seemly to do ought until ye see all the rest do so too; wherefore it commonly happens that in great emergencies ye do nothing though each telleth his fellow that something must be done. I ask you not for worship, but for silence. Let not your men speak nor your women cough; for I am come to draw you back two thousand years over the graves of sixty generations. Ye poor posterity, think not that ye are the first. Other fools before ye have seen the sun rise and set, and the moon change her shape and her hour. As they were so ye are; and yet not so great; for the pyramids my people built stand to this day; whilst the dustheaps on which ye slave, and which ye call empires, scatter in the wind even as ye pile your dead sons' bodies on them to make yet more dust.

Hearken to me then, oh ye compulsorily educated ones. Know that even as there is an old England and a new, and ye stand perplexed between the twain; so in the days when I was worshipped was there an old Rome and a new, and men standing perplexed between them. And the old Rome was poor and little, and greedy and fierce, and evil in many ways; but because its mind was little and its work was simple, it knew its own mind and did its own work; and the gods pitied it and helped it and strengthened it and shielded it; for the gods are patient with littleness. Then the old Rome, like the beggar on horseback, presumed on the favor of the gods, and said, "Lo! there is neither riches nor greatness in our littleness: the road to riches and greatness is through robbery of the poor and slaughter of the weak." So they robbed their own poor until they became great masters of that art, and knew by what laws it could be made to appear seemly and honest. And when they had squeezed their own poor dry, they robbed the poor of other lands, and added those lands to Rome until there came a new Rome, rich and huge. And I, Ra, laughed; for the minds of the Romans remained the same size whilst their dominion spread over the earth.

Now mark me, that ye may understand what ye are presently to see. Whilst the Romans still stood between the old Rome and the new, there arose among them a mighty soldier: Pompey the Great. And the way of the soldier is the way of death; but the way of the gods is the way of life; and so it comes that a god at the end of his way is wise and a soldier at the end of his way is a fool. So Pompey held by the old Rome, in which only soldiers could become great; but the gods turned to the new Rome, in which any man with wit enough could become what he would. And Pompey's friend Julius Cæsar was on the side of the gods; for he saw that Rome had passed beyond the control of the little old Romans. This Cæsar was a great talker and a politician: he bought men with words and with gold, even as ye are bought. And when they would not be satisfied with words and gold, and demanded also the glories of war, Cæsar in his middle age turned his hand to that trade; and they that were against him when he sought their welfare, bowed down before him when he became a slayer and a conqueror; for such is the nature of you mortals. And as for Pompey, the gods grew tired of his triumphs and his airs of being himself a god; for he talked of law and duty and other matters that concerned not a mere human worm. And the gods smiled on Cæsar; for he lived the life they had given him boldly, and was not forever rebuking us for our indecent ways of creation, and hiding our handiwork as a shameful thing. Ye know well what I mean; for this is one of your own sins.

And thus it fell out between the old Rome and the new, that Cæsar said, "Unless I break the law of old Rome, I cannot take my share in ruling her; and the gift of ruling that the gods gave me will perish without fruit." But Pompey said, "The law is above all; and if thou break it thou shalt die." Then said Cæsar, "I will break it: kill me who can." And he broke it. And Pompey went for him, as ye say, with a great army to slay him and uphold the old Rome. So Cæsar fled across the Adriatic sea; for the high gods had a lesson to teach him, which lesson they shall also teach you in due time if ye continue to forget them and to worship that cad among gods, Mammon. Therefore before they raised Cæsar to be master of the world, they were minded to throw him down into the dust, even beneath the feet of Pompey, and blacken his face before the nations. And Pompey they raised higher than ever, he and his laws and his high mind that aped the gods, so that his fall might be the more terrible. And Pompey followed Cæsar, and overcame him with all the majesty of old Rome, and stood over him and over the whole world even as ye stand over it with your fleet that covers thirty miles of the sea. And when Cæsar was brought down to utter nothingness, he made a last stand to die honorably, and did not despair; for he said, "Against me there is Pompey, and the old Rome, and the law and the legions: all against me; but high above these are the gods; and Pompey is a fool." And the gods laughed and approved; and on the field of Pharsalia the impossible came to pass; the blood and iron ye pin your faith on fell before the spirit of man; for the spirit of man is the will of the gods; and Pompey's power crumbled in his hand, even as the power of imperial Spain crumbled when it was set against your fathers in the days when England was little, and knew her own mind, and had a mind to know instead of a circulation of newspapers. Wherefore look to it, lest some little people whom ye would enslave rise up and become in the hand of God the scourge of your boastings and your injustices and your lusts and stupidities.

And now, would ye know the end of Pompey, or will ye sleep while a god speaks? Heed my words well; for Pompey went where ye have gone, even to Egypt, where there was a Roman occupation even as there was but now a British one. And Cæsar pursued Pompey to Egypt; a Roman fleeing, and a Roman pursuing: dog eating dog. And the Egyptians said, "Lo: those Romans which have lent money to our kings and levied a distraint upon us with their arms, call for ever upon us to be loyal to them by betraying our own country to them. But now behold two Romes! Pompey's Rome and Cæsar's

Rome! To which of the twain shall we pretend to be loyal?" So they turned in their perplexity to a soldier that had once served Pompey, and that knew the ways of Rome and was full of her lusts. And they said to him, "Lo: in thy country dog eats dog; and both dogs are coming to eat us: what counsel hast thou to give us?" And this soldier, whose name was Lucius Septimius, and whom ye shall presently see before ye, replied, "Ye shall diligently consider which is the bigger dog of the two; and ye shall kill the other dog for his sake and thereby earn his favor." And the Egyptians said, "Thy counsel is expedient; but if we kill a man outside the law we set ourselves in the place of the gods; and this we dare not do. But thou, being a Roman, art accustomed to this kind of killing; for thou hast imperial instincts. Wilt thou therefore kill the lesser dog for us?" And he said, "I will; for I have made my home in Egypt; and I desire consideration and influence among you." And they said, "We knew well thou wouldst not do it for nothing: thou shalt have thy reward." Now when Pompey came, he came alone in a little galley, putting his trust in the law and the constitution. And it was plain to the people of Egypt that Pompey was now but a very small dog. So when he set his foot on the shore he was greeted by his old comrade Lucius Septimius, who welcomed him with one hand and with the other smote off his head, and kept it as it were a pickled cabbage to make a present to Cæsar. And mankind shuddered; but the gods laughed; for Septimius was but a knife that Pompey had sharpened; and when it turned against his own throat they said that Pompey had better have made Septimius a ploughman than so brave and ready-handed a slayer. Therefore again I bid you beware, ye who would all be Pompeys if ye dared; for war is a wolf that may come to your own door.

Are ye impatient with me? Do ye crave for a story of an unchaste woman? Hath the name of Cleopatra tempted ye hither? Ye foolish ones; Cleopatra is as yet but a child that is whipped by her nurse. And what I am about to shew you for the good of your souls is how Cæsar, seeking Pompey in Egypt, found Cleopatra; and how he received that present of a pickled cabbage that was once the head of Pompey; and what things happened between the old Cæsar and the child queen before he left Egypt and battled his way back to Rome to be slain there as Pompey was slain, by men in whom the spirit of Pompey still lived. All this ye shall see; and ye shall marvel, after your ignorant manner, that men twenty centuries ago were already just such as you, and spoke and lived as ye speak and live, no worse and no better, no wiser and no sillier. And the two thousand years that have past are to me, the god Ra, but a moment; nor is this day any other than the day in which Cæsar set foot in the land of my people. And now I leave you; for ye are a dull folk, and instruction is wasted on you; and I had not spoken so much but that it is in the nature of a god to struggle for ever with the dust and the darkness, and to drag from them, by the force of his longing for the divine, more life and more light. Settle ye therefore in your seats and keep silent; for ye are about to hear a man speak, and a great man he was, as ye count greatness. And fear not that I shall speak to you again: the rest of the story must ye learn from them that lived it. Farewell; and do not presume to applaud me.

(*The temple vanishes in utter darkness.*)

AN ALTERNATIVE TO THE PROLOGUE

(*An October night on the Syrian border of Egypt towards the end of the XXXIII Dynasty, in the year 706 by Roman computation, afterwards reckoned by Christian computation at 48 B.C. A great radiance of silver fire, the dawn of a moonlit night, is rising in the east. The stars and the cloudless sky are our own contemporaries, nineteen and a half centuries younger than we know them; but you would not guess that from their appearance. Below them are two notable drawbacks of civilization: a palace, and soldiers. The palace, an old, low, Syrian building of whitened mud, is not so ugly as Buckingham Palace; and the officers in the courtyard are more highly civilized than modern English officers: for example, they do not dig up the corpses of their dead enemies and mutilate them, as we dug up Cromwell and the Mahdi. They are in two groups: one intent on the gambling of their captain BELZANOR, a warrior of fifty, who, with his spear on the ground beside his knee, is stooping to throw dice with a sly-looking young PERSIAN recruit; the other gathered about a guardsman who has just finished telling a naughty story (still current in English barracks) at which they are laughing uproariously. They are about a dozen in number, all highly aristocratic young Egyptian GUARDSMEN, handsomely equipped with weapons and armor, very unEnglish in point of not being ashamed of and uncomfortable in their professional dress; on the contrary, rather ostentatiously and arrogantly warlike, as valu- ing themselves on their military caste.*

BELZANOR *is a typical veteran, tough and wilful; prompt, capable and crafty where brute force will serve; helpless and boyish when it will not: an effective sergeant, an incompetent general, a deplora-*

ble dictator. Would, if influentially connected, he employed in the two last capacities by a modern European State on the strength of his success in the first. Is rather to be pitied just now in view of the fact that JULIUS CÆSAR *is invading his country. Not knowing this, is intent on his game with the* PERSIAN, *whom, as a foreigner, he considers quite capable of cheating him.*

His subalterns are mostly handsome young fellows whose interest in the game and the story symbolize with tolerable completeness the main interests in life of which they are conscious. Their spears are leaning against the walls, or lying on the ground ready to their hands. The corner of the courtyard forms a triangle of which one side is the front of the palace, with a doorway, the other a wall with a gateway. The storytellers are on the palace side: the gamblers, on the gateway side. Close to the gateway, against the wall, is a stone block high enough to enable a Nubian SENTINEL, *standing on it, to look over the wall. The yard is lighted by a torch stuck in the wall. As the laughter from the group round the storyteller dies away, the kneeling* PERSIAN, *winning the throw, snatches up the stake from the ground.*)

BELZANOR: By Apis, Persian, thy gods are good to thee.

PERSIAN: Try yet again, O captain. Double or quits!

BELZANOR: No more. I am not in the vein.

SENTINEL (*poising his javelin as he peers over the wall*): Stand. Who goes there?

(*They all start, listening. A strange* VOICE *replies from without.*)

VOICE: The bearer of evil tidings.

BELZANOR (*calling to the sentry*): Pass him.

SENTINEL (*grounding his javelin*): Draw near, O bearer of evil tidings.

BELZANOR (*pocketing the dice and picking up his spear*): Let us receive this man with honor. He bears evil tidings.

(*The* GUARDSMEN *seize their spears and gather about the gate, leaving a way through for the* NEW COMER.)

PERSIAN (*rising from his knee*): Are evil tidings, then, so honorable?

BELZANOR: O barbarous Persian, hear my instruction. In Egypt the bearer of good tidings is sacrificed to the gods as a thank offering; but no god will accept the blood of the messenger of evil. When we have good tidings, we are careful to send them in the mouth of the cheapest slave we can find. Evil tidings are borne by young noblemen who desire to bring themselves into notice. (*They join the rest at the gate.*)

SENTINEL: Pass, O young captain; and bow the head in the House of the Queen.

VOICE: Go anoint thy javelin with fat of swine, O Blackamoor; for before morning the Romans will make thee eat it to the very butt.

(*The owner of the* VOICE, *a fairhaired dandy, dressed in a different fashion from that affected by the* GUARDSMEN, *but no less extravagantly, comes through the gateway laughing. He is somewhat battlestained; and his left forearm, bandaged, comes through a torn sleeve. In his right hand he carries a Roman sword in its sheath. He swaggers down the courtyard, the* PERSIAN *on his right,* BELZANOR *on his left, and the* GUARDSMEN *crowding down behind him.*)

BELZANOR: Who are thou that laughest in the House of Cleopatra the Queen, and in the teeth of Belzanor, the captain of her guard?

NEW COMER: I am Bel Affris, descended from the gods.

BELZANOR (*ceremoniously*): Hail, cousin!

ALL (*except the* PERSIAN): Hail, cousin!

PERSIAN: All the Queen's guards are descended from the gods, O stranger, save myself. I am Persian, and descended from many kings.

BEL AFFRIS (*to the* GUARDSMEN): Hail, cousins! (*To the* PERSIAN, *condescendingly.*) Hail, mortal!

BELZANOR: You have been in battle, Bel Affris; and you are a soldier among soldiers. You will not let the Queen's women have the first of your tidings.

BEL AFFRIS: I have no tidings, except that we shall have our throats cut presently, women, soldiers, and all.

PERSIAN (*to* BELZANOR): I told you so.

SENTINEL (*who has been listening*): Woe, alas!

BEL AFFRIS (*calling to him*): Peace, peace, poor Ethiop: destiny is with the gods who painted thee black. (*To* BELZANOR.) What has this mortal (*indicating the* PERSIAN) told you?

BELZANOR: He says that the Roman Julius Cæsar, who has landed on our shores with a handful of followers, will make himself master of Egypt. He is afraid of the Roman soldiers. (*The* GUARDSMEN *laugh with boisterous scorn.*) Peasants, brought up to scare crows and follow the plough! Sons of smiths and millers and tanners! And we nobles, consecrated to arms, descended from the gods!

PERSIAN: Belzanor: the gods are not always good to their poor relations.

BELZANOR (*hotly, to the* PERSIAN): Man to man, are we worse than the slaves of Cæsar?

BEL AFFRIS (*stepping between them*): Listen, cousin. Man to man, we Egyptians are as gods above the Romans.

GUARDSMEN (*exultantly*): Aha!

BEL AFFRIS: But this Cæsar does not pit man against man: he throws a legion at you where you are weakest as he throws a stone from a catapult; and that legion is as a man with one head, a thousand arms, and no religion. I have fought against them; and I know.

BELZANOR (*derisively*): Were you frightened, cousin?

(*The* GUARDSMEN *roar with laughter, their eyes sparkling at the wit of their captain.*)

BEL AFFRIS: No, cousin; but I was beaten. They were frightened (perhaps); but they scattered us like chaff.

(*The* GUARDSMEN, *much damped, utter a growl of contemptuous disgust.*)

BELZANOR: Could you not die?

BEL AFFRIS: No: that was too easy to be worthy of a descendant of the gods. Besides, there was no time: all was over in a moment. The attack came just where we least expected it.

BELZANOR: That shews that the Romans are cowards.

BEL AFFRIS: They care nothing about cowardice, these Romans: they fight to win. The pride and honor of war are nothing to them.

PERSIAN: Tell us the tale of the battle. What befell?

GUARDSMEN (*gathering eagerly round* BEL AFFRIS): Ay: the tale of the battle.

BEL AFFRIS: Know then, that I am a novice in the guard of the temple of Ra in Memphis, serving neither Cleopatra nor her brother Ptolemy, but only the high gods. We went a journey to inquire of Ptolemy why he had driven Cleopatra into Syria, and how we of Egypt should deal with the Roman Pompey, newly come to our shores after his defeat by Cæsar at Pharsalia. What, think ye, did we learn? Even that Cæsar is coming also in hot pursuit of his foe, and that Ptolemy has slain Pompey, whose severed head he holds in readiness to present to the conqueror. (*Sensation among the* GUARDSMEN). Nay, more: we found that Cæsar is already come; for we had not made half a day's journey on our way back when we came upon a city rabble flying from his legions, whose landing they had gone out to withstand.

BELZANOR: And ye, the temple guard! did ye not withstand these legions?

BEL AFFRIS: What a man could that we did. But there came the sound of a trumpet whose voice was as the cursing of a black mountain. Then saw we a moving wall of shields coming towards us. You know how the heart burns when you charge a fortified wall; but how if the fortified wall were to charge *you*?

PERSIAN (*exulting in having told them so*): Did I not say it?

BEL AFFRIS: When the wall came nigh, it changed into a line of men — common fellows enough, with helmets, leather tunics, and breast-plates. Every man of them flung his javelin: the one that came my way drove through my shield as through a papyrus — lo there! (*he points to the bandage on his left arm*) and would have gone through my neck had I not stooped. They were charging at the double then, and were upon us with short swords almost as soon as their javelins. When a man is close to you with such a sword, you can do nothing with our weapons: they are all too long.

PERSIAN: What did you do?

BEL AFFRIS: Doubled my fist and smote my Roman on the sharpness of his jaw. He was but mortal after all: he lay down in a stupor; and I took his sword and laid it on. (*Drawing the sword.*) Lo! a Roman sword with Roman blood on it!

GUARDSMEN (*approvingly*): Good! (*They take the sword and hand it round, examining it curiously.*)

PERSIAN: And your men?

BEL AFFRIS: Fled. Scattered like sheep.

BELZANOR (*furiously*): The cowardly slaves! Leaving the descendants of the gods to be butchered!

BEL AFFRIS (*with acid coolness*): The descendants of the gods did not stay to be butchered, cousin. The battle was not to the strong; but the race was to the swift. The Romans, who have no chariots, sent a cloud of horsemen in pursuit, and slew multitudes. Then our high priest's captain rallied a dozen descendants of the gods and exhorted us to die fighting. I said to myself: surely it is safer to stand than to lose my breath and be stabbed in the back; so I joined our captain and stood. Then the Romans treated us with respect; for no man attacks a lion when the field is full of sheep, except for the pride and honor of war, of which these Romans know nothing. So we escaped with our lives; and I am come to warn you that you must open your gates to Cæsar; for his advance guard is scarce an hour behind me; and not an Egyptian warrior is left standing between you and his legions.

SENTINEL: Woe, alas! (*He throws down his javelin and flies into the palace.*)

BELZANOR: Nail him to the door, quick! (*The GUARDSMEN rush for him with their spears; but he is too quick for them.*) Now this news will run through the palace like fire through stubble.

BEL AFFRIS: What shall we do to save the women from the Romans?

BELZANOR: Why not kill them?

PERSIAN: Because we should have to pay blood money for some of them. Better let the Romans kill them: it is cheaper.

BELZANOR (*awestruck at his brain power*): O subtle one! O serpent!

BEL AFFRIS: But your Queen?

BELZANOR: True: we must carry off Cleopatra.

BEL AFFRIS: Will ye not await her command?

BELZANOR: Command! a girl of sixteen! Not we. At Memphis ye deem her a Queen: here we know better. I will take her on the crupper of my horse. When we soldiers have carried her out of Cæsar's reach, then the priests and the nurses and the rest of them can pretend she is a Queen again, and put their commands into her mouth.

PERSIAN: Listen to me, Belzanor.

BELZANOR: Speak, O subtle beyond thy years.

PERSIAN: Cleopatra's brother Ptolemy is at war with her. Let us sell her to him.

GUARDSMEN: O subtle one! O serpent!

BELZANOR: We dare not. We are descended from the gods; but Cleopatra is descended from the river Nile; and the lands of our fathers will grow no grain if the Nile rises not to water them. Without our father's gifts we should live the lives of dogs.

PERSIAN: It is true: the Queen's guard cannot live on its pay. But hear me further, O ye kinsmen of Osiris.

GUARDSMEN: Speak, O subtle one. Hear the serpent-begotten!

PERSIAN: Have I heretofore spoken truly to you of Cæsar, when you thought I mocked you?

GUARDSMEN: Truly, truly.

BELZANOR (*reluctantly admitting it*): So Bel Affris says.

PERSIAN: Hear more of him, then. This Cæsar is a great lover of women: he makes them his friends and counsellors.

BELZANOR: Faugh! This rule of women will be the ruin of Egypt!

PERSIAN: Let it rather be the ruin of Rome! Cæsar grows old now: he is past fifty and full of labors and battles. He is too old for the young women; and the old women are too wise to worship him.

BEL AFFRIS: Take heed, Persian. Cæsar is by this time almost within earshot.

PERSIAN: Cleopatra is not yet a woman: neither is she wise. But she already troubles men's wisdom.

BELZANOR: Ay: that is because she is descended from the river Nile and a black kitten of the sacred White Cat. What then?

PERSIAN: Why, sell her secretly to Ptolemy, and then offer ourselves to Cæsar as volunteers to fight for the overthrow of her brother and the rescue of our Queen, the Great Granddaughter of the Nile.

GUARDSMEN: O serpent!

PERSIAN: He will listen to us if we come with her picture in our mouths. He will conquer and kill her brother, and reign in Egypt with Cleopatra for his Queen. And we shall be her guard.

GUARDSMEN: O subtlest of all the serpents! O admiration! O wisdom!

BEL AFFRIS: He will also have arrived before you have done talking, O word spinner.

BELZANOR: That is true. (*An affrighted uproar in the palace interrupts him.*) Quick: the flight has begun: guard the door. (*They rush to the door and form a cordon before it with their spears. A mob of women-servants and nurses surges out. Those in front recoil from the spears, screaming to those behind to keep back.* BELZANOR'S *voice dominates the disturbance as he shouts.*) Back there. In again, unprofitable cattle.

GUARDSMEN: Back, unprofitable cattle.

BELZANOR: Send us out Ftatateeta, the Queen's chief nurse.

THE WOMEN (*calling into the palace*): Ftatateeta, Ftatateeta. Come, come. Speak to Belzanor.

A WOMAN: Oh, keep back. You are thrusting me on the spearheads.

(*A huge grim woman, her face covered with a network of tiny wrinkles, and her eyes old, large, and wise; sinewy handed, very tall, very strong; with the mouth of a bloodhound and the jaws of a bulldog, appears on the threshold. She is dressed like a person of consequence in the palace, and confronts the* GUARDSMEN *insolently.*)

FTATATEETA: Make way for the Queen's chief nurse.

BELZANOR (*with solemn arrogance*): Ftatateeta: I am Belzanor, the captain of the Queen's guard, descended from the gods.

FTATATEETA (*retorting his arrogance with interest*): Belzanor: I am Ftatateeta, the Queen's chief nurse; and your divine ancestors were proud to be painted on the wall in the pyramids of the kings whom my fathers served.

(*The* WOMEN *laugh triumphantly.*)

BELZANOR (*with grim humor*): Ftatateeta: daughter of a long-tongued, swivel-eyed chameleon, the Romans are at hand. (*A cry of terror from the* WOMEN: *they would fly but for the spears.*) Not even the descendants of the gods can resist them; for they have each man seven arms, each carrying seven spears. The blood in their veins is boiling quicksilver; and their wives become mothers in three hours, and are slain and eaten the next day.

(*A shudder of horror from the* WOMEN. FTATATEETA, *despising them and scorning the soldiers, pushes her way through the crowd and confronts the spear points undismayed.*)

FTATATEETA: Then fly and save yourselves, O cowardly sons of the cheap clay gods that are sold to fish porters; and leave us to shift for ourselves.

BELZANOR: Not until you have first done our bidding, O terror of manhood. Bring out Cleopatra the Queen to us; and then go whither you will.

FTATATEETA (*with a derisive laugh*): Now I know why the gods have taken her out of our hands. (*The* GUARDSMEN *start and look at one another.*) Know, thou foolish soldier, that the Queen has been missing since an hour past sundown.

BELZANOR (*furious*): Hag: you have hidden her to sell to Cæsar or her brother. (*He grasps her by the left wrist, and drags her, helped by a few of the* GUARD, *to the middle of the courtyard, where, as they fling her on her knees, he draws a murderous looking knife.*) Where is she? Where is she? or — (*He threatens to cut her throat.*)

FTATATEETA (*savagely*): Touch me, dog; and the Nile will not rise on your fields for seven times seven years of famine.

BELZANOR (*frightened, but desperate*): I will sacrifice: I will pay. Or stay. (*To the* PERSIAN.) You, O subtle one: your father's lands lie far from the Nile. Slay her.

PERSIAN (*threatening her with his knife*): Persia has but one god; yet he loves the blood of old women. Where is Cleopatra?

FTATATEETA: Persian: as Osiris lives, I do not know. I chid her for bringing evil days upon us by talking to the sacred cats of the priests, and carrying them in her arms. I told her she would be left alone here when the Romans came as a punishment for her disobedience. And now she is gone — run away — hidden. I speak the truth. I call Osiris to witness —

THE WOMEN (*protesting officiously*): She speaks the truth, Belzanor.

BELZANOR: You have frightened the child: she is hiding. Search — quick — into the palace — search every corner.

(*The* GUARDS, *led by* BELZANOR, *shoulder their way into the palace through the flying crowd of* WOMEN, *who escape through the courtyard gate.*)

FTATATEETA (*screaming*): Sacrilege! Men in the Queen's chambers! Sa — (*Her voice dies away as the* PERSIAN *puts his knife to her throat.*)

BEL AFFRIS (*laying a hand on* FTATATEETA's *left shoulder*): Forbear her

yet a moment, Persian. (*To* FTATATEETA, *very significantly.*) Mother:
your gods are asleep or away hunting; and the sword is at your throat.
Bring us to where the Queen is hid, and you shall live.

FTATATEETA (*contemptuously*): Who shall stay the sword in the hand
of a fool, if the high gods put it there? Listen to me, ye young men
without understanding. Cleopatra fears me; but she fears the Romans
more. There is but one power greater in her eyes than the wrath of
the Queen's nurse and the cruelty of Cæsar; and that is the power of
the Sphinx that sits in the desert watching the way to the sea. What
she would have it know, she tells into the ears of the sacred cats; and
on her birthday she sacrifices to it and decks it with poppies. Go ye
therefore into the desert and seek Cleopatra in the shadow of the
Sphinx; and on your heads see to it that no harm comes to her.

BEL AFFRIS (*to the* PERSIAN): May we believe this, O subtle one?

PERSIAN: Which way come the Romans?

BEL AFFRIS: Over the desert, from the sea, by this very Sphinx.

PERSIAN (*to* FTATATEETA): O mother of guile! O aspic's tongue! You
have made up this tale so that we two may go into the desert and
perish on the spears of the Romans. (*Lifting his knife.*) Taste death.

FTATATEETA: Not from thee, baby. (*She snatches his ankle from under
him and flies stooping along the palace wall, vanishing in the darkness within its precinct.* BEL AFFRIS *roars with laughter as the* PERSIAN
tumbles. The GUARDSMEN *rush out of the palace with* BELZANOR *and
a mob of fugitives, mostly carrying bundles.*)

PERSIAN: Have you found Cleopatra?

BELZANOR: She is gone. We have searched every corner.

SENTINEL (*appearing at the door of the palace*): Woe! Alas! Fly, fly!

BELZANOR: What is the matter now?

SENTINEL: The sacred white cat has been stolen.

ALL: Woe! woe! (*General panic. They all fly with cries of consternation. The torch is thrown down and extinguished in the rush. The
noise of the fugitives dies away. Darkness and dead silence.*)

ACT ONE

(*The same darkness into which the temple of Ra and the Syrian palace vanished. The same silence. Suspense. Then the blackness and
stillness break softly into silver mist and strange airs as the windswept harp of Memnon plays at the dawning of the moon. It rises
full over the desert; and a vast horizon comes into relief, broken by a
huge shape which soon reveals itself in the spreading radiance as a*

Sphinx pedestalled on the sands. The light still clears, until the up-raised eyes of the image are distinguished looking straight forward and upward in infinite fearless vigil, and a mass of color between its great paws defines itself as a heap of red poppies on which a girl lies motionless, her silken vest heaving gently and regularly with the breathing of a dreamless sleeper, and her braided hair glittering in a shaft of moonlight like a bird's wing.

Suddenly there comes from afar a vaguely fearful sound (it might be the bellow of a Minotaur softened by great distance) and Memnon's music stops. Silence: then a few faint high-ringing trumpet notes. Then silence again. Then a man comes from the south with stealing steps, ravished by the mystery of the night, all wonder, and halts, lost in contemplation, opposite the left flank of the Sphinx, whose bosom, with its burden, is hidden from him by its massive shoulder.)

THE MAN: Hail, Sphinx: salutation from Julius Cæsar! I have wandered in many lands, seeking the lost regions from which my birth into this world exiled me, and the company of creatures such as I myself. I have found flocks and pastures, men and cities, but no other Cæsar, no air native to me, no man kindred to me, none who can do my day's deed, and think my night's thought. In the little world yonder, Sphinx, my place is as high as yours in this great desert; only I wander, and you sit still; I conquer, and you endure; I work and wonder, you watch and wait; I look up and am dazzled, look down and am darkened, look round and am puzzled, whilst your eyes never turn from looking out — out of the world — to the lost region — the home from which we have strayed. Sphinx, you and I, strangers to the race of men, are no strangers to one another: have I not been conscious of you and of this place since I was born? Rome is a madman's dream: this is my Reality. These starry lamps of yours I have seen from afar in Gaul, in Britain, in Spain, in Thessaly, signalling great secrets to some eternal sentinel below, whose post I never could find. And here at last is their sentinel — an image of the constant and immortal part of my life, silent, full of thoughts, alone in the silver desert. Sphinx, Sphinx: I have climbed mountains at night to hear in the distance the stealthy footfall of the winds that chase your sands in forbidden play — our invisible children, O Sphinx, laughing in whispers. My way hither was the way of destiny; for I am he of whose genius you are the symbol: part brute, part woman, and part god — nothing of man in me at all. Have I read your riddle, Sphinx?

THE GIRL (*who has wakened, and peeped cautiously from her nest to see who is speaking*): Old gentleman.

CÆSAR (*staring violently, and clutching his sword*): Immortal gods!

THE GIRL: Old gentleman: dont run away.

CÆSAR (*stupefied*): "Old gentleman: dont run away"!!! This! to Julius Cæsar!

THE GIRL (*urgently*): Old gentleman.

CÆSAR: Sphinx: you presume on your centuries. I am younger than you, though your voice is but a girl's voice as yet.

THE GIRL: Climb up here, quickly; or the Romans will come and eat you.

CÆSAR (*running forward past the Sphinx's shoulder, and seeing her*): A child at its breast! a divine child!

THE GIRL: Come up quickly. You must get up at its side and creep round.

CÆSAR (*amazed*): Who are you?

THE GIRL: Cleopatra, Queen of Egypt.

CÆSAR: Queen of the Gypsies, you mean.

CLEOPATRA: You must not be disrespectful to me, or the Sphinx will let the Romans eat you. Come up. It is quite cosy here.

CÆSAR (*to himself*): What a dream! What a magnificent dream! Only let me not wake, and I will conquer ten continents to pay for dreaming it out to the end. (*He climbs to the Sphinx's flank, and presently reappears to her on the pedestal, stepping round its right shoulder.*)

CLEOPATRA: Take care. Thats right. Now sit down: you may have its other paw. (*She seats herself comfortably on its left paw.*) It is very powerful and will protect us; but (*shivering, and with plaintive loneliness*) it would not take any notice of me or keep me company. I am glad you have come: I was very lonely. Did you happen to see a white cat anywhere?

CÆSAR (*sitting slowly down on the right paw in extreme wonderment*): Have you lost one?

CLEOPATRA: Yes: the sacred white cat: is it not dreadful? I brought him here to sacrifice him to the Sphinx; but when we got a little way from the city a black cat called him, and he jumped out of my arms and ran away to it. Do you think that the black cat can have been my great-great-great-grandmother?

CÆSAR (*staring at her*): Your great-great-great-grandmother! Well, why not? Nothing would surprise me on this night of nights.

CLEOPATRA: I think it must have been. My great-grandmother's great-grandmother was a black kitten of the sacred white cat; and the river Nile made her his seventh wife. That is why my hair is so wavy. And I always want to be let do as I like, no matter whether it is the will of the gods or not: that is because my blood is made with Nile water.

CÆSAR: What are you doing here at this time of night? Do you live here?

CLEOPATRA: Of course not: I am the Queen; and I shall live in the palace at Alexandria when I have killed my brother, who drove me out of it. When I am old enough I shall do just what I like. I shall be able to poison the slaves and see them wriggle, and pretend to Ftatateeta that she is going to be put into the fiery furnace.

CÆSAR: Hm! Meanwhile why are you not at home and in bed?

CLEOPATRA: Because the Romans are coming to eat us all. You are not at home and in bed either.

CÆSAR (*with conviction*): Yes I am. I live in a tent; and I am now in that tent, fast asleep and dreaming. Do you suppose that I believe you are real, you impossible little dream witch?

CLEOPATRA (*giggling and leaning trustfully towards him*): You are a funny old gentleman. I like you.

CÆSAR: Ah, that spoils the dream. Why dont you dream that I am young?

CLEOPATRA: I wish you were; only I think I should be more afraid of you. I like men, especially young men with round strong arms; but I am afraid of them. You are old and rather thin and stringy; but you have a nice voice; and I like to have somebody to talk to, though I think you are a little mad. It is the moon that makes you talk to yourself in that silly way.

CÆSAR: What! you heard that, did you? I was saying my prayers to the great Sphinx.

CLEOPATRA: But this isnt the great Sphinx.

CÆSAR (*much disappointed, looking up at the statue*): What!

CLEOPATRA: This is only a dear little kitten of a Sphinx. Why, the great Sphinx is so big that it has a temple between its paws. This is my pet Sphinx. Tell me: do you think the Romans have any sorcerers who could take us away from the Sphinx by magic?

CÆSAR: Why? Are you afraid of the Romans?

CLEOPATRA (*very seriously*): Oh, they would eat us if they caught us. They are barbarians. Their chief is called Julius Cæsar. His father was a tiger and his mother a burning mountain; and his nose is like an elephant's trunk. (CÆSAR *involuntarily rubs his nose.*) They all have long noses, and ivory tusks, and little tails, and seven arms with a hundred arrows in each; and they live on human flesh.

CÆSAR: Would you like me to shew you a real Roman?

CLEOPATRA (*terrified*): No. You are frightening me.

CÆSAR: No matter: this is only a dream —

CLEOPATRA (*excitedly*): It is not a dream: it is not a dream. See, see.

(*She plucks a pin from her hair and jabs it repeatedly into his arm.*)

CÆSAR: Ffff — Stop. (*Wrathfully.*) How dare you?

CLEOPATRA (*abashed*): You said you were dreaming. (*Whimpering.*) I only wanted to shew you —

CÆSAR (*gently*): Come, come: dont cry. A queen mustnt cry. (*He rubs his arm, wondering at the reality of the smart.*) Am I awake? (*He strikes his hand against the Sphinx to test its solidity. It feels so real that he begins to be alarmed, and says perplexedly.*) Yes, I — (*quite panic-stricken*) no: impossible: madness, madness! (*Desperately.*) Back to camp — to camp. (*He rises to spring down from the pedestal.*)

CLEOPATRA (*flinging her arms in terror round him*): No: you shant leave me. No, no, no: dont go. I'm afraid — afraid of the Romans.

CÆSAR (*as the conviction that he is really awake forces itself on him*): Cleopatra: can you see my face well?

CLEOPATRA: Yes. It is so white in the moonlight.

CÆSAR: Are you sure it is the moonlight that makes me look whiter than an Egyptian? (*Grimly.*) Do you notice that I have a rather long nose?

CLEOPATRA (*recoiling, paralysed by a terrible suspicion*): Oh!

CÆSAR: It is a Roman nose, Cleopatra.

CLEOPATRA: Ah! (*With a piercing scream she springs up; darts round the left shoulder of the Sphinx; scrambles down to the sand; and falls on her knees in frantic supplication, shrieking.*) Bite him in two, Sphinx: bite him in two. I meant to sacrifice the white cat — I did indeed — I (CÆSAR, *who has slipped down from the pedestal, touches her on the shoulder.*) — Ah! (*She buries her head in her arms.*)

CÆSAR: Cleopatra: Shall I teach you a way to prevent Cæsar from eating you?

CLEOPATRA (*clinging to him piteously*): Oh do, do, do. I will steal Ftatateeta's jewels and give them to you. I will make the river Nile water your lands twice a year.

CÆSAR: Peace, peace, my child. Your gods are afraid of the Romans: you see the Sphinx dare not bite me, nor prevent me carrying you off to Julius Cæsar.

CLEOPATRA (*in pleading murmurings*): You wont, you wont. You said you wouldnt.

CÆSAR: Cæsar never eats women.

CLEOPATRA (*springing up full of hope*): What!

CÆSAR (*impressively*): But he eats girls (*she relapses*) and cats. Now you are a silly little girl; and you are descended from the black kitten. You are both a girl and a cat.

CLEOPATRA (*trembling*): And will he eat *me?*

CÆSAR: Yes; unless you make him believe that you are a woman.

CLEOPATRA: Oh, you must get a sorcerer to make a woman of me. Are you a sorcerer?

CÆSAR: Perhaps. But it will take a long time; and this very night you must stand face to face with Cæsar in the palace of your fathers.

CLEOPATRA: No, no. I darent.

CÆSAR: Whatever dread may be in your soul — however terrible Cæsar may be to you — you must confront him as a brave woman and a great queen; and you must feel no fear. If your hand shakes: if your voice quavers; then — night and death! (*She moans.*) But if he thinks you worthy to rule, he will set you on the throne by his side and make you the real ruler of Egypt.

CLEOPATRA (*despairingly*): No: he will find me out: he will find me out.

CÆSAR (*rather mournfully*): He is easily deceived by women. Their eyes dazzle him; and he sees them not as they are, but as he wishes them to appear to him.

CLEOPATRA (*hopefully*): Then we will cheat him. I will put on Ftatateeta's head-dress; and he will think me quite an old woman.

CÆSAR: If you do that he will eat you at one mouthful.

CLEOPATRA: But I will give him a cake with my magic opal and seven hairs of the white cat baked in it; and —

CÆSAR (*abruptly*): Pah! you are a little fool. He will eat your cake and you too. (*He turns contemptuously from her.*)

CLEOPATRA (*running after him and clinging to him*): Oh please, *please!* I will do whatever you tell me. I will be good. I will be your slave. (*Again the terrible bellowing note sounds across the desert, now closer at hand. It is the bucina, the Roman war trumpet.*)

CÆSAR: Hark!

CLEOPATRA (*trembling*): What was that?

CÆSAR: Cæsar's voice.

CLEOPATRA (*pulling at his hand*): Let us run away. Come. Oh, come.

CÆSAR: You are safe with me until you stand on your throne to receive Cæsar. Now lead me thither.

CLEOPATRA (*only too glad to get away*): I will, I will. (*Again the bucina.*) Oh come, come, come: the gods are angry. Do you feel the earth shaking?

CÆSAR: It is the tread of Cæsar's legions.

CLEOPATRA (*drawing him away*): This way, quickly. And let us look for the white cat as we go. It is he that has turned you into a Roman.

CÆSAR: Incorrigible, oh, incorrigible! Away! (*He follows her, the bucina sounding louder as they steal across the desert. The moonlight wanes:*

*the horizon again shows black against the sky, broken only by the
fantastic silhouette of the Sphinx. The sky itself vanishes in darkness,
from which there is no relief until the gleam of a distant torch falls
on great Egyptian pillars supporting the roof of a majestic corridor.
At the further end of this corridor a Nubian slave appears carrying
the torch.* CÆSAR, *still led by* CLEOPATRA, *follows him. They come
down the corridor,* CÆSAR *peering keenly about at the strange architecture, and at the pillar shadows between which, as the passing torch
makes them hurry noiselessly backwards, figures of men with wings
and hawks' heads, and vast black marble cats, seem to flit in and out
of ambush. Further along, the wall turns a corner and makes a spacious transept in which* CÆSAR *sees, on his right, a throne, and behind
the throne a door. On each side of the throne is a slender pillar with
a lamp on it.*)

CÆSAR: What place is this?

CLEOPATRA: This is where I sit on the throne when I am allowed to
wear my crown and robes. (*The slave holds his torch to shew the
throne.*)

CÆSAR: Order the slave to light the lamps.

CLEOPATRA (*shyly*): Do you think I may?

CÆSAR: Of course. You are the Queen. (*She hesitates.*) Go on.

CLEOPATRA (*timidly, to the slave*): Light all the lamps.

FTATATEETA (*suddenly coming from behind the throne*): Stop. (*The
slave stops. She turns sternly to* CLEOPATRA, *who quails like a naughty
child.*) Who is this you have with you; and how dare you order the
lamps to be lighted without my permission? (CLEOPATRA *is dumb
with apprehension.*)

CÆSAR: Who is she?

CLEOPATRA: Ftatateeta.

FTATATEETA (*arrogantly*): Chief nurse to —

CÆSAR (*cutting her short*): I speak to the Queen. Be silent. (*To* CLEO-
PATRA.) Is this how your servants know their places? Send her away;
and do you (*to the slave*) do as the Queen has bidden. (*The slave
lights the lamps. Meanwhile* CLEOPATRA *stands hesitating, afraid of*
FTATATEETA.) You are the Queen: send her away.

CLEOPATRA (*cajoling*): Ftatateeta, dear: you must go away — just for
a little.

CÆSAR: You are not commanding her to go away: you are begging her.
You are no Queen. You will be eaten. Farewell. (*He turns to go.*)

CLEOPATRA (*clutching him*): No, no, no. Dont leave me.

CÆSAR: A Roman does not stay with queens who are afraid of their
slaves.

CLEOPATRA: I am not afraid. Indeed I am not afraid.

FTATATEETA: We shall see who is afraid here. (*Menacingly.*) Cleopatra —

CÆSAR: On your knees, woman: am I also a child that you dare trifle with me? (*He points to the floor at* CLEOPATRA'S *feet.* FTATATEETA, *half cowed, half savage, hesitates.* CÆSAR *calls to the* NUBIAN.) Slave. (*The* NUBIAN *comes to him.*) Can you cut off a head? (*The* NUBIAN *nods and grins ecstatically, showing all his teeth.* CÆSAR *takes his sword by the scabbard, ready to offer the hilt to the* NUBIAN, *and turns again to* FTATATEETA, *repeating his gesture.*) Have you remembered yourself, mistress?

(FTATATEETA, *crushed, kneels before* CLEOPATRA, *who can hardly believe her eyes.*)

FTATATEETA (*hoarsely*): O Queen, forget not thy servant in the days of thy greatness.

CLEOPATRA (*blazing with excitement*): Go. Begone. Go away. (FTATATEETA *rises with stooped head, and moves backwards towards the door.* CLEOPATRA *watches her submission eagerly, almost clapping her hands, which are trembling. Suddenly she cries.*) Give me something to beat her with. (*She snatches a snake-skin from the throne and dashes after* FTATATEETA, *whirling it like a scourge in the air.* CÆSAR *makes a bound and manages to catch her and hold her while* FTATATEETA *escapes.*)

CÆSAR: You scratch, kitten, do you?

CLEOPATRA (*breaking from him*): I *will* beat somebody. I will beat him. (*She attacks the slave.*) There, there, there! (*The slave flies for his life up the corridor and vanishes. She throws the snake-skin away and jumps on the step of the throne with her arms waving, crying.*) I am a real Queen at last — a real, real Queen! Cleopatra the Queen! (CÆSAR *shakes his head dubiously, the advantage of the change seeming open to question from the point of view of the general welfare of Egypt. She turns and looks at him exultantly. Then she jumps down from the steps, runs to him, and flings her arms round him rapturously, crying.*) Oh, I love you for making me a Queen.

CÆSAR: But queens love only kings.

CLEOPATRA: I will make all the men I love kings. I will make you a king. I will have many young kings, with round strong arms; and when I am tired of them I will whip them to death; but you shall always be my king: my nice, kind, wise, good old king.

CÆSAR: Oh, my wrinkles, my wrinkles! And my child's heart! You will be the most dangerous of all Cæsar's conquests.

CLEOPATRA (*appalled*): Cæsar! I forgot Cæsar. (*Anxiously.*) You will tell him that I am a Queen, will you not? — a real Queen. Listen!

(*stealthily coaxing him*) let us run away and hide until Cæsar is gone.

CÆSAR: If you fear Cæsar, you are no true queen; and though you were to hide beneath a pyramid, he would go straight to it and lift it with one hand. And then — ! (*He chops his teeth together.*)

CLEOPATRA (*trembling*): Oh!

CÆSAR: Be afraid if you dare. (*The note of the bucina resounds again in the distance. She moans with fear.* CÆSAR *exults in it, exclaiming.*) Aha! Cæsar approaches the throne of Cleopatra. Come: take your place. (*He takes her hand and leads her to the throne. She is too downcast to speak.*) Ho, there, Teetatota. How do you call your slaves?

CLEOPATRA (*spiritlessly, as she sinks on the throne and cowers there, shaking*): Clap your hands.

(*He claps his hands.* FTATATEETA *returns.*)

CÆSAR: Bring the Queen's robes, and her crown, and her women; and prepare her.

CLEOPATRA (*eagerly — recovering herself a little*): Yes, the crown, Ftatateeta: I shall wear the crown.

FTATATEETA: For whom must the Queen put on her state?

CÆSAR: For a citizen of Rome. A king of kings, Totateeta.

CLEOPATRA (*stamping at her*): How dare you ask questions? Go and do as you are told. (FTATATEETA *goes out with a grim smile.* CLEOPATRA *goes on eagerly, to* CÆSAR.) Cæsar will know that I am a Queen when he sees my crown and robes, will he not?

CÆSAR: No. How shall he know that you are not a slave dressed up in the Queen's ornaments?

CLEOPATRA: You must tell him.

CÆSAR: He will not ask me. He will know Cleopatra by her pride, her courage, her majesty, and her beauty. (*She looks very doubtful.*) Are you trembling?

CLEOPATRA (*shivering with dread*): No, I — I — (*in a very sickly voice*) No.

(FTATATEETA *and three* WOMEN *come in with the regalia.*)

FTATATEETA: Of all the Queen's women, these three alone are left. The rest are fled. (*They begin to deck* CLEOPATRA, *who submits, pale and motionless.*)

CÆSAR: Good, good. Three are enough. Poor Cæsar generally has to dress himself.

FTATATEETA (*contemptuously*): The Queen of Egypt is not a Roman barbarian. (*To* CLEOPATRA.) Be brave, my nursling. Hold up your head before this stranger.

CÆSAR (*admiring* CLEOPATRA, *and placing the crown on her head*): Is it sweet or bitter to be a Queen, Cleopatra?

CLEOPATRA: Bitter.

CÆSAR: Cast out fear; and you will conquer Cæsar. Tota: are the Romans at hand?

FTATATEETA: They are at hand; and the guard has fled.

THE WOMEN (*wailing subduedly*): Woe to us!

(*The* NUBIAN *comes running down the hall.*)

NUBIAN: The Romans are in the courtyard. (*He bolts through the door. With a shriek, the* WOMEN *fly after him.* FTATATEETA'S *jaw expresses savage resolution: she does not budge.* CLEOPATRA *can hardly restrain herself from following them.* CÆSAR *grips her wrist, and looks steadfastly at her. She stands like a martyr.*)

CÆSAR: The Queen must face Cæsar alone. Answer "So be it."

CLEOPATRA (*white*): So be it.

CÆSAR (*releasing her*): Good.

(*A tramp and tumult of armed men is heard.* CLEOPATRA'S *terror increases. The bucina sounds close at hand, followed by a formidable clangor of trumpets. This is too much for* CLEOPATRA: *she utters a cry and darts towards the door.* FTATATEETA *stops her ruthlessly.*)

FTATATEETA: You are my nursling. You have said "So be it"; and if you die for it, you must make the Queen's word good. (*She hands* CLEOPATRA *to* CÆSAR, *who takes her back, almost beside herself with apprehension, to the throne.*)

CÆSAR: Now, if you quail — ! (*He seats himself on the throne.*)

(*She stands on the step, all but unconscious, waiting for death. The Roman soldiers troop in tumultuously through the corridor, headed by their ensign with his eagle, and their bucinator, a burly fellow with his instrument coiled round his body, its brazen bell shaped like the head of a howling wolf. When they reach the transept, they stare in amazement at the throne; dress into ordered rank opposite it; draw their swords and lift them in the air with a shout of* Hail, Cæsar. CLEOPATRA *turns and stares wildly at* CÆSAR; *grasps the situation; and, with a great sob of relief, falls into his arms.*)

ACT TWO

(*Alexandria. A hall on the first floor of the Palace, ending in a log-gia approached by two steps. Through the arches of the loggia the Mediterranean can be seen, bright in the morning sun. The clean lofty walls, painted with a procession of the Egyptian theocracy, presented in profile as flat ornament, and the absence of mirrors, sham perspectives, stuffy upholstery and textiles, make the place handsome, wholesome, simple and cool, or, as a rich English manu-facturer would express it, poor, bare, ridiculous and unhomely. For Tottenham Court Road civilization is to this Egyptian civilization as glass bead and tattoo civilization is to Tottenham Court Road.*

The young king PTOLEMY DIONYSUS (*aged ten*) *is at the top of the steps, on his way in through the loggia, led by his guardian* POTHINUS, *who has him by the hand. The court is assembled to receive him. It is made up of men and women* (*some of the women being officials*) *of various complexions and races, mostly Egyptian; some of them, comparatively fair, from lower Egypt, some, much darker, from upper Egypt; with a few Greeks and Jews. Prominent in a group on* PTOLEMY'S *right hand is* THEODOTUS, PTOLEMY'S *tutor. Another group, on* PTOLEMY'S *left, is headed by* ACHILLAS, *the general of* PTOLEMY'S *troops.* THEODOTUS *is a little old man, whose features are as cramped and wizened as his limbs, except his tall straight forehead, which occupies more space than all the rest of his face. He maintains an air of magpie keenness and pro-fundity, listening to what the others say with the sarcastic vigilance of a philosopher listening to the exercises of his disciples.* ACHILLAS *is a tall handsome man of thirty-five, with a fine black beard curled like the coat of a poodle. Apparently not a clever man, but distin-guished and dignified.* POTHINUS *is a vigorous man of fifty, a eunuch, passionate, energetic and quick witted, but of common mind and character; impatient and unable to control his temper. He has fine tawny hair, like fur.* PTOLEMY, *the King, looks much older than an English boy of ten; but he has the childish air, the habit of being in leading strings, the mixture of impotence and petulance, the appearance of being excessively washed, combed and dressed by other hands, which is exhibited by court-bred princes of all ages.*

All receive the King with reverences. He comes down the steps to a chair of state which stands a little to his right, the only seat in the hall. Taking his place before it, he looks nervously for in-structions to POTHINUS, *who places himself at his left hand.*)

POTHINUS: The King of Egypt has a word to speak.

THEODOTUS (*in a squeak which he makes impressive by sheer self-opinionativeness*): Peace for the King's word!

PTOLEMY (*without any vocal inflexions: he is evidently repeating a lesson*): Take notice of this all of you. I am the first-born son of Auletes the Flute Blower who was your King. My sister Berenice drove him from his throne and reigned in his stead but — but — (*he hesitates*) —

POTHINUS (*stealthily prompting*): — but the gods would not suffer —

PTOLEMY: Yes — the gods would not suffer — not suffer — (*He stops; then, crestfallen.*) I forget what the gods would not suffer.

THEODOTUS: Let Pothinus, the King's guardian, speak for the King.

POTHINUS (*suppressing his impatience with difficulty*): The King wished to say that the gods would not suffer the impiety of his sister to go unpunished.

PTOLEMY (*hastily*): Yes: I remember the rest of it. (*He resumes his monotone.*) Therefore the gods sent a stranger one Mark Antony a Roman captain of horsemen across the sands of the desert and he set my father again upon the throne. And my father took Berenice my sister and struck her head off. And now that my father is dead yet another of his daughters my sister Cleopatra would snatch the kingdom from me and reign in my place. But the gods would not suffer — (POTHINUS *coughs admonitorily*) — the gods — the gods would not suffer —

POTHINUS (*prompting*): — will not maintain —

PTOLEMY: Oh yes — will not maintain such iniquity they will give her head to the axe even as her sister's. But with the help of the witch Ftatateeta she hath cast a spell on the Roman Julius Cæsar to make him uphold her false pretence to rule in Egypt. Take notice then that I will not suffer — that I will not suffer — (*Pettishly, to* POTHINUS.) What is it that I will not suffer?

POTHINUS (*suddenly exploding with all the force and emphasis of political passion*): The King will not suffer a foreigner to take from him the throne of our Egypt. (*A shout of applause.*) Tell the King, Achillas, how many soldiers and horsemen follow the Roman?

THEODOTUS: Let the King's general speak!

ACHILLAS: But two Roman legions, O King. Three thousand soldiers and scarce a thousand horsemen.

(*The court breaks into derisive laughter; and a great chattering begins, amid which* RUFIO, *a Roman officer, appears in the loggia. He is a burly, black-bearded man of middle age, very blunt, prompt and rough, with small clear eyes, and plump nose and cheeks, which, however, like the rest of his flesh, are in iron-hard condition.*)

RUFIO (*from the steps*): Peace, ho! (*The laughter and chatter cease abruptly.*) Cæsar approaches.

THEODOTUS (*with much presence of mind*): The King permits the Roman commander to enter!

(CÆSAR, *plainly dressed, but wearing an oak wreath to conceal his baldness, enters from the loggia, attended by* BRITANNUS, *his secretary, a Briton, about forty, tall, solemn, and already slightly bald, with a heavy, drooping, hazel-coloured moustache trained so as to lose its ends in a pair of trim whiskers. He is carefully dressed in blue, with portfolio, inkhorn, and reed pen at his girdle. His serious air and sense of the importance of the business in hand is in marked contrast to the kindly interest of* CÆSAR, *who looks at the scene, which is new to him, with the frank curiosity of a child, and then turns to the King's chair:* BRITANNUS *and* RUFIO *posting themselves near the steps at the other side.*)

CÆSAR (*looking at* POTHINUS *and* PTOLEMY): Which is the King? the man or the boy?

POTHINUS: I am Pothinus, the guardian of my lord the King.

CÆSAR (*patting* PTOLEMY *kindly on the shoulder*): So you are the King. Dull work at your age, eh? (*To* POTHINUS.) Your servant, Pothinus. (*He turns away unconcernedly and comes slowly along the middle of the hall, looking from side to side at the courtiers until he reaches* ACHILLAS.) And this gentleman?

THEODOTUS: Achillas, the King's general.

CÆSAR (*to* ACHILLAS, *very friendly*): A general, eh? I am a general myself. But I began too old, too old. Health and many victories, Achillas!

ACHILLAS: As the gods will, Cæsar.

CÆSAR (*turning to* THEODOTUS): And you, sir, are — ?

THEODOTUS: Theodotus, the King's tutor.

CÆSAR: You teach men how to be kings, Theodotus. That is very clever of you. (*Looking at the gods on the walls as he turns away from* THEODOTUS *and goes up again to* POTHINUS.) And this place?

POTHINUS: The council chamber of the chancellors of the King's treasury, Cæsar.

CÆSAR: Ah! that reminds me. I want some money.

POTHINUS: The King's treasury is poor, Cæsar.

CÆSAR: Yes: I notice that there is but one chair in it.

RUFIO (*shouting gruffly*): Bring a chair there, some of you, for Cæsar.

PTOLEMY (*rising shyly to offer his chair*): Cæsar —

CÆSAR (*kindly*): No, no, my boy: that is your chair of state. Sit down.

(*He makes* PTOLEMY *sit down again. Meanwhile* RUFIO, *looking about him, sees in the nearest corner an image of the god Ra, represented as a seated man with the head of a hawk. Before the image is a bronze tripod, about as large as a three-legged stool, with a stick of incense burning on it.* RUFIO, *with Roman resourcefulness and indifference to foreign superstitions, promptly seizes the tripod; shakes off the incense; blows away the ash; and dumps it down behind* CÆSAR, *nearly in the middle of the hall.*)

RUFIO: Sit on that, Cæsar.

(*A shiver runs through the court, followed by a hissing whisper of* Sacrilege!)

CÆSAR (*seating himself*): Now, Pothinus, to business. I am badly in want of money.

BRITANNUS (*disapproving of these informal expressions*): My master would say that there is a lawful debt due to Rome by Egypt, contracted by the King's deceased father to the Triumvirate; and that it is Cæsar's duty to his country to require immediate payment.

CÆSAR (*blandly*): Ah, I forgot. I have not made my companions known here. Pothinus: this is Britannus, my secretary. He is an islander from the western end of the world, a day's voyage from Gaul. (BRITANNUS *bows stiffly.*) This gentleman is Rufio, my comrade in arms. (RUFIO *nods.*) Pothinus: I want 1,600 talents.

(*The courtiers, appalled, murmur loudly, and* THEODOTUS *and* ACHILLAS *appeal mutely to one another against so monstrous a demand.*)

POTHINUS (*aghast*): Forty million sesterces! Impossible. There is not so much money in the King's treasury.

CÆSAR (*encouragingly*): Only 1,600 talents, Pothinus. Why count it in sesterces? A sestertius is only worth a loaf of bread.

POTHINUS: And a talent is worth a racehorse. I say it is impossible. We have been at strife here, because the King's sister Cleopatra falsely claims his throne. The King's taxes have not been collected for a whole year.

CÆSAR: Yes they have, Pothinus. My officers have been collecting them all morning. (*Renewed whisper and sensation, not without some stifled laughter, among the courtiers.*)

RUFIO (*bluntly*): You must pay, Pothinus. Why waste words? You are getting off cheaply enough.

POTHINUS (*bitterly*): Is it possible that Cæsar, the conqueror of the world, has time to occupy himself with such a trifle as our taxes?

CÆSAR: My friend: taxes are the chief business of a conqueror of the world.

POTHINUS: Then take warning, Cæsar. This day, the treasures of the temple and the gold of the King's treasury shall be sent to the mint to be melted down for our ransom in the sight of the people. They shall see us sitting under bare walls and drinking from wooden cups. And their wrath be on your head, Caesar, if you force us to this sacrilege!

CÆSAR: Do not fear, Pothinus: the people know how well wine tastes in wooden cups. In return for your bounty, I will settle this dispute about the throne for you, if you will. What say you?

POTHINUS: If I say no, will that hinder you?

RUFIO (*defiantly*): No.

CÆSAR: You say the matter has been at issue for a year, Pothinus. May I have ten minutes at it?

POTHINUS: You will do your pleasure, doubtless.

CÆSAR: Good! But first, let us have Cleopatra here.

THEODOTUS: She is not in Alexandria: she is fled into Syria.

CÆSAR: I think not. (*To* RUFIO.) Call Totateeta.

RUFIO (*calling*): Ho there, Teetatota.

(FTATATEETA *enters the loggia, and stands arrogantly at the top of the steps.*)

FTATATEETA: Who pronounces the name of Ftatateeta, the Queen's chief nurse?

CÆSAR: Nobody can pronounce it, Tota, except yourself. Where is your mistress?

(CLEOPATRA, *who is hiding behind* FTATATEETA, *peeps out at them laughing.* CÆSAR *rises.*)

CÆSAR: Will the Queen favor us with her presence for a moment?

CLEOPATRA (*pushing* FTATATEETA *aside and standing haughtily on the brink of the steps*): Am I to behave like a Queen?

CÆSAR: Yes.

(CLEOPATRA *immediately comes down to the chair of state; seizes* PTOLEMY; *drags him out of his seat; then takes his place in the chair.* FTATATEETA *seats herself on the steps of the loggia, and sits there, watching the scene with sibylline intensity.*)

PTOLEMY (*mortified, and struggling with his tears*): Cæsar: this is how she treats me always. If I am a king why is she allowed to take everything from me?

CLEOPATRA: You are not to be King, you little cry-baby. You are to be eaten by the Romans.

CÆSAR (*touched by* PTOLEMY'S *distress*): Come here, my boy, and stand by me.

(PTOLEMY *goes over to* CÆSAR, *who, resuming his seat on the tripod, takes the boy's hand to encourage him.* CLEOPATRA, *furiously jealous, rises and glares at them.*)

CLEOPATRA (*with flaming cheeks*): Take your throne: I dont want it. (*She flings away from the chair, and approaches* PTOLEMY, *who shrinks from her.*) Go this instant and sit down in your place.

CÆSAR: Go, Ptolemy. Always take a throne when it is offered to you.

RUFIO: I hope you will have the good sense to follow your own advice when we return to Rome, Cæsar.

(PTOLEMY *slowly goes back to the throne, giving* CLEOPATRA *a wide berth, in evident fear of her hands. She takes his place beside* CÆSAR.)

CÆSAR: Pothinus —

CLEOPATRA (*interrupting him*): Are you not going to speak to me?

CÆSAR: Be quiet. Open your mouth again before I give you leave and you shall be eaten.

CLEOPATRA: I am not afraid. A queen must not be afraid. Eat my husband there, if you like: *he* is afraid.

CÆSAR (*starting*): Your husband! What do you mean?

CLEOPATRA (*pointing to* PTOLEMY): That little thing.

(*The two Romans and the Briton stare at one another in amazement.*)

THEODOTUS: Cæsar: you are a stranger here, and not conversant with our laws. The kings and queens of Egypt may not marry except with their own royal blood. Ptolemy and Cleopatra are born king and consort just as they are born brother and sister.

BRITANNUS (*shocked*): Cæsar: this is not proper.

THEODOTUS (*outraged*): How!

CÆSAR (*recovering his self-possession*): Pardon him, Theodotus: he is a barbarian, and thinks that the customs of his tribe and island are the laws of nature.

BRITANNUS: On the contrary, Cæsar, it is these Egyptians who are barbarians; and you do wrong to encourage them. I say it is a scandal.

CÆSAR: Scandal or not, my friend, it opens the gate of peace. (*He addresses* POTHINUS *seriously.*) Pothinus: hear what I propose.

RUFIO: Hear Cæsar there.

CÆSAR: Ptolemy and Cleopatra shall reign jointly in Egypt.

ACHILLAS: What of the King's younger brother and Cleopatra's younger sister?

RUFIO (*explaining*): There is another little Ptolemy, Cæsar: so they tell me.

CÆSAR: Well, the little Ptolemy can marry the other sister; and we will make them both a present of Cyprus.

POTHINUS (*impatiently*): Cyprus is of no use to anybody.

CÆSAR: No matter: you shall have it for the sake of peace.

BRITTANUS (*unconsciously anticipating a later statesman*): Peace with honor, Pothinus.

POTHINUS (*mutinously*): Cæsar: be honest. The money you demand is the price of our freedom. Take it; and leave us to settle our own affairs.

THE BOLDER COURTIERS (*encouraged by* POTHINUS'S *tone and* CÆSAR'S *quietness*): Yes, yes. Egypt for the Egyptians!

(*The conference now becomes an altercation, the Egyptians becoming more and more heated.* CÆSAR *remains unruffled; but* RUFIO *grows fiercer and doggeder, and* BRITANNUS *haughtily indignant.*)

RUFIO (*contemptuously*): Egypt for the Egyptians! Do you forget that there is a Roman army of occupation here, left by Aulus Gabinius when he set up your toy king for you?

ACHILLAS (*suddenly asserting himself*): And now under *my* command. I am the Roman general here, Cæsar.

CÆSAR (*tickled by the humor of the situation*): And also the Egyptian general, eh?

POTHINUS (*triumphantly*): That is so, Cæsar.

CÆSAR (*to* ACHILLAS): So you can make war on the Egyptians in the name of Rome, and on the Romans — on me, if necessary — in the name of Egypt?

ACHILLAS: That is so, Cæsar.

CÆSAR: And which side are you on at present, if I may presume to ask, general?

ACHILLAS: On the side of the right and of the gods.

CÆSAR: Hm! How many men have you?

ACHILLAS: That will appear when I take the field.

RUFIO (*truculently*): Are your men Romans? If not, it matters not how many there are, provided you are no stronger than 500 to ten.

POTHINUS: It is useless to try to bluff us, Rufio. Caesar has been defeated before and may be defeated again. A few weeks ago Caesar was flying for his life before Pompey: a few months hence he may be flying for his life before Cato and Juba of Numidia, the African King.

ACHILLAS (*following up* POTHINUS's *speech menacingly*): What can you do with 4,000 men?

THEODOTUS (*following up* ACHILLAS's *speech with a raucous squeak*): And without money? Away with you.

ALL THE COURTIERS (*shouting fiercely and crowding towards* CÆSAR): Away with you. Egypt for the Egyptians! Begone

(RUFIO *bites his beard, too angry to speak.* CÆSAR *sits as comfortably as if he were at breakfast, and the cat were clamoring for a piece of Finnan-haddie.*)

CLEOPATRA: Why do you let them talk to you like that, Cæsar? Are you afraid?

CÆSAR: Why, my dear, what they say is quite true.

CLEOPATRA: But if you go away, I shall not be Queen.

CÆSAR: I shall not go away until you are Queen.

POTHINUS: Achillas: if you are not a fool, you will take that girl whilst she is under your hand.

RUFIO (*daring them*): Why not take Cæsar as well, Achillas?

POTHINUS (*retorting the defiance with interest*): Well said, Rufio. Why not?

RUFIO: Try, Achillas. (*Calling.*) Guard there.

(*The loggia immediately fills with* CÆSAR's *soldiers, who stand, sword in hand, at the top of the steps, waiting the word to charge from their centurion, who carries a cudgel. For a moment the Egyptians face them proudly: then they retire sullenly to their former places.*)

BRITANNUS: You are Cæsar's prisoners, all of you.

CÆSAR (*benevolently*): Oh no, no, no. By no means. Cæsar's guests, gentlemen.

CLEOPATRA: Wont you cut their heads off?

CÆSAR: What! Cut off your brother's head?

CLEOPATRA: Why not? He would cut off mine, if he got the chance. Wouldnt you, Ptolemy?

PTOLEMY (*pale and obstinate*): I would. I will, too, when I grow up.

(CLEOPATRA *is rent by a struggle between her newly-acquired dignity as a queen, and a strong impulse to put out her tongue at him. She takes no part in the scene which follows, but watches it with curiosity and wonder, fidgeting with the restlessness of a child, and sitting down on* CÆSAR'S *tripod when he rises.*)

POTHINUS: Cæsar: if you attempt to detain us —

RUFIO: He will succeed, Egyptian: make up your mind to that. We hold the palace, the beach, and the eastern harbor. The road to Rome is open; and you shall travel it if Cæsar chooses.

CÆSAR (*courteously*): I could do no less, Pothinus, to secure the retreat of my own soldiers. I am accountable for every life among them. But you are free to go. So are all here, and in the palace.

RUFIO (*aghast at this clemency*): What! Renegades and all?

CÆSAR (*softening the expression*): Roman army of occupation and all, Rufio.

POTHINUS (*bewildered*): But — but — but —

CÆSAR: Well, my friend?

POTHINUS: You are turning us out of our own palace into the streets; and you tell us with a grand air that we are free to go! It is for you to go.

CÆSAR: Your friends are in the street, Pothinus. You will be safer there.

POTHINUS: This is a trick. I am the King's guardian: I refuse to stir. I stand on my right here. Where is your right?

CÆSAR: It is in Rufio's scabbard, Pothinus. I may not be able to keep it there if you wait too long.

(*Sensation.*)

POTHINUS (*bitterly*): And this is Roman justice!

THEODOTUS: But not Roman gratitude, I hope.

CÆSAR: Gratitude! Am I in your debt for any service, gentlemen?

THEODOTUS: Is Cæsar's life of so little account to him that he forgets that we have saved it?

CÆSAR: My life! Is that all?

THEODOTUS: Your life. Your laurels. Your future.

POTHINUS: It is true. I can call a witness to prove that but for us, the Roman army of occupation, led by the greatest soldier in the world, would now have Cæsar at its mercy. (*Calling through the loggia.*) Ho, there, Lucius Septimius (CÆSAR *starts, deeply moved*): if my voice can reach you, come forth and testify before Cæsar.

CÆSAR (*shrinking*): No, no.

THEODOTUS: Yes, I say. Let the military tribune bear witness.

(LUCIUS SEPTIMIUS, *a clean-shaven, trim athlete of about 40, with symmetrical features, resolute mouth, and handsome, thin Roman nose, in the dress of a Roman officer, comes in through the loggia and confronts* CÆSAR, *who hides his face with his robe for a moment; then, mastering himself, drops it, and confronts the tribune with dignity.*)

POTHINUS: Bear witness, Lucius Septimius. Cæsar came hither in pursuit of his foe. Did we shelter his foe?

LUCIUS: As Pompey's foot touched the Egyptian shore, his head fell by the stroke of my sword.

THEODOTUS (*with viperish relish*): Under the eyes of his wife and child! Remember that, Cæsar! They saw it from the ship he had just left. We have given you a full and sweet measure of vengeance.

CÆSAR (*with horror*): Vengeance!

POTHINUS: Our first gift to you, as your galley came into the roadstead, was the head of your rival for the empire of the world. Bear witness, Lucius Septimius: is it not so?

LUCIUS: It is so. With this hand, that slew Pompey, I placed his head at the feet of Cæsar.

CÆSAR: Murderer! So would you have slain Cæsar, had Pompey been victorious at Pharsalia.

LUCIUS: Woe to the vanquished, Cæsar! When I served Pompey, I slew as good men as he, only because he conquered them. His turn came at last.

THEODOTUS (*flatteringly*): The deed was not yours, Cæsar, but ours — nay, mine; for it was done by my counsel. Thanks to us, you keep your reputation for clemency, and have your vengeance too.

CÆSAR: Vengeance! Vengeance!! Oh, if I could stoop to vengeance, what would I not exact from you as the price of this murdered man's blood? (*They shrink back, appalled and disconcerted.*) Was he not my son-in-law, my ancient friend, for 20 years the master of great Rome, for 30 years the compeller of victory? Did not I, as a Roman, share his glory? Was the Fate that forced us to fight for the mastery of the world, of our making? Am I Julius Cæsar, or am I a wolf, that you fling to me the grey head of the old soldier, the laurelled conqueror, the mighty Roman, treacherously struck down by this callous ruffian, and then claim my gratitude for it! (*To* LUCIUS SEPTIMIUS.) Begone: you fill me with horror.

LUCIUS (*cold and undaunted*): Pshaw! You have seen severed heads before, Cæsar, and severed right hands too, I think; some thousands of them, in Gaul, after you vanquished Vercingetorix. Did you spare him, with all your clemency? Was that vengeance?

CÆSAR: No, by the gods! would that it had been! Vengeance at least is human. No, I say: those severed right hands, and the brave Vercingetorix basely strangled in a vault beneath the Capitol, were (*with shuddering satire*) a wise severity, a necessary protection to the commonwealth, a duty of statesmanship — follies and fictions ten times bloodier than honest vengeance! What a fool was I then! To think that men's lives should be at the mercy of such fools! (*Humbly.*) Lucius Septimius, pardon me: why should the slayer of Vercingetorix rebuke the slayer of Pompey? You are free to go with the rest. Or stay if you will: I will find a place for you in my service.

LUCIUS: The odds are against you, Cæsar. I go. (*He turns to go out through the loggia.*)

RUFIO (*full of wrath at seeing his prey escaping*): That means that he is a Republican.

LUCIUS (*turning defiantly on the loggia steps*): And what are you?

RUFIO: A Cæsarian, like all Cæsar's soldiers.

CÆSAR (*courteously*): Lucius: believe me, Cæsar is no Cæsarian. Were Rome a true republic, then were Cæsar the first of Republicans. But you have made your choice. Farewell.

LUCIUS: Farewell. Come, Achillas, whilst there is yet time.

(CÆSAR, *seeing that* RUFIO's *temper threatens to get the worse of him, puts his hand on his shoulder and brings him down the hall out of harm's way,* BRITANNUS *accompanying them and posting himself on* CÆSAR's *right hand. This movement brings the three in a little group to the place occupied by* ACHILLAS, *who moves haughtily away and joins* THEODOTUS *on the other side.* LUCIUS SEPTIMIUS *goes out through the soldiers in the loggia.* POTHINUS, THEODOTUS *and* ACHILLAS *follow him with the courtiers, very mistrustful of the soldiers, who close up in their rear and go out after them, keeping them moving without much ceremony. The King is left in his chair, piteous, obstinate, with twitching face and fingers. During these movements* RUFIO *maintains an energetic grumbling, as follows: —*)

RUFIO (*as* LUCIUS *departs*): Do you suppose he would let us go if he had our heads in his hands?

CÆSAR: I have no right to suppose that his ways are any baser than mine.

RUFIO: Pshaw!

CÆSAR: Rufio: if I take Lucius Septimius for my model, and become exactly like him, ceasing to be Cæsar, will you serve me still?

BRITANNUS: Cæsar: this is not good sense. Your duty to Rome demands that her enemies should be prevented from doing further mischief.

(CÆSAR, *whose delight in the moral eye-to-business of his British secretary is inexhaustible, smiles indulgently.*)

RUFIO: It is no use talking to him, Britannus: you may save your breath to cool your porridge. But mark this, Cæsar. Clemency is very well for you; but what is it for your soldiers, who have to fight to-morrow the men you spared yesterday? You may give what orders you please; but I tell you that your next victory will be a massacre, thanks to your clemency. I, for one, will take no prisoners. I will kill my enemies in the field; and then you can preach as much clemency as you please: I shall never have to fight them again. And now, with your leave, I will see these gentry off the premises. (*He turns to go.*)

CÆSAR (*turning also and seeing* PTOLEMY): What! have they left the boy alone! Oh shame, shame!

RUFIO (*taking* PTOLEMY's *hand and making him rise*): Come, your majesty!

PTOLEMY (*to* CÆSAR, *drawing away his hand from* RUFIO): Is he turning me out of my palace?

RUFIO (*grimly*): You are welcome to stay if you wish.

CÆSAR (*kindly*): Go, my boy. I will not harm you but you will be safer away, among your friends. Here you are in the lion's mouth.

PTOLEMY (*turning to go*): It is not the lion I fear, but (*looking at* RUFIO) the jackal. (*He goes out through the loggia.*)

CÆSAR (*laughing approvingly*): Brave boy!

CLEOPATRA (*jealous of* CÆSAR's *approbation, calling after* PTOLEMY): Little silly. You think that very clever.

CÆSAR: Britannus: attend the King. Give him in charge to that Pothinus fellow. (BRITANNUS *goes out after* PTOLEMY.)

RUFIO (*pointing to* CLEOPATRA): And this piece of goods? What is to be done with *her*? However, I suppose I may leave that to you. (*He goes out through the loggia.*)

CLEOPATRA (*flushing suddenly and turning on* CÆSAR): Did you mean me to go with the rest?

CÆSAR (*a little preoccupied, goes with a sigh to* PTOLEMY's *chair, whilst she waits for his answer with red cheeks and clenched fist*): You are free to do just as you please, Cleopatra.

CLEOPATRA: Then you do not care whether I stay or not?

CÆSAR (*smiling*): Of course I had rather you stayed.

CLEOPATRA: Much, *much* rather?

CÆSAR (*nodding*): Much, much rather.

CLEOPATRA: Then I consent to stay, because I am asked. But I do not want to, mind.

CÆSAR: That is quite understood. (*Calling.*) Totateeta.

(FTATATEETA, *still seated, turns her eyes on him with a sinister expression, but does not move.*)

CLEOPATRA (*with a splutter of laughter*): Her name is not Totateeta: it is Ftatateeta. (*Calling.*) Ftatateeta. (FTATATEETA *instantly rises and comes to* CLEOPATRA.)

CÆSAR (*stumbling over the name*): Tfatafeeta will forgive the erring tongue of a Roman. Tota: the Queen will hold her state here in Alexandria. Engage women to attend upon her; and do all that is needful.

FTATATEETA: Am I then the mistress of the Queen's household?

CLEOPATRA (*sharply*): No: *I* am the mistress of the Queen's household. Go and do as you are told, or I will have you thrown into the Nile this very afternoon, to poison the poor crocodiles.

CÆSAR (*shocked*): Oh no, no.

CLEOPATRA: Oh yes, yes. You are very sentimental, Cæsar; but you are clever; and if you do as I tell you, you will soon learn to govern.

(CÆSAR, *quite dumbfounded by this impertinence, turns in his chair and stares at her.* FTATATEETA, *smiling grimly, and showing a splendid set of teeth, goes, leaving them alone together.*)

CÆSAR: Cleopatra: I really think I must eat you, after all.

CLEOPATRA (*kneeling beside him and looking at him with eager interest, half real, half affected to shew how intelligent she is*): You must not talk to me now as if I were a child.

CÆSAR: You have been growing up since the Sphinx introduced us the other night; and you think you know more than I do already.

CLEOPATRA (*taken down, and anxious to justify herself*): No: that would be very silly of me: of course I know that. But — (*suddenly*) are you angry with me?

CÆSAR: No.

CLEOPATRA (*only half believing him*): Then why are you so thoughful?

CÆSAR (*rising*): I have work to do, Cleopatra.

CLEOPATRA (*drawing back*): Work! (*Offended.*) You are tired of talking to me; and that is your excuse to get away from me.

CÆSAR (*sitting down again to appease her*): Well, well: another minute. But then — work!

CLEOPATRA: Work! what nonsense! You must remember that you are a king now: I have made you one. Kings dont work.

CÆSAR: Oh! Who told you that, little kitten? Eh?

CLEOPATRA: My father was King of Egypt; and he never worked. But he was a great king, and cut off my sister's head because she rebelled against him and took the throne from him.

CÆSAR: Well; and how did he get his throne back again?

CLEOPATRA (*eagerly, her eyes lighting up*): I will tell you. A beautiful young man, with strong round arms, came over the desert with many horsemen, and slew my sister's husband and gave my father back his throne. (*Wistfully.*) I was only twelve then. Oh, I wish he would come again, now that I am a queen. I would make him my husband.

CÆSAR: It might be managed, perhaps; for it was I who sent that beautiful young man to help your father.

CLEOPATRA (*enraptured*): You know him!

CÆSAR (*nodding*): I do.

CLEOPATRA: Has he come with you? (CÆSAR *shakes his head: she is cruelly disappointed.*) Oh, I wish he had, I wish he had. If only I were a little older; so that he might not think me a mere kitten, as you do! But perhaps that is because *you* are old. He is many, *many* years younger than you, is he not?

CÆSAR (*as if swallowing a pill*): He is somewhat younger.

CLEOPATRA: Would he be my husband, do you think, if I asked him?

CÆSAR: Very likely.

CLEOPATRA: But I should not like to ask him. Could you not persuade him to ask me — without knowing that I wanted him to?

CÆSAR (*touched by her innocence of the beautiful young man's character*): My poor child!

CLEOPATRA: Why do you say that as if you were sorry for me? Does he love anyone else?

CÆSAR: I am afraid so.

CLEOPATRA (*tearfully*): Then I shall not be his first love.

CÆSAR: Not quite the first. He is greatly admired by women.

CLEOPATRA: I wish I could be the first. But if he loves me, I will make him kill all the rest. Tell me: is he still beautiful? Do his strong round arms shine in the sun like marble?

CÆSAR: He is in excellent condition — considering how much he eats and drinks.

CLEOPATRA: Oh, you must not say common, earthly things about him; for I love him. He is a god.

CÆSAR: He is a great captain of horsemen, and swifter of foot than any other Roman.

CLEOPATRA: What is his real name?

CÆSAR (*puzzled*): His *real* name?

CLEOPATRA: Yes. I always call him Horus, because Horus is the most beautiful of our gods. But I want to know his real name.

CÆSAR: His name is Mark Antony.

CLEOPATRA (*musically*): Mark Antony, Mark Antony, Mark Antony! What a beautiful name! (*She throws her arms round* CÆSAR's *neck.*)

Oh, how I love you for sending him to help my father! Did you love my father very much?

CÆSAR: No, my child; but your father, as you say, never worked. I always work. So when he lost his crown he had to promise me 16,000 talents to get it back for him.

CLEOPATRA: Did he ever pay you?

CÆSAR: Not in full.

CLEOPATRA: He was quite right: it was too dear. The whole world is not worth 16,000 talents.

CÆSAR: That is perhaps true, Cleopatra. Those Egyptians who work paid as much of it as he could drag from them. The rest is still due. But as I most likely shall not get it, I must go back to my work. So you must run away for a little and send my secretary to me.

CLEOPATRA (*coaxing*): No: I want to stay and hear you talk about Mark Antony.

CÆSAR: But if I do not get to work, Pothinus and the rest of them will cut us off from the harbor; and then the way from Rome will be blocked.

CLEOPATRA: No matter: I dont want you to go back to Rome.

CÆSAR: But you want Mark Antony to come from it.

CLEOPATRA (*springing up*): Oh yes, yes, yes: I forgot. Go quickly and work, Cæsar; and keep the way over the sea open for my Mark Antony. (*She runs out through the loggia, kissing her hand to Mark Antony across the sea.*)

CÆSAR (*going briskly up the middle of the hall to the loggia steps*): Ho, Britannus. (*He is startled by the entry of a wounded Roman* SOLDIER, *who confronts him from the upper step.*) What now?

SOLDIER (*pointing to his bandaged head*): This, Cæsar; and two of my comrades killed in the market place.

CÆSAR (*quiet, but attending*): Ay. Why?

SOLDIER: There is an army come to Alexandria, calling itself the Roman army.

CÆSAR: The Roman army of occupation. Ay?

SOLDIER: Commanded by one Achillas.

CÆSAR: Well?

SOLDIER: The citizens rose against us when the army entered the gates. I was with two others in the market place when the news came. They set upon us. I cut my way out; and here I am.

CÆSAR: Good. I am glad to see you alive. (RUFIO *enters the loggia hastily, passing behind the soldier to look out through one of the arches at the quay beneath.*) Rufio: we are besieged.

RUFIO: What! Already?

CÆSAR: Now or to-morrow: what does it matter? We *shall* be besieged.

(BRITANNUS *runs in.*)

BRITANNUS: Cæsar —

CÆSAR (*anticipating him*): Yes: I know. (RUFIO *and* BRITANNUS *come down the hall from the loggia at opposite sides, past* CÆSAR, *who waits for a moment near the step to say to the soldier:*) Comrade: give the word to turn out on the beach and stand by the boats. Get your wounded attended to. Go. (*The* SOLDIER *hurries out.* CÆSAR *comes down the hall between* RUFIO *and* BRITANNUS.) Rufio: we have some ships in the west harbor. Burn them.

RUFIO (*staring*): Burn them!!

CÆSAR: Take every boat we have in the east harbor, and seize the Pharos — that island with the lighthouse. Leave half our men behind to hold the beach and the quay outside this palace: that is the way home.

RUFIO (*disapproving strongly*): Are we to give up the city?

CÆSAR: We have not got it, Rufio. This palace we have; and — what is that building next door?

RUFIO: The theatre.

CÆSAR: We will have that too: it commands the strand. For the rest, Egypt for the Egyptians!

RUFIO: Well, you know best, I suppose. Is that all?

CÆSAR: That is all. Are those ships burnt yet?

RUFIO: Be easy: I shall waste no more time. (*He runs out.*)

BRITANNUS: Cæsar: Pothinus demands speech of you. In my opinion he needs a lesson. His manner is most insolent.

CÆSAR: Where is he?

BRITANNUS: He waits without.

CÆSAR: Ho there! admit Pothinus.

(POTHINUS *appears in the loggia, and comes down the hall very haughtily to* CÆSAR's *left hand.*)

CÆSAR: Well, Pothinus?

POTHINUS: I have brought you our ultimatum, Cæsar.

CÆSAR: Ultimatum! The door was open: you should have gone out through it before you declared war. You are my prisoner now. (*He goes to the chair and loosens his toga.*)

POTHINUS (*scornfully*): I *your* prisoner! Do you know that you are in Alexandria, and that King Ptolemy, with an army outnumbering your little troop a hundred to one, is in possession of Alexandria?

CÆSAR (*unconcernedly taking off his toga and throwing it on the chair*): Well, my friend, get out if you can. And tell your friends not to kill any more Romans in the market place. Otherwise my soldiers, who do not share my celebrated clemency, will probably kill you. Britannus: pass the word to the guard; and fetch my armor. (BRITANNUS *runs out*, RUFIO *returns*.) Well?

RUFIO (*pointing from the loggia to a cloud of smoke drifting over the harbor*): See there! (POTHINUS *runs eagerly up the steps to look out*.)

CÆSAR: What, ablaze already! Impossible!

RUFIO: Yes, five good ships, and a barge laden with oil grappled to each. But it is not my doing: the Egyptians have saved me the trouble. They have captured the west harbor.

CÆSAR (*anxiously*): And the east harbor? The lighthouse, Rufio?

RUFIO (*with a sudden splutter of raging ill usage, coming down to* CÆSAR *and scolding him*): Can I embark a legion in five minutes? The first cohort is already on the beach. We can do no more. If you want faster work, come and do it yourself.

CÆSAR (*soothing him*): Good, good. Patience, Rufio, patience.

RUFIO: Patience! Who is impatient here, you or I? Would I be here, if I could not oversee them from that balcony?

CÆSAR: Forgive me, Rufio; and (*anxiously*) hurry them as much as —

(*He is interrupted by an outcry as of an old man in the extremity of misfortune. It draws near rapidly; and* THEODOTUS *rushes in, tearing his hair, and squeaking the most lamentable exclamations.* RUFIO *steps back to stare at him, amazed at his frantic condition.* POTHINUS *turns to listen.*)

THEODOTUS (*on the steps, with uplifted arms*): Horror unspeakable! Woe, alas! Help!

RUFIO: What now?

CÆSAR (*frowning*): Who is slain?

THEODOTUS: Slain! Oh, worse than the death of ten thousand men! Loss irreparable to mankind!

RUFIO: What has happened, man?

THEODOTUS (*rushing down the hall between them*): The fire has spread from your ships. The first of the seven wonders of the world perishes. The library of Alexandria is in flames.

RUFIO: Pshaw! (*Quite relieved, he goes up to the loggia and watches the preparations of the troops on the beach.*)

CÆSAR: Is that all?

THEODOTUS (*unable to believe his senses*): All! Cæsar: will you go down to posterity as a barbarous soldier too ignorant to know the value of books?

CÆSAR: Theodotus: I am an author myself; and I tell you it is better that the Egyptians should live their lives than dream them away with the help of books.

THEODOTUS (*kneeling, with genuine literary emotion: the passion of the pedant*): Cæsar: once in ten generations of men, the world gains an immortal book.

CÆSAR (*inflexible*): If it did not flatter mankind, the common executioner would burn it.

THEODOTUS: Without history, death will lay you beside your meanest soldier.

CÆSAR: Death will do that in any case. I ask no better grave.

THEODOTUS: What is burning there is the memory of mankind.

CÆSAR: A shameful memory. Let it burn.

THEODOTUS (*wildly*): Will you destroy the past?

CÆSAR: Ay, and build the future with its ruins. (THEODOTUS, *in despair, strikes himself on the temples with his fists.*) But hearken, Theodotus, teacher of kings: you who valued Pompey's head no more than a shepherd values an onion, and who now kneel to me, with tears in your old eyes, to plead for a few sheepskins scrawled with errors. I cannot spare you a man or a bucket of water just now; but you shall pass freely out of the palace. Now, away with you to Achillas; and borrow his legions to put out the fire. (*He hurries him to the steps.*)

POTHINUS (*significantly*): You understand. Theodotus: I remain a prisoner.

THEODOTUS: A prisoner!

CÆSAR: Will you stay to talk whilst the memory of mankind is burning? (*Calling through the loggia.*) Ho there! Pass Theodotus out. (*To* THEODOTUS.) Away with you.

THEODOTUS (*to* POTHINUS): I must go to save the library. (*He hurries out.*)

CÆSAR: Follow him to the gate, Pothinus. Bid him urge your people to kill no more of my soldiers, for your sake.

POTHINUS: My life will cost you dear if you take it, Cæsar. (*He goes out after* THEODOTUS.)

(RUFIO, *absorbed in watching the embarkation, does not notice the departure of the two Egyptians.*)

RUFIO (*shouting from the loggia to the beach*): All ready, there?

CENTURION (*from below*): All ready. We wait for Cæsar.

CÆSAR: Tell them Cæsar is coming — the rogues! (*Calling.*) Britannicus. (*This magniloquent version of his secretary's name is one of* CÆSAR's *jokes. In later years it would have meant, quite seriously and officially, Conqueror of Britain.*)

RUFIO (*calling down*): Push off, all except the longboat. Stand by it to embark, Cæsar's guard there. (*He leaves the balcony and comes down into the hall.*) Where are those Egyptians? Is this more clemency? Have you let them go?

CÆSAR (*chuckling*): I have let Theodotus go to save the library. We must respect literature, Rufio.

RUFIO (*raging*): Folly on folly's head! I believe if you could bring back all the dead of Spain, Gaul, and Thessaly to life, you would do it that we might have the trouble of fighting them over again.

CÆSAR: Might not the gods destroy the world if their only thought were to be at peace next year? (RUFIO, *out of all patience, turns away in anger.* CÆSAR *suddenly grips his sleeve, and adds slyly in his ear.*) Besides, my friend: every Egyptian we imprison means imprisoning two Roman soldiers to guard him. Eh?

RUFIO: Agh! I might have known there was some fox's trick behind your fine talking. (*He gets away from* CÆSAR *with an ill-humored shrug, and goes to the balcony for another look at the preparations; finally goes out.*)

CÆSAR: Is Britannus asleep? I sent him for my armor an hour ago. (*Calling.*) Britannicus, thou British islander. Britannicus!

(CLEOPATRA *runs in through the loggia with* CÆSAR's *helmet and sword, snatched from* BRITANNUS, *who follows her with a cuirass and greaves. They come down to* CÆSAR, *she to his left hand,* BRITANNUS *to his right.*)

CLEOPATRA: I am going to dress you, Cæsar. Sit down. (*He obeys.*) These Roman helmets are so becoming! (*She takes off his wreath.*) Oh! (*She bursts out laughing at him.*)

CÆSAR: What are you laughing at?

CLEOPATRA: Youre bald (*beginning with a big B, and ending with a splutter.*)

CÆSAR (*almost annoyed*): Cleopatra! (*He rises, for the convenience of* BRITANNUS, *who puts the cuirass on him.*)

CLEOPATRA: So that is why you wear the wreath — to hide it.

BRITANNUS: Peace, Egyptian: they are the bays of the conqueror. (*He buckles the cuirass.*)

CLEOPATRA: Peace, thou: islander! (*To* CÆSAR.) You should rub your head with strong spirits of sugar, Cæsar. That will make it grow.

CÆSAR (*with a wry face*): Cleopatra: do you like to be reminded that you are very young?

CLEOPATRA (*pouting*): No.

CÆSAR (*sitting down again, and setting out his leg for* BRITANNUS, *who kneels to put on his greaves*): Neither do I like to be reminded that I am — middle aged. Let me give you ten of my superfluous years.

That will make you 26, and leave me only — no matter. Is it a bargain?

CLEOPATRA: Agreed. 26, mind. (*She puts the helmet on him.*) Oh! How nice! You look only about 50 in it!

BRITANNUS (*looking up severely at* CLEOPATRA): You must not speak in this manner to Cæsar.

CLEOPATRA: Is it true that when Cæsar caught you on that island, you were painted all over blue?

BRITANNUS: Blue is the colour worn by all Britons of good standing. In war we stain our bodies blue; so that though our enemies may strip us of our clothes and our lives, they cannot strip us of our respectability. (*He rises.*)

CLEOPATRA (*with* CÆSAR's *sword*): Let me hang this on. Now you look splendid. Have they made any statues of you in Rome?

CÆSAR: Yes, many statues.

CLEOPATRA: You must send for one and give it to me.

RUFIO (*coming back into the loggia, more impatient than ever*): Now Cæsar: have you done talking? The moment your foot is aboard there will be no holding our men back: the boats will race one another for the lighthouse.

CÆSAR (*drawing his sword and trying the edge*): Is this well set today, Britannicus? At Pharsalia it was as blunt as a barrel-hoop.

BRITANNUS: It will split one of the Egyptian's hairs today, Cæsar. I have set it myself.

CLEOPATRA (*suddenly throwing her arms in terror round* CÆSAR): Oh, you are not really going into battle to be killed?

CÆSAR: No, Cleopatra. No man goes to battle to be killed.

CLEOPATRA: But they do get killed. My sister's husband was killed in battle. You must not go. Let *him* go. (*Pointing to* RUFIO. *They all laugh at her.*) Oh please, *please* dont go. What will happen to me if you never come back?

CÆSAR (*gravely*): Are you afraid?

CLEOPATRA (*shrinking*): No.

CÆSAR (*with quiet authority*): Go to the balcony; and you shall see us take the Pharos. You must learn to look on battles. Go. (*She goes, downcast, and looks out from the balcony.*) That is well. Now, Rufio. March.

CLEOPATRA (*suddenly clapping her hands*): Oh, you will not be able to go!

CÆSAR: Why? What now?

CLEOPATRA: They are drying up the harbor with buckets — a multitude of soldiers — over there (*pointing out across the sea to her left*) — they are dipping up the water.

RUFIO (*hastening to look*): It is true. The Egyptian army! Crawling over the edge of the west harbor like locusts. (*With sudden anger he strides down to* CÆSAR.) This is your accursed clemency, Cæsar. Theodotus has brought them.

CÆSAR (*delighted at his own cleverness*): I meant him to, Rufio. They have come to put out the fire. The library will keep them busy whilst we seize the lighthouse. Eh? (*He rushes out buoyantly through the loggia, followed by* BRITANNUS.)

RUFIO (*disgustedly*): More foxing! Agh! (*He rushes off. A shout from the soldiers announces the appearance of* CÆSAR *below.*)

CENTURION (*below*): All aboard. Give way there. (*Another shout.*)

CLEOPATRA (*waving her scarf through the loggia arch*): Goodbye, goodbye, dear Cæsar. Come back safe. Goodbye!

ACT THREE

(*The edge of the quay in front of the palace, looking out west over the east harbor of Alexandria to Pharos island, just off the end of which, and connected with it by a narrow mole, is the famous lighthouse, a gigantic square tower of white marble diminishing in size storey by storey to the top, on which stands a cresset beacon. The island is joined to the main land by the Heptastadium, a great mole or causeway five miles long bounding the harbor on the south.*

In the middle of the quay a Roman SENTINEL *stands on guard pilum in hand, looking out to the lighthouse with strained attention, his left hand shading his eyes. The pilum is a stout wooden shaft 4½ feet long, with an iron spit about three feet long fixed in it. The* SENTINEL *is so absorbed that he does not notice the approach from the north end of the quay of four Egyptian market* PORTERS *carrying rolls of carpet, preceded by* FTATATEETA *and* APOLLODORUS *the Sicilian.* APOLLODORUS *is a dashing young man of about 24, handsome and debonair, dressed with deliberate æstheticism in the most delicate purples and dove greys, with ornaments of bronze, oxidized silver, and stones of jade and agate. His sword, designed as carefully as a medieval cross, has a blue blade showing through an openwork scabbard of purple leather and filigree. The* PORTERS, *conducted by* FTATATEETA, *pass along the quay behind the* SENTINEL *to the steps of the palace, where they put down their bales and squat on the ground.* APOLLODORUS *does not pass along with them: he halts, amused by the preoccupation of the* SENTINEL.)

APOLLODORUS (*calling to the* SENTINEL): Who goes there, eh?

SENTINEL (*starting violently and turning with his pilum at the charge, revealing himself as a small, wiry, sandy-haired, conscientious young man with an elderly face*): Whats this? Stand. Who are you?

APOLLODORUS: I am Apollodorus the Sicilian. Why, man, what are you dreaming of? Since I came through the lines beyond the theatre there, I have brought my caravan past three sentinels, all so busy staring at the lighthouse that not one of them challenged me. Is this Roman discipline?

SENTINEL: We are not here to watch the land but the sea. Cæsar has just landed on the Pharos. (*Looking at* FTATATEETA.) What have you here? Who is this piece of Egyptian crockery?

FTATATEETA: Apollodorus: rebuke this Roman dog; and bid him bridle his tongue to the presence of Ftatateeta, the mistress of the Queen's household.

APOLLODORUS: My friend: this is a great lady, who stands high with Cæsar.

SENTINEL (*not at all impressed, pointing to the carpets*): And what is all this truck?

APOLLODORUS: Carpets for the furnishing of the Queen's apartments in the palace. I have picked them from the best carpets in the world; and the Queen shall choose the best of my choosing.

SENTINEL: So you are the carpet merchant?

APOLLODORUS (*hurt*): My friend: I am a patrician.

SENTINEL: A patrician! A patrician keeping a shop instead of following arms!

APOLLODORUS: I do not keep a shop. Mine is a temple of the arts. I am a worshipper of beauty. My calling is to choose beautiful things for beautiful queens. My motto is Art for Art's sake.

SENTINEL: That is not the password.

APOLLODORUS: It is a universal password.

SENTINEL: I know nothing about universal passwords. Either give me the password for the day or get back to your shop.

(FTATATEETA, *roused by his hostile tone, steals towards the edge of the quay with the step of a panther, and gets behind him.*)

APOLLODORUS: How if I do neither?

SENTINEL: Then I will drive this pilum through you.

APOLLODORUS: At your service, my friend. (*He draws his sword, and springs to his guard with unruffled grace.*)

FTATATEETA (*suddenly seizing the* SENTINEL'S *arms from behind*): Thrust your knife into the dog's throat, Apollodorus. (*The chivalrous* APOLLODORUS *laughingly shakes his head; breaks ground away from the* SENTINEL *towards the palace; and lowers his point.*)

SENTINEL (*struggling vainly*): Curse on you! Let me go. Help ho!

FTATATEETA (*lifting him from the ground*): Stab the little Roman reptile. Spit him on your sword.

(*A couple of Roman soldiers, with a* CENTURION, *come running along the edge of the quay from the north end. They rescue their comrade, and throw off* FTATATEETA, *who is sent reeling away on the left hand of the* SENTINEL.)

CENTURION (*an unattractive man of fifty, short in his speech and manners, with a vinewood cudgel in his hand*): How now? What is all this?

FTATATEETA (*to* APOLLODORUS): Why did you not stab him? There was time!

APOLLODORUS: Centurion: I am here by order of the Queen to —

CENTURION (*interrupting him*): The Queen! Yes, yes: (*to the* SENTINEL) pass him in. Pass all these bazaar people in to the Queen, with their goods. But mind you pass no one out that you have not passed in — not even the Queen herself.

SENTINEL: This old woman is dangerous: she is as strong as three men. She wanted the merchant to stab me.

APOLLODORUS: Centurion: I am not a merchant. I am a patrician and a votary of art.

CENTURION: Is the woman your wife?

APOLLODORUS (*horrified*): No, no! (*Correcting himself politely.*) Not that the lady is not a striking figure in her own way. But (*emphatically*) she is *not* my wife.

FTATATEETA (*to the* CENTURION): Roman: I am Ftatateeta, the mistress of the Queen's household.

CENTURION: Keep your hands off our men, mistress; or I will have you pitched into the harbor, though you were as strong as ten men. (*To his men.*) To your posts: march! (*He returns with his men the way they came.*)

FTATATEETA (*looking malignantly after him*): We shall see whom Isis loves best: her servant Ftatateeta or a dog of a Roman.

SENTINEL (*to* APOLLODORUS, *with a wave of his pilum towards the palace*): Pass in there; and keep your distance. (*Turning to* FTATATEETA.) Come within a yard of me, you old crocodile; and I will give you this (*the pilum*) in your jaws.

CLEOPATRA (*calling from the palace*): Ftatateeta, Ftatateeta.

FTATATEETA (*looking up, scandalized*): Go from the window, go from the window. There are men here.

CLEOPATRA: I am coming down.

FTATATEETA (*distracted*): No, no. What are you dreaming of? O ye gods, ye gods! Apollodorus: bid your men pick up your bales; and in with me quickly.

APOLLODORUS: Obey the mistress of the Queen's household.

FTATATEETA (*impatiently, as the porters stoop to lift the bales*): Quick, quick: she will be out upon us. (CLEOPATRA *comes from the palace and across the quay to* FTATATEETA.) Oh that ever I was born!

CLEOPATRA (*eagerly*): Ftatateeta: I have thought of something. I want a boat — at once.

FTATATEETA: A boat! No, no: you cannot. Apollodorus: speak to the Queen.

APOLLODORUS (*gallantly*): Beautiful queen: I am Apollodorus the Sicilian, your servant, from the bazaar. I have brought you the three most beautiful Persian carpets in the world to choose from.

CLEOPATRA: I have no time for carpets to-day. Get me a boat.

FTATATEETA: What whim is this? You cannot go on the water except in the royal barge.

APOLLODORUS: Royalty, Ftatateeta, lies not in the barge but in the Queen. (*To* CLEOPATRA.) The touch of your majesty's foot on the gunwale of the meanest boat in the harbor will make it royal. (*He turns to the harbor and calls seaward.*) Ho there, boatman! Pull in to the steps.

CLEOPATRA: Apollodorus: you are my perfect knight; and I will always buy my carpets through you. (APOLLODORUS *bows joyously. An oar appears above the quay; and the* BOATMAN, *a bullet-headed, vivacious, grinning fellow, burnt almost black by the sun, comes up a flight of steps from the water on the* SENTINEL's *right, oar in hand, and waits at the top.*) Can you row, Appollodorus?

APOLLODORUS: My oars shall be your majesty's wings. Whither shall I row my Queen?

CLEOPATRA: To the lighthouse. Come. (*She makes for the steps.*)

SENTINEL (*opposing her with his pilum at the charge*): Stand. You cannot pass.

CLEOPATRA (*flushing angrily*): How dare you? Do you know that I am the Queen?

SENTINEL: I have my orders. You cannot pass.

CLEOPATRA: I will make Cæsar have you killed if you do not obey me.

SENTINEL: He will do worse to me if I disobey my officer. Stand back.

CLEOPATRA: Ftatateeta: strangle him.

SENTINEL (*alarmed — looking apprehensively at* FTATATEETA, *and brandishing his pilum*): Keep off, there.

CLEOPATRA (*running to* APOLLODORUS): Apollodorus: make your slaves help us.

APOLLODORUS: I shall not need their help, lady. (*He draws his sword.*) Now, soldier: choose which weapon you will defend yourself with. Shall it be sword against pilum, or sword against sword?

SENTINEL: Roman against Sicilian, curse you. Take that. (*He hurls his pilum at* APOLLODORUS, *who drops expertly on one knee. The pilum passes whizzing over his head and falls harmless.* APOLLODORUS, *with a cry of triumph, springs up and attacks the* SENTINEL, *who draws his sword and defends himself, crying:*) Ho there, guard. Help!

(CLEOPATRA, *half frightened, half delighted, takes refuge near the palace, where the porters are squatting among the bales. The* BOAT-MAN, *alarmed, hurries down the steps out of harm's way, but stops, with his head just visible above the edge of the quay, to watch the fight. The* SENTINEL *is handicapped by his fear of an attack in the rear from* FTATATEETA. *His swordsmanship, which is of a rough and ready sort, is heavily taxed, as he has occasionally to strike at her to keep her off between a blow and a guard with* APOLLODORUS. *The* CENTURION *returns with several soldiers.* APOLLODORUS *springs back towards* CLEOPATRA *as this reinforcement confronts him.*)

CENTURION (*coming to the* SENTINEL's *right hand*): What is this? What now?

SENTINEL (*panting*): I could do well enough by myself if it werent for the old woman. Keep her off me: this is all the help I need.

CENTURION: Make your report, soldier. What has happened?

FTATATEETA: Centurion: he would have slain the Queen.

SENTINEL (*bluntly*): I would, sooner than let her pass. She wanted to take a boat, and go — so she said — to the lighthouse. I stopped her, as I was ordered to; and she set this fellow on me. (*He goes to pick up his pilum and returns to his place with it.*)

CENTURION (*turning to* CLEOPATRA): Cleopatra: I am loth to offend you; but without Cæsar's express order we dare not let you pass beyond the Roman lines.

APOLLODORUS: Well, Centurion; and has not the lighthouse been within the Roman lines since Cæsar landed there?

CLEOPATRA: Yes, yes. Answer that, if you can.

CENTURION (*to* APOLLODORUS): As for you, Apollodorus, you may thank the gods that you are not nailed to the palace door with a pilum for your meddling.

APOLLODORUS (*urbanely*): My military friend, I was not born to be slain by so ugly a weapon. When I fall, it will be (*holding up his sword*) by this white queen of arms, the only weapon fit for an artist. And now that you are convinced that we do not want to go beyond the lines, let me finish killing your sentinel and depart with the Queen.

CENTURION (*as the* SENTINEL *makes an angry demonstration*): Peace there, Cleopatra: I must abide by my orders, and not by the subtleties of this Sicilian. You must withdraw into the palace and examine your carpets there.

CLEOPATRA (*pouting*): I will not: I am the Queen. Cæsar does not speak to me as you do. Have Cæsar's centurions changed manners with his scullions?

CENTURION (*sulkily*): I do my duty. That is enough for me.

APOLLODORUS: Majesty: when a stupid man is doing something he is ashamed of, he always declares that it is his duty.

CENTURION (*angry*): Apollodorus —

APOLLODORUS (*interrupting him with defiant elegance*): I will make amends for that insult with my sword at fitting time and place. Who says artist, says duellist. (*To* CLEOPATRA.) Hear my counsel, star of the east. Until word comes to these soldiers from Cæsar himself, you are a prisoner. Let me go to him with a message from you, and a present; and before the sun has stooped half way to the arms of the sea, I will bring you back Cæsar's order of release.

CENTURION (*sneering at him*): And you will sell the Queen the present, no doubt.

APOLLODORUS: Centurion: the Queen shall have from me, without payment, as the unforced tribute of Sicilian taste to Egyptian beauty, the richest of these carpets for her present to Cæsar.

CLEOPATRA (*exultantly, to the* CENTURION): Now you see what an ignorant common creature you are!

CENTURION (*curtly*): Well, a fool and his wares are soon parted. (*He turns to his men.*) Two more men to this post here; and see that no one leaves the palace but this man and his merchandise. If he draws his sword again inside the lines, kill him. To your posts. March.

(*He goes out, leaving two* AUXILIARY SENTINELS *with the other.*)

APOLLODORUS (*with polite goodfellowship*): My friends: will you not enter the palace and bury our quarrel in a bowl of wine? (*He takes out his purse, jingling the coins in it.*) The Queen has presents for you all.

SENTINEL (*very sulkily*): You heard our orders. Get about your business.

FIRST AUXILIARY: Yes: you ought to know better. Off with you.

SECOND AUXILIARY (*looking longingly at the purse — this sentinel is a hooknosed man, unlike his comrade, who is squab faced*): Do not tantalize a poor man.

APOLLODORUS (*to* CLEOPATRA): Pearl of Queens: the centurion is at hand; and the Roman soldier is incorruptible when his officer is looking. I must carry your word to Cæsar.

CLEOPATRA (*who has been meditating among the carpets*): Are these carpets very heavy?

APOLLODORUS: It matters not how heavy. There are plenty of porters.

CLEOPATRA: How do they put the carpets into boats? Do they throw them down?

APOLLODORUS: Not into small boats, majesty. It would sink them.

CLEOPATRA: Not into that man's boat, for instance? (*Pointing to the* BOATMAN.)

APOLLODORUS: No. Too small.

CLEOPATRA: But you can take a carpet to Cæsar in it if I send one?

APOLLODORUS: Assuredly.

CLEOPATRA: And you will have it carried gently down the steps and take great care of it?

APOLLODORUS: Depend on me.

CLEOPATRA: Great, *great* care?

APOLLODORUS: More than of my own body.

CLEOPATRA: You will promise me not to let the porters drop it or throw it about?

APOLLODORUS: Place the most delicate glass goblet in the palace in the heart of the roll, Queen; and if it be broken, my head shall pay for it.

CLEOPATRA: Good. Come, Ftatateeta. (FTATATEETA *comes to her.* APOLLODORUS *offers to squire them into the palace.*) No, Apollodorus, you must not come. I will choose a carpet for myself. You must wait here. (*She runs into the palace.*)

APOLLODORUS (*to the* PORTERS): Follow this lady (*indicating* FTATATEETA); and obey her.

(*The* PORTERS *rise and take up their bales.*)

FTATATEETA (*addressing the* PORTERS *as if they were vermin*): This way. And take your shoes off before you put your feet on those stairs.

(*She goes in, followed by the* PORTERS *with the carpets. Meanwhile* APOLLODORUS *goes to the edge of the quay and looks out over the harbor. The* SENTINELS *keep their eyes on him malignantly.*)

APOLLODORUS (*addressing the* SENTINEL): My friend —

SENTINEL (*rudely*): Silence there.

FIRST AUXILIARY: Shut your muzzle, you.

SECOND AUXILIARY (*in a half whisper, glancing apprehensively towards the north end of the quay*): Cant you wait a bit?

APOLLODORUS: Patience, worthy three-headed donkey. (*They mutter ferociously; but he is not at all intimidated.*) Listen: were you set here to watch me, or to watch the Egyptians?

SENTINEL: We know our duty.

APOLLODORUS: Then why dont you do it? There is something going on over there. (*Pointing southwestward to the mole.*)

SENTINEL (*sulkily*): I do not need to be told what to do by the like of you.

APOLLODORUS: Blockhead. (*He begins shouting.*) Ho there, Centurion. Hoiho!

SENTINEL: Curse your meddling. (*Shouting.*) Hoiho! Alarm! Alarm!

FIRST AND SECOND AUXILIARIES: Alarm! Alarm! Hoiho!

(*The* CENTURION *comes running in with his guard.*)

CENTURION: What now? Has the old woman attacked you again? (*Seeing* APOLLODORUS.) Are *you* here still?

APOLLODORUS (*pointing as before*): See there. The Egyptians are moving. They are going to recapture the Pharos. They will attack by sea and land: by land along the great mole; by sea from the west harbor. Stir yourselves, my military friends: the hunt is up. (*A clangor of trumpets from several points along the quay.*) Aha! I told you so.

CENTURION (*quickly*): The two extra men pass the alarm to the south posts. One man keep guard here. The rest with me — quick.

(*The two* AUXILIARY SENTINELS *run off to the south. The* CENTURION *and his guard run off northward; and immediately afterwards the bucina sounds. The four* PORTERS *come from the palace carrying a carpet, followed by* FTATATEETA.)

SENTINEL (*handling his pilum apprehensively*): You again! (*The* PORTERS *stop.*)

FTATATEETA: Peace, Roman fellow: you are now singlehanded. Apollodorus: this carpet is Cleopatra's present to Cæsar. It has rolled up in it ten precious goblets of the thinnest Iberian crystal, and a hundred eggs of the sacred blue pigeon. On your honor, let not one of them be broken.

APOLLODORUS: On my head be it! (*To the* PORTERS.) Into the boat with them carefully.

(*The* PORTERS *carry the carpet to the steps.*)

FIRST PORTER (*looking down at the boat*): Beware what you do, sir. Those eggs of which the lady speaks must weigh more than a pound apiece. This boat is too small for such a load.

BOATMAN (*excitedly rushing up the steps*): Oh thou injurious porter!

Oh thou unnatural son of a she-camel! (*To* APOLLODORUS.) My boat, sir, hath often carried five men. Shall it not carry your lordship and a bale of pigeon's eggs? (*To the* PORTER.) Thou mangy dromedary, the gods shall punish thee for this envious wickedness.

FIRST PORTER (*stolidly*): I cannot quit this bale now to beat thee; but another day I will lie in wait for thee.

APOLLODORUS (*going between them*): Peace there. If the boat were but a single plank, I would get to Cæsar on it.

FTATATEETA (*anxiously*): In the name of the gods, Apollodorus, run no risks with that bale.

APOLLODORUS: Fear not, thou venerable grotesque: I guess its great worth. (*To the* PORTERS.) Down with it, I say; and gently; or ye shall eat nothing but stick for ten days.

(*The* BOATMAN *goes down the steps, followed by the* PORTERS *with the bale:* FTATATEETA *and* APOLLODORUS *watching from the edge.*)

APOLLODORUS: Gently, my sons, my children — (*with sudden alarm*) gently, ye dogs. Lay it level in the stern — so — tis well.

FTATATEETA (*screaming down at one of the* PORTERS): Do not step on it, do not step on it. Oh thou brute beast!

FIRST PORTER (*ascending*): Be not excited, mistress: all is well.

FTATATEETA (*panting*): All well! Oh, thou hast given my heart a turn! (*She clutches her side, gasping.*)

(*The four* PORTERS *have now come up and are waiting at the stair-head to be paid.*)

APOLLODORUS: Here, ye hungry ones. (*He gives money to the* FIRST PORTER, *who holds it in his hand to shew to the others. They crowd greedily to see how much it is, quite prepared, after the Eastern fashion, to protest to heaven against their patron's stinginess. But his liberality overpowers them.*)

FIRST PORTER: O bounteous prince!

SECOND PORTER: O lord of the bazaar!

THIRD PORTER: O favored of the gods!

FOURTH PORTER: O father to all the porters of the market!

SENTINEL (*enviously, threatening them fiercely with his pilum*): Hence, dogs: off. Out of this. (*They fly before him northward along the quay.*)

APOLLODORUS: Farewell, Ftatateeta. I shall be at the lighthouse before the Egyptians. (*He descends the steps.*)

FTATATEETA: The gods speed thee and protect my nursling!

(*The* SENTRY *returns from chasing the* PORTERS *and looks down at the boat, standing near the stairhead lest* FTATATEETA *should attempt to escape.*)

APOLLODORUS (*from beneath, as the boat moves off*): Farewell, valiant pilum pitcher.

SENTINEL: Farewell, shopkeeper.

APOLLODORUS: Ha, ha! Pull, thou brave boatman, pull. Soho-o-o-o-o! (*He begins to sing in barcarolle measure to the rhythm of the oars.*)

> My heart, my heart, spread out thy wings:
> Shake off thy heavy load of love —

Give me the oars, O son of a snail.

SENTINEL (*threatening* FTATATEETA): Now mistress: back to your henhouse. In with you.

FTATATEETA (*falling on her knees and stretching her hands over the waters*): Gods of the seas, bear her safely to the shore!

SENTINEL: Bear *who* safely? What do you mean?

FTATATEETA (*looking darkly at him*): Gods of Egypt and of Vengeance, let this Roman fool be beaten like a dog by his captain for suffering her to be taken over the waters.

SENTINEL: Accursed one: is she then in the boat? (*He calls over the sea.*) Hoiho, there, boatman! Hoiho!

APOLLODORUS (*singing in the distance*)

> My heart, my heart, be whole and free:
> Love is thine only enemy.

(*Meanwhile* RUFIO, *the morning's fighting done, sits munching dates on a faggot of brushwood outside the door of the lighthouse, which towers gigantic to the clouds on his left. His helmet, full of dates, is between his knees; and a leathern bottle of wine is by his side. Behind him the great stone pedestal of the lighthouse is shut in from the open sea by a low stone parapet, with a couple of steps in the middle of the broad coping. A huge chain with a hook hangs down from the lighthouse crane above his head. Faggots like the one he sits on lie beneath it ready to be drawn up to feed the beacon.* CÆSAR *is standing on the step at the parapet looking out anxiously, evidently ill at ease.* BRITANNUS *comes out of the lighthouse door.*)

RUFIO: Well, my British islander. Have you been up to the top?

BRITANNUS: I have. I reckon it at 200 feet high.

RUFIO: Anybody up there?

BRITANNUS: One elderly Tyrian to work the crane; and his son, a well conducted youth of 14.

RUFIO (*looking at the chain*): What! An old man and a boy work that! Twenty men, you mean.

BRITANNUS: Two only, I assure you. They have counterweights, and a machine with boiling water in it which I do not understand: it is not of British design. They use it to haul up barrels of oil and faggots to burn in the brazier on the roof.

RUFIO: But —

BRITANNUS: Excuse me: I came down because there are messengers coming along the mole to us from the island. I must see what their business is. (*He hurries out past the lighthouse.*)

CÆSAR (*coming away from the parapet, shivering and out of sorts*): Rufio: this has been a mad expedition. We shall be beaten. I wish I knew how our men are getting on with that barricade across the great mole.

RUFIO (*angrily*): Must I leave my food and go starving to bring you a report?

CÆSAR (*soothing him nervously*): No, Rufio, no. Eat, my son, eat. (*He takes another turn,* RUFIO *chewing dates meanwhile.*) The Egyptians cannot be such fools as not to storm the barricade and swoop down on us here before it is finished. It is the first time I have ever run an avoidable risk. I should not have come to Egypt.

RUFIO: An hour ago you were all for victory.

CÆSAR (*apologetically*): Yes: I was a fool — rash, Rufio — boyish.

RUFIO: Boyish! Not a bit of it. Here (*offering him a handful of dates*).

CÆSAR: What are these for?

RUFIO: To eat. Thats whats the matter with you. When a man comes to your age, he runs down before his midday meal. Eat and drink; and then have another look at our chances.

CÆSAR (*taking the dates*): My age! (*He shakes his head and bites a date.*) Yes, Rufio: I am an old man — worn out now — true, quite true. (*He gives way to melancholy contemplation, and eats another date.*) Achillas is still in his prime: Ptolemy is a boy. (*He eats another date, and plucks up a little.*) Well, every dog has his day; and I have had mine: I cannot complain. (*With sudden cheerfulness.*) These dates are not bad, Rufio. (BRITANNUS *returns, greatly excited, with a leathern bag.* CÆSAR *is himself again in a moment.*) What now?

BRITANNUS (*triumphantly*): Our brave Rhodian mariners have captured a treasure. There! (*He throws the bag down at* CÆSAR's *feet.*) Our enemies are delivered into our hands.

CÆSAR: In that bag?

BRITANNUS: Wait till you hear, Cæsar. This bag contains all the letters which have passed between Pompey's party and the army of occupation here.

CÆSAR: Well?

BRITANNUS (*impatient of* CÆSAR's *slowness to grasp the situation*): Well, we shall now know who your foes are. The name of every man who has plotted against you since you crossed the Rubicon may be in these papers, for all we know.

CÆSAR: Put them in the fire.

BRITANNUS: Put them — (*he gasps*)!!!!

CÆSAR: In the fire. Would you have me waste the next three years of my life in proscribing and condemning men who will be my friends when I have proved that my friendship is worth more than Pompey's was — than Cato's is. O incorrigible British islander: am I a bull dog, to seek quarrels merely to shew how stubborn my jaws are?

BRITANNUS: But your honor — the honor of Rome —

CÆSAR: I do not make human sacrifices to my honor, as your Druids do. Since you will not burn these, at least I can drown them. (*He picks up the bag and throws it over the parapet into the sea.*)

BRITANNUS: Cæsar: this is mere eccentricity. Are traitors to be allowed to go free for the sake of a paradox?

RUFIO (*rising*): Cæsar: when the islander has finished preaching, call me again. I am going to have a look at the boiling water machine.

(*He goes into the lighthouse.*)

BRITANNUS (*with genuine feeling*): O Cæsar, my great master, if I could but persuade you to regard life seriously, as men do in my country!

CÆSAR: Do they truly do so, Britannus?

BRITANNUS: Have you not been there? Have you not seen them? What Briton speaks as you do in your moments of levity? What Briton neglects to attend the services at the sacred grove? What Briton wears clothes of many colors as you do, instead of plain blue, as all solid, well esteemed men should? These are moral questions with us.

CÆSAR: Well, well, my friend: some day I shall settle down and have a blue toga, perhaps. Meanwhile, I must get on as best I can in my flippant Roman way. (APOLLODORUS *comes past the lighthouse.*) What now?

BRITANNUS (*turning quickly, and challenging the stranger with official haughtiness*): What is this? Who are you? How did you come here?

APOLLODORUS: Calm yourself, my friend: I am not going to eat you. I have come by boat, from Alexandria, with precious gifts for Cæsar.

CÆSAR: From Alexandria!

BRITANNUS (*severely*): That is Cæsar, sir.

RUFIO (*appearing at the lighthouse door*): Whats the matter now?

APOLLODORUS: Hail, great Cæsar! I am Apollodorus the Sicilian, an artist.

BRITANNUS: An artist! Why have they admitted this vagabond?

CÆSAR: Peace, man. Apollodorus is a famous patrician amateur.

BRITANNUS (*disconcerted*): I crave the gentleman's pardon. (*To* CÆSAR.) I understood him to say that he was a professional. (*Somewhat out of countenance, he allows* APOLLODORUS *to approach* CÆSAR, *changing places with him.* RUFIO, *after looking* APOLLODORUS *up and down with marked disparagement, goes to the other side of the platform.*)

CÆSAR: You are welcome, Apollodorus. What is your business?

APOLLODORUS: First, to deliver to you a present from the Queen of Queens.

CÆSAR: Who is that?

APOLLODORUS: Cleopatra of Egypt.

CÆSAR (*taking him into his confidence in his most winning manner*): Apollodorus: this is no time for playing with presents. Pray you, go back to the Queen, and tell her that if all goes well I shall return to the palace this evening.

APOLLODORUS: Cæsar: I cannot return. As I approached the lighthouse, some fool threw a great leathern bag into the sea. It broke the nose of my boat; and I had hardly time to get myself and my charge to the shore before the poor little cockleshell sank.

CÆSAR: I am sorry, Apollodorus. The fool shall be rebuked. Well, well: what have you brought me? The Queen will be hurt if I do not look at it.

RUFIO: Have we time to waste on this trumpery? The Queen is only a child.

CÆSAR: Just so: that is why we must not disappoint her. What is the present, Apollodorus?

APOLLODORUS: Cæsar: it is a Persian carpet — a beauty! And in it are — so I am told — pigeons' eggs and crystal goblets and fragile precious things. I dare not for my head have it carried up that narrow ladder from the causeway.

RUFIO: Swing it up by the crane, then. We will send the eggs to the cook, drink our wine from the goblets; and the carpet will make a bed for Cæsar.

APOLLODORUS: The crane! Cæsar: I have sworn to tender this bale of carpets as I tender my own life.

CÆSAR (*cheerfully*): Then let them swing you up at the same time; and if the chain breaks, you and the pigeons' eggs will perish together.

(*He goes to the chain and looks up along it, examining it curiously.*)

APOLLODORUS (*to* BRITANNUS): Is Cæsar serious?

BRITANNUS: His manner is frivolous because he is an Italian; but he means what he says.

APOLLODORUS: Serious or not, he spake well. Give me a squad of soldiers to work the crane.

BRITANNUS: Leave the crane to me. Go and await the descent of the chain.

APOLLODORUS: Good. You will presently see me there (*turning to them all and pointing with an eloquent gesture to the sky above the parapet*) rising like the sun with my treasure.

(*He goes back the way he came.* BRITANNUS *goes into the lighthouse.*)

RUFIO (*ill-humoredly*): Are you really going to wait here for this foolery, Cæsar?

CÆSAR (*backing away from the crane as it gives signs of working*): Why not?

RUFIO: The Egyptians will let you know why not if they have the sense to make a rush from the shore end of the mole before our barricade is finished. And here we are waiting like children to see a carpet full of pigeons' eggs.

(*The chain rattles, and is drawn up high enough to clear the parapet. It then swings round out of sight behind the lighthouse.*)

CÆSAR: Fear not, my son Rufio. When the first Egyptian takes his first step along the mole, the alarm will sound; and we two will reach the barricade from our end before the Egyptians reach it from their end — we two, Rufio: I, the old man, and you, his biggest boy. And the old man will be there first. So peace; and give me some more dates.

APOLLODORUS (*from the causeway below*): Soho, haul away. So-ho-o-o-o! (*The chain is drawn up and comes round again from behind the lighthouse.* APOLLODORUS *is swinging in the air with his bale of carpet at the end of it. He breaks into song as he soars above the parapet.*)

> Aloft, aloft, behold the blue
> That never shone in woman's eyes —

Easy there: stop her. (*He ceases to rise.*) Further round! (*The chain comes forward above the platform.*)

RUFIO (*calling up*): Lower away there. (*The chain and its load begin to descend.*)

APOLLODORUS (*calling up*): Gently — slowly — mind the eggs.

RUFIO (*calling up*): Easy there — slowly — slowly.

(APOLLODORUS *and the bale are deposited safely on the flags in the middle of the platform.* RUFIO *and* CÆSAR *help* APOLLODORUS *to cast off the chain from the bale.*)

RUFIO: Haul up.

(*The chain rises clear of their heads with a rattle.* BRITANNUS *comes from the lighthouse and helps them to uncord the carpet.*)

APOLLODORUS (*when the cords are loose*): Stand off, my friends: let Cæsar see. (*He throws the carpet open.*)

RUFIO: Nothing but a heap of shawls. Where are the pigeons' eggs?

APOLLODORUS: Approach, Cæsar; and search for them among the shawls.

RUFIO (*drawing his sword*): Ha, treachery. Keep back, Cæsar: I saw the shawl move: there is something alive in there.

BRITANNUS (*drawing his sword*): It is a serpent.

APOLLODORUS: Dares *Cæsar* thrust his hand into the sack where the serpent moves?

RUFIO (*turning on him*): Treacherous dog —

CÆSAR: Peace. Put up your swords. Apollodorus: your serpent seems to breathe very regularly. (*He thrusts his hand under the shawls and draws out a bare arm.*) This is a pretty little snake.

RUFIO (*drawing out the other arm*): Let us have the rest of you.

(*They pull* CLEOPATRA *up by the wrists into a sitting position.* BRITANNUS, *scandalized, sheathes his sword with a drive of protest.*)

CLEOPATRA (*gasping*): Oh, I'm smothered. Oh, Cæsar, a man stood on me in the boat; and a great sack of something fell upon me out of the sky; and then the boat sank; and then I was swung up into the air and bumped down.

CÆSAR (*petting her as she rises and takes refuge on his breast*): Well, never mind: here you are safe and sound at last.

RUFIO: Ay, and now that she *is* here, what are we to do with her?

BRITANNUS: She cannot stay here, Cæsar, without the companionship of some matron.

CLEOPATRA (*jealously, to* CÆSAR, *who is obviously perplexed*): Arent you glad to see me?

CÆSAR: Yes, yes; I am very glad. But Rufio is very angry; and Britannus is shocked.

CLEOPATRA (*contemptuously*): You can have their heads cut off, can you not?

CÆSAR: They would not be so useful with their heads cut off as they are now, my sea bird.

RUFIO (*to* CLEOPATRA): We shall have to go away presently and cut some of your Egyptians' heads off. How will you like being left here with the chance of being captured by that little brother of yours if we are beaten?

CLEOPATRA: But you mustnt leave me alone. Cæsar: you will not leave me alone, will you?

RUFIO: What! not when the trumpet sounds and all our lives depend on Cæsar's being at the barricade before the Egyptians reach it? Eh?

CLEOPATRA: Let them lose their lives: they are only soldiers.

CÆSAR (*gravely*): Cleopatra: when that trumpet sounds, we must take every man his life in his hand, and throw it in the face of Death. And of my soldiers who have trusted me there is not one whose hand I shall not hold more sacred than your head. (CLEOPATRA *is overwhelmed. Her eyes fill with tears.*) Apollodorus: you must take her back to the palace.

APOLLODORUS: Am I a dolphin, Cæsar, to cross the seas with young ladies on my back? My boat is sunk: all yours are either at the barricade or have returned to the city. I will hail one if I can: that is all I can do. (*He goes back to the causeway.*)

CLEOPATRA (*struggling with her tears*): It does not matter. I will not go back. Nobody cares for me.

CÆSAR: Cleopatra —

CLEOPATRA: You want me to be killed.

CÆSAR (*still more gravely*): My poor child: your life matters little here to anyone but yourself. (*She gives way altogether at this, casting herself down on the faggots weeping. Suddenly a great tumult is heard in the distance, bucinas and trumpets sounding through a storm of shouting.* BRITTANUS *rushes to the parapet and looks along the mole.* CÆSAR *and* RUFIO *turn to one another with quick intelligence.*)

CÆSAR: Come, Rufio.

CLEOPATRA (*scrambling to her knees and clinging to him*): No, no. Do not leave me, Cæsar. (*He snatches his skirt from her clutch.*) Oh!

BRITANNUS (*from the parapet*): Cæsar: we are cut off. The Egyptians have landed from the west harbor between us and the barricade!!!

RUFIO (*running to see*): Curses! It is true. We are caught like rats in a trap.

CÆSAR (*ruthfully*): Rufio, Rufio: my men at the barricade are between the sea party and the shore party. I have murdered them.

RUFIO (*coming back from the parapet to* CÆSAR'S *right hand*): Ay: that comes of fooling with this girl here.

APOLLODORUS (*coming up quickly from the causeway*): Look over the parapet, Cæsar.

CÆSAR: We have looked, my friend. We must defend ourselves here.

APOLLODORUS: I have thrown the ladder into the sea. They cannot get in without it.

RUFIO: Ay; and we cannot get out. Have you thought of that?

APOLLODORUS: Not get out! Why not? You have ships in the east harbor.

BRITANNUS (*hopefully, at the parapet*): The Rhodian galleys are standing in towards us already. (CÆSAR *quickly joins* BRITANNUS *at the parapet.*)

RUFIO (*to* APOLLODORUS, *impatiently*): And by what road are we to walk to the galleys, pray?

APOLLODORUS (*with gay, defiant rhetoric*): By the road that leads everywhere — the diamond path of the sun and moon. Have you never seen the child's shadow play of The Broken Bridge? "Ducks and geese with ease get over" — eh? (*He throws away his cloak and cap, and binds his sword on his back.*)

RUFIO: What are you talking about?

APOLLODORUS: I will shew you. (*Calling to* BRITANNUS.) How far off is the nearest galley?

BRITANNUS: Fifty fathom.

CÆSAR: No, no: they are further off than they seem in this clear air to your British eyes. Nearly quarter of a mile, Apollodorus.

APOLLODORUS: Good. Defend yourselves here until I send you a boat from that galley.

RUFIO: Have you wings, perhaps?

APOLLODORUS: Water wings, soldier. Behold!

(*He runs up the steps between* CÆSAR *and* BRITANNUS *to the coping of the parapet; springs into the air; and plunges head foremost into the sea.*)

CÆSAR (*like a schoolboy — wildly excited*): Bravo, bravo! (*Throwing off his cloak.*) By Jupiter, I will do that too.

RUFIO (*seizing him*): You are mad. You shall not.

CÆSAR: Why not? Can I not swim as well as he?

RUFIO (*frantic*): Can an old fool dive and swim like a young one? He is twenty-five and you are fifty.

CÆSAR (*breaking loose from* RUFIO): Old!!!

BRITANNUS (*shocked*): Rufio: you forget yourself.

CÆSAR: I will race you to the galley for a week's pay, father Rufio.

CLEOPATRA: But me! me!!! me!!! what is to become of me?

CÆSAR: I will carry you on my back to the galley like a dolphin. Rufio:

when you see me rise to the surface, throw her in: I will answer for her. And then in with you after her, both of you.

CLEOPATRA: No, no, NO. I shall be drowned.

BRITANNUS: Cæsar: I am a man and a Briton, not a fish. I must have a boat. I cannot swim.

CLEOPATRA: Neither can I.

CÆSAR (*to* BRITANNUS): Stay here, then, alone, until I recapture the lighthouse: I will not forget you. Now, Rufio.

RUFIO: You have made up your mind to this folly?

CÆSAR: The Egyptians have made it up for me. What else is there to do? And mind where you jump: I do not want to get your fourteen stone in the small of my back as I come up. (*He runs up the steps and stands on the coping.*)

BRITANNUS (*anxiously*): One last word, Cæsar. Do not let yourself be seen in the fashionable part of Alexandria until you have changed your clothes.

CÆSAR (*calling over the sea*): Ho, Apollodorus. (*He points skyward and quotes the barcarolle.*)

The white upon the blue above —

APOLLODORUS (*swimming in the distance*):

Is purple on the green below —

CÆSAR (*exultantly*): Aha! (*He plunges into the sea.*)

CLEOPATRA (*running excitedly to the steps*): Oh, let me see. He will be drowned (RUFIO *seizes her.*) — Ah — ah — ah — ah! (*He pitches her screaming into the sea.* RUFIO *and* BRITANNUS *roar with laughter.*)

RUFIO (*looking down after her*): He has got her. (*To* BRITANNUS.) Hold the fort, Briton. Cæsar will not forget you. (*He springs off.*)

BRITANNUS (*running to the steps to watch them as they swim*): All safe, Rufio?

RUFIO (*swimming*): All safe.

CÆSAR (*swimming further off*): Take refuge up there by the beacon; and pile the fuel on the trap door, Britannus.

BRITANNUS (*calling in reply*): I will first do so, and then commend myself to my country's gods. (*A sound of cheering from the sea.* BRITANNUS *gives full vent to his excitement.*) The boat has reached him: Hip, hip, hip, hurrah!

ACT FOUR

(CLEOPATRA'S *sousing in the east harbor of Alexandria was in October 48 B.C. In March 47 she is passing the afternoon in her boudoir in the palace, among a bevy of her ladies, listening to a slave girl who is playing the harp in the middle of the room. The harpist's master, an old* MUSICIAN, *with a lined face, prominent brows, white beard, moustache and eyebrows twisted and horned at the ends, and a consciously keen and pretentious expression, is squatting on the floor close to her on her right, watching her performance.* FTATATEETA *is in attendance near the door, in front of a group of female slaves. Except the harp player all are seated:* CLEOPATRA *in a chair opposite the door on the other side of the room; the rest on the ground.* CLEOPATRA'S *ladies are all young, the most conspicuous being* CHARMIAN *and* IRAS, *her favorites.* CHARMIAN *is a hatchet faced, terra cotta colored little goblin, swift in her movements, and neatly finished at the hands and feet.* IRAS *is a plump, goodnatured creature, rather fatuous, with a profusion of red hair, and a tendency to giggle on the slightest provocation.*)

CLEOPATRA: Can I —

FTATATEETA (*insolently, to the player*): Peace, thou! The Queen speaks. (*The player stops.*)

CLEOPATRA (*to the old* MUSICIAN): I want to learn to play the harp with my own hands. Cæsar loves music. Can you teach me?

MUSICIAN: Assuredly I and no one else can teach the Queen. Have I not discovered the lost method of the ancient Egyptians, who could make a pyramid tremble by touching a bass string? All the other teachers are quacks: I have exposed them repeatedly.

CLEOPATRA: Good: you shall teach me. How long will it take?

MUSICIAN: Not very long: only four years. Your Majesty must first become proficient in the philosophy of Pythagoras.

CLEOPATRA: Has she (*indicating the slave*) become proficient in the philosophy of Pythagoras?

MUSICIAN: Oh, she is but a slave. She learns as a dog learns.

CLEOPATRA: Well, then, I will learn as a dog learns; for she plays better than you. You shall give me a lesson every day for a fortnight. (*The* MUSICIAN *hastily scrambles to his feet and bows profoundly.*) After that, whenever I strike a false note you shall be flogged; and if I strike so many that there is not time to flog you, you shall be thrown

into the Nile to feed the crocodiles. Give the girl a piece of gold; and
send them away.

MUSICIAN (*much taken aback*): But true art will not be thus forced.

FTATATEETA (*pushing him out*): What is this? Answering the Queen,
forsooth. Out with you.

(*He is pushed out by* FTATATEETA, *the girl following with her
harp, amid the laughter of the ladies and slaves.*)

CLEOPATRA: Now, can any of you amuse me? Have you any stories or
any news?

IRAS: Ftatateeta —

CLEOPATRA: Oh. Ftatateeta, Ftatateeta, always Ftatateeta. Some new
tale to set me against her.

IRAS: No: this time Ftatateeta has been virtuous. (*All the ladies laugh
— not the slaves.*) Pothinus has been trying to bribe her to let him
speak with you.

CLEOPATRA (*wrathfully*): Ha! you all sell audiences with me, as if I
saw whom you please, and not whom I please. I should like to know
how much of her gold piece that harp girl will have to give up before
she leaves the palace.

IRAS: We can easily find that out for you.

(*The ladies laugh.*)

CLEOPATRA (*frowning*): You laugh; but take care, take care. I will find
out some day how to make myself served as Cæsar is served.

CHARMIAN: Old hooknose! (*They laugh again.*)

CLEOPATRA (*revolted*): Silence. Charmian: do not you be a silly little
Egyptian fool. Do you know why I allow you all to chatter imper-
tinently just as you please, instead of treating you as Ftatateeta would
treat you if she were Queen?

CHARMIAN: Because you try to imitate Cæsar in everything; and he
lets everybody say what they please to him.

CLEOPATRA: No; but because I asked him one day why he did so; and
he said "Let your women talk; and you will learn something from
them." What have I to learn from them? I said. "What they are,"
said he; and oh! you should have seen his eye as he said it. You
would have curled up, you shallow things. (*They laugh. She turns
fiercely on* IRAS.) At whom are you laughing — at me or at Cæsar?

IRAS: At Cæsar.

CLEOPATRA: If you were not a fool, you would laugh at me; and if you
were not a coward you would not be afraid to tell me so. (FTATA-
TEETA *returns.*) Ftatateeta: they tell me that Pothinus has offered
you a bribe to admit him to my presence.

FTATATEETA (*protesting*): Now by my father's gods —

CLEOPATRA (*cutting her short despotically*): Have I not told you not to deny things? You would spend the day calling your father's gods to witness to your virtues if I let you. Go take the bribe; and bring in Pothinus. (FTATATEETA *is about to reply.*) Dont answer me. Go.

(FTATATEETA *goes out; and* CLEOPATRA *rises and begins to prowl to and fro between her chair and the door, meditating. All rise and stand.*)

IRAS (*as she reluctantly rises*): Heigho! I wish Cæsar were back in Rome.

CLEOPATRA (*threateningly*): It will be a bad day for you all when he goes. Oh, if I were not ashamed to let him see that I am as cruel at heart as my father, I would make you repent that speech! Why do you wish him away?

CHARMIAN: He makes you so terribly prosy and serious and learned and philosophical. It is worse than being religious, at *our* ages. (*The ladies laugh.*)

CLEOPATRA: Cease that endless cackling, will you. Hold your tongues.

CHARMIAN (*with mock resignation*): Well, well: we must try to live up to Cæsar.

(*They laugh again.* CLEOPATRA *rages silently as she continues to prowl to and fro.* FTATATEETA *comes back with* POTHINUS, *who halts on the threshold.*)

FTATATEETA (*at the door*): Pothinus craves the ear of the —

CLEOPATRA: There, there: that will do: let him come in. (*She resumes her seat. All sit down except* POTHINUS, *who advances to the middle of the room.* FTATATEETA *takes her former place.*) Well, Pothinus: what is the latest news from your rebel friends?

POTHINUS (*haughtily*): I am no friend of rebellion. And a prisoner does not receive news.

CLEOPATRA: You are no more a prisoner than I am — than Cæsar is. These six months we have been besieged in this palace by my subjects. You are allowed to walk on the beach among the soldiers. Can I go further myself, or can Cæsar?

POTHINUS: You are but a child, Cleopatra, and do not understand these matters.

(*The ladies laugh.* CLEOPATRA *looks inscrutably at him.*)

CHARMIAN: I see you do not know the latest news, Pothinus.

POTHINUS: What is that?

CHARMIAN: That Cleopatra is no longer a child. Shall I tell you how to grow much older, and much, *much* wiser in one day?

POTHINUS: I should prefer to grow wiser without growing older.

CHARMIAN: Well, go up to the top of the lighthouse; and get somebody to take you by the hair and throw you into the sea. (*The ladies laugh.*)

CLEOPATRA: She is right, Pothinus: you will come to the shore with much conceit washed out of you. (*The ladies laugh.* CLEOPATRA *rises impatiently.*) Begone, all of you. I will speak with Pothinus alone. Drive them out, Ftatateeta. (*They run out laughing.* FTATATEETA *shuts the door on them.*) What are *you* waiting for?

FTATATEETA: It is not meet that the Queen remain alone with —

CLEOPATRA (*interrupting her*): Ftatateeta: must I sacrifice you to your father's gods to teach you that I am Queen of Egypt, and not you?

FTATATEETA (*indignantly*): You are like the rest of them. You want to be what these Romans call a New Woman. (*She goes out, banging the door.*)

CLEOPATRA (*sitting down again*): Now, Pothinus: why did you bribe Ftatateeta to bring you hither?

POTHINUS (*studying her gravely*): Cleopatra: what they tell me is true. You are changed.

CLEOPATRA: Do you speak with Cæsar every day for six months: and *you* will be changed.

POTHINUS: It is the common talk that you are infatuated with this old man?

CLEOPATRA: Infatuated? What does that mean? Made foolish, is it not? Oh no: I wish I were.

POTHINUS: You wish you were made foolish! How so?

CLEOPATRA: When I was foolish, I did what I liked, except when Ftatateeta beat me; and even then I cheated her and did it by stealth. Now that Cæsar has made we wise, it is no use my liking or disliking: I do what must be done, and have no time to attend to myself. That is not happiness; but it is greatness. If Cæsar were gone, I think I could govern the Egyptians; for what Cæsar is to me, I am to the fools around me.

POTHINUS (*looking hard at her*): Cleopatra: this may be the vanity of youth.

CLEOPATRA: No, no: it is not that I am so clever, but that the others are so stupid.

POTHINUS (*musingly*): Truly, that is the great secret.

CLEOPATRA: Well, now tell me what you came to say?

POTHINUS (*embarrassed*): I! Nothing.

CLEOPATRA: Nothing!

POTHINUS: At least — to beg for my liberty: that is all.

CLEOPATRA: For that you would have knelt to Cæsar. No, Pothinus: you came with some plan that depended on Cleopatra being a little nursery kitten. Now that Cleopatra is a Queen, the plan is upset.

POTHINUS (*bowing his head submissively*): It is so.

CLEOPATRA (*exultant*): Aha!

POTHINUS (*raising his eyes keenly to hers*): Is Cleopatra then indeed a Queen, and no longer Cæsar's prisoner and slave?

CLEOPATRA: Pothinus: we are all Cæsar's slaves — all we in this land of Egypt — whether we will or no. And she who is wise enough to know this will reign when Cæsar departs.

POTHINUS: You harp on Cæsar's departure.

CLEOPATRA: What if I do?

POTHINUS: Does he not love you?

CLEOPATRA: Love me! Pothinus: Cæsar loves no one. Who are those we love. Only those whom we do not hate: all people are strangers and enemies to us except those we love. But it is not so with Cæsar. He has no hatred in him: he makes friends with everyone as he does with dogs and children. His kindness to me is a wonder; neither mother, father, nor nurse have ever taken so much care for me, or thrown open their thoughts to me so freely.

POTHINUS: Well: is not this love?

CLEOPATRA: What! when he will do as much for the first girl he meets on his way back to Rome? Ask his slave, Britannus: he has been just as good to him. Nay, ask his very horse! His kindness is not for anything in me: it is in his own nature.

POTHINUS: But how can you be sure that he does not love you as men love women?

CLEOPATRA: Because I cannot make him jealous. I have tried.

POTHINUS: Hm! Perhaps I should have asked, then, do *you* love *him*?

CLEOPATRA: Can one love a god? Besides, I love another Roman: one whom I saw long before Cæsar — no god, but a man — one who can love and hate — one whom I can hurt and who would hurt me.

POTHINUS: Does Cæsar know this?

CLEOPATRA: Yes.

POTHINUS: And he is not angry?

CLEOPATRA: He promises to send him to Egypt to please me!

POTHINUS: I do not understand this man.

CLEOPATRA (*with superb contempt*): *You* understand Cæsar! How could you? (*Proudly.*) I do — by instinct.

POTHINUS (*deferentially, after a moment's thought*): Your Majesty caused me to be admitted to-day. What message has the Queen for me?

CLEOPATRA: This. You think that by making my brother king, you will rule in Egypt, because you are his guardian and he is a little silly.

POTHINUS: The Queen is pleased to say so.

CLEOPATRA: The Queen is pleased to say this also. That Cæsar will eat up you, and Achillas, and my brother, as a cat eats up mice; and that he will put on this land of Egypt as a shepherd puts on his garment. And when he has done that, he will return to Rome, and leave Cleopatra here as his viceroy.

POTHINUS (*breaking out wrathfully*): That he shall never do. We have a thousand men to his ten; and we will drive him and his beggarly legions into the sea.

CLEOPATRA (*with scorn, getting up to go*): You rant like any common fellow. Go, then, and marshal your thousands; and make haste; for Mithridates of Pergamos is at hand with reinforcements for Cæsar. Cæsar has held you at bay with two legions: we shall see what he will do with twenty.

POTHINUS: Cleopatra —

CLEOPATRA: Enough, enough: Cæsar has spoiled me for talking to weak things like you. (*She goes out.* POTHINUS, *with a gesture of rage, is following, when* FTATATEETA *enters and stops him.*)

POTHINUS: Let me go forth from this hateful place.

FTATATEETA: What angers you?

POTHINUS: The curse of all the gods of Egypt be upon her! She has sold her country to the Roman, that she may buy it back from him with her kisses.

FTATATEETA: Fool: did she not tell you that she would have Cæsar gone?

POTHINUS: You listened?

FTATATEETA: I took care that some honest woman should be at hand whilst you were with her.

POTHINUS: Now by the gods —

FTATATEETA: Enough of your gods! Cæsar's gods are all powerful here. It is no use *you* coming to Cleopatra: you are only an Egyptian. She will not listen to any of her own race: she treats us all as children.

POTHINUS: May she perish for it!

FTATATEETA (*balefully*): May your tongue wither for that wish! Go! send for Lucius Septimius, the slayer of Pompey. He is a Roman: may be she will listen to him. Begone!

POTHINUS (*darkly*): I know to whom I must go now.

FTATATEETA (*suspiciously*): To whom, then?

POTHINUS: To a greater Roman than Lucius. And mark this, mistress. You thought, before Cæsar came, that Egypt should presently be ruled by you and your crew in the name of Cleopatra. I set myself against it —

FTATATEETA (*interrupting him — wrangling*): Ay; that it might be ruled by you and *your* crew in the name of Ptolemy.

POTHINUS: Better me, or even you, than a woman with a Roman heart; and that is what Cleopatra is now become. Whilst I live, she shall never rule. So guide yourself accordingly. (*He goes out.*)

(*It is by this time drawing on to dinner time. The table is laid on the roof of the palace; and thither* RUFIO *is now climbing, ushered by a majestic palace* OFFICIAL, *wand of office in hand, and followed by a* SLAVE *carrying an inlaid stool. After many stairs they emerge at last into a massive colonnade on the roof. Light curtains are drawn between the columns on the north and east to soften the westering sun. The* OFFICIAL *leads* RUFIO *to one of these shaded sections. A cord for pulling the curtains apart hangs down between the pillars.*)

OFFICIAL (*bowing*): The Roman commander will await Cæsar here.

(*The* SLAVE *sets down the stool near the southernmost column, and slips out through the curtains.*)

RUFIO (*sitting down, a little blown*): Pouf! That was a climb. How high have we come?

OFFICIAL: We are on the palace roof, O Beloved of Victory!

RUFIO: Good! the Beloved of Victory has no more stairs to get up.

(*A* SECOND OFFICIAL *enters from the opposite end, walking backwards.*)

SECOND OFFICIAL: Cæsar approaches.

(*CÆSAR, fresh from the bath, clad in a new tunic of purple silk, comes in, beaming and festive, followed by two* SLAVES *carrying a light couch, which is hardly more than an elaborately designed bench. They place it near the northmost of the two curtained columns. When this is done they slip out through the curtains; and the two* OFFICIALS, *formally bowing, follow them.* RUFIO *rises to receive* CÆSAR.)

CÆSAR (*coming over to him*): Why, Rufio! (*Surveying his dress with an air of admiring astonishment.*) A new baldrick! A new golden pommel to your sword! And you have had your hair cut. But not your beard — ? impossible! (*He sniffs at* RUFIO's *beard.*) Yes, per-fumed, by Jupiter Olympus!

RUFIO (*growling*): Well: is it to please myself?

CÆSAR (*affectionately*): No, my son Rufio, but to please me — to cele-brate my birthday.

RUFIO (*contemptuously*): Your birthday! You always have a birthday when there is a pretty girl to be flattered or an ambassador to be conciliated. We had seven of them in ten months last year.

CÆSAR (*contritely*): It is true, Rufio! I shall never break myself of these petty deceits.

RUFIO: Who is to dine with us — besides Cleopatra?

CÆSAR: Apollodorus the Sicilian.

RUFIO: That popinjay!

CÆSAR: Come! the popinjay is an amusing dog — tells a story; sings a song; and saves us the trouble of flattering the Queen. What does she care for old politicians and camp-fed bears like us? No: Apollo-dorus is good company, Rufio, good company.

RUFIO: Well, he can swim a bit and fence a bit: he might be worse, if he only knew how to hold his tongue.

CÆSAR: The gods forbid he should ever learn! Oh, this military life! this tedious, brutal life of action! That is the worst of us Romans: we are mere doers and drudgers: a swarm of bees turned into men. Give me a good talker — one with wit and imagination enough to live without continually doing something!

RUFIO: Ay! a nice time he would have of it with you when dinner was over! Have you noticed that I am before my time?

CÆSAR: Aha! I thought that meant something. What is it?

RUFIO: Can we be overheard here?

CÆSAR: Our privacy invites eavesdropping. I can remedy that. (*He claps his hands twice. The curtains are drawn, revealing the roof gar-den with a banqueting table set across in the middle for four persons, one at each end, and two side by side. The side next* CÆSAR *and* RUFIO *is blocked with golden wine vessels and basins. A gorgeous* MAJOR-DOMO *is superintending the laying of the table by a staff of* SLAVES. *The colonnade goes round the garden at both sides to the further end, where a gap in it, like a great gateway, leaves the view open to the sky beyond the western edge of the roof, except in the middle, where a life size image of Ra, seated on a huge plinth, towers up, with hawk head and crown of asp and disk. His altar, which stands at his feet, is a single white stone.*) Now everybody can see us, nobody will think of listening to us. (*He sits down on the bench left by the two* SLAVES.)

RUFIO (*sitting down on his stool*): Pothinus wants to speak to you. I advise you to see him: there is some plotting going on here among the women.

CÆSAR: Who is Pothinus?

RUFIO: The fellow with hair like squirrel's fur — the little King's bear leader, whom you kept prisoner.

CÆSAR (*annoyed*): And has he not escaped?

RUFIO: No.

CÆSAR (*rising imperiously*): Why not? You have been guarding this man instead of watching the enemy. Have I not told you always to let prisoners escape unless there are special orders to the contrary? Are there not enough mouths to be fed without him?

RUFIO: Yes; and if you would have a little sense and let me cut his throat, you would save his rations. Anyhow, he *wont* escape. Three sentries have told him they would put a pilum through him if they saw him again. What more can they do? He prefers to stay and spy on us. So would I if I had to do with generals subject to fits of clemency.

CÆSAR (*resuming his seat, argued down*): Hm! And so he wants to see me.

RUFIO: Ay. I have brought him with me. He is waiting there (*jerking his thumb over his shoulder*) under guard.

CÆSAR: And you want me to see him?

RUFIO (*obstinately*): I dont want anything. I daresay you will do what you like. Dont put it on to me.

CÆSAR (*with an air of doing it expressly to indulge* RUFIO): Well, well: let us have him.

RUFIO (*calling*): Ho there, guard! Release your man and send him up. (*Beckoning.*) Come along!

(POTHINUS *enters and stops mistrustfully between the two, looking from one to the other.*)

CÆSAR (*graciously*): Ah, Pothinus! You are welcome. And what is the news this afternoon?

POTHINUS: Cæsar: I come to warn you of a danger, and to make you an offer.

CÆSAR: Never mind the danger. Make the offer.

RUFIO: Never mind the offer. Whats the danger?

POTHINUS: Cæsar: you think that Cleopatra is devoted to you.

CÆSAR (*gravely*): My friend: I already know what I think. Come to your offer.

POTHINUS: I will deal plainly. I know not by what strange gods you have been enabled to defend a palace and a few yards of beach against a city and an army. Since we cut you off from Lake Mareotis, and you dug wells in the salt sea sand and brought up buckets of fresh water from them, we have known that your gods are irresistible, and that you are a worker of miracles. I no longer threaten you —

RUFIO (*sarcastically*): Very handsome of you, indeed.

POTHINUS: So be it: you are the master. Our gods sent the north west winds to keep you in our hands; but you have been too strong for them.

CÆSAR (*gently urging him to come to the point*): Yes, yes, my friend. But what then?

RUFIO: Spit it out, man. What have you to say?

POTHINUS: I have to say that you have a traitress in your camp. Cleopatra —

MAJOR-DOMO (*at the table, announcing*): The Queen! (CÆSAR *and* RUFIO *rise.*)

RUFIO (*aside to* POTHINUS): You should have spat it out sooner, you fool. Now it is too late.

(CLEOPATRA, *in gorgeous raiment, enters in state through the gap in the colonnade, and comes down past the image of Ra and past the table to* CÆSAR. *Her retinue, headed by* FTATATEETA, *joins the staff at the table.* CÆSAR *gives* CLEOPATRA *his seat, which she takes.*)

CLEOPATRA (*quickly, seeing* POTHINUS): What is he doing here?

CÆSAR (*seating himself beside her, in the most amiable of tempers*): Just going to tell me something about you. You shall hear it. Proceed, Pothinus.

POTHINUS (*disconcerted*): Cæsar — (*He stammers.*)

CÆSAR: Well, out with it.

POTHINUS: What I have to say is for your ear, not for the Queen's.

CLEOPATRA (*with subdued ferocity*): There are means of making you speak. Take care.

POTHINUS (*defiantly*): Cæsar does not employ those means.

CÆSAR: My friend: when a man has anything to tell in this world, the difficulty is not to make him tell it, but to prevent him from telling it too often. Let me celebrate my birthday by setting you free. Farewell: we shall not meet again.

CLEOPATRA (*angrily*): Cæsar: this mercy is foolish.

POTHINUS (*to* CÆSAR): Will you not give me a private audience? Your life may depend on it. (CÆSAR *rises loftily.*)

RUFIO (*aside to* POTHINUS): Ass! Now we shall have some heroics.

CÆSAR (*oratorically*): Pothinus —

RUFIO (*interrupting him*): Cæsar: the dinner will spoil if you begin preaching your favorite sermon about life and death.

CLEOPATRA (*priggishly*): Peace, Rufio. I desire to hear Cæsar.

RUFIO (*bluntly*): Your Majesty has heard it before. You repeated it to Apollodorus last week; and he thought it was all your own. (CÆSAR's *dignity collapses. Much tickled, he sits down again and looks roguishly at* CLEOPATRA, *who is furious.* RUFIO *calls as before.*) Ho there, guard! Pass the prisoner out. He is released. (*To* POTHINUS.) Now off with you. You have lost your chance.

POTHINUS (*his temper overcoming his prudence*): I *will* speak.

CÆSAR (*to* CLEOPATRA): You see. Torture would not have wrung a word from him.

POTHINUS: Cæsar: you have taught Cleopatra the arts by which the Romans govern the world.

CÆSAR: Alas! they cannot even govern themselves. What then?

POTHINUS: What then? Are you so besotted with her beauty that you do not see that she is impatient to reign in Egypt alone, and that her heart is set on your departure?

CLEOPATRA (*rising*): Liar!

CÆSAR (*shocked*): What! Protestations! Contradictions!

CLEOPATRA (*ashamed, but trembling with suppressed rage*): No. I do not deign to contradict. Let him talk. (*She sits down again.*)

POTHINUS: From her own lips I have heard it. You are to be her catspaw: you are to tear the crown from her brother's head and set it on her own, delivering us all into her hand — delivering yourself also. And then Cæsar can return to Rome, or depart through the gate of death, which is nearer and surer.

CÆSAR (*calmly*): Well, my friend; and is not this very natural?

POTHINUS (*astonished*): Natural! Then you do not resent treachery?

CÆSAR: Resent! O thou foolish Egyptian, what have I to do with resentment? Do I resent the wind when it chills me, or the night when it makes me stumble in the darkness? Shall I resent youth when it turns from age, and ambition when it turns from servitude? To tell me such a story as this is but to tell me that the sun will rise to-morrow.

CLEOPATRA (*unable to contain herself*): But it is false — false. I swear it.

CÆSAR: It is true, though you swore it a thousand times, and believed all you swore. (*She is convulsed with emotion. To screen her, he rises and takes* POTHINUS *to* RUFIO, *saying:*) Come, Rufio: let us see Pothinus past the guard. I have a word to say to him. (*Aside to them.*) We must give the Queen a moment to recover herself.

(*Aloud.*) Come. (*He takes* POTHINUS *and* RUFIO *out with him, conversing with them meanwhile.*) Tell your friends, Pothinus, that they must not think I am opposed to a reasonable settlement of the country's affairs — (*They pass out of hearing.*)

CLEOPATRA (*in a stifled whisper*): Ftatateeta, Ftatateeta.

FTATATEETA (*hurrying to her from the table and petting her*): Peace, child: be comforted —

CLEOPATRA (*interrupting her*): Can they hear us?

FTATATEETA: No, dear heart, no.

CLEOPATRA: Listen to me. If he leaves the Palace alive, never see my face again.

FTATATEETA: He? Poth —

CLEOPATRA (*striking her on the mouth*): Strike his life out as I strike his name from your lips. Dash him down from the wall. Break him on the stones. Kill, kill, *kill* him.

FTATATEETA (*shewing all her teeth*): The dog shall perish.

CLEOPATRA: Fail in this, and you go out from before me for ever.

FTATATEETA (*resolutely*): So be it. You shall not see my face until his eyes are darkened.

(CÆSAR *comes back, with* APOLLODORUS, *exquisitely dressed, and* RUFIO.)

CLEOPATRA (*to* FTATATEETA): Come soon — soon. (FTATATEETA *turns her meaning eyes for a moment on her mistress; then goes grimly away past Ra and out.* CLEOPATRA *runs like a gazelle to* CÆSAR.) So you have come back to me, Cæsar. (*Caressingly.*) I thought you were angry. Welcome, Apollodorus. (*She gives him her hand to kiss, with her other arm about* CÆSAR.)

APOLLODORUS: Cleopatra grows more womanly beautiful from week to week.

CLEOPATRA: Truth, Apollodorus?

APOLLODORUS: Far, far short of the truth! Friend Rufio threw a pearl into the sea: Cæsar fished up a diamond.

CÆSAR: Cæsar fished up a touch of rheumatism, my friend. Come: to dinner! to dinner! (*They move towards the table.*)

CLEOPATRA (*skipping like a young fawn*): Yes, to dinner. I have ordered *such* a dinner for you, Cæsar!

CÆSAR: Ay? What are we to have?

CLEOPATRA: Peacocks' brains.

CÆSAR (*as if his mouth watered*): Peacocks' brains, Apollodorus!

APOLLODORUS: Not for me. I prefer nightingales' tongues. (*He goes to one of the two covers set side by side*).

CLEOPATRA: Roast boar, Rufio!

RUFIO (*gluttonously*): Good! (*He goes to the seat next* APOLLODORUS, *on his left.*)

CÆSAR (*looking at his seat, which is at the end of the table, to Ra's left hand*): What has become of my leathern cushion?

CLEOPATRA (*at the opposite end*): I have got new ones for you.

MAJOR-DOMO: These cushions, Cæsar, are of Maltese gauze, stuffed with rose leaves.

CÆSAR: Rose leaves! Am I a caterpillar? (*He throws the cushions away and seats himself on the leather mattress underneath.*)

CLEOPATRA: What a shame! My new cushions!

MAJOR-DOMO (*at* CÆSAR's *elbow*): What shall we serve to whet Cæsar's appetite?

CÆSAR: What have you got?

MAJOR-DOMO: Sea hedgehogs, black and white sea acorns, sea nettles, beccaficoes, purple shellfish —

CÆSAR: Any oysters?

MAJOR-DOMO: Assuredly.

CÆSAR: *British* oysters?

MAJOR-DOMO (*assenting*): British oysters, Cæsar.

CÆSAR: Oysters, then. (*The* MAJOR-DOMO *signs to a* SLAVE *at each order; and the* SLAVE *goes out to execute it.*) I have been in Britain — that western land of romance — the last piece of earth on the edge of the ocean that surrounds the world. I went there in search of its famous pearls. The British pearl was a fable; but in searching for it I found the British oyster.

APOLLODORUS: All posterity will bless you for it. (*To the* MAJOR-DOMO.) Sea hedgehogs for me.

RUFIO: Is there nothing solid to begin with?

MAJOR-DOMO: Fieldfares with asparagus —

CLEOPATRA (*interrupting*): Fattened fowls! have some fattened fowls, Rufio.

RUFIO: Ay, that will do.

CLEOPATRA (*greedily*): Fieldfares for me.

MAJOR-DOMO: Cæsar will deign to choose his wine? Sicilian, Lesbian, Chian —

RUFIO (*contemptuously*): All Greek.

APOLLODORUS: Who would drink Roman wine when he could get Greek. Try the Lesbian, Cæsar.

CÆSAR: Bring me my barley water.

RUFIO (*with intense disgust*): Ugh! Bring *me* my Falernian. (*The Falernian is presently brought to him.*)

CLEOPATRA (*pouting*): It is waste of time giving you dinners, Cæsar. My scullions would not condescend to your diet.

CÆSAR (*relenting*): Well, well: let us try the Lesbian. (*The* MAJOR-DOMO *fills* CÆSAR's *goblet; then* CLEOPATRA's *and* APOLLODORUS's.) But when I return to Rome, I will make laws against these extravagances. I will even get the laws carried out.

CLEOPATRA (*coaxing*): Never mind. To-day you are to be like other people: idle, luxurious, and kind. (*She stretches her hand to him along the table.*)

CÆSAR: Well, for once I will sacrifice my comfort — (*kissing her hand*) there! (*He takes a draught of wine.*) Now are you satisfied?

CLEOPATRA: And you no longer believe that I long for your departure for Rome?

CÆSAR: I no longer believe anything. My brains are asleep. Besides, who knows whether I shall return to Rome?

RUFIO (*alarmed*): How? Eh? What?

CÆSAR: What has Rome to shew me that I have not seen already? One year of Rome is like another, except that I grow older, whilst the crowd in the Appian Way is always the same age.

APOLLODORUS: It is no better here in Egypt. The old men, when they are tired of life, say "We have seen everything except the source of the Nile."

CÆSAR (*his imagination catching fire*): And why not see that? Cleopatra: will you come with me and track the flood to its cradle in the heart of the regions of mystery? Shall we leave Rome behind us — Rome, that has achieved greatness only to learn how greatness destroys nations of men who are not great! Shall I make you a new kingdom, and build you a holy city there in the great unknown?

CLEOPATRA (*rapturously*): Yes, yes. You shall.

RUFIO: Ay: now he will conquer Africa with two legions before we come to the roast boar.

APOLLODORUS: Come: no scoffing. This is a noble scheme: in it Cæsar is no longer merely the conquering soldier, but the creative poet-artist. Let us name the holy city, and consecrate it with Lesbian wine.

CÆSAR: Cleopatra shall name it herself.

CLEOPATRA: It shall be called Cæsar's Gift to his Beloved.

APOLLODORUS: No, no. Something vaster than that — something universal, like the starry firmament.

CÆSAR (*prosaically*): Why not simply The Cradle of the Nile?

CLEOPATRA: No: the Nile is my ancestor; and he is a god. Oh! I have thought of something. The Nile shall name it himself. Let us call upon him. (*To the* MAJOR-DOMO.) Send for him. (*The three men stare at one another; but the* MAJOR-DOMO *goes out as if he had received the most matter-of-fact order.*) And (*to the retinue*) away with you all.

(*The retinue withdraws, making obeisance. A priest enters, carrying a miniature Sphinx with a tiny tripod before it. A morsel of incense is smoking in the tripod. The priest comes to the table and places the image in the middle of it. The light begins to change to the magenta purple of the Egyptian sunset, as if the god had brought a strange colored shadow with him. The three men are determined not to be impressed; but they feel curious in spite of themselves.*)

CÆSAR: What hocus-pocus is this?

CLEOPATRA: You shall see. And it is *not* hocus-pocus. To do it properly, we should kill something to please him; but perhaps he will answer Cæsar without that if we spill some wine to him.

APOLLODORUS (*turning his head to look up over his shoulder at Ra*): Why not appeal to our hawkheaded friend here?

CLEOPATRA (*nervously*): Sh! He will hear you and be angry.

RUFIO (*phlegmatically*): The source of the Nile is out of his district, I expect.

CLEOPATRA: No: I will have my city named by nobody but my dear little Sphinx, because it was in its arms that Cæsar found me asleep. (*She languishes at* CÆSAR *then turns curtly to the priest.*) Go. I am a priestess, and have power to take your charge from you. (*The priest makes a reverence and goes out.*) Now let us call on the Nile altogether. Perhaps he will rap on the table.

CÆSAR: What! table rapping! Are such superstitions still believed in this year 707 of the Republic?

CLEOPATRA: It is no superstition: our priests learn lots of things from the tables. Is it not so, Apollodorus?

APOLLODORUS: Yes: I profess myself a converted man. When Cleopatra is priestess, Apollodorus is devotee. Propose the conjuration.

CLEOPATRA: You must say with me "Send us thy voice, Father Nile."

ALL FOUR (*holding their glasses together before the idol*): Send us thy voice, Father Nile.

(*The death cry of a man in mortal terror and agony answers them. Appalled, the men set down their glasses, and listen. Silence. The purple deepens in the sky.* CÆSAR, *glancing at* CLEOPATRA, *catches her pouring out her wine before the god, with gleaming eyes, and*) *mute assurances of gratitude and worship.* APOLLODORUS *springs up and runs to the edge of the roof to peer down and listen.*)

CÆSAR (*looking piercingly at* CLEOPATRA): What was that?

CLEOPATRA (*petulantly*): Nothing. They are beating some slave.

CÆSAR: Nothing.

RUFIO: A man with a knife in him, I'll swear.

CÆSAR (*rising*): A murder.

APOLLODORUS (*at the back, waving his hand for silence*): S-sh! Silence. Did you hear that?

CÆSAR: Another cry?

APOLLODORUS (*returning to the table*): No, a thud. Something fell on the beach, I think.

RUFIO (*grimly, as he rises*): Something with bones in it, eh?

CÆSAR (*shuddering*): Hush, hush, Rufio. (*He leaves the table and returns to the colonnade:* RUFIO *following at his left elbow, and* APOLLODORUS *at the other side.*)

CLEOPATRA (*still in her place at the table*): Will you leave me, Cæsar? Apollodorus: are you going?

APOLLODORUS: Faith, dearest Queen, my appetite is gone.

CÆSAR: Go down to the courtyard, Apollodorus; and find out what has happened.

(APOLLODORUS *nods and goes out, making for the staircase by which* RUFIO *ascended.*)

CLEOPATRA: Your soldiers have killed somebody, perhaps. What does it matter?

(*The murmur of a crowd rises from the beach below.* CÆSAR *and* RUFIO *look at one another.*)

CÆSAR: This must be seen to. (*He is about to follow* APOLLODORUS *when* RUFIO *stops him with a hand on his arm as* FTATATEETA *comes back by the far end of the roof, with dragging steps, a drowsy satiety in her eyes and in the corners of the bloodhound lips. For a moment* CÆSAR *suspects that she is drunk with wine. Not so* RUFIO: *he knows well the red vintage that has inebriated her.*)

RUFIO (*in a low tone*): There is some mischief between those two.

FTATATEETA: The Queen looks again on the face of her servant.

(CLEOPATRA *looks at her for a moment with an exultant reflection of her murderous expression. Then she flings her arms round her; kisses her repeatedly and savagely; and tears off her jewels and heaps them on her. The two men turn from the spectacle to look at one another.* FTATATEETA *drags herself sleepily to the altar; kneels before Ra; and remains there in prayer.* CÆSAR *goes to* CLEOPATRA, *leaving* RUFIO *in the colonnade.*)

CÆSAR (*with searching earnestness*): Cleopatra: what has happened?

CLEOPATRA (*in mortal dread of him, but with her utmost cajolery*): Nothing, dearest Cæsar. (*With sickly sweetness, her voice almost failing.*) Nothing. I am innocent. (*She approaches him affectionately.*) Dear Cæsar: are you angry with me? Why do you look at me so? I have been here with you all the time. How can I know what has happened?

CÆSAR (*reflectively*): That is true.

CLEOPATRA (*greatly relieved, trying to caress him*): Of course it is true. (*He does not respond to the caress.*) You know it is true, Rufio.

(*The murmur without suddenly swells to a roar and subsides.*)

RUFIO: I shall know presently. (*He makes for the altar in the burly trot that serves him for a stride, and touches* FTATATEETA *on the shoulder.*) Now, mistress: I shall want you. (*He orders her, with a gesture, to go before him.*)

FTATATEETA (*rising and glowering at him*): My place is with the Queen.

CLEOPATRA: She has done no harm, Rufio.

CÆSAR (*to* RUFIO): Let her stay.

RUFIO (*sitting down on the altar*): Very well. Then my place is here too; and you can see what is the matter for yourself. The city is in a pretty uproar, it seems.

CÆSAR (*with grave displeasure*): Rufio: there is a time for obedience.

RUFIO: And there is a time for obstinacy. (*He folds his arms doggedly.*)

CÆSAR (*to* CLEOPATRA): Send her away.

CLEOPATRA (*whining in her eagerness to propitiate him*): Yes, I will. I will do whatever you ask me, Cæsar, always, because I love you. Ftatateeta: go away.

FTATATEETA: The Queen's word is my will. I shall be at hand for the Queen's call. (*She goes out past Ra, as she came.*)

RUFIO (*following her*): Remember, Cæsar, your bodyguard also is within call. (*He follows her out.*)

(CLEOPATRA, *presuming upon* CÆSAR's *submission to* RUFIO, *leaves the table and sits down on the bench in the colonnade.*)

CLEOPATRA: Why do you allow Rufio to treat you so? You should teach him his place.

CÆSAR: Teach him to be my enemy, and to hide his thoughts from me as you are now hiding yours.

CLEOPATRA (*her fears returning*): Why do you say that, Cæsar? Indeed, indeed, I am not hiding anything. You are wrong to treat me like this. (*She stifles a sob.*) I am only a child; and you turn into stone because you think some one has been killed. I cannot bear it. (*She purposely breaks down and weeps. He looks at her with profound sadness and complete coldness. She looks up to see what effect she is producing. Seeing that he is unmoved, she sits up, pretending to struggle with her emotion and to put it bravely away.*) But there: I know you hate tears: you shall not be troubled with them. I know you are not angry, but only sad; only I am so silly, I cannot help being hurt when you speak coldly. Of course you are quite right: it is dreadful to think of anyone being killed or even hurt; and I hope nothing really serious has — (*Her voice dies away under his contemptuous penetration.*)

CÆSAR: What has frightened you into this? What have you done? (*A trumpet sounds on the beach below.*) Aha! that sounds like the answer.

CLEOPATRA (*sinking back trembling on the bench and covering her face with her hands*): I have not betrayed you, Cæsar: I swear it.

CÆSAR: I know that. I have not trusted you. (*He turns from her, and is about to go out when* APOLLODORUS *and* BRITANNUS *drag in* LUCIUS SEPTIMIUS *to him.* RUFIO *follows.* CÆSAR *shudders.*) Again, Pompey's murderer!

RUFIO: The town has gone mad, I think. They are for tearing the palace down and driving us into the sea straight away. We laid hold of this renegade in clearing them out of the courtyard.

CÆSAR: Release him. (*They let go his arms.*) What has offended the citizens, Lucius Septimius?

LUCIUS: What did you expect, Cæsar? Pothinus was a favorite of theirs.

CÆSAR: What has happened to Pothinus? I set him free, here, not half an hour ago. Did they not pass him out?

LUCIUS: Ay, through the gallery arch sixty feet above ground, with three inches of steel in his ribs. He is as dead as Pompey. We are quits now, as to killing — you and I.

CÆSAR (*shocked*): Assassinated! — our prisoner, our guest! (*He turns reproachfully on* RUFIO.) Rufio —

RUFIO (*emphatically — anticipating the question*): Whoever did it was a wise man and a friend of yours (CLEOPATRA *is greatly emboldened*); but none of us had a hand in it. So it is no use to frown at me. (CÆSAR *turns and looks at* CLEOPATRA.)

CLEOPATRA (*violently — rising*): He was slain by order of the Queen of Egypt. I am not Julius Cæsar the dreamer, who allows every slave to insult him. Rufio has said I did well: now the others shall judge me too. (*She turns to the others.*) This Pothinus sought to make me conspire with him to betray Cæsar to Achillas and Ptolemy. I refused; and he cursed me and came privily to Cæsar to accuse me of his own treachery. I caught him in the act; and he insulted me — *me*, the Queen! to my face. Cæsar would not avenge me: he spoke him fair and set him free. Was I right to avenge myself? Speak, Lucius.

LUCIUS: I do not gainsay it. But you will get little thanks from Cæsar for it.

CLEOPATRA: Speak, Apollodorus. Was I wrong?

APOLLODORUS: I have only one word of blame, most beautiful. You should have called upon me, your knight; and in fair duel I should have slain the slanderer.

CLEOPATRA (*passionately*): I will be judged by your very slave, Cæsar. Britannus: speak. Was I wrong?

BRITANNUS: Were treachery, falsehood, and disloyalty left unpunished, society must become like an arena full of wild beasts, tearing one another to pieces. Cæsar is in the wrong.

CÆSAR (*with quiet bitterness*): And so the verdict is against me, it seems.

CLEOPATRA (*vehemently*): Listen to me, Cæsar. If one man in all Alexandria can be found to say that I did wrong, I swear to have myself crucified on the door of the palace by my own slaves.

CÆSAR: If one man in all the world can be found, now or forever, to *know* that you did wrong, that man will have either to conquer the world as I have, or be crucified by it. (*The uproar in the streets again reaches them.*) Do you hear? These knockers at your gate are also believers in vengeance and in stabbing. You have slain their leader: it is right that they shall slay you. If you doubt it, ask your four counsellors here. And then in the name of that *right* (*he emphasizes the word with great scorn*) shall I not slay them for murdering their Queen, and be slain in my turn by their countrymen as the invader of their fatherland? Can Rome do less then than slay these slayers, too, to shew the world how Rome avenges her sons and her honor. And so, to the end of history, murder shall breed murder, always in the name of right and honor and peace, until the gods are tired of blood and create a race that can understand. (*Fierce uproar.* CLEOPATRA *becomes white with terror.*) Hearken, you who must not be insulted. Go near enough to catch their words: you will find them bitterer than the tongue of Pothinus. (*Loftily, wrapping himself up in an impenetrable dignity.*) Let the Queen of Egypt now give her orders

for vengeance, and take her measures for defence; for she has renounced Cæsar. (*He turns to go.*)

CLEOPATRA (*terrified, running to him and falling on her knees*): You
will not desert me, Cæsar. You will defend the palace.

CÆSAR: You have taken the powers of life and death upon you. I am
only a dreamer.

CLEOPATRA: But they will kill me.

CÆSAR: And why not?

CLEOPATRA: In pity —

CÆSAR: Pity! What! has it come to this so suddenly, that nothing can
save you now but pity? Did it save Pothinus?

(*She rises, wringing her hands, and goes back to the bench in
despair.* APOLLODORUS *shews his sympathy with her by quietly
posting himself behind the bench. The sky has by this time become the most vivid purple, and soon begins to change to a glowing pale orange, against which the colonnade and the great image
shew darklier and darklier.*)

RUFIO: Cæsar: enough of preaching. The enemy is at the gate.

CÆSAR (*turning on him and giving way to his wrath*): Ay; and what
has held him baffled at the gate all these months? Was it my folly,
as you deem it, or your wisdom? In this Egyptian Red Sea of blood,
whose hand has held all your heads above the waves? (*Turning on*
CLEOPATRA.) And yet, when Cæsar says to such an one, "Friend, go
free," you, clinging for your little life to my sword, dare steal out and
stab him in the back? And you, soldiers and gentlemen, and honest
servants as you forget that you are, applaud this assassination, and
say "Cæsar is in the wrong." By the gods, I am tempted to open my
hand and let you all sink into the flood.

CLEOPATRA (*with a ray of cunning hope*): But, Cæsar, if you do, you
will perish yourself.

(CÆSAR'S *eyes blaze.*)

RUFIO (*greatly alarmed*): Now, by great Jove, you filthy little Egyptian
rat, that is the very word to make him walk out alone into the city
and leave us here to be cut to pieces. (*Desperately, to* CÆSAR.) Will
you desert us because we are a parcel of fools? I mean no harm by
killing: I do it as a dog kills a cat, by instinct. We are all dogs at
your heels; but we have served you faithfully.

CÆSAR (*relenting*): Alas, Rufio, my son, my son: as dogs we are like to
perish now in the streets.

APOLLODORUS (*at his post behind* CLEOPATRA'S *seat*): Cæsar: what you
say has an Olympian ring in it: it must be right; for it is fine art.

But I am still on the side of Cleopatra. If we must die, she shall not want the devotion of a man's heart nor the strength of a man's arm.

CLEOPATRA (*sobbing*): But I dont want to die.

CÆSAR (*sadly*): Oh, ignoble, ignoble!

LUCIUS (*coming forward between* CÆSAR *and* CLEOPATRA): Hearken to me, Cæsar. It may be ignoble; but I also mean to live as long as I can.

CÆSAR: Well, my friend, you are likely to outlive Cæsar. Is it any magic of mine, think you, that has kept your army and this whole city at bay for so long? Yesterday, what quarrel had they with me that they should risk their lives against me? But today we have flung them down their hero, murdered; and now every man of them is set upon clearing out this nest of assassins — for such we are and no more. Take courage then; and sharpen your sword. Pompey's head has fallen; and Cæsar's head is ripe.

APOLLODORUS: Does Cæsar despair?

CÆSAR (*with infinite pride*): He who has never hoped can never despair. Cæsar, in good or bad fortune, looks his fate in the face.

LUCIUS: Look it in the face, then; and it will smile as it always has on Cæsar.

CÆSAR (*with involuntary haughtiness*): Do you presume to encourage me?

LUCIUS: I offer you my services. I will change sides if you will have me.

CÆSAR (*suddenly coming down to earth again, and looking sharply at him, divining that there is something behind the offer*): What! At this point?

LUCIUS (*firmly*): At this point.

RUFIO: Do you suppose Cæsar is mad, to trust you?

LUCIUS: I do not ask him to trust me until he is victorious. I ask for my life, and for a command in Cæsar's army. And since Cæsar is a fair dealer, I will pay in advance.

CÆSAR: Pay! How?

LUCIUS: With a piece of good news for you.

(CÆSAR *divines the news in a flash.*)

RUFIO: What news?

CÆSAR (*with an elated and buoyant energy which makes* CLEOPATRA *sit up and stare*): What news! What news, did you say, my son Rufio? The relief has arrived: what other news remains for us? Is it not so, Lucius Septimius? Mithridates of Pergamos is on the march.

LUCIUS: He has taken Pelusium.

CÆSAR (*delighted*): Lucius Septimius: you are henceforth my officer. Rufio: the Egyptians must have sent every soldier from the city to prevent Mithridates crossing the Nile. There is nothing in the streets now but mob — mob!

LUCIUS: It is so. Mithridates is marching by the great road to Memphis to cross above the Delta. Achillas will fight him there.

CÆSAR (*all audacity*): Achillas shall fight Cæsar there. See, Rufio. (*He runs to the table; snatches a napkin; and draws a plan on it with his finger dipped in wine, whilst* RUFIO *and* LUCIUS SEPTIMIUS *crowd about him to watch, all looking closely, for the light is now almost gone.*) Here is the palace (*pointing to his plan*): here is the theatre. You (*to* RUFIO) take twenty men and pretend to go by *that* street (*pointing it out*); and whilst they are stoning you, out go the cohorts by this and this. My streets are right, are they, Lucius?

LUCIUS: Ay, that is the fig market —

CÆSAR (*too much excited to listen to him*): I saw them the day we arrived. Good! (*He throws the napkin on the table, and comes down again into the colonnade.*) Away, Britannus: tell Petronius that within an hour half our forces must take ship for the western lake. See to my horse and armor. (BRITANNUS *runs out.*) With the rest, I shall march round the lake and up the Nile to meet Mithridates. Away, Lucius; and give the word. (LUCIUS *hurries out after* BRITANNUS.) Apollodorus: lend me your sword and your right arm for this campaign.

APOLLODORUS: Ay, and my heart and life to boot.

CÆSAR (*grasping his hand*): I accept both. (*Mighty handshake.*) Are you ready for work?

APOLLODORUS: Ready for Art — the Art of War. (*He rushes out after* LUCIUS, *totally forgetting* CLEOPATRA.)

RUFIO: Come! this is something like business.

CÆSAR (*buoyantly*): Is it not, my only son? (*He claps his hands. The* SLAVES *hurry in to the table.*) No more of this mawkish revelling: away with all this stuff: shut it out of my sight and be off with you. (*The* SLAVES *begin to remove the table; and the curtains are drawn, shutting in the colonnade.*) You understand about the streets, Rufio?

RUFIO: Ay, I think I do. I will get through them, at all events.

(*The bucina sounds busily in the courtyard beneath.*)

CÆSAR: Come, then: we must talk to the troops and hearten them. You down to the beach: I to the courtyard. (*He makes for the staircase.*)

CLEOPATRA (*rising from her seat, where she has been quite neglected all this time, and stretching out her hands timidly to him*): Cæsar.

CÆSAR (*turning*): Eh?

CLEOPATRA: Have you forgotten me?

CÆSAR (*indulgently*): I am busy now, my child, busy. When I return your affairs shall be settled. Farewell; and be good and patient.

(*He goes, preoccupied and quite indifferent. She stands with clenched fists, in speechless rage and humiliation.*)

RUFIO: That game is played and lost, Cleopatra. The woman always gets the worst of it.

CLEOPATRA (*haughtily*): Go. Follow your master.

RUFIO (*in her ear, with rough familiarity*): A word first. Tell your executioner that if Pothinus had been properly killed — in the *throat* — he would not have called out. Your man bungled his work.

CLEOPATRA (*enigmatically*): How do you know it was a man?

RUFIO (*startled, and puzzled*): It was not you: you were with us when it happened. (*She turns her back scornfully on him. He shakes his head, and draws the curtains to go out. It is now a magnificent moon-lit night. The table has been removed.* FTATATEETA *is seen in the light of the moon and stars, again in prayer before the white altar-stone of Ra.* RUFIO *starts; closes the curtains again softly; and says in a low voice to* CLEOPATRA.) Was it she? with her own hand?

CLEOPATRA (*threateningly*): Whoever it was, let my enemies beware of her. Look to it, Rufio, you who dare make the Queen of Egypt a fool before Cæsar.

RUFIO (*looking grimly at her*): I will look to it, Cleopatra. (*He nods in confirmation of the promise, and slips out through the curtains, loosening his sword in its sheath as he goes.*)

ROMAN SOLDIERS (*in the courtyard below*): Hail, Cæsar! Hail, hail!

(CLEOPATRA *listens. The bucina sounds again, followed by several trumpets.*)

CLEOPATRA (*wringing her hands and calling*): Ftatateeta. Ftatateeta. It is dark; and I am alone. Come to me. (*Silence.*) Ftatateeta. (*Louder.*) Ftatateeta. (*Silence. In a panic she snatches the cord and pulls the curtains apart.* FTATATEETA *is lying dead on the altar of Ra, with her throat cut. Her blood deluges the white stone.*)

ACT FIVE

(*High noon. Festival and military pageant on the esplanade before the palace. In the east harbor* CÆSAR's *galley, so gorgeously decorated that it seems to be rigged with flowers, is alongside the quay, close to the steps* APOLLODORUS *descended when he embarked with*

the carpet. A Roman GUARD *is posted there in charge of a gangway,
whence a red floorcloth is laid down the middle of the esplanade,
turning off to the north opposite the central gate in the palace
front, which shuts in the esplanade on the south side. The broad
steps of the gate, crowded with* CLEOPATRA'S *ladies, all in their gay-
est attire, are like a flower garden. The façade is lined by her guard,
officered by the same gallants to whom* BEL AFFRIS *announced the
coming of* CÆSAR *six months before in the old palace on the Syrian
border. The north side is lined by Roman* SOLDIERS, *with the
townsfolk on tiptoe behind them, peering over their heads at the
cleared esplanade, in which the* OFFICERS *stroll about, chatting.
Among these are* BELZANOR *and the* PERSIAN; *also the* CENTURION,
*vinewood cudgel in hand, battle worn, thick-booted and much
outshone, both socially and decoratively, by the Egyptian officers.*

   APOLLODORUS *makes his way through the townsfolk and calls to
the officers from behind the Roman line.*)

APOLLODORUS: Hullo! May I pass?

CENTURION: Pass Apollodorus the Sicilian there! (*The* SOLDIERS *let him
   through.*)

BELZANOR: Is Cæsar at hand?

APOLLODORUS: Not yet. He is still in the market place. I could not
   stand any more of the roaring of the soldiers! After half an hour of
   the enthusiasm of an army, one feels the need of a little sea air.

PERSIAN: Tell us the news. Hath he slain the priests?

APOLLODORUS: Not he. They met him in the market place with ashes
   on their heads and their gods in their hands. They placed the gods at
   his feet. The only one that was worth looking at was Apis: a miracle
   of gold and ivory work. By my advice he offered the chief priest two
   talents for it.

BELZANOR (*appalled*): Apis the all-knowing for two talents! What said
   the Priest?

APOLLODORUS: He invoked the mercy of Apis, and asked for five.

BELZANOR: There will be famine and tempest in the land for this.

PERSIAN: Pooh! Why did not Apis cause Cæsar to be vanquished by
   Achillas? Any fresh news from the war, Apollodorus?

APOLLODORUS: The little King Ptolemy was drowned.

BELZANOR: Drowned! How?

APOLLODORUS: With the rest of them. Cæsar attacked them from three
   sides at once and swept them into the Nile. Ptolemy's barge sank.

BELZANOR: A marvellous man, this Cæsar! Will he come soon, think
   you?

APOLLODORUS: He was settling the Jewish question when I left.

(*A flourish of trumpets from the north, and commotion among the townsfolk, announces the approach of* CÆSAR.)

PERSIAN: He has made short work of them. Here he comes. (*He hurries to his post in front of the Egyptian lines.*)

BELZANOR (*following him*): Ho there! Cæsar comes.

(*The* SOLDIERS *stand at attention, and dress their lines.* APOLLODORUS *goes to the Egyptian line.*)

CENTURION (*hurrying to the gangway* GUARD): Attention there! Cæsar comes.

(CÆSAR *arrives in state with* RUFIO: BRITANNUS *following. The* SOLDIERS *receive him with enthusiastic shouting.*)

CÆSAR: I see my ship awaits me. The hour of Cæsar's farewell to Egypt has arrived. And now, Rufio, what remains to be done before I go?

RUFIO (*at his left hand*): You have not yet appointed a Roman governor for this province.

CÆSAR (*looking whimsically at him, but speaking with perfect gravity*): What say you to Mithridates of Pergamos, my reliever and rescuer, the great son of Eupator?

RUFIO: Why, that you will want him elsewhere. Do you forget that you have some three or four armies to conquer on your way home?

CÆSAR: Indeed! Well, what say you to yourself?

RUFIO (*incredulously*): I! I a governor! What are you dreaming of? Do you not know that I am only the son of a freedman?

CÆSAR (*affectionately*): Has not Cæsar called you his son? (*Calling to the whole assembly.*) Peace awhile there; and hear me.

ROMAN SOLDIERS: Hear Cæsar.

CÆSAR: Hear the service, quality, rank and name of the Roman governor. By service, Cæsar's shield; by quality, Cæsar's friend; by rank, a Roman soldier. (*The Roman* SOLDIERS *give a triumphant shout.*) By name, Rufio. (*They shout again.*)

RUFIO (*kissing* CÆSAR'S *hand*): Ay: I am Cæsar's shield; but of what use shall I be when I am no longer on Cæsar's arm? Well, no matter — (*He becomes husky, and turns away to recover himself.*)

CÆSAR: Where is that British Islander of mine?

BRITANNUS (*coming forward on* CÆSAR'S *right hand*): Here, Cæsar.

CÆSAR: Who bade you, pray, thrust yourself into the battle of the Delta, uttering the barbarous cries of your native land, and affirming yourself a match for any four of the Egyptians, to whom you applied unseemly epithets?

BRITANNUS: Cæsar: I ask you to excuse the language that escaped me in the heat of the moment.

CÆSAR: And how did you, who cannot swim, cross the canal with us when we stormed the camp?

BRITANNUS: Cæsar: I clung to the tail of your horse.

CÆSAR: These are not the deeds of a slave, Britannicus, but of a free man.

BRITANNUS: Cæsar: I was born free.

CÆSAR: But they call you Cæsar's slave.

BRITANNUS: Only as Cæsar's slave have I found real freedom.

CÆSAR (*moved*): Well said. Ungrateful that I am, I was about to set you free; but now I will not part from you for a million talents. (*He claps him friendly on the shoulder.* BRITANNUS, *gratified, but a trifle shamefaced, takes his hand and kisses it sheepishly.*)

BELZANOR (*to the* PERSIAN): This Roman knows how to make men serve him.

PERSIAN: Ay: men too humble to become dangerous rivals to him.

BELZANOR: O subtle one! O cynic!

CÆSAR (*seeing* APOLLODORUS *in the Egyptian corner, and calling to him*): Apollodorus: I leave the art of Egypt in your charge. Remember: Rome loves art and will encourage it ungrudgingly.

APOLLODORUS: I understand, Cæsar. Rome will produce no art itself; but it will buy up and take away whatever the other nations produce.

CÆSAR: What! Rome produce no art! Is peace not an art? is war not an art? is government not an art? is civilization not an art? All these we give you in exchange for a few ornaments. You will have the best of the bargain. (*Turning to* RUFIO.) And now, what else have I to do before I embark? (*Trying to recollect.*) There is something I cannot remember: what *can* it be? Well, well: it must remain undone: we must not waste this favorable wind. Farewell, Rufio.

RUFIO: Cæsar: I am loth to let you go to Rome without your shield. There are too many daggers there.

CÆSAR: It matters not: I shall finish my life's work on my way back; and then I shall have lived long enough. Besides: I have always disliked the idea of dying: I had rather be killed. Farewell.

RUFIO (*with a sigh, raising his hands and giving* CÆSAR *up as incorrigible.*) Farewell. (*They shake hands.*)

CÆSAR (*waving his hand to* APOLLODORUS): Farewell, Apollodorus, and my friends, all of you. Aboard!

(*The gangway is run out from the quay to the ship. As* CÆSAR *moves towards it,* CLEOPATRA, *cold and tragic, cunningly dressed in black, without ornaments or decoration of any kind, and thus mak-*

*ing a striking figure among the brilliantly dressed bevy of ladies as
she passes through it, comes from the palace and stands on the
steps.* CÆSAR *does not see her until she speaks.*)

CLEOPATRA: Has Cleopatra no part in this leavetaking?

CÆSAR (*enlightened*): Ah, I *knew* there was something. (*To* RUFIO.)
How could you let me forget her, Rufio? (*Hastening to her.*) Had I
gone without seeing you, I should never have forgiven myself. (*He
takes her hands, and brings her into the middle of the esplanade.
She submits stonily.*) Is this mourning for me?

CLEOPATRA: No.

CÆSAR (*remorsefully*): Ah, that was thoughtless of me! It is for your
brother.

CLEOPATRA: No.

CÆSAR: For whom, then?

CLEOPATRA: Ask the Roman governor whom you have left us.

CÆSAR: Rufio?

CLEOPATRA: Yes: Rufio. (*She points at him with deadly scorn.*) He
who is to rule here in Cæsar's name, in Cæsar's way, according to
Cæsar's boasted laws of life.

CÆSAR (*dubiously*): He is to rule as he can, Cleopatra. He has taken
the work upon him, and will do it in his own way.

CLEOPATRA: Not in your way, then?

CÆSAR (*puzzled*): What do you mean by my way?

CLEOPATRA: Without punishment. Without revenge. Without judgment.

CÆSAR (*approvingly*): Ay: that is the right way, the great way, the only
possible way in the end. (*To* RUFIO.) Believe it Rufio, if you can.

RUFIO: Why, I believe it, Cæsar. You have convinced me of it long
ago. But look you. You are sailing for Numidia today. Now tell me:
if you meet a hungry lion there, you will not punish it for wanting to
eat you?

CÆSAR (*wondering what he is driving at*): No.

RUFIO: Nor revenge upon it the blood of those it has already eaten.

CÆSAR: No.

RUFIO: Nor judge it for its guiltiness.

CÆSAR: No.

RUFIO: What, then, will you do to save your life from it?

CÆSAR (*promptly*): Kill it, man, without malice, just as it would kill
me. What does this parable of the lion mean?

RUFIO: Why, Cleopatra had a tigress that killed men at her bidding. I
thought she might bid it kill you some day. Well, had I not been
Cæsar's pupil, what pious things might I not have done to that

tigress! I might have punished it. I might have revenged Pothinus on it.

CÆSAR (*interjects*): Pothinus!

RUFIO (*continuing*): I might have judged it. But I put all these follies behind me; and, without malice, only cut its throat. And that is why Cleopatra comes to you in mourning.

CLEOPATRA (*vehemently*): He has shed the blood of my servant Fta-tateeta. On your head be it as upon his, Cæsar, if you hold him free of it.

CÆSAR (*energetically*): On my head be it, then; for it was well done. Rufio: had you set yourself in the seat of the judge, and with hateful ceremonies and appeals to the gods handed that woman over to some hired executioner to be slain before the people in the name of justice, never again would I have touched your hand without a shudder. But this was natural slaying: I feel no horror at it.

(RUFIO, *satisfied, nods at* CLEOPATRA, *mutely inviting her to mark that.*)

CLEOPATRA (*pettish and childish in her impotence*): No: not when a Roman slays an Egyptian. All the world will now see how unjust and corrupt Cæsar is.

CÆSAR (*taking her hands coaxingly*): Come: do not be angry with me. I am sorry for that poor Totateeta. (*She laughs in spite of herself.*) Aha! you are laughing. Does that mean reconciliation?

CLEOPATRA (*angry with herself for laughing*): No, no, NO!! But it is so ridiculous to hear you call her Totateeta.

CÆSAR: What! As much a child as ever, Cleopatra! Have I not made a woman of you after all?

CLEOPATRA: Oh, it is you who are a great baby: you make me seem silly because you will not behave seriously. But you have treated me badly; and I do not forgive you.

CÆSAR: Bid me farewell.

CLEOPATRA: I will not.

CÆSAR (*coaxing*): I will send you a beautiful present from Rome.

CLEOPATRA (*proudly*): Beauty from Rome to Egypt indeed! What can Rome give *me* that Egypt cannot give me?

APOLLODORUS: That is true, Cæsar. If the present is to be really beautiful, I shall have to buy it for you in Alexandria.

CÆSAR: You are forgetting the treasures for which Rome is most famous, my friend. You cannot buy *them* in Alexandria.

APOLLODORUS: What are they, Cæsar?

CÆSAR: Her sons. Come, Cleopatra: forgive me and bid me farewell; and I will send you a man, Roman from head to heel and Roman of the noblest; not old and ripe for the knife; not lean in the arms and cold in the heart; not hiding a bald head under his conqueror's laurels; not stooped with the weight of the world on his shoulders; but brisk and fresh, strong and young, hoping in the morning, fighting in the day, and revelling in the evening. Will you take such an one in exchange for Cæsar?

CLEOPATRA (*palpitating*): His name, his name?

CÆSAR: Shall it be Mark Antony? (*She throws herself into his arms.*)

RUFIO: You are a bad hand at a bargain, mistress, if you will swop Cæsar for Antony.

CÆSAR: So now you are satisfied.

CLEOPATRA: You will not forget.

CÆSAR: I will not forget. Farewell: I do not think we shall meet again. Farewell. (*He kisses her on the forehead. She is much affected and begins to sniff. He embarks.*)

ROMAN SOLDIERS (*as he sets his foot on the gangway*): Hail, Cæsar; and farewell!

(*He reaches the ship and returns* RUFIO's *wave of the hand.*)

APOLLODORUS (*to* CLEOPATRA): No tears, dearest Queen: they stab your servant to the heart. He will return some day.

CLEOPATRA: I hope not. But I cant help crying, all the same.

(*She waves her handkerchief to* CÆSAR; *and the ship begins to move.*)

ROMAN SOLDIERS (*drawing their swords and raising them in the air*): Hail, Cæsar!

〰 CÆSAR AND CLEOPATRA was written in 1898. Shaw was sick with an infected foot during much of the time he worked on the play, but there is hardly evidence of sickness in it — unless the mellow resignation of Cæsar's wit be so considered. It was first performed in Chicago in 1901. The first London production, in 1907, was not a success, but later productions were. In 1913 Shaw added Ra's prologue. Today *Cæsar and Cleopatra* ranks among the dozen or so plays that by general consent make up Shaw's major canon. It was first published in 1901 in a collection entitled *Three Plays for Puritans*.

As Puritans notoriously abominated plays, the title is a paradox, though not a hard one. *Cæsar and Cleopatra*, according to Shaw's preface to the volume, is "for Puritans," first, because it ignores the conventional premise of the popular theater that since romance is mankind's main business the function of plays is to titillate the sensual imagination (but decorously, since this is a polite age), and, second, because it does not smother dialogue in expensive pageantry in the manner of contemporary productions of historical plays. But, as is commonly the case with Shaw, the explanation of one paradox only raises a larger one: here, a play about Cæsar and Cleopatra that is unheroic and unromantic. *This* paradox is the heart of the play. We may approach it by way of Shaw's prefatory objection to pageantry.

The objection may seem strange, since *Cæsar and Cleopatra* itself is excellent pageantry. Any one of Shaw's stage directions introducing the several acts will reveal his unfailing sense for scenic architecture, the fineness of his artist's eye, and his relish for tasteful and appropriate color and texture in dress and sets. Once one has enjoyed the glorious athleticism of the theatrically superb (though dramatically thin) Act III, or has seen, actually or imaginatively, the moonlit desert scene in Act I, with Cleopatra asleep between the paws of the Sphinx on "a heap of red poppies," while the conqueror of the world apostrophizes the silvery stillness, the popular notion that Shaw is a purely cerebral writer vanishes forever. Shaw was intelligent, witty, argumentative, didactic, and paradoxical, but his greatness as playright is at least as much a matter of his masterful command of theater space as of the lucid, speakable stage prose by which he communicates pointed meaning with graceful ease.

His objection is simply that when pageantry becomes an end in itself drama dies. In the London theater of late Victorian times Shakespeare's dialogue was cut to make room for what producers and audiences thought of as genuine Shakespearean spectacle: processions and battles and tiny stage business for the sake of authentic atmosphere — the products of painstaking research into medieval and Elizabethan costuming, armory, choreography, furniture, architecture, and details of domestic life. Such showy historicity enraged Shaw. He admitted pageantry only as an appropriate setting for the play of ideas which to him was always the drama's sole reason for being. ". . . new ideas," he wrote in the Preface, "make their technique as water makes its channel; and the technician without ideas is as useless as the canal constructor without water, though he may do very skillfully what the Mississippi does very rudely."

In *Cæsar and Cleopatra* the Shavian ideas amount to a refutation of the kind of activity which the exotic splendors of the historical setting and the glamorous aura surrounding the famous names invite and seem proper to. The action keeps failing to deliver the high drama of passion and conquest which title and locale and even the facts of history promise. After all, Cæsar and Cleopatra *were* lovers; they even had a child together. Then why won't Shaw give us the romance we expect to see? Not just because paradox is his manner and he aims to disoblige by deglamorizing history and debunking golden legend. *Why* is it his manner? The reason is not flippant. He wants to show us the unheroic, unromantic contemporaneity of the past. Idea is ironically played off against spectacle, and in our disappointed expectation of seeing staged for us the rich associations that encrust fact and legend, the moral fable we *do* get seems all the more sardonically telling. Pageantry, in short, helps to convey the history lesson which is Shaw's theme.

In general, literature uses history in one of two ways. Fictitious main characters may be placed in a setting of fact, in which the principals and circumstance of true history function as parts of the authenticating backdrop. This is Thackeray's method in *Henry Esmond* and Tolstoy's in *War and Peace* (except in the Napoleon and Kutuzov scenes). Or historical figures may be made protagonists in a more or less imaginative treatment of the facts. This is Shakespeare's method in his history plays and Shaw's in *The Man of Destiny, Cæsar and Cleopatra,* and *Saint Joan.*

Neither one wrote an antiquarian's kind of historical play, disengaged and meticulous, respectfully and learnedly observing chronology and authentic language. Museum pieces don't come alive by being made to move on a stage. By Shakespeare's and Shaw's example, a history play is an evocation of an image of the past for useful contemplation by the present. We see reflected in Shakespeare's dramatizations of royal English history in (roughly) the 15th century the political ideals of an enlightened Elizabethan. The plays are about the responsibilities of kingship, the blessings of a strong and sanctified monarchy, and the horrors of usurpation and civil war. Perhaps Shakespeare's conscious aim was simply to supply attractive entertainment for London audiences from the storehouse of Hall's and Holinshed's chronicles. Nevertheless, the plays, singly and in sequence, express what scholars call "the Tudor myth." They amount to a loyal patriot's concerned comment on past national anarchy that might return. Shakespeare's Henry V may seem more Tudor than Lancaster and his environment more late 16th century than early 15th century. But what else could he be?

One section of Shaw's Preface to *Three Plays for Puritans* is headed, "Better Than Shakespeare?" (hostile critics have ignored the question mark). The comparison is inevitable, since Shaw's title characters in *Cæsar and Cleopatra* are title characters in Shakespeare, too (though not together). Drama for Shaw was not art if it was not didactic, and his alleged arrogance is his suggestion that his Victorian view of

Cæsar and Cleopatra may be better for — that is, more relevant to the particular problems of — the Victorian age than Shakespeare's Elizabethan view. To deny that there is an issue here at all, says Shaw, is to be a victim of bardolatry; *i.e.*, the conviction that as a dramatist Shakespeare was not subject to human limitations. Bardolatry is bad for the worshipper, bad for drama, and bad even for Shakespeare, since it feeds on invincible ignorance. Doing Cæsar better than Shakespeare did is not to disparage Shakespeare, and it is not just a matter of making use of the discoveries and insights of historical scholarship (though Shaw acknowledges his debt to the German historian Theodor Mommsen for his conception of Cæsar). It is, like Shakespeare, to search the past for political allegory of present relevance. Shaw turns Shakespeare's practice into critical tenet and holds that every age must reinterpret the past by its own lights. The question that has prompted his play is: What, for us, is the truth about the historical Julius Cæsar?

Shaw's truth about Cæsar-in-Egypt is a twofold lesson of history: that the record of the past is nothing but a record of our own current errors (it is because he knows this that Cæsar so calmly can receive the news that the library of Alexandria is burning) and that moral progress — the only kind that matters — in public affairs must await the world's conversion to Cæsar's system of political ethics.

As only an anachronistic King Henry V could serve Shakespeare's political fable, so Shaw, too, writes anachronistically. In fact, he capitalizes on anachronisms; they are his chief dramatic metaphor. The dialogue is full of them: "Double or quits," "Egypt for the Egyptians," "Peace with honor," "Art for art's sake." And so is the characterization. Britannus is probably the most striking example. Shaw's solemn declaration in the Notes to the contrary, Britannus is only a likeness of the decent, insularly bigoted Englishman of some 2,000 years after Cæsar's time. But no more than the deglamorization of the legend are the anachronisms mere irreverence. By definition, an anachronism is a confusion of past and present. In *Cæsar and Cleopatra* they are recurrent symptoms in the characters' speech and manners of what the whole play argues, viz., that progress is a myth. If past and present are alike, if, as the god Ra says in the Prologue, "men twenty centuries ago were already just such as you, and spoke and lived as ye speak and live, no worse and no better, no wiser and no sillier," then even the pedant's objections fall to the ground. How can there be anachronism where there has been no change?

The main conflict in *Cæsar and Cleopatra* is not between Rome and Egypt. The siege, the politics, the military moves are nothing but events on which Shaw hangs his lesson of history. Nor is the conflict the more sophisticated one between the imperial love story we might have had and the quaint father–daughter, teacher–pupil relationship we actually get. The main conflict is, not in a romantic, but in a pedagogic situation. It ends in the separation, literal and figurative, of tutor and tutored. The separating issue is the murder of Pothinus. Cleopatra calls Cæsar a dreamer because he refuses to take revenge on his enemies. Pothinus and Britannus have at different times been equally astonished at his strange clemency. But events show him to be more practical and efficient than anyone else in the play. He out-fights, out-talks, and out-foxes the Egyptians whenever he wants. He approves of necessary killing. But he does not believe in murderous passion parading as justice, virtue, and honor. When Cleopatra seeks to vindicate the murder of Pothinus, she is supported by Cæsar's own men. Inasmuch as the honest soldier Rufio, the brave moralist Britannus, and the gay artist Apollodorus collectively represent a sampling of the world's vital values, their support darkens the moral issue between Cleopatra and Cæsar and is one of the reasons why the play is felt to transcend the ideological simplemindedness and dogmatism that limit most thesis plays to a kind of dramatic journalism. Encouraged, and still heated with her righteous vengeance, Cleopatra shifts from defense to attack:

CLEOPATRA (*vehemently*): Listen to me, Cæsar. If one man in all Alexandria can be found to say that I did wrong, I swear to have myself crucified on the door of the palace by my own slaves.

CÆSAR: If one man in all the world can be found, now or forever, to know that you did wrong, that man will have either to conquer the world as I have or be crucified by it.

The allusion to Christ is probably the most discreet anachronism in the play, but it is also its most important one. It enriches the earlier associations of Cæsar with divinity: in Ra's Prologue, in Cæsar's claiming kinship with the immortal Sphinx, in the boy–king Ptolemy's assumption that it was the gods who sent Mark Antony to Egypt, and in Cleopatra's identification of Cæsar with a god in her talk with Pothinus early in Act IV. It is noteworthy that except for an occasional pompous phrase by the Egyptian leaders the only examples of noncolloquial language in the play are the god Ra's prologue and Cæsar's apostrophe to the Sphinx. Both speakers represent eternal values, and the Cæsar–Cleopatra conflict could also be defined as one between divine permanence of reason and of universal love and the impermanence of man's exclusive passions. One of the paradoxes of

Shaw's theme is that Cæsar, who seeks change, represents timelessness, whereas the world, which refuses to change, is in continuous flux. If the play's middle (Acts II-IV) seems disorderly and diffuse, there is a good reason for it. It translates into stage action the irony of the moral inertia of melodramatic busyness.

Ironic, too, is the fact that even the apparently more successful of the two alternative saviors of the world that Cæsar mentions fails and that his failure is due to the changes time brings. His mortality betrays his divinity. Balding and wrinkled, he is no lover for Cleopatra. Their first scene together obliquely anticipates his failure. It is not a scene of a god–conqueror solving the Sphinx' riddle but only of an "old gentleman" pointlessly addressing "a little kitten of a Sphinx," a "pet" Sphinx. When Pothinus asks Cleopatra in Act IV whether she is in love with Cæsar, she counters with another question: "Can one love a god?" She is wise enough to wish she *were* in love with him, but not wise enough to realize that her rejoinder is an inadequate answer. To the question of why one cannot love a godlike Cæsar, a Cleopatra answers, "Because he is not a beautiful young man with strong, round arms" — and at that moment the world slips from grace. Cleopatra's education toward ideal queenship has gone far, as her words to Pothinus early in Act IV show. Already by the end of Act I Cæsar has taught her to make herself obeyed, and when Rufio pitches her into the sea at the end of Act III it is as if she were being baptized into a new maturity. But the murder of Pothinus shows that it has not gone far enough. The kitten has only grown claws. She founders on passion. And the sulking, giggle-prone Cleopatra of Act V is closer to the silly, charming girl of Act I than to the wise and humble queen she seemed to have become by Act IV. Time present is still time past.

As the play has a Prologue (and an "Alternative to the Prologue") to the action of Cleopatra's truncated education, so it also has an epilogue: Act V. Soon after Cæsar's disillusionment with his pupil the stage once more becomes busy with military and political affairs, and the moral drama ends. When he is about to embark for Rome he almost forgets to say goodbye to Cleopatra. But the light, almost burlesque, tone of the departure scene is made ominous with hints of the daggers waiting in Rome. Cæsar, we know, falls, and the world reverts to its Pompeian and Antonian ways after the Cæsarian interlude, to "the way of the soldier . . . the way of death," as Ra calls it, after Cæsar's "way of the gods . . . the way of life." And so, Rome remains "a madman's dream." As the doomed Cæsar resigns Cleopatra to her young lover–soldier and to her deathless fate as siren, history's old, passionate melodrama resumes. Two thousand years have done nothing to disprove Cæsar's prophecy:

. . . And so, to the end of history, murder shall breed murder, always in the name of right and honor and peace, until the gods are tired of blood and create a race that can understand.

Here is Shaw's earliest reference in drama to the Superman whom he later celebrated as John Tanner in *Man and Superman* (1903) and as the wise Ancients in *Back to Methuselah* (1921), the two plays which have been called the trunk of his dramatic canon, on which all the other plays are branches. Joan of Arc in *Saint Joan* (1924) is, like Cæsar, a historical example of the superman race. Superman's (or -woman's) superiority over ordinary men is his commitment, conscious or unconscious, to the service of the Life Force, the vital principle in what Shaw called Creative Evolution toward ever higher forms of contemplative intelligence. Cæsar, says Shaw in his Notes, "is greater off the battle field than on it." This seems like a paradox in the eyes of the world and will till the world learns from its violent past not to reject its Superman saviors — its Cæsars, its Christs, and its saints. "He will return some day," says Apollodorus as Cæsar leaves. "I hope not," replies Cleopatra. "But I cant help crying, all the same." Between her hope and her tears is the world's impasse.

Cæsar and Cleopatra is a thesis play, if by a thesis play is meant a play in which the playwright tells us something which he hopes will change our ways. Nevertheless, it is not irrelevant to ask whether it ends as a kind of comedy or as a kind of tragedy. It is, however, a difficult question.

Anton Chekhov

THE CHERRY ORCHARD

Translated by Stark Young

Characters

RANEVSKAYA, LYUBOFF ANDREEVNA, *a landowner*
ANYA, *her daughter, seventeen years old*
VARYA, *her adopted daughter, twenty-four years old*
GAYEFF, LEONID ANDREEVICH, *brother of Ranevskaya*
LOPAHIN, YERMOLAY ALEXEEVICH, *a merchant*
TROFIMOFF, PYOTR SERGEEVICH, *a student*
SEMYONOFF-PISHTCHIK, BORIS BORISOVICH, *a landowner*
CHARLOTTA IVANOVNA, *a governess*
EPIHODOFF, SEMYON PANTELEEVICH, *a clerk*
DUNYASHA, *a maid*
FIERS, *a valet, an old man of eighty-seven*
YASHA, *a young valet*
A PASSERBY *or* STRANGER
THE STATIONMASTER
A POST-OFFICE CLERK
VISITORS, SERVANTS

SCENE: *The action takes place on the estate of* L. A. RANEVSKAYA.

ACT ONE

(*A room that is still called the nursery. One of the doors leads into* ANYA's *room. Dawn, the sun will soon be rising. It is May, the cherry trees are in blossom but in the orchard it is cold, with a morning frost. The windows in the room are closed. Enter* DUN-YASHA *with a candle and* LOPAHIN *with a book in his hand.*)

LOPAHIN: The train got in, thank God! What time is it?

DUNYASHA: It's nearly two. (*Blows out her candle.*) It's already daylight.

LOPAHIN: But how late was the train? Two hours at least. (*Yawning and stretching.*) I'm a fine one, I am, look what a fool thing I did! I drove her on purpose just to meet them at the station, and then all of a sudden I'd overslept myself! Fell asleep in my chair. How provoking! — You could have waked me up.

DUNYASHA: I thought you had gone. (*Listening.*) Listen, I think they are coming now.

LOPAHIN (*listening*): No — No, there's the luggage and one thing and another. (*A pause.*) Lyuboff Andreevna has been living abroad five years. I don't know what she is like now — She is a good woman. An easy-going, simple woman. I remember when I was a boy about fifteen, my father, who is at rest — in those days he ran a shop here in the village — hit me in the face with his fist, my nose was bleeding — We'd come to the yard together for something or other, and he was a little drunk. Lyuboff Andreevna, I can see her now, still so young, so slim, led me to the washbasin here in this very room, in the nursery. "Don't cry," she says, "little peasant, it will be well in time for your wedding" — (*A pause.*) Yes, little peasant — My father was a peasant truly, and here I am in a white waistcoat and yellow shoes. Like a pig rooting in a pastry shop — I've got this rich, lots of money, but if you really stop and think of it, I'm just a peasant — (*Turning the pages of a book.*) Here I was reading a book and didn't get a thing out of it. Reading and went to sleep. (*A pause.*)

DUNYASHA: And all night long the dogs were not asleep, they know their masters are coming.

LOPAHIN: What is it, Dunyasha, you're so —

DUNYASHA: My hands are shaking. I'm going to faint.

LOPAHIN: You're just so delicate, Dunyasha. And all dressed up like a lady, and your hair all done up! Mustn't do that. Must know your place.

(*Enter* EPIHODOFF, *with a bouquet: he wears a jacket and highly polished boots with a loud squeak. As he enters he drops the bouquet.*)

EPIHODOFF (*picking up the bouquet*): Look, the gardener sent these, he says to put them in the dining room. (*Giving the bouquet to* DUNYASHA.)

LOPAHIN: And bring me some kvass.

DUNYASHA: Yes, sir. (*Goes out.*)

EPIHODOFF: There is a morning frost now, three degrees of frost (*sighing*) and the cherries all in bloom. I cannot approve of our climate — I cannot. Our climate can never quite rise to the occasion. Listen, Yermolay Alexeevich, allow me to subtend, I bought myself, day before yesterday, some boots and they, I venture to assure you, squeak so that it is impossible. What could I grease them with?

LOPAHIN: Go on. You annoy me.

EPIHODOFF: Every day some misfortune happens to me. But I don't complain, I am used to it and I even smile.

(DUNYASHA *enters, serves* LOPAHIN *the kvass.*)

EPIHODOFF: I'm going. (*Stumbling over a chair and upsetting it.*) There (*as if triumphant*), there, you see, pardon the expression, a circumstance like that, among others — It is simply quite remarkable. (*Goes out.*)

DUNYASHA: And I must tell you, Yermolay Alexeevich, that Epihodoff has proposed to me.

LOPAHIN: Ah!

DUNYASHA: I don't know really what to — He is a quiet man but sometimes when he starts talking, you can't understand a thing he means. It's all very nice, and full of feeling, but just doesn't make any sense. I sort of like him. He loves me madly. He's a man that's unfortunate, every day there's something or other. They tease him around here, call him twenty-two misfortunes —

LOPAHIN (*cocking his ear*): Listen, I think they are coming —

DUNYASHA: They are coming! But what's the matter with me — I'm cold all over.

LOPAHIN: They're really coming. Let's go meet them. Will she recognize me? It's five years we haven't seen each other.

DUNYASHA (*excitedly*): I'm going to faint this very minute. Ah, I'm going to faint!

(*Two carriages can be heard driving up to the house.* LOPAHIN *and* DUNYASHA *hurry out. The stage is empty. In the adjoining rooms a noise begins.* FIERS *hurries across the stage, leaning on a stick; he has been to meet* LYUBOFF ANDREEVNA, *and wears an old-fashioned livery and a high hat; he mutters something to himself, but you cannot understand a word of it. The noise offstage gets louder and louder. A voice: "Look! Let's go through here—"* LYUBOFF ANDREEVNA, ANYA *and* CHARLOTTA IVANOVNA, *with a little dog on a chain, all of them dressed for traveling,* VARYA, *in a coat and kerchief,* GAYEFF, SEMYONOFF-PISHTCHIK, LOPAHIN, DUN-YASHA, *with a bundle and an umbrella,* SERVANTS *with pieces of luggage—all pass through the room.*)

ANYA: Let's go through here. Mama, do you remember what room this is?

LYUBOFF ANDREEVNA (*happily, through her tears*): The nursery!

VARYA: How cold it is, my hands are stiff. (*To* LYUBOFF ANDREEVNA.) Your rooms, the white one and the violet, are just the same as ever, Mama.

LYUBOFF ANDREEVNA: The nursery, my dear beautiful room—I slept here when I was little—(*Crying.*) And now I am like a child—(*Kisses her brother and* VARYA, *then her brother again.*) And Varya is just the same as ever, looks like a nun. And I knew Dunyasha—(*Kisses* DUNYASHA.)

GAYEFF: The train was two hours late. How's that? How's that for good management?

CHARLOTTA (*to* PISHTCHIK): My dog he eats nuts too.

PISHTCHIK (*astonished*): Think of that!

(*Everybody goes out except* ANYA *and* DUNYASHA.)

DUNYASHA: We waited so long—(*Taking off* ANYA'S *coat and hat.*)

ANYA: I didn't sleep all four nights on the way. And now I feel so chilly.

DUNYASHA: It was Lent when you left, there was some snow then, there was frost, and now? My darling (*laughing and kissing her*), I waited so long for you, my joy, my life—I'm telling you now, I can't keep from it another minute.

ANYA (*wearily*): There we go again—

DUNYASHA: The clerk Epihodoff, proposed to me after Holy Week.

ANYA: You're always talking about the same thing—(*Arranging her hair.*) I've lost all my hairpins—(*She is tired to the point of staggering.*)

DUNYASHA: I just don't know what to think. He loves me, loves me so!

ANYA (*looks in through her door, tenderly*): My room, my windows, it's just as if I had never been away. I'm home! Tomorrow morning

I'll get up, I'll run into the orchard — Oh, if I only could go to sleep! I haven't slept all the way, I was tormented by anxiety.

DUNYASHA: Day before yesterday, Pyotr Sergeevich arrived.

ANYA (*joyfully*): Petya!

DUNYASHA: He's asleep in the bathhouse, he lives there. I am afraid, he says, of being in the way. (*Taking her watch from her pocket and looking at it.*) Somebody ought to wake him up. It's only that Varvara Mikhailovna told us not to. Don't you wake him up, she said.

VARYA (*enter* VARYA *with a bunch of keys at her belt*): Dunyasha, coffee, quick — Mama is asking for coffee.

DUNYASHA: This minute. (*Goes out.*)

VARYA: Well, thank goodness, you've come back. You are home again. (*Caressingly.*) My darling is back! My precious is back!

ANYA: I've had such a time.

VARYA: I can imagine!

ANYA: I left during Holy Week, it was cold then. Charlotta talked all the way and did her tricks. Why did you fasten Charlotta on to me — ?

VARYA: But you couldn't have traveled alone, darling; not at seventeen!

ANYA: We arrived in Paris, it was cold there and snowing. I speak terrible French. Mama lived on the fifth floor; I went to see her; there were some French people in her room, ladies, an old priest with his prayer book, and the place was full of tobacco smoke — very dreary. Suddenly I began to feel sorry for Mama, so sorry, I drew her to me, held her close and couldn't let her go. Then Mama kept hugging me, crying — yes —

VARYA (*tearfully*): Don't — oh, don't —

ANYA: Her villa near Mentone she had already sold, she had nothing left, nothing. And I didn't have a kopeck left. It was all we could do to get here. And Mama doesn't understand! We sit down to dinner at a station and she orders, insists on the most expensive things and gives the waiters rouble tips. Charlotta does the same. Yasha too demands his share; it's simply dreadful. Mama has her butler, Yasha, we've brought him here —

VARYA: I saw the wretch.

ANYA: Well, how are things? Has the interest on the mortgage been paid?

VARYA: How could we?

ANYA: Oh, my God, my God — !

VARYA: In August the estate is to be sold —

ANYA: My God — !

LOPAHIN (*looking in through the door and mooing like a cow*): Moo-o-o — (*Goes away.*)

VARYA (*tearfully*): I'd land him one like that — (*Shaking her fist.*)

ANYA (*embracing* VARYA *gently*): Varya, has he proposed? (VARYA *shakes her head.*) But he loves you — Why don't you have it out with him, what are you waiting for?

VARYA: I don't think anything will come of it for us. He is very busy, he hasn't any time for me — And doesn't notice me. God knows, it's painful for me to see him — Everybody talks about our marriage, everybody congratulates us, and the truth is, there's nothing to it — it's all like a dream — (*In a different tone.*) You have a brooch looks like a bee.

ANYA (*sadly*): Mama bought it. (*Going toward her room, speaking gaily, like a child.*) And in Paris I went up in a balloon!

VARYA: My darling is back! My precious is back! (DUNYASHA *has returned with the coffee pot and is making coffee.* VARYA *is standing by the door.*) Darling, I'm busy all day long with the house and I go around thinking things. If only you could be married to a rich man, I'd be more at peace too, I would go all by myself to a hermitage — then to Kiev — to Moscow, and I'd keep going like that from one holy place to another — I would go on and on. Heavenly!

ANYA: The birds are singing in the orchard. What time is it now?

VARYA: It must be after two. It's time you were asleep, darling. (*Going into* ANYA's *room.*) Heavenly!

YASHA (YASHA *enters with a lap robe and a traveling bag. Crossing the stage airily*): May I go through here?

DUNYASHA: We'd hardly recognize you, Yasha; you've changed so abroad!

YASHA: Hm — And who are you?

DUNYASHA: When you left here, I was like that — (*Her hand so high from the floor.*) I'm Dunyasha, Fyodor Kozoyedoff's daughter. You don't remember!

YASHA: Hm — You little peach! (*Looking around before he embraces her; she shrieks and drops a saucer;* YASHA *hurries out.*)

VARYA (*at the door, in a vexed tone*): And what's going on here?

DUNYASHA (*tearfully*): I broke a saucer —

VARYA: That's good luck.

ANYA (*emerging from her room*): We ought to tell Mama beforehand: Petya is here —

VARYA: I told them not to wake him up.

ANYA (*pensively*): Six years ago our father died, a month later our brother Grisha was drowned in the river, such a pretty little boy, just seven. Mama couldn't bear it, she went away, went away without ever looking back — (*Shuddering.*) How I understand her, if she only knew I did. (*A pause.*) And Petya Trofimoff was Grisha's tutor, he might remind —

FIERS (*enter* FIERS; *he is in a jacket and white waistcoat. Going to the coffee urn, busy with it*): The mistress will have her breakfast here — (*Putting on white gloves.*) Is the coffee ready? (*To* DUNYASHA, *sternly.*) You! What about the cream?

DUNYASHA: Oh, my God — (*Hurrying out.*)

FIERS (*busy at the coffee urn*): Oh, you good-for-nothing — ! (*Muttertering to himself.*) Come back from Paris — And the master used to go to Paris by coach — (*Laughing.*)

VARYA: Fiers, what are you — ?

FIERS: At your service. (*Joyfully.*) My mistress is back! It's what I've been waiting for! Now I'm ready to die — (*Crying for joy.*)

(LYUBOFF ANDREEVNA, GAYEFF *and* SEMYONOFF-PISHTCHIK *enter;* SEMYONOFF-PISHTCHIK *is in a podyovka of fine cloth and sharovary.* GAYEFF *enters; he makes gestures with his hands and body as if he were playing billiards.*)

LYUBOFF ANDREEVNA: How is it? Let me remember — Yellow into the corner! Duplicate in the middle!

GAYEFF: I cut into the corner. Sister, you and I slept here in this very room once, and now I am fifty-one years old, strange as that may seem —

LOPAHIN: Yes, time passes.

GAYEFF: What?

LOPAHIN: Time, I say, passes.

GAYEFF: And it smells like patchouli here.

ANYA: I'm going to bed. Good night, Mama. (*Kissing her mother.*)

LYUBOFF ANDREEVNA: My sweet little child. (*Kissing her hands.*) You're glad you are home? I still can't get myself together.

ANYA: Good-by, Uncle.

GAYEFF (*kissing her face and hands*): God be with you. How like your mother you are! (*To his sister.*) Lyuba, at her age you were exactly like her.

(ANYA *shakes hands with* LOPAHIN *and* PISHTCHIK, *goes out and closes the door behind her.*)

LYUBOFF ANDREEVNA: She's very tired.

PISHTCHIK: It is a long trip, I imagine.

VARYA (*to* LOPAHIN *and* PISHTCHIK): Well, then, sirs? It's going on three o'clock, time for gentlemen to be going

LYUBOFF ANDREEVNA (*laughing*): The same old Varya. (*Drawing her to her and kissing her.*) There, I'll drink my coffee, then we'll all go. (FIERS *puts a small cushion under her feet.*) Thank you, my dear. I am used to coffee. Drink it day and night. Thank you, my dear old soul. (*Kissing* FIERS.)

VARYA: I'll go see if all the things have come. (*Goes out.*)

LYUBOFF ANDREEVNA: Is it really me sitting here? (*Laughing.*) I'd like to jump around and wave my arms. (*Covering her face with her hands.*) But I may be dreaming! God knows I love my country, love it deeply, I couldn't look out of the car window, I just kept crying. (*Tearfully.*) However, I must drink my coffee. Thank you, Fiers, thank you, my dear old friend. I'm so glad you're still alive.

FIERS: Day before yesterday.

GAYEFF: He doesn't hear well.

LOPAHIN: And I must leave right now. It's nearly five o'clock in the morning, for Kharkov. What a nuisance! I wanted to look at you — talk — You are as beautiful as ever.

PISHTCHIK (*breathing heavily*): Even more beautiful — In your Paris clothes — It's a feast for the eyes —

LOPAHIN: Your brother, Leonid Andreevich here, says I'm a boor, a peasant money grubber, but that's all the same to me, absolutely. Let him say it. All I wish is you'd trust me as you used to, and your wonderful, touching eyes would look at me as they did. Merciful God! My father was a serf; belonged to your grandfather and your father; but you, your own self, you did so much for me once that I've forgotten all that and love you like my own kin — more than my kin.

LYUBOFF ANDREEVNA: I can't sit still — I can't. (*Jumping up and walking about in great excitement.*) I'll never live through this happiness — Laugh at me, I'm silly — My own little bookcase —! (*Kissing the bookcase.*) My little table!

GAYEFF: And in your absence the nurse here died.

LYUBOFF ANDREEVNA (*sitting down and drinking coffee*): Yes, may she rest in Heaven! They wrote me.

GAYEFF: And Anastasy died. Cross-eyed Petrushka left me and lives in town now at the police officer's. (*Taking out of his pocket a box of hard candy and sucking a piece.*)

PISHTCHIK: My daughter, Dashenka — sends you her greetings —

LOPAHIN: I want to tell you something very pleasant, cheerful. (*Glancing at his watch.*) I'm going right away. There's no time for talking. Well, I'll make it two or three words. As you know, your cherry orchard is to be sold for your debts; the auction is set for August twenty-second, but don't you worry, my dear, you just sleep in peace, there's a way out of it. Here's my plan. Please listen to me. Your estate is only thirteen miles from town. They've run the railroad by it. Now if the cherry orchard and the land along the river were cut up into building lots and leased for summer cottages, you'd have at the very lowest twenty-five thousand roubles per year income.

GAYEFF: Excuse me, what rot!

LYUBOFF ANDREEVNA: I don't quite understand you, Yermolay Alexeevich.

LOPAHIN: At the very least you will get from the summer residents twenty-five roubles per year for a two-and-a-half acre lot and if you post a notice right off, I'll bet you anything that by autumn you won't have a single patch of land free, everything will be taken. In a word, my congratulations, you are saved. The location is wonderful, the river's so deep. Except, of course, it all needs to be tidied up, cleared — For instance, let's say, tear all the old buildings down and this house, which is no good any more, and cut down the old cherry orchard —

LYUBOFF ANDREEVNA: Cut down? My dear, forgive me, you don't understand at all. If there's one thing in the whole province that's interesting — not to say remarkable — it's our cherry orchard.

LOPAHIN: The only remarkable thing about this cherry orchard is that it's very big. There's a crop of cherries once every two years and even that's hard to get rid of. Nobody buys them.

GAYEFF: This orchard is even mentioned in the encyclopedia.

LOPAHIN (*glancing at his watch*): If we don't cook up something and don't get somewhere, the cherry orchard and the entire estate will be sold at auction on the twenty-second of August. Do get it settled then! I swear there is no other way out. Not a one!

FIERS: There was a time, forty-fifty years ago when the cherries were dried, soaked, pickled, cooked into jam and it used to be —

GAYEFF: Keep quiet, Fiers.

FIERS: And it used to be that the dried cherries were shipped by the wagon-load to Moscow and to Kharkov. And the money there was! And the dried cherries were soft then, juicy, sweet, fragrant — They had a way of treating them then —

LYUBOFF ANDREEVNA: And where is that way now?

FIERS: They have forgotten it. Nobody remembers it.

PISHTCHIK (*to* LYUBOFF ANDREEVNA): What's happening in Paris? How is everything? Did you eat frogs?

LYUBOFF ANDREEVNA: I ate crocodiles.

PISHTCHIK: Think of it — !

LOPAHIN: Up to now in the country there have been only the gentry and the peasants, but now in summer the villa people too are coming in. All the towns, even the least big ones, are surrounded with cottages. In about twenty years very likely the summer resident will multiply enormously. He merely drinks tea on the porch now, but it might well happen that on this two-and-a-half acre lot of his, he'll go in for farming, and then your cherry orchard would be happy, rich, splendid —

GAYEFF (*getting hot*): What rot!

(*Enter* VARYA *and* YASHA.)

VARYA: Here, Mama. Two telegrams for you. (*Choosing a key and opening the old bookcase noisily.*) Here they are.

LYUBOFF ANDREEVNA: From Paris (*Tearing up the telegrams without reading them.*) Paris, that's all over —

GAYEFF: Do you know how old this bookcase is, Lyuba? A week ago I pulled out the bottom drawer and looked, and there the figures were burned on it. The bookcase was made exactly a hundred years ago. How's that? Eh? You might celebrate its jubilee. It's an in-animate object, but all the same, be that as it may, it's a bookcase.

PISHTCHIK (*in astonishment*): A hundred years — ! Think of it — !

GAYEFF: Yes — quite something — (*Shaking the bookcase.*) Dear, hon-ored bookcase! I saluted your existence, which for more than a hundred years has been directed toward the clear ideals of goodness and justice; your silent appeal to fruitful endeavor has not flagged in all the course of a hundred years, sustaining (*tearfully*) through the generations of our family, our courage and our faith in a better future and nurturing in us ideals of goodness and of a social con-sciousness.

(*A pause.*)

LOPAHIN: Yes.

LYUBOFF ANDREEVNA: You're the same as ever, Lenya.

GAYEFF (*slightly embarrassed*): Carom to the right into the corner pocket. I cut into the side pocket!

LOPAHIN (*glancing at his watch*): Well, it's time for me to go.

YASHA (*handing medicine to* LYUBOFF ANDREEVNA): Perhaps you'll take the pills now —

PISHTCHIK: You should never take medicaments, dear madam — They do neither harm nor good — Hand them here, dearest lady. (*He takes the pillbox, shakes the pills out into his palm, blows on them, puts them in his mouth and washes them down with kvass.*) There! Now!

LYUBOFF ANDREEVNA (*startled*): Why, you've lost your mind!

PISHTCHIK: I took all the pills.

LOPAHIN: Such a glutton!

(*Everyone laughs.*)

FIERS: The gentleman stayed with us during Holy Week, he ate half a bucket of pickles — (*Muttering.*)

LYUBOFF ANDREEVNA: What is he muttering about?

VARYA: He's been muttering like that for three years. We're used to it.

YASHA: In his dotage.

(CHARLOTTA IVANOVNA *in a white dress — she is very thin, her corset laced very tight — with a lorgnette at her belt, crosses the stage.*)

LOPAHIN: Excuse me, Charlotta Ivanovna, I haven't had a chance yet to welcome you. (*Trying to kiss her hand.*)

CHARLOTTA (*drawing her hand away*): If I let you kiss my hand, 'twould be my elbow next, then my shoulder —

LOPAHIN: No luck for me today. (*Everyone laughs.*) Charlotta Ivanovna, show us a trick!

CHARLOTTA: No. I want to go to bed. (*Exit.*)

LOPAHIN: In three weeks we shall see each other. (*Kissing* LYUBOFF ANDREEVNA's *hand.*) Till then, good-by. It's time. (*To* GAYEFF.) See you soon. (*Kissing* PISHTCHIK.) See you soon. (*Shaking* VARYA's *hand, then* FIERS' *and* YASHA's.) I don't feel like going. (*To* LYUBOFF ANDREEVNA.) If you think it over and make up your mind about the summer cottages, let me know and I'll arrange a loan of something like fifty thousand roubles. Think it over seriously.

VARYA (*angrily*): Do go on, anyhow, will you!

LOPAHIN: I'm going, I'm going — (*Exit.*)

GAYEFF: Boor. However, pardon — Varya is going to marry him, it's Varya's little fiancé.

VARYA: Don't talk too much, Uncle.

LYUBOFF ANDREEVNA: Well, Varya, I should be very glad. He's a good man.

PISHTCHIK: A man, one must say truthfully — A most worthy — And my Dashenka — says also that — she says all sorts of things — (*Snoring but immediately waking up.*) Nevertheless, dearest lady, oblige me — With a loan of two hundred and forty roubles — To-morrow the interest on my mortgage has got to be paid —

VARYA (*startled*): There's not any money, none at all.

LYUBOFF ANDREEVNA: Really, I haven't got anything.

PISHTCHIK: I'll find it, somehow. (*Laughing.*) I never give up hope. There, I think to myself, all is lost, I am ruined and lo and behold — a railroad is put through my land and — they paid me. And then, just watch, something else will turn up — if not today, then tomorrow — Dashenka will win two hundred thousand — She has a ticket.

LYUBOFF ANDREEVNA: We've finished the coffee, now we can go to bed.

FIERS (*brushing* GAYEFF's *clothes, reprovingly*): You put on the wrong trousers again. What am I going to do with you!

VARYA (*softly*): Anya is asleep. (*Opening the window softly.*) Already the sun's rising — it's not cold. Look, Mama! What beautiful trees! My Lord, what air! The starlings are singing!

GAYEFF (*opening another window*): The orchard is all white. You haven't forgotten, Lyuba? That long lane there runs straight — as a strap stretched out. It glistens on moonlight nights. Do you remember? You haven't forgotten it?

LYUBOFF ANDREEVNA (*looking out of the window on to the orchard*): Oh, my childhood, my innocence! I slept in this nursery and looked out on the orchard from here, every morning happiness awoke with me, it was just as it is now, then, nothing has changed. (*Laughing with joy.*) All, all white! Oh, my orchard! After a dark, rainy autumn and cold winter, you are young again and full of happiness. The heavenly angels have not deserted you — If I only could lift the weight from my breast, from my shoulders, if I could only forget my past!

GAYEFF: Yes, and the orchard will be sold for debt, strange as that may seem.

LYUBOFF ANDREEVNA: Look, our dear mother is walking through the orchard — In a white dress! (*Laughing happily.*) It's she.

GAYEFF: Where?

VARYA: God be with you, Mama!

LYUBOFF ANDREEVNA: There's not anybody, it only seemed so. To the right, as you turn to the summerhouse, a little white tree is leaning there, looks like a woman — (*Enter* TROFIMOFF, *in a student's uniform, well worn, and glasses.*) What a wonderful orchard? The white masses of blossoms, the sky all blue.

TROFIMOFF: Lyuboff Andreevna! (*She looks around at him.*) I will just greet you and go immediately. (*Kissing her hand warmly.*) I was told to wait until morning, but I hadn't the patience —

(LYUBOFF ANDREEVNA *looks at him puzzled.*)

VARYA (*tearfully*): This is Petya Trofimoff —

TROFIMOFF: Petya Trofimoff, the former tutor of your Grisha — Have I really changed so?

(LYUBOFF ANDREEVNA *embraces him; and crying quietly.*)

GAYEFF (*embarrassed*): There, there, Lyuba.

VARYA (*crying*): I told you, Petya, to wait till tomorrow.

LYUBOFF ANDREEVNA: My Grisha — My boy — Grisha — Son —

VARYA: What can we do, Mama? It's God's will.

TROFIMOFF (*in a low voice, tearfully*): There, there —

LYUBOFF ANDREEVNA (*weeping softly*): My boy was lost, drowned — Why? Why, my friend? (*More quietly.*) Anya is asleep there, and I am talking so loud — Making so much noise — But why, Petya? Why have you lost your looks? Why do you look so much older?

TROFIMOFF: A peasant woman on the train called me a mangy-looking gentleman.

LYUBOFF ANDREEVNA: You were a mere boy then, a charming young student, and now your hair's not very thick any more and you wear glasses. Are you really a student still? (*Going to the door.*)

TROFIMOFF: Very likely I'll be a perennial student.

LYUBOFF ANDREEVNA (*kissing her brother, then* VARYA): Well, go to bed — You've grown older too, Leonid.

PISHTCHIK (*following her*): So that's it, we are going to bed now. Oh, my gout! I'm staying here — I'd like, Lyuboff Andreevna, my soul, tomorrow morning — Two hundred and forty roubles —

GAYEFF: He's still at it.

PISHTCHIK: Two hundred and forty roubles — To pay interest on the mortgage.

LYUBOFF ANDREEVNA: I haven't any money, my dove.

PISHTCHIK: I'll pay it back, my dear — It's a trifling sum —

LYUBOFF ANDREEVNA: Oh, very well, Leonid will give — You give it to him, Leonid.

GAYEFF: Oh, certainly, I'll give it to him. Hold out your pockets.

LYUBOFF ANDREEVNA: What can we do, give it, he needs it — He'll pay it back.

(LYUBOFF ANDREEVNA, TROFIMOFF, PISHTCHIK *and* FIERS *go out.* GAYEFF, VARYA *and* YASHA *remain.*)

GAYEFF: My sister hasn't yet lost her habit of throwing money away. (*To* YASHA.) Get away, my good fellow, you smell like hens.

YASHA (*with a grin*): And you are just the same as you used to be, Leonid Andreevich.

GAYEFF: What? (*To* VARYA.) What did he say?

VARYA (*to* YASHA): Your mother has come from the village, she's been sitting in the servants' hall ever since yesterday, she wants to see you —

YASHA: The devil take her!

VARYA: Ach, shameless creature!

YASHA: A lot I need her! She might have come tomorrow. (*Goes out.*)

VARYA: Mama is just the same as she was, she hasn't changed at all. If she could, she'd give away everything she has.

GAYEFF: Yes — If many remedies are prescribed for an illness, you may know the illness is incurable. I keep thinking, I rack my brains, I have many remedies, a great many, and that means, really, I haven't any at all. It would be fine to inherit a fortune from somebody, it would be fine to marry off our Anya to a very rich man, it would be fine to go to Yaroslavl and try our luck with our old aunt, the Countess. Auntie is very, very rich.

VARYA (*crying*): If God would only help us!

GAYEFF: Don't bawl! Auntie is very rich but she doesn't like us. To begin with, Sister married a lawyer, not a nobleman — (ANYA *appears at the door.*) Married not a nobleman and behaved herself, you could say, not very virtuously. She is good, kind, nice, I love her very much, but no matter how much you allow for the extenuating circumstances, you must admit she's a depraved woman. You feel it in her slightest movement.

VARYA (*whispering*): Anya is standing in the door there.

GAYEFF: What? (*A pause.*) It's amazing, something got in my right eye. I am beginning to see poorly. And on Thursday, when I was in the District Court —

(ANYA *enters.*)

VARYA: But why aren't you asleep, Anya?

ANYA: I don't feel like sleeping. I can't.

GAYEFF: My little girl — (*Kissing* ANYA's *face and hands.*) My child — (*Tearfully.*) You are not my niece, you are my angel, you are everything to me. Believe me, believe —

ANYA: I believe you, Uncle. Everybody loves you, respects you — But dear Uncle, you must keep quiet, just keep quiet — What were you saying, just now, about my mother, about your own sister? What did you say that for?

GAYEFF: Yes, yes — (*Putting her hand up over his face.*) Really, it's terrible! My God! Oh, God, save me! And today I made a speech to the bookcase — So silly! And it was only when I finished it that I could see it was silly.

VARYA: It's true, Uncle, you ought to keep quiet. Just keep quiet. That's all.

ANYA: If you kept quiet, you'd have more peace.

GAYEFF: I'll keep quiet. (*Kissing* ANYA's *and* VARYA's *hands.*) I'll keep quiet. Only this, it's about business. On Thursday I was in the District Court; well, a few of us gathered around and a conversation began about this and that, about lots of things; apparently it will be possible to arrange a loan on a promissory note to pay the bank the interest due.

VARYA: If the Lord would only help us!

GAYEFF: Tuesday I shall go and talk it over again. (*To* VARYA.) Don't bawl! (*To* ANYA.) Your mother will talk to Lopahin; of course, he won't refuse her . . . And as soon as you rest up, you will go to Yaroslavl to your great-aunt, the Countess. There, that's how we will move from three directions, and the business is in the bag. We'll pay the interest. I am convinced of that — (*Putting a hard candy in his mouth.*) On my honor I'll swear, by anything you like, that the estate shall not be sold! (*Excitedly.*) By my happiness, I swear! Here's my hand, call me a worthless, dishonorable man, if I allow it to come up for auction! With all my soul I swear it!

ANYA (*a quieter mood returns to her; she is happy*): How good you are, Uncle, how clever! (*Embracing her uncle.*) I feel easy now! I feel easy! I'm happy!

FIERS (FIERS *enters, reproachfully*): Leonid Andreevich, have you no fear of God? When are you going to bed?

GAYEFF: Right away, right away. You may go, Fiers. For this once I'll undress myself. Well, children, beddy bye — More details tomorrow, and now, go to bed. (*Kissing* ANYA *and* VARYA.) I am a man of the eighties — It is a period that's not admired, but I can say, nevertheless, that I've suffered no little for my convictions in the course of my life. It is not for nothing that the peasant loves me. One must know the peasant! One must know from what —

ANYA: Again, Uncle!

VARYA: You, Uncle dear, keep quiet.

FIERS (*angrily*): Leonid Andreevich!

GAYEFF: I'm coming, I'm coming — Go to bed. A double bank into the side pocket! A clean shot — (*Goes out,* FIERS *hobbling after him.*)

ANYA: I feel easy now. I don't feel like going to Yaroslavl; I don't like Great-aunt, but still I feel easy. Thanks to Uncle. (*Sits down.*)

VARYA: I must get to sleep. I'm going. And there was unpleasantness here during your absence. In the old servants' quarters, as you know, live only the old servants: Yephemushka, Polya, Yevstignay, well, and Karp. They began to let every sort of creature spend the night with them — I didn't say anything. But then I hear they've spread the rumor that I'd given orders to feed them nothing but beans. Out of stinginess, you see — And all that from Yevstignay — Very well, I think to myself. If that's the way it is, I think to myself, then you just wait. I call in Yevstignay — (*Yawning.*) He comes — How is it, I say, that you, Yevstignay — You're such a fool — (*Glancing at* ANYA.) Anitchka! — (*A pause.*) Asleep! (*Takes* ANYA *by her arm.*) Let's go to bed — Come on! — (*Leading her.*) My little darling fell asleep! Come on — (*They go. Far away beyond the orchard a shepherd is playing on a pipe.* TROFIMOFF *walks across the stage and, seeing* VARYA *and* ANYA, *stops.*) Shh — She is asleep — asleep — Let's go, dear.

ANYA (*softly, half dreaming*): I'm so tired — All the bells! — Uncle — dear — And Mama and Uncle — Varya.

VARYA: Come on, my dear, come on. (*They go into* ANYA's *room.*)

TROFIMOFF (*tenderly*): My little sun! My spring!

ACT TWO

(*A field. An old chapel, long abandoned, with crooked walls, near it a well, big stones that apparently were once tombstones, and an old bench. A road to the estate of* GAYEFF *can be seen. On one side poplars rise, casting their shadows, the cherry orchard begins there. In the distance a row of telegraph poles; and far, far away, faintly traced on the horizon, is a large town, visible only in the clearest weather. The sun will soon be down.* CHARLOTTA, YASHA *and* DUNYASHA *are sitting on the bench;* EPIHODOFF *is standing near and playing the guitar; everyone sits lost in thought.* CHARLOTTA *wears an old peak cap* (fourrage); *she has taken a rifle from off her shoulders and is adjusting the buckle on the strap.*)

CHARLOTTA (*pensively*): I have no proper passport, I don't know how old I am — it always seems to me I'm very young. When I was a little girl, my father and mother traveled from fair to fair and gave performances, very good ones. And I did *salto mortale* and different tricks. And when Papa and Mama died, a German lady took me to live with her and began teaching me. Good. I grew up. And became a governess. But where I came from and who am I don't know — Who my parents were, perhaps they weren't even married — I don't know. (*Taking a cucumber out of her pocket and beginning to eat it.*) I don't know a thing. (*A pause.*) I'd like so much to talk but there's not anybody. I haven't anybody.

EPIHODOFF (*playing the guitar and singing*): "What care I for the noisy world, what care I for friends and foes." — How pleasant it is to play the mandolin!

DUNYASHA: That's a guitar, not a mandolin. (*Looking into a little mirror and powdering her face.*)

EPIHODOFF: For a madman who is in love this is a mandolin — (*Singing.*) "If only my heart were warm with the fire of requited love."

(YASHA *sings with him.*)

CHARLOTTA: How dreadfully these people sing — Phooey! Like jackals.

DUNYASHA (*to* YASHA): All the same what happiness to have been abroad.

YASHA: Yes, of course. I cannot disagree with you. (*Yawning and then lighting a cigar.*)

EPIHODOFF: That's easily understood. Abroad everything long since attained its complete development.

YASHA: That's obvious.

EPIHODOFF: I am a cultured man. I read all kinds of remarkable books, but the trouble is I cannot discover my own inclinations, whether to live or to shoot myself, but nevertheless, I always carry a revolver on me. Here it is — (*Showing a revolver.*)

CHARLOTTA: That's done. Now I am going. (*Slinging the rifle over her shoulder.*) You are a very clever man, Epihodoff, and a very terrible one; the women must love you madly. Brrrr-r-r-r! (*Going.*) These clever people are all so silly, I haven't anybody to talk with. I'm always alone, alone, I have nobody and — Who I am, why I am, is unknown — (*Goes out without hurrying.*)

EPIHODOFF: Strictly speaking, not touching on other subjects, I must state about myself, in passing, that fate treats me mercilessly, as a storm does a small ship. If, let us suppose, I am mistaken, then why, to mention one instance, do I wake up this morning, look and there on my chest is a spider of terrific size — There, like that. (*Showing the size with both hands.*) And also I take some kvass to drink and in it I find something in the highest degree indecent, such as a cockroach. (*A pause.*) Have you read Buckle? (*A pause.*) I desire to trouble you, Avdotya Feodorovna, with a couple of words.

DUNYASHA: Speak.

EPIHODOFF: I have a desire to speak with you alone — (*Sighing.*)

DUNYASHA (*embarrassed*): Very well — But bring me my cape first — by the cupboard — It's rather damp here —

EPIHODOFF: Very well — I'll fetch it — Now I know what I should do with my revolver — (*Takes the guitar and goes out playing.*)

YASHA: Twenty-two misfortunes! Between us he's a stupid man, it must be said. (*Yawning.*)

DUNYASHA: God forbid he should shoot himself. (*A pause.*) I've grown so uneasy, I'm always fretting. I was only a girl when I was taken into the master's house, and now I've lost the habit of simple living — and here are my hands white, white as a-lady's. I've become so delicate, fragile, ladylike, afraid of everything — Frightfully so. And, Yasha, if you deceive me, I don't know what will happen to my nerves.

YASHA (*kissing her*): You little cucumber! Of course every girl must behave properly. What I dislike above everything is for a girl to conduct herself badly.

DUNYASHA: I have come to love you passionately, you are educated, you can discuss anything. (*A pause.*)

YASHA (*yawning*): Yes, sir — To my mind it is like this: If a girl loves someone, it means she is immoral. (*A pause.*) It is pleasant to smoke a cigar in the clear air — (*Listening.*) They are coming here — It is the ladies and gentlemen —

(DUNYASHA *impulsively embraces him.*)

YASHA: Go to the house, as though you had been to bathe in the river, go by this path, otherwise, they might meet you and suspect me of making a rendezvous with you. That I cannot tolerate.

DUNYASHA (*with a little cough*): Your cigar has given me the headache. (*Goes out.*)

(YASHA *remains, sitting near the chapel.* LYUBOFF ANDREEVNA, GAYEFF *and* LOPAHIN *enter.*)

LOPAHIN: We must decide definitely, time doesn't wait. Why, the matter's quite simple. Are you willing to lease your land for summer cottages or are you not? Answer in one word, yes or no? Just one word!

LYUBOFF ANDREEVNA: Who is it smokes those disgusting cigars out here — ? (*Sitting down.*)

GAYEFF: The railroad running so near is a great convenience. (*Sitting down.*) We made a trip to town and lunched there — Yellow in the side pocket! Perhaps I should go in the house first and play one game —

LYUBOFF ANDREEVNA: You'll have time.

LOPAHIN: Just one word! (*Imploringly.*) Do give me your answer!

GAYEFF (*yawning*): What?

LYUBOFF ANDREEVNA (*looking in her purse*): Yesterday there was lots of money in it. Today there's very little. My poor Varya! For the sake of economy she feeds everybody milk soup, and in the kitchen the old people get nothing but beans, and here I spend money — senselessly — (*Dropping her purse and scattering gold coins.*) There they go scattering! (*She is vexed.*)

YASHA: Allow me, I'll pick them up in a second. (*Picking up the coins.*)

LYUBOFF ANDREEVNA: If you will, Yasha. And why did I go in town for lunch — ? Your restaurant with its music is trashy, the tablecloths smell of soap — Why drink so much, Lyonya? Why eat so much? Why talk so much? Today in the restaurant you were talking a lot again, and all of it beside the point. About the seventies, about the decadents. And to whom? Talking to waiters about the decadents!

LOPAHIN: Yes.

GAYEFF (*waving his hand*): I am incorrigible, that's evident — (*To* YASHA, *irritably.*) What is it? — You are forever swirling around in front of us!

YASHA (*laughing*): I cannot hear your voice without laughing.

GAYEFF (*to his sister*): Either I or he —

LYUBOFF ANDREEVNA: Go away, Yasha. Go on —

YASHA (*giving* LYUBOFF ANDREEVNA *her purse*): I am going right away. (*Barely suppressing his laughter.*) This minute. (*Goes out.*)

LOPAHIN: The rich Deriganoff intends to buy your estate. They say he is coming personally to the auction.

LYUBOFF ANDREEVNA: And where did you hear that?

LOPAHIN: In town they are saying it.

GAYEFF: Our Yaroslavl aunt promised to send us something, but when and how much she will send, nobody knows —

LOPAHIN: How much will she send? A hundred thousand? Two hundred?

LYUBOFF ANDREEVNA: Well — maybe ten, fifteen thousand — we'd be thankful for that.

LOPAHIN: Excuse me, but such light-minded people as you are, such odd, unbusinesslike people, I never saw. You are told in plain Russian that your estate is being sold up and you just don't seem to take it in.

LYUBOFF ANDREEVNA: But what are we to do? Tell us what?

LOPAHIN: I tell you every day. Every day I tell you the same thing. Both the cherry orchard and the land have got to be leased for summer cottages, it has to be done right now, quick — The auction is right under your noses. Do understand! Once you finally decide that there are to be summer cottages, you will get all the money you want, and then you'll be saved.

LYUBOFF ANDREEVNA: Summer cottages and summer residents — it is so trivial, excuse me.

GAYEFF: I absolutely agree with you.

LOPAHIN: I'll either burst out crying, or scream, or faint. I can't bear it! You are torturing me! (*To* GAYEFF.) You're a perfect old woman!

GAYEFF: What?

LOPAHIN: A perfect old woman! (*About to go.*)

LYUBOFF ANDREEVNA (*alarmed*): No, don't go, stay, my lamb, I beg you. Perhaps we will think of something!

LOPAHIN: What is there to think about?

LYUBOFF ANDREEVNA: Don't go, I beg you. With you here it is more cheerful anyhow — (*A pause.*) I keep waiting for something, as if the house were about to tumble down on our heads.

GAYEFF (*deep in thought*): Double into the corner pocket — Bank into the side pocket —

LYUBOFF ANDREEVNA: We have sinned so much —

LOPAHIN: What sins have you — ?

GAYEFF (*puts a hard candy into his mouth*): They say I've eaten my fortune up in hard candies — (*Laughing.*)

LYUBOFF ANDREEVNA: Oh, my sins — I've always thrown money around like mad, recklessly, and I married a man who accumulated nothing but debts. My husband died from champagne — he drank fearfully — and to my misfortune I fell in love with another man. I lived with him, and just at that time — it was my first punishment — a blow over the head: right here in the river my boy was drowned and I went abroad — went away for good, never to return, never to see this river again — I shut my eyes, ran away, beside myself, and he after me — mercilessly, brutally. I bought a villa near Menton, because he fell ill there, and for three years I knew no rest day or night, the sick man exhausted me, my soul dried up. And last year when the villa was sold for debts, I went to Paris and there he robbed me of everything, threw me over, took up with another woman; I tried to poison myself — so stupid, so shameful — And suddenly I was seized with longing for Russia, for my own country, for my little girl — (*Wiping away her tears.*) Lord, Lord, have mercy, forgive me my sins! Don't punish me any more! (*Getting a telegram out of her pocket.*) I got this today from Paris, he asks forgiveness, begs me to return — (*Tears up the telegram.*) That sounds like music somewhere. (*Listening.*)

GAYEFF: It is our famous Jewish orchestra. You remember, four violins, a flute and double bass.

LYUBOFF ANDREEVNA: Does it still exist? We ought to get hold of it sometime and give a party.

LOPAHIN (*listening*): Can't hear it — (*Singing softly.*) "And for money the Germans will frenchify a Russian." (*Laughing.*) What a play I saw yesterday at the theatre, very funny!

LYUBOFF ANDREEVNA: And most likely there was nothing funny about it. You shouldn't look at plays, but look oftener at yourselves. How gray all your lives are, what a lot of idle things you say!

LOPAHIN: That's true. It must be said frankly this life of ours is idiotic — (*A pause.*) My father was a peasant, an idiot, he understood nothing, he taught me nothing, he just beat me in his drunken fits and always with a stick. At bottom I am just as big a dolt and idiot as he was. I wasn't taught anything, my handwriting is vile, I write like a pig — I am ashamed for people to see it.

LYUBOFF ANDREEVNA: You ought to get married, my friend.

LOPAHIN: Yes — That's true.

LYUBOFF ANDREEVNA: To our Varya, perhaps. She is a good girl.

LOPAHIN: Yes.

LYUBOFF ANDREEVNA: She comes from simple people, and she works all day long, but the main thing is she loves you. And you, too, have liked her a long time.

LOPAHIN: Why not? I am not against it — She's a good girl. (*A pause.*)

GAYEFF: They are offering me a position in a bank. Six thousand a year — Have you heard that?

LYUBOFF ANDREEVNA: Not you! You stay where you are —

FIERS (FIERS *enters, bringing an overcoat. To* GAYEFF): Pray, Sir, put this on, it's damp.

GAYEFF (*putting on the overcoat*): You're a pest, old man.

FIERS: That's all right — This morning you went off without letting me know. (*Looking him over.*)

LYUBOFF ANDREEVNA: How old you've grown, Fiers!

FIERS: At your service.

LOPAHIN: She says you've grown very old!

FIERS: I've lived a long time. They were planning to marry me off before your papa was born. (*Laughing.*) And at the time the serfs were freed I was already the head footman. I didn't want to be freed then, I stayed with the masters — (*A pause.*) And I remember, everybody was happy, but what they were happy about they didn't know themselves.

LOPAHIN: In the old days it was fine. At least they flogged.

FIERS (*not hearing*): But, of course. The peasants stuck to the masters, the masters stuck to the peasants, and now everything is all smashed up, you can't tell about anything.

GAYEFF: Keep still, Fiers. Tomorrow I must go to town. They have promised to introduce me to a certain general who might make us a loan.

LOPAHIN: Nothing will come of it. And you can rest assured you won't pay the interest.

LYUBOFF ANDREEVNA: He's just raving on. There aren't any such generals.

(TROFIMOFF, ANYA *and* VARYA *enter.*)

GAYEFF: Here they come.

ANYA: There is Mama sitting there.

LYUBOFF ANDREEVNA (*tenderly*): Come, come — My darlings — (*Em-*

bracing ANYA *and* VARYA.) If you only knew how I love you both! Come sit by me — there — like that.

(*Everybody sits down.*)

LOPAHIN: Our perennial student is always strolling with the young ladies.

TROFIMOFF: It's none of your business.

LOPAHIN: He will soon be fifty and he's still a student.

TROFIMOFF: Stop your stupid jokes.

LOPAHIN: But why are you so peevish, you queer duck?

TROFIMOFF: Don't you pester me.

LOPAHIN (*laughing*): Permit me to ask you, what do you make of me?

TROFIMOFF: Yermolay Alexeevich, I make this of you: you are a rich man, you'll soon be a millionaire. Just as it is in the metabolism of nature, a wild beast is needed to eat up everything that comes his way; so you, too, are needed.

(*Everyone laughs.*)

VARYA: Petya, you'd better tell us about the planets.

LYUBOFF ANDREEVNA: No, let's go on with yesterday's conversation.

TROFIMOFF: What was it about?

GAYEFF: About the proud man.

TROFIMOFF: We talked a long time yesterday, but didn't get anywhere. In a proud man, in your sense of the word, there is something mystical. Maybe you are right, from your standpoint, but if we are to discuss it in simple terms, without whimsy, then what pride can there be, is there any sense in it, if man physiologically is poorly constructed, if in the great majority he is crude, unintelligent, profoundly miserable. One must stop admiring oneself. One must only work.

GAYEFF: All the same, you will die.

TROFIMOFF: Who knows? And what does it mean — you will die? Man may have a hundred senses, and when he dies only the five that are known to us may perish, and the remaining ninety-five go on living.

LYUBOFF ANDREEVNA: How clever you are, Petya!

LOPAHIN (*ironically*): Terribly!

TROFIMOFF: Humanity goes forward, perfecting its powers. Everything that's unattainable now will some day become familiar, understandable; it is only that one must work and must help with all one's might those who seek the truth. With us in Russia so far only a very few work. The great majority of the intelligentsia that I know are looking for nothing, doing nothing, and as yet have no capacity for work. They call themselves intelligentsia, are free and easy with the servants, treat the peasants like animals, educate themselves poorly, read nothing seriously, do absolutely nothing; about science they just talk and about art they understand very little. Every one of them is serious, all have stern faces; they all talk of nothing but important things, philosophize, and all the time everybody can see that the workmen eat abominably, sleep without any pillows, thirty or forty to a room, and everywhere there are bedbugs, stench, dampness, moral uncleanness — And apparently with us, all the fine talk is only to divert the attention of ourselves and of others. Show me where we have the day nurseries they are always talking so much about, where are the reading rooms? They only write of these in novels, for the truth is there are not any at all. There is only filth, vulgarity, orientalism — I am afraid of very serious faces and dislike them. I'm afraid of serious conversations. Rather than that let's just keep still.

LOPAHIN: You know I get up before five o'clock in the morning and work from morning till night. Well, I always have money, my own and other people's, on hand, and I see what the people around me are. One has only to start doing something to find out how few honest and decent people there are. At times when I can't go to sleep, I think: Lord, thou gavest us immense forests, unbounded fields and the widest horizons, and living in the midst of them we should indeed be giants —

LYUBOFF ANDREEVNA: You feel the need for giants — They are good only in fairy tales, anywhere else they only frighten us.

(At the back of the stage EPIHODOFF passes by, playing the guitar.)

LYUBOFF ANDREEVNA (*lost in thought*): Epihodoff is coming —

ANYA (*lost in thought*): Epihodoff is coming.

GAYEFF: The sun has set, ladies and gentlemen.

TROFIMOFF: Yes.

GAYEFF (*not loud and as if he were declaiming*): Oh, Nature, wonderful, you gleam with eternal radiance, beautiful and indifferent, you, whom we call Mother, combine in yourself both life and death, you give life and you take it away.

VARYA (*beseechingly*): Uncle!

ANYA: Uncle, you're doing it again!

TROFIMOFF: You'd better bank the yellow into the side pocket.

GAYEFF: I'll be quiet, quiet.

(All sit absorbed in their thoughts. There is only the silence. FIERS is heard muttering to himself softly. Suddenly a distant *sound is heard, as if from the sky, like the sound of a snapped string, dying away, mournful.*)

LYUBOFF ANDREEVNA: What's that?

LOPAHIN: I don't know. Somewhere far off in a mine shaft a bucket fell. But somewhere very far off.

GAYEFF: And it may be some bird — like a heron.

TROFIMOFF: Or an owl —

LYUBOFF ANDREEVNA (*shivering*): It's unpleasant, somehow. (*A pause.*)

FIERS: Before the disaster it was like that. The owl hooted and the samovar hummed without stopping, both.

GAYEFF: Before what disaster?

FIERS: Before the emancipation. (*A pause.*)

LYUBOFF ANDREEVNA: You know, my friends, let's go. Twilight is falling. (*To* ANYA.) You have tears in your eyes — What is it, my dear little girl? (*Embracing her.*)

ANYA: It's just that, Mama. It's nothing.

TROFIMOFF: Somebody is coming.

(*A* STRANGER *appears in a shabby white cap, and an overcoat; he is a little drunk.*)

THE STRANGER: Allow me to ask you, can I go straight through here to the station?

GAYEFF: You can. Go by that road.

THE STRANGER: I am heartily grateful to you. (*Coughing.*) The weather is splendid — (*Declaiming.*) Brother of mine, suffering brother — Go out to the Volga, whose moans — (*To* VARYA.) Mademoiselle, grant a hungry Russian man some thirty kopecks —

(VARYA *is frightened and gives a shriek.*)

LOPAHIN (*angrily*): There's a limit to everything.

LYUBOFF ANDREEVNA (*flustered*): Take this — Here's this for you — (*Searching in her purse.*) No silver — It's all the same, here's a gold piece for you —

THE STRANGER: I am heartily grateful to you. (*Goes out. Laughter.*)

VARYA (*frightened*): I'm going — I'm going — Oh, Mama, you poor little Mama! There's nothing in the house for people to eat, and you gave him a gold piece.

LYUBOFF ANDREEVNA: What is to be done with me, so silly? I shall give you all I have in the house. Yermolay Alexeevich, you will lend me some this once more! —

LOPAHIN: Agreed.

LYUBOFF ANDREEVNA: Let's go, ladies and gentlemen, it's time. And here, Varya, we have definitely made a match for you, I congratulate you.

VARYA (*through her tears*): Mama, that's not something to joke about.

LOPAHIN: Achmelia, get thee to a nunnery.

GAYEFF: And my hands are trembling; it is a long time since I have played billiards.

LOPAHIN: Achmelia, oh nymph, in thine orisons be all my sins remember'd —

LYUBOFF ANDREEVNA: Let's go, my dear friends, it will soon be supper-time.

VARYA: He frightened me. My heart is thumping so!

LOPAHIN: I remind you, ladies and gentlemen: August twenty-second the cherry orchard will be auctioned off. Think about that! — Think! —

(*All go out except* TROFIMOFF *and* ANYA.)

ANYA (*laughing*): My thanks to the stranger, he frightened Varya, now we are alone.

TROFIMOFF: Varya is afraid we might begin to love each other and all day long she won't leave us to ourselves. With her narrow mind she cannot understand that we are above love. To sidestep the petty and illusory, which prevent our being free and happy, that is the aim and meaning of our life. Forward! We march on irresistibly toward the bright star that burns there in the distance. Forward! Do not fall behind, friends!

ANYA (*extending her arms upward*): How well you talk! (*A pause.*) It's wonderful here today!

TROFIMOFF: Yes, the weather is marvelous.

ANYA: What have you done to me, Petya, why don't I love the cherry orchard any longer the way I used to? I loved it so tenderly, it seemed to me there was not a better place on earth than our orchard.

TROFIMOFF: All Russia is our orchard. The earth is immense and beautiful, and on it are many wonderful places. (*A pause.*) Just think, Anya: your grandfather, great-grandfather and all your ancestors were slave owners, in possession of living souls, and can you doubt that from every cherry in the orchard, from every leaf, from every trunk, human beings are looking at you, can it be that you don't hear their voices? To possess living souls, well, that depraved all of you who lived before and who are living now, so that your mother and you, and your uncle no longer notice that you live by debt, at somebody else's expense, at the expense of those very people whom you wouldn't let past your front door — We are at least two hundred years behind the times, we have as yet absolutely nothing, we have no definite attitude toward the past, we only philosophize, complain of our sadness or drink vodka. Why, it is quite clear that to begin to live in the present we must first atone for our past, must be done with it; and we can atone for it only through suffering, only through uncommon, incessant labor. Understand that, Anya.

ANYA: The house we live in ceased to be ours long ago, and I'll go away, I give you my word.

TROFIMOFF: If you have the household keys, throw them in the well and go away. Be free as the wind.

ANYA (*transported*): How well you said that!

TROFIMOFF: Believe me, Anya, believe me! I am not thirty yet, I am young, I am still a student, but I have already borne so much! Every winter I am hungry, sick, anxious, poor as a beggar, and — where has destiny not chased me, where haven't I been! And yet, my soul has always, every minute, day and night, been full of inexplicable premonitions. I have a premonition of happiness, Anya, I see it already —

ANYA (*pensively*): The moon is rising.

(EPIHODOFF *is heard playing on the guitar, always the same sad song. The moon rises. Somewhere near the poplars* VARYA *is looking for* ANYA *and calling:* "Anya! Where are you?")

TROFIMOFF: Yes, the moon is rising. (*A pause.*) Here is happiness, here it comes, comes always nearer and nearer, I hear its footsteps now. And if we shall not see it, shall not come to know it, what does that matter? Others will see it!

VARYA (*off*): Anya! Where are you?

TROFIMOFF: Again, that Varya! (*Angrily.*) It's scandalous!

ANYA: Well, let's go to the river. It's lovely there.

TROFIMOFF: Let's go. (*They go out.*)

VARYA (*off*): Anya! Anya!

ACT THREE

(*The drawing room, separated by an arch from the ballroom. A chandelier is lighted. A Jewish orchestra is playing — the same that was mentioned in Act Two. Evening. In the ballroom they are dancing grand rond. The voice of* SEMYONOFF-PISHTCHIK: "Promenade à une paire!" *They enter the drawing room; in the first couple are* PISHTCHIK *and* CHARLOTTA IVANOVNA; *in the second,* TROFIMOFF *and* LYUBOFF ANDREEVNA; *in the third,* ANYA *with the* POST-OFFICE CLERK; *in the fourth,* VARYA *with the* STA-

TIONMASTER, *et cetera* — VARYA *is crying softly and wipes away her tears while she is dancing.* DUNYASHA *is in the last couple through the drawing room,* PISHTCHIK *shouts: "Grand rond, balancez!" and "Les Cavaliers à genoux et remerciez vos dames!"*

FIERS *in a frock coat goes by with seltzer water on a tray.* PISHTCHIK *and* TROFIMOFF *come into the drawing room.*)

PISHTCHIK: I am full-blooded, I have had two strokes already, and dancing is hard for me, but as they say, if you are in a pack of dogs, you may bark and bark, but you must still wag your tail. At that, I have the health of a horse. My dear father — he was a great joker — may he dwell in Heaven — used to talk as if our ancient line, the Semyonoff-Pishtchiks, were descended from the very horse that Caligula made a Senator — (*Sitting down.*) But here's my trouble: I haven't any money. A hungry dog believes in nothing but meat — (*Snoring but waking at once.*) And the same way with me — I can't talk about anything but money.

TROFIMOFF: Well, to tell you the truth, there is something of a horse about your figure.

PISHTCHIK: Well — a horse is a fine animal — You can sell a horse —

(*The sound of playing billiards comes from the next room.* VARYA *appears under the arch to the ballroom.*)

TROFIMOFF (*teasing*): Madam Lopahin! Madam Lopahin!

VARYA (*angrily*): A mangy-looking gentleman!

TROFIMOFF: Yes, I am a mangy-looking gentleman, and proud of it!

VARYA (*in bitter thought*): Here we have gone and hired musicians and what are we going to pay them with? (*Goes out.*)

TROFIMOFF (*to* PISHTCHIK): If the energy you have wasted in the course of your life trying to find money to pay the interest had gone into something else, you could very likely have turned the world upside down before you were done with it.

PISHTCHIK: Nietzsche — the philosopher — the greatest — the most celebrated — a man of tremendous mind — says in his works that one may make counterfeit money.

TROFIMOFF: And have you read Nietzsche?

PISHTCHIK: Well — Dashenka told me. And I'm in such a state now that I could make counterfeit money myself — Day after tomorrow three hundred and ten roubles must be paid — one hundred and thirty I've on hand — (*Feeling in his pockets, alarmed.*) The money is gone! I have lost the money! (*Tearfully.*) Where is the money? (*Joyfully.*) Here it is, inside the lining — I was in quite a sweat —

(LYUBOFF ANDREEVNA *and* CHARLOTTA IVANOVNA *come in.*)

LYUBOFF ANDREEVNA (*humming lazginka, a Georgian dance*): Why does Leonid take so long? What's he doing in town? (*To* DUNYASHA.) Dunyasha, offer the musicians some tea —

TROFIMOFF: In all probability the auction did not take place.

LYUBOFF ANDREEVNA: And the musicians came at an unfortunate moment and we planned the ball at an unfortunate moment — Well, it doesn't matter. (*Sitting down and singing softly.*)

CHARLOTTA (*gives* PISHTCHIK *a deck of cards*): Here is a deck of cards for you, think of some one card.

PISHTCHIK: I have thought of one.

CHARLOTTA: Now, shuffle the deck. Very good. Hand it here; oh, my dear Monsieur Pishtchik. *Ein, zwei, drei!* Now look for it, it's in your coat pocket —

PISHTCHIK (*getting a card out of his coat pocket*): The Eight of Spades, that's absolutely right! (*Amazed.*) Fancy that!

CHARLOTTA (*holding a deck of cards in her palm; to* TROFIMOFF): Tell me quick now, which card is on top?

TROFIMOFF: What is it? Well — the Queen of Spades.

CHARLOTTA: Right! (*To* PISHTCHIK.) Well? Which card's on top?

PISHTCHIK: The Ace of Hearts.

CHARLOTTA: Right! (*Strikes the deck against her palm; the deck of cards disappears.*) And what beautiful weather we are having today!

(*A mysterious feminine voice answers her, as if from under the floor: "Oh, yes. The weather is splendid, madame." "You are so nice, you're my ideal —" The voice: "Madame, you too please me greatly."*)

THE STATIONMASTER (*applauding*): Madam Ventriloquist, bravo!

PISHTCHIK (*amazed*): Fancy that! Most charming Charlotta Ivanovna — I am simply in love with you.

CHARLOTTA: In love? (*Shrugging her shoulders.*) Is it possible that you can love? *Guter menschaber schlachter musikant.*

TROFIMOFF (*slapping* PISHTCHIK *on the shoulder*): You horse, you —

CHARLOTTA: I beg your attention, one more trick. (*Taking a lap robe from the chair.*) Here is a very fine lap robe — I want to sell it — (*Shaking it out.*) Wouldn't somebody like to buy it?

PISHTCHIK (*amazed*): Fancy that!

CHARLOTTA: *Ein, zwei, drei!*

(*She quickly raises the lowered robe, behind it stands* ANYA, *who curtseys, runs to her mother, embraces her and runs back into the ballroom amid the general delight.*)

LYUBOFF ANDREEVNA (*applauding*): Bravo, bravo — !

CHARLOTTA: Now again! *Ein, zwei, drei!*

(*Lifting the robe: behind it stands* VARYA, *she bows.*)

PISHTCHIK (*amazed*): Fancy that!

CHARLOTTA: That's all. (*Throwing the robe at* PISHTCHIK, *curtseying and running into the ballroom.*)

PISHTCHIK (*hurrying after her*): You little rascal — What a girl! What a girl! (*Goes out.*)

LYUBOFF ANDREEVNA: And Leonid is not here yet. What he's doing in town so long, I don't understand! Everything is finished there, either the estate is sold by now, or the auction didn't take place. Why keep it from us so long?

VARYA (*trying to comfort her*): Uncle has bought it, I am sure of that.

TROFIMOFF (*mockingly*): Yes.

VARYA: Great-aunt sent him power of attorney to buy it in her name and transfer the debt. She did this for Anya. And I feel certain, God willing, that Uncle will buy it.

LYUBOFF ANDREEVNA: Our Yaroslavl great-aunt has sent fifteen thousand to buy the estate in her name — She doesn't trust us, but that wouldn't be enough to pay the interest even — (*Covering her face with her hands.*) Today my fate will be decided, my fate —

TROFIMOFF (*teasing* VARYA): Madam Lopahin!

VARYA (*angrily*): Perennial student! You have already been expelled from the University twice.

LYUBOFF ANDREEVNA: But why are you angry, Varya? He teases you about Lopahin, what of it? Marry Lopahin if you want to, he is a good man, interesting. If you don't want to, don't marry him; darling, nobody is making you do it.

VARYA: I look at this matter seriously, Mama, one must speak straight out. He's a good man, I like him.

LYUBOFF ANDREEVNA: Then marry him. What there is to wait for I don't understand!

VARYA: But I can't propose to him myself, Mama. It's two years now; everyone has been talking to me about him, everyone talks, and he either remains silent or jokes. I understand. He's getting rich, he's busy with his own affairs, and has no time for me. If there were money, ever so little, even a hundred roubles, I would drop everything, and go far away. I'd go to a nunnery.

TROFIMOFF: How saintly!

VARYA (*to* TROFIMOFF): A student should be intelligent! (*In a low voice, tearfully.*) How homely you have grown, Petya, how old you've got. (*To* LYUBOFF ANDREEVNA, *no longer crying.*) It is just that I can't live without working, Mama. I must be doing something every minute.

YASHA (YASHA *enters. Barely restraining his laughter.*): Epihodoff has broken a billiard cue! — (*Goes out.*)

VARYA: But why is Epihodoff here? Who allowed him to play billiards? I don't understand these people — (*Goes out.*)

LYUBOFF ANDREEVNA: Don't tease her, Petya; you can see she has troubles enough without that.

TROFIMOFF: She is just too zealous. Sticking her nose into things that are none of her business. All summer she gave us no peace, neither me nor Anya; she was afraid a romance would spring up between us. What business is that of hers? And besides I haven't shown any signs of it. I am so remote from triviality. We are above love!

LYUBOFF ANDREEVNA: Well, then, I must be beneath love. (*Very anxiously.*) Why isn't Leonid here? Just to tell us whether the estate is sold or not? Calamity seems to me so incredible that I don't know what to think, I'm lost — I could scream this minute — I could do something insane. Save me, Petya. Say something, do say. . . .

TROFIMOFF: Whether the estate is sold today or is not sold — is it not the same? There is no turning back, the path is all grown over. Calm yourself, my dear, all that was over long ago. One mustn't deceive oneself, one must for once at least in one's life look truth straight in the eye.

LYUBOFF ANDREEVNA: What truth? You see where the truth is and where the untruth is, but as for me, it's as if I had lost my sight, I see nothing. You boldly decide all important questions, but tell me, my dear boy, isn't that because you are young and haven't had time yet to suffer through any one of your problems? You look boldly ahead, and isn't that because you don't see and don't expect anything terrible, since life is still hidden from your young eyes? You are braver, more honest, more profound than we are, but stop and think, be magnanimous, have a little mercy on me, just a little. Why, I was born here. My father and mother lived here and my grandfather. I love this house, I can't imagine my life without the cherry orchard and if it is very necessary to sell it, then sell me along with the orchard — (*Embracing* TROFIMOFF *and kissing him on the forehead.*) Why, my son was drowned here — (*Crying.*) Have mercy on me, good, kind man.

TROFIMOFF: You know I sympathize with you from the bottom of my heart.

LYUBOFF ANDREEVNA: But that should be said differently, differently — (*Taking out her handkerchief; a telegram falls on the floor.*) My heart is heavy today, you can't imagine how heavy. It is too noisy for me here, my soul trembles at every sound, I tremble all over and yet I can't go off to myself, when I am alone the silence frightens me. Don't blame me, Petya — I love you as one of my own. I should gladly have given you Anya's hand, I assure you, only, my dear, you must study and finish your course. You do nothing. Fate simply flings you about from place to place, and that's so strange — Isn't that so? Yes? And you must do something about your beard, to make it grow somehow — (*Laughing.*) You look funny!

TROFIMOFF (*picking up the telegram*): I do not desire to be beautiful.

LYUBOFF ANDREEVNA: This telegram is from Paris. I get one every day. Yesterday and today too. That wild man has fallen ill again, something is wrong again with him — He asks forgiveness, begs me to come, and really I ought to make a trip to Paris and stay awhile near him. Your face looks stern, Petya, but what is there to do, my dear, what am I to do, he is ill, he is alone, unhappy and who will look after him there, who will keep him from doing the wrong thing, who will give him his medicine on time? And what is there to hide or keep still about? I love him, that's plain. I love him, love him — It's a stone about my neck, I'm sinking to the bottom with it, but I love that stone and live without it I cannot. (*Pressing* TROFIMOFF's *hand.*) Don't think harshly of me, Petya, don't say anything to me, don't —

TROFIMOFF (*tearfully*): Forgive my frankness, for God's sake! Why, he picked your bones.

LYUBOFF ANDREEVNA: No, no, no, you must not talk like that. (*Stopping her ears.*)

TROFIMOFF: But he is a scoundrel, only you, you are the only one that doesn't know it. He is a petty scoundrel, a nonentity —

LYUBOFF ANDREEVNA (*angry but controlling herself*): You are twenty-six years old or twenty-seven, but you are still a schoolboy in the second grade!

TROFIMOFF: Very well!

LYUBOFF ANDREEVNA: You should be a man — at your age you should understand people who love. And you yourself should love someone — you should fall in love! (*Angrily.*) Yes, yes! And there is no purity in you; you are simply smug, a ridiculous crank, a freak —

TROFIMOFF (*horrified*): What is she saying!

LYUBOFF ANDREEVNA: "I am above love!" You are not above love, Petya, you are, as our Fiers would say, just a good-for-nothing. Imagine, at your age, not having a mistress — !

TROFIMOFF (*horrified*): This is terrible! What is she saying! (*Goes *quickly into the ballroom, clutching his head.*) This is horrible — I can't bear it, I am going — (*Goes out but immediately returns.*) All is over between us. (*Goes out into the hall.*)

LYUBOFF ANDREEVNA (*shouting after him*): Petya, wait! You funny creature, I was joking! Petya! (*In the hall you hear someone running up the stairs and suddenly falling back down with a crash. You hear* ANYA *and* VARYA *scream but immediately you hear laughter.*) What's that?

ANYA (ANYA *runs in. Laughing*): Petya fell down the stairs! (*Runs out.*)

LYUBOFF ANDREEVNA: What a funny boy that Petya is — ! (*The* STA-TIONMASTER *stops in the center of the ballroom and begins to recite* "The Sinner" *by A. Tolstoi. They listen to him but he has recited only a few lines when the strains of a waltz are heard from the hall and the recitation is broken off. They all dance.* TROFIMOFF, ANYA, VARYA *and* LYUBOFF ANDREEVNA *come in from the hall.*) But, Petya — but, dear soul — I beg your forgiveness — Let's go dance. (*She dances with* TROFIMOFF. ANYA *and* VARYA *dance.* FIERS *enters, leaving his stick by the side door.* YASHA *also comes into the drawing room and watches the dancers.*)

YASHA: What is it, Grandpa?

FIERS: I don't feel very well. In the old days there were generals, barons, admirals dancing at our parties, and now we send for the post-office clerk and the stationmaster, and even they are none too anxious to come. Somehow I've grown feeble. The old master, the grandfather, treated everybody with sealing-wax for all sicknesses. I take sealing-wax every day, have done so for twenty-odd years or more; it may be due to that that I'm alive.

YASHA: You are tiresome, Grandpa. (*Yawning.*) Why don't you go off and die?

FIERS: Aw, you — good-for-nothing! — (*Muttering.*)

(TROFIMOFF *and* LYUBOFF ANDREEVNA *dance in the ballroom and then in the drawing room.*)

LYUBOFF ANDREEVNA: Merci. I'll sit down awhile — (*Sitting down.*) I'm tired.

ANYA (ANYA *enters. Agitated*): And just now in the kitchen some man was saying that the cherry orchard had been sold today.

LYUBOFF ANDREEVNA: Sold to whom?

ANYA: He didn't say who to. He's gone.

(*Dancing with* TROFIMOFF, *they pass into the ballroom.*)

YASHA: It was some old man babbling there. A stranger.

FIERS: And Leonid Andreevich is still not here, he has not arrived. The overcoat he has on is light, midseason — let's hope he won't catch cold. Ach, these young things!

LYUBOFF ANDREEVNA: I shall die this minute. Go, Yasha, find out who it was sold to.

YASHA: But he's been gone a long time, the old fellow. (*Laughing.*)

LYUBOFF ANDREEVNA (*with some annoyance*): Well, what are you laughing at? What are you so amused at?

YASHA: Epihodoff is just too funny. An empty-headed man. Twenty-two misfortunes!

LYUBOFF ANDREEVNA: Fiers, if the estate is sold, where will you go?

FIERS: Wherever you say, there I'll go.

LYUBOFF ANDREEVNA: Why do you look like that? Aren't you well? You know you ought to go to bed —

FIERS: Yes — (*With a sneer.*) I go to bed and without me who's going to serve, who'll take care of things? I'm the only one in the whole house.

YASHA (*to* LYUBOFF ANDREEVNA): Lyuboff Andreevna, let me ask a favor of you, do be so kind! If you ever go back to Paris, take me with you, please do! It's impossible for me to stay here. (*Looking around him, and speaking in a low voice.*) Why talk about it? You can see for yourself it's an uncivilized country, an immoral people and not only that, there's the boredom of it. The food they give us in that kitchen is abominable and there's that Fiers, too, walking about and muttering all kinds of words that are out of place. Take me with you, be so kind!

PISHTCHIK (*enters*): Allow me to ask you — for a little waltz, most beautiful lady — (LYUBOFF ANDREEVNA *goes with him.*) Charming lady, I must borrow a hundred and eighty roubles from you — will borrow — (*dancing*) a hundred and eighty roubles — (*They pass into the ballroom.*)

YASHA (*singing low*): "Wilt thou know the unrest in my soul!"

(*In the ballroom a figure in a gray top hat and checked trousers waves both hands and jumps about; there are shouts of "Bravo, Charlotta Ivanovna!"*)

DUNYASHA (*stopping to powder her face*): The young lady orders me to dance — there are a lot of gentlemen and very few ladies — but dancing makes my head swim and my heart thump. Fiers Nikolae-vich, the post-office clerk said something to me just now that took my breath away.

(*The music plays more softly.*)

FIERS: What did he say to you?

DUNYASHA: You are like a flower, he says.

YASHA (*yawning*): What ignorance — ! (*Goes out.*)

DUNYASHA: Like a flower — I am such a sensitive girl, I love tender words awfully.

FIERS: You'll be getting your head turned.

(EPIHODOFF *enters.*)

EPIHODOFF: Avdotya Feodorovna, you don't want to see me — It's as if I were some sort of insect. (*Sighing.*) Ach, life!

DUNYASHA: What do you want?

EPIHODOFF: Undoubtedly you may be right. (*Sighing.*) But of course, if one considers it from a given point of view, then you, I will allow myself so to express it, forgive my frankness, absolutely led me into a state of mind. I know my fate, every day some misfortune happens to me, but I have long since become accustomed to that, and so I look on my misfortunes with a smile. You gave me your word and, although I —

DUNYASHA: I beg you, we'll talk later on, but leave me now in peace. I'm in a dream now. (*Playing with her fan.*)

EPIHODOFF: I have a something wrong happens every day — I will allow myself so to express it — I just smile, I even laugh.

VARYA (*enters from the ballroom*): You are not gone yet, Semyon? What a really disrespectful man you are! (*To* DUNYASHA.) Get out of here, Dunyasha. (*To* EPIHODOFF.) You either play billiards and break a cue or you walk about the drawing room like a guest.

EPIHODOFF: Allow me to tell you, you cannot make any demands on me.

VARYA: I'm not making any demands on you, I'm talking to you. All you know is to walk from place to place but not do any work. We keep a clerk, but what for, nobody knows.

EPIHODOFF (*offended*): Whether I work, whether I walk, whether I eat, or whether I play billiards are matters to be discussed only by people of understanding and my seniors.

VARYA: You dare to say that to me! (*Flying into a temper.*) You dare? So I don't understand anything? Get out of here! This minute!

EPIHODOFF (*alarmed*): I beg you to express yourself in a delicate manner.

VARYA (*beside herself*): This very minute, get out of here! Get out! (*He goes to the door; she follows him.*) Twenty-two misfortunes! Don't you dare breathe in here! Don't let mè set eyes on you! (EPIHODOFF *has gone out, but his voice comes from outside the door:* "I shall complain about you.") Ah, you are coming back? (*Grabbing the stick that* FIERS *put by the door.*) Come on, come —

come on, I'll show you — Ah, you are coming? You are coming? Take that then — !

(*She swings the stick, at the very moment when* LOPAHIN *is coming in.*)

LOPAHIN: Most humbly, I thank you.

VARYA (*angrily and ironically*): I beg your pardon!

LOPAHIN: It's nothing at all. I humbly thank you for the pleasant treat.

VARYA: It isn't worth your thanks. (*Moving away, then looking back and asking gently.*) I haven't hurt you?

LOPAHIN: No, it's nothing. There's a great bump coming though.

(*Voices in the balllroom:* "Lopahin has come back." "Yermolay Alexeevich!")

PISHTCHIK (*enters*): See what we see, hear what we hear — ! (*He and* LOPAHIN *kiss one another.*) You smell slightly of cognac, my dear, my good old chap. And we are amusing ourselves here too.

LYUBOFF ANDREEVNA (*enters*): It that you, Yermolay Alexeevich? Why were you so long? Where is Leonid?

LOPAHIN: Leonid Andreevich got back when I did, he's coming.

LYUBOFF ANDREEVNA (*agitated*): Well, what? Was there an auction? Do speak!

LOPAHIN (*embarrassed, afraid of showing the joy he feels*): The auction was over by four o'clock — We were late for the train, had to wait till half-past nine. (*Sighing heavily.*) Ugh, my head's swimming a bit!

(GAYEFF *enters; with his right hand he carries his purchases, with his left he wipes away his tears.*)

LYUBOFF ANDREEVNA: Lyona, what? Lyona, eh? (*Impatiently, with tears in her eyes.*) Quick, for God's sake —

GAYEFF (*not answering her, merely waving his hand; to* FIERS, *crying*): Here, take it — There are anchovies, some Kertch herrings — I haven't eaten anything all day — What I have suffered! (*The door into the billiard room is open; you hear the balls clicking and* YASHA'S *voice:* "Seven and eighteen!" GAYEFF'S *expression changes, he is no longer crying.*) I'm terribly tired. You help me change, Fiers. (*Goes to his room through the ballroom,* FIERS *behind him.*)

PISHTCHIK: What happened at the auction? Go on, tell us!

LYUBOFF ANDREEVNA: Is the cherry orchard sold?

LOPAHIN: It's sold.

LYUBOFF ANDREEVNA: Who bought it?

LOPAHIN: I bought it. (*A pause.* LYUBOFF ANDREEVNA *is overcome. She would have fallen had she not been standing near the chair and table.* VARYA *takes the keys from her belt, throws them on the floor in the middle of the drawing room and goes out.*) I bought it. Kindly wait a moment, ladies and gentlemen, everything is muddled up in my head, I can't speak — (*Laughing.*) We arrived at the auction, Deriganoff was already there. Leonid Andreevich had only fifteen thousand and Deriganoff right off bids thirty over and above indebtedness. I see how things are, I match him with forty thousand. He forty-five. I fifty-five. That is to say he raises it by fives, I by tens — So it ended. Over and above the indebtedness, I bid up to ninety thousand, it was knocked down to me. The cherry orchard is mine now. Mine! (*Guffawing.*) My God, Lord, the cherry orchard is mine! Tell me I'm drunk, out of my head, that I'm imagining all this — (*Stamps his feet.*) Don't laugh at me! If only my father and grandfather could rise from their graves and see this whole business, see how their Yermolay, beaten, half-illiterate Yermolay, who used to run around barefoot in winter, how that very Yermolay has bought an estate that nothing in the world can beat. I bought the estate where grandfather and father were slaves, where you wouldn't even let me in the kitchen. I am asleep, it's only some dream of mine, it only seems so to me — That's nothing but the fruit of your imagination, covered with the darkness of the unknown — (*Picking up the keys, with a gentle smile.*) She threw down the keys, wants to show she is not mistress any more — (*Jingling the keys.*) Well, it's all the same. (*The orchestra is heard tuning up.*) Hey, musicians, play, I want to hear you! Come on, everybody, and see how Yermolay Lopahin will swing the ax in the cherry orchard, how the trees will fall to the ground! We are going to build villas and our grandsons and great-grandsons will see a new life here — Music, play! (*The music is playing.* LYUBOFF ANDREEVNA *has sunk into a chair, crying bitterly.* LOPAHIN *reproachfully.*) Why, then, didn't you listen to me? My poor dear, it can't be undone now. (*With tears.*) Oh, if this could all be over soon, if somehow our awkward, unhappy life would be changed!

PISHTCHIK (*taking him by the arm, in a low voice*): She is crying. Come on in the ballroom, let her be by herself — Come on — (*Taking him by the arm and leading him into the ballroom.*)

LOPAHIN: What's the matter? Music, there, play up! (*Sarcastically.*) Everything is to be as I want it! Here comes the new squire, the owner of the cherry orchard. (*Quite accidentally, he bumps into the little table, and very nearly upsets the candelabra.*) I can pay for everything!

(*Goes out with* PISHTCHIK. *There is nobody left either in the ball-room or the drawing room but* LYUBOFF ANDREEVNA, *who sits all huddled up and crying bitterly. The music plays softly.* ANYA *and* TROFIMOFF *enter hurriedly.* ANYA *comes up to her mother and kneels in front of her.* TROFIMOFF *remains at the ballroom door.*)

ANYA: Mama — ! Mama, you are crying? My dear, kind, good Mama, my beautiful, I love you — I bless you. The cherry orchard is sold, it's not ours any more, that's true, true; but don't cry, Mama, you've your life still left you, you've your good, pure heart ahead of you — Come with me, come on, darling, away from here, come on — We will plant a new orchard, finer than this one, you'll see it, you'll understand; and joy, quiet, deep joy will sink into your heart, like the sun at evening, and you'll smile, Mama! Come, darling, come on!

ACT FOUR

(*The same setting as in Act One. There are neither curtains on the windows nor are there any pictures on the walls. Only a little furniture remains piled up in one corner as if for sale. A sense of emptiness is felt. Near the outer door, at the rear of the stage, is a pile of suitcases, traveling bags, and so on. The door on the left is open, and through it* VARYA'S *and* ANYA'S *voices are heard.* LOPAHIN *is standing waiting.* YASHA *is holding a tray with glasses of champagne. In the hall* EPIHODOFF *is tying up a box, offstage at the rear there is a hum. It is the peasants who have come to say good-by.* GAYEFF'S *voice: "Thanks, brothers, thank you."*)

YASHA: The simple folk have come to say good-by. I am of the opinion, Yermolay Alexeevich, that the people are kind enough but don't understand anything.

(*The hum subsides.* LYUBOFF ANDREEVNA *enters through the hall with* GAYEFF; *she is not crying, but is pale, her face quivers, she is not able to speak.*)

GAYEFF: You gave them your purse, Lyuba. Mustn't do that! Mustn't do that!

LYUBOFF ANDREEVNA: I couldn't help it! I couldn't help it!

(*Both go out.*)

LOPAHIN (*calling through the door after them*): Please, I humbly beg you! A little glass at parting. I didn't think to bring some from town, and at the station I found just one bottle. Please! (*A pause.*) Well, then, ladies and gentlemen! You don't want it? (*Moving away from the door.*) If I'd known that, I wouldn't have bought it. Well, then I won't drink any either. (YASHA *carefully sets the tray down on a chair.*) At least, you have some, Yasha.

YASHA: To those who are departing! Pleasant days to those who stay behind! (*Drinking.*) This champagne is not the real stuff, I can assure you.

LOPAHIN: Eight roubles a bottle. (*A pause.*) It's devilish cold in here.

YASHA: They didn't heat up today, we are leaving anyway. (*Laughing.*)

LOPAHIN: What are you laughing about?

YASHA: For joy.

LOPAHIN: Outside it's October, but it's sunny and still, like summer. Good for building. (*Looking at his watch, then through the door.*) Ladies and gentlemen, bear in mind we have forty-six minutes in all till train time! Which means you have to go to the station in twenty minutes. Hurry up a little.

TROFIMOFF (*in an overcoat, entering from outside*): Seems to me it is time to go. The carriages are ready. The devil knows where my rubbers are. They've disappeared. (*In the door.*) Anya, my rubbers are not here! I can't find them.

LOPAHIN: And I have to go to Harkoff. I'm going on the same train with you. I'm going to live in Harkoff all winter. I've been dilly-dallying along with you, I'm tired of doing nothing. I can't be without work, look, I don't know what to do with my hands here, see, they are dangling somehow, as if they didn't belong to me.

TROFIMOFF: We are leaving right away, and you'll set about your useful labors again.

LOPAHIN: Here, drink a glass.

TROFIMOFF: I shan't.

LOPAHIN: It's to Moscow now?

TROFIMOFF: Yes. I'll see them off to town, and tomorrow to Moscow.

LOPAHIN: Yes — Maybe the professors are not giving their lectures. I imagine they are waiting till you arrive.

TROFIMOFF: That's none of your business.

LOPAHIN: How many years is it you've been studying at the University?

TROFIMOFF: Think of something newer. This is old and flat. (*Looking for his rubbers.*) You know, perhaps, we shall not see each other again; therefore, permit me to give you one piece of advice at parting! Don't wave your arms! Cure yourself of that habit — of arm waving. And also of building summer cottages, figuring that the summer residents will in time become individual landowners; figuring like that is arm waving too — Just the same, however, I like you.

You have delicate soft fingers like an artist, you have a delicate soft heart —

LOPAHIN (*embracing him*): Good-by, my dear boy. Thanks for everything. If you need it, take some money from me for the trip.

TROFIMOFF: Why should I? There's no need for it.

LOPAHIN: But you haven't any!

TROFIMOFF: I have. Thank you. I got some for a translation. Here it is in my pocket. (*Anxiously.*) But my rubbers are gone.

VARYA (*from another room*): Take your nasty things! (*Throws a pair of rubbers on to the stage.*)

TROFIMOFF: But what are you angry about, Varya? Hm — Why, these are not my rubbers.

LOPAHIN: In the spring I planted twenty-seven hundred acres of poppies and now I've made forty thousand clear. And when my poppies were in bloom, what a picture it was! So look, as I say, I've made forty thousand, which means I'm offering you a loan because I can afford to. Why turn up your nose? I'm a peasant — I speak straight out.

TROFIMOFF: Your father was a peasant, mine — an apothecary — and from that absolutely nothing follows. (LOPAHIN *takes out his wallet.*) Leave it alone, leave it alone — If you gave me two hundred thousand even, I wouldn't take it. I am a free man. And everything that you all value so highly and dearly, both rich man and beggars, has not the slightest power over me, it's like a mere feather floating in the air. I can get along without you, I can pass you by, I am strong and proud. Humanity is moving toward the loftiest truth, toward the loftiest happiness that is possible on earth and I am in the front ranks.

LOPAHIN: Will you get there?

TROFIMOFF: I'll get there. (*A pause.*) I'll get there, or I'll show the others the way to get there.

(*In the distance is heard the sound of an ax on a tree.*)

LOPAHIN: Well, good-by, my dear boy. It's time to go. We turn up our noses at one another, but life keeps on passing. When I work a long time without stopping, my thoughts are clearer, and it seems as if I, too, know what I exist for, and, brother, how many people are there in Russia who exist, nobody knows for what? Well, all the same, it's not that that keeps things circulating. Leonid Andreevich, they say, has accepted a position — he'll be in a bank, six thousand a year — the only thing is he won't stay there, he's very lazy —

ANYA (*in the doorway*): Mama begs of you until she's gone, not to cut down the orchard.

TROFIMOFF: Honestly, haven't you enough tact to — (*Goes out through the hall.*)

LOPAHIN: Right away, right away — What people, really! (*Goes out after him.*)

ANYA: Has Fiers been sent to the hospital?

YASHA: I told them to this morning. They must have sent him.

ANYA (*to* EPIHODOFF, *who is passing through the room*): Semyon Panteleevich, please inquire whether or not they have taken Fiers to the hospital.

YASHA (*huffily*): This morning, I told Igor. Why ask ten times over!

EPIHODOFF: The venerable Fiers, according to my conclusive opinion, is not worth mending, he ought to join his forefathers. And I can only envy him. (*Putting a suitcase on a hatbox and crushing it.*) Well, there you are, of course. I knew it. (*Goes out.*)

YASHA (*mockingly*): Twenty-two misfortunes —

VARYA (*on the other side of the door*): Have they taken Fiers to the hospital?

ANYA: They have.

VARYA: Then why didn't they take the letter to the doctor?

ANYA: We must send it on after them — (*Goes out.*)

VARYA (*from the next room*): Where is Yasha? Tell him his mother has come, she wants to say good-by to him.

YASHA (*waving his hand*): They merely try my patience.

(DUNYASHA *has been busying herself with the luggage; now when* YASHA *is left alone, she goes up to him.*)

DUNYASHA: If you'd only look at me once, Yasha. You are going away — leaving me — (*Crying and throwing herself on his neck.*)

YASHA: Why are you crying? (*Drinking champagne.*) In six days I'll be in Paris again. Tomorrow we will board the express train and dash off out of sight; somehow, I can't believe it. *Vive la France!* It doesn't suit me here — I can't live here — Can't help that. I've seen enough ignorance — enough for me. (*Drinking champagne.*) Why do you cry? Behave yourself properly, then you won't be crying.

DUNYASHA (*powdering her face, looking into a small mirror*): Send me a letter from Paris. I loved you, Yasha, you know, loved you so! I am a tender creature, Yasha!

YASHA: They are coming here. (*Bustling about near the suitcases, humming low.*)

(LYUBOFF ANDREEVNA, GAYEFF, ANYA *and* CHARLOTTA IVANOVNA *enter.*)

GAYEFF: We should be going. There is very little time left. (*Looking at* YASHA.) Who is it smells like herring!

LYUBOFF ANDREEVNA: In about ten minutes let's be in the carriage — (*Glancing around the room.*) Good-by, dear house, old Grandfather. Winter will pass, spring will be here, but you won't be here any longer, they'll tear you down. How much these walls have seen! (*Kissing her daughter warmly.*) My treasure, you are beaming, your eyes are dancing like two diamonds. Are you happy? Very?

ANYA: Very! It's the beginning of a new life, Mama!

GAYEFF (*gaily*): Yes, indeed, everything is fine now. Before the sale of the cherry orchard, we all were troubled, distressed, and then when the question was settled definitely, irrevocably, we all calmed down and were even cheerful — I'm a bank official. I am a financier now — Yellow ball into the side pocket, anyway, Lyuba, you look better, no doubt about that.

LYUBOFF ANDREEVNA: Yes. My nerves are better, that's true. (*They hand her her hat and coat.*) I sleep well. Carry out my things, Yasha. It's time. (*To* ANYA.) My little girl, we shall see each other again soon — I am going to Paris, I shall live there on the money your Yaroslavl great-aunt sent for the purchase of the estate — long live Great-aunt! But that money won't last long.

ANYA: Mama, you'll come back soon, soon — Isn't that so? I'll prepare myself, pass the examination at high school, and then I'll work, I will help you. We'll read all sorts of books together. Mama, isn't that so? (*Kissing her mother's hands.*) We'll read in the autumn evenings, read lots of books, and a new, wonderful world will open up before us — (*Daydreaming.*) Mama, do come —

LYUBOFF ANDREEVNA: I'll come, my precious. (*Embracing her daughter.*)

(LOPAHIN *enters with* CHARLOTTA *who is softly humming a song.*)

GAYEFF: Lucky Charlotta: she's singing!

CHARLOTTA (*taking a bundle that looks like a baby wrapped up*): My baby, bye, bye — (*A baby's cry is heard: Ooah, ooah —* !) Hush, my darling, my dear little boy. (*Ooah, ooah —* !) I am so sorry for you! (*Throwing the bundle back.*) Will you please find me a position? I cannot go on like this.

LOPAHIN: We will find something, Charlotta Ivanovna, don't worry.

GAYEFF: Everybody is dropping us, Varya is going away. — All of a sudden we are not needed.

CHARLOTTA: I have no place in town to live. I must go away. (*Humming.*) It's all the same —

(PISHTCHIK *enters.*)

LOPAHIN: The freak of nature — !

PISHTCHIK (*out of breath*): Ugh, let me catch my breath — I'm exhausted — My honored friends — Give me some water —

GAYEFF: After money, I suppose? This humble servant will flee from sin! (*Goes out.*)

PISHTCHIK: It's a long time since I was here — Most beautiful lady — (*To* LOPAHIN.) You here — ? Glad to see you — a man of the greatest intellect — Here — Take it — (*Giving* LOPAHIN *some money.*) Four hundred roubles — That leaves eight hundred and forty I still owe you —

LOPAHIN (*with astonishment, shrugging his shoulders*): I must be dreaming. But where did you get it?

PISHTCHIK: Wait — I'm hot — Most extraordinary event. Some Englishmen came and found on my land some kind of white clay — (*To* LYUBOFF ANDREEVNA.) And four hundred for you — Beautiful lady — Wonderful lady — (*Handing over the money.*) The rest later. (*Taking a drink of water.*) Just now a young man was saying on the train that some great philosopher recommends jumping off roofs — "Jump!" he says, and "therein lies the whole problem." (*With astonishment.*) You don't say! Water!

LOPAHIN: And what Englishmen were they?

PISHTCHIK: I leased them the parcel of land with the clay for twenty-four years — And now, excuse me, I haven't time — I must run along — I'm going to Znoykoff's — To Kardamonoff's — I owe everybody — (*Drinking.*) I wish you well — I'll drop in on Thursday —

LYUBOFF ANDREEVNA: We are moving to town right away, and tomorrow I'm going abroad —

PISHTCHIK: What? (*Alarmed.*) Why to town? That's why I see furniture — Suitcases — Well, no matter — (*Tearfully.*) No matter — Men of the greatest minds — those Englishmen — No matter — Good luck! God will help you — No matter — Everything in this world comes to an end — (*Kissing* LYUBOFF ANDREEVNA'S *hand.*) And should the report reach you that my end has come, think of that well-known horse and say: "There was once on earth a so and so — Semyonoff Pishtchik — The kingdom of Heaven be his." Most remarkable weather — yes — (*Going out greatly disconcerted, but immediately returning and speaking from the door.*) Dashenka sends her greetings! (*Goes out.*)

LYUBOFF ANDREEVNA: And now we can go. I am leaving with two worries. First, that Fiers is sick. (*Glancing at her watch.*) We still have five minutes —

ANYA: Mama, Fiers has already been sent to the hospital. Yasha sent him off this morning.

LYUBOFF ANDREEVNA: My second worry — is Varya. She is used to getting up early and working, and now without any work she is like a fish out of water. She has grown thin, pale and cries all the time, poor thing — (*A pause.*) You know this, Yermolay Alexeevich: I dreamed — of marrying her to you. And there was every sign of your getting married. (*Whispering to* ANYA, *who beckons to* CHARLOTTA; *both go out.*) She loves you, you are fond of her, and I don't know, don't know why it is you seem to avoid each other — I don't understand it!

LOPAHIN: I don't understand it either, I must confess. It's all strange somehow — If there's still time, I am ready right now even — Let's finish it up — and *basta*, but without you I feel I won't propose.

LYUBOFF ANDREEVNA: But that's excellent. Surely it takes only a minute. I'll call her at once.

LOPAHIN: And to fit the occasion there's the champagne. (*Looking at the glasses.*) Empty, somebody has already drunk them. (YASHA *coughs.*) That's what's called lapping it up —

LYUBOFF ANDREEVNA (*vivaciously*): Splendid! We'll go out — Yasha, *allez!* I'll call her — (*Through the door.*) Varya, drop everything and come here. Come on! (*Goes out with* YASHA.)

LOPAHIN (*looking at his watch*): Yes —

(*A pause. Behind the door you hear smothered laughter, whispering, finally* VARYA *enters.*)

VARYA (*looking at the luggage a long time*): That's strange, I just can't find it —

LOPAHIN: What are you looking for?

VARYA: I packed it myself and don't remember where. (*A pause.*)

LOPAHIN: Where do you expect to go now, Varvara Mikhailovna?

VARYA: I? To Regulin's. I agreed to go there to look after the house — As a sort of housekeeper.

LOPAHIN: That's in Yashnevo? It's nigh on to seventy miles. (*A pause.*) And here ends life in this house —

VARYA (*examining the luggage*): But where is it? Either I put it in the trunk, perhaps — Yes, life in this house is ended — it won't be any more —

LOPAHIN: And I am going to Harkoff now — By the next train. I've a lot to do. And I am leaving Epihodoff — on the ground here — I've hired him.

VARYA: Well!

LOPAHIN: Last year at this time it had already been snowing, if you remember, and now it's quiet, it's sunny. It's only that it's cold, about three degrees of frost.

VARYA: I haven't noticed. (*A pause.*) And besides our thermometer is broken — (*A pause. A voice from the yard through the door.*) Yermolay Alexeevich —

LOPAHIN (*as if he had been expecting this call for a long time*): This minute! (*Goes out quickly.*)

(*VARYA, sitting on the floor, putting her head on a bundle of clothes, sobs quietly. The door opens, LYUBOFF ANDREEVNA enters cautiously.*)

VARYA (*she is not crying any longer, and has wiped her eyes*): Yes, it's time, Mama. I can get to Regulin's today, if we are just not too late for the train — (*Through the door.*) Anya, put your things on! (*ANYA, then GAYEFF and CHARLOTTA IVANOVNA enter. GAYEFF has on a warm overcoat, with a hood. The servants gather, also the drivers. EPIHODOFF busies himself with the luggage.*) Now we can be on our way.

ANYA (*joyfully*): On our way!

GAYEFF: My friends, my dear, kind friends! Leaving this house forever, can I remain silent, can I restrain myself from expressing, as we say, farewell, those feelings that fill now my whole being —

ANYA (*beseechingly*): Uncle!

VARYA: Dear Uncle, don't!

GAYEFF (*dejectedly*): Bank the yellow into the side pocket — I am silent —

(*TROFIMOFF and then LOPAHIN enter.*)

TROFIMOFF: Well, ladies and gentlemen, it's time to go!

LOPAHIN: Epihodoff, my coat!

LYUBOFF ANDREEVNA: I'll sit here just a minute more. It's as if I had never seen before what the walls in this house are like, what kind of ceilings, and now I look at them greedily, with such tender love —

GAYEFF: I remember when I was six years old, on Trinity Day, I sat in this window and watched my father going to Church —

LYUBOFF ANDREEVNA: Are all the things taken out?

LOPAHIN: Everything, I think. (*Putting on his overcoat. To EPIHODOFF.*) Epihodoff, you see that everything is in order.

EPIHODOFF (*talking in a hoarse voice*): Don't worry, Yermolay Alexeevich!

LOPAHIN: Why is your voice like that?

EPIHODOFF: Just drank some water, swallowed something.

YASHA (*with contempt*): The ignorance —

LYUBOFF ANDREEVNA: We are going and there won't be a soul left here —

LOPAHIN: Till spring.

VARYA (*she pulls an umbrella out from a bundle, it looks as if she were going to hit someone;* LOPAHIN *pretends to be frightened*): What do you, what do you — I never thought of it.

TROFIMOFF: Ladies and gentlemen, let's get in the carriages — It's time! The train is coming any minute.

VARYA: Petya, here they are, your rubbers, by the suitcase. (*Tearfully.*) And how dirty yours are, how old — !

TROFIMOFF (*putting on the rubbers*): Let's go, ladies and gentlemen!

GAYEFF (*greatly embarrassed, afraid he will cry*): The train — The station — Cross into the side, combination off the white into the corner —

LYUBOFF ANDREEVNA: Let's go!

LOPAHIN: Everybody here? Nobody there? (*Locking the side door on the left.*) Things are stored here, it must be locked up, let's go!

ANYA: Good-by, house! Good-by, the old life!

TROFIMOFF: Long live the new life!

(*Goes out with* ANYA. VARYA *casts a glance around the room and, without hurrying, goes out.* YASHA *and* CHARLOTTA, *with her dog, go out.*)

LOPAHIN: And so, till spring. Out, ladies and gentlemen — Till we meet. (*Goes out.*)

(LYUBOFF ANDREEVNA *and* GAYEFF *are left alone. As if they had been waiting for this, they throw themselves on one another's necks sobbing, but smothering their sobs as if afraid of being heard.*)

GAYEFF (*in despair*): Oh, Sister, Sister —

LYUBOFF ANDREEVNA: Oh, my dear, my lovely, beautiful orchard! My life, my youth, my happiness, good-by!

ANYA (ANYA's *voice, gaily, appealingly*): Mama — !

TROFIMOFF (TROFIMOFF's *voice, gaily, excitedly*): Aaooch!

LYUBOFF ANDREEVNA: For the last time, just to look at the walls, at the window — My dear mother used to love to walk around in this room —

GAYEFF: Oh, Sister, Sister — !

ANYA (ANYA's *voice*): Mama — !

TROFIMOFF (TROFIMOFF's *voice*): Aaooch — !

LYUBOFF ANDREEVNA: We are coming! (*They go out.*)

(*The stage is empty. You hear the keys locking all the doors, then the carriages drive off. It grows quiet. In the silence you hear the dull thud of an ax on a tree, a lonely, mournful sound. Footsteps are heard. From the door on the right* FIERS *appears. He is dressed as usual, in a jacket and a white waistcoat, slippers on his feet. He is sick.*)

FIERS (*going to the door and trying the knob*): Locked. They've gone. (*Sitting down on the sofa.*) They forgot about me — No matter — I'll sit here awhile — And Leonid Andreevich, for sure, didn't put on his fur coat, he went off with his topcoat — (*Sighing anxiously.*) And I didn't see to it — The young saplings! (*He mutters something that cannot be understood.*) Life has gone by, as if I hadn't lived at all — (*Lying down.*) I'll lie down awhile — You haven't got any strength, nothing is left, nothing — Ach, you — good-for-nothing — (*He lies still.*)

(*There is a far-off sound as if out of the sky, the sound of a snapped string, dying away, sad. A stillness falls, and there is only the thud of an ax on a tree, far away in the orchard.*)

✒ The beginning of the second act of *The Cherry Orchard* is a particularly concise collocation of characteristics found in all of Chekhov's last four plays. Since the plays are so often misunderstood and since a main cause of misunderstanding is the failure to realize what Chekhov was doing and the assumption that he was trying to do something else, the passage may repay a closer look.

Its four characters are all employed in the Ranevskaya household, and all are minor: Charlotta, a governess of indeterminate youthfulness and cosmopolitan circus background; Epihodoff, a foolish clerk, whose dignity of speech and bearing continually collapses in pratfalls and jammed syntax; the maid Dunyasha, with whom Epihodoff is in love; and the brash young valet Yasha, Epihodoff's successful rival. They are together for no particular purpose. There is a touch of pathos in Charlotta's situation and perhaps in Epihodoff's, but none of the four is really an attractive character. They do not know each other very well and do not establish any close rapport. Their words bound off other words or drop, echoless, in a void of indifference and self-absorption. When Charlotta ends her opening monologue with a plea for human contact, Epihodoff breaks into song on the all-sufficiency of love. He is joined in singing by his rival Yasha. Dunyasha tells them they sound "like jackals." Alone with Yasha Dunyasha tells him she loves him. Yasha replies that he considers a girl who is in love immoral. Talk is desultory, punctuated by pauses and yawns. The constant changes in topic are incoherent: foreign travel, suicide, a cockroach in a glass of beer, an early Victorian philosopher. The setting is desolate: sunset among forgotten tombstones near an abandoned chapel, the cherry orchard on one side and a large town looming on the horizon.

One hesitates calling such a passage a "scene," because "scene" suggests a distinct unit within a larger plot dynamic. But no plot is furthered by this casual group, no phase of action marked, no issue raised or concluded, no climax prepared. The impression of aimless and listless small talk remains even when the passage is seen in the context of the whole play. At its end Charlotta is as lost and lonely as she is here, and Epihodoff neither kills himself nor ever stops stumbling over or crushing things or tangling his sentences. Neither her rifle nor his revolver is ever mentioned again, let alone fired. The Epihodoff–Dunyasha–Yasha triangle ends in stalemate, like the other two tentative romances in the play, Lopahin's and Varya's, and Anya's and Trofimoff's. None of the four characters here influences the issue of whether or not the estate is to be sold or otherwise affects the destiny of the major characters.

To people used to the taut, significant action patterns of western drama from Sophocles through Shakespeare and Ibsen, Chekhov's status as major dramatist may seem puzzling. The tension between Mme Ranevskaya and her equally vague and ineffectual brother Gayeff on the one hand and the concerned and practical merchant Lopahin on the other on how to save the mortgaged estate provides *The Cherry Orchard* with more suspense and plot coherence than Chekhov's other important plays. Nevertheless, what coherence the play possesses is rather in the nature of frame than of substance. As in *The Sea-Gull*, *Uncle Vanya*, and *Three Sisters* most of the drama proceeds, like our sample passage, by incongruent juxtapositions of little banalities and irrelevancies, fatuities and incoherences — random fragments of life lifted on stage from a continuing flow of trivia to make an irregular, languid rhythm of inconsequence. Take the episode in Act I when Pishtchik swallows Mme Ranevskaya's (Lyuboff Andreevna's) pills.

PISHTCHIK: You should never take medicament, dear madam — They do neither harm nor good — Hand them here, dearest lady. (*He takes the pillbox, shakes the pills out into his palm, blows on them, puts them in his mouth and washes them down with kvass.*) There! Now!

LYUBOFF ANDREEVNA (*Startled*): Why, you've lost your mind!

PISHTCHIK: I took all the pills.
LOPAHIN: Such a glutton!
  (*Everyone laughs.*)

And that is the end of the episode. The pills are not missed, we are
never told what Mme Ranevskaya takes pills for, Pishtchik does not
get sick, they do not alter his behavior in any way, nobody ever refers
to them again. By the rules of sound play construction one should be
shocked by such casualness and waste and demand to know the relevance of the incident. But its relevance is its non-relevance to anything
beyond its own inanity. Of such isolated bits of humdrum life, as
startling as they are pointless, is Chekhov's world made. No wonder
he did not find Ibsen simple enough and refused him status as a dramatist for not "knowing life." To judge by his own plays, what he objected to in the Norwegian was his careful arrangement of the rich and
immediate chaos of experience to the demands of tightly plotted melodrama of thematic import, in which every event is a link in a causal
chain and every speech reveals character or contributes to the theme.
Economy of means to a significant end is the Ibsen hallmark. Chekhov
is lavish with apparently useless character and incident. His plays are
not unplanned, and their quality of improvised rambling is the result
of scrupulous craftsmanship, but his realism is of the inclusive kind
that not only can afford but needs items that have no other function
than to make a moment of live drama. Near the close of Act II there
is heard, "as if from the sky," a "mournful" sound, "like the sound of a
snapped string." A few moments later, a drunken beggar appears. If
only because of mere proximity, is there a connection between sound
and man? What do they mean? How do they function in the drama?
The questions are unanswerable, even — in the sense in which they
usually are asked — impertinent. We can only say that without the
sound and the beggar a dimension of reality would be gone from the
scene. Instead of Ibsen's stripped and strictly functional casts Chekhov
prodigally peoples the Ranevskaya estate with a chorus of semi-gro-
tesque retainers and hangers-on, for whom there is no more a definite
function in the plot than there appears to be in the running of the
household. The quartet in the opening of Act II are just four of them.
He further diffuses the outline of his cast with unseen characters in a
kind of ghostly attendance on those on stage: Mme Ranevskaya's dead
little boy Grisha, her Paris lover, Gayeff's rich old aunt in Yaroslavl,
Pishtchik's clever daughter Dashenka. Swayed by the dead and the absent, the characters we *do* see appear more real and less strong.

  Thus, Chekhov builds drama by a kind of pointillism. If we look
too close we see only specks of reality, but at a distance a pattern

emerges. As sentiment is about to become pathos and tension approaches tragic intensity, a sudden incongruity deflates theme and mood — a moment of slapstick, a change in tempo, an unattuned image or speech, a new topic of conversation. In Act I, when Varya tells Anya of the family's precarious financial position — "In August the estate is to be sold" — Lopahin suddenly sticks his head through the door and moos like a cow. "I'd land him one like that," threatens Varya tearfully, shaking her fist. In Act III she does almost exactly that, by unlucky timing hitting him over the head with a broomstick just as he enters to tell the family that he has bought the estate. In Chekhov, typically, farce impinges on the peripety of the main drama. Lopahin's allusions to Hamlet and Ophelia represent the third coordinate in the system that defines his and Varya's abortive romance in terms partly farcical and partly poignant. Just as Lopahin, the serf's son, impatient with procrastination and a businessman of action himself, is no Prince Hamlet, so is the Ranevskaya estate which he seeks to set right both a more innocent and a pettier world than the realm of Denmark. And poor Varya is only a formidable and rather foolish nun. Tragic grandeur is further deflated by Lopahin's consistent failure to remember Ophelia's name.*

From such discord and ambivalence the play builds its larger patterns. Old Fiers considers the emancipation of the serfs in 1863 a disaster. In contrast, Trofimoff, the muddled revolutionary idealist, envisions a brighter Russian future built by liberty and dignified labor. Between past and future the present moves by ceaseless ebb and flow. In Act I, Mme Ranevskaya comes home; in Act IV she goes away. Arrival–departure frames the collection of discordant moments here as in Chekhov's other late plays. But departure is not conclusion. Though something passes, something also comes. The cherry trees fall by the blows of the axe that new enterprise wields. But how great is the loss? After all, the old recipe for drying cherries and keeping them "soft, . . . juicy, sweet, fragrant" is forgotten. But, then, is the main value of the orchard commercial? The beauty of the old order, but also its foolishness and gentle decadence, give way to Lopahin, the entrepreneur, the reluctant heir of the feudal past, including his own childhood and — though he does not know it — the old serf Fiers.

The pattern of change is framed by a still larger pattern. The play begins with Lopahin waking up and ends with Fiers falling asleep. What happens in the interval?

---

* He also misquotes Shakespeare's lines, a fact which the English translation here does not take notice of. See David Magarshack, *Chekhov the Dramatist* (New York, 1960), pp. 278-279.

> We are such stuff
> As dreams are made on, and our little life
> Is rounded with a sleep.

That is, nothing — and everything. Is it just another odd fact that the first and the last act both take place in a room called "the Nursery" and that it is furnished in Act I and bare in Act IV? To Fiers at the end it is as if life has gone by and left him with a feeling of not having lived at all. Is *The Cherry Orchard* Chekhov's *Tempest* in a deeper sense than by being his last play? Lopahin has been taken to represent the new economic man, the proletarian become a rising merchant, a bourgeois forerunner of the Soviet revolution. Perhaps he is. There certainly is irony in his unawareness of his artistic inclinations and in his inability to escape his serf origin long enough to get himself a genteel wife, either Varya or her foster mother, Mme Ranevskaya herself, who is — as certain of his speeches hint — the woman he really loves. But to seize upon socio-economic symbolism or on Lopahin's psychology as main theme is to lock Chekhov's kaleidoscope in one or the other of only two of its myriad constellations. Life may be "little" in Chekhov, as it is for most people, but the drama in which it is recorded is not impoverished. When people complain that "nothing happens" in Chekhov, one may agree to see what they have in mind. But they are quite wrong.

What is true, however, is that Chekhov's manner of drama is one that makes heavy demands on the *reader*. Few great playwrights gain more from performance than he. His distinctive tonality is muted on the page. In the absence of exciting scenes and strong plot, interest has to depend on imaginative evocation of spectacle, movement, and voice, and this, for most of us, is a new and difficult challenge. If we fail to meet it, bewilderment first and then boredom may follow. The strangeness and the number of the Rusian names are further obstacles.

But even in the theater there are people who find Chekhov too wanly elegiac, slow, and indefinite. Chekhov realized the danger himself and quarreled with the two directors of the Moscow Art Theater for not guarding sufficiently against it. One of them was Konstantin Stanislavsky, whose naturalistic staging of *The Sea-Gull* in 1898 had established Chekhov's reputation as a dramatist and whose painstaking rehearsals, emphasis on ensemble acting, and insistence that the actor engage himself imaginatively and emotionally in his part (we call all this "Method" acting today) were to make him the single most important influence on modern acting. But to Chekhov he was the man who had "ruined" his *Cherry Orchard*. In an effort, perhaps, to avert the disaster he saw was coming he wrote to Stanislavsky's wife even before rehearsals began, in October, 1903: "I'm afraid my play has turned out to be not a drama but a comedy, and in places even a farce, and I fear Nemirovich-Danchenko [the literary director of the Theater] will never forgive me for that." What actually happened was, from Chekhov's point of view, even worse. So far from feeling any need for forgiving Chekhov for having written a comedy, it did not even occur to the two directors that he had not written a tragedy. Some weeks after the first performance of *The Cherry Orchard* in January, 1904, and about four months before his death, Chekhov wrote to his wife about the Stanislavsky production:

> Take my *Cherry Orchard*. Is it my *Cherry Orchard*? With the ex- ception of one or two parts nothing in it is mine. I am describing life, ordinary life, and not blank despondency. They either make me into a cry-baby or a bore. They invent something about me out of their own heads, anything they like, something I never thought of or dreamed about. This is beginning to make me angry.

There is in principle no reason why Stanislavsky and Nemirovich-Danchenko cannot have perceived the nature of *The Cherry Orchard* more clearly than Chekhov himself. But did they? Most producers have heeded the playwright's protests against a tragic *Cherry Orchard*, but few have staged it as a comedy or agreed with Chekhov that Lopahin's part is comical and the whole play "gay and frivolous." For most people, on either side of the footlights, Chekhov remains the twilight voice of old Russia, a bittersweet realist poet of mood and atmosphere, the sympathetic–ironic chronicler of the heartaches and frustrations and failures of decent but foolishly weak and confused people. What comedy there is in Chekhov is in a very minor key indeed, at most arch and acid, very rarely hearty. Trofimoff, for example, is an un-doubted fool, and yet he is made the spokesman of genuine values: the blessings of work and love. Other visionary idealists in Chekhov are also presented as fatuous escapists into vague and wordy optimism.

From the vantage point of today we may wonder whether Chekhov, were he still alive, would have persisted in using "comedy" and "farce" as labels for *The Cherry Orchard*. To turn again to the open-ing of Act II, consider the following exchange:

CHARLOTTA: . . . Who my parents were, perhaps they weren't even married — I don't know. (*Taking a cucumber out of her pocket and beginning to eat it*) I don't know a thing. (*A pause.*) I'd like so much to talk but there's not anybody. I haven't anybody.

EPIHODOFF (*playing the guitar and singing*): "What care I for the noisy world, what care I for friends and foes." — How pleasant it is to play the mandolin!

DUNYASHA: That's a guitar, not a mandolin. (*Looking in a little mirror and powdering her face.*)

EPIHODOFF: For a madman who is in love this is a mandolin — (*Singing.*) "If only my heart were warm with the fire of requited love."

(YASHA *sings with him.*)

This is quintessential Chekhov, but it might have come from a contemporary play of the absurd theater. Without a "proper passport" and with her sense of lostness and isolation in a meaningless existence — "Who I am, why I am, is unknown" — Charlotta becomes an almost Kafkaesque figure in a parable of modern man's existential agony. In her military cap, tinkering with a rifle, eating a cucumber, holding forth in unhappy monologue, she is a figure of pathetic farce as well. The incongruity is "absurd" in the modern, literary, sense. She and Epihodoff are equally lonely, but their monodies produce only discord. The scenic and verbal imagery of guitar and cigar, guns and pocket mirror, jackals, spider, cockroach, and a serving-maid's lily white, ladylike hands belongs in an odd, vaguely disturbing dream. "Absurd" also is people's failure to relate through language. Charlotta's sudden vaudeville tricks come to seem less like farcical interruptions than like symptoms of an isolation desperately battered by the inarticulate prisoner within. Epihodoff reads important books he cannot understand and which fail to convince him that life is worth living. For lack of human respondents Gayeff apostrophizes bookcases and Nature and hides his embarrassment in billiard jargon and candy. As means to overcome a breakdown in communication his antics resemble Charlotta's tricks. Since experience is wholly subjective, there can be no stable relationship between word and meaning:

DUNYASHA: That's a guitar, not a mandolin. . . .

EPIHODOFF: For a madman who is in love this is a mandolin — . . .

Even the lovers fail to communicate:

DUNYASHA: I have come to love you passionately, you are educated, you can discuss anything. (*A pause.*)

YASHA (*yawning*): Yes sir — . . .

Certainly there is comedy here, even farce, but is that *all* there is?

The point is not that Chekhov anticipated the absurd theater some sixty years ago or that today's absurdists are indebted to him — not even, though this is true, that the absurd manner is not the invention of existential playwrights of the last decade. The point of Chekhov's "absurdity" is the more general one that art always "is" and does not "mean" and that modern art has made a fetish and a program of what previous generations of artists tacitly took for granted.

Not that Chekhov, of course, is "meaningless" — literally — any more than are playwrights like Beckett and Genet. Art cannot be "meaningless" — literally — and still remain art (which is why people who make nothing of the absurdists quite properly deny them status as dramatists). "Absurd" is a silly epithet for drama that takes reality too seriously to presume to subject it to interpretation or judgment or to arrangement by laws of narrative. The dictum that art be without meaning means that its meaning should be inviolately implicit and centripetal. The artist's image of reality does not derive its authority from a non-art original and does not justify itself by any intention of altering such an original, for however commendable an end. Chekhov was occasionally provoked into claiming for his plays a pragmatic value for lethargic, end-of-the-century Russian inelligentsia — object lessons in how *not* to manage the business of life — but their uncompromising objectivity suggests that the claim was only an effort to speak a language that dull producers could understand. With reference to this specific case: in the opening of Act II of *The Cherry Orchard* Chekhov is not telling us that life is trivial, futile, and solitary or asking us to do something about it. He is showing us some trivial, futile, and solitary moments in a scenic imitation of life. The distinction is all-important: ultimately that between an election poster and Rembrandt. "You ask me what life is?" he once wrote to his wife. "It is like asking what a carrot is. A carrot is a carrot; that's all we know." The artist records facts: people, places, things, words. But held in the artist's vision, they catch the comical or frightening but always vulnerable human pose — "the lust of the flesh and the soul's incurable loneliness" — between the quaint, incontrovertible events of birth and death. Our most vital drama, old and contemporary, claims to do no more and no less.

J. M. Synge

THE PLAYBOY
OF THE WESTERN WORLD

ACT I

(*Country public-house or shebeen,*[1] *very rough and untidy. There is a sort of counter on the right with shelves, holding many bottles and jugs, just seen above it. Empty barrels stand near the counter. At back, a little to left of counter, there is a door into the open air, then, more to the left, there is a settle with shelves above it, with more jugs, and a table beneath a window. At the left there is a large open fireplace, with turf fire, and a small door into inner room.* PEGEEN, *a wild-looking but fine girl, of about twenty, is writing at table. She is dressed in the usual peasant dress.*)

PEGEEN (*slowly as she writes*): Six yards of stuff for to make a yellow gown. A pair of lace boots with lengthy heels on them and brassy eyes. A hat is suited [2] for a wedding-day. A fine-tooth comb. To be sent with three barrels of porter in Jimmy Farrell's creel cart on the evening of the coming Fair to Mister Michael James Flaherty. With the best compliments of this season. Margaret Flaherty.

SHAWN KEOGH (*a fat and fair young man comes in as she signs, looks round awkwardly, when he sees she is alone*): Where's himself?

PEGEEN (*without looking at him*): He's coming. (*She directs letter.*) To Mister Sheamus Mulroy, Wine and Spirit Dealer, Castlebar.

SHAWN (*uneasily*): I didn't see him on the road.

PEGEEN: How would you see him (*licks stamp and puts it on letter*) and it dark night this half-hour gone by?

SHAWN (*turning towards door again*): I stood a while outside wondering would I have a right to pass on or to walk in and see you, Pegeen

---

[1] tavern   [2] that is suitable

282

Mike (*comes to fire*), and I could hear the cows breathing and sighing in the stillness of the air, and not a step moving any place from this gate to the bridge.

PEGEEN (*putting letter in envelope*): It's above at the crossroads he is, meeting Philly Cullen and a couple more are going along with him to Kate Cassidy's wake.

SHAWN (*looking at her blankly*): And he's going that length in the dark night.

PEGEEN (*impatiently*): He is surely, and leaving me lonesome on the scruff of the hill. (*She gets up and puts envelope on dresser, then winds clock.*) Isn't it long the nights are now, Shawn Keogh, to be leaving a poor girl with her own self counting the hours to the dawn of day?

SHAWN (*with awkward humour*): If it is, when we're wedded in a short while you'll have no call to complain, for I've little will to be walking off to wakes or weddings in the darkness of the night.

PEGEEN (*with rather scornful good-humour*): You're making mighty certain Shaneen, that I'll wed you now.

SHAWN: Aren't we after making a good bargain, the way we're only waiting these days on Father Reilly's dispensation from the bishops, or the Court of Rome.

PEGEEN (*looking at him teasingly, washing up at dresser*): It's a wonder, Shaneen, the Holy Father'd be taking notice of the likes of you; for if I was him I wouldn't bother with this place where you'll meet none but Red Linahan, has a squint in his eye, and Patcheen is lame in his heel, or the mad Mulrannies were driven from California and they lost in their wits. We're a queer lot these times to go troubling the Holy Father on his sacred seat.

SHAWN (*scandalized*): If we are, we're as good this place as another, maybe, and as good these times as we were for ever.

PEGEEN (*with scorn*): As good, is it? Where now will you meet the like of Daneen Sullivan knocked the eye from a peeler; [3] or Marcus Quin, God rest him, got six months for maiming ewes, and he a great warrant to tell stories of holy Ireland till he'd have the old women shedding down tears about their feet. Where will you find the like of them, I'm saying?

SHAWN (*timidly*): If you don't, it's a good job, maybe; for (*with peculiar emphasis on the words*) Father Reilly has small conceit [4] to have that kind walking around and talking to the girls.

PEGEEN (*impatiently throwing water from basin out of the door*): Stop tormenting me with Father Reilly (*imitating his voice*) when I'm

---

[3] policeman, "bobby"   [4] doesn't like

asking only what way I'll pass these twelve hours of dark, and not take my death with the fear. (*Looking out of door.*)

SHAWN (*timidly*): Would I fetch you the Widow Quin, maybe?

PEGEEN: Is it the like of that murderer? You'll not, surely.

SHAWN (*going to her, soothingly*): Then I'm thinking himself will stop along with you when he sees you taking on; for it'll be a long night-time with great darkness, and I'm after feeling a kind of fellow above in the furzy ditch, groaning wicked like a maddening dog, the way it's good cause you have, maybe, to be fearing now.

PEGEEN (*turning on him sharply*): What's that? Is it a man you seen?

SHAWN (*retreating*): I couldn't see him at all; but I heard him groaning out, and breaking his heart. It should have been a young man from his words speaking.

PEGEEN (*going after him*): And you never went near to see was he hurted or what ailed him at all?

SHAWN: I did not, Pegeen Mike. It was a dark, lonesome place to be hearing the like of him.

PEGEEN: Well, you're a daring fellow, and if they find his corpse stretched above in the dews of dawn, what'll you say then to the peelers, or the Justice of the Peace?

SHAWN (*thunderstruck*): I wasn't thinking of that. For the love of God, Pegeen Mike, don't let on I was speaking of him. Don't tell your father and the men is coming above; for if they heard that story they'd have great blabbing this night at the wake.

PEGEEN: I'll maybe tell them, and I'll maybe not.

SHAWN: They are coming at the door. Will you whisht,[5] I'm saying?

PEGEEN: Whisht yourself.

(*She goes behind counter.* MICHAEL JAMES, *fat jovial publican, comes in followed by* PHILLY CULLEN, *who is thin and mistrusting, and* JIMMY FARRELL, *who is fat and amorous, about forty-five.*)

MEN (*together*): God bless you! The blessing of God on this place!

PEGEEN: God bless you kindly.

MICHAEL (*to men, who go to the counter*): Sit down now, and take your rest. (*Crosses to* SHAWN *at the fire.*) And how is it you are, Shawn Keogh? Are you coming over the sands to Kate Cassidy's wake?

SHAWN: I am not, Michael James. I'm going home the short cut to my bed.

PEGEEN (*speaking across the counter*): He's right, too, and have you

---

[5] be quiet, shut up

no shame, Michael James, to be quitting off for the whole night, and leaving myself lonesome in the shop?

MICHAEL (*good-humouredly*): Isn't it the same whether I go for the whole night or a part only? and I'm thinking it's a queer daughter you are if you'd have me crossing backward through the Stooks[6] of the Dead Women, with a drop taken.

PEGEEN: If I am a queer daughter, it's a queer father'd be leaving me lonesome these twelve hours of dark, and I piling the turf with the dogs barking, and the calves mooing, and my own teeth rattling with the fear.

JIMMY (*flatteringly*): What is there to hurt you, and you a fine, hardy girl would knock the head of any two men in the place?

PEGEEN (*working herself up*): Isn't there the harvest boys with their tongues red for drink, and the ten tinkers is camped in the east glen, and the thousand militia — bad cess[7] to them! — walking idle through the land. There's lots surely to hurt me, and I won't stop alone in it, let himself do what he will.

MICHAEL: If you're that afeard, let Shawn Keogh stop along with you. It's the will of God, I'm thinking, himself should be seeing to you now.

(*They all turn on* SHAWN.)

SHAWN (*in horrified confusion*): I would and welcome, Michael James, but I'm afeard of Father Reilly; and what at all would the Holy Father and the Cardinals of Rome be saying if they heard I did the like of that?

MICHAEL (*with contempt*): God help you! Can't you sit in by the hearth with the light lit and herself beyond in the room? You'll do that surely, for I've heard tell there's a queer fellow above, going mad or getting his death, maybe, in the gripe[8] of the ditch, so she'd be safer this night with a person here.

SHAWN (*with plaintive despair*): I'm afeard of Father Reilly, I'm saying. Let you not be tempting me, and we near married itself.

PHILLY (*with cold contempt*): Lock him in the west room. He'll stay then and have no sin to be telling to the priest.

MICHAEL (*to* SHAWN, *getting between him and the door*): Go up now.

SHAWN (*at the top of his voice*): Don't stop me, Michael James. Let me out of the door, I'm saying, for the love of the Almighty God. Let me out. (*Trying to dodge past him.*) Let me out of it, and may God grant you His indulgence in the hour of need.

MICHAEL (*loudly*): Stop your noising, and sit down by the hearth.

6 bundles of sheaves, shocks, of cut grain ("Stooks of the Dead Women" = a local place name)   7 luck   8 trough.

(*Gives him a push and goes to counter laughing.*)

SHAWN (*turning back, wringing his hands*): Oh, Father Reilly, and the saints of God, where will I hide myself today? Oh, St. Joseph and St. Patrick and St. Brigid and St. James, have mercy on me now! (SHAWN *turns round, sees door clear, and makes a rush for it.*)

MICHAEL (*catching him by the coat-tail*): You'd be going, is it?

SHAWN (*screaming*): Leave me go, Michael James, leave me go, you old Pagan, leave me go, or I'll get the curse of the priests on you, and of the scarlet-coated bishops of the Courts of Rome. (*With a sudden movement he pulls himself out of his coat, and disappears out of the door, leaving his coat in* MICHAEL's *hands.*)

MICHAEL (*turning round, and holding up coat*): Well, there's the coat of a Christian man. Oh, there's sainted glory this day in the lonesome west; and by the will of God I've got you a decent man, Pegeen, you'll have no call to be spying after if you've a score of young girls, maybe, weeding in your fields.

PEGEEN (*taking up the defence of her property*): What right have you to be making game of a poor fellow for minding the priest, when it's your own the fault is, not paying a penny pot-boy to stand along with me and give me courage in the doing of my work? (*She snaps the coat away from him, and goes behind counter with it.*)

MICHAEL (*taken aback*): Where would I get a pot-boy? Would you have me send the bellman screaming in the streets of Castlebar?

SHAWN (*opening the door a chink and putting in his head, in a small voice*): Michael James!

MICHAEL (*imitating him*): What ails you?

SHAWN: The queer dying fellow's beyond looking over the ditch. He's come up, I'm thinking, stealing your hens. (*Looks over his shoulder.*) God help me, he's following me now (*he runs into room*), and if he's heard what I said, he'll be having my life, and I going home lonesome in the darkness of the night.

(*For a perceptible moment they watch the door with curiosity. Someone coughs outside. Then* CHRISTY MAHON, *a slight young man, comes in very tired and frightened and dirty.*)

CHRISTY (*in a small voice*): God save all here!

MEN: God save you kindly!

CHRISTY (*going to the counter*): I'd trouble you for a glass of porter, woman of the house.

(*He puts down coin.*)

PEGEEN (*serving him*): You're one of the tinkers, young fellow, is beyond camped in the glen?

CHRISTY: I am not; but I'm destroyed walking.

MICHAEL (*patronizingly*): Let you come up then to the fire. You're looking famished with the cold.

CHRISTY: God reward you. (*He takes up his glass and goes a little way across to the left, then stops and looks about him.*) Is it often the polis do be coming into this place, master of the house?

MICHAEL: If you'd come in better hours, you'd have seen "Licensed for the Sale of Beer and Spirits, to be Consumed on the Premises," written in white letters above the door, and what would the polis want spying on me, and not a decent house within four miles, the way every living Christian is a bona fide,[9] saving one widow alone?

CHRISTY (*with relief*): It's a safe house, so. (*He goes over to the fire, sighing and moaning. Then he sits down, putting his glass beside him, and begins gnawing a turnip, too miserable to feel the others staring at him with curiosity.*)

MICHAEL (*going after him*): Is it yourself is fearing the polis? You're wanting,[10] maybe?

CHRISTY: There's many wanting.

MICHAEL: Many, surely, with the broken harvest and the ended wars. (*He picks up some stockings, etc., that are near the fire, and carries them away furtively.*) It should be larceny, I'm thinking?

CHRISTY (*dolefully*): I had it in my mind it was a different word and a bigger.

PEGEEN: There's a queer lad. Were you never slapped in school, young fellow, that you don't know the name of your deed?

CHRISTY (*bashfully*): I'm slow at learning, a middling scholar only.

MICHAEL: If you're a dunce itself, you'd have a right to know that larceny's robbing and stealing. Is it for the like of that you're wanting?

CHRISTY (*with a flash of family pride*): And I the son of a strong farmer (*with a sudden qualm*), God rest his soul, could have bought up the whole of your old house a while since, from the butt of his tail-pocket, and not have missed the weight of it gone.

MICHAEL (*impressed*): If it's not stealing, it's maybe something big.

CHRISTY (*flattered*): Aye; it's maybe something big.

JIMMY: He's a wicked-looking young fellow. Maybe he followed after a young woman on a lonesome night.

CHRISTY (*shocked*): Oh, the saints forbid, mister; I was all times a decent lad.

PHILLY (*turning on* JIMMY): You're a silly man, Jimmy Farrell. He said his father was a farmer a while since, and there's himself now

---

[9] *i.e.*, a traveler. Only "travelers" (anyone living more than four miles from a licensed house) could be served drinks all around the clock. *Cf.* p. 302

[10] wanted (by the police)

in a poor state. Maybe the land was grabbed from him, and he did what any decent man would do.

MICHAEL (*to* CHRISTY, *mysteriously*): Was it bailiffs?

CHRISTY: The divil a one.

MICHAEL: Agents?

CHRISTY: The divil a one.

MICHAEL: Landlords?

CHRISTY (*peevishly*): Ah, not at all, I'm saying. You'd see the like of them stories on any little paper of a Munster town. But I'm not calling to mind any person, gentle, simple, judge or jury, did the like of me.

(*They all draw nearer with delighted curiosity.*)

PHILLY: Well, that lad's a puzzle-the-world.

JIMMY: He'd beat Dan Davies' circus, or the holy missioners making sermons on the villainy of man. Try him again, Philly.

PHILLY: Did you strike golden guineas out of solder, young fellow, or shilling coins itself?

CHRISTY: I did not, mister, not sixpence nor a farthing coin.

JIMMY: Did you marry three wives maybe? I'm told there's a sprinkling have done that among the holy Luthers of the preaching north.

CHRISTY (*shyly*): I never married with one, let alone with a couple or three.

PHILLY: Maybe he went fighting for the Boers, the like of the man beyond, was judged to be hanged, quartered, and drawn. Were you off east, young fellow, fighting bloody wars for Kruger and the freedom of the Boers?

CHRISTY: I never left my own parish till Tuesday was a week.

PEGEEN (*coming from counter*): He's done nothing, so. (*To* CHRISTY.) If you didn't commit murder or a bad, nasty thing; or false coining, or robbery, or butchery, or the like of them, there isn't anything that would be worth your troubling for to run from now. You did nothing at all.

CHRISTY (*his feelings hurt*): That's an unkindly thing to be saying to a poor orphaned traveller, has a prison behind him, and hanging before, and hell's gap gaping below.

PEGEEN (*with a sign to the men to be quiet*): You're only saying it. You did nothing at all. A soft lad the like of you wouldn't slit the windpipe of a screeching sow.

CHRISTY (*offended*): You're not speaking the truth.

PEGEEN (*in mock rage*): Not speaking the truth, is it? Would you have me knock the head of you with the butt of the broom?

CHRISTY (*twisting round on her with a sharp cry of horror*): Don't strike me. I killed my poor father, Tuesday was a week, for doing the like of that.

PEGEEN (*with blank amazement*): Is it killed your father?

CHRISTY (*subsiding*): With the help of God I did, surely, and that the Holy Immaculate Mother may intercede for his soul.

PHILLY (*retreating with* JIMMY): There's a daring fellow.

JIMMY: Oh, glory be to God!

MICHAEL (*with great respect*): That was a hanging crime, mister honey. You should have had good reason for doing the like of that.

CHRISTY (*in a very reasonable tone*): He was a dirty man, God forgive him, and he getting old and crusty, the way I couldn't put up with him at all.

PEGEEN: And you shot him dead?

CHRISTY (*shaking his head*): I never used weapons. I've no licence, and I'm a law-fearing man.

MICHAEL: It was with a hilted knife maybe? I'm told, in the big world, it's bloody knives they use.

CHRISTY (*loudly, scandalized*): Do you take me for a slaughter-boy?

PEGEEN: You never hanged him, the way Jimmy Farrell hanged his dog from the licence, and had it screeching and wriggling three hours at the butt of a string, and himself swearing it was a dead dog, and the peelers swearing it had life?

CHRISTY: I did not, then. I just riz the loy[11] and let fall the edge of it on the ridge of his skull, and he went down at my feet like an empty sack, and never let a grunt or groan from him at all.

MICHAEL (*making a sign to* PEGEEN *to fill* CHRISTY's *glass*): And what way weren't you hanged, mister? Did you bury him then?

CHRISTY (*considering*): Aye. I buried him then. Wasn't I digging spuds in the field?

MICHAEL: And the peelers never followed after you the eleven days that you're out?

CHRISTY (*shaking his head*): Never a one of them, and I walking forward facing hog, dog, or divil on the highway of the road.

PHILLY (*nodding wisely*): It's only with a common weekday kind of a murderer them lads would be trusting their carcase, and that man should be a great terror when his temper's roused.

MICHAEL: He should then. (*To* CHRISTY.) And where was it, mister honey, that you did the deed?

CHRISTY (*looking at him with suspicion*): Oh, a distant place, master of the house, a windy corner of high, distant hills.

---

[11] raised the spade

PHILLY (*nodding with approval*): He's a close man, and he's right, surely.

PEGEEN: That'd be a lad with a sense of Solomon to have for a pot-boy, Michael James, if it's the truth you're seeking one at all.

PHILLY: The peelers is fearing him, and if you'd that lad in the house there isn't one of them would come smelling around if the dogs itself were lapping poteen[12] from the dung-pit of the yard.

JIMMY: Bravery's a treasure in a lonesome place, and a lad would [13] kill his father, I'm thinking, would face a foxy divil with a pitchpike on the flags of hell.

PEGEEN: It's the truth they're saying, and if I'd that lad in the house, I wouldn't be fearing the looséd kharki[14] cut-throats, or the walking dead.

CHRISTY (*swelling with surprise and triumph*): Well, glory be to God!

MICHAEL (*with deference*): Would you think well to stop here and be pot-boy, mister honey, if we gave you good wages, and didn't destroy you with the weight of work.

SHAWN (*coming forward uneasily*): That'd be a queer kind to bring into a decent, quiet household with the like of Pegeen Mike.

PEGEEN (*very sharply*): Will you whisht? Who's speaking to you?

SHAWN (*retreating*): A bloody-handed murderer the like of . . .

PEGEEN (*snapping at him*): Whisht, I am saying; we'll take no fooling from your like at all. (*To* CHRISTY *with a honeyed voice.*) And you, young fellow, you'd have a right to stop, I'm thinking, for we'd do our all and utmost to content your needs.

CHRISTY (*overcome with wonder*): And I'd be safe this place from the searching law?

MICHAEL: You would, surely. If they're not fearing you, itself, the peelers in this place is decent, drouthy poor fellows, wouldn't touch a cur dog and not give warning in the dead of night.

PEGEEN (*very kindly and persuasively*): Let you stop a short while anyhow. Aren't you destroyed walking with your feet in bleeding blisters, and your whole skin needing washing like a Wicklow sheep.

CHRISTY (*looking round with satisfaction*): It's a nice room, and if it's not humbugging me you are, I'm thinking that I'll surely stay.

JIMMY (*jumps up*): Now, by the grace of God, herself will be safe this night, with a man killed his father holding danger from the door, and let you come on, Michael James, or they'll have the best stuff drunk at the wake.

MICHAEL (*going to the door with men*): And begging your pardon,

[12] illegally distilled whisky, moonshine   [13] who would   [14] khaki, *i.e.,* British soldiers

mister, what name will we call you, for we'd like to know?

CHRISTY: Christopher Mahon.

MICHAEL: Well, God bless you, Christy, and a good rest till we meet again when the sun'll be rising to the noon of day.

CHRISTY: God bless you all.

MEN: God bless you.

(*They go out, except* SHAWN, *who lingers at the door.*)

SHAWN (*to* PEGEEN): Are you wanting me to stop along with you and keep you from harm?

PEGEEN (*gruffly*): Didn't you say you were fearing Father Reilly?

SHAWN: There'd be no harm staying now, I'm thinking, and himself in it too.

PEGEEN: You wouldn't stay when there was need for you, and let you step off nimble this time when there's none.

SHAWN: Didn't I say it was Father Reilly . . .

PEGEEN: Go on, then, to Father Reilly (*in a jeering tone*), and let him put you in the holy brotherhoods, and leave that lad to me.

SHAWN: If I meet the Widow Quin . . .

PEGEEN: Go on, I'm saying, and don't be waking this place with your noise. (*She hustles him out and bolts door.*) That lad would wear the spirits from the saints of peace. (*Bustles about, then takes off her apron and pins it up in the window as a blind,* CHRISTY *watching her timidly. Then she comes to him and speaks with bland good-humour.*) Let you stretch out now by the fire, young fellow. You should be destroyed travelling.

CHRISTY (*shyly again, drawing off his boots*): I'm tired surely, walking wild eleven days, and waking fearful in the night. (*He holds up one of his feet, feeling his blisters, and looking at them with compassion.*)

PEGEEN (*standing beside him, watching him with delight*): You should have had great people in your family, I'm thinking, with the little, small feet you have, and you with a kind of a quality name, the like of what you'd find on the great powers and potentates of France and Spain.

CHRISTY (*with pride*): We were great, surely, with wide and windy acres of rich Munster land.

PEGEEN: Wasn't I telling you, and you a fine, handsome young fellow with a noble brow?

CHRISTY (*with a flash of delighted surprise*): Is it me?

PEGEEN: Aye. Did you never hear that from the young girls where you come from in the west or south?

CHRISTY (*with venom*): I did not, then. Oh, they're bloody liars in the naked parish where I grew a man.

PEGEEN: If they are itself, you've heard it these days, I'm thinking, and you walking the world telling out your story to young girls or old.

CHRISTY: I've told my story no place till this night, Pegeen Mike, and it's foolish I was here, maybe, to be talking free; but you're decent people, I'm thinking, and yourself a kindly woman, the way I wasn't fearing you at all.

PEGEEN (*filling a sack with straw*): You've said the like of that, maybe, in every cot and cabin where you've met a young girl on your way.

CHRISTY (*going over to her, gradually raising his voice*): I've said it nowhere till this night, I'm telling you; for I've seen none the like of you the eleven long days I am walking the world, looking over a low ditch or a high ditch on my north or south, into stony, scattered fields, or scribes[15] of bog, where you'd see young, limber girls, and fine, prancing women making laughter with the men.

PEGEEN: If you weren't destroyed travelling, you'd have as much talk and streeleen,[16] I'm thinking, as Owen Roe O'Sullivan or the poets of the Dingle Bay; and I've heard all times it's the poets are your like — fine, fiery fellows with great rages when their temper's roused.

CHRISTY (*drawing a little nearer to her*): You've a power of rings, God bless you, and would there be any offence if I was asking are you single now?

PEGEEN: What would I want wedding so young?

CHRISTY (*with relief*): We're alike, so.

PEGEEN (*she puts sack on settle and beats it up*): I never killed my father. I'd be afeard to do that, except I was the like of yourself with blind rages tearing me within, for I'm thinking you should have had great tussling when the end was come.

CHRISTY (*expanding with delight at the first confidential talk he has ever had with a woman*): We had not then. It was a hard woman was come over the hill; and if he was always a crusty kind when he'd a hard woman setting him on, not the divil himself or his four fathers could put up with him at all.

PEGEEN (*with curiosity*): And isn't it a great wonder that one wasn't fearing you?

CHRISTY (*very confidentially*): Up to the day I killed my father, there wasn't a person in Ireland knew the kind I was, and I there drinking, waking, eating, sleeping, a quiet, simple poor fellow with no man giving me heed.

[15] patches   [16] small talk, chatter

PEGEEN (*getting a quilt out of cupboard and putting it on the sack*):
It was the girls were giving you heed, maybe, and I'm thinking it's
most conceit you'd have to be gaming with their like.

CHRISTY (*shaking his head, with simplicity*): Not the girls itself, and
I won't tell you a lie. There wasn't anyone heeding me in that place
saving only the dumb beasts of the field. (*He sits down at fire.*)

PEGEEN (*with disappointment*): And I thinking you should have been
living the like of a king of Norway or the eastern world. (*She comes
and sits beside him after placing bread and mug of milk on the
table.*)

CHRISTY (*laughing piteously*): The like of a king, is it? And I after
toiling, moiling, digging, dodging from the dawn till dusk; with never
a sight of joy or sport saving only when I'd be abroad in the dark
night poaching rabbits on hills, for I was a divil to poach, God forgive me (*very naïvely*), and I near got six months for going with a
dung fork and stabbing a fish.

PEGEEN: And it's that you'd call sport, is it, to be abroad in the darkness with yourself alone?

CHRISTY: I did, God help me, and there I'd be as happy as the sunshine of St. Martin's Day, watching the light passing the north or
the patches of fog, till I'd hear a rabbit starting to screech and I'd go
running in the furze. Then, when I'd my full share, I'd come walking down where you'd see the ducks and geese stretched sleeping
on the highway of the road, and before I'd pass the dunghill, I'd
hear himself snoring out — a loud, lonesome snore he'd be making
all times, the while he was sleeping; and he a man'd be raging all
times, the while he was waking, like a gaudy officer you'd hear
cursing and damning and swearing oaths.

PEGEEN: Providence and Mercy, spare us all!

CHRISTY: It's that you'd say surely if you seen him and he after drinking for weeks, rising up in the red dawn, or before it maybe, and
going out into the yard as naked as an ash-tree in the moon of May,
and shying clods against the visage of the stars till he'd put the fear
of death into the banbhs[17] and the screeching sows.

PEGEEN: I'd be well-nigh afeard of that lad myself, I'm thinking. And
there was no one in it but the two of you alone?

CHRISTY: The divil a one, though he'd sons and daughters walking all
great states and territories of the world, and not a one of them, to
this day, but would say their seven curses on him, and they rousing
up to let a cough or sneeze, maybe, in the deadness of the night.

PEGEEN (*nodding her head*): Well, you should have been a queer lot.

---

[17] suckling pigs

I never cursed my father the like of that, though I'm twenty and more years of age.

CHRISTY: Then you'd have cursed mine, I'm telling you, and he a man never gave peace to any, saving when he'd get two months or three, or be locked in the asylums for battering peelers or assaulting men (*with depression*), the way it was a bitter life he led me till I did up a Tuesday and halve his skull.

PEGEEN (*putting her hand on his shoulder*): Well, you'll have peace in this place, Christy Mahon, and none to trouble you, and it's near time a fine lad like you should have your good share of the earth.

CHRISTY: It's time surely, and I a seemly fellow with great strength in me and bravery of . . . (*Someone knocks.*)

CHRISTY (*clinging to* PEGEEN): Oh, glory! it's late for knocking, and this last while I'm in terror of the peelers, and the walking dead. (*Knocking again.*)

PEGEEN: Who's there?

VOICE (*outside*): Me.

PEGEEN: Who's me?

VOICE: The Widow Quin.

PEGEEN (*jumping up and giving him the bread and milk*): Go on now with your supper, and let on to be sleepy, for if she found you were such a warrant to talk, she'd be stringing gabble till the dawn of day.

(*He takes bread and sits shyly with his back to the door.*)

PEGEEN (*opening the door, with temper*): What ails you, or what is it you're wanting at this hour of the night?

WIDOW QUIN (*coming in a step and peering at* CHRISTY): I'm after meeting Shawn Keogh and Father Reilly below, who told me of your curiosity man, and they fearing by this time he was maybe roaring, romping on your hands with drink.

PEGEEN (*pointing to* CHRISTY): Look now is he roaring, and he stretched out drowsy with his supper and his mug of milk. Walk down and tell that to Father Reilly and to Shaneen Keogh.

WIDOW QUIN (*coming forward*): I'll not see them again, for I've their word to lead that lad forward for to lodge with me.

PEGEEN (*in blank amazement*): This night is it?

WIDOW QUIN (*going over*): This night. "It isn't fitting," says the priesteen, "to have his likeness lodging with an orphaned girl." (*To* CHRISTY.) God save you, mister!

CHRISTY (*shyly*): God save you kindly!

WIDOW QUIN (*looking at him with half-amused curiosity*): Well, aren't you a little smiling fellow? It should have been great and bitter torments did rouse your spirits to a deed of blood.

CHRISTY (*doubtfully*): It should, maybe.

WIDOW QUIN: It's more than "maybe" I'm saying, and it'd soften my heart to see you sitting so simple with your cup and cake, and you fitter to be saying your catechism than slaying your da.[18]

PEGEEN (*at counter, washing glasses*): There's talking when any'd see he's fit to be holding his head high with the wonders of the world. Walk on from this, for I'll not have him tormented, and he destroyed travelling since Tuesday was a week.

WIDOW QUIN (*peaceably*): We'll be walking surely when his supper's done, and you'll find we're great company, young fellow, when it's of the like of you and me you'd hear the penny poets singing in an August Fair.

CHRISTY (*innocently*): Did you kill your father?

PEGEEN (*contemptuously*): She did not. She hit himself with a worn pick, and the rusted poison did corrode his blood the way he never overed [19] it, and died after. That was a sneaky kind of murder did win small glory with the boys itself. (*She crosses to* CHRISTY's *left.*)

WIDOW QUIN (*with good humour*): If it didn't, maybe all knows a widow woman has buried her children and destroyed her man is a wiser comrade for a young lad than a girl, the like of you, who'd go helter-skeltering after any man would let you a wink upon the road.

PEGEEN (*breaking out into wild rage*): And you'll say that, Widow Quin, and you gasping with the rage you had racing the hill beyond to look on his face.

WIDOW QUIN (*laughing derisively*): Me, is it? Well, Father Reilly has cuteness to divide you now. (*She pulls* CHRISTY *up.*) There's great temptation in a man did slay his da, and we'd best be going, young fellow; so rise up and come with me.

PEGEEN (*seizing his arm*): He'll not stir. He's pot-boy in this place, and I'll not have him stolen off and kidnapped while himself's abroad.

WIDOW QUIN: It'd be a crazy pot-boy'd lodge him in the shebeen where he works by day, so you'd have a right to come on, young fellow, till you see my little houseen, a perch off on the rising hill.

PEGEEN: Wait till morning, Christy Mahon. Wait till you lay eyes on her leaky thatch is growing more pasture for her buck goat than her square of fields, and she without a tramp itself to keep in order her place at all.

WIDOW QUIN: When you see me contriving in my little gardens, Christy Mahon, you'll swear the Lord God formed me to be living lone, and that there isn't my match in Mayo for thatching, or mowing, or shearing a sheep.

18 father   19 got over

PEGEEN (*with noisy scorn*): It's true the Lord God formed you to contrive indeed. Doesn't the world know you reared a black ram at your own breast, so that the Lord Bishop of Connaught felt the elements of a Christian, and he eating it after in a kidney stew? Doesn't the world know you've been seen shaving the foxy skipper from France for a threepennybit and a sop of grass tobacco would wring the liver from a mountain goat you'd meet leaping the hills?

WIDOW QUIN (*with amusement*): Do you hear her now, young fellow? Do you hear the way she'll be rating at your own self when a week is by?

PEGEEN (*to* CHRISTY): Don't heed her. Tell her to go on into her pigsty and not plague us here.

WIDOW QUIN: I'm going; but he'll come with me.

PEGEEN (*shaking him*): Are you dumb, young fellow?

CHRISTY (*timidly to* WIDOW QUIN): God increase you; but I'm pot-boy in this place, and it's here I liefer stay.

PEGEEN (*triumphantly*): Now you have heard him, and go on from this.

WIDOW QUIN (*looking round the room*): It's lonesome this hour crossing the hill, and if he won't come along with me, I'd have a right maybe to stop this night with yourselves. Let me stretch out on the settle, Pegeen Mike; and himself can lie by the hearth.

PEGEEN (*short and fiercely*): Faith, I won't. Quit off or I will send you now.

WIDOW QUIN (*gathering her shawl up*): Well, it's a terror to be aged a score. (*To* CHRISTY.) God bless you now, young fellow, and let you be wary, or there's right torment will await you here if you go romancing with her like, and she waiting only, as they bade me say, on a sheepskin parchment to be wed with Shawn Keogh of Killakeen.

CHRISTY (*going to* PEGEEN *as she bolts door*): What's that she's after saying?

PEGEEN: Lies and blather, you've no call to mind. Well, isn't Shawn Keogh an impudent fellow to send up spying on me? Wait till I lay hands on him. Let him wait, I'm saying.

CHRISTY: And you're not wedding him at all?

PEGEEN: I wouldn't wed him if a bishop came walking for to join us here.

CHRISTY: That God in glory may be thanked for that.

PEGEEN: There's your bed now. I've put a quilt upon you I'm after quilting a while since with my own two hands, and you'd best stretch out now for your sleep, and may God give you a good rest till I call you in the morning when the cocks will crow.

CHRISTY (*as she goes to inner room*): May God and Mary and St.

Patrick bless you and reward you for your kindly talk. (*She shuts the door behind her. He settles his bed slowly, feeling the quilt with immense satisfaction.*) Well, it's a clean bed and soft with it, and it's great luck and company I've won me in the end of time — two fine women fighting for the likes of me — till I'm thinking this night wasn't I a foolish fellow not to kill my father in the years gone by.

ACT II

(*Scene as before. Brilliant morning light.* CHRISTY, *looking bright and cheerful, is cleaning a girl's boots.*)

CHRISTY (*to himself, counting jugs on dresser*): Half a hundred beyond. Ten there. A score that's above. Eighty jugs. Six cups and a broken one. Two plates. A power of glasses. Bottles, a schoolmaster'd be hard set to count, and enough in them, I'm thinking, to drunken all the wealth and wisdom of the county Clare. (*He puts down the boot carefully.*) There's her boots now, nice and decent for her evening use, and isn't it grand brushes she has? (*He puts them down and goes by degrees to the looking-glass.*) Well, this'd be a fine place to be my whole life talking out with swearing Christians, in place of my old dogs and cat; and I stalking around, smoking my pipe and drinking my fill, and never a day's work but drawing a cork an odd time, or wiping a glass, or rinsing out a shiny tumbler for a decent man. (*He takes the looking-glass from the wall and puts it on the back of a chair; then sits down in front of it and begins washing his face.*) Didn't I know rightly, I was handsome, though it was the divil's own mirror we had beyond, would twist a squint across an angel's brow; and I'll be growing fine from this day, the way I'll have a soft lovely skin on me and won't be the like of the clumsy young fellows do be ploughing all times in the earth and dung. (*He starts.*) Is she coming again? (*He looks out.*) Stranger girls. God help me, where'll I hide myself away and my long neck naked to the world? (*He looks out.*) I'd best go to the room maybe till I'm dressed again.

(*He gathers up his coat and the looking-glass, and runs into the inner room. The door is pushed open, and* SUSAN BRADY *looks in, and knocks on door.*)

SUSAN: There's nobody in it. (*Knocks again.*)
NELLY (*pushing her in and following her, with* HONOR BLAKE *and* SARA TANSEY): It'd be early for them both to be out walking the hill.

SUSAN: I'm thinking Shawn Keogh was making game of us, and there's no such man in it at all.

HONOR (*pointing to straw and quilt*): Look at that. He's been sleeping there in the night. Well, it'll be a hard case if he's gone off now, the way we'll never set our eyes on a man killed his father, and we after rising early and destroying ourselves running fast on the hill.

NELLY: Are you thinking them's his boots?

SARA (*taking them up*): If they are, there should be his father's track on them. Did you never read in the papers the way murdered men do bleed and drip?

SUSAN: Is that blood there, Sara Tansey?

SARA (*smelling it*): That's bog water, I'm thinking; but it's his own they are, surely, for I never seen the like of them for whitey mud, and red mud, and turf on them, and the fine sands of the sea. That man's been walking, I'm telling you. (*She goes down right, putting on one of his boots.*)

SUSAN (*going to window*): Maybe he's stolen off to Belmullet with the boots of Michael James, and you'd have a right so to follow after him, Sara Tansey, and you the one yoked the ass cart and drove ten miles to set your eyes on the man bit the yellow lady's nostril on the northern shore. (*She looks out.*)

SARA (*running to window, with one boot on*): Don't be talking, and we fooled today. (*Putting on the other boot.*) There's a pair do fit me well and I'll be keeping them for walking to the priest, when you'd be ashamed this place, going up winter and summer with nothing worth while to confess at all.

HONOR (*who has been listening at door*): Whisht! there's someone inside the room. (*She pushes door a chink open.*) It's a man.

(SARA *kicks off boots and puts them where they were. They all stand in a line looking through chink.*)

SARA: I'll call him. Mister! Mister! (*He puts in his head.*) Is Pegeen within?

CHRISTY (*coming in as meek as a mouse, with the looking-glass held behind his back*): She's above on the cnuceen,[20] seeking the nanny goats, the way she'd have a sup of goats' milk for to colour my tea.

SARA: And asking your pardon, is it you's the man killed his father?

CHRISTY (*sidling towards the nail where the glass was hanging*): I am, God help me!

SARA (*taking eggs she has brought*): Then my thousand welcomes to you, and I've run up with a brace of duck's eggs for your food to-day.

[20] hill

Pegeen's ducks is no use, but these are the real rich sort. Hold out your hand and you'll see it's no lie I'm telling you.

CHRISTY (*coming forward shyly, and holding out his left hand*): They're a great and weighty size.

SUSAN: And I run up with a pat of butter, for it'd be a poor thing to have you eating your spuds dry, and you after running a great way since you did destroy your da.

CHRISTY: Thank you kindly.

HONOR: And I brought you a little cut of a cake, for you should have a thin stomach on you, and you that length walking the world.

NELLY: And I brought you a little laying pullet — boiled and all she is — was crushed at the fall of night by the curate's car. Feel the fat of that breast, mister.

CHRISTY: It's bursting, surely. (*He feels it with back of his hand, in which he holds the presents.*)

SARA: Will you pinch it? Is your right hand too sacred for to use at all? (*She slips round behind him.*) It's a glass he has. Well, I never seen to this day a man with a looking-glass held to his back. Them that kills their fathers is a vain lot surely.

(GIRLS *giggle.*)

CHRISTY (*smiling innocently and piling presents on glass*): I'm very thankful to you all to-day. . . .

WIDOW QUIN (*coming in quickly, at door*): Sara Tansey, Susan Brady, Honor Blake! What in glory has you here at this hour of day?

GIRLS (*giggling*): That's the man killed his father.

WIDOW QUIN (*coming to them*): I know well it's the man; and I'm after putting him down in the sports below for racing, leaping, pitching, and the Lord knows what.

SARA (*exuberantly*): That's right, Widow Quin. I'll bet my dowry that he'll lick the world.

WIDOW QUIN: If you will, you'd have a right to have him fresh and nourished in place of nursing a feast. (*Taking presents.*) Are you fasting or fed, young fellow?

CHRISTY: Fasting, if you please.

WIDOW QUIN (*loudly*): Well, you're the lot. Stir up now and give him his breakfast. (*To* CHRISTY.) Come here to me (*she puts him on bench beside her while the girls make tea and get his breakfast*), and let you tell us your story before Pegeen will come, in place of grinning your ears off like the moon of May.

CHRISTY (*beginning to be pleased*): It's a long story; you'd be destroyed listening.

WIDOW QUIN: Don't be letting on to be shy, a fine, gamey, treacherous lad the like of you. Was it in your house beyond you cracked his skull?

CHRISTY (*shy but flattered*): It was not. We were digging spuds in his cold, sloping, stony, divil's patch of a field.

WIDOW QUIN: And you went asking money of him, or making talk of getting a wife would drive him from his farm?

CHRISTY: I did not, then; but there I was digging and digging, and "You squinting idiot," says he, "let you walk down now and tell the priest you'll wed the Widow Casey in a score of days."

WIDOW QUIN: And what kind was she?

CHRISTY (*with horror*): A walking terror from beyond the hills, and she two score and five years, and two hundred-weights and five pounds in the weighing scales, with a limping leg on her, and a blinded eye, and she a woman of noted misbehaviour with the old and young.

GIRLS (*clustering round him, serving him*): Glory be.

WIDOW QUIN: And what did he want driving you to wed with her? (*She takes a bit of the chicken.*)

CHRISTY (*eating with growing satisfaction*): He was letting on I was wanting a protector from the harshness of the world, and he without a thought the whole while but how he'd have her hut to live in and her gold to drink.

WIDOW QUIN: There's maybe worse than a dry hearth and a widow woman and your glass at night. So you hit him then?

CHRISTY (*getting almost excited*): I did not. "I won't wed her," says I, "when all know she did suckle me for six weeks when I came into the world, and she a hag this day with a tongue on her has the crows and seabirds scattered, the way they wouldn't cast a shadow on her garden with the dread of her curse."

WIDOW QUIN (*teasingly*): That one should be right company.

SARA (*eagerly*): Don't mind her. Did you kill him then?

CHRISTY: "She's too good for the like of you," says he, "and go on now or I'll flatten you out like a crawling beast has passed under a dray." "You will not if I can help it," says I. "Go on," says he, "or I'll have the divil making garters of your limbs tonight." "You will not if I can help it," says I. (*He sits up brandishing his mug.*)

SARA: You were right surely.

CHRISTY (*impressively*): With that the sun came out between the cloud and the hill, and it shining green in my face. "God have mercy on your soul," says he, lifting a scythe. "Or on your own," said I, raising the loy.

SUSAN: That's a grand story.

HONOR: He tells it lovely.

CHRISTY (*flattered and confident, waving bone*): He gave a drive with the scythe, and I gave a lep to the east. Then I turned around with my back to the north, and I hit a blow on the ridge of his skull, laid him stretched out, and he split to the knob of his gullet. (*He raises the chicken bone to his Adam's apple.*)

GIRLS (*together*): Well, you're a marvel! Oh, God bless you! You're the lad, surely!

SUSAN: I'm thinking the Lord God sent him this road to make a second husband to the Widow Quin, and she with a great yearning to be wedded, though all dread her here. Lift him on her knee, Sara Tansey.

WIDOW QUIN: Don't tease him.

SARA (*going over to dresser and counter very quickly, and getting two glasses and porter*): You're heroes, surely, and let you drink a supeen with your arms linked like the outlandish lovers in the sailor's song. (*She links their arms and gives them the glasses.*) There now. Drink a health to the wonders of the western world, the pirates, preachers, poteen-makers, with the jobbing jockies; [21] parching peelers, and the juries fill their stomachs selling judgments of the English law. (*Brandishing the bottle.*)

WIDOW QUIN: That's a right toast, Sara Tansey. Now, Christy.

(*They drink with their arms linked, he drinking with his left hand, she with her right. As they are drinking,* PEGEEN MIKE *comes in with a milk-can and stands aghast. They all spring away from* CHRISTY. *He goes down left.* WIDOW QUIN *remains seated.*)

PEGEEN (*angrily, to* SARA): What is it you're wanting?

SARA (*twisting her apron*): An ounce of tobacco.

PEGEEN: Have you tuppence?

SARA: I've forgotten my purse.

PEGEEN: Then you'd best be getting it and not be fooling us here. (*To the* WIDOW QUIN, *with more elaborate scorn.*) And what is it you're wanting, Widow Quin?

WIDOW QUIN (*insolently*): A penn'orth of starch.

PEGEEN (*breaking out*). And you without a white shift or a shirt in your whole family since the drying of the flood. I've no starch for the like of you, and let you walk on now to Killamuck.

WIDOW QUIN (*turning to* CHRISTY, *as she goes out with the* GIRLS): Well, you're mighty huffy this day, Pegeen Mike, and you, young fellow, let you not forget the sports and racing when the noon is by. (*They go out.*)

[21] swindling peddlers

PEGEEN (*imperiously*): Fling out that rubbish and put them cups away. (CHRISTY *tidies away in great haste.*) Shove in the bench by the wall. (*He does so.*) And hang that glass on the nail. What disturbed it at all?

CHRISTY (*very meekly*): I was making myself decent only, and this a fine country for young lovely girls.

PEGEEN (*sharply*): Whisht your talking of girls. (*Goes to counter on right.*)

CHRISTY: Wouldn't any wish to be decent in a place . . .

PEGEEN: Whisht, I'm saying.

CHRISTY (*looks at her face for a moment with great misgivings, then as a last effort takes up a loy, and goes towards her, with feigned assurance*): It was with a loy the like of that I killed my father.

PEGEEN (*still sharply*): You've told me that story six times since the dawn of day.

CHRISTY (*reproachfully*): It's a queer thing you wouldn't care to be hearing it and them girls after walking four miles to be listening to me now.

PEGEEN (*turning round astonished*): Four miles?

CHRISTY (*apologetically*): Didn't himself say there were only bona fides living in the place?

PEGEEN: It's bona fides by the road they are, but that lot came over the river lepping the stones. It's not three perches[22] when you go like that, and I was down this morning looking on the papers the post-boy does have in his bag. (*With meaning and emphasis.*) For there was great news this day, Christopher Mahon. (*She goes into room on left.*)

CHRISTY (*suspiciously*): Is it news of my murder?

PEGEEN (*inside*): Murder, indeed.

CHRISTY (*loudly*): A murdered da?

PEGEEN (*coming in again and crossing right*): There was not, but a story filled half a page of the hanging of a man. Ah, that should be a fearful end, young fellow, and it worst of all for a man destroyed his da; for the like of him would get small mercies, and when it's dead he is they'd put him in a narrow grave, with cheap sacking wrapping him round, and pour down quicklime on his head, the way you'd see a woman pouring any frish-frash[23] from a cup.

CHRISTY (*very miserably*): Oh, God help me. Are you thinking I'm safe? You were saying at the fall of night I was shut of jeopardy and I here with yourselves.

PEGEEN (*severely*): You'll be shut of jeopardy no place if you go

[22] units of measurement, 16½ feet long   [23] dregs

talking with a pack of wild girls the like of them do be walking
abroad with the peelers, talking whispers at the fall of night.

CHRISTY (*with terror*): And you're thinking they'd tell?

PEGEEN (*with mock sympathy*): Who knows, God help you?

CHRISTY (*loudly*): What joy would they have to bring hanging to the
likes of me?

PEGEEN: It's queer joys they have, and who knows the thing they'd
do, if it'd make the green stones cry itself to think of you swaying
and swiggling at the butt of a rope, and you with a fine, stout neck,
God bless you! the way you'd be a half an hour, in great anguish,
getting your death.

CHRISTY (*getting his boots and putting them on*): If there's that terror
of them, it'd be best, maybe, I went on wandering like Esau or Cain
and Abel on the sides of Neifin or the Erris plain.

PEGEEN (*beginning to play with him*): It would, maybe, for I've heard
the Circuit Judges this place is a heartless crew.

CHRISTY (*bitterly*): It's more than Judges this place is a heartless crew.
(*Looking up at her.*) And isn't it a poor thing to be starting again,
and I a lonesome fellow will be looking out on women and girls the
way the needy fallen spirits do be looking on the Lord?

PEGEEN: What call have you to be that lonesome when there's poor
girls walking Mayo in their thousands now?

CHRISTY (*grimly*): It's well you know what call I have. It's well you
know it's a lonesome thing to be passing small towns with the lights
shining sideways when the night is down, or going in strange places
with a dog noising before you and a dog noising behind, or drawn
to the cities where you'd hear a voice kissing and talking deep love
in every shadow of the ditch, and you passing on with an empty,
hungry stomach failing from your heart.

PEGEEN: I'm thinking you're an odd man, Christy Mahon. The oddest
walking fellow I ever set my eyes on to this hour today.

CHRISTY: What would any be but odd men and they living lonesome
in the world?

PEGEEN: I'm not odd, and I'm my whole life with my father only.

CHRISTY (*with infinite admiration*): How would a lovely, handsome
woman the like of you be lonesome when all men should be throng-
ing around to hear the sweetness of your voice, and the little infant
children should be pestering your steps, I'm thinking, and you walking the roads.

PEGEEN: I'm hard set to know what way a coaxing fellow the like of
yourself should be lonesome either.

CHRISTY: Coaxing.

PEGEEN: Would you have me think a man never talked with the girls

would have the words you've spoken today? It's only letting on you
are to be lonesome, the way you'd get around me now.

CHRISTY: I wish to God I was letting on; but I was lonesome all times,
and born lonesome, I'm thinking, as the moon of dawn. (*Going to
door.*)

PEGEEN (*puzzled by his talk*): Well, it's a story I'm not understanding
at all why you'd be worse than another, Christy Mahon, and you a
fine lad with the great savagery to destroy your da.

CHRISTY: It's little I'm understanding myself, saving only that my
heart's scalded this day, and I going off stretching out the earth between us, the way I'll not be waking near you another dawn of the
year till the two of us do arise to hope or judgment with the saints
of God, and now I'd best be going with my wattle[24] in my hand, for
hanging is a poor thing (*turning to go*), and it's little welcome only
is left me in this house today.

PEGEEN (*sharply*): Christy. (*He turns round.*) Come here to me. (*He
goes towards her.*) Lay down that switch and throw some sods on
the fire. You're pot-boy in this place, and I'll not have you mitch[25]
off from us now.

CHRISTY: You were saying I'd be hanged if I stay.

PEGEEN (*quite kindly at last*): I'm after going down and reading the
fearful crimes of Ireland for two weeks or three, and there wasn't
a word of your murder. (*Getting up and going over to the counter.*)
They've likely not found the body. You're safe so with ourselves.

CHRISTY (*astonished, slowly*): It's making game of me you were (*following her with fearful joy*), and I can stay so, working at your side,
and I not lonesome from this mortal day.

PEGEEN: What's to hinder you staying, except the widow woman or
the young girls would inveigle you off?

CHRISTY (*with rapture*): And I'll have your words from this day filling
my ears, and that look is come upon you meeting my two eyes, and
I watching you loafing around in the warm sun, or rinsing your
ankles when the night is come.

PEGEEN (*kindly, but a little embarrassed*): I'm thinking you'll be a
loyal young lad to have working around, and if you vexed me a while
since with your leaguing with the girls, I wouldn't give a thraneen[26]
for a lad hadn't a mighty spirit in him and a gamey heart.

(SHAWN KEOGH *runs in carrying a cleeve*[27] *on his back, followed by
the* WIDOW QUIN.)

[24] switch　　[25] sneak　　[26] straw　　[27] basket

SHAWN (*to* PEGEEN): I was passing below, and I seen your mountainy sheep eating cabbages in Jimmy's field. Run up or they'll be bursting, surely.

PEGEEN: Oh, God mend them!

(*She puts a shawl over her head and runs out.*)

CHRISTY (*looking from one to the other. Still in high spirits*): I'd best go to her aid maybe. I'm handy with ewes.

WIDOW QUIN (*closing the door*): She can do that much, and there is Shaneen has long speeches for to tell you now. (*She sits down with an amused smile.*)

SHAWN (*taking something from his pocket and offering it to* CHRISTY): Do you see that, mister?

CHRISTY (*looking at it*): The half of a ticket to the Western States!

SHAWN (*trembling with anxiety*): I'll give it to you and my new hat (*pulling it out of hamper*); and my breeches with the double seat (*pulling it out*); and my new coat is woven from the blackest shearings for three miles around (*giving him the coat*); I'll give you the whole of them, and my blessing, and the blessing of Father Reilly itself, maybe, if you'll quit from this and leave us in the peace we had till last night at the fall of dark.

CHRISTY (*with a new arrogance*): And for what is it you're wanting to get shut of me?

SHAWN (*looking to the* WIDOW *for help*): I'm a poor scholar with middling faculties to coin a lie, so I'll tell you the truth, Christy Mahon. I'm wedding with Pegeen beyond, and I don't think well of having a clever, fearless man the like of you dwelling in her house.

CHRISTY (*almost pugnaciously*): And you'd be using bribery for to banish me?

SHAWN (*in an imploring voice*): Let you not take it badly, mister honey; isn't beyond the best place for you, where you'll have golden chains and shiny coats and you riding upon hunters with the ladies of the land. (*He makes an eager sign to the* WIDOW QUIN *to come to help him.*)

WIDOW QUIN (*coming over*): It's true for him, and you'd best quit off and not have that poor girl setting her mind on you, for there's Shaneen thinks she wouldn't suit you, though all is saying that she'll wed you now.

(CHRISTY *beams with delight.*)

SHAWN (*in terrified earnest*): She wouldn't suit you, and she with the divil's own temper the way you'd be strangling one another in a score of days. (*He makes the movement of strangling with his hands.*) It's the like of me only that she's fit for; a quiet simple fellow wouldn't raise a hand upon her if she scratched itself.

WIDOW QUIN (*putting* SHAWN's *hat on* CHRISTY): Fit them clothes on you anyhow, young fellow, and he'd maybe loan them to you for the sports. (*Pushing him towards inner door.*) Fit them on and you can give your answer when you have them tried.

CHRISTY (*beaming, delighted with the clothes*): I will then. I'd like herself to see me in them tweeds and hat. (*He goes into room and shuts the door.*)

SHAWN (*in great anxiety*): He'd like herself to see them. He'll not leave us, Widow Quin. He's a score of divils in him the way it's well-nigh certain he will wed Pegeen.

WIDOW QUIN (*jeeringly*): It's true all girls are fond of courage and do hate the like of you.

SHAWN (*walking about in desperation*): Oh, Widow Quin, what'll I be doing now? I'd inform again him, but he'd burst from Kilmainham[28] and he'd be sure and certain to destroy me. If I wasn't so God-fearing, I'd near have courage to come behind him and run a pike into his side. Oh, it's a hard case to be an orphan and not to have your father that you're used to, and you'd easy kill and make yourself a hero in the sight of all. (*Coming up to her.*) Oh, Widow Quin, will you find me some contrivance when I've promised you a ewe?

WIDOW QUIN: A ewe's a small thing, but what would you give me if I did wed him and did save you so?

SHAWN (*with astonishment*): You?

WIDOW QUIN: Aye. Would you give me the red cow you have and the mountainy ram, and the right of way across your rye path, and a load of dung at Michaelmas, and turbary[29] upon the western hill?

SHAWN (*radiant with hope*): I would, surely, and I'd give you the wedding-ring I have, and the loan of a new suit, the way you'd have him decent on the wedding-day. I'd give you two kids for your dinner, and a gallon of poteen, and I'd call the piper on the long car to your wedding from Crossmolina or from Ballina. I'd give you . . .

WIDOW QUIN: That'll do, so, and let you whisht, for he's coming now again.

(CHRISTY *comes in very natty in the new clothes.* WIDOW QUIN *goes to him admiringly.*)

WIDOW QUIN: If you seen yourself now, I'm thinking you'd be too proud to speak to at all, and it'd be a pity surely to have your like sailing from Mayo to the western world.

[28] prison near Dublin   [29] right to cut turf

CHRISTY (*as proud as a peacock*): I'm not going. If this is a poor place itself, I'll make myself contented to be lodging here.

(WIDOW QUIN *makes a sign to* SHAWN *to leave them.*)

SHAWN: Well, I'm going measuring the racecourse while the tide is low, so I'll leave you the garments and my blessing for the sports to-day. God bless you! (*He wriggles out.*)

WIDOW QUIN (*admiring* CHRISTY): Well, you're mighty spruce, young fellow. Sit down now while you're quiet till you talk with me.

CHRISTY (*swaggering*): I'm going abroad on the hillside for to seek Pegeen.

WIDOW QUIN: You'll have time and plenty for to seek Pegeen, and you heard me saying at the fall of night the two of us should be great company.

CHRISTY: From this out I'll have no want of company when all sorts is bringing me their food and clothing (*he swaggers to the door, tightening his belt*), the way they'd set their eyes upon a gallant orphan cleft his father with one blow to the breeches belt. (*He opens door, then staggers back.*) Saints of glory! Holy angels from the throne of light!

WIDOW QUIN (*going over*): What ails you?

CHRISTY: It's the walking spirit of my murdered da!

WIDOW QUIN (*looking out*): Is it that tramper?

CHRISTY (*wildly*): Where'll I hide my poor body from that ghost of hell?

(*The door is pushed open, and* OLD MAHON *appears on threshold.* CHRISTY *darts in behind door.*)

WIDOW QUIN (*in great amusement*): God save you, my poor man.

MAHON (*gruffly*): Did you see a young lad passing this way in the early morning or the fall of night?

WIDOW QUIN: You're a queer kind to walk in not saluting at all.

MAHON: Did you see the young lad?

WIDOW QUIN (*stiffly*): What kind was he?

MAHON: An ugly young streeler[30] with a murderous gob[31] on him, and a little switch in his hand. I met a tramper seen him coming this way at the fall of night.

WIDOW QUIN: There's harvest hundreds do be passing these days for the Sligo boat. For what is it you're wanting him, my poor man?

MAHON: I want to destroy him for breaking the head on me with the clout of a loy. (*He takes off a big hat, and shows his head in a mass*

---

[30] vagabond   [31] "mug"

of bandages and plaster, with some pride.) It was he did that, and amn't I a great wonder to think I've traced him ten days with that rent in my crown?

WIDOW QUIN (*taking his head in both hands and examining it with extreme delight*): That was a great blow. And who hit you? A robber maybe?

MAHON: It was my own son hit me, and he the divil a robber, or anything else, but a dirty, stuttering lout.

WIDOW QUIN (*letting go his skull and wiping her hands in her apron*): You'd best be wary of a mortified scalp, I think they call it, lepping around with that wound in the splendour of the sun. It was a bad blow, surely, and you should have vexed him fearful to make him strike that gash in his da.

MAHON: Is it me?

WIDOW QUIN (*amusing herself*): Aye. And isn't it a great shame when the old and hardened do torment the young?

MAHON (*raging*): Torment him, is it? And I after holding out with the patience of a martyred saint till there's nothing but destruction on, and I'm driven out in my old age with none to aid me.

WIDOW QUIN (*greatly amused*): It's a sacred wonder the way that wickedness will spoil a man.

MAHON: My wickedness, is it? Amn't I after saying it is himself has me destroyed, and he a lier on walls, a talker of folly, a man you'd see stretched the half of the day in the brown ferns with his belly to the sun.

WIDOW QUIN: Not working at all?

MAHON: The divil a work, or if he did itself, you'd see him raising up a haystack like the stalk of a rush, or driving our last cow till he broke her leg at the hip, and when he wasn't at that he'd be fooling over little birds he had — finches and felts[32] — or making mugs at his own self in the bit of a glass we had hung on the wall.

WIDOW QUIN (*looking at* CHRISTY): What way was he so foolish? It was running wild after the girls maybe?

MAHON (*with a shout of derision*): Running wild, is it? If he seen a red petticoat coming swinging over the hill, he'd be off to hide in the sticks, and you'd see him shooting out his sheep's eyes between the little twigs and the leaves, and his two ears rising like a hare looking out through a gap. Girls, indeed!

WIDOW QUIN: It was drink maybe?

MAHON: And he a poor fellow would get drunk on the smell of a pint. He'd a queer rotten stomach, I'm telling you, and when I gave him

[32] thrushes

three pulls from my pipe a while since, he was taken with contortions till I had to send him in the ass-cart to the females' nurse.

WIDOW QUIN (*clasping her hands*): Well, I never, till this day, heard tell of a man the like of that!

MAHON: I'd take a mighty oath you didn't, surely, and wasn't he the laughing joke of every female woman where four baronies meet, the way the girls would stop their weeding if they seen him coming the road to let a roar at him, and call him the looney of Mahon's.

WIDOW QUIN: I'd give the world and all to see the like of him. What kind was he?

MAHON: A small, low fellow.

WIDOW QUIN: And dark?

MAHON: Dark and dirty.

WIDOW QUIN (*considering*): I'm thinking I seen him.

MAHON (*eagerly*): An ugly young blackguard.

WIDOW QUIN: A hideous, fearful villain, and the spit of you.

MAHON: What way is he fled?

WIDOW QUIN: Gone over the hills to catch a coasting steamer to the north or south.

MAHON: Could I pull up on him now?

WIDOW QUIN: If you'll cross the sands below where the tide is out, you'll be in it as soon as himself, for he had to go round ten miles by the top of the bay. (*She points to the door.*) Strike down by the head beyond and then follow on the roadway to the north and east.

(MAHON *goes abruptly.*)

WIDOW QUIN (*shouting after him*): Let you give him a good vengeance when you come up with him, but don't put yourself in the power of the law, for it'd be a poor thing to see a judge in his black cap reading out his sentence on a civil warrior the like of you. (*She swings the door to and looks at* CHRISTY, *who is cowering in terror, for a moment, then she bursts into a laugh.*) Well, you're the walking Playboy of the Western World, and that's the poor man you had divided to his breeches belt.

CHRISTY (*looking out; then, to her*): What'll Pegeen say when she hears that story? What'll she be saying to me now?

WIDOW QUIN: She'll knock the head of you, I'm thinking, and drive you from the door. God help her to be taking you for a wonder, and you a little schemer making up a story you destroyed your da.

CHRISTY (*turning to the door, nearly speechless with rage, half to himself*): To be letting on he was dead, and coming back to his life, and following after me like an old weasel tracing a rat, and coming in here laying desolation between my own self and the fine women of

Ireland, and he a kind of carcase that you'd fling upon the sea. . . .

WIDOW QUIN (*more soberly*): There's talking for a man's one only son.

CHRISTY (*breaking out*): His one son, is it? May I meet him with one
tooth and it aching, and one eye to be seeing seven and seventy divils
in the twists of the road, and one old timber leg on him to limp into
the scalding grave. (*Looking out.*) There he is now crossing the
strands, and that the Lord God would send a high wave to wash him
from the world.

WIDOW QUIN (*scandalized*): Have you no shame? (*Putting her hand on
his shoulder and turning him round.*) What ails you? Near crying,
is it?

CHRISTY (*in despair and grief*): Amn't I after seeing the love-light of
the star of knowledge shining from her brow, and hearing words
would put you thinking on the holy Brigid speaking to the infant
saints, and now she'll be turning again, and speaking hard words to
me, like an old woman with a spavindy[33] ass she'd have, urging on a
hill.

WIDOW QUIN: There's poetry talk for a girl you'd see itching and scratching, and she with a stale stink of poteen on her from selling in the
shop.

CHRISTY (*impatiently*): It's her like is fitted to be handling merchandise in the heavens above, and what'll I be doing now, I ask you, and
I a kind of wonder was jilted by the heavens when a day was by.

(*There is a distant noise of* GIRLS' *voices.* WIDOW QUIN *looks from
window and comes to him, hurriedly.*)

WIDOW QUIN: You'll be doing like myself, I'm thinking, when I did de-
troy my man, for I'm above many's the day, odd times in great
spirits, abroad in the sunshine, darning a stocking or stitching a
shift; and odd times again looking out on the schooners, hookers,
trawlers is sailing the sea, and I thinking on the gallant hairy fellows are drifting beyond, and myself long years living alone.

CHRISTY (*interested*): You're like me, so.

WIDOW QUIN: I am your like, and it's for that I'm taking a fancy to
you, and I with my little houseen above where there'd be myself
to tend you, and none to ask were you a murderer or what at all.

CHRISTY: And what would I be doing if I left Pegeen?

WIDOW QUIN: I've nice jobs you could be doing — gathering shells to
make a white-wash for our hut within, building up a little goose-
house, or stretching a new skin on an old curagh[34] I have, and if my
hut is far from all sides, it's there you'll meet the wisest old men, I

[33] lame   [34] boat

tell you, at the corner of my wheel, and it's there yourself and me will have great times whispering and hugging. . . .

VOICES (*outside, calling far away*): Christy! Christy Mahon! Christy!

CHRISTY: Is it Pegeen Mike?

WIDOW QUIN: It's the young girls, I'm thinking, coming to bring you to the sports below, and what is it you'll have me to tell them now?

CHRISTY: Aid me for to win Pegeen. It's herself only that I'm seeking now. (WIDOW QUIN *gets up and goes to window.*) Aid me for to win her, and I'll be asking God to stretch a hand to you in the hour of death, and lead you short cuts through the Meadows of Ease, and up the floor of Heaven to the Footstool of the Virgin's Son.

WIDOW QUIN: There's praying!

VOICES (*nearer*): Christy! Christy Mahon!

CHRISTY (*with agitation*): They're coming. Will you swear to aid and save me, for the love of Christ?

WIDOW QUIN (*looks at him for a moment*): If I aid you, will you swear to give me a right of way I want, and a mountainy ram, and a load of dung at Michaelmas, the time that you'll be master here?

CHRISTY: I will, by the elements and stars of night.

WIDOW QUIN: Then we'll not say a word of the old fellow, the way Pegeen won't know your story till the end of time.

CHRISTY: And if he chances to return again?

WIDOW QUIN: We'll swear he's a maniac and not your da. I could take an oath I seen him raving on the sands today.

(GIRLS *run in.*)

SUSAN: Come on to the sports below. Pegeen says you're to come.

SARA TANSEY: The lepping's beginning, and we've a jockey's suit to fit upon you for the mule race on the sands below.

HONOR: Come on, will you?

CHRISTY: I will then if Pegeen's beyond.

SARA: She's in the boreen[35] making game of Shaneen Keogh.

CHRISTY: Then I'll be going to her now. (*He runs out, followed by the* GIRLS.)

WIDOW QUIN: Well, if the worst comes in the end of all, it'll be great game to see there's none to pity him but a widow woman, the like of me, has buried her children and destroyed her man. (*She goes out.*)

[35] lane

ACT III

(*Scene as before. Later in the day.* JIMMY *comes in, slightly drunk.*)

JIMMY (*calls*): Pegeen! (*Crosses to inner door.*) Pegeen Mike! (*Comes back again into the room.*) Pegeen! (PHILLY *comes in in the same state. To* PHILLY.) Did you see herself?

PHILLY: I did not; but I sent Shawn Keogh with the ass-cart for to bear him home. (*Trying cupboards, which are locked.*) Well, isn't he a nasty man to get into such staggers at a morning wake; and isn't herself the divil's daughter for locking, and she so fussy after that young gaffer, you might take your death with drouth and none to heed you?

JIMMY: It's little wonder she'd be fussy, and he after bringing bank-rupt ruin on the roulette man, and the trick-o'-the-loop man, and breaking the nose of the cockshot-man, and winning all in the sports below, racing, lepping, dancing, and the Lord knows what! He's right luck, I'm telling you.

PHILLY: If he has, he'll be rightly hobbled yet, and he not able to say ten words without making a brag of the way he killed his father, and the great blow he hit with the loy.

JIMMY: A man can't hang by his own informing, and his father should be rotten by now.

(OLD MAHON *passes window slowly.*)

PHILLY: Supposing a man's digging spuds in that field with a long spade, and supposing he flings up the two halves of that skull, what'll be said then in the papers and the courts of law?

JIMMY: They'd say it was an old Dane, maybe, was drowned in the flood. (OLD MAHON *comes in and sits down near door listening.*) Did you never hear tell of the skulls they have in the city of Dublin, ranged out like blue jugs in a cabin of Connaught?

PHILLY: And you believe that?

JIMMY (*pugnaciously*): Didn't a lad see them and he after coming from harvesting in the Liverpool boat? "They have them there," says he, "making a show of the great people there was one time walking the world. White skulls and black skulls and yellow skulls, and some with full teeth, and some haven't only but one."

PHILLY: It was no lie, maybe, for when I was a young lad there was a graveyard beyond the house with the remnants of a man who had thighs as long as your arm. He was a horrid man, I'm telling you, and there was many a fine Sunday I'd put him together for fun, and he with shiny bones, you wouldn't meet the like of these days in the cities of the world.

MAHON (*getting up*): You wouldn't, is it? Lay your eyes on that skull, and tell me where and when there was another the like of it, is splintered only from the blow of a loy.

PHILLY: Glory be to God! And who hit you at all?

MAHON (*triumphantly*): It was my own son hit me. Would you believe that?

JIMMY: Well, there's wonders hidden in the heart of man!

PHILLY (*suspiciously*): And what way was it done?

MAHON (*wandering about the room*): I'm after walking hundreds and long scores of miles, winning clean beds and the fill of my belly four times in the day, and I doing nothing but telling stories of that naked truth. (*He comes to them a little aggressively.*) Give me a supeen and I'll tell you now.

(WIDOW QUIN *comes in and stands aghast behind him. He is facing* JIMMY *and* PHILLY, *who are on the left.*)

JIMMY: Ask herself beyond. She's the stuff hidden in her shawl.

WIDOW QUIN (*coming to* MAHON *quickly*): You here, is it? You didn't go far at all?

MAHON: I seen the coasting steamer passing, and I got a drouth upon me and a cramping leg, so I said, "The divil go along with him," and turned again. (*Looking under her shawl.*) And let you give me a supeen, for I'm destroyed travelling since Tuesday was a week.

WIDOW QUIN (*getting a glass, in a cajoling tone*): Sit down then by the fire and take your ease for a space. You've a right to be destroyed indeed, with your walking, and fighting, and facing the sun. (*Giving him poteen from a stone jar she has brought in.*) There now is a drink for you, and may it be to your happiness and length of life.

MAHON (*taking glass greedily, and sitting down by fire*): God increase you!

WIDOW QUIN (*taking men to the right stealthily*): Do you know what? That man's raving from his wound today, for I met him a while since telling a rambling tale of a tinker had him destroyed. Then he heard of Christy's deed, and he up and says it was his son had cracked his skull. Oh, isn't madness a fright, for he'll go killing someone yet, and he thinking it's the man has struck him so?

JIMMY (*entirely convinced*): It's a fright surely. I knew a party was kicked in the head by a red mare, and he went killing horses a great while, till he eat the insides of a clock and died after.

PHILLY (*with suspicion*): Did he see Christy?

WIDOW QUIN: He didn't (*With a warning gesture.*) Let you not be putting him in mind of him, or you'll be likely summoned if there's murder done. (*Looking round at* MAHON.) Whisht! He's listening. Wait now till you hear me taking him easy and unravelling all. (*She goes to* MAHON.) And what way are you feeling, mister? Are you in contentment now?

MAHON (*slightly emotional from his drink*): I'm poorly only, for it's a hard story the way I'm left today, when it was I did tend him from his hour of birth, and he a dunce never reached his second book, the way he'd come from school, many's the day, with his legs lamed under him, and he blackened with his beatings like a tinker's ass. It's a hard story, I'm saying, the way some do have their next and nighest raising up a hand of murder on them, and some is lonesome getting their death with lamentation in the dead of night.

WIDOW QUIN (*not knowing what to say*): To hear you talking so quiet, who'd know you were the same fellow we seen pass today?

MAHON: I'm the same surely. The wrack and ruin of three-score years; and it's a terror to live that length, I tell you, and to have your sons going to the dogs against you, and you wore out scolding them, and skelping[36] them, and God knows what.

PHILLY (*to* JIMMY): He's not raving. (*To* WIDOW QUIN.) Will you ask him what kind was his son?

WIDOW QUIN (*to* MAHON, *with a peculiar look*): Was your son that hit you a lad of one year and a score maybe, a great hand at racing and lepping and licking the world?

MAHON (*turning on her with a roar of rage*): Didn't you hear me say he was the fool of men, the way from this out he'll know the orphan's lot, with old and young making game of him, and they swearing, raging, kicking at him like a mangy cur.

(*A great burst of cheering outside, some way off.*)

MAHON (*putting his hands to his ears*): What in the name of God do they want roaring below?

WIDOW QUIN (*with the shade of a smile*): They're cheeting a young lad, the champion Playboy of the Western World.

(*More cheering.*)

MAHON (*going to window*): It'd split my heart to hear them, and I with pulses in my brain-pan for a week gone by. Is it racing they are?

JIMMY (*looking from door*): It is, then. They are mounting him for

[36] beating

the mule race will be run upon the sands. That's the playboy on the winkered [37] mule.

MAHON (*puzzled*): That lad, is it? If you said it was a fool he was, I'd have laid a mighty oath he was the likeness of my wandering son. (*Uneasily, putting his hand to his head.*) Faith, I'm thinking I'll go walking for to view the race.

WIDOW QUIN (*stopping him, sharply*): You will not. You'd best take the road to Belmullet, and not be dilly-dallying in this place where there isn't a spot you could sleep.

PHILLY (*coming forward*): Don't mind her. Mount there on the bench and you'll have a view of the whole. They're hurrying before the tide will rise, and it'd be near over if you went down the pathway through the crags below.

MAHON (*mounts on bench,* WIDOW QUIN *beside him*): That's a right view again the edge of the sea. They're coming now from the point. He's leading. Who is he at all?

WIDOW QUIN: He's the champion of the world, I tell you, and there isn't a hap'orth[38] isn't falling lucky to his hands today.

PHILLY (*looking out, interested in the race*): Look at that. They're pressing him now.

JIMMY: He'll win it yet.

PHILLY: Take your time, Jimmy Farrell. It's too soon to say.

WIDOW QUIN (*shouting*): Watch him taking the gate. There's riding.

JIMMY (*cheering*): More power to the young lad!

MAHON: He's passing the third.

JIMMY: He'll lick them yet.

WIDOW QUIN: He'd lick them if he was running races with a score itself.

MAHON: Look at the mule he has, kicking the stars.

WIDOW QUIN: There was a lep! (*Catching hold of* MAHON *in her excitement.*) He's fallen? He's mounted again! Faith, he's passing them all!

JIMMY: Look at him skelping her!

PHILLY: And the mountain girls hooshing him on!

JIMMY: It's the last turn! The post's cleared for them now!

MAHON: Look at the narrow place. He'll be into the bogs! (*With a yell.*) Good rider! He's through it again!

JIMMY: He neck and neck!

PHILLY: Good boy to him! Flames, but he's in! (*Great cheering, in which all join.*)

MAHON (*with hesitation*): What's that? They're raising him up.

---

[37] blinkered   [38] ha'pennyworth, *i.e.*, merest trifle

They're coming this way. (*With a roar of rage and astonishment.*) It's Christy, by the stars of God! I'd know his way of spitting and he astride the moon. (*He jumps down and makes a run for the door, but* WIDOW QUIN *catches him and pulls him back.*)

WIDOW QUIN: Stay quiet, will you? That's not your son. (*To* JIMMY.) Stop him, or you'll get a month for the abetting of manslaughter and be fined as well.

JIMMY: I'll hold him.

MAHON (*struggling*): Let me out! Let me out, the lot of you, till I have my vengeance on his head today.

WIDOW QUIN (*shaking him, vehemently*): That's not your son. That's a man is going to make a marriage with the daughter of this house, a place with fine trade, with a licence, and with poteen too.

MAHON (*amazed*): That man marrying a decent and a moneyed girl! Is it mad yous are? Is it in a crazy-house for females that I'm landed now?

WIDOW QUIN: It's mad yourself is with the blow upon your head. That lad is the wonder of the western world.

MAHON: I seen it's my son.

WIDOW QUIN: You seen that you're mad. (*Cheering outside.*) Do you hear them cheering him in the zig-zags of the road? Aren't you after saying that your son's a fool, and how would they be cheering a true idiot born?

MAHON (*getting distressed*): It's maybe out of reason that that man's himself. (*Cheering again.*) There's none surely will go cheering him. Oh, I'm raving with a madness that would fright the world! (*He sits down with his hand to his head.*) There was one time I seen ten scarlet divils letting on they'd cork my spirit in a gallon can; and one time I seen rats as big as badgers sucking the lifeblood from the butt of my lug; [39] but I never till this day confused that dribbling idiot with a likely man. I'm destroyed surely.

WIDOW QUIN: And who'd wonder when it's your brain-pan that is gaping now?

MAHON: Then the blight of the sacred drouth upon myself and him, for I never went mad to this day, and I not three weeks with the Limerick girls drinking myself silly and parlatic[40] from the dusk to dawn. (*To* WIDOW QUIN, *suddenly.*) Is my visage astray?

WIDOW QUINN: It is, then. You're a sniggering maniac, a child could see.

MAHON (*getting up more cheerfully*): Then I'd best be going to the union[41] beyond, and there'll be a welcome before me, I tell you (*with*

[39] lobe of my ear   [40] paralytic   [41] parish work house

great pride), and I a terrible and fearful case, the way that there I was one time, screeching in a straightened waistcoat, with seven doctors writing out my sayings in a printed book. Would you believe that?

WIDOW QUIN: If you're a wonder itself, you'd best be hasty, for them lads caught a maniac one time and pelted the poor creature till he ran out, raving and foaming, and was drowned in the sea.

MAHON (*with philosophy*): It's true mankind is the divil when your head's astray. Let me out now and I'll slip down the boreen, and not see them so.

WIDOW QUIN (*showing him out*): That's it. Run to the right, and not a one will see. (*He runs off.*)

PHILLY (*wisely*): You're at some gaming, Widow Quin; but I'll walk after him and give him his dinner and a time to rest, and I'll see then if he's raving or as sane as you.

WIDOW QUIN (*annoyed*): If you go near that lad, let you be wary of your head, I'm saying. Didn't you hear him telling he was crazed at times?

PHILLY: I heard him telling a power; and I'm thinking we'll have right sport before night will fall. (*He goes out.*)

JIMMY: Well, Philly's a conceited and foolish man. How could that madman have his senses and his brain-pan slit? I'll go after them and see him turn on Philly now.

(*He goes;* WIDOW QUIN *hides poteen behind counter. Then hubbub outside.*)

VOICES: There you are! Good jumper! Grand lepper! Darlint boy! He's the racer! Bear him on, will you!

(CHRISTY *comes in, in jockey's dress, with* PEGEEN MIKE, SARA, *and other* GIRLS *and* MEN.)

PEGEEN (*to crowd*): Go on now and don't destroy him and he drenching with sweat. Go along, I'm saying, and have your tug-of-warring till he's dried his skin.

CROWD: Here's his prizes! A bagpipes! A fiddle was played by a poet in the years gone by! A flat and three-thorned blackthorn would lick the scholars out of Dublin town!

CHRISTY (*taking prizes from the* MEN): Thank you kindly, the lot of you. But you'd say it was little only I did this day if you'd seen me a while since striking my one single blow.

TOWN CRIER (*outside ringing a bell*): Take notice, last event of this day! Tug-of-warring on the green below! Come on, the lot of you! Great achievements for all Mayo men!

PEGEEN: Go on and leave him for to rest and dry. Go on, I tell you, for he'll do no more.

(*She hustles crowd out;* WIDOW QUIN *following them.*)

MEN (*going*): Come on, then. Good luck for the while!

PEGEEN (*radiantly, wiping his face with her shawl*): Well, you're the lad, and you'll have great times from this out when you could win that wealth of prizes, and you sweating in the heat of noon!

CHRISTY (*looking at her with delight*): I'll have great times if I win the crowning prize I'm seeking now, and that's your promise that you'll wed me in a fortnight, when our banns is called.

PEGEEN (*backing away from him*): You've right daring to go ask me that, when all knows you'll be starting to some girl in your own townland, when your father's rotten in four months, or five.

CHRISTY (*indignantly*): Starting from you, it it? (*He follows her.*) I will not, then, and when the airs is warming, in four months or five, it's then yourself and me should be pacing Neifin in the dews of night, the times sweet smells do be rising, and you'd see a little, shiny new moon, maybe, sinking on the hills.

PEGEEN (*looking at him playfully*): And it's that kind of a poacher's love you'd make, Christy Mahon, on the sides of Neifin, when the night is down?

CHRISTY: It's little you'll think if my love's a poacher's, or an earl's itself, when you'll feel my two hands stretched around you, and I squeezing kisses on your puckered lips, till I'd feel a kind of pity for the Lord God is all ages sitting lonesome in His golden chair.

PEGEEN: That'll be right fun, Christy Mahon, and any girl would walk her heart out before she'd meet a young man was your like for eloquence, or talk at all.

CHRISTY (*encouraged*): Let you wait, to hear me talking, till we're astray in Erris, when Good Friday's by, drinking a sup from a well, and making mighty kisses with our wetted mouths, or gaming in a gap of sunshine, with yourself stretched back unto your necklace, in the flowers of the earth.

PEGEEN (*in a low voice, moved by his tone*): I'd be nice so, is it?

CHRISTY (*with rapture*): If the mitred bishops seen you that time, they'd be the like of the holy prophets, I'm thinking, do be straining the bars of Paradise to lay eyes on the Lady Helen of Troy, and she abroad, pacing back and forward, with a nosegay in her golden shawl.

PEGEEN (*with real tenderness*): And what is it I have, Christy Mahon, to make me fitting entertainment for the like of you, that has such poet's talking, and such bravery of heart.

CHRISTY (*in a low voice*): Isn't there the light of seven heavens in your heart alone, the way you'll be an angel's lamp to me from this out, and I abroad in the darkness, spearing salmons in the Owen or the Carrowmore?

PEGEEN: If I was your wife I'd be along with you those nights, Christy Mahon, the way you'd see I was a great hand at coaxing bailiffs, or coining funny nicknames for the stars of night.

CHRISTY: You, is it? Taking your death in the hailstones, or in the fogs of dawn.

PEGEEN: Yourself and me would shelter easy in a narrow bush (*with a qualm of dread*); but we're only talking, maybe, for this would be a poor, thatched place to hold a fine lad is the like of you.

CHRISTY (*putting his arm round her*): If I wasn't a good Christian, it's on my naked knees I'd be saying my prayers and paters to every jack-straw you have roofing your head, and every stony pebble is paving the laneway to your door.

PEGEEN (*radiantly*): If that's the truth I'll be burning candles from this out to the miracles of God that have brought you from the south to-day, and I with my gowns bought ready, the way that I can wed you, and not wait at all.

CHRISTY: It's miracles, and that's the truth. Me there toiling a long while, and walking a long while, not knowing at all I was drawing all times nearer to this holy day.

PEGEEN: And myself, a girl, was tempted often to go sailing the seas till I'd marry a Jew-man, with ten kegs of gold, and I not knowing at all there was the like of you drawing nearer, like the stars of God.

CHRISTY: And to think I'm long years hearing women talking that talk, to all bloody fools, and this the first time I've heard the like of your voice talking sweetly for my own delight.

PEGEEN: And to think it's me is talking sweetly, Christy Mahon, and I the fright of seven townlands for my biting tongue. Well, the heart's a wonder; and, I'm thinking, there won't be our like in Mayo, for gallant lovers, from this hour today. (*Drunken singing is heard outside.*) There's my father coming from the wake, and when he's had his sleep we'll tell him, for he's peaceful then. (*They separate.*)

MICHAEL (*singing outside*):

> The jailer and the turnkey
> They quickly ran us down,
> And brought us back as prisoners
> Once more to Cavan town.

(*He comes in supported by* SHAWN.)

There we lay bewailing
All in a prison bound.´ . . .

(*He sees* CHRISTY. *Goes and shakes him drunkenly by the hand,
while* PEGEEN *and* SHAWN *talk on the left.*)

MICHAEL (*to* CHRISTY): The blessing of God and the holy angels on
your head, young fellow. I hear tell you're after winning all in the
sports below; and wasn't it a shame I didn't bear you along with me
to Kate Cassidy's wake, a fine, stout lad, the like of you, for you'd
never see the match of it for flows of drink, the way when we sunk
her bones at noon-day in her narrow grave, there were five men, aye,
and six men, stretched out retching speechless on the holy stones.

CHRISTY (*uneasily, watching* PEGEEN): Is that the truth?

MICHAEL: It is, then; and aren't you a louty schemer to go burying your
poor father unbeknownst when you'd a right to throw him on the
crupper of a Kerry mule and drive him westwards, like holy Joseph in
the days gone by, the way we could have given him a decent burial,
and not have him rotting beyond, and not a Christian drinking a
smart drop to the glory of his soul?

CHRISTY (*gruffly*): It's well enough he's lying, for the likes of him.

MICHAEL (*slapping him on the back*): Well, aren't you a hardened
slayer? It'll be a poor thing for the household man where you go
sniffing for a female wife; and (*pointing to* SHAWN) look beyond at
that shy and decent Christian I have chosen for my daughter's hand,
and I after getting the gilded dispensation this day for to wed them
now.

CHRISTY: And you'll be wedding them this day, is it?

MICHAEL (*drawing himself up*): Aye. Are you thinking, if I'm drunk itself, I'd leave my daughter living single with a little frisky rascal is
the like of you?

PEGEEN (*breaking away from* SHAWN): Is it the truth the dispensation's
come?

MICHAEL (*triumphantly*): Father Reilly's after reading it in gallous[42]
Latin, and "It's come in the nick of time," says he; "so I'll wed them
in a hurry, dreading that young gaffer who'd capsize the stars."

PEGEEN (*fiercely*): He's missed his nick of time, for it's that lad,
Christy Mahon, that I'm wedding now.

MICHAEL (*loudly, with horror*): You'd be making him a son to me,
and he wet and crusted with his father's blood?

PEGEEN: Aye. Wouldn't it be a bitter thing for a girl to go marrying

[42] an intensive: "bloody," "great"

the like of Shaneen, and he a middling kind of a scarecrow, with no savagery or fine words in him at all?

MICHAEL (*gasping and sinking on a chair*): Oh, aren't you a heathen daughter to go shaking the fat of my heart, and I swamped and drownded with the weight of drink? Would you have them turning on me the way that I'd be roaring to the dawn of day with the wind upon my heart? Have you not a word to aid me, Shaneen? Are you not jealous at all?

SHAWN (*in great misery*): I'd be afeard to be jealous of a man did slay his da.

PEGEEN: Well, it'd be a poor thing to go marrying your like. I'm seeing there's a world of peril for an orphan girl, and isn't it a great blessing I didn't wed you before himself came walking from the west or south?

SHAWN: It's a queer story you'd go picking a dirty tramp up from the highways of the world.

PEGEEN (*playfully*): And you think you're a likely beau to go straying along with the shiny Sundays of the opening year, when it's sooner on a bullock's liver you'd put a poor girl thinking than on the lily or the rose?

SHAWN: And have you no mind of my weight of passion, and the holy dispensation, and the drift of heifers I'm giving, and the golden ring?

PEGEEN: I'm thinking you're too fine for the like of me, Shawn Keogh of Killakeen, and let you go off till you'd find a radiant lady with droves of bullocks on the plains of Meath, and herself bedizened in the diamond jewelleries of Pharaoh's ma. That'd be your match, Shaneen. So God save you now! (*She retreats behind* CHRISTY.)

SHAWN: Won't you hear me telling you . . . ?

CHRISTY (*with ferocity*): Take yourself from this, young fellow, or I'll maybe add a murder to my deeds today.

MICHAEL (*springing up with a shriek*): Murder, is it? Is it mad yous are? Would you go making murder in this place, and it piled with poteen for our drink to-night? Go on to the foreshore if it's fighting you want, where the rising tide will wash all traces from the memory of man. (*Pushing* SHAWN *towards* CHRISTY.)

SHAWN (*shaking himself free, and getting behind* MICHAEL): I'll not fight him, Michael James. I'd liefer live a bachelor, simmering in passions to the end of time, than face a lepping savage the like of him has descended from the Lord knows where. Strike him yourself, Michael James, or you'll lose my drift of heifers and my blue bull from Sneem.

MICHAEL: Is it me fight him, when it's father-slaying he's bred to now? (*Pushing* SHAWN.) Go on, you fool, and fight him now.

SHAWN (*coming forward a little*): Will I strike him with my hand?

MICHAEL: Take the loy is on your western side.

SHAWN: I'd be afeard of the gallows if I struck with that.

CHRISTY (*taking up the loy*): Then I'll make you face the gallows or quit off from this. (SHAWN *flies out of the door.*)

CHRISTY: Well, fine weather be after him (*going to* MICHAEL, *coaxingly*), and I'm thinking you wouldn't wish to have that quaking blackguard in your house at all. Let you give us your blessing and hear her swear her faith to me, for I'm mounted on the spring-tide of the stars of luck, the way it'll be good for any to have me in the house.

PEGEEN (*at the other side of* MICHAEL): Bless us now, for I swear to God I'll wed him, and I'll not renege.

MICHAEL (*standing up in the centre, holding on to both of them*): It's the will of God, I'm thinking, that all should win an easy or a cruel end, and it's the will of God that all should rear up lengthy families for the nurture of the earth. What's a single man, I ask you, eating a bit in one house and drinking a sup in another, and he with no place of his own, like an old braying jackass strayed upon the rocks? (*To* CHRISTY.) It's many would be in dread to bring your like into their house for to end them, maybe, with a sudden end; but I'm a decent man of Ireland, and I liefer face the grave untimely and I seeing a score of grandsons growing up little gallant swearers by the name of God, than go peopling my bedside with puny weeds the like of what you'd breed, I'm thinking, out of Shaneen Keogh. (*He joins their hands.*) A daring fellow is the jewel of the world, and a man did split his father's middle with a single clout should have the bravery of ten, so may God and Mary and St. Patrick bless you, and increase you from this mortal day.

CHRISTY *and* PEGEEN: Amen, O Lord!

(*Hubbub outside.* OLD MAHON *rushes in, followed by all the crowd, and* WIDOW QUIN. *He makes a rush at* CHRISTY, *knocks him down, and begins to beat him.*)

PEGEEN (*dragging back his arm*): Stop that, will you? Who are you at all?

MAHON: His father, God forgive me!

PEGEEN (*drawing back*): Is it rose from the dead?

MAHON: Do you think I look so easy quenched with the tap of a loy?

(*Beats* CHRISTY *again.*)

PEGEEN (*glaring at* CHRISTY): And it's lies you told, letting on you had him slitted, and you nothing at all.

CHRISTY (*catching* MAHON's *stick*): He's not my father. He's a raving maniac would scare the world. (*Pointing to* WIDOW QUIN.) Herself knows it is true.

CROWD: You're fooling Pegeen! The Widow Quin seen him this day, and you likely knew! You're a liar!

CHRISTY (*dumbfounded*): It's himself was a liar, lying stretched out with an open head on him, letting on he was dead.

MAHON: Weren't you off racing the hills before I got my breath with the start I had seeing you turn on me at all?

PEGEEN: And to think of the coaxing glory we had given him, and he after doing nothing but hitting a soft blow and chasing northward in a sweat of fear. Quit off from this.

CHRISTY (*piteously*): You've seen my doings this day, and let you save me from the old man; for why would you be in such a scorch of haste to spur me to destruction now?

PEGEEN: It's there your treachery is spurring me, till I'm hard set to think you're the one I'm after lacing in my heart-strings half an hour gone by. (*To* MAHON.) Take him on from this, for I think bad the world should see me raging for a Munster liar, and the fool of men.

MAHON: Rise up now to retribution, and come on with me.

CROWD (*jeeringly*): There's the playboy! There's the lad thought he'd rule the roost in Mayo! Slate him now, mister.

CHRISTY (*getting up in shy terror*): What is it drives you to torment me here, when I'd asked the thunders of the might of God to blast me if I ever did hurt to any saving only that one single blow.

MAHON (*loudly*): If you didn't, you're a poor good-for-nothing, and isn't it by the like of you the sins of the whole world are committed?

CHRISTY (*raising his hands*): In the name of the Almighty God . . .

MAHON: Leave troubling the Lord God. Would you have Him sending down drouths, and fevers, and the old hen and the cholera morbus?

CHRISTY (*to* WIDOW QUIN): Will you come between us and protect me now?

WIDOW QUIN: I've tried a lot, God help me, and my share is done.

CHRISTY (*looking round in desperation*): And I must go back into my torment, is it, or run off like a vagabond straying through the unions with the dust of August making mudstains in the gullet of my throat; or the winds of March blowing on me till I'd take an oath I felt them making whistles of my ribs within?

SARA: Ask Pegeen to aid you. Her like does often change.

CHRISTY: I will not, then, for there's torment in the splendour of her like, and she a girl any moon of midnight would take pride to meet, facing southwards on the heaths of Keel. But what did I want crawling forward to scorch my understanding at her flaming brow?

PEGEEN (*to* MAHON, *vehemently, fearing she will break into tears*): Take him on from this or I'll set the young lads to destroy him here.

MAHON (*going to him, shaking his stick*): Come on now if you wouldn't have the company to see you skelped.

PEGEEN (*half-laughing, through her tears*): That's it, now the world will see him pandied,[43] and he an ugly liar was playing off the hero, and the fright of men.

CHRISTY (*to* MAHON, *very sharply*): Leave me go!

CROWD: That's it. Now, Christy. If them two set fighting, it will lick the world.

MAHON (*making a grab at* CHRISTY): Come here to me.

CHRISTY (*more threatening*): Leave me go, I'm saying.

MAHON: I will, maybe, when your legs is limping, and your back is blue.

CROWD: Keep it up, the two of you. I'll back the old one. Now the play-boy.

CHRISTY (*in low and intense voice*): Shut your yelling, for if you're after making a mighty man of me this day by the power of a lie, you're setting me now to think if it's a poor thing to be lonesome it's worse, maybe, go mixing with the fools of earth.

(MAHON *makes a movement towards him.*)

CHRISTY (*almost shouting*): Keep off . . . lest I do show a blow unto the lot of you would set the guardian angels winking in the clouds above. (*He swings round with a sudden rapid movement and picks up a loy.*)

CROWD (*half-frightened, half-amused*): He's going mad! Mind yourselves! Run from the idiot!

CHRISTY: If I am an idiot, I'm after hearing my voice this day saying words would raise the top-knot on a poet in a merchant's town. I've won your racing, and your lepping, and . . .

MAHON: Shut your gullet and come on with me.

CHRISTY: I'm going, but I'll stretch you first.

(*He runs at* OLD MAHON *with the loy, chases him out of the door, followed by crowd and* WIDOW QUIN. *There is a great noise outside, then a yell, and dead silence for a moment.* CHRISTY *comes in, half-dazed, and goes to fire.*)

[43] beaten

WIDOW QUIN (*coming in hurriedly, and going to him*): They're turning again you. Come on, or you'll be hanged, indeed.

CHRISTY: I'm thinking, from this out, Pegeen'll be giving me praises, the same as in the hours gone by.

WIDOW QUIN (*impatiently*): Come by the back door. I'd think bad to have you stifled on the gallows tree.

CHRISTY (*indignantly*): I will not, then. What good'd be my lifetime if I left Pegeen?

WIDOW QUIN: Come on, and you'll be no worse than you were last night; and you with a double murder this time to be telling to the girls.

CHRISTY: I'll not leave Pegeen Mike.

WIDOW QUIN (*impatiently*): Isn't there the match of her in every parish public, from Binghamstown unto the plain of Meath? Come on, I tell you, and I'll find you finer sweethearts at each waning moon.

CHRISTY: It's Pegeen I'm seeking only, and what'd I care if you brought me a drift of chosen females, standing in their shifts itself, maybe, from this place to the eastern world?

SARA (*runs in, pulling off one of her petticoats*): They're going to hang him. (*Holding out petticoat and shawl.*) Fit these upon him, and let him run off to the east.

WIDOW QUIN: He's raving now; but we'll fit them on him, and I'll take him to the ferry to the Achill boat.

CHRISTY (*struggling feebly*): Leave me go, will you? when I'm thinking of my luck today, for she will wed me surely, and I a proven hero in the end of all.

(*They try to fasten petticoat round him.*)

WIDOW QUIN: Take his left hand, and we'll pull him now. Come on, young fellow.

CHRISTY (*suddenly starting up*): You'll be taking me from her? You're jealous, is it, of her wedding me? Go on from this. (*He snatches up a stool, and threatens them with it.*)

WIDOW QUIN (*going*): It's in the madhouse they should put him, not in jail, at all. We'll go by the back door to call the doctor, and we'll save him so.

(*She goes out, with* SARA, *through inner room.* MEN *crowd in the doorway.* CHRISTY *sits down again by the fire.*)

MICHAEL (*in a terrified whisper*): Is the old lad killed surely?

PHILLY: I'm after feeling the last gasps quitting his heart. (*They peer in at* CHRISTY.)

MICHAEL (*with a rope*): Look at the way he is. Twist a hangman's knot on it, and slip it over his head, while he's not minding at all.

PHILLY: Let you take it, Shaneen. You're the soberest of all that's here.

SHAWN: Is it me to go near him, and he the wickedest and the worst with me? Let you take it, Pegeen Mike.

PEGEEN: Come on, so. (*She goes forward with the others, and they drop the double hitch over his head.*)

CHRISTY: What ails you?

SHAWN (*triumphantly, as they pull the rope tight on his arms*): Come on to the peelers, till they stretch you now.

CHRISTY: Me!

MICHAEL: If we took pity on you the Lord God would, maybe, bring us ruin from the law today, so you'd best come easy, for hanging is an easy and a speedy end.

CHRISTY: I'll not stir. (*To* PEGEEN.) And what is it you'll say to me, and I after doing it this time in the face of all?

PEGEEN: I'll say, a strange man is a marvel, with his mighty talk; but what's a squabble in your backyard, and the blow of a loy, have taught me that there's a great gap between a gallous story and a dirty deed. (*To* MEN.) Take him on from this, or the lot of us will be likely put on trial for his deed to-day.

CHRISTY (*with horror in his voice*): And it's yourself will send me off, to have a horny-fingered hangman hitching his bloody slipknots at the butt of my ear.

MEN (*pulling rope*): Come on, will you?

(*He is pulled down on the floor.*)

CHRISTY (*twisting his legs round the table*): Cut the rope, Pegeen, and I'll quit the lot of you, and live from this out, like the madmen of Keel, eating muck and green weeds on the faces of the cliffs.

PEGEEN: And leave us to hang, is it, for a saucy liar, the like of you? (*To* MEN.) Take him on, out from this.

SHAWN: Pull a twist on his neck, and squeeze him so.

PHILLY: Twist yourself. Sure he cannot hurt you, if you keep your distance from his teeth alone.

SHAWN: I'm afeard of him. (*To* PEGEEN.) Lift a lighted sod, will you, and scorch his leg.

PEGEEN (*blowing the fire with a bellows*): Leave go now, young fellow, or I'll scorch your shins.

CHRISTY: You're blowing for to torture me. (*His voice rising and growing stronger.*) That's your kind, is it? Then let the lot of you be wary, for, if I've to face the gallows, I'll have a gay march down, I tell you, and shed the blood of some of you before I die.

SHAWN (*in terror*): Keep a good hold, Philly. Be wary, for the love of God. For I'm thinking he would liefest wreak his pains on me.

CHRISTY (*almost gaily*): If I do lay my hands on you, it's the way you'll be at the fall of night, hanging as a scarecrow for the fowls of hell. Ah, you'll have a gallous jaunt, I'm saying, coaching out through Limbo with my father's ghost.

SHAWN (*to* PEGEEN): Make haste, will you? Oh, isn't he a holy terror, and isn't it true for Father Reilly, that all drink's a curse that has the lot of you so shaky and uncertain now?

CHRISTY: If I can wring a neck among you, I'll have a royal judgment looking on the trembling jury in the courts of law. And won't there be crying out in Mayo the day I'm stretched upon the rope, with ladies in their silks and satins snivelling in their lacy kerchiefs, and they rhyming songs and ballads on the terror of my fate? (*He squirms round on the floor and bites* SHAWN's *leg*.)

SHAWN (*shrieking*): My leg's bit on me. He's the like of a mad dog, I'm thinking, the way that I will surely die.

CHRISTY (*delighted with himself*): You will, then, the way you can shake out hell's flags of welcome for my coming in two weeks or three, for I'm thinking Satan hasn't many have killed their da in Kerry, and in Mayo too.

(OLD MAHON *comes in behind on all fours and looks on unnoticed*.)

MEN (*to* PEGEEN): Bring the sod, will you?

PEGEEN (*coming over*): God help him so. (*Burns his leg*.)

CHRISTY (*kicking and screaming*): Oh, glory be to God! (*He kicks loose from the table, and they all drag him towards the door*.)

JIMMY (*seeing* OLD MAHON): Will you look what's come in?

(*They all drop* CHRISTY *and run left*.)

CHRISTY (*scrambling on his knees face to face with* OLD MAHON): Are you coming to be killed a third time, or what ails you now?

MAHON: For what is it they have you tied?

CHRISTY: They're taking me to the peelers to have me hanged for slaying you.

MICHAEL (*apologetically*): It is the will of God that all should guard their little cabins from the treachery of law, and what would my daughter be doing if I was ruined or was hanged itself?

MAHON (*grimly, loosening* CHRISTY): It's little I care if you put a bag on her back, and went picking cockles till the hour of death; but my son and myself will be going our own way, and we'll have great times from this out telling stories of the villainy of Mayo, and the fools is here. (*To* CHRISTY, *who is freed.*) Come on now.

CHRISTY: Go with you, is it? I will then, like a gallant captain with his heathen slave. Go on now and I'll see you from this day stewing my oatmeal and washing my spuds, for I'm master of all fights from now. (*Pushing* MAHON.) Go on, I'm saying.

MAHON: Is it me?

CHRISTY: Not a word out of you. Go on from this.

MAHON (*walking out and looking back at* CHRISTY *over his shoulder*): Glory be to God! (*With a broad smile.*) I am crazy again. (*Goes.*)

CHRISTY: Ten thousand blessings upon all that's here, for you've turned me a likely gaffer in the end of all, the way I'll go romancing through a romping lifetime from this hour to the dawning of the judgment day. (*He goes out.*)

MICHAEL: By the will of God, we'll have peace now for our drinks. Will you draw the porter, Pegeen?

SHAWN (*going up to her*): It's a miracle Father Reilly can wed us in the end of all, and we'll have none to trouble us when his vicious bite is healed.

PEGEEN (*hitting him a box on the ear*): Quit my sight. (*Putting her shawl over her head and breaking out into wild lamentations.*) Oh, my grief, I've lost him surely. I've lost the only Playboy of the Western World.

⌐ AN ENTERPRISING journalist interviewed Synge during the opening-night riots of the week-long disturbance that attended the original run of *The Playboy of the Western World* * at Dublin's Abbey Theatre, January 26–February 2, 1907. "In art," Synge told him, defending his play, "a spade must be called a spade." "But the complaint is, Mr. Synge," replied the journalist, "that you have called it a bloody shovel."

The pun neatly pinpointed the trouble. What the rioters objected to in Synge's play was blasphemy and indecency of language and brutality of incident. Piety flinched when Christy, in his ardor for Pegeen, felt pity "for the Lord God is all ages sitting lonesome in His golden chair," and virtue blushed at his vision of "a drift of chosen females,

---

* The title has irrelevant connotations in contemporary colloquial American. It refers neither to Christy's delight in pretty girls nor to Shawn's offer to ship him off to the States. "Playboy" means both one who is good at games, and a hoaxer. "Western world" is an old Irish poeticism for western Ireland.

standing in their shifts itself, maybe." * Parricide failed to seem amusing, and the burning of Christy's leg on stage seemed — not unnaturally — merely shocking. The next day the Nationalist newspapers blasted the performance as an "unmitigated, protracted libel upon Irish peasant men and worse still upon Irish peasant girlhood." "Squalid . . . offensive . . . incongruously called a comedy . . . barbarous jargon . . . elaborate and incessant cursings . . . repulsive creatures . . . vile and inhuman story . . . the foulest language" set their general tone. Behind their indignation was the feeling that Synge had unpatriotically betrayed the public image of a mature and enlightened nation, long since ready for self-rule.

The reaction is understandable in the political context of the time, but in the calm nonpartisanship that distance breeds the rioters seem bigoted and insensitive. No Scotchman feels that his country has been slurred because Macbeth is a murderer. Shakespeare's erring heroes are redeemed in our eyes by the fineness of feeling of which the matchless poetry they have been given to speak is proof. Similarly, Christy's natural way with rich words saves him from being merely a murderous backyard squabbler. Poetic imagination alters and makes reality. But by the token of this romantic theme Synge seems unconvincing in his role of martyr in the cause of realism. Calling a spade a spade is almost exactly what he does not do. Rather, his play shows the temporary triumph of eloquence over fact. Language is the real hero of *Playboy*. And the number of versions Synge wrote of his play proves that it was no impromptu copy of reality. He lettered each version. The final one of Act I was G, of Act II, I, and of Act III, K.

Realism is rarely a simple quality in art. That Synge based his play on an actual case and that it may well be true that he used, as he said in his Preface, "one or two words only that I have not heard among the country people of Ireland, or spoken in my nursery before I could read the newspapers" do not guarantee authenticity in the sense that the play faithfully reflects the realities of west-Irish peasants in the early years of the century. The quality of a dramatic action based on fact is not necessarily identical with that of its real-life origin, and there is more to dramatic speech than diction. And if *Playboy* is felt to be less than fully realistic, the reason, perhaps, is not that it is implausible that a whole village would lionize a confessed father-slayer and turn against him when his alleged victim turns up alive, or that rough peasants talk readily in lovely lilt and image, but that the tone of village life seems imaginatively heightened in the intense and exclusive concern with the romantic stranger. The play commands belief as reality, but it is less

* "Mayo girls" were substituted for "chosen females" in performance. Even so, the speech set the first-night audience hissing.

the reality of a documentary than that of a successfully realized imaginative world. It is a world of such ubiquitous grace and power of lyrical speech that at times it barely accommodates Synge's plot. Christy's distinction over Shawn Keogh, who has "no savagery or fine words in him at all," is a basic plot premise. Pegeen and the other villagers infer Christy's savagery from his words. But Shawn is occasionally given speeches as fine as many of Christy's. "Let you not take it badly, mister honey" (he says to Christy); "isn't beyond the best place for you, where you'll have golden chains and shiny coats and you riding upon hunters with the ladies of the land."

The issue of "reality" in *Playboy* is further complicated by its affiliations with naturalistic theory. However wrong the hooters and hissers may have been in feeling that Synge vilified Irish peasantry, they were not wrong in sensing the larger, communal implications of his story of Christy's growth into manhood. For the metamorphosis of a "dirty, stuttering lout" into a girl's marvel of a poet, one of the "fine, fiery fellows with great rages when their temper's roused," of sordid fact into heroic legend, is a function not just of language but of the particular community into which Christy is taken. From "a windy corner of high, distant hills" he comes to a place of furze and ditch and peat bog, scrawny potato patches and leaky thatch, ruled by priests and peelers, a place of violence and gossip, hard work and meagre living, young men gone to America and girls like Pegeen left in the stale stink of liquor to marry funks like Shawn Keogh. The idiosyncrasies of the local group, the collective ethos, is a main character. *Playboy*, that is to say, is a folk play, and to the extent it is, the riots, unlike many theatrical battles, may be said to have concerned a fact of the play and not some extrinsic circumstance of production.

The naturalism implicit in this concept of the playboy character as the product, in part, of a folk environment that first "makes" Christy and then completes his self-discovery by becoming his antagonist is evidence of the strength of the naturalistic influence on the drama of the time. For Synge was opposed to naturalism — not so much, perhaps, to its mechanistic philosophy as to its language. The turn-of-the-century Irish literary revival saw in the prevailing Ibsenite naturalism of English and Continental drama nothing but prosy didacticism and ugly copies of mean urban life. In conscious reaction it sought the spontaneous beauty and intensity of native song and legend and fairy tale, symbolism and ritual.

Like the other leaders of the Irish renaissance, Synge was cool to the efforts of the Nationalist extremists to replace English with Gaelic as national language. In the Preface to *Playboy* he assumes that the English of the Irish peasant is the proper speech for the Irish stage. "For a few years more," he says, Irish peasant speech, the voice of "a popular imagination that is fiery, and magnificent, and tender," will continue to supply the "reality," which musical comedy has falsified, and the "joy," which the "pallid words" of "the intellectual modern drama" have failed to furnish. Naturalism is on principle committed to "reality," and though it is true that naturalistic plays generally are more grim than joyous, there is really no reason why blind determinism cannot play happy as well as sad games with the human pawn. In other words, although *Playboy* is less a dialect play, by strict naturalistic norms, than a play in standard English with dialect elements, Synge's language is not in conflict with the naturalistic implications of its theme and characterization.*

Speech carries the burden of the play. It evokes the larger world of wakes and games and prisons, of weather, and of landscape of places with names like "the Stooks of the Dead Women." Actual stage setting is limited to the interior of the pub, which serves as a public place for Christy to tell his story in and to suggest that Christy, like poteen, is an antidote to boredom. Plot, too, is mainly an occasion for speech. The Abbey actor who grumbled that the play lacked plot was not right, but it is true that there is little movement between Christy's arrival early in Act I and Old Mahon's in the middle of Act II and between the middle of Act II and the row at the end of the last act, which ends in the departure of both father and son. Until Old Mahon's arrival in the middle of Act II Christy's fortunes are rising. Between that climactic midpoint in the play and Pegeen's confrontation with Old Mahon near the end of Act III we more or less know that Christy is living on borrowed time. But this pattern is almost the whole extent of the plot. Widow Quin's alliance with Shawn in an effort to win Christy for herself and her later attempt to save Christy from being exposed do not amount to much of an intrigue, and her unruffled good sense and good

---

* Some of the more striking features of Synge's prose in *Playboy* may be noted. There are items of specifically Irish syntax and idiom: the use of progressive for simple verb forms ("It should be larceny, I'm thinking"), the omission of relatives ("I'd feel a kind of pity for the Lord God is all ages sitting lonesome"), inversion ("It's above at the crossroads he is"), co-ordination with "and" for more logically exact subordination ("What is there to hurt you, and you a fine, hardy girl"), "after" to indicate completed action ("I'm after feeling a kind of fellow above"), insertions ("surely," "I'm thinking," vocatives), and "himself" and "itself" (the latter in the sense of "even" or "actually"). Stylistic characteristics include strong non-periodicity (the voice, as if self-entranced, trailing off into upbeat image or speech tag after the completion of the sense), frequent simile (and hardly a single metaphor), landscape and religious imagery, Old Testament cadence and naive–solemn circumstantial concreteness, and irregularly spaced clusters of stressed and unstressed syllables producing lilting speech rhythms.

temper fail to provide exciting drama. Shawn only frets and whimpers. Pegeen's fits of jealousy hardly deserve to be called even minor episodes. The main function of the lesser characters is choric. Michael Flaherty and his two wake companions are Christy's rapt audience in the murky flicker of the turf fire in Act I, just as are the girls in the "brilliant morning light" of Act II. The contrast in light is scenically effective and appropriate to the two kinds of audience, but it only emphasizes their subordinate function in the story of the making of the playboy personality.

Synge's art is objective, and the story means what the stage shows. One could read it as allegory and say that the trouble with the Irish is that they, like Pegeen, take more kindly to a poetic fable of rebellious bravado than to an act of real rebellion, or that Old Mahon represents England and Christy Ireland belatedly discovering her identity and throwing off English authority, or that the parricide suggests the archetypal action of every son who in self-fulfilment seeks to kill his father. This, perhaps, is neither mistaken nor irrelevant. But it is to diminish, simplify, render abstract, and hence to distort, the solid and various totality of speech and spectacle. A play can be allegory only if it is drama first. A view that in *Playboy* sees only satire on Irish national character, or political allegory, or allegory on the nation's need to find its own voice in art, or the operation of the unsublimated, Jungian unconscious, and not a play about Christy Mahon and Pegeen Mike, is looking at something else than drama.

The surface story should not be "taken for granted" and probed for "hidden meanings." It has plenty of overt meaning. Pegeen reflects Christy's growth and is partly responsible for it. Her love represents the community's affection for the heroic newcomer, but it is also, simply, a girl's love. Her spite of Shawn is a form of longing for the hero she deserves and for whom she is — though she hardly knows it — waiting. Where now, she asks, in these smaller times, do you find a man "the like of Daneen Sullivan knocked the eye from a peeler; or Marcus Quin, God rest him, got six months for maiming ewes, and he a great warrant to tell stories of holy Ireland till he'd have the old women shedding down tears about their feet." As if in answer, Christy walks in with his "hanging crime."

Christy's transformation begins when his words change murder into heroic deed for Pegeen and the others. Act and word belong to different worlds. We laugh at Jimmy Farrell telling Pegeen's father that "herself will be safe tonight, with a man killed his father holding danger from the door." But he is only proving the truth of Pegeen's reply to Christy's question why they all turn against him now that he has killed his father in plain sight of all: ". . . what's a squabble in your backyard, and the blow of a loy, have taught me that there's a great gap between a gallous story and a dirty deed."

This might only have been a wholesome, though bitter, lesson for Pegeen to learn and for all of us to take home with us from the theater. But the irony of the ending will not permit such patness. Christy's change is as much a reality as the ugly assault. And it is the gallous story that the assault presumably cancels that has made Christy what he has now become. By the time Pegeen and the others lose their illusions about him, illusion has turned itself into reality: Christy has become what the village thought he was, because its belief has become his own. He has every reason to bless those who turn him out. He leaves as the hero of his own glorious fable, timid lout turned "likely gaffer," bullying his proud father, and rich enough in the promise of his "romping lifetime" to afford to lose even a girl like Pegeen. With Christy gone, Michael calls on Pegeen to "draw the porter." Shawn assumes that everything is as before Christy came and that the wedding will take place now that Father Reilly has got the dispensation. But Pegeen breaks into "wild lamentations."

No purely comic view can hold her final grief. Christy and Pegeen, like Cleopatra in Shaw's play, both undergo an education. But while the non-comic element in Shaw is the breaking off of Cleopatra's development toward wise and virtuous queenship, in *Playboy* it is the irreconcilability of squalid fact and brave imagination, the cost of that awakening into reality that marks the completion of the education. The cost is partly Christy's; he loses Pegeen. But he has gained his manhood and independence, and there will be other girls. Mainly, the cost is Pegeen's, who grieves for the loss of "the only Playboy of the Western World" — that is, she has lost, not just a lover, but an ideal. Cleopatra speaks for a world which, Shaw implies, could change if it chose to. Pegeen's disenchantment seems as inevitable as the awakening from a dream. In Shaw, world history takes a decisive turn; in Synge some west-coast villagers turn out a violent vagrant. But it is a question as to which play is the richer in tragic implications. And despite chronology and historical event, Synge's shifting, unresolved ambiguities of illusion and reality seem closer to the postwar drama of relativism and scepticism (like Pirandello's) than to the essential optimism of a Shavian thesis play of moral reform.

Synge was not always unfortunate in his comments on *Playboy*. It is, he once said, "perfectly serious when looked at in a certain light." He went on: "That is often the case, I think, with comedy, and no one is quite sure today whether Shylock and Alceste should be played seriously or not."

W. B. Yeats

THE HOUR-GLASS

Persons in the Play

A WISE MAN   TEIGUE, *a Fool*
BRIDGET, *his wife*   ANGEL

CHILDREN *and* PUPILS

*(The stage is brought out into the orchestra so as to leave a wide
space in front of the stage curtain. PUPILS come in and stand before the stage curtain, which is still closed. ONE PUPIL carries a
book.)*

FIRST PUPIL: He said we might choose the subject for the lesson.

SECOND PUPIL: There is none of us wise enough to do that.

THIRD PUPIL: It would need a great deal of wisdom to know what it is
we want to know.

FOURTH PUPIL: I will question him.

FIFTH PUPIL: You?

is no God and no soul — maybe, if there is not much of either,
there is yet some tatters, some tag on the wind — so to speak —

FOURTH PUPIL: Last night I dreamt that some one came and told me
to question him. I was to say to him, "You were wrong to say there
some rag upon a bush, some bob-tail of a god." I will argue with
him — nonsense though it be — according to my dream, and you
will see how well I can argue, and what thoughts I have.

FIRST PUPIL: I'd as soon listen to dried peas in a bladder as listen to your thoughts.

(TEIGUE *the Fool comes in.*)

FOOL: Give me a penny.

SECOND PUPIL: Let us choose a subject by chance. Here is his big book. Let us turn over the pages slowly. Let one of us put down his finger without looking. The passage his finger lights on will be the subject for the lesson.

FOOL: Give me a penny.

THIRD PUPIL (*taking up book*): How heavy it is!

FOURTH PUPIL: Spread it on Teigue's back, and then we can all stand round and see the choice.

SECOND PUPIL: Make him spread out his arms.

FOURTH PUPIL: Down on your knees. Hunch up your back. Spread your arms out now, and look like a golden eagle in a church. Keep still, keep still.

FOOL: Give me a penny.

THIRD PUPIL: Is that the right cry for an eagle-cock?

SECOND PUPIL: I'll turn the pages — you close your eyes and put your finger down.

THIRD PUPIL: That's it, and then he cannot blame us for the choice.

FIRST PUPIL: There, I have chosen. Fool, keep still — and if what's wise is strange and sounds like nonsense, we've made a good choice.

FIFTH PUPIL: The Master has come.

FOOL: Will anybody give a penny to a fool?

(*One of the* PUPILS *draws back the stage curtains showing the* MASTER *sitting at his desk. There is an hour-glass upon his desk or in a bracket on the wall.* ONE PUPIL *puts the book before him.*)

FIRST PUPIL: We have chosen the passage for the lesson, Master. "There are two living countries, one visible and one invisible, and when it is summer there, it is winter here, and when it is November with us, it is lambing-time there."

WISE MAN: That passage, that passage! What mischief has there been since yesterday?

FIRST PUPIL: None, Master.

WISE MAN: Oh yes, there has; some craziness has fallen from the wind, or risen from the graves of old men, and made you choose that subject. — Diem noctemque contendo, sed quos elegi, quos amavi, in tirocinium vel hi labuntur.[1]

---

[1] I struggle day and night, but even those I have chosen, those I have loved, keep slipping into inexperience.

FOURTH PUPIL: I knew that it was folly, but they would have it.

THIRD PUPIL: Had we not better say we picked it by chance?

SECOND PUPIL: No; he would say we were children still.

FIRST PUPIL: I have found a sentence under that one that says — as though to show it had a hidden meaning — a beggar wrote it upon the walls of Babylon.

WISE MAN: Then find some beggar and ask him what it means, for I will have nothing to do with it.

FOURTH PUPIL: Come, Teigue, what is the old book's meaning when it says that there are sheep that drop their lambs in November?

FOOL: To be sure — everybody knows, everybody in the world knows, when it is spring with us, the trees are withering there, when it is summer with us, the snow is falling there, and have I not myself heard the lambs that are there all bleating on a cold November day — to be sure, does not everybody with an intellect know that? And maybe when it's night with us, it is day with them, for many a time I have seen the roads lighted before me.

WISE MAN: The beggar who wrote that on Babylon wall meant that there is a spiritual kingdom that cannot be seen or known till the faculties, whereby we master the kingdom of this world, wither away like green things in winter. A monkish thought, the most mischievous thought that ever passed out of a man's mouth. — Virgas ut partus educant colligunt aves, mens hominis nugas.[2]

FIRST PUPIL: If he meant all that, I will take an oath that he was spindle-shanked, and cross-eyed, and had a lousy itching shoulder, and that his heart was crosser than his eyes, and that he wrote it out of malice.

SECOND PUPIL: Let's come away and find a better subject.

FOURTH PUPIL: And maybe now you'll let me choose.

FIRST PUPIL: Come.

WISE MAN: Were it but true, 'twould alter everything
Until the stream of the world had changed its course,
And that and all our thoughts had run
Into some cloudy thunderous spring
They dream to be its source —
Aye, to some frenzy of the mind;
And all that we have done would be undone,
Our speculation but as the wind.   (*A pause.*)
I have dreamed it twice.

FIRST PUPIL: Something has troubled him.   (PUPILS *go out.*)

WISE MAN: Twice have I dreamed it in a morning dream,

---

[2] Birds gather twigs together to bring up their young; the mind of man gathers trifles.

Now nothing serves my pupils but to come
With a like thought. Reason is growing dim;
A moment more and Frenzy will beat his drum
And laugh aloud and scream;
And I must dance in the dream.
No, no, but it is like a hawk, a hawk of the air,
It has swooped down — and this swoop makes the third —
And what can I, but tremble like a bird?

FOOL: Give me a penny.

WISE MAN: That I should dream it twice, and after that, that they should pick it out!

FOOL: Won't you give me a penny?

WISE MAN: What do you want? What can it matter to you whether the words I am reading are wisdom or sheer folly?

FOOL: Such a great, wise teacher will not refuse a penny to a fool.

WISE MAN: Seeing that everybody is a fool when he is asleep and dreaming, why do you call me wise?

FOOL: O, I know, — I know, I know what I have seen.

WISE MAN: Well, to see rightly is the whole of wisdom, whatever dreams be with us.

FOOL: When I went by Kilcluan, where the bells used to be ringing at the break of every day, I could hear nothing but the people snoring in their houses. When I went by Tubber-vanach, where the young men used to be climbing the hill to the blessed well, they were sitting at the cross-roads playing cards. When I went by Carrick-orus, where the friars used to be fasting and serving the poor, I saw them drinking wine and obeying their wives. And when I asked what misfortune had brought all these changes, they said it was no misfortune, but that it was the wisdom they had learned from your teaching.

WISE MAN: And you too have called me wise — you would be paid for that good opinion doubtless. — Run to the kitchen; my wife will give you food and drink.

FOOL: That's foolish advice for a wise man to give.

WISE MAN: Why, Fool?

FOOL: What is eaten is gone — I want pennies for my bag. I must buy bacon in the shops, and nuts in the market, and strong drink for the time the sun is weak, and snares to catch the rabbits and the hares, and a big pot to cook them in.

WISE MAN: I have more to think about than giving pennies to your like, so run away.

FOOL: Give me a penny and I will bring you luck. The fishermen let me sleep among their nets in the loft because I bring them luck;

and in the summer-time, the wild creatures let me sleep near their nests and their holes. It is lucky even to look at me, but it is much more lucky to give me a penny. If I was not lucky I would starve.

WISE MAN: What are the shears for?

FOOL: I won't tell you. If I told you, you would drive them away.

WISE MAN: Drive them away! Whom would I drive away?

FOOL: I won't tell you.

WISE MAN: Not if I give you a penny?

FOOL: No.

WISE MAN: Not if I give you two pennies?

FOOL: You will be very lucky if you give me two pennies, but I won't tell you.

WISE MAN: Three pennies?

FOOL: Four, and I will tell you.

WISE MAN: Very well — four, but from this out I will not call you Teigue the Fool.

FOOL: Let me come close to you, where nobody will hear me; but first you must promise not to drive them away. (WISE MAN *nods*.) Every day men go out dressed in black and spread great black nets over the hills, great black nets.

WISE MAN: A strange place that to fish in.

FOOL: They spread them out on the hills that they may catch the feet of the angels; but every morning, just before the dawn, I go out and cut the nets with the shears and the angels fly away.

WISE MAN (*speaking with excitement*): Ah, now I know that you are Teigue the Fool. You say that I am wise, and yet I say there are no angels.

FOOL: I have seen plenty of angels.

WISE MAN: No, no, you have not.

FOOL: They are plenty if you but look about you. They are like the blades of grass.

WISE MAN: They are plenty as the blades of grass — I heard that phrase when I was but a child and was told folly.

FOOL: When one gets quiet. When one is so quiet that there is not a thought in one's head maybe, there is something that wakes up inside one, something happy and quiet, and then all in a minute one can smell summer flowers, and tall people go by, happy and laughing, but they will not let us look at their faces. O no, it is not right that we should look at their faces.

WISE MAN: You have fallen asleep upon a hill; yet even those that used to dream of angels dream now of other things.

FOOL: I saw one but a moment ago — that is because I am lucky. It was coming behind me, but it was not laughing.

WISE MAN: There's nothing but what men can see when they are
    awake. Nothing, nothing.
FOOL: I knew you would drive them away.
WISE MAN: Pardon me, Fool.
    I had forgotten whom I spoke to.
    Well, there are your four pennies — Fool you are called,
    And all day long they cry, "Come hither, Fool."
                            (*The* FOOL *goes close to him.*)
    Or else it's, "Fool, be gone."   (*The* FOOL *goes further off.*)
    Or, "Fool, stand there."   (*The* FOOL *straightens himself up.*)
    Or, "Fool, go sit in the corner."   (*The* FOOL *sits in the corner.*)
                                And all the while
    What were they all but fools before I came?
    What are they now but mirrors that seem men
    Because of my image? Fool, hold up your head. (*The* FOOL *does so.*)
    What foolish stories they have told of the ghosts
    That fumbled with the clothes upon the bed,
    Or creaked and shuffled in the corridor,
    Or else, if they were pious bred,
    Of angels from the skies,
    That coming through the door,
    Or, it may be, standing there,
    Would solidly out-stare
    The steadiest eyes with their unnatural eyes,
    Aye, on a man's own floor.

(*An* ANGEL *has come in. It may be played by a man if a man can
be found with the right voice, and in that case "she" should be
changed to "he" throughout, and may wear a little golden dom-
ino and a halo made of metal. Or the whole face may be a beautiful mask, in which case the sentence in lines 38 and 39 on page
338 should not be spoken.*)

    Yet it is strange, the strangest thing I have known,
    That I should still be haunted by the notion
    That there's a crisis of the spirit wherein
    We get new sight, and that they know some trick
    To turn our thoughts for their own needs to frenzy.
    Why do you put your finger to your lip,
    And creep away?   (*The* FOOL *goes out.*)
    (WISE MAN *sees* ANGEL.) What are you? Who are you?
    I think I saw some like you in my dreams,
    When but a child. That thing about your head, —

That brightness in your hair — that flowery branch;
But I have done with dreams, I have done with dreams.

ANGEL: I am the crafty one that you have called.

WISE MAN: How that I called?

ANGEL: I am the messenger.

WISE MAN: What message could you bring to one like me?

ANGEL (*turning the hour-glass*): That you will die when the last grain
     of sand
Has fallen through this glass.

WISE MAN: I have a wife,
Children and pupils that I cannot leave:
Why must I die, my time is far away?

ANGEL: You have to die because no soul has passed
The heavenly threshold since you have opened school,
But grass grows there, and rust upon the hinge;
And they are lonely that must keep the watch.

WISE MAN: And whither shall I go when I am dead?

ANGEL: You have denied there is a Purgatory,
Therefore that gate is closed; you have denied
There is a Heaven, and so that gate is closed.

WISE MAN: Where then? For I have said there is no Hell.

ANGEL: Hell is the place of those who have denied;
They find there what they planted and what dug,
A Lake of Spaces, and a Wood of Nothing,
And wander there and drift, and never cease
Wailing for substance.

WISE MAN: Pardon me, blessed Angel,
I have denied and taught the like to others.
But how could I believe before my sight
Had come to me?

ANGEL: It is too late for pardon.

WISE MAN: Had I but met your gaze as now I meet it —
But how can you that live but where we go
In the uncertainty of dizzy dreams
Know why we doubt? Parting, sickness, and death,
The rotting of the grass, tempest, and drouth,
These are the messengers that came to me.
Why are you silent? You carry in your hands
God's pardon, and you will not give it me.
Why are you silent? Were I not afraid,
I'd kiss your hands — no, no, the hem of your dress.

ANGEL: Only when all the world has testified,
May soul confound it, crying out in joy,

And laughing on its lonely precipice.
What's dearth and death and sickness to the soul
That knows no virtue but itself? Nor could it,
So trembling with delight and mother-naked,
Live unabashed if the arguing world stood by.

WISE MAN: It is as hard for you to understand
Why we have doubted as it is for us
To banish doubt. — What folly have I said?
There can be nothing that you do not know.
Give me a year — a month — a week — a day,
I would undo what I have done — an hour —
Give me until the sand has run in the glass.

ANGEL: Though you may not undo what you have done,
I have this power — if you but find one soul,
Before the sands have fallen, that still believes,
One fish to lie and spawn among the stones
Till the great Fisher's net is full again,
You may, the purgatorial fire being passed,
Spring to your peace.

(PUPILS *sing in the distance.*)

> Who stole your wits away
> And where are they gone?

WISE MAN: My pupils come.
Before you have begun to climb the sky
I shall have found that soul. They say they doubt,
But what their mothers dinned into their ears
Cannot have been so lightly rooted up;
Besides, I can disprove what I once proved —
And yet give me some thought, some argument,
More mighty than my own.

ANGEL: Farewell — farewell,
For I am weary of the weight of time.

(ANGEL *goes out.* WISE MAN *makes a step to follow and pauses. Some of his* PUPILS *come in at the other side of the stage.*)

FIRST PUPIL: Master, Master, you must choose the subject.

(*Enter other* PUPILS *with* FOOL, *about whom they dance; all the* PUPILS *may have little cushions on which presently they seat themselves.*)

SECOND PUPIL: Here is a subject — Where have the Fool's wits gone?

(*singing*)

Who dragged your wits away
Where no one knows?
Or have they run off
On their own pair of shoes?

FOOL: Give me a penny.

FIRST PUPIL: The Master will find your wits.

SECOND PUPIL: And when they are found, you must not beg for pennies.

THIRD PUPIL: They are hidden somewhere in the badger's hole,
But you must carry an old candle-end
If you would find them.

FOURTH PUPIL: They are up above the clouds.

FOOL: Give me a penny, give me a penny.

FIRST PUPIL (*singing*):

I'll find your wits again.
Come, for I saw them roll
To where old badger mumbles
In the black hole.

SECOND PUPIL (*singing*):

No, but an angel stole them
The night that you were born,
And now they are but a rag
On the moon's horn.

WISE MAN: Be silent.

FIRST PUPIL: Can you not see that he is troubled?

(*All the* PUPILS *are seated.*)

WISE MAN: Nullum esse deum dixi, nullam dei matrem: mentitus vero: nam recte intelligenti sunt et deus et dei mater.[3]

FIRST PUPIL: Argumentis igitur proba; nam argumenta poscit qui rationis est particeps.[4]

WISE MAN: Pro certo habeo e vobis unum quidem in fide perstitisse, unum altius quam me vidisse.[5]

SECOND PUPIL: You answer for us.

THIRD PUPIL (*in a whisper to* FIRST PUPIL): Be careful what you say; If he persuades you to an argument,
He will but turn us all to mockery.

---

[3] I have said there is no God, no Mother of God, but I have lied: for the truly wise both God and the Mother of God exist.

[4] Prove it, then, by arguments, for the sharer in reason demands arguments.

[5] I know for certain that one of you has remained firm in his faith, that one has seen higher than I.

FIRST PUPIL: We had no minds until you made them for us.

WISE MAN: Quae destruxi necesse est omnia reaedificem.[6]

FIRST PUPIL: Haec rationibus nondum natis opinabamur: nunc vero adolevimus: exuimus incunabula.[7]

WISE MAN: You are afraid to tell me what you think
Because I am hot and angry when I am crossed.
I do not blame you for it; but have no fear,
For if there's one that sat on smiling there
As though my arguments were sweet as milk,
Yet found them bitter, I will thank him for it,
If he but speak his mind.

FIRST PUPIL: There is no one, Master.
There is not one but found them sweet as milk.

WISE MAN: The things that have been told us in our childhood
Are not so fragile.

SECOND PUPIL: We are not children now.

FIRST PUPIL: Non iam pueri sumus; corpus tantummodo ex matre fictum est.[8]

SECOND PUPIL: Docuisti; et nobis persuadetur.[9]

WISE MAN: Mendaciis vos imbui, mentisque simulacris.[10]

SECOND PUPIL: Nulli non persuasisti.[11]

OTHER PUPILS (*speaking together*): Nulli, nulli, nulli.[12]

WISE MAN: I have deceived you — where shall I go for words? —
I have no thoughts — my mind has been swept bare.
The messengers that stand in the fiery cloud
Fling themselves out, if we but dare to question,
And after that the Babylonian moon
Blots all away.

FIRST PUPIL (*to other* PUPILS): I take his words to mean
That visionaries and martyrs, when they are raised
Above translunary things, and there enlightened,
As the contention is, may lose the light,
And flounder in their speech when the eyes open.

SECOND PUPIL: How well he imitates their trick of speech.

THIRD PUPIL: Their air of mystery.

---

[6] It is necessary that I rebuild all that I have destroyed.
[7] Of these things we never thought when we were little, but now we have grown up; we have left our swaddling clothes.
[8] We are not boys now; only the body is born from the mother.
[9] You have taught, and we are convinced.
[10] I have filled you with lies and your mind with shadows.
[11] There is none you have not convinced.
[12] None, none, none.

FOURTH PUPIL: Their empty gaze
As though they'd looked upon some wingéd thing,
And would not condescend to mankind after.

FIRST PUPIL: Master, we all have learnt that truth is learnt
When the intellect's deliberate and cold,
As it were a polished mirror that reflects
An unchanged world; not when the steel dissolves
Bubbling and hissing, till there's naught but fume.

WISE MAN: When it is melted, when it all fumes up,
They walk as when beside those three in the furnace
The form of the fourth.

FIRST PUPIL: Master, there's none among us
That has not heard your mockery of these,
Or thoughts like these, and we have not forgot.

WISE MAN: Something incredible has happened — some one has come
Suddenly like a grey hawk out of the air,
And all that I declared untrue is true.

FIRST PUPIL (*to other* PUPILS): You'd think, the way he says it, that
he felt it.
There's not a mummer to compare with him.
He's something like a man.

SECOND PUPIL: Argumentum, domine, profer.[13]

WISE MAN: What proof have I to give, but that an angel
An instant ago was standing on that spot? (*The* PUPILS *rise.*)

THIRD PUPIL: You dreamed it.

WISE MAN: I was awake as I am now.

FIRST PUPIL (*to the others*): I may be dreaming now for all I know.
He wants to show we have no certain proof
Of anything in the world.

SECOND PUPIL: There is this proof
That shows we are awake — we have all one world
While every dreamer has a world of his own,
And sees what no one else can.

THIRD PUPIL: Teigue sees angels.
So when the Master says he has seen an angel,
He may have seen one.

FIRST PUPIL: Both may still be dreamers,
Unless it's proved the angels were alike.

SECOND PUPIL: What sort are the angels, Teigue?

THIRD PUPIL: That will prove nothing,
Unless we are sure prolonged obedience

[13] Give proof, O teacher.

Has made one angel like another angel
As they were eggs.

FIRST PUPIL: The Master's silent now:
For he has found that to dispute with us —
Seeing that he has taught us what we know —
Is but to reason with himself. Let us away,
And find if there is one believer left.

WISE MAN: Yes, Yes. Find me but one that still can say:
Credo in patrem et filium et spiritum sanctum.[14]

THIRD PUPIL: He'll mock and maul him.

FOURTH PUPIL: From the first I knew
He wanted somebody to argue with.   (*They go.*)

WISE MAN: I have no reason left. All dark, all dark!

(PUPILS *return laughing. They push forward* FOURTH PUPIL.)

FIRST PUPIL: Here, Master, is the very man you want.
He said, when we were studying the book,
That maybe after all the monks were right,
And you mistaken, and if we but gave him time,
He'd prove that it was so.

FOURTH PUPIL: I never said it.

WISE MAN: Dear friend, dear friend, do you believe in God?

FOURTH PUPIL: Master, they have invented this to mock me.

WISE MAN: You are afraid of me.

FOURTH PUPIL: They know well, Master,
That all I said was but to make them argue.
They've pushed me in to make a mock of me,
Because they know I could take either side
And beat them at it.

WISE MAN: If you can say the creed
With but a grain, a mustard-grain of faith,
You are my soul's one friend.   (PUPILS *laugh.*)
                    Mistress or wife
Can give us but our good or evil luck
Amid the howling world, but you shall give
Eternity, and those sweet-throated things
That drift above the moon.

(PUPILS *look at one another and are silent.*)

SECOND PUPIL: How strange he is!

[14] I believe in the Father, the Son, and the Holy Spirit.

WISE MAN: The angel that stood there upon that spot
  Said that my soul was lost unless I found
  One that had faith.

FOURTH PUPIL: Cease mocking at me, Master,
  For I am certain that there is no God
  Nor immortality, and they that said it
  Made a fantastic tale from a starved dream
  To plague our hearts. Will that content you, Master?

WISE MAN: The giddy glass is emptier every moment,
  And you stand there, debating, laughing and wrangling.
  Out of my sight! Out of my sight, I say.   (*He drives them out.*)
  I'll call my wife, for what can women do,
  That carry us in the darkness of their bodies,
  But mock the reason that lets nothing grow
  Unless it grow in light? Bridget, Bridget!
  A woman never gives up all her faith,
  Say what we will. Bridget, come quickly, Bridget.

(BRIDGET *comes in wearing her apron. Her sleeves are turned up
from her arms, which are covered with flour.*)

Wife, what do you believe in? Tell me the truth,
And not — as is the habit with you all —
Something you think will please me. Do you pray?
Sometimes when you're along in the house, do you pray?

BRIDGET: Prayers — no, you taught me to leave them off long ago. At
first I was sorry, but I am glad now, for I am sleepy in the evenings.

WISE MAN: Do you believe in God?

BRIDGET: O, a good wife only believes in what her husband tells her.

WISE MAN: But sometimes, when the children are asleep
  And I am in the school, do you not think
  About the martyrs and the saints and the angels,
  And all the things that you believed in once?

BRIDGET: I think about nothing. Sometimes I wonder if the linen is
bleaching white, or I go out to see if the crows are picking up the
chickens' food.

WISE MAN: My God, — my God! I will go out myself.
  My pupils said they would find a man
  Whose faith I never shook — they may have found him.
  Therefore I will go out — but if I go,
  The glass will let the sands run out unseen.
  I cannot go — I cannot leave the glass.
  Go call my pupils — I can explain all now.
  Only when all our hold on life is troubled,

Only in spiritual terror can the Truth
Come through the broken mind — as the pease burst
Out of a broken pease-cod. (*He clutches* BRIDGET *as she is going.*)
             Say to them
That Nature would lack all in her most need,
Could not the soul find truth as in a flash,
Upon the battle-field, or in the midst
Of overwhelming waves, and say to them —
But no, they would but answer as I bid.

BRIDGET: You want somebody to get up an argument with.

WISE MAN: Look out and see if there is any one
There in the street — I cannot leave the glass,
For somebody might shake it, and the sand
If it were shaken might run down on the instant.

BRIDGET: I don't understand a word you are saying.
There's a crowd of people talking to your pupils.

WISE MAN: Go out and find if they have found a man
Who did not understand me when I taught,
Or did not listen.

BRIDGET: It is a hard thing to be married to a man of learning that
must always be having arguments.   (*She goes out.*)

WISE MAN: Strange that I should be blind to the great secret,
And that so simple a man might write it out
Upon a blade of grass with the juice of a berry,
And laugh and cry, because it was so simple.

(*Enter* BRIDGET *followed by the* FOOL.)

FOOL: Give me something; give me a penny to buy bacon in the shops
and nuts in the market, and strong drink for the time when the
sun is weak.

BRIDGET: I have no pennies. (*To* WISE MAN.) Your pupils cannot find
anybody to argue with you. There's nobody in the whole country
with religion enough for a lover's oath. Can't you be quiet now,
and not always wanting to have arguments? It must be terrible to
have a mind like that.

WISE MAN: Then I am lost indeed.

BRIDGET: Leave me alone now, I have to make the bread for you and
the children.   (*She goes into kitchen. The* FOOL *follows her.*)

WISE MAN: Children, children!

BRIDGET: Your father wants you, run to him.   (CHILDREN *run in.*)

WISE MAN: Come to me, Children. Do not be afraid.
I want to know if you believe in Heaven,
God or the soul — no, do not tell me yet;

You need not be afraid I shall be angry;
Say what you please — so that it is your thought —
I wanted you to know before you spoke
That I shall not be angry.

FIRST CHILD: We have not forgotten, father.

SECOND CHILD: O no, father.

BOTH CHILDREN (*as if repeating a lesson*): There is nothing we cannot
see, nothing we cannot touch.

FIRST CHILD: Foolish people used to say that there was, but you have
taught us better.

WISE MAN: Go to your mother, go — yet do not go.
What can she say? If I am dumb you are lost;
And yet, because the sands are running out,
I have but a moment to show it all in. Children,
The sap would die out of the blades of grass
Had they a doubt. They understand it all,
Being the fingers of God's certainty,
Yet can but make their sign into the air;
But could they find their tongues they'd show it all;
But what am I to say that am but one,
When they are millions and they will not speak? —

(CHILDREN *have run out.*)

But they are gone; what made them run away?

(*The* FOOL *comes in with a dandelion.*)

Look at me, tell me if my face is changed,
Is there a notch of the Fiend's nail upon it
Already? Is it terrible to sight
Because the moment's near? (*Going to glass.*)

I dare not look,
I dare not know the moment when they come.
No, no, I dare not. (*Covers glass.*) Will there be a footfall,
Or will there be a sort of rending sound,
Or else a cracking, as though an iron claw
Had gripped the threshold-stone?

(*The* FOOL *has begun to blow the dandelion.*)

What are you doing?

FOOL: Wait a minute — four — five — six —

WISE MAN: What are you doing that for?

FOOL: I am blowing the dandelion to find out what hour it is.

WISE MAN: You have heard everything and that is why
You'd find what hour it is — you'd find that out
That you may look upon a fleet of devils

Dragging my soul away. You shall not stop,
I will have no one here when they come in,
I will have no one sitting there — no one!
And yet — and yet — there is something strange about you.
I half remember something. What is it?
Do you believe in God and in the soul?

FOOL: So you ask me now. I thought when you were asking your pupils, "Will he ask Teigue the Fool? Yes, he will, he will; no, he will not — yes, he will." But Teigue will say nothing. Teigue will say nothing.

WISE MAN: Tell me quickly.

FOOL: I said, "Teigue knows everything, not even the green-eyed cats and the hares that milk the cows have Teigue's wisdom"; but Teigue will not speak, he says nothing.

WISE MAN: Speak, speak, for underneath the cover there
The sand is running from the upper glass,
And when the last grain's through, I shall be lost.

FOOL: I will not speak. I will not tell you what is in my mind. I will not tell you what is in my bag. You might steal away my thoughts. I met a bodach on the road yesterday, and he said, "Teigue, tell me how many pennies are in your bag; I will wager three pennies that there are not twenty pennies in your bag; let me put in my hand and count them." But I gripped the bag the tighter and when I go to sleep at night I hide the bag where nobody knows.

WISE MAN: There's but one pinch of sand, and I am lost
If you are not he I seek.

FOOL: O, what a lot the Fool knows, but he says nothing.

WISE MAN: Yes, I remember now. You spoke of angels.
You said but now that you have seen an angel.
You are the one I seek, and I am saved.

FOOL: O no. How could poor Teigue see angels? O, Teigue tells one tale here, another there, and everybody give him pennies. If Teigue had not his tales he would starve.   (*He breaks away and goes out.*)

WISE MAN: The last hope is gone,
And now that it's too late I see it all:
We perish into God and sink away
Into reality — the rest's a dream.

(*The* FOOL *comes back.*)

FOOL: There was one there — there by the threshold, waiting there; and he said, "Go in, Teigue, and tell him everything that he asks you. He will give you a penny if you tell him."

WISE MAN: I know enough, that know God's will prevails.

FOOL: Waiting till the moment had come — That is what the one out there was saying, but I might tell you what you asked. That is what he was saying.

WISE MAN: Be silent. May God's will prevail on the instant,
Although His will be my eternal pain.
I have no question:
It is enough, I know what fixed the station
Of star and cloud.
And knowing all, I cry
That whatso God has willed
On the instant be fulfilled,
Though that be my damnation.
The stream of the world has changed its course,
And with the stream my thoughts have run
Into some cloudy thunderous spring
That is its mountain source —
Aye, to some frenzy of the mind,
For all that we have done's undone,
Our speculation but as the wind.   (*He dies.*)

FOOL: Wise Man — Wise Man, wake up and I will tell you everything for a penny. It is I, poor Teigue the Fool. Why don't you wake up, and say, "There is a penny for you, Teigue"? No, no, you will say nothing. You and I, we are the two fools, we know everything, but we will not speak.

(ANGEL *enters holding a casket.*)

O, look what has come from his mouth! O, look what has come from his mouth — the white butterfly! He is dead, and I have taken his soul in my hands; but I know why you open the lid of that golden box. I must give it to you. There then (*he puts butterfly in casket*), he has gone through his pains, and you will open the lid in the Garden of Paradise. (*He closes curtain and remains outside it.*) He is gone, he is gone, he is gone, but come in, everybody in the world, and look at me.

> I hear the wind a-blow,
> I hear the grass a-grow,
> And all that I know, I know.

But I will not speak, I will run away.   (*He goes out.*)

THE END

⟋ THE "crisis of the spirit" that informs the action of *The Hour-Glass* — the conflict of soul and matter, dream and reason, inner and outer life — was a theme that Yeats returned to again and again in both drama and poetry. Like Synge, he revolted against the contemporary naturalistic theater with its emphasis on character and real-life problems and its commitment to a dialogue that reproduced as faithfully as possible the inarticulateness of ordinary people. He thought it a meaningless and unlovely "mimicry of the restless surface of reality." It seems significant that he wrote two main versions of *The Hour-Glass*, the first all in prose, the second partly in prose, partly in verse, and that the versions were separated by one of the most formative decades in his literary life, a period in which he began to develop the succinct and pregnant verse idiom, the highly personal mythic imagery, and the complexity of thought that mark his greatest achievements in both genres in the 1920's and '30's. His later plays came close to realizing his ideal of a spiritual drama, a pure form that would be an end in itself because it would tap the roots of man's primeval consciousness, a dance-like ritual, deliberately distancing itself from the beholder, a symbolic, characterless, nonpopular drama for small and select audiences. He found his inspiration and model in the aristocratic plays of the Japanese Noh theater, highly stylized and formalized in gesture and chant, using masks rather than mimicry and make-up, relying for communication as much on qualities of the speaking voice as on the words themselves. The architecture, mode, and language of *The Hour-Glass* show him already moving toward his final dramatic form.

The prose version was written in 1902. By the time it was published the next year Yeats had already begun to plan a poetic version, but first there intervened a series of minor revisions of the original play between 1904 and 1913. In that year appeared the expanded play in mixed prose and verse that has been reprinted here. The play was first performed in Dublin in 1903 by the Irish National Theatre Society, the company that the following year began to give plays in Dublin's Abbey Theatre. The final version of the play was first produced by the Abbey players late in 1912.

The prose version possesses a naivistic strength and simplicity that have been somewhat muted in the lyricism and the sophistication of religious thought of the later version. And although Yeats's addition of Latin phrases lends an air of solemnity and erudition and a note of irony in the use of Church language for a dialectic on materialism, they

With the permission of *The Explicator* (University of North Carolina), these comments are based, to some extent, upon Professor Reinert's notes on "The Hour Glass" as published in the December 1956 issue of *The Explicator* (Vol. XV, No. 3).

are a dubious gain dramatically. Still, most critics have found the final, "mixed," version of the play superior. The substance of the Wise Man's opening soliloquy in the original play is now rendered dramatically in dialogue. While in the early version the Wise Man was saved by the Fool's confession of faith and the play ended with the pupils kneeling by the body of their dead master, in the revision the Fool either does not understand the Wise Man's pleading or refuses to save him, and by the time the Angel sends him back to the Wise Man with the command that he give him the answer he wants, the latter has already renounced the world of reason and submitted himself to the will of God. The new salvation appears less gratuitous (and less predictable) than the old. It is prepared for in the Angel's identification of himself in reply to the Wise Man's question. His answer, "I am the crafty one that you have called," originally read, "I am the Angel of the Most High God." What the revised line loses in majesty it gains in significance and depth. The implication now is that the believing soul that saves the Wise Man is his own and that his dilemma really is self-sought: "I have dreamed it twice." The spiritual rescue of a man of reason is work for angelic "craft," a matter of subtle strategy disguising itself as "some craziness . . . fallen from the wind." The play resolves itself in Christ's paradox that he who seeks death shall find his life — a piece of rank paradox to reason. And the new ending avoids the diversion of dramatic interest away from the Wise Man to his pupils, who, kneeling, presumably were converted at the end of the prose version. Nothing is now said about their ultimate fate.

The prose play was subtitled "a morality." Yeats later removed the subtitle, quite likely because he had come to realize that the obvious needs no spelling out. At stake here, as in the Christian moralities of the middle ages, is the destiny of a soul, and the Wise Man has some of the pride of intellect and some of the agony of an educated and imaginative and poetically gifted mind contemplating perdition that belong to Marlowe's Doctor Faustus, the hero of the greatest Renaissance treatment of the old morality theme. As in Ibsen's Peer Gynt, another modern morality, a kind of post-medieval Everyman (Peer Gynt is a prudent egoist, the Wise Man an empiricist-intellectual) is confronted by an agent of the supernatural with a radical challenge to set his house in order. Also like Ibsen, Yeats based his fable on an old folk tale, the story of an apostate priest who is saved by an innocent's belief — in the tale, a child's "from a far country" — and whose escaping soul becomes the "first butterfly that was ever seen in Ireland." If, as is virtually certain, Yeats was not influenced by Peer Gynt, the parallel is all the more meaningful in suggesting that finding matter for an existential fable in native folklore was an aspect of the lingering romanticism of the late 1800's. Yeats's method is less starkly allegorical than that of the old moralities. His characters are not personifications of abstract virtues and vices, or, at least, they are not *just* that, and the main ones are developed far beyond schematic allegory. Bridget, the wife, perhaps represents soulless materialism, the children the stultified imaginations that are the heirs (in Yeats's view) of rationalism and science, and the pupils arid logic (with the possible exception of the Fourth, who in an early passage dimly glimpses the spiritual truth behind physical appearances). But the Fool (for whom there is no prototype in the folk tale) seems Shakespearean in the terrible mordancy of his crazed wit — one thinks of Lear's Fool — and the Angel, despite the traditional function of the "Good Angel" in the moralities, is less an admonitory Christian conscience than the impersonal executor of God's will. If he belongs in the morality tradition at all, it is as a figure something like summoning Death in *Everyman* — or, again, like the Button-moulder in *Peer Gynt*. And the conflict in the play is not so much between good and evil or right and wrong belief as between ways of seeking and perceiving truth and between realms of being. Yeats himself called his play "a parable of the conscious and the subconscious life." If we abstract the clearly irrelevant Freudian associations from the dichotomy, it accurately describes the conflict and accounts for the way in which the overt drama between the Wise Man and his two antagonists and his converts intersect his inner spiritual struggle. Still, the antithetical structure, the eschatological issue, the movement toward Christian salvation, the polarization of values, the allegorical implications, and the symbolism, all clearly establish a morality pattern.

Paradoxical inversion of the values represented by the "two living countries" in antithesis is the intellectual and imagistic form in which Yeats has cast his parable. Its "meaning," put briefly, is that in the realm of faith wisdom is folly and folly wisdom. The first part of the action takes place in the world of reason, the second in the world of faith. In the former the Fool is foolish and the Wise Man wise; in the latter the Fool is wise and the Wise Man foolish. The transposition of values is hinted at in one of the play's first speeches, the Third Pupil's, "It would need a great deal of wisdom to know what it is we want to know." It is anticipated in the scene in which the pupils tell the Fool to spread his arms and "look like a golden eagle in a church" so that they can use his back as a table for the "big book" from which they will select a passage for debate, and in the First Pupil's comment on their selection: "if what's wise is strange and sounds like nonsense, we've made a good choice." The moment of peripety is also the moment of recognition. It comes when the Angel turns the hour-glass and the

Wise Man learns that before the hour is up he must find a soul who still believes or else be damned forever.

The hour-glass is emblematic of the two-phased action and the two worlds. It is a conventional symbol of the shortness of earthly life, of the tragic experience of transitoriness, of

Parting, sickness, and death,
The rotting of the grass, tempest, and drouth,

that are the only "messengers" that come to him who ignores the soul's dreams for the passing phenomena of the actual. Reality has been illusion and illusion reality for the Wise Man, but he has enough of a soul to have suffered the disillusion that attends all terrestrial experience and to hear in his pupils' clever discourse only the dry, damning echoes of his own voice. His soul is salvagable because it is worth saving.

The shape of the hour-glass represents the two sets of antithetical values. When the Angel turns the glass the two worlds and the two main characters change their relative position: high becomes low and low high — as in an early image May and November are interchangeable seasons. The sand of wisdom no longer runs into folly. Instead, the sand of folly fills the void that is wisdom. Before the turning of the glass the Fool begs pennies from the Wise Man, an act that ironically foreshadows the reversal-recognition, for though money is not the proper thing to ask of wisdom, paltry alms are in fact all that wisdom can give. After the glass has been turned the Wise Man, now knowing, begs for salvation from the Fool, while the Fool practises his mock begging only on the pupils, who are still foolishly wise. At the end, the void of wisdom (God's angels escape its nets) is filled with the folly of faith, and the Wise Man dies a fool, truly wise, his soul a butterfly in angelic keeping. Perished into God and sunk away into reality, his end is the silence of that existence which the world of reason and sensation considers to be no existence at all. "There is nothing we cannot see, nothing we cannot touch," parrot the well-taught children. "You and I," says the Fool at the end, "we are the two fools, we know everything, but we will not speak." As there is a reality behind reality, so there is a wisdom beyond words. Denial has become affirmation.

In the hour-glass, his title property, Yeats has concentrated an image of the rich interplay of antitheses and paradoxes that constitute his drama. It is his main means toward achieving his ideal "visible" play.

Luigi Pirandello

SIX CHARACTERS IN SEARCH
OF AN AUTHOR

A Comedy in the Making

English Version by Edward Storer

Characters of the Comedy in the Making

THE FATHER

THE MOTHER

THE STEP-DAUGHTER

THE SON

THE BOY

THE CHILD

(*The last two do not speak*)

MADAME PACE

Actors of the Company

THE MANAGER

LEADING LADY

LEADING MAN

SECOND LADY .

LEAD

L'INGÉNUE

JUVENILE LEAD

OTHER ACTORS AND ACTRESSES

PROPERTY MAN

PROMPTER

MACHINIST

MANAGER'S SECRETARY

DOOR-KEEPER

SCENE-SHIFTERS

SCENE: *Daytime. The stage of a theater.*

N. B. *The Comedy is without acts or scenes. The performance is interrupted once, without the curtain being lowered, when the*

From the book *Naked Masks: Five Plays* by Luigi Pirandello, edited by Eric Bentley. Copyright, 1922, by E. P. Dutton & Co., Inc. Renewal, 1950, in the names of Stefano, Fausto & Lietta Pirandello. Dutton Paperback Series. Reprinted by permission of the publishers.

355

manager and the chief characters withdraw to arrange a scenario. A second interruption of the action takes place when, by mistake, the stage hands let the curtain down.

ACT I

(*The spectators will find the curtain raised and the stage as it usually is during the day time. It will be half dark, and empty, so that from the beginning the public may have the impression of an impromptu performance.*

Prompter's box and a small table and chair for the MANAGER.

Two other small tables and several chairs scattered about as during rehearsals.

The ACTORS *and* ACTRESSES *of the company enter from the back of the stage: first one, then another, then two together; nine or ten in all. They are about to rehearse a Pirandello play: Mixing It Up.* Some of the company move off towards their dressing rooms. The* PROMPTER, *who has the "book" under his arm, is waiting for the* MANAGER *in order to begin the rehearsal.*

The ACTORS *and* ACTRESSES, *some standing, some sitting, chat and smoke. One perhaps reads a paper; another cons his part.*

Finally, the MANAGER *enters and goes to the table prepared for him. His* SECRETARY *brings him his mail, through which he glances. The* PROMPTER *takes his seat, turns on a light, and opens the "book.")*

THE MANAGER (*throwing a letter down on the table*): I can't see. (To PROPERTY MAN.) Let's have a little light, please!

PROPERTY MAN: Yes sir, yes, at once. (*A light comes down on to the stage.*)

THE MANAGER (*clapping his hands*): Come along! Come along! Second act of "Mixing It Up." (*Sits down.*)

(*The* ACTORS *and* ACTRESSES *go from the front of the stage to the wings, all except the three who are to begin the rehearsal.*)

THE PROMPTER (*reading the "book"*): "Leo Gala's house. A curious room serving as dining-room and study."

THE MANAGER (*to* PROPERTY MAN): Fix up the old red room.

PROPERTY MAN (*noting it down*): Red set. All right!

THE PROMPTER (*continuing to read from the "book"*): "Table already

* i.e. *Il giuoco delle parti.*

laid and writing desk with books and papers. Book-shelves. Exit rear
to Leo's bedroom. Exit left to kitchen. Principal exit to right."

THE MANAGER (*energetically*): Well, you understand: The principal
exit over there; here, the kitchen. (*Turning to actor who is to play
the part of* SOCRATES.) You make your entrances and exits here. (*To*
PROPERTY MAN.) The baize doors at the rear, and curtains.

PROPERTY MAN (*noting it down*): Right!

PROMPTER (*reading as before*): "When the curtain rises, Leo Gala,
dressed in cook's cap and apron is busy beating an egg in a cup.
Philip, also dressed as a cook, is beating another egg. Guido Venanzi
is seated and listening."

LEADING MAN (*to* MANAGER): Excuse me, but must I absolutely wear
a cook's cap?

THE MANAGER (*annoyed*): I imagine so. It says so there anyway.
(*Pointing to the "book."*)

LEADING MAN: But it's ridiculous!

THE MANAGER (*jumping up in a rage*): Ridiculous? Ridiculous? Is it
my fault if France won't send us any more good comedies, and we
are reduced to putting on Pirandello's works, where nobody understands anything, and where the author plays the fool with us all?
(*The* ACTORS *grin. The* MANAGER *goes to* LEADING MAN *and shouts.*)
Yes sir, you put on the cook's cap and beat eggs. Do you suppose
that with all this egg-beating business you are on an ordinary stage?
Get that out of your head. You represent the shell of the eggs you
are beating! (*Laughter and comments among the* ACTORS.) Silence!
and listen to my explanations, please! (*To* LEADING MAN.) "The
empty form of reason without the fullness of instinct, which is
blind." — You stand for reason, your wife is instinct. It's a mixing
up of the parts, according to which you who act your own part become the puppet of yourself. Do you understand?

LEADING MAN: I'm hanged if I do.

THE MANAGER: Neither do I. But let's get on with it. It's sure to be a
glorious failure anyway. (*Confidentially.*) But I say, please face
three-quarters. Otherwise, what with the abstruseness of the dialogue,
and the public that won't be able to hear you, the whole thing will
go to hell. Come on! come on!

PROMPTER: Pardon sir, may I get into my box? There's a bit of a
draught.

THE MANAGER: Yes, yes, of course!

(*At this point, the* DOOR-KEEPER *has entered from the stage door
and advances towards the* MANAGER's *table, taking off his braided
cap. During this manoeuvre, the* SIX CHARACTERS *enter, and stop*

by the door at back of stage, so that when the DOOR-KEEPER *is about to announce their coming to the* MANAGER, *they are already on the stage. A tenuous light surrounds them, almost as if irradiated by them — the faint breath of their fantastic reality.*

This light will disappear when they come forward towards the actors. They preserve, however, something of the dream lightness in which they seem almost suspended; but this does not detract from the essential reality of their forms and expressions.

He who is known as THE FATHER *is a man of about 50: hair, reddish in color, thin at the temples; he is not bald, however; thick moustaches, falling over his still fresh mouth, which often opens in an empty and uncertain smile. He is fattish, pale; with an especially wide forehead. He has blue, oval-shaped eyes, very clear and piercing. Wears light trousers and a dark jacket. He is alternatively mellifluous and violent in his manner.*

THE MOTHER *seems crushed and terrified as if by an intolerable weight of shame and abasement. She is dressed in modest black and wears a thick widow's veil of crêpe. When she lifts this, she reveals a wax-like face. She always keeps her eyes downcast.*

THE STEP-DAUGHTER *is dashing, almost impudent, beautiful. She wears mourning too, but with great elegance. She shows contempt for the timid half-frightened manner of the wretched* BOY *(14 years old, and also dressed in black); on the other hand, she displays a lively tenderness for her little sister, THE* CHILD *(about four), who is dressed in white, with a black silk sash at the waist.*

THE SON *(22) tall, severe in his attitude of contempt for* THE FATHER, *supercilious and indifferent to* THE MOTHER. *He looks as if he had come on the stage against his will.)*

DOOR-KEEPER *(cap in hand)*: Excuse me, sir . . .

THE MANAGER *(rudely)*: Eh? What is it?

DOOR-KEEPER *(timidly)*: These people are asking for you, sir.

THE MANAGER *(furious)*: I am rehearsing, and you know perfectly well no one's allowed to come in during rehearsals! *(Turning to the* CHARACTERS.) Who are you, please? What do you want?

THE FATHER *(coming forward a little, followed by the others who seem embarrassed)*: As a matter of fact . . . we have come here in search of an author . . .

THE MANAGER *(half angry, half amazed)*: An author? What author?

THE FATHER: Any author, sir.

THE MANAGER: But there's no author here. We are not rehearsing a new piece.

THE STEP-DAUGHTER (*vivaciously*): So much the better, so much the better! We can be your new piece.

AN ACTOR (*coming forward from the others*): Oh, do you hear that?

THE FATHER (*to* STEP-DAUGHTER): Yes, but if the author isn't here . . . (*To* MANAGER.) unless you would be willing . . .

THE MANAGER: You are trying to be funny.

THE FATHER: No, for Heaven's sake, what are you saying? We bring you a drama, sir.

THE STEP-DAUGHTER: We may be your fortune.

THE MANAGER: Will you oblige me by going away? We haven't time to waste with mad people.

THE FATHER (*mellifluously*): Oh sir, you know well that life is full of infinite absurdities, which, strangely enough, do not even need to appear plausible, since they are true.

THE MANAGER: What the devil is he talking about?

THE FATHER: I say that to reverse the ordinary process may well be considered a madness: that is, to create credible situations, in order that they may appear true. But permit me to observe that if this be madness, it is the sole *raison d'être* of your profession, gentlemen. (*The* ACTORS *look hurt and perplexed.*)

THE MANAGER (*getting up and looking at him*): So our profession seems to you one worthy of madmen then?

THE FATHER: Well, to make seem true that which isn't true . . . without any need . . . for a joke as it were . . . Isn't that your mission, gentlemen: to give life to fantastic characters on the stage?

THE MANAGER (*interpreting the rising anger of the* COMPANY): But I would beg you to believe, my dear sir, that the profession of the comedian is a noble one. If today, as things go, the playwrights give us stupid comedies to play and puppets to represent instead of men, remember we are proud to have given life to immortal works here on these very boards! (*The* ACTORS, *satisfied, applaud their* MANAGER.)

THE FATHER (*interrupting furiously*): Exactly, perfectly, to living beings more alive than those who breathe and wear clothes: beings less real perhaps, but truer! I agree with you entirely. (*The* ACTORS *look at one another in amazement.*)

THE MANAGER: But what do you mean? Before, you said . . .

THE FATHER: No, excuse me, I meant it for you, sir, who were crying out that you had no time to lose with madmen, while no one better than yourself knows that nature uses the instrument of human fantasy in order to pursue her high creative purpose.

THE MANAGER: Very well, — but where does all this take us?

THE FATHER: Nowhere! It is merely to show you that one is born to life in many forms, in many shapes, as tree, or as stone, as water, as butterfly, or as woman. So one may also be born a character in a play.

THE MANAGER (*with feigned comic dismay*): So you and these other friends of yours have been born characters?

THE FATHER: Exactly, and alive as you see! (MANAGER *and* ACTORS *burst out laughing.*)

THE FATHER (*hurt*): I am sorry you laugh, because we carry in us a drama, as you can guess from this woman here veiled in black.

THE MANAGER (*losing patience at last and almost indignant*): Oh, chuck it! Get away please! Clear out of here! (*To* PROPERTY MAN.) For Heaven's sake, turn them out!

THE FATHER (*resisting*): No, no, look here, we . . .

THE MANAGER (*roaring*): We come here to work, you know.

LEADING ACTOR: One cannot let oneself be made such a fool of.

THE FATHER (*determined, coming forward*): I marvel at your incredulity, gentlemen. Are you not accustomed to see the characters created by an author spring to life in yourselves and face each other? Just because there is no "book" (*pointing to the* PROMPTER'S box) which contains us, you refuse to believe . . .

THE STEP-DAUGHTER (*advances towards* MANAGER, *smiling and coquettish*): Believe me, we are really six most interesting characters, sir; side-tracked however.

THE FATHER: Yes, that is the word! (*To* MANAGER *all at once.*) In the sense, that is, that the author who created us alive no longer wished, or was no longer able, materially to put us into a work of art. And this was a real crime, sir; because he who has had the luck to be born a character can laugh even at death. He cannot die. The man, the writer, the instrument of the creation will die, but his creation does not die. And to live for ever, it does not need to have extraordinary gifts or to be able to work wonders. Who was Sancho Panza? Who was Don Abbondio? Yet they live eternally because — live germs as they were — they had the fortune to find a fecundating matrix, a fantasy which could raise and nourish them: make them live for ever!

THE MANAGER: That is quite all right. But what do you want here, all of you?

THE FATHER: We want to live.

THE MANAGER (*ironically*): For Eternity?

THE FATHER: No, sir, only for a moment . . . in you.

AN ACTOR: Just listen to him!

LEADING LADY: They want to live, in us . . . !

JUVENILE LEAD (*pointing to the* STEP-DAUGHTER): I've no objection, as far as that one is concerned!

THE FATHER: Look here! look here! The comedy has to be made. (*To the* MANAGER.) But if you and your actors are willing, we can soon concert it among ourselves.

THE MANAGER (*annoyed*): But what do you want to concert? We don't go in for concerts here. Here we play dramas and comedies!

THE FATHER: Exactly! That is just why we have come to you.

THE MANAGER: And where is the "book"?

THE FATHER: It is in us! (*The* ACTORS *laugh.*) The drama is in us, and we are the drama. We are impatient to play it. Our inner passion drives us on to this.

THE STEP-DAUGHTER (*disdainful, alluring, treacherous, full of impudence*): My passion, sir! Ah, if you only knew! My passion for him! (*Points to the* FATHER *and makes a pretence of embracing him. Then she breaks out into a loud laugh.*)

THE FATHER (*angrily*): Behave yourself! And please don't laugh in that fashion.

THE STEP-DAUGHTER: With your permission, gentlemen, I, who am a two months' orphan, will show you how I can dance and sing. (*Sings and then dances* Prenez garde à Tchou-Tchin-Tchou.)

> Les chinois sont un peuple malin,
> De Shangaî à Pékin,
> Ils ont mis des écriteaux partout:
> Prenez garde à Tchou-Tchin-Tchou.

ACTORS *and* ACTRESSES: Bravo! Well done! Tip-top!

THE MANAGER: Silence! This isn't a café concert, you know! (*Turning to the* FATHER *in consternation.*) Is she mad?

THE FATHER: Mad? No, she's worse than mad.

THE STEP-DAUGHTER (*to* MANAGER): Worse? Worse? Listen! Stage this drama for us at once! Then you will see that at a certain moment I . . . when this little darling here. . . . (*Takes the* CHILD *by the hand and leads her to the* MANAGER.) Isn't she a dear? (*Takes her up and kisses her.*) Darling! Darling! (*Puts her down again and adds feelingly.*) Well, when God suddenly takes this dear little child away from that poor mother there; and this imbecile here (*seizing hold of the* BOY *roughly and pushing him forward*) does the stupidest things, like the fool he is, you will see me run away. Yes, gentlemen, I shall be off. But the moment hasn't arrived yet. After what has taken place between him and me (*indicates the*

FATHER *with a horrible wink*) I can't remain any longer in this society, to have to witness the anguish of this mother here for that fool. . . . (*Indicates the* SON.) Look at him! Look at him! See how indifferent, how frigid he is, because he is the legitimate son. He despises me, despises him (*pointing to the* BOY), despises this baby here; because . . . we are bastards. (*Goes to the* MOTHER *and embraces her.*) And he doesn't want to recognize her as his mother — she who is the common mother of us all. He looks down upon her as if she were only the mother of us three bastards. Wretch! (*She says all this very rapidly, excitedly. At the word "bastards" she raises her voice, and almost spits out the final "Wretch!"*)

THE MOTHER (*to the* MANAGER, *in anguish*): In the name of these two little children, I beg you. . . . (*She grows faint and is about to fall.*) Oh God!

THE FATHER (*coming forward to support her as do some of the* ACTORS): Quick, a chair, a chair for this poor widow!

THE ACTORS: Is it true? Has she really fainted?

THE MANAGER: Quick, a chair! Here!

(*One of the* ACTORS *brings a chair, the* OTHERS *proffer assistance. The* MOTHER *tries to prevent the* FATHER *from lifting the veil which covers her face.*)

THE FATHER: Look at her! Look at her!

THE MOTHER: No, no; stop it please!

THE FATHER (*raising her veil*): Let them see you!

THE MOTHER (*rising and covering her face with her hands, in desperation*): I beg you, sir, to prevent this man from carrying out his plan which is loathsome to me.

THE MANAGER (*dumbfounded*): I don't understand at all. What is the situation? Is this lady your wife? (*To the* FATHER.)

THE FATHER: Yes, gentlemen: my wife!

THE MANAGER: But how can she be a widow if you are alive? (*The* ACTORS *find relief for their astonishment in a loud laugh.*)

THE FATHER: Don't laugh! Don't laugh like that, for Heaven's sake. Her drama lies just here in this: she has had a lover, a man who ought to be here.

THE MOTHER (*with a cry*): No! No!

THE STEP-DAUGHTER: Fortunately for her, he is dead. Two months ago as I said. We are in mourning, as you see.

THE FATHER: He isn't here you see, not because he is dead. He isn't here — look at her a moment and you will understand — because her drama isn't a drama of the love of two men for whom she was incapable of feeling anything except possibly a little gratitude —

gratitude not for me but for the other. She isn't a woman, she is a mother, and her drama — powerful sir, I assure you — lies, as a matter of fact, all in these four children she has had by two men.

THE MOTHER: I had them? Have you got the courage to say that I wanted them? (*To the* COMPANY.) It was his doing. It was he who gave me that other man, who forced me to go away with him.

THE STEP-DAUGHTER: It isn't true.

THE MOTHER (*startled*): Not true, isn't it?

THE STEP-DAUGHTER: No, it isn't true, it just isn't true.

THE MOTHER: And what can you know about it?

THE STEP-DAUGHTER: It isn't true. Don't believe it. (*To* MANAGER.) Do you know why she says so? For that fellow there. (*Indicates the* SON.) She tortures herself, destroys herself on account of the neglect of that son there; and she wants him to believe that if she abandoned him when he was only two years old, it was because he (*indicates the* FATHER) made her do so.

THE MOTHER (*vigorously*): He forced me to it, and I call God to witness it. (*To the* MANAGER.) Ask him (*indicates* HUSBAND) if it isn't true. Let him speak. You (*to* DAUGHTER) are not in a position to know anything about it.

THE STEP-DAUGHTER: I know you lived in peace and happiness with my father while he lived. Can you deny it?

THE MOTHER: No, I don't deny it. . . .

THE STEP-DAUGHTER: He was always full of affection and kindness for you. (*To the* BOY, *angrily*.) It's true, isn't it? Tell them! Why don't you speak, you little fool?

THE MOTHER: Leave the poor boy alone. Why do you want to make me appear ungrateful, daughter? I don't want to offend your father. I have answered him that I didn't abandon my house and my son through any fault of mine, nor from any wilful passion.

THE FATHER: It is true. It was my doing.

LEADING MAN (*to the* COMPANY): What a spectacle!

LEADING LADY: We are the audience this time.

JUVENILE LEAD: For once, in a way.

THE MANAGER (*beginning to get really interested*): Let's hear them out. Listen!

THE SON: Oh yes, you're going to hear a fine bit now. He will talk to you of the Demon of Experiment.

THE FATHER: You are a cynical imbecile. I've told you so already a hundred times. (*To the* MANAGER.) He tries to make fun of me on account of this expression which I have found to excuse myself with.

THE SON (*with disgust*): Yes, phrases! phrases!

THE FATHER: Phrases! Isn't everyone consoled when faced with a trouble or fact he doesn't understand, by a word, some simple word, which tells us nothing and yet calms us?

THE STEP-DAUGHTER: Even in the case of remorse. In fact, especially then.

THE FATHER: Remorse? No, that isn't true. I've done more than use words to quieten the remorse in me.

THE STEP-DAUGHTER: Yes, there was a bit of money too. Yes, yes, a bit of money. There were the hundred lire he was about to offer me in payment, gentlemen. . . . (*Sensation of horror among the* ACTORS.)

THE SON (*to the* STEP-DAUGHTER): This is vile.

THE STEP-DAUGHTER: Vile? There they were in a pale blue envelope on a little mahogany table in the back of Madame Pace's shop. You know Madame Pace — one of those ladies who attract poor girls of good family into their ateliers, under the pretext of their selling *robes et manteaux*.

THE SON: And he thinks he has bought the right to tyrannize over us all with those hundred lire he was going to pay; but which, fortunately — note this, gentlemen — he had no chance of paying.

THE STEP-DAUGHTER: It was a near thing, though, you know! (*Laughs ironically.*)

THE MOTHER (*protesting*): Shame, my daughter, shame!

THE STEP-DAUGHTER: Shame indeed! This is my revenge! I am dying to live that scene . . . The room . . . I see it . . . Here is the window with the mantles exposed, there the divan, the looking-glass, a screen, there in front of the window the little mahogany table with the blue envelope containing one hundred lire. I see it. I see it. I could take hold of it. . . . But you, gentlemen, you ought to turn your backs now: I am almost nude, you know. But I don't blush: I leave that to him. (*Indicating* FATHER.)

THE MANAGER: I don't understand this at all.

THE FATHER: Naturally enough. I would ask you, sir, to exercise your authority a little here, and let me speak before you believe all she is trying to blame me with. Let me explain.

THE STEP-DAUGHTER: Ah yes, explain it in your own way.

THE FATHER: But don't you see that in the whole trouble lies here? In words, words. Each one of us has within him a whole world of things, each man of us his own special world. And how can we ever come to an understanding if I put in the words I utter the sense and value of things as I see them; while you who listen to me must inevitably translate them according to the conception of things each one of you has within himself. We think we understand each other, but we never really do. Look here! This woman (*indicating the* MOTHER) takes all my pity for her as a specially ferocious form of cruelty.

THE MOTHER: But you drove me away.

THE FATHER: Do you hear her? I drove her away! She believes I really sent her away.

THE MOTHER: You know how to talk, and I don't; but, believe me, sir (*to* MANAGER), after he had married me . . . who knows why? . . . I was a poor insignificant woman. . . .

THE FATHER: But, good Heavens! it was just for your humility that I married you. I loved this simplicity in you. (*He stops when he sees she makes signs to contradict him, opens his arms wide in sign of desperation, seeing how hopeless it is to make himself understood.*) You see she denies it. Her mental deafness, believe me, is phenomenal, the limit: (*touches his forehead*) deaf, deaf, mentally deaf! She has plenty of feeling. Oh yes, a good heart for the children; but the brain — deaf, to the point of desperation ——!

THE STEP-DAUGHTER: Yes, but ask him how his intelligence has helped us.

THE FATHER: If we could see all the evil that may spring from good, what should we do? (*At this point the* LEADING LADY, *who is biting her lips with rage at seeing the* LEADING MAN *flirting with the* STEP-DAUGHTER, *comes forward and speaks to the* MANAGER.)

LEADING LADY: Excuse me, but are we going to rehearse today?

MANAGER: Of course, of course; but let's hear them out.

JUVENILE LEAD: This is something quite new.

L'INGÉNUE: Most interesting!

LEADING LADY: Yes, for the people who like that kind of thing. (*Casts a glance at* LEADING MAN.)

THE MANAGER (*to* FATHER): You must please explain yourself quite clearly. (*Sits down.*)

THE FATHER: Very well then: listen! I had in my service a poor man, a clerk, a secretary of mine, full of devotion, who became friends with her. (*Indicating the* MOTHER.) They understood one another, were kindred souls in fact, without, however, the least suspicion of any evil existing. They were incapable even of thinking of it.

THE STEP-DAUGHTER: So he thought of it — for them!

THE FATHER: That's not true. I meant to do good to them — and to myself, I confess, at the same time. Things had come to the point that I could not say a word to either of them without their making a mute appeal, one to the other, with their eyes. I could see them silently asking each other how I was to be kept in countenance, how I was to be kept quiet. And this, believe me, was just about enough of itself to keep me in a constant rage, to exasperate me beyond measure.

THE MANAGER: And why didn't you send him away then — this secretary of yours?

THE FATHER: Precisely what I did, sir. And then I had to watch this poor woman drifting forlornly about the house like an animal without a master, like an animal one has taken in out of pity.

THE MOTHER: Ah yes . . . !

THE FATHER (*suddenly turning to the* MOTHER): It's true about the son anyway, isn't it?

THE MOTHER: He took my son away from me first of all.

THE FATHER: But not from cruelty. I did it so that he should grow up healthy and strong by living in the country.

THE STEP-DAUGHTER (*pointing to him ironically*): As one can see.

THE FATHER (*quickly*): Is it my fault if he has grown up like this? I sent him to a wet nurse in the country, a peasant, as *she* did not seem to me strong enough, though she is of humble origin. That was, anyway, the reason I married her. Unpleasant all this may be, but how can it be helped? My mistake possibly, but there we are! All my life I have had these confounded aspirations towards a certain moral sanity. (*At this point the* STEP-DAUGHTER *bursts into a noisy laugh.*) Oh, stop it! Stop it! I can't stand it.

THE MANAGER: Yes, please stop it, for Heaven's sake.

THE STEP-DAUGHTER: But imagine moral sanity from him, if you please — the client of certain ateliers like that of Madame Pace!

THE FATHER: Fool! That is the proof that I am a man! This seeming contradiction, gentlemen, is the strongest proof that I stand here a live man before you. Why, it is just for this very incongruity in my nature that I have had to suffer what I have. I could not live by the side of that woman (*indicating the* MOTHER) any longer; but not so much for the boredom she inspired me with as for the pity I felt for her.

THE MOTHER: And so he turned me out —.

THE FATHER: — well provided for! Yes, I sent her to that man, gentlemen . . . to let her go free of me.

THE MOTHER: And to free himself.

THE FATHER: Yes, I admit it. It was also a liberation for me. But great evil has come of it. I meant well when I did it; and I did it more for her sake than mine. I swear it. (*Crosses his arms on his chest; then turns suddenly to the* MOTHER.) Did I ever lose sight of you until that other man carried you off to another town, like the angry fool he was? And on account of my pure interest in you

. . . my pure interest, I repeat, that had no base motive in it . . . I watched with the tenderest concern the new family that grew up around her. She can bear witness to this. (*Points to the* STEP-DAUGHTER.)

THE STEP-DAUGHTER: Oh yes, that's true enough. When I was a kiddie, so so high, you know, with plaits over my shoulders and knickers longer than my skirts, I used to see him waiting outside the school for me to come out. He came to see how I was growing up.

THE FATHER: This is infamous, shameful!

THE STEP-DAUGHTER: No. Why?

THE FATHER: Infamous! infamous! (*Then excitedly to* MANAGER *explaining.*) After she (*indicating* MOTHER) went away, my house seemed suddenly empty. She was my incubus, but she filled my house. I was like a dazed fly alone in the empty rooms. This boy here (*indicating the* SON) was educated away from home, and when he came back, he seemed to me to be no more mine. With no mother to stand between him and me, he grew up entirely for himself, on his own, apart, with no tie of intellect or affection binding him to me. And then — strange but true — I was driven, by curiosity at first and then by some tender sentiment, towards her family, which had come into being through my will. The thought of her began gradually to fill up the emptiness I felt all around me. I wanted to know if she were happy in living out the simple daily duties of life. I wanted to think of her as fortunate and happy because far away from the complicated torments of my spirit. And so, to have proof of this, I used to watch that child coming out of school.

THE STEP-DAUGHTER: Yes, yes. True. He used to follow me in the street and smiled at me, waved his hand, like this. I would look at him with interest, wondering who he might be. I told my mother, who guessed at once. (*The* MOTHER *agrees with a nod.*) Then she didn't want to send me to school for some days; and when I finally went back, there he was again — looking so ridiculous — with a paper parcel in his hands. He came close to me, caressed me, and drew out a fine straw hat from the parcel, with a bouquet of flowers — all for me!

THE MANAGER: A bit discursive this, you know!

THE SON (*contemptuously*): Literature! Literature!

THE FATHER: Literature indeed! This is life, this is passion!

THE MANAGER: It may be, but it won't act.

THE FATHER: I agree. This is only the part leading up. I don't suggest this should be staged. She (*pointing to the* STEP-DAUGHTER), as you see, is no longer the flapper with plaits down her back —.

THE STEP-DAUGHTER: — and the knickers showing below the skirt!

THE FATHER: The drama is coming now, sir; something new, complex, most interesting.

THE STEP-DAUGHTER: As soon as my father died . . .

THE FATHER: — there was absolute misery for them. They came back here, unknown to me. Through her stupidity! (*Pointing to the* MOTHER.) It is true she can barely write her own name; but she could anyhow have got her daughter to write to me that they were in need . . .

THE MOTHER: And how was I to divine all this sentiment in him?

THE FATHER: That is exactly your mistake, never to have guessed any of my sentiments.

THE MOTHER: After so many years apart, and all that had happened . . .

THE FATHER: Was it my fault if that fellow carried you away? It happened quite suddenly; for after he had obtained some job or other, I could find no trace of them; and so, not unnaturally, my interest in them dwindled. But the drama culminated unforeseen and violent on their return, when I was impelled by my miserable flesh that still lives. . . . Ah! what misery, what wretchedness is that of the man who is alone and disdains debasing *liaisons!* Not old enough to do without women, and not young enough to go and look for one without shame. Misery? It's worse than misery; it's a horror; for no woman can any longer give him love; and when a man feels this. . . . One ought to do without, you say? Yes, yes, I know. Each of us when he appears before his fellows is clothed in a certain dignity. But every man knows what unconfessable things pass within the secrecy of his own heart. One gives way to the temptation, only to rise from it again, afterwards, with a great eagerness to re-establish one's dignity, as if it were a tombstone to place on the grave of one's shame, and a monument to hide and sign the memory of our weaknesses. Everybody's in the same case. Some folks haven't the courage to say certain things, that's all!

THE STEP-DAUGHTER: All appear to have the courage to do them though.

THE FATHER: Yes, but in secret. Therefore, you want more courage to say these things. Let a man but speak these things out, and folks at once label him a cynic. But it isn't true. He is like all the others, better indeed, because he isn't afraid to reveal with the light of the intelligence the red shame of human bestiality on which most men close their eyes so as not to see it.

Woman — for example, look at her case! She turns tantalizing inviting glances on you. You seize her. No sooner does she feel

herself in your grasp than she closes her eyes. It is the sign of her
mission, the sign by which she says to man: "Blind yourself, for
I am blind."

THE STEP-DAUGHTER: Sometimes she can close them no more: when
she no longer feels the need of hiding her shame to herself, but
dry-eyed and dispassionately, sees only that of the man who has
blinded himself without love. Oh, all these intellectual complica-
tions make me sick, disgust me — all this philosophy that uncovers
the beast in man, and then seeks to save him, excuse him . . . I
can't stand it, sir. When a man seeks to "simplify" life bestially,
throwing aside every relic of humanity, every chaste aspiration,
every pure feeling, all sense of ideality, duty, modesty, shame . . .
then nothing is more revolting and nauseous than a certain kind
of remorse — crocodiles' tears, that's what it is.

THE MANAGER: Let's come to the point. This is only discussion.

THE FATHER: Very good, sir! But a fact is like a sack which won't
stand up when it's empty. In order that it may stand up, one has
to put into it the reason and sentiment which have caused it to
exist. I couldn't possibly know that after the death of that man,
they had decided to return here, that they were in misery, and that
she (*pointing to the* MOTHER) had gone to work as a modiste, and
at a shop of the type of that of Madame Pace.

THE STEP-DAUGHTER: A real high-class modiste, you must know, gentlemen. In appearance, she works for the leaders of the best society;
but she arranges matters so that these elegant ladies serve her
purpose . . . without prejudice to other ladies who are . . . well
. . . only so so.

THE MOTHER: You will believe me, gentlemen, that it never entered
my mind that the old hag offered me work because she had her
eye on my daughter.

THE STEP-DAUGHTER: Poor mamma! Do you know, sir, what that
woman did when I brought her back the work my mother had
finished? She would point out to me that I had torn one of my
frocks, and she would give it back to my mother to mend. It was
I who paid for it, always I; while this poor creature here believed
she was sacrificing herself for me and these two children here,
sitting up at night sewing Madame Pace's robes.

THE MANAGER: And one day you met there . . .

THE STEP-DAUGHTER: Him, him. Yes sir, an old client. There's a scene
for you to play! Superb!

THE FATHER: She, the Mother arrived just then . . .

THE STEP-DAUGHTER (*treacherously*): Almost in time!

THE FATHER (*crying out*): No, in time! in time! Fortunately I recognized her . . . in time. And I took them back home with me to my house. You can imagine now her position and mine; she, as you see her; and I who cannot look her in the face.

THE STEP-DAUGHTER: Absurd! How can I possibly be expected — after that — to be a modest young miss, a fit person to go with his con- founded aspirations for "a solid moral sanity"?

THE FATHER: For the drama lies all in this — in the conscience that I have, that each one of us has. We believe this conscience to be a single thing, but it is many-sided. There is one for this person, and another for that. Diverse consciences. So we have this illusion of being one person for all, of having a personality that is unique in all our acts. But it isn't true. We perceive this when, tragically perhaps, in something we do, we are as it were, suspended, caught up in the air on a kind of hook. Then we perceive that all of us was not in that act, and that it would be an atrocious injustice to judge us by that action alone, as if all our existence were summed up in that one deed. Now do you understand the perfidy of this girl? She surprised me in a place, where she ought not to have known me, just as I could not exist for her; and she now seeks to attach to me a reality such as I could never suppose I should have to assume for her in a shameful and fleeting moment of my life. I feel this above all else. And the drama, you will see, acquires a tremendous value from this point. Then there is the position of the others . . . his. . . . (*Indicating the* SON.)

THE SON (*shrugging his shoulders scornfully*): Leave me alone! I don't come into this.

THE FATHER: What? You don't come into this?

THE SON: I've got nothing to do with it, and don't want to have; because you know well enough I wasn't made to be mixed up in all this with the rest of you.

THE STEP-DAUGHTER: We are only vulgar folk! He is the fine gentle- man. You may have noticed, Mr. Manager, that I fix him now and again with a look of scorn while he lowers his eyes — for he knows the evil he has done me.

THE SON (*scarcely looking at her*): I?

THE STEP-DAUGHTER: You! you! I owe my life on the streets to you. Did you or did you not deny us, with your behavior, I won't say the intimacy of home, but even that mere hospitality which makes guests feel at their ease? We were intruders who had come to dis- turb the kingdom of your legitimacy. I should like to have you witness, Mr. Manager, certain scenes between him and me. He says I have tyrannized over everyone. But it was just his behavior which made me insist on the reason for which I had come into the house, — this reason he calls "vile" — into his house, with my mother who is his mother too. And I came as mistress of the house.

THE SON: It's easy for them to put me always in the wrong. But imagine, gentlemen, the position of a son, whose fate it is to see arrive one day at his home a young woman of impudent bearing, a young woman who inquires for his father, with whom who knows what business she has. This young man has then to witness her return bolder than ever, accompanied by that child there. He is obliged to watch her treat his father in an equivocal and confidential manner. She asks money of him in a way that lets one suppose he must give it to her, *must*, do you understand, because he has every obligation to do so.

THE FATHER: But I have, as a matter of fact, this obligation. I owe it to your mother.

THE SON: How should I know? When had I ever seen or heard of her? One day there arrive with her (*indicating* STEP-DAUGHTER) that lad and this baby here. I am told: "This is *your* mother too, you know." I divine from her manner (*indicating* STEP-DAUGHTER *again*) why it is they have come home. I had rather not say what I feel and think about it. I shouldn't even care to confess to myself. No action can therefore be hoped for from me in this affair. Believe me, Mr. Manager, I am an "unrealized" character, dramatically speaking; and I find myself not at all at ease in their company. Leave me out of it, I beg you.

THE FATHER: What? It is just because you are so that . . .

THE SON: How do you know what I am like? When did you ever bother your head about me?

THE FATHER: I admit it. I admit it. But isn't that a situation in itself? This aloofness of yours which is so cruel to me and to your mother, who returns home and sees you almost for the first time grown up, who doesn't recognize you but knows you are her son. . . . (*Pointing out the* MOTHER *to the* MANAGER.) See, she's crying!

THE STEP-DAUGHTER (*angrily, stamping her foot*): Like a fool!

THE FATHER (*indicating* STEP-DAUGHTER): She can't stand him you know. (*Then referring again to the* SON.) He says he doesn't come into the affair, whereas he is really the hinge of the whole action. Look at that lad who is always clinging to his mother, frightened and humiliated. It is on account of this fellow here. Possibly his situation is the most painful of all. He feels himself a stranger more than the others. The poor little chap feels mortified, humiliated at being brought into a home out of charity as it were. (*In con-*

fidence.) He is the image of his father. Hardly talks at all. Humble and quiet.

THE MANAGER: Oh, we'll cut him out. You've no notion what a nuisance boys are on the stage. . . .

THE FATHER: He disappears soon, you know. And the baby too. She is the first to vanish from the scene. The drama consists finally in this: when that mother re-enters my house, her family born outside of it, and shall we say superimposed on the original, ends with the death of the little girl, the tragedy of the boy and the flight of the elder daughter. It cannot go on, because it is foreign to its surroundings. So after much torment, we three remain: I, the mother, that son. Then, owing to the disappearance of that extraneous family, we too find ourselves strange to one another. We find we are living in an atmosphere of mortal desolation which is the revenge, as he (*indicating* SON) scornfully said of the Demon of Experiment, that unfortunately hides in me. Thus, sir, you see when faith is lacking, it becomes impossible to create certain states of happiness, for we lack the necessary humility. Vaingloriously, we try to substitute ourselves for this faith, creating thus for the rest of the world a reality which we believe after their fashion, while, actually, it doesn't exist. For each one of us has his own reality to be respected before God, even when it is harmful to one's very self.

THE MANAGER: There is something in what you say. I assure you all this interests me very much. I begin to think there's the stuff for a drama in all this, and not a bad drama either.

THE STEP-DAUGHTER (*coming forward*): When you've got a character like me.

THE FATHER (*shutting her up, all excited to learn the decision of the* MANAGER): You be quiet!

THE MANAGER (*reflecting, heedless of interruption*): It's new . . . hem . . . yes. . . .

THE FATHER: Absolutely new!

THE MANAGER: You've got a nerve though, I must say, to come here and fling it at me like this . . .

THE FATHER: You will understand, sir, born as we are for the stage . . .

THE MANAGER: Are you amateur actors then?

THE FATHER: No. I say born for the stage, because . . .

THE MANAGER: Oh, nonsense. You're an old hand, you know.

THE FATHER: No sir, no. We act that rôle for which we have been cast, that rôle which we are given in life. And in my own case, passion itself, as usually happens, becomes a trifle theatrical when it is exalted.

THE MANAGER: Well, well, that will do. But you see, without an author. . . . I could give you the address of an author if you like . . .

THE FATHER: No, no. Look here! You must be the author.

THE MANAGER: I? What are you talking about?

THE FATHER: Yes, you, you! Why not?

THE MANAGER: Because I have never been an author: that's why.

THE FATHER: Then why not turn author now? Everybody does it. You don't want any special qualities. Your task is made much easier by the fact that we are all here alive before you. . . .

THE MANAGER: It won't do.

THE FATHER: What? When you see us live our drama. . . .

THE MANAGER: Yes, that's all right. But you want someone to write it.

THE FATHER: No, no. Someone to take it down, possibly, while we play it, scene by scene! It will be enough to sketch it out at first, and then try it over.

THE MANAGER: Well . . . I am almost tempted. It's a bit of an idea. One might have a shot at it.

THE FATHER: Of course. You'll see what scenes will come out of it. I can give you one, at once . . .

THE MANAGER: By Jove, it tempts me. I'd like to have a go at it. Let's try it out. Come with me to my office. (*Turning to the* ACTORS.) You are at liberty for a bit, but don't step out of the theatre for long. In a quarter of an hour, twenty minutes, all back here again! (*To the* FATHER.) We'll see what can be done. Who knows if we don't get something really extraordinary out of it?

THE FATHER: There's no doubt about it. They (*indicating the* CHARACTERS) had better come with us too, hadn't they?

THE MANAGER: Yes, yes. Come on! come on! (*Moves away and then turning to the* ACTORS.) Be punctual, please! (MANAGER *and the* SIX CHARACTERS *cross the stage and go off. The other* ACTORS *remain, looking at one another in astonishment.*)

LEADING MAN: Is he serious? What the devil does he want to do?

JUVENILE LEAD: This is rank madness.

THIRD ACTOR: Does he expect to knock up a drama in five minutes?

JUVENILE LEAD: Like the improvisers!

LEADING LADY: If he thinks I'm going to take part in a joke like this. . . .

JUVENILE LEAD: I'm out of it anyway.

FOURTH ACTOR: I should like to know who they are. (*Alludes to* CHARACTERS.)

THIRD ACTOR: What do you suppose? Madmen or rascals!

JUVENILE LEAD: And he takes them seriously!

L'INGÉNUE: Vanity! He fancies himself as an author now.

LEADING MAN: It's absolutely unheard of. If the stage has come to this . . . well I'm . . .

FIFTH ACTOR: It's rather a joke.

THIRD ACTOR: Well, we'll see what's going to happen next.

(*Thus talking, the* ACTORS *leave the stage; some going out by the little door at the back; others retiring to their dressing-rooms.*
The curtain remains up.
The action of the play is suspended for twenty minutes.)

ACT II

The stage call-bells ring to warn the company that the play is about to begin again.

The STEP-DAUGHTER *comes out of the* MANAGER'S *office along with the* CHILD *and the* BOY. *As she comes out of the office, she cries:* —

Nonsense! nonsense! Do it yourselves! I'm not going to mix myself up in this mess. (*Turning to the* CHILD *and coming quickly with her on to the stage.*) Come on, Rosetta, let's run!

(*The* BOY *follows them slowly, remaining a little behind and seeming perplexed.*)

THE STEP-DAUGHTER (*stops, bends over the* CHILD *and takes the latter's face between her hands*): My little darling! You're frightened, aren't you? You don't know where we are, do you? (*Pretending to reply to a question of the* CHILD.) What is the stage? It's a place, baby, you know, where people play at being serious, a place where they act comedies. We've got to act a comedy now, dead serious, you know; and you're in it also, little one. (*Embraces her, pressing the little head to her breast, and rocking the* CHILD *for a moment.*) Oh darling, darling, what a horrid comedy you've got to play! What a wretched part they've found for you! A garden . . . a fountain . . . look . . . just suppose, kiddie, it's here. Where, you say? Why, right here in the middle. It's all pretense you know. That's the trouble, my pet: it's all make-believe here. It's better to imagine it though, because if they fix it up for you, it'll only be painted cardboard, painted cardboard for the rockery, the water, the plants. . . . Ah, but I think a baby like this one would sooner have a make-believe fountain than a real one, so she could play with it. What a joke it'll be for the others! But for you, alas! not quite such a joke: you who are real, baby dear, and really play by a real fountain that is big and green and beautiful, with ever so many bamboos around it that are reflected in the water, and a whole lot of little ducks swimming about. . . . No, Rosetta, no, your mother doesn't bother about you on account of that wretch of a son there. I'm in the devil of a temper, and as for that lad. . . . (*Seizes* BOY *by the arm to force him to take one of his hands out of his pockets.*) What have you got there? What are you hiding? (*Pulls his hand out of his pocket, looks into it and catches the glint of a revolver.*) Ah! where did you get this? (*The* BOY, *very pale in the face, looks at her, but does not answer.*) Idiot! If I'd been in your place, instead of killing myself, I'd have shot one of those two, or both of them: father and son.

(*The* FATHER *enters from the office, all excited from his work. The* MANAGER *follows him.*)

THE FATHER: Come on, come on dear! Come here for a minute! We've arranged everything. It's all fixed up.

THE MANAGER (*also excited*): If you please, young lady, there are one or two points to settle still. Will you come along?

THE STEP-DAUGHTER (*following him towards the office*): Ouff! what's the good, if you've arranged everything.

(*The* FATHER, MANAGER *and* STEP-DAUGHTER *go back into the office again* [*off*] *for a moment. At the same time, the* SON *followed by the* MOTHER, *comes out.*)

THE SON (*looking at the three entering office*): Oh this is fine, fine! And to think I can't even get away!

(*The* MOTHER *attempts to look at him, but lowers her eyes immediately when he turns away from her. She then sits down. The* BOY *and the* CHILD *approach her. She casts a glance again at the* SON, *and speaks with humble tones, trying to draw him into conversation.*)

THE MOTHER: And isn't my punishment the worst of all? (*Then seeing from the* SON's *manner that he will not bother himself about her.*) My God! Why are you so cruel? Isn't it enough for one person to support all this torment? Must you then insist on others seeing it also?

THE SON (*half to himself, meaning the* MOTHER *to hear, however*): And they want to put it on the stage! If there was at least a reason for it! He thinks he has got at the meaning of it all. Just as if each one of us in every circumstance of life couldn't find his own explanation of it! (*Pauses.*) He complains he was discovered in a place where he ought not to have been seen, in a moment of his life which ought to have remained hidden and kept out of the reach of that convention which he has to maintain for other people. And what about my case? Haven't I had to reveal what no son ought ever to reveal: how father and mother live and are man and wife for themselves quite apart from that idea of father and mother which we give them? When this idea is revealed, our life is then linked at one point only to that man and that woman; and as such it should shame them, shouldn't it?

(*The* MOTHER *hides her face in her hands. From the dressing-rooms and the little door at the back of the stage the* ACTORS *and* STAGE MANAGER *return, followed by the* PROPERTY MAN, *and the* PROMPTER. *At the same moment, the* MANAGER *comes out of his office, accompanied by the* FATHER *and the* STEP-DAUGHTER.)

THE MANAGER: Come on, come on, ladies and gentlemen! Heh! you there, machinist!

MACHINIST: Yes sir?

THE MANAGER: Fix up the white parlor with the floral decorations. Two wings and a drop with a door will do. Hurry up!

(*The* MACHINIST *runs off at once to prepare the scene, and arranges it while the* MANAGER *talks with the* STAGE MANAGER, *the* PROPERTY MAN, *and the* PROMPTER *on matters of detail.*)

THE MANAGER (*to* PROPERTY MAN): Just have a look, and see if there isn't a sofa or divan in the wardrobe . . .

PROPERTY MAN: There's the green one.

THE STEP-DAUGHTER: No no! Green won't do. It was yellow, ornamented with flowers — very large! and most comfortable!

PROPERTY MAN: There isn't one like that.

THE MANAGER: It doesn't matter. Use the one we've got.

THE STEP-DAUGHTER: Doesn't matter? It's most important!

THE MANAGER: We're only trying it now. Please don't interfere. (*To* PROPERTY MAN.) See if we've got a shop window — long and narrowish.

THE STEP-DAUGHTER: And the little table! The little mahogany table for the pale blue envelope!

PROPERTY MAN (*to* MANAGER): There's that little gilt one.

THE MANAGER: That'll do fine.

THE FATHER: A mirror.

THE STEP-DAUGHTER: And the screen! We must have a screen. Otherwise how can I manage?

PROPERTY MAN: That's all right, Miss. We've got any amount of them.

THE MANAGER (*to the* STEP-DAUGHTER): We want some clothes pegs too, don't we?

THE STEP-DAUGHTER: Yes, several, several!

THE MANAGER: See how many we've got and bring them all.

PROPERTY MAN: All right!

(*The* PROPERTY MAN *hurries off to obey his orders. While he is putting the things in their places, the* MANAGER *talks to the* PROMPTER *and then with the* CHARACTERS *and the* ACTORS.)

THE MANAGER (*to* PROMPTER): Take your seat. Look here: this is the outline of the scenes, act by act. (*Hands him some sheets of paper.*) And now I'm going to ask you to do something out of the ordinary.

PROMPTER: Take it down in shorthand?

THE MANAGER (*pleasantly surprised*): Exactly! Can you do shorthand?

PROMPTER: Yes, a little.

THE MANAGER: Good! (*Turning to a* STAGE HAND.) Go and get some paper from my office, plenty, as much as you can find.

(*The* STAGE HAND *goes off, and soon returns with a handful of paper which he gives to the* PROMPTER.)

THE MANAGER (*to* PROMPTER): You follow the scenes as we play them, and try and get the points down, at any rate the most important ones. (*Then addressing the* ACTORS.) Clear the stage, ladies and gentlemen! Come over here (*pointing to the left*) and listen attentively.

LEADING LADY: But, excuse me, we. . . .

THE MANAGER (*guessing her thought*): Don't worry! You won't have to improvise.

LEADING MAN: What have we to do then?

THE MANAGER: Nothing. For the moment you just watch and listen. Everybody will get his part written out afterwards. At present we're going to try the thing as best we can. They're going to act now.

THE FATHER (*as if fallen from the clouds into the confusion of the stage*): We? What do you mean, if you please, by a rehearsal?

THE MANAGER: A rehearsal for them. (*Points to the* ACTORS.)

THE FATHER: But since we are the characters . . .

THE MANAGER: All right: "characters" then, if you insist on calling yourselves such. But here, my dear sir, the characters don't act. Here the actors do the acting. The characters are there, in the "book" (*pointing towards* PROMPTER's *box*) — when there is a "book"!

THE FATHER: I won't contradict you; but excuse me, the actors aren't the characters. They want to be, they pretend to be, don't they? Now if these gentlemen here are fortunate enough to have us alive before them . . .

THE MANAGER: Oh this is grand! You want to come before the public yourselves then?

THE FATHER: As we are. . . .

THE MANAGER: I can assure you it would be a magnificent spectacle!

LEADING MAN: What's the use of us here anyway then?

THE MANAGER: You're not going to pretend that you can act? It makes me laugh! (*The* ACTORS *laugh.*) There, you see, they are laughing at the notion. But, by the way, I must cast the parts. That won't be difficult. They cast themselves. (*To the* SECOND LADY LEAD.) You play the Mother. (*To the* FATHER.) We must find her a name.

THE FATHER: Amalia, sir.

THE MANAGER: But that is the real name of your wife. We don't want to call her by her real name.

THE FATHER: Why ever not, if it is her name? . . . Still, perhaps, if that lady must. . . . (*Makes a slight motion of the hand to indicate the* SECOND LADY LEAD.) I see this woman here (*means the* MOTHER) as Amalia. But do as you like. (*Gets more and more confused.*) I don't know what to say to you. Already, I begin to hear my own words ring false, as if they had another sound. . . .

THE MANAGER: Don't you worry about it. It'll be our job to find the right tones. And as for her name, if you want her Amalia, Amalia it shall be; and if you don't like it, we'll find another! For the moment though, we'll call the characters in this way: (*To* JUVENILE LEAD.) You are the Son. (*To the* LEADING LADY.) You naturally are the Step-Daughter. . . .

THE STEP-DAUGHTER (*excitedly*): What? what? I, that woman there? (*Bursts out laughing.*)

THE MANAGER (*angry*): What is there to laugh at?

LEADING LADY (*indignant*): Nobody has ever dared to laugh at me. I insist on being treated with respect; otherwise I go away.

THE STEP-DAUGHTER: No, no, excuse me . . . I am not laughing at you. . . .

THE MANAGER (*to* STEP-DAUGHTER): You ought to feel honored to be played by. . .

LEADING LADY (*at once, contemptuously*): "That woman there" . . .

THE STEP-DAUGHTER: But I wasn't speaking of you, you know. I was speaking of myself — whom I can't see at all in you! That is all. I don't know . . . but . . . you . . . aren't in the least like me. . . .

THE FATHER: True. Here's the point. Look here, sir, our temperaments, our souls. . . .

THE MANAGER: Temperament, soul, be hanged! Do you suppose the spirit of the piece is in you? Nothing of the kind!

THE FATHER: What, haven't we our own temperaments, our own souls?

THE MANAGER: Not at all. Your soul or whatever you like to call it takes shape here. The actors give body and form to it, voice and gesture. And my actors — I may tell you — have given expression to much more lofty material than this little drama of yours, which may or may not hold up on the stage. But if it does, the merit of it, believe me, will be due to my actors.

THE FATHER: I don't dare contradict you, sir; but, believe me, it is a terrible suffering for us who are as we are, with these bodies of ours, these features to see. . . .

THE MANAGER (*cutting him short and out of patience*): Good heavens! The make-up will remedy all that, man, the make-up. . . .

THE FATHER: Maybe. But the voice, the gestures . . .

THE MANAGER: Now, look here! On the stage, you as yourself, cannot exist. The actor here acts you, and that's an end to it!

THE FATHER: I understand. And now I think I see why our author who conceived us as we are, all alive, didn't want to put us on the stage after all. I haven't the least desire to offend your actors. Far from it! But when I think that I am to be acted by . . . I don't know by whom. . . .

LEADING MAN (*on his dignity*): By me, if you've no objection!

THE FATHER (*humbly, mellifluously*): Honored, I assure you, sir. (*Bows.*) Still, I must say that try as this gentleman may, with all his good will and wonderful art, to absorb me into himself. . . .

LEADING MAN: Oh chuck it! "Wonderful art!" Withdraw that, please!

THE FATHER: The performance he will give, even doing his best with make-up to look like me. . . .

LEADING MAN: It will certainly be a bit difficult! (*The* ACTORS *laugh.*)

THE FATHER: Exactly! It will be difficult to act me as I really am. The effect will be rather — apart from the make-up — according as to how he supposes I am, as he senses me — if he does sense me — and not as I inside of myself feel myself to be. It seems to me then that account should be taken of this by everyone whose duty it may become to criticize us. . . .

THE MANAGER: Heavens! The man's starting to think about the critics now! Let them say what they like. It's up to us to put on the play if we can. (*Looking around.*) Come on! come on! Is the stage set? (*To the* ACTORS *and* CHARACTERS.) Stand back — stand back! Let me see, and don't let's lose any more time! (*To the* STEP-DAUGHTER.) Is it all right as it is now?

THE STEP-DAUGHTER: Well, to tell the truth, I don't recognize the scene.

THE MANAGER: My dear lady, you can't possibly suppose that we can construct that shop of Madame Pace piece by piece here? (*To the* FATHER.) You said a white room with flowered wall paper, didn't you?

THE FATHER: Yes.

THE MANAGER: Well then. We've got the furniture right more or less. Bring that little table a bit further forward. (*The* STAGE HANDS *obey the order. To* PROPERTY MAN.) You go and find an envelope, if possible, a pale blue one; and give it to that gentleman. (*Indicates* FATHER.)

PROPERTY MAN: An ordinary envelope?

MANAGER *and* FATHER: Yes, yes, an ordinary envelope.

PROPERTY MAN: At once, sir (*Exit.*)

THE MANAGER: Ready, everyone! First scene — the Young Lady. (*The* LEADING LADY *comes forward.*) No, no, you must wait. I meant her. (*Indicating the* STEP-DAUGHTER.) You just watch —

THE STEP-DAUGHTER (*adding at once*): How I shall play it, how I shall live it! . . .

LEADING LADY (*offended*): I shall live it also, you may be sure, as soon as I begin!

THE MANAGER (*with his hands to his head*): Ladies and gentlemen, if you please! No more useless discussions! Scene I: the young lady with Madame Pace: Oh! (*Looks around as if lost.*) And this Madame Pace, where is she?

THE FATHER: She isn't with us, sir.

THE MANAGER: Then what the devil's to be done?

THE FATHER: But she is alive too.

THE MANAGER: Yes, but where is she?

THE FATHER: One minute. Let me speak! (*Turning to the* ACTRESSES.) If these ladies would be so good as to give me their hats for a moment. . . .

THE ACTRESSES (*half surprised, half laughing, in chorus*): What? Why? Our hats? What does he say?

THE MANAGER: What are you going to do with the ladies' hats? (*The* ACTORS *laugh.*)

THE FATHER: Oh nothing. I just want to put them on these pegs for a moment. And one of the ladies will be so kind as to take off her mantle. . . .

THE ACTORS: Oh, what d'you think of that? Only the mantle? He must be mad.

SOME ACTRESSES: But why? Mantles as well?

THE FATHER: To hang them up here for a moment. Please be so kind, will you?

THE ACTRESSES (*taking off their hats, one or two also their cloaks, and going to hang them on the racks*): After all, why not? There you are! This is really funny. We've got to put them on show.

THE FATHER: Exactly; just like that, on show.

THE MANAGER: May we know why?

THE FATHER: I'll tell you. Who knows if, by arranging the stage for her, she does not come here herself, attracted by the very articles of her trade? (*Inviting the* ACTORS *to look towards the exit at back of stage.*) Look! Look!

(*The door at the back of stage opens and* MADAME PACE *enters and takes a few steps forward. She is a fat, oldish woman with puffy oxygenated hair. She is rouged and powdered, dressed with a comical elegance in black silk. Round her waist is a long silver chain from which hangs a pair of scissors. The* STEP-DAUGHTER *runs over to her at once amid the stupor of the* ACTORS.)

THE STEP-DAUGHTER (*turning towards her*): There she is! There she is!

THE FATHER (*radiant*): It's she! I said so, didn't I? There she is!

THE MANAGER (*conquering his surprise, and then becoming indignant*): What sort of a trick is this?

LEADING MAN (*almost at the same time*): What's going to happen next?

JUVENILE LEAD: Where does *she* come from?

L'INGÉNUE: They've been holding her in reserve, I guess.

LEADING LADY: A vulgar trick!

THE FATHER (*dominating the protests*): Excuse me, all of you! Why are you so anxious to destroy in the name of a vulgar, common-place sense of truth, this reality which comes to birth attracted and formed by the magic of the stage itself, which has indeed more right to live here than you, since it is much truer than you — if you don't mind my saying so? Which is the actress among you who is to play Madame Pace? Well, here is Madame Pace herself. And you will allow, I fancy, that the actress who acts her will be less true than this woman here, who is herself in person. You see my daughter recognized her and went over to her at once. Now you're going to witness the scene!

(*But the scene between the* STEP-DAUGHTER *and* MADAME PACE *has already begun despite the protest of the actors and the reply of the* FATHER. *It has begun quietly, naturally, in a manner impossible for the stage. So when the* ACTORS, *called to attention by the* FATHER, *turn round and see* MADAME PACE, *who has placed one hand under the* STEP-DAUGHTER's *chin to raise her head, they observe her at first with great attention, but hearing her speak in an unintelligible manner their interest begins to wane.*)

THE MANAGER: Well? well?

LEADING MAN: What does she say?

LEADING LADY: One can't hear a word.

JUVENILE LEAD: Louder! Louder please!

THE STEP-DAUGHTER (*leaving* MADAME PACE, *who smiles a Sphinx-like smile, and advancing towards the* ACTORS): Louder? Louder? What are you talking about? These aren't matters which can be shouted at the top of one's voice. If I have spoken them out loud, is was to shame him and have my revenge. (*Indicates* FATHER.) But for Madame it's quite a different matter.

THE MANAGER: Indeed? indeed? But here, you know, people have got to make themselves heard, my dear. Even we who are on the stage can't hear you. What will it be when the public's in the theatre? And anyway, you can very well speak up now among yourselves, since we shan't be present to listen to you as we are now. You've got to pretend to be alone in a room at the back of a shop where no one can hear you.

(*The* STEP-DAUGHTER *coquettishly and with a touch of malice makes a sign of disagreement two or three times with her finger.*)

THE MANAGER: What do you mean by no?

THE STEP-DAUGHTER (*sotto voce, mysteriously*): There's someone who will hear us if she (*indicating* MADAME PACE) speaks out loud.

THE MANAGER (*in consternation*): What? Have you got someone else to spring on us now? (*The* ACTORS *burst out laughing.*)

THE FATHER: No, no sir. She is alluding to me. I've got to be here — there behind that door, in waiting; and Madame Pace knows it. In fact, if you will allow me, I'll go there at once, so I can be quite ready. (*Moves away.*)

THE MANAGER (*stopping him*): No! Wait! wait! We must observe the conventions of the theatre. Before you are ready. . . .

THE STEP-DAUGHTER (*interrupting him*): No, get on with it at once!

I'm just dying, I tell you, to act this scene. If he's ready, I'm more than ready.

THE MANAGER (*shouting*): But, my dear young lady, first of all, we must have the scene between you and this lady. . . . (*Indicates* MADAME PACE.) Do you understand? . . .

THE STEP-DAUGHTER: Good Heavens! She's been telling me what you know already: that mamma's work is badly done again, that the material's ruined; and that if I want her to continue to help us in our misery I must be patient. . . .

MADAME PACE (*coming forward with an air of great importance*): Yes indeed, sir, I no wanta take advantage of her, I no wanta be hard. . . .

(*Note.* MADAME PACE *is supposed to talk in a jargon half Italian, half English.*)

THE MANAGER (*alarmed*): What? What? She talks like that? (*The* ACTORS *burst out laughing again.*)

THE STEP-DAUGHTER (*also laughing*): Yes yes, that's the way she talks, half English, half Italian! Most comical it is!

MADAME PACE: Itta seem not verra polite gentlemen laugha atta me eeff I trya best speaka English.

THE MANAGER: *Diamine!* Of course! Of course! Let her talk like that! Just what we want. Talk just like that, Madame, if you please! The effect will be certain. Exactly what was wanted to put a little comic relief into the crudity of the situation. Of course she talks like that! Magnificent!

THE STEP-DAUGHTER: Magnificent? Certainly! When certain suggestions are made to one in language of that kind, the effect is certain, since it seems almost a joke. One feels inclined to laugh when one hears her talk about an "old signore" "who wanta talka nicely with you." Nice old signore, eh, Madame?

MADAME PACE: Not so old my dear, not so old! And even if you no lika him, he won't make any scandal!

THE MOTHER (*jumping up amid the amazement and consternation of the* ACTORS *who had not been noticing her. They move to restrain her*): You old devil! You murderess!

THE STEP-DAUGHTER (*running over to calm her* MOTHER): Calm yourself, Mother, calm yourself! Please don't. . . .

THE FATHER (*going to her also at the same time*): Calm yourself! Don't get excited! Sit down now!

THE MOTHER: Well then, take that woman away out of my sight!

THE STEP-DAUGHTER (*to* MANAGER): It is impossible for my mother to remain here.

THE FATHER (*to* MANAGER): They can't be here together. And for this reason, you see: that woman there was not with us when we came. . . . If they are on together, the whole thing is given away inevitably, as you see.

THE MANAGER: It doesn't matter. This is only a first rough sketch — just to get an idea of the various points of the scene, even confusedly. . . . (*Turning to the* MOTHER *and leading her to her chair.*) Come along, my dear lady, sit down now, and let's get on with the scene. . . .

(*Meanwhile, the* STEP-DAUGHTER, *coming forward again, turns to* MADAME PACE.)

THE STEP-DAUGHTER: Come on, Madame, come on!

MADAME PACE (*offended*): No, no, *grazie*. I not do anything witha your mother present.

THE STEP-DAUGHTER: Nonsense! Introduce this "old signore" who wants to talk nicely to me. (*Addressing the* COMPANY *imperiously.*) We've got to do this scene one way or another, haven't we? Come on! (*To* MADAME PACE.) You can go!

MADAME PACE: Ah yes! I go'way! I go'way! Certainly! (*Exits furious.*)

THE STEP-DAUGHTER (*to the* FATHER): Now you make your entry. No. you needn't go over here. Come here. Let's suppose you've already come in. Like that, yes! I'm here with bowed head, modest like. Come on! Out with your voice! Say "Good morning, Miss" in that peculiar tone, that special tone. . . .

THE MANAGER: Excuse me, but are you the Manager, or am I? (*To the* FATHER, *who looks undecided and perplexed.*) Get on with it, man! Go down there to the back of the stage. You needn't go off. Then come right forward here.

(*The* FATHER *does as he is told, looking troubled and perplexed at first. But as soon as he begins to move, the reality of the action affects him, and he begins to smile and to be more natural. The* ACTORS *watch intently.*)

THE MANAGER (*sotto voce, quickly to the* PROMPTER *in his box*): Ready! ready? Get ready to write now.

THE FATHER (*coming forward and speaking in a different tone*): Good afternoon, Miss!

THE STEP-DAUGHTER (*head bowed down slightly, with restrained disgust*): Good afternoon!

THE FATHER (*looks under her hat which partly covers her face. Perceiving she is very young, he makes an exclamation, partly of surprise, partly of fear lest he compromise himself in a risky ad-*

venture): Ah . . . but . . . ah . . . I say . . . this is not the first time that you have come here, is it?

THE STEP-DAUGHTER (*modestly*): No sir.

THE FATHER: You've been here before, eh? (*Then seeing her nod agreement.*) More than once? (*Waits for her to answer, looks under her hat, smiles, and then says.*) Well then, there's no need to be so shy, is there? May I take off your hat?

THE STEP-DAUGHTER (*anticipating him and with veiled disgust*): No sir . . . I'll do it myself. (*Takes it off quickly.*)

(*The* MOTHER, *who watches the progress of the scene with the* SON *and the other two children who cling to her, is on thorns; and follows with varying expressions of sorrow, indignation, anxiety, and horror the words and actions of the other two. From time to time she hides her face in her hands and sobs.*)

THE MOTHER: Oh, my God, my God!

THE FATHER (*playing his part with a touch of gallantry*): Give it to me! I'll put it down. (*Takes hat from her hands.*) But a dear little head like yours ought to have a smarter hat. Come and help me choose one from the stock, won't you?

L'INGÉNUE (*interrupting*): I say . . . those are our hats you know.

THE MANAGER (*furious*): Silence! silence! Don't try and be funny, if you please. . . . We're playing the scene now I'd have you notice. (*To the* STEP-DAUGHTER.) Begin again, please!

THE STEP-DAUGHTER (*continuing*): No thank you, sir.

THE FATHER: Oh, come now. Don't talk like that. You must take it. I shall be upset if you don't. There are some lovely little hats here; and then — Madame will be pleased. She expects it, anyway, you know.

THE STEP-DAUGHTER: No, no! I couldn't wear it!

THE FATHER: Oh, you're thinking about what they'd say at home if they saw you come in with a new hat? My dear girl, there's always a way round these little matters, you know.

THE STEP-DAUGHTER (*all keyed up*): No, it's not that. I couldn't wear it because I am . . . as you see . . . you might have noticed . . . (*Showing her black dress.*)

THE FATHER: . . . in mourning! Of course: I beg your pardon: I'm frightfully sorry. . . .

THE STEP-DAUGHTER (*forcing herself to conquer her indignation and nausea*): Stop! Stop! It's I who must thank you. There's no need for you to feel mortified or specially sorry. Don't think any more of what I've said. (*Tries to smile.*) I must forget that I am dressed so. . . .

THE MANAGER (*interrupting and turning to the* PROMPTER): Stop a minute! Stop! Don't write that down. Cut out that last bit. (*Then to the* FATHER *and* STEP-DAUGHTER.) Fine! it's going fine! (*To the* FATHER *only.*) And now you can go on as we arranged. (*To the* ACTORS.) Pretty good that scene, where he offers her the hat, eh?

THE STEP-DAUGHTER: The best's coming now. Why can't we go on?

THE MANAGER: Have a little patience! (*To the* ACTORS.) Of course, it must be treated rather lightly.

LEADING MAN: Still, with a bit of go in it!

LEADING LADY: Of course! It's easy enough! (*To* LEADING MAN.) Shall you and I try it now?

LEADING MAN: Why, yes! I'll prepare my entrance. (*Exit in order to make his entrance.*)

THE MANAGER (*to* LEADING LADY): See here! The scene between you and Madame Pace is finished. I'll have it written out properly after. You remain here . . . oh, where are you going?

LEADING LADY: One minute. I want to put my hat on again. (*Goes over to hat-rack and puts her hat on her head.*)

THE MANAGER: Good! You stay here with your head bowed down a bit.

THE STEP-DAUGHTER: But she isn't dressed in black.

LEADING LADY: But I shall be, and much more effectively than you.

THE MANAGER (*to* STEP-DAUGHTER): Be quiet please, and watch! You'll be able to learn something. (*Clapping his hands.*) Come on! come on! Entrance, please!

(*The door at rear of stage opens, and the* LEADING MAN *enters with the lively manner of an old gallant. The rendering of the scene by the* ACTORS *from the very first words is seen to be quite a different thing, though it has not in any way the air of a parody. Naturally, the* STEP-DAUGHTER *and the* FATHER, *not being able to recognize themselves in the* LEADING LADY *and the* LEADING MAN, *who deliver their words in different tones and with a different psychology, express, sometimes with smiles, sometimes with gestures, the impression they receive.*)

LEADING MAN: Good afternoon, Miss. . . .

THE FATHER (*at once unable to contain himself*): No!

(*The* STEP-DAUGHTER *noticing the way the* LEADING MAN *enters, bursts out laughing.*)

THE MANAGER (*furious*): Silence! And you please just stop that laughing. If we go on like this, we shall never finish.

THE STEP-DAUGHTER: Forgive me, sir, but it's natural enough. This lady (*indicating* LEADING LADY) stands there still; but if she is supposed to be me, I can assure you that if I heard anyone say "Good afternoon" in that manner and in that tone, I should burst out laughing as I did.

THE FATHER: Yes, yes, the manner, the tone. . . .

THE MANAGER: Nonsense! Rubbish! Stand aside and let me see the action.

LEADING MAN: If I've got to represent an old fellow who's coming into a house of an equivocal character. . . .

THE MANAGER: Don't listen to them, for Heaven's sake! Do it again! It goes fine. (*Waiting for the* ACTORS *to begin again.*) Well?

LEADING MAN: Good afternoon, Miss.

LEADING LADY: Good afternoon.

LEADING MAN (*imitating the gesture of the* FATHER *when he looked under the hat, and then expressing quite clearly first satisfaction and then fear*): Ah, but . . . I say . . . this is not the first time that you have come here, is it?

THE MANAGER: Good, but not quite so heavily. Like this. (*Acts himself.*) "This isn't the first time that you have come here" . . . (*To* LEADING LADY.) And you say: "No, sir."

LEADING LADY: No, sir.

LEADING MAN: You've been here before, more than once.

THE MANAGER: No, no, stop! Let her nod "yes" first. "You've been here before, eh?" (*The* LEADING LADY *lifts up her head slightly and closes her eyes as though in disgust. Then she inclines her head twice.*)

THE STEP-DAUGHTER (*unable to contain herself*): Oh my God! (*Puts a hand to her mouth to prevent herself from laughing.*)

THE MANAGER (*turning round*): What's the matter?

THE STEP-DAUGHTER: Nothing, nothing!

THE MANAGER (*to* LEADING MAN): Go on!

LEADING MAN: You've been here before, eh? Well then, there's no need to be so shy, is there? May I take off your hat?

(*The* LEADING MAN *says this last speech in such a tone and with such gestures that the* STEP-DAUGHTER, *though she has her hand to her mouth, cannot keep from laughing.*)

LEADING LADY (*indignant*): I'm not going to stop here to be made a fool of by that woman there.

LEADING MAN: Neither am I! I'm through with it!

THE MANAGER (*shouting to* STEP-DAUGHTER): Silence! for once and all, I tell you!

THE STEP-DAUGHTER: Forgive me! forgive me!

THE MANAGER: You haven't any manners: that's what it is! You go too far.

THE FATHER (*endeavoring to intervene*): Yes, it's true, but excuse her. . . .

THE MANAGER: Excuse what? It's absolutely disgusting.

THE FATHER: Yes, sir, but believe me, it has such a strange effect when. . . .

THE MANAGER: Strange? Why strange? Where is it strange?

THE FATHER: No, sir; I admire your actors — this gentleman here, this lady; but they are certainly not us!

THE MANAGER: I should hope not. Evidently they cannot be you, if they are actors.

THE FATHER: Just so: actors! Both of them act our parts exceedingly well. But, believe me, it produces quite a different effect on us. They want to be us, but they aren't, all the same.

THE MANAGER: What is it then anyway?

THE FATHER: Something that is . . . that is theirs — and no longer ours . . .

THE MANAGER: But naturally, inevitably. I've told you so already.

THE FATHER: Yes, I understand . . . I understand . . .

THE MANAGER: Well then, let's have no more of it! (*Turning to the* ACTORS.) We'll have the rehearsals by ourselves, afterwards, in the ordinary way. I never could stand rehearsing with the author present. He's never satisfied! (*Turning to* FATHER *and* STEP-DAUGHTER.) Come on! Let's get on with it again; and try and see if you can't keep from laughing.

THE STEP-DAUGHTER: Oh, I shan't laugh any more. There's a nice little bit coming for me now: you'll see.

THE MANAGER: Well then: when she says "Don't think any more of what I've said, I must forget, etc.," you (*addressing the* FATHER) come in sharp with "I understand, I understand"; and then you ask her . . .

THE STEP-DAUGHTER (*interrupting*): What?

THE MANAGER: Why she is in mourning.

THE STEP-DAUGHTER: Not at all! See here: when I told him that it was useless for me to be thinking about my wearing mourning, do you know how he answered me? "Ah well," he said, "then let's take off this little frock."

THE MANAGER: Great! Just what we want, to make a riot in the theatre!

THE STEP-DAUGHTER: But it's the truth!

THE MANAGER: What does that matter? Acting is our business here. Truth up to a certain point, but no further.

THE STEP-DAUGHTER: What do you want to do then?

THE MANAGER: You'll see, you'll see! Leave it to me.

THE STEP-DAUGHTER: No sir! What you want to do is to piece together a little romantic sentimental scene out of my disgust, out of all the reasons, each more cruel and viler than the other, why I am what I am. He is to ask me why I'm in mourning; and I'm to answer with tears in my eyes, that it is just two months since papa died. No sir, no! He's got to say to me; as he did say: "Well, let's take off this little dress at once." And I, with my two months' mourning in my heart, went there behind that screen, and with these fingers tingling with shame . . .

THE MANAGER (*running his hands through his hair*): For Heaven's sake! What are you saying?

THE STEP-DAUGHTER (*crying out excitedly*): The truth! The truth!

THE MANAGER: It may be. I don't deny it, and I can understand all your horror; but you must surely see that you can't have this kind of thing on the stage. It won't go.

THE STEP-DAUGHTER: Not possible, eh? Very well! I'm much obliged to you — but I'm off!

THE MANAGER: Now be reasonable! Don't lose your temper!

THE STEP-DAUGHTER: I won't stop here! I won't! I can see you've fixed it all up with him in your office. All this talk about what is possible for the stage . . . I understand! He wants to get at his complicated "cerebral drama," to have his famous remorses and torments acted; but I want to act my part, *my part*!

THE MANAGER (*annoyed, shaking his shoulders*): Ah! Just *your* part! But, if you will pardon me, there are other parts than yours: His (*indicating the* FATHER) and hers (*indicating the* MOTHER)! On the stage you can't have a character becoming too prominent and overshadowing all the others. The thing is to pack them all into a neat little framework and then act what is actable. I am aware of the fact that everyone has his own interior life which he wants very much to put forward. But the difficulty lies in this fact: to set out just so much as is necessary for the stage, taking the other characters into consideration, and at the same time hint at the unrevealed interior life of each. I am willing to admit, my dear young lady, that from your point of view it would be a fine idea if each character could tell the public all his troubles in a nice monologue or a regular one hour lecture. (*Good humoredly.*) You must restrain yourself, my dear, and in your own interest, too; because this fury of yours, this exaggerated disgust you show, may make a bad impression, you know. After you have confessed to me that there were others before him at Madame Pace's and more than once . . .

THE STEP-DAUGHTER (*bowing her head, impressed*): It's true. But remember those others mean him for me all the same.

THE MANAGER (*not understanding*): What? The others? What do you mean?

THE STEP-DAUGHTER: For one who has gone wrong, sir, he who was responsible for the first fault is responsible for all that follow. He is responsible for my faults, was, even before I was born. Look at him, and see if it isn't true!

THE MANAGER: Well, well! And does the weight of so much responsibility seem nothing to you? Give him a chance to act it, to get it over!

THE STEP-DAUGHTER: How? How can he act all his "noble remorses," all his "moral torments," if you want to spare him the horror of being discovered one day — after he had asked her what he did ask her — in the arms of her, that already fallen woman, that child, sir, that child he used to watch come out of school? (*she is moved.*)

(*The* MOTHER *at this point is overcome with emotion, and breaks out into a fit of crying. All are touched. A long pause.*)

THE STEP-DAUGHTER (*as soon as the* MOTHER *becomes a little quieter, adds resolutely and gravely*): At present, we are unknown to the public. Tomorrow, you will act us as you wish, treating us in your own manner. But do you really want to see drama, do you want to see it flash out as it really did?

THE MANAGER: Of course! That's just what I do want, so I can use as much of it as is possible.

THE STEP-DAUGHTER: Well then, ask that Mother there to leave us.

THE MOTHER (*changing her low plaint into a sharp cry*): No! No! Don't permit it, sir, don't permit it!

THE MANAGER: But it's only to try it.

THE MOTHER: I can't bear it. I can't.

THE MANAGER: But since it has happened already . . . I don't understand!

THE MOTHER: It's taking place now. It happens all the time. My torment isn't a pretended one. I live and feel every minute of my torture. Those two children there — have you heard them speak? They can't speak any more. They cling to me to keep up my torment actual and vivid for me. But for themselves, they do not exist, they aren't any more. And she (*indicating the* STEP-DAUGHTER) has run away, she has left me, and is lost. If I now see her here before me, it is only to renew for me the tortures I have suffered for her too.

THE FATHER: The eternal moment! She (*indicating the* STEP-DAUGH-TER) is here to catch me, fix me, and hold me eternally in the stocks for that one fleeting and shameful moment of my life. She can't give it up! And you sir, cannot either fairly spare me it.

THE MANAGER: I never said I didn't want to act it. It will form, as a matter of fact, the nucleus of the whole first act right up to her surprise. (*Indicates the* MOTHER.)

THE FATHER: Just so! This is my punishment: the passion in all of us that must culminate in her final cry.

THE STEP-DAUGHTER: I can hear it still in my ears. It's driven me mad, that cry! — You can put me on as you like; it doesn't matter. Fully dressed, if you like — provided I have at least the arm bare; because, standing like this (*she goes close to the* FATHER *and leans her head on his breast*) with my head so, and my arms round his neck, I saw a vein pulsing in my arm here; and then, as if that live vein had awakened disgust in me, I closed my eyes like this, and let my head sink on his breast. (*Turning to the* MOTHER.) Cry out mother! Cry out! (*Buries head in* FATHER's *breast, and with her shoulders raised as if to prevent her hearing the cry, adds in tones of intense emotion.*) Cry out as you did then!

THE MOTHER (*coming forward to separate them*): No! My daughter, my daughter! (*And after having pulled her away from him.*) You brute! you brute! She is my daughter! Don't you see she's my daughter?

THE MANAGER (*walking backwards towards footlights*): Fine! fine! Damned good! And then, of course — curtain!

THE FATHER (*going towards him excitedly*): Yes, of course, because that's the way it really happened.

THE MANAGER (*convinced and pleased*): Oh, yes, no doubt about it. Curtain here, curtain!

(*At the reiterated cry of the* MANAGER, *the* MACHINIST *lets the curtain down, leaving the* MANAGER *and the* FATHER *in front of it before the footlights.*)

THE MANAGER: The darned idiot! I said "curtain" to show the act should end there, and he goes and lets it down in earnest. (*To the* FATHER, *while he pulls the curtain back to go on to the stage again.*) Yes, yes, it's all right. Effect certain! That's the right ending. I'll guarantee the first act at any rate.

ACT III

When the curtain goes up again, it is seen that the stage hands have shifted the bit of scenery used in the last part, and have rigged up instead at the back of the stage a drop, with some trees, and one or two wings. A portion of a fountain basin is visible. The MOTHER *is sitting on the right with the two children by her side. The* SON *is on the same side, but away from the others. He seems bored, angry, and full of shame. The* FATHER *and the* STEP-DAUGHTER *are also seated towards the right front. On the other side (left) are the* ACTORS, *much in the positions they occupied before the curtain was lowered. Only the* MANAGER *is standing up in the middle of the stage, with his hand closed over his mouth in the act of meditating.*

THE MANAGER (*shaking his shoulders after a brief pause*): Ah yes: the second act! Leave it to me, leave it all to me as we arranged, and you'll see! It'll go fine!

THE STEP-DAUGHTER: Our entry into his house (*indicates* FATHER) in spite of him . . . (*indicates the* SON).

THE MANAGER (*out of patience*): Leave it to me, I tell you!

THE STEP-DAUGHTER: Do let it be clear, at any rate, that it is in spite of my wishes.

THE MOTHER (*from her corner, shaking her head*): For all the good that's come of it. . . .

THE STEP-DAUGHTER (*turning towards her quickly*): It doesn't matter. The more harm done us, the more remorse for him.

THE MANAGER (*impatiently*): I understand! Good Heavens! I understand! I'm taking it into account.

THE MOTHER (*supplicatingly*): I beg you, sir, to let it appear quite plain that for conscience' sake I did try in every way. . . .

THE STEP-DAUGHTER (*interrupting indignantly and continuing for the* MOTHER): . . . to pacify me, to dissuade me from spiting him. (*To* MANAGER.) Do as she wants: satisfy her, because it is true! I enjoy it immensely. Anyhow, as you can see, the meeker she is, the more she tries to get at his heart, the more distant and aloof does he become.

THE MANAGER: Are we going to begin this second act or not?

THE STEP-DAUGHTER: I'm not going to talk any more now. But I must tell you this: you can't have the whole action take place in the garden, as you suggest. It isn't possible!

THE MANAGER: Why not?

THE STEP-DAUGHTER: Because he (*indicates the* SON *again*) is always shut up alone in his room. And then there's all the part of that poor dazed-looking boy there which takes place indoors.

THE MANAGER: Maybe! On the other hand, you will understand — we can't change scenes three or four times in one act.

THE LEADING MAN: They used to once.

THE MANAGER: Yes, when the public was up to the level of that child there.

THE LEADING LADY: It makes the illusion easier.

THE FATHER (*irritated*): The illusion! For Heaven's sake, don't say illusion. Please don't use that word, which is particularly painful for us.

THE MANAGER (*astounded*): And why, if you please?

THE FATHER: It's painful, cruel, really cruel; and you ought to understand that.

THE MANAGER: But why? What ought we to say then? The illusion, I tell you, sir, which we've got to create for the audience. . . .

THE LEADING MAN: With our acting.

THE MANAGER: The illusion of a reality.

THE FATHER: I understand; but you, perhaps, do not understand us. Forgive me! You see . . . here for you and your actors, the thing is only — and rightly so . . . a kind of game. . . .

THE LEADING LADY (*interrupting indignantly*): A game! We're not children here, if you please! We are serious actors.

THE FATHER: I don't deny it. What I mean is the game, or play, of your art, which has to give, as the gentleman says, a perfect illusion of reality.

THE MANAGER: Precisely — !

THE FATHER: Now, if you consider the fact that we (*indicates himself and the other five* CHARACTERS), as we are, have no other reality outside of this illusion. . . .

THE MANAGER (*astonished, looking at his* ACTORS, *who are also amazed*): And what does that mean?

THE FATHER (*after watching them for a moment with a wan smile*): As I say, sir, that which is a game of art for you is our sole reality. (*Brief pause. He goes a step or two nearer the* MANAGER *and adds.*) But not only for us, you know, by the way. Just you think it over well. (*Looks him in the eyes.*) Can you tell me who you are?

THE MANAGER (*perplexed, half smiling*): What? Who am I? I am myself.

THE FATHER: And if I were to tell you that that isn't true, because you and I . . . ?

THE MANAGER: I should say you were mad — ! (*The* ACTORS *laugh.*)

THE FATHER: You're quite right to laugh: because we are all making believe here. (*To* MANAGER.) And you can therefore object that it's only for a joke that that gentleman there (*indicates the* LEADING MAN), who naturally is himself, has to be me, who am on the contrary myself — this thing you see here. You see I've caught you in a trap! (*The* ACTORS *laugh.*)

THE MANAGER (*annoyed*): But we've had all this over once before. Do you want to begin again?

THE FATHER: No, no! That wasn't my meaning! In fact, I should like to request you to abandon this game of art (*looking at the* LEADING LADY *as if anticipating her*) which you are accustomed to play here with your actors, and to ask you seriously once again: who are you?

THE MANAGER (*astonished and irritated, turning to his* ACTORS): If this fellow here hasn't got a nerve! A man who calls himself a character comes and asks me who I am!

THE FATHER (*with dignity, but not offended*): A character, sir, may always ask a man who he is. Because a character has really a life of his own, marked with his especial characteristics; for which reason he is always "somebody." But a man — I'm not speaking of you now — may very well be "nobody."

THE MANAGER: Yes, but you are asking these questions of me, the boss, the manager! Do you understand?

THE FATHER: But only in order to know if you, as you really are now, see yourself as you once were with all the illusions that were yours then, with all the things both inside and outside of you as they seemed to you — as they were then indeed for you. Well, sir, if you think of all those illusions that mean nothing to you now, of all those things which don't even *seem* to you to exist any more, while once they *were* for you, don't you feel that — I won't say these boards — but the very earth under your feet is sinking away from you when you reflect that in the same way this *you* as you feel it today — all this present reality of yours — is fated to seem a mere illusion to you tomorrow?

THE MANAGER (*without having understood much, but astonished by the specious argument*): Well, well! And where does all this take us anyway?

THE FATHER: Oh, nowhere! It's only to show you that if we (*indicating the* CHARACTERS) have no other reality beyond the illusion, you too must not count overmuch on your reality as you feel it today, since, like that of yesterday, it may prove an illusion for you tomorrow.

THE MANAGER (*determining to make fun of him*): Ah, excellent!

Then you'll be saying next that you, with this comedy of yours
that you brought here to act, are truer and more real than I am.

THE FATHER (*with the greatest seriousness*): But of course; without
doubt!

THE MANAGER: Ah, really?

THE FATHER: Why, I thought you'd understand that from the beginning.

THE MANAGER: More real than I?

THE FATHER: If your reality can change from one day to another. . . .

THE MANAGER: But everyone knows it can change. It is always changing, the same as anyone else's.

THE FATHER (*with a cry*): No, sir, not ours! Look here! That is the
very difference! Our reality doesn't change: it can't change! It
can't be other than what it is, because it is already fixed for ever.
It's terrible. Ours is an immutable reality which should make you
shudder when you approach us if you are really conscious of the
fact that your reality is a mere transitory and fleeting illusion, taking this form today and that tomorrow, according to the conditions,
according to your will, your sentiments, which in turn are controlled by an intellect that shows them to you today in one manner
and tomorrow. . . . who knows how? . . . Illusions of reality
represented in this fatuous comedy of life that never ends, nor can
ever end! Because if tomorrow it were to end . . . then why, all
would be finished.

THE MANAGER: Oh for God's sake, will you *at least* finish with this
philosophizing and let us try and shape this comedy which you
yourself have brought me here? You argue and philosophize a bit
too much, my dear sir. You know you seem to me almost, almost. . . . (*Stops and looks him over from head to foot.*) Ah,
by the way, I think you introduced yourself to me as a — what
shall . . . we say — a "character," created by an author who did
not afterward care to make a drama of his own creations.

THE FATHER: It is the simple truth, sir.

THE MANAGER: Nonsense! Cut that out, please! None of us believes
it, because it isn't a thing, as you must recognize yourself, which
one can believe seriously. If you want to know, it seems to me
you are trying to imitate the manner of a certain author whom I
heartily detest — I warn you — although I have unfortunately
bound myself to put on one of his works. As a matter of fact, I
was just starting to rehearse it, when you arrived. (*Turning to the*
ACTORS.) And this is what we've gained — out of the frying-pan
into the fire!

THE FATHER: I don't know to what author you may be alluding, but believe me I feel what I think; and I seem to be philosophizing only for those who do not think what they feel, because they blind themselves with their own sentiment. I know that for many people this self-blinding seems much more "human"; but the contrary is really true. For man never reasons so much and becomes so introspective as when he suffers; since he is anxious to get at the cause of his sufferings, to learn who has produced them, and whether it is just or unjust that he should have to bear them. On the other hand, when he is happy, he takes his happiness as it comes and doesn't analyze it, just as if happiness were his right. The animals suffer without reasoning about their sufferings. But take the case of a man who suffers and begins to reason about it. Oh no! it can't be allowed! Let him suffer like an animal, and then — ah yet, he is "human"!

THE MANAGER: Look here! Look here! You're off again, philosophizing worse than ever.

THE FATHER: Because I suffer, sir! I'm not philosophizing: I'm crying aloud the reason of my sufferings.

THE MANAGER (*makes brusque movement as he is taken with a new idea*): I should like to know if anyone has ever heard of a character who gets right out of his part and perorates and speechifies as you do. Have you ever heard of a case? I haven't.

THE FATHER: You have never met such a case, sir, because authors, as a rule, hide the labor of their creations. When the characters are really alive before their author, the latter does nothing but follow them in their action, in other words, in the situations which they suggest to him; and he has to will them the way they will themselves — for there's trouble if he doesn't. When a character is born, he acquires at once such an independence, even of his own author, that he can be imagined by everybody even in many other situations where the author never dreamed of placing him; and so he acquires for himself a meaning which the author never thought of giving him.

THE MANAGER: Yes, yes, I know this.

THE FATHER: What is there then to marvel at in us? Imagine such a misfortune for characters as I have described to you: to be born of an author's fantasy, and be denied life by him; and then answer me if these characters left alive, and yet without life, weren't right in doing what they did do and are doing now, after they have attempted everything in their power to persuade him to give them their stage life. We've all tried him in turn, I, she (*indicating the* STEP-DAUGHTER) and she (*indicating the* MOTHER).

THE STEP-DAUGHTER: It's true. I too have sought to tempt him, many,

many times, when he has been sitting at his writing table, feeling a bit melancholy, at the twilight hour. He would sit in his armchair too lazy to switch on the light, and all the shadows that crept into his room were full of our presence coming to tempt him. (*As if she saw herself still there by the writing table, and was annoyed by the presence of the* ACTORS.) Oh, if you would only go away, go away and leave us alone — mother here with that son of hers — I with that Child — that Boy there always alone — and then I with him (*just hints at the* FATHER) — and then I alone, alone . . . in those shadows! (*Makes a sudden movement as if in the vision she has of herself illuminating those shadows she wanted to seize hold of herself.*) Ah! my life! my life! Oh, what scenes we proposed to him — and I tempted him more than any of the others!

THE FATHER: Maybe. But perhaps it was your fault that he refused to give us life: because you were too insistent, too troublesome.

THE STEP-DAUGHTER: Nonsense! Didn't he make me so himself? (*Goes close to the* MANAGER *to tell him as if in confidence.*) In my opinion he abandoned us in a fit of depression, of disgust for the ordinary theatre as the public knows it and likes it.

THE SON: Exactly what it was, sir; exactly that!

THE FATHER: Not at all! Don't believe it for a minute. Listen to me! You'll be doing quite right to modify, as you suggest, the excesses both of this girl here, who wants to do too much, and of this young man, who won't do anything at all.

THE SON: No, nothing!

THE MANAGER: You too get over the mark occasionally, my dear sir, if I may say so.

THE FATHER: I? When? Where?

THE MANAGER: Always! Continuously! Then there's this insistence of yours in trying to make us believe you are a character. And then too, you must really argue and philosophize less, you know, much less.

THE FATHER: Well, if you want to take away from me the possibility of representing the torment of my spirit which never gives me peace, you will be suppressing me: that's all. Every true man, sir, who is a little above the level of the beasts and plants does not live for the sake of living, without knowing how to live; but he lives so as to give a meaning and a value of his own to life. For me this is *everything*. I cannot give up this, just to represent a mere fact as she (*indicating the* STEP-DAUGHTER) wants. It's all very well for her, since her "vendetta" lies in the "fact." I'm not going to do it. It destroys my *raison d'être*.

THE MANAGER: Your *raison d'être!* Oh, we're going ahead fine! First she starts off, and then you jump in. At this rate, we'll never finish.

THE FATHER: Now, don't be offended! Have it your own way — provided, however, that within the limits of the parts you assign us each one's sacrifice isn't too great.

THE MANAGER: You've got to understand that you can't go on arguing at your own pleasure. Drama is action, sir, action and not confounded philosophy.

THE FATHER: All right. I'll do just as much arguing and philosophizing as everybody does when he is considering his own torments.

THE MANAGER: If the drama permits! But for Heaven's sake, man, let's get along and come to the scene.

THE STEP-DAUGHTER: It seems to me we've got too much action with our coming into his house. (*Indicating* FATHER.) You said, before, you couldn't change the scene every five minutes.

THE MANAGER: Of course not. What we've got to do is to combine and group up all the facts in one simultaneous, close-knit, action. We can't have it as you want, with your little brother wandering like a ghost from room to room, hiding behind doors and meditating a project which — what did you say it did to him?

THE STEP-DAUGHTER: Consumes him, sir, wastes him away!

THE MANAGER: Well, it may be. And then at the same time, you want the little girl there to be playing in the garden . . . one in the house, and the other in the garden: isn't that it?

THE STEP-DAUGHTER: Yes, in the sun, in the sun! That is my only pleasure: to see her happy and careless in the garden after the misery and squalor of the horrible room where we all four slept together. And I had to sleep with her — I, do you understand? — with my vile contaminated body next to hers; with her folding me fast in her loving little arms. In the garden, whenever she spied me, she would run to take me by the hand. She didn't care for the big flowers, only the little ones; and she loved to show me them and pet me.

THE MANAGER: Well then, we'll have it in the garden. Everything shall happen in the garden; and we'll group the other scenes there. (*Calls a* STAGE HAND.) Here, a backcloth with trees and something to do as a fountain basin. (*Turning round to look at the back of the stage.*) Ah, you've fixed it up. Good! (*To* STEP-DAUGHTER.) This is just to give an idea, of course. The Boy, instead of hiding behind the doors, will wander about here in the garden, hiding behind the trees. But it's going to be rather difficult to find a child to do that scene with you where she shows you the flowers. (*Turning to the* BOY.) Come forward a little, will you please? Let's try it now! Come along! come along! (*Then seeing him come shyly forward, full of fear and looking lost.*) It's a nice business, this lad here. What's the matter with him? We'll have to give him a word or two to say. (*Goes close to him, puts a hand on his shoulders, and leads him behind one of the trees.*) Come on! come on! Let me see you a little! Hide here . . . yes, like that. Try and show your head just a little as if you were looking for someone. . . . (*Goes back to observe the effect, when the* BOY *at once goes through the action.*) Excellent! fine! (*Turning to* STEP-DAUGHTER.) Suppose the little girl there were to surprise him as he looks round, and run over to him, so we could give him a word or two to say?

THE STEP-DAUGHTER: It's useless to hope he will speak, as long as that fellow there is here. . . . (*Indicates the* SON.) You must send him away first.

THE SON (*jumping up*): Delighted! Delighted! I don't ask for anything better. (*Begins to move away.*)

THE MANAGER (*at once stopping him*): No! No! Where are you going? Wait a bit!

(*The* MOTHER *gets up alarmed and terrified at the thought that he is really about to go away. Instinctively she lifts her arms to prevent him, without, however, leaving her seat.*)

THE SON (*to* MANAGER *who stops him*): I've got nothing to do with this affair. Let me go please! Let me go!

THE MANAGER: What do you mean by saying you've got nothing to do with this?

THE STEP-DAUGHTER (*calmly, with irony*): Don't bother to stop him: he won't go away.

THE FATHER: He has to act the terrible scene in the garden with his mother.

THE SON (*suddenly resolute and with dignity*): I shall act nothing at all. I've said so from the very beginning. (*To the* MANAGER.) Let me go!

THE STEP-DAUGHTER (*going over to the* MANAGER): Allow me? (*Puts down the* MANAGER's *arm which is restraining the* SON.) Well, go away then, if you want to! (*The* SON *looks at her with contempt and hatred. She laughs and says.*) You see, he can't, he can't go away! He is obliged to stay here, indissolubly bound to the chain. If I, who fly off when that happens which has to happen, because I can't bear him — if I am still here and support that face and expression of his, you can well imagine that he is unable to move. He has to remain here, has to stop with that nice father of his, and that mother whose only son he is. (*Turning to the* MOTHER.) Come on, mother, come along! (*Turning to* MANAGER *to indicate her.*) You see, she was getting up to keep him back. (*To the* MOTHER, *beckoning her with her hand.*) Come on! come on! (*Then to* MANAGER.) You can imagine how little she wants to show these actors of yours what she really feels; but so eager is she to get near him that. . . . There, you see? She is willing to act her part. (*And in fact, the* MOTHER *approaches him; and as soon as the* STEP-DAUGHTER *has finished speaking, opens her arms to signify that she consents.*)

THE SON (*suddenly*): No! no! If I can't go away, then I'll stop here; but I repeat: I act nothing!

THE FATHER (*to* MANAGER *excitedly*): You can force him, sir.

THE SON: Nobody can force me.

THE FATHER: I can.

THE STEP-DAUGHTER: Wait a minute, wait . . . First of all, the baby has to go to the fountain. . . . (*Runs to take the* CHILD *and leads her to the fountain.*)

THE MANAGER: Yes, yes of course; that's it. Both at the same time.

(*The* SECOND LADY LEAD *and the* JUVENILE LEAD *at this point separate themselves from the group of* ACTORS. *One watches the* MOTHER *attentively; the other moves about studying the movements and manner of the* SON *whom he will have to act.*)

THE SON (*to* MANAGER): What do you mean by both at the same time? It isn't right. There was no scene between me and her. (*Indicates the* MOTHER.) Ask her how it was!

THE MOTHER: Yes, it's true. I had come into his room. . . .

THE SON: Into my room, do you understand? Nothing to do with the garden.

THE MANAGER: It doesn't matter. Haven't I told you we've got to group the action?

THE SON (*observing the* JUVENILE LEAD *studying him*): What do you want?

THE JUVENILE LEAD: Nothing! I was just looking at you.

THE SON (*turning towards the* SECOND LADY LEAD): Ah! she's at it too: to re-act her part! (*Indicating the* MOTHER.)

THE MANAGER: Exactly! And it seems to me that you ought to be grateful to them for their interest.

THE SON: Yes, but haven't you yet perceived that it isn't possible to live in front of a mirror which not only freezes us with the image of ourselves, but throws our likeness back at us with a horrible grimace?

THE FATHER: That is true, absolutely true. You must see that.

THE MANAGER (*to* SECOND LADY LEAD *and* JUVENILE LEAD): He's right! Move away from them!

THE SON: Do as you like. I'm out of this!

THE MANAGER: Be quiet, you, will you? And let me hear your mother! (*To* MOTHER.) You were saying you had entered. . . .

THE MOTHER: Yes, into his room, because I couldn't stand it any longer. I went to empty my heart to him of all the anguish that tortures me. . . . But as soon as he saw me come in. . . .

THE SON: Nothing happened! There was no scene. I went away, that's all! I don't care for scenes!

THE MOTHER: It's true, true. That's how it was.

THE MANAGER: Well now, we've got to do this bit between you and him. It's indispensable.

THE MOTHER: I'm ready . . . when you are ready. If you could only find a chance for me to tell him what I feel here in my heart.

THE FATHER (*going to* SON *in a great rage*): You'll do this for your mother, for your mother, do you understand?

THE SON (*quite determined*): I do nothing!

THE FATHER (*taking hold of him and shaking him*): For God's sake, do as I tell you! Don't you hear your mother asking you for a favor? Haven't you even got the guts to be a son?

THE SON (*taking hold of the* FATHER): No! No! And for God's sake stop it, or else. . . . (*General agitation. The* MOTHER, *frightened, tries to separate them.*)

THE MOTHER (*pleading*): Please! please!

THE FATHER (*not leaving hold of the* SON): You've got to obey, do you hear?

THE SON (*almost crying from rage*): What does it mean, this madness you've got? (*They separate.*) Have you no decency, that you insist on showing everyone our shame? I won't do it! I won't! And I stand for the will of our author in this. He didn't want to put us on the stage, after all!

THE MANAGER: Man alive! You came here . . .

THE SON (*indicating* FATHER): He did! I didn't!

THE MANAGER: Aren't you here now?

THE SON: It was his wish, and he dragged us along with him. He's told you not only the things that did happen, but also things that have never happened at all.

THE MANAGER: Well, tell me then what did happen. You went out of your room without saying a word?

THE SON: Without a word, so as to avoid a scene!

THE MANAGER: And then what did you do?

THE SON: Nothing . . . walking in the garden. . . . (*Hesitates for a moment with expression of gloom.*)

THE MANAGER (*coming closer to him, interested by his extraordinary reserve*): Well, well . . . walking in the garden. . . .

THE SON (*exasperated*): Why on earth do you insist? It's horrible!

(*The* MOTHER *trembles, sobs, and looks towards the fountain.*)

THE MANAGER (*slowly observing the glance and turning towards the* SON *with increasing apprehension*): The baby?

THE SON: There in the fountain. . . .

THE FATHER (*pointing with tender pity to the* MOTHER): She was following him at the moment. . . .

THE MANAGER (*to the* SON *anxiously*): And then you. . . .

THE SON: I ran over to her; I was jumping in to drag her out when I saw something that froze my blood . . . the boy standing stock still, with eyes like a madman's, watching his little drowned sister, in the fountain! (*The* STEP-DAUGHTER *bends over the fountain to hide the* CHILD. *She sobs.*) Then. . . . (*A revolver shot rings out behind the trees where the* BOY *is hidden.*)

THE MOTHER (*with a cry of terror runs over in that direction together with several of the* ACTORS *amid general confusion*): My son! My son! (*Then amid the cries and exclamations one hears her voice.*) Help! Help!

THE MANAGER (*pushing the* ACTORS *aside while they lift up the* BOY *and carry him off*): Is he really wounded?

SOME ACTORS: He's dead! dead!

OTHER ACTORS: No, no, it's only make believe, it's only pretense!

THE FATHER (*with a terrible cry*): Pretense? Reality, sir, reality!

THE MANAGER: Pretense? Reality? To hell with it all! Never in my life has such a thing happened to me. I've lost a whole day over these people, a whole day!

━━━━━━━━━━━

〜◁ *Six Characters in Search of an Author* (1921) remains in the memory as the image of the real-life theater of illusionism invaded by the "fantastic reality" of imaginative truth. Pirandello, perhaps as thinking a playwright as there ever was, yet subordinates philosophy to action — the action of the six characters usurping the stage. That he does is the secret of the play's success as play of ideas. We contemplate facing mirrors. The eye is lost, the mind reels, in the infinitely reciprocal vistas of play and reality, actors and characters, illusion and truth. And the play's brilliance as drama is the containment of all its riddles and paradoxes within the one image of the invaded theater.

Not surprisingly, *Six Characters* has been provocative and controversial ever since its first appearance. Though it established Pirandello's fame, there were some, then as now, whom it irritated as a scoreless cerebral game. Others, friendly or hostile, saw in it only a new way of presenting the old middle-class domestic tragedy of past guilt and present anguish — Ibsen with a gimmick. Such views appear inadequate to explain the fact that *Six Characters* has been one of the most seminal plays of our time. In America it has influenced such theatricalist pieces as O'Neill's *Great God Brown* and *Marco Millions,* Thornton Wilder's *Our Town,* and Tennessee Williams' *Glass Menagerie.* It has anticipated much of the mood and manner of today's "absurd" drama. It has been partly responsible for the current scorn of straightforward realism in the theater as unimaginative and old-fashioned photographism. But its family connections run backward, too, for even the avant-garde has a way of slipping into place in the continuum of our dramatic tradition. The play-within-the-play device is traditional. The play's form has been partly suggested by that of the sixteenth- and seventeenth-century Italian *commedia dell' arte,* a playful, earthy drama of dialogue improvisation over stock characters, situations, and plots. Like expressionistic drama *Six Characters* shatters the surface of experience without abandoning the fragments in pursuit of symbol and myth. Its immediate historical context was the "grotesque" theater movement in Italy during and immediately after World War I, whose leader was Luigi Chiarelli and the aim and method of which was to mock and shock conventional sensibilities and institutions while proclaiming universal meaninglessness. But most significant of all is the play's relationship to the serious naturalistic drama of the previous generation.

That drama — Ibsenism and Chekhovianism rather than Ibsen's and Chekhov's own plays — stimulated Pirandello into revolutionizing dramatic form, but he did not simply react against it. He applied to it a new viewpoint. In a sense, what *Six Characters in Search of an Author* does is to put on trial the reality the nineteenth century had taken for granted: the reality of positivist science, matter in motion governed by discoverable, stable laws. It does not bring in a verdict of guilt; Pirandello's thought and art are both too subtle for that. It gives a vote of no confidence. In an important preface to the play, which he wrote in 1925, Pirandello contrasts playwrights to whom it is "enough to present a man or a woman and what is special and characteristic about them simply for the pleasure of presenting them" with those "others, who, beyond such pleasure, feel a more profound spiritual need on whose account they admit only figures, affairs, landscapes which have been soaked, so to speak, in a particular sense of life and acquire from it a universal value." Among these latter, "philosophical," writers he includes himself. His plays suggest that we should interpret this to mean that the concatenation of scene, event, and character that constitutes theme or mood within the realistic convention of scenic and psychological plausibility yielded no "particular sense of life" for him. Just as Strindberg's expressionistic chamber plays today seem more contemporary with our own sense of life than his historical and his naturalistic plays, so is the peculiar quality of Pirandello's modernity precisely his disaffection with the realistic theater of the first generation of modern masters. The particular sense of life that animates *Six Characters* derives from Pirandello's use of the theater itself to challenge the reality his predecessors had made it their artistic end to record as honestly as possible. His making playwriting conscious of itself as medium has been his most important original contribution to modern drama. Ever since, we have been getting plays of double vision: not just (to paraphrase Francis Fergusson) the stage seen as real-life parlor, but the real-life parlor seen as stage — a shifting and multiple stage at that. It is not Pirandello's fault that much of this drama has been mere toying with cleverness. Rather, the number of imitations suggests that the theatricalist convention invites and sometimes allows expression of a reality particularly meaningful to an age haunted by disaster, space, and relativity.

When the Manager, at the end of the play, complains that he has "lost a whole day," his sentiment strikes us as ironic, because our view is more inclusive than his. It is Pirandello's theatricalism that provides that more inclusive view. The Manager is interested in the play the six characters bring him only as long as he senses a hit. At the end he abandons them to the strange limbo in which their author left them. But *we* see that the aborted play-within is not the whole play. The burden of the whole is the tension and interplay between the framing and the framed action — not the family agony, but the family agony *seeking expression in the theater*. Hence, "A Comedy in the Making." The plot that unites the six characters, the web of jealousy, shame, scorn, guilt, rage, and inarticulate, childish sorrow, the demonstration that good intentions may have evil consequences, all this is neither comic nor in the making. The tragedy is rather that the script is finished and can never more be changed. But the Manager's effort to reduce raw suffering to a play *is* comic, because it offers the incongruous spectacle of the irascible, confident, bustlingly effective man of the theater being defeated by a play more real, in the Platonic sense, than reality itself. Since the core of the larger play is here, the point will bear illustration.

The curtain that falls at the end of Act II falls simultaneously in two distinct plays and, falling, brings them together without reconciling them. The crude matter-of-factness of the physical stage and its personnel dispels the purer reality of the family torment. Theatrical expedience, "effective drama," interrupts the characters' "eternal moment" of agony, the terrible scene in Madame Pace's shop that is a debased version of the recognition scene in older tragedy (recognition of identity bringing about recognition of unwitting guilt in an incestuous situation). The ironies proliferate as one ponders the scene. Beings who have no life except as characters in a play are betrayed by heavy-handed theatrical technique. The Manager does not believe in the reality only his craft can bestow. He loses his temper with an underling who is only trying to translate the projected play into theatrical actuality (itself a concept of ironic paradox). The psychological and moral realities of the inner play suddenly accommodate box office demands for a thrilling act climax, with the result that everything comes to a screeching halt. Where does reality end and art begin? The characters rehearse their reality, while the real-life troupe distort it into an actable play and finally close the curtain on both. We witness simultaneously a play about a rehearsal and one about a husband who ceded his wife to her lover with dreadful consequences for husband, wife, lover, and both sets of children. Clearly, there is a sense in which the rehearsal of *Mixing It Up* (there is such a play, Pirandello wrote it in 1918) has not been interrupted at all! The end impression is fireworks rather than incandescence.

But the bewildering doubt, the teasing skepticism, is the play's metaphysical point. The image of the invaded theater is a dramatization of relativism. And the built-in paradox of philosophical relativism is that any assertion of its validity necessarily forgoes all claim to being considered absolutely valid. For to hold that the statement "Everything is relative" is true is also to hold that no truth is absolute, including the assertion of relativity itself. This, of course, is a sophism, and people who don't like to be made dizzy by sophisms don't like Pirandello. What they fail to see is the disturbing truth of the drama of relativity: that it is man's doom to live with and in the metaphysical uncertainty. The passion (as distinct from the intellectualism) of a Pirandello play is man's cry of protest against his condition: perched on the sharp edge of paradox.

What is more, the metaphysical sophism has an esthetic counterpart. To consider it we must begin with a point of ethics. As ethics, the play implies a radical doctrine of human irresponsibility. For if identity is discontinuous, as the Father insists, no one is accountable for his past. The Father refuses to be judged by the degrading moment in the dress shop, because the visitor to Madame Pace's establishment was not his "true" self. In fact, he has no true self; there is no such thing. Art (ethics becoming esthetics), says the Father, is permanence, life ceaseless change, and it is his misfortune that as "character," a figure of literary art, he has been arrested in a single, disgraceful moment. The sordid assignation, the child in the fountain — these are forever. And like the figures on Keats' Grecian urn, only grimly so, these too do "tease us out of thought/As doth eternity." But if, as "character," the Father can rightly claim to be "less real perhaps, but truer" than the Manager and everyone else in the empirical, non-art reality of change, it follows — and this is the sophism — that the truth of art necessarily falsifies life, for when flux freezes as "eternal moment" it is no longer flux. The very essence of experience forever eludes art.

And so *Six Characters in Search of an Author* may be said to embody also the artist's unresolvable dilemma. The primary dramatic conflict between company and characters, invaded and invader, is a fable of artistic creation, with the Manager as a kind of semi-comical middle man, resentful, interested, again resentful, a mocking but painful self-portrait of the author haunted by shapes he can neither give life to nor exorcise.

"All that lives," says Pirandello in the Preface, "by the fact of living, has a form, and by the same token must die — except the work of art which lives forever in so far as it *is* form." Again paradox. His play, according to his own account, grew out of his futile search for a form for the six characters of his imagination. He made living art out of his inability to do so.)‿⁓

Michel de Ghelderode

CHRONICLES OF HELL

Translated by George Hauger

Characters

JAN IN EREMO, *Bishop of Lapideopolis*
VENERANDA, *a servant*
SIMON LAQUEDEEM, *auxiliary bishop*
SODOMATI, *the nuncio's secretary*
KRAKENBUS, *vicar-general*
REAL-TREMBLOR, *archdeacon*
DOM PIKKEDONCKER, *pleban (rural dean)*
CARNIBOS, *chaplain*
DUVELHOND, *guardian of the holy relics*
THE MASTER OF THE BUTCHERS
THE BUTCHERS
AN ARQUEBUSIER
FOUR SWISS
THE CROWD

SCENE: *A decaying episcopal palace in bygone Flanders around which an invisible and threatening crowd snarls persistently during the whole of this tragedy. At the back, a wide double door, framed between columns that support a pediment, and reached by some steps. There is a Gothic doorway to the left, and farther downstage a low and narrow exit. To the right, a glass bay window looking onto the public square, through which breaks the morbid light of a stormy summer dusk. Tapestries hang in shreds on the walls, to which portraits of prelates are fastened, very high up. Everywhere at the base of the walls there are piles of baroque objects, idols, suns, witches' masks, multicolored devils, totems, stakes, and instruments of torture. But in the foreground stands a heavy table with a crimson velvet cloth, sumptuously laden with silver plate and crystal.*

(*The chaplain goes around the table shiftily, stealing pieces of meat and swallowing them, while the vicar-general, who has taken up position on the steps at the back, looks through the keyhole.*)

CARNIBOS: Yum . . . yum . . . I'm nibbling . . . yum . . . I've done nothing! Mutton! Good! Veal! Lovely! Yum, yum, yum. . . . What hunger, what hunger! Nibble here, nibble there, oop! It's the first time so much meat has been seen at the palace. For twenty years, eh, Krakenbus? I've withered. You fed yourself on the fat in your hump, didn't you? Never any meat! I used to cry *Miserere nobis!* each day. Never, while in the town they used to set up altars in the market, bearing tottering sacrifices of rich red meats — used to hang up huge oxen, droves of them . . . Ho! Krakenbus, I saw that, and the skinny people, so skinny they frightened you, like me, murmured yum, yum, yum, before these tantalizing displays! . . . (*He puffs.*) What time are we going to eat, Krakenbus, or is this a show table that will be carried away, load and all? I'm hungry! Say nothing, since you haven't seen what I haven't done. I was setting the cold meats in order! (*He is seized by a violent cough.*) Swallowed the wrong way . . . so . . . Ach! Ouf! (*He spits a piece of meat into his hand.*) Yum! (*And eats it again.*)

KRAKENBUS (*who has stopped spying, gazes at this scene*): Heaven has punished you, ravener! This clacking of your jaws is a profanation, Carnibos, a scandal! And the only thing that can be heard of your prayers, Carnibos, is yum, yum, yum. . . . Stop, you devourer! When there's nothing else left, you'll swallow the knives and the cloth. . . . Your sin —

CARNIBOS: My illness, not my sin! Look, Krakenbus, a chicken. Ho, this leg! (*With his mouth full.*) Those who have a stomach, eat; those who have a hump, glue themselves to keyholes.

KRAKENBUS (*who has come close to the table*): It's a pious service that I perform! Take care, my hump contains a second brain, and venom! . . . I am as spiteful as I am humped, as humped as I am spiteful, meat thief! You shall suffer! You shall eat your dirty feet, your knotted guts, your spongy heart! You shall trim yourself to the bone. Put that fowl back in its place and go and wash your hands, your sticky hands. Lick those hands whose marks one finds on sacred cloths that are polluted forevermore. . . .

CARNIBOS (*humble*): Yes, reverend hump. My punishment! I once dreamed I was on all fours eating refuse in a charnel house. Yum, yum, yum . . . But tell me, dear doctor of humpology, is what we do in our dreams reckoned against us?

KRAKENBUS: No, it all depends, chaplain. Yes indeed, when one's head is full of sticky water, greenish pus, like yours. (*He laughs unpleasantly.*) Gnaw your nails, which are too long, as well, chaplain. There are little worms under them. And close your lipless mouth, chaplain. Your breath breeds violet flies. . . . (*He is close to* CARNIBOS.) You will confess these foul dreams to me. I demand it. . . . No? (*With a sudden stamp of his heel, he crushes* CARNIBOS' *foot.*)

CARNIBOS: Ow!

KRAKENBUS: Suffer in silence! And let me have your other foot! I'm going to bruise it in its turn; one pain may drive out the other. . . . No? (*In a smooth voice.*) Talking about feet, I have just seen something philosophical. (*Drawing close to* CARNIBOS.) Sorry yet, glutton? (*He lays hold of a slice of meat.*) Open your mouth! (*And he puts the meat in.*) Give thanks, cockroach! Thanks!

CARNIBOS (*devouring it*): Thanks, holy hump! . . . Ivory hump! . . . Miraculous hump! . . . (*Having finished, he puffs.*) This spectacle? You must teach me to watch through keyholes. . . . Which eye does one use? Left? Right? They say that in time one's eye becomes shaped like a keyhole. I prefer eavesdropping. There! See my ear, a delicate shell. . . .

(*The two priests have gone toward the back and have stopped on steps leading to the double door.*)

KRAKENBUS: Bend down, look, and not with half an eye. Look with all your eyes, for you will never again see anything like it!

CARNIBOS (*watching through the keyhole*): Yum, yum, yum!

KRAKENBUS: What do you see?

CARNIBOS: Meat! Nothing but meat! A hairy bear. No, it has feet. It's a man. (*Standing upright.*) A dead man!

KRAKENBUS: Right! And what is a dead man?

CARNIBOS: Meat.

KRAKENBUS: No, chaplain. A dead man is two feet! A human being has to be dead for anyone to notice that he has feet. I like seeing dead people. And I've seen some! Men, women too. But never, I swear, was it given to me to see a dead person like this one! Like this one!

CARNIBOS: You couldn't say he's naked, hairy as he is. (*Chuckles.*) A moral in that? When men die, they are chucked into lime. Beasts? Carved up and eaten. As for game, it's decently buried, so that it takes on its flavor. (*He pushes* KRAKENBUS *who has begun spying again.*)

KRAKENBUS (*standing up, hustles the chaplain*): The dead man is still warm. Cross yourself, dipping crumbs!

CARNIBOS: After you. . . . (*He avoids* KRAKENBUS, *who is seeking to crush his foot with a stamp of the heel.*) Hi! My feet are alive. Peace!

KRAKENBUS: Peace! . . . Let us embrace.

(*They go toward each other to embrace, lower their heads, and bang their foreheads together. Double laughter. The pleban enters from the left.*)

DOM PIKKEDONCKER: He, he, and I . . .

CARNIBOS: And the dead man make four.

KRAKENBUS: A dead man is nobody. Good evening, pleban.

DOM PIKKEDONCKER: They told me they were sounding passing bells, and I couldn't hear them at all, not at all. . . . Poor, yes. . . . For a bishop — Holy Virgin! — they should ring royally! Ding-dang-dongs well struck. Not thin-mouthed bells, great thick-lipped ones that go (*motion of pulling the rope*) boo-oo-oom! . . . Boo-oo-oom! . . . I'm sweating from it!

KRAKENBUS: You are an old fool, Dom Pikkedoncker!

DOM PIKKEDONCKER (*putting a trumpet to his right ear*): What did you say?

KRAKENBUS: I pledge my word that a bishop may not be worth a chime of pots and pans! (*Mocking.*) That talks of setting the great bells ringing, and it wouldn't hear the walls of Jericho fall.

CARNIBOS (*pulling* KRAKENBUS' *sleeve*): Take care of the deaf one! . . . He hears nothing of what you shout and overhears everything you whisper.

DOM PIKKEDONCKER: Exactly. I shall say that display, whose custom is falling into disuse, is necessary. I love ceremony. Even Hell displays such. . . .

KRAKENBUS: He has been there. . . .

DOM PIKKEDONCKER (*who has heard*): Yes. . . . To buy a place there for you, in a noxious dungeon where you will crush slugs, krak, krak, Krakenbus! . . . (*Shaken by laughter.*) And the deceased? . . .

CARNIBOS: They're rigging it out in priestly fashion. You'll have display! . . . It's the rule. For myself, I'm of the opinion that a sack was enough. . . .

DOM PIKKEDONCKER (*counting*): So many candles, so many succentors, so many clerics. . . . A coffin of some size will be needed, you know. . . .

CARNIBOS: I say a sack would do!

DOM PIKKEDONCKER: Such a body! What did he weigh? And dead, twice as much as when alive. . . . What were you saying?

KRAKENBUS: You trickster! Is this trumpet at your ear for listening to thoughts?

DOM PIKKEDONCKER: A marvelous little horn, my friends, made by a renowned physician, and with which I hear all I want, and even what I don't want. A dead man would be less deaf than me, my friends. Try it. Tell me something!

KRAKENBUS: How is your rural deanery, dear rural dean?

DOM PIKKEDONCKER: Not bad, I say. . . .

CARNIBOS: Do you hear music as well? Listen. . . . (*He sings into the trumpet.*)

> That old man Noah one day
> Had drunk more than his fill.
> I heard his daughter say —
> She who liked him ill —

DOM PIKKEDONCKER (*singing*):
> "I'll have the breeches off the fool!
> Come, sister dear, and help me pull."

Be quiet! If God had a trumpet like mine! . . . Do you hear bells, at last, bells? (*He lays hold of a knife and strikes the crystal glasses on the table.*) Ting . . . tang . . . Saint Donatus'! Clang, Saint Walburga's! Her name is Maria. . . .

KRAKENBUS (*who has meanwhile filled several glasses*): What of it? No. Glasses, I empty them, I do. . . . (*He drinks.*)

CARNIBOS (*drinking*): I no longer say yum, yum, but glug, glug. . . .

DOM PIKKEDONCKER (*drinking*): Believe me, brethren, I'm in favor of bells and towers, square towers crammed with bells. There are not enough towers being built, there are not enough bells being cast, and that is why religion is losing its allure. When Flanders is bristling all over with towers, Jesus will enter the cities of stone and bronze to the sound of the chimes. And not along the streets, no! He will walk on the towers. . . . (*Senile laugh.*) I'm not drunk, not at all. You will be, today. A great day for the lesser clergy, isn't that so? Wine! Tell me, what did we come here to do?

KRAKENBUS: To cry! When the shepherd is gone, the sheep go baa-aa! Bleat! Let us bleat! . . .

CARNIBOS: May the Most High bring it about that the new shepherd does not molest his flock and that he wields a crook rather than a

bludgeon! What did we come to do? I know: eat! This light repast
is for the vigil. In three days, the triumphal banquet! Then . . .
then will be the time for ringing the bells, the great bells. The occasion? Eating in this palace! Starving priests who have come running
in packs from all the parishes! Historic day! One used to eat on the
sly in this place. I used to go and eat in the privy. . . .

DOM PIKKEDONCKER: Already? . . . I hear them rumbling, the priests,
their innards . . .

CARNIBOS: It's the crowd gathering.

DOM PIKKEDONCKER: What does it expect, to eat as well?

KRAKENBUS: The crowd expects a corpse, a corpse to gaze at. Death,
the sight of death, what more gorgeous!

(DUVELHOND *has come in and, with hands outstretched, he goes
toward the other three.*)

DUVELHOND: Mi — mi — miserere! D — D — Death is ne — is ne —
is never. . . .

CARNIBOS (*imitating him*): Who's this? The guar — guar — guardian
of the holy relics? (*And as* DUVELHOND *stands with mouth agape,
the chaplain thrusts in a piece of meat.*) Swallow it!

DUVELHOND (*choking*): Ah! . . . Ouf! . . . Pfaugh! . . . Ouf! . . . Ah!

DOM PIKKEDONCKER: Listen to the stammerer! He's giving His Highness' funeral oration! As a deaf man, I find it eloquent.

KRAKENBUS: That? Already on the way to hew relics from His Highness' remains? They're yours, Duvelhond, yours. . . . His hair, his
nails . . .

CARNIBOS: His last gasp. . . . The last gasp that he belched up. . . .

DOM PIKKEDONCKER: What?

CARNIBOS: Oh, worthy of him! One didn't expect less of His Highness
in that supreme moment. What was the word? No, I shan't tell it
to you, not me!

KRAKENBUS: Nor me! Why are you growing pale, pleban? Could you
have heard this word in your wooden ear?

DOM PIKKEDONCKER: The thickest walls must have heard it. It's your
hump that's growing pale, vicar. And your rat's snout, chaplain.
Candle color . . .

CARNIBOS: I'm pale with hunger, yum!

DUVELHOND (*interposing*): His High — Highness said as he died . . .

KRAKENBUS (*crushing* DUVELHOND'S *foot with a swift stamp of the
heel*): Deo gratias!

CARNIBOS: Quick! He has two feet!

DUVELHOND (*limping and moaning, makes off to the left, shaking his
fists*): Curse you!

(*He bumps into a newcomer,* REAL-TREMBLOR, *whom he almost knocks over.*)

DUVELHOND: Look out! . . . Your fee — eet! . . . Krak — Krak —

(*The rest and the newcomer laugh unrestrainedly. Crestfallen,* DUVELHOND *comes back.*)

REAL-TREMBLOR: I'm not laughing, you know. . . . (*Hilariously.*) Ho, ho! And in a mortuary! Ho, ho! My feet . . . (*in consternation*) . . . bore me to this place, which is made majestic by the presence . . .

KRAKENBUS: Of rhetoric? Good evening, archdeacon. Good evening is what is wished.

REAL-TREMBLOR: Good evening, your reverends. . . . A thousand pardons, I was upset. . . . Have you slept these last nights of His Highness' great death agony? The knells that nothing could assuage! . . . The public lamentations! . . . And the august deceased, tell me, have you seen him? . . .

CARNIBOS: Come here, Real-Tremblor. Why are you quaking?

REAL-TREMBLOR: Strongly affected, you know. . . . Death . . . dead people . . . very frightened, very frightened of them. . . .

DUVELHOND: G — go! . . . They are going to . . .

KRAKENBUS (*barring the way to* REAL-TREMBLOR, *who was attempting to step to the left*): Stop! You are going to salute His Highness. . . . A terrifying corpse! . . . Eyes still open . . . sagging jaw that will have to be wedged with a breviary. . . . Let's drag him there! Let's shut him up with the dreadful corpse! . . .

REAL-TREMBLOR (*struggling*): No, no! He was wicked. . . . No! Hated me! Used to say to me, sneak . . . dirty sneak . . . each time!

KRAKENBUS: How truly he spoke! (*Loosing the archdeacon.*) Is it also true that you were castrated in your young days?

CARNIBOS: Let's not torment this tormented fellow! . . . What more tormented than a spy? What tale did you come to tell us? Hum, hornet. . . . In return, you won't go to the dead wicked man. . . .

REAL-TREMBLOR: What to tell you? I went in quest of information.

KRAKENBUS: You have run about the town to take a collection of rumors and remarks. Open your bag!

CARNIBOS: What is the crowd murmuring?

KRAKENBUS: The common people . . .

REAL-TREMBLOR: That a saint has just died!

DOM PIKKEDONCKER (*who has heard*): That was foreseen! The crowd canonizes! It does in a moment what Rome takes centuries to do!

The crowd makes a saint of a mountebank! A saint! . . . What a disgrace sentiment is!

KRAKENBUS: Come on . . . the bottom of the bag!

REAL-TREMBLOR: Here's the filth. . . . Delight yourselves. . . . (*He waits.*)

KRAKENBUS (*raising his heel to crush the archdeacon's foot*): For the sneak, eh?

REAL-TREMBLOR: I was saying . . .

DOM PIKKEDONCKER: You weren't saying anything. . . .

REAL-TREMBLOR: The common folk were saying, in their jargon, that God had nothing to do with the bishop's passing away. . . . Consequently, they are babbling no longer. They are clenching their teeth and snarling, are the common people. What more do I know? The truth is that at the moment of the passing, the sun's sky suddenly darkened — it's not very light, notice — and grisly storm clouds came and piled up above the town, where they are yet, haunting in their motionlessness. For the crowds, no more is needed. . . .

KRAKENBUS: Never mind the crowd! But the storm seems to me disturbing. Where is Monsignor tarrying? Does the auxiliary see that the heavens are threatening to fall on our heads?

REAL-TREMBLOR: Monsignor must be in conference with the governor of the Old Town. They are calling out the men under arms. Why? To do the honors — and from other motives. No doubt the governor will order the closing of the city gates as well. . . .

CARNIBOS: That's the least that can be done, with these masses who know how to read the clouds. Won't they say that the plague will break out, that it's going to rain fiery swords and burning stones? That would be the limit!

DOM PIKKEDONCKER: The masses are afraid, the masses to whom all occasions for fear are good, like all those for being angry!

DUVELHOND: Would you be priests if the ma — masses weren't af — af — raid?

KRAKENBUS: Let them be afraid. Later, we shall give them festivities, consecration festivities! And if they are not satisfied with all this blessing, there will be butchery. There's real politics! Blessing and butchery!

DOM PIKKEDONCKER: Is yon Krakenbus uttering abuse?

CARNIBOS: The storm is responsible.

REAL-TREMBLOR: May the storm be without effect on Monsignor's bowels! Let us ask nothing more!

KRAKENBUS: Let Monsignor come. It's urgent. Let him push his belly on the balcony and offer it to the admiration of the crowd! And the nuncio we're expecting! It's urgent that the crowd have something to look at. . . . Something other than the canopies of the storm to look at!

REAL-TREMBLOR: In actual fact, the air is heavy, vibrant with gnats. News from without? Not very reassuring, and how right you are . . .

CARNIBOS: Is anyone asking your opinion? It's enough that the storm's tainting the meat.

REAL-TREMBLOR (*turning his back on the interrupter*): . . . for nothing augurs well. As soon as the bishop's death was known, the burgomaster, who knew the crowd was tired out with three days and nights of waiting, called upon the brotherhoods to put on their cowls and to keep moving in an endless procession, very much reckoning that the crowd would fall into step with the penitents, as happens with us. A crowd that walks slowly, intoning psalms, behind crosses and lanterns, becomes the best, the most good-natured of crowds, doesn't it? Without taking into account that they are, at the time, escorted by armed men. But what was the reply to the magistrates from the emissaries of the people? That the people weren't troubling themselves about the threatening storm, and that they wouldn't budge, even at the risk of being struck down on the spot by lightning; that they were pleased to go in procession in honor of the bishop, but without priests or sacristans, and only in company with the carnival giants and dragons, all in silence and with dignity. This rabble has imagination! . . .

KRAKENBUS: Enough, weak mouth! You stink of fear. You are shivering in your shoes and you want your shivers to spread to the universe. . . . Since you tell your tales so badly, I resolve that you go and lick the dead man's nose. Bind him! . . .

(*The others rush at the archdeacon, who throws himself flat on his belly on the ground.*)

DUVELHOND (*shouting*): Mon — Mon — Monsignor! . . .

(*Row. They all give a jump.* SIMON LAQUEDEEM *enters from the left and swoops down on the group, which immediately breaks up.*)

SIMON LAQUEDEEM (*tracing blessings*): Bless you . . . And you, you, you. . . .

CARNIBOS: He blesses as if he were boxing your ears!

SIMON LAQUEDEEM: And that thing? (*He kicks* REAL-TREMBLOR, *who is still lying flat on the ground.*) I have blessed you, drunkard! . . .

REAL-TREMBLOR (*standing up and bowing*): I have not had anything to drink, Monsignor. . . .

SIMON LAQUEDEEM: Are you greeting my stomach? (*He shakes* REAL-TREMBLOR *and pushes him toward the others, who laugh shamelessly. With a sharp gesture,* LAQUEDEEM *stops this courtiers' laughter dead.*) What are you laughing at? (*Sternly.*) Alter your faces! You shall laugh later, and the good last of all. (*Raising his voice.*) For we shall be the last to laugh! (*Smooth-tongued.*) Don't chuckle, don't get excited; assume the bearing of people overwhelmed by an infinite stupor; stick your noses out; let your arms hang down and walk trembling on your feet like Barbary apes after love-making; have your eyes lusterless and full of gray water, and from time to time raise them skyward like blind men counting the stars. You, pleban, with the truffle-nosing snout, try it. Compose your features into this circumstantial mask, which the others will imitate. . . .

DOM PIKKEDONCKER: Is Monsignor talking to us about his health? In my opinion, nothing is as good as a clyster. . . .

SIMON LAQUEDEEM: For the time being, swallow your bowel-washings, you deaf old man! My bowels are my business. For the present, it's the diocese that needs purging of what is obstructing it. The corpse, where is it? Is it prepared?

KRAKENBUS: Must be. We are waiting for you, Monsignor. And the crowd is waiting. . . .

SIMON LAQUEDEEM: I know. . . . The squares will be purged as well. . . . We know our duties. . . . Let the nuncio get here. (*He walks up and down, talking to himself.*) I shall purge the palace of these idols. I understand, I do. And I shall drive his shadow away, obliterate him even to the trace of his footsteps! . . . And sweep out these debauched underlings. . . . (*He stops and holds his stomach, his face suddenly drawn.*) Ah!

REAL-TREMBLOR: Poor Monsignor. . . . Monsignor's poor stomach!

SIMON LAQUEDEEM (*mumbling*). My stomach! . . . Calvary of a stomach! . . . The thorns, the nails, and the lance in it. . . . (*Big sigh.*) Ouf . . . it's working loose!

CARNIBOS: An angel has passed by. . . . The wind from his wing . . .

SIMON LAQUEDEEM: *Laus Deo!* (*He mops his brow. Flashes of silent lightning quiver on the panes of the balcony.*) Who has been in the chamber? None of you? Are they taking hours over embalming him? Are you frightened to go near him dead? He won't bite you any more, my good fellows. . . . (*He goes toward the steps at the back.*) He shan't have the funeral he asked for, in open ground and without a shroud, in the outcasts' enclosure. He will be clad in iron, in lead, and in oak; he will be hidden in the deepest crypt — and the cathedral will press down with all its weight on his bones! (*Hav-*

ing turned toward the archdeacon.) Go and see if the nuncio is coming to us, Real-Tremblor!

(REAL-TREMBLOR *goes out swiftly at the left.* SIMON LAQUEDEEM *is preparing to open the double door at the back when it half-opens. A little black shape comes into view through it.*)

KRAKENBUS: The servant! (*The little shape hugs the walls, seeking to run away. The priests encircle it.*) Catch the crow!

SIMON LAQUEDEEM (*apostrophizing the little old woman*): Have you done your funeral task? (*Pause.*) Oh simplicity! She is weeping! The paradise of the innocent will be yours, old servant: you shall have your wages. . . . Vanish into your garret. Henceforth your master will have no further need of you. Let go of her!

DUVELHOND: Impru — pru — dence!

SIMON LAQUEDEEM: I say let her make ready her bits of clothes. She has the right to attend the services. Afterward . . .

CARNIBOS (*shaking the servant*): What is she muttering in her patois?

VENERANDA (*frightened and in a toneless voice*): *Bid voor de ziel!*

SIMON LAQUEDEEM: Pray for the soul? By all means! Go! Let us not see you again! (VENERANDA *is pushed, without consideration, to the left, and disappears.*) I am afraid that, although she is unaware of it, this ninety-year-old knows too much. . . . Imprudence, someone said? No. The staircases in this palace are decrepit. . . . One false step. . . . (*Flashes of lightning outside. A silence during which the crowd is heard snarling.*) Darkness is going to fall. . . . And this storm that seems to be holding itself back for the night! . . . And this nuncio! . . . (*Arrogantly.*) Is there no longer any give and take with Heaven?

(*Noise at the left, from which direction* REAL-TREMBLOR *returns, preceding a young priest.*

SIMON LAQUEDEEM: Him? Greetings, bambino! And the nuncio? Are you hiding him under your robe? Come, let me embrace you! (*He embraces the new arrival who shields himself.*)

SODOMATI: Don't suffocate me! . . . (*Bowing and scraping to all.*) My compliments, Monsignor! And to you, revered, very worthy, learned, and inspired gentlemen. . . . Here we are at last! What den are you drawing me into? The crowd surrounded my carriage. Gallows birds hurled foul words at me. Imagine! They shouted "*Rok af!*" at me. What does that mean?

CARNIBOS: "Tear off his gown!" . . . nothing else.

SODOMATI: Horror!

SIMON LAQUEDEEM: No doubt the people thought to see a pretty girl. Never mind that. . . . Have you brought the nuncio to me?

SODOMATI: Became unexpectedly ill on learning of the decease of the bishop. Understand? I am acting as his substitute. Have the time to make an appearance, then I'm off, understand? I don't like dramatic ceremonials the way they carry them out in this country. Is this a way of doing things? A bishop dies . . .

KRAKENBUS: And what a bishop, too!

SODOMATI: . . . whom I indeed regret not having known alive! The nuncio became crimson when he was spoken to about this apostle. . . . (*Indicating the wall at the back.*) I can imagine the person, incarnated by these abominations, these idols. . . . Bah! . . . What bad form!

SIMON LAQUEDEEM: His friends. . . .

CARNIBOS: His only friends. . . .

SIMON LAQUEDEEM: His court. He was fond of these idols, these monsters, yes, which, he said, consoled him for the hideousness of our human faces. He liked the false gods, his victims, he said, and gazed on them with a culpable pride, like a barbaric warrior counting his trophies. . . .

KRAKENBUS: We have got to admit that he converted savages, and of a dangerous sort. He had his ways: beating and barking! . . . Poor savages converted in this way to a hard life, and all their gods stolen! Why didn't this formidable zealot stay on the other side of the globe!

CARNIBOS: More than that! . . . He drew a subtle argument from these idols. "Men of the Church, my savages were nearer to the divine truth in adoring these untrue gods than you, the anointed, who pretend to adore the true god!" he said. . . .

SODOMATI: Oh, the shameless creature! He said that?

SIMON LAQUEDEEM: Said? No! Shouted . . . bawled . . . howled!

SODOMATI: How I pity you, brethren, how I pity you! Free yourselves as quickly as possible from these symbols of Evil. Bury them with your bishop, or, better, burn them. . . . The nuncio spoke to me about them. It is not rash to assert that wooden and metal devils possess baleful powers, and may have been masters of your bishop's mind; not rash to assert that these idols have operated, causing the absurd and foolish actions of your bewitched bishop. . . . The nuncio maintains that this palace is under a spell — and I believe it! Make a colossal pile of faggots. Burn these appurtenances of idolatry. The nuncio even believes that these poisonous powers are spreading, contagiously reaching the town, the country, the whole diocese. And I believe it! . . . Only look at the way the crowd be-

haves since the death of the wonder-worker, I mean the bishop, the
wretch . . . I mean the late Monsignor, whom the Almighty will
forgive by reason of his faith and zeal, which were worthy of past
ages, but no longer of ours. . . .

SIMON LAQUEDEEM: We shall burn them, bambino. . . . These idols
were truly the bishop's mistresses, and they ruled the town and the
diocese! Burn? It's the whole poisoned population that should be
thrown on the pile, a pile as vast as the diocese . . . (*his voice
chokes*) . . . to destroy these packs of wolves — for our pastor's
sheep are fierce wolves, believe me!

SODOMATI: Calm yourself, auxiliary! . . . If fire can cleanse the diocese, burn, burn. . . . But will the fire change these wolves into
lambs? I doubt it. A strange race in this land of marshes, free-
thinking, subversive, yes, violent, unmanageable! Among you here,
heresiarchs spring up like tares! . . . Ungodly race!

KRAKENBUS: We belong to it, if you don't mind!

SODOMATI: You belong to it! I was thinking so as I watched you making faces. And since you admit it . . . It's obvious the idols have
taken possession of you as of the others. You make unsightly grimaces like men possessed. You are the suspect priests of a people of
possessed souls!

SIMON LAQUEDEEM: All that because they wanted to tear off your
gown, bambino? Calm yourself, pretty secretary! We shall do our
burning. We shall burn the sodomites as well. We know how to
behave and how to lead our flocks without the advice of the nuncio,
pretty secretary! We shall burn the seed of the heresiarch, and lilies
shall sprout in the frog-filled marshes. Our pestilential bogs shall
become mystical meadows, ineffable gardens of the nunciature,
where little angels with chubby buttocks shall dance. . . .

SODOMATI (*superciliously*): I beg your pardon, Simon Laquedeem!
. . . I beg your pardon for having confused you! . . . You are not
of this race. . . . I was forgetting. You are indisputably descended
from kings and prophets, which I would not have believed had I not
read your disclaimer of your ancestors written in Hebrew on a fore-
skin! . . . Burn the sodomites and the heresiarchs. In addition,
burn the Jews, the filthy Jews, since this diocese is overflowing with
them, Simon Laquedeem — since it is not known by what operation
of unwonted charity this diocese receives them, Simon Laquedeem,
to the extent of resembling a huge ghetto. . . .

SIMON LAQUEDEEM (*furious, rushes at* SODOMATI): *Rok af!* Strip him!

(*Uproar.* REAL-TREMBLOR *intervenes and holds the auxiliary
bishop back. Outside, flashes of silent lightning.*)

REAL-TREMBLOR: The storm . . . oh! . . . Everything is going wrong!

KRAKENBUS: They will become so excited that they'll draw down a thunderbolt! Instead of calming the crowd! . . . Give me the aspergillum, well soaked. . . .

SIMON LAQUEDEEM (*pulling himself up*): That is right. We are delaying a great deal. Let us show ourselves on the balcony and give blessing. This action may have results. And no doubt the crowd will think we are warding off the storm. Prepare yourselves! Get on my left, Sodomati. The presence of a Roman witness has its importance in these difficult moments.

(*The group forms up,* CARNIBOS *remaining behind, near the table, and* KRAKENBUS *hastening to the right where he goes to open the balcony windows with a crash. At once, the distant murmur outside comes in, amplified, and a harsh though gloomy light floods the room. Slowly, after having drawn themselves up, the priests, with the auxiliary leading, move to the right and disappear on the balcony.* CARNIBOS *does not follow them and sets about stealing pieces of meat which he devours swiftly. Flashes of lightning, nearer and bluish, follow each other in silence. And suddenly a fierce clamor breaks out: booing, whistling, barking, laughter — the violent crowd is insulting the priests. The latter fall back inside in disorder. The balcony windows shut once more; the clamor diminishes. The priests look at one another and, in the chiaroscuro, seem to be counting their number. This confusion does not last long,* SODOMATI *taking the attention of everyone by a disordered gesticulation. Before long, he bursts out.*)

SODOMATI: We are being booed, do you hear? And for greeting, these sheaves of bare arms, these bundles of fists held out to us! The riffraff of Jerusalem didn't rage more in affronting the Messiah and calling for his execution!

DOM PIKKEDONCKER: Worthy folk! What riffraff! Alleluia! They cried out, "Alleluia!"

SODOMATI: That's what your prestige is capable of, Monsignor! (*Indicating the idols.*) And that is what the prestige of these devils can do! Is it clear enough in this doubtful evening? These devils, unchained by the disappearance of their suzerain, have overcome the vast collection of the crowd, the crowd that will fell you!

SIMON LAQUEDEEM: Am I responsible for the civil order? Have I authority to disperse crowds and control storms?

SODOMATI: The crowd that will fell you! It will serve you right. And don't reckon on being granted the benefit of martyrdom!

SIMON LAQUEDEEM: Go, and may God give you an escort of archangels! Go quickly: this moment is perilous, and those that are coming. For the time being, the crowd will content itself with making water against your coach. Later, you might leap in the air like a puppet and fall down again, impaled through the bottom, on a picket. We are familiar with our people and their humors. . . .

SODOMATI: I shall not leave until the obsequies are over, seen by my own eyes. . . .

SIMON LAQUEDEEM: Then you will leave without delay, and you will see nothing of the carnival that follows, for the corpse will soon have tumbled down into the vault; go. . . .

SODOMATI: Prudence, Monsignor! . . . There have been refractory corpses that would not allow themselves to be interred with ease. As for your carnival, no, I shall not see anything of it; but you are not at all certain of superintending it. . . .

SIMON LAQUEDEEM: Will you explain yourself?

SODOMATI: The Holy See might become concerned about your bowels. . . . It is acknowledged that this great belly is ill and contains enough stinking breaths to infect all the nearby countries more thoroughly than heresy . . .

SIMON LAQUEDEEM (*bursting out laughing*): Really? Has it been smelled as far as Rome? What a sense of smell, bambino! . . . (*He rubs his belly.*) And if I gave off floral perfumes, wouldn't the cry be, "A miracle"? Tell me, bambino, what is your favorite flower?

KRAKENBUS: The guard.

(FOUR SWISS *carrying halberds have just come in and stand waiting.*)

SIMON LAQUEDEEM (*going toward the* SWISS): These, guards? Four vergers rigged out for the occasion. You, Swiss, will station yourselves at each corner of the funeral couch and will not budge from there. Your vigil will not last long, since the corpse will go to lie in the choir of the cathedral when night falls. Don't look at the jugs. You shall have drink, but later. . . .

CARNIBOS: Those who keep vigil in a death chamber are sometimes subject to hallucinations.

REAL-TREMBLOR: Let's set our minds at rest: vergers have never been sensitive to the supernatural. Come, Switzers. . . .

(*Followed by the* FOUR SWISS, REAL-TREMBLOR *makes his way to the back and climbs the steps. He opens the double door a little way, makes the men slip through one after the other, and observes the interior. Then, after a moment, he turns toward the company again.*)

REAL-TREMBLOR: *Facta est!* (*He indicates the door.*) Would it not be fitting to gaze in a spirit of Christian sorrow on the mortal remains of Monsignor Jan in Eremo, Bishop of Lapideopolis?

SIMON LAQUEDEEM (*after a short pause during which he has questioned his confederates by his gaze*): Struck by Christian sorrow, we wish to gaze on the mortal remains of Monsignor John of Eremo, Bishop of what you said. . . .

(*And, with the auxiliary leading, the priests take several steps toward the double door which* REAL-TREMBLOR *opens with a calculated slowness. When the door is open, a chamber is revealed, blazingly illuminated by a hundred candles which light up a tilted funeral couch on which, clothed in his canonicals, mitered, and with his crook, lies a man of remarkable height and breadth, with a grayish and shining face, and all angular, like a recumbent figure cut in stone — the mortal remains of Monsignor* JAN IN EREMO, *Bishop of Lapideopolis. The* SWISS *stand rigid at the corners of the funeral couch. Above the couch, a great crucifix. At the foot of the bed, a coat of arms showing the bearings of the bishop, anchors sable on a field of gold.*)

SIMON LAQUEDEEM (*with authority*): *Flectamus genua!* . . . (*At this command, the priests kneel, turned toward the chamber. The auxiliary goes up the steps and stops at the threshold. After a long pause.*) He looks still more formidable dead than living! (*He turns away and comes down the steps and prays aloud.*) *Agnus Dei, qui tollis.* . . . (*He yawns and mumbles the Latin words.*)

THE OTHERS (*confusedly making responses*): *Dona eis requiem* . . .

SIMON LAQUEDEEM (*with authority*): *Levate!* . . .

(*On the command, the priests get up.* REAL-TREMBLOR *shuts the double door again. Now, after this brief illumination, the gloom has taken on a thickness that the lightning from outside hachures almost continuously.*)

KRAKENBUS: We need lights. . . .

SIMON LAQUEDEEM: The servants will bring them when they come for the body. It was my wish that from now until then the windows of the palace should remain dark. Haven't you the most extraordinary illumination dispensed to us from the heavens?

CARNIBOS: Enough to find one's mouth. I feel weak. . . .

SIMON LAQUEDEEM: Sit down! (*The priests take stools from under the table and settle down.* SIMON LAQUEDEEM *remains standing and from time to time walks about.*) Who has played havoc with the food? You, you beast of prey?

REAL-TREMBLOR: The idols. . . . But the jugs are untouched, and the flasks. . . .

SIMON LAQUEDEEM: Eat. Drink. In silence, if possible. Silence would be fitting after what we have just seen.

SODOMATI: Impressive, what we have just seen! I am unaware of what this man was in life; I know what he is in death, somebody! Tell us about him, Laquedeem. I can't abide silence, particularly in this place, particularly this evening. . . .

SIMON LAQUEDEEM: What do you want me to say, since you have said everything? Somebody! There is no other comment. . . .

SODOMATI: You seem to be dreaming, Laquedeem. Are you entering into meditation when your clergy are not missing a mouthful? . . .

SIMON LAQUEDEEM: I was thinking about the inscrutability of the designs of Providence, the strangeness of certain destinies. . . . Somebody! whose shadow weighs on us, in whose shadow we live crushed down. Somebody. . . .

KRAKENBUS: He was called Jan Eremo. . . .

SODOMATI: Will you tell us his legend?

SIMON LAQUEDEEM: No, his true history — the reality is prodigious enough without adding to it. I shall relate it since you dread the silence. It will displease you, as our fogs displease you, and our marshes. . . .

SODOMATI: Your storms . . . your gloom . . .

KRAKENBUS: He was called Jan Eremo. . . .

SIMON LAQUEDEEM: Jan in Eremo was his name. . . . John in the desert, in memory of the sand hills where he was found — a child of an unknown mother, a child without a name — by the monks from the monastery of the Dunes, whom his haunting cries had alerted. It is more than seventy years since John was born in the desert, John, son of the sea and the sand, who used to say, "I am solitude" — which he was!

REAL-TREMBLOR: The people say that he was born of the fornication of a monk and a mermaid!

SIMON LAQUEDEEM: And when did that happen? (*He drinks a cup of wine and throws the dregs in the interrupter's face.*) Not much is known of how this accursed being grew up in the monastery, of what his young life was like up to the day of his ordination. He was a rugged pioneer, and a daring fisherman. His brethren looked on him as being attacked by a strange insanity, and were not surprised when, once, they saw him put out to sea on an equinoctial day in a boat he had dug up from the mud, put out to sea and disappear in the foaming tempest. When their brother did not return, they believed he had perished and sang the office for the dead.

(*Satisfied at his beginning,* LAQUEDEEM *gazes on the company. During the short silence, a rumble of thunder, still distant, is heard. All prick up their ears.*)

DOM PIKKEDONCKER: Your belly, Monsignor?

SIMON LAQUEDEEM: The bowels of the storm. The sky's grumbling pleases me, for what I am relating to you doesn't call for the song of the nightingale, I assure you, but the heart-rending cry of the sea gulls. How far had I gotten with this man?

KRAKENBUS: You had just sent him to the bottom, and the monks were singing the office for the dead. . . .

SIMON LAQUEDEEM: But it was written that the man whom the tempests and the cannibals did not want would come back to us some time, after a long, long while, on a day of calamity, a terrible day when the world and Flanders appeared to be doomed to end. . . . He came into view in a worm-eaten boat that the ocean shattered on the beach and whose sides let fall idols. The tides had submerged the ground inland, and it was by walking on the dykes, as if he were walking on the waters, that this man reached the town, this town decimated by the Plague. . . .

SODOMATI: In which chronicles are these horrors recorded?

SIMON LAQUEDEEM: In my memory. Indeed, I lived through those baleful days, and I too thought the world was going to end!

CARNIBOS: That will happen tonight.

SIMON LAQUEDEEM: Eat, Carnibos! At the time I am calling to mind, you would have done the same as the wretched inhabitants of this town, you would have devoured purple flesh from the graveyard, fighting with the rats and the dogs over it, and dying forthwith, to be devoured in your turn! . . . After the Plague, Famine and Madness took office in this town shrouded in opaque yellow mists, our town from which both the count and the bishop had fled, both the priests and the physicians, and where I, a young deacon, remained alone to comfort the dying and drag the blackened corpses to the fire. (*Pause.*) It was then that he appeared, suddenly looming out of the mists, bowed beneath a huge cross made from tarred planks. That was how he appeared! And the plague-stricken, filled with terror at this apparition, had only one word . . .

REAL-TREMBLOR: The Antichrist!

SIMON LAQUEDEEM: The Antichrist was the word that sprang from dying lips as this wild processionary passed by. He certainly had that appearance.

SODOMATI: Where was your crucifer going?

SIMON LAQUEDEEM: Straight to the market square, where a huge fire was crackling, in which corpses writhed in horrible attitudes. Was he going to walk in the flames, after having walked on the waters? The plague-stricken followed him, moaning pitifully from hope or fear. . . . And then what did he do? Threw the huge cross into the fire. A pillar of flame rose up, a glowing pillar, lifting the mists. . . . A marvel? Yes! The Plague was vanquished at once. The yellow mists broke up, the pure sky appeared, and the wind, the great blue wind, drove away the deadly miasmas. A marvel! I can still hear the crackling of the cross, the outcry of that raving crowd, above all the bells, the panic-stricken bells. . . . The survivors had rushed to the churches and had hung themselves in bunches to the ropes, and the bells began ringing, driving other bells crazy — and in the open country, the bells gave as good as they got, rolling the news around the four corners of the horizon, the astounding news of the end of the Scourge. . . .

SODOMATI: And the author of the marvel?

SIMON LAQUEDEEM: Priest John worked another miracle. Not content with having bound the Plague in chains, he ran the Famine to earth. This inspired, or simply astute, man had discovered the siege stores in the town vaults, casks of wine and beer, salt meats, dried fish, flour, all of which was thrown to the hungry. At night, the moribund were drunk and sang and danced as at fair time. At dawn, the women were pregnant. Life was carrying on. The town had a master, Priest John! The corpses buried, the streets cleaned, the craftsmen at work, life carried on. . . . (*Pause.*) And when, after some weeks, the count came back, the bishop, the clergy, the physicians, the notables, and all those who had fled the Plague, they ran up against the master of the town and didn't know what to do. The bishop and the clergy wanted to recover this palace from which they had fled, and ran up against Priest John — what am I saying? — against Bishop John, Bishop Jan in Eremo, sent by the tempest. . . .

SODOMATI: He was, certainly! He was!

SIMON LAQUEDEEM: He was! This priest in his madness had rigged himself out in the miter, had laid hold of the crook, the crook with which he dealt out blows like a hardened trooper to the old bishop and his runaway priests, uttering the most abominable abuse that clerical ears have ever heard. And Bishop John remained in the palace, a triumphant impostor protected against all justice by the vicious adoration of the butchers and the fullers, until the day that Rome, this Rome with designs more inscrutable than those of Providence, consecrated the imposture . . .

SODOMATI: The History is written, don't amend it!

SIMON LAQUEDEEM (*forcefully*): . . . consecrated the imposture!
. . . You know the rest.

SODOMATI: Not at all! I know the beginning, from your so striking
evocation, which must leave you tired. Tell me the end, how he
died. . . .

SIMON LAQUEDEEM: By God! Are you unaware of that, seeing that you
are writing the History? He died a godly death, that's all. . . .

KRAKENBUS: When does an ecclesiastic die otherwise, even if he gives
up the ghost calling on Beelzebub? . . .

SIMON LAQUEDEEM: He died a godly death, but in an unusual way;
and could it be otherwise? This man who had his life, had to have
his death. He had it! And the end was worthy of the beginning. . . .

SODOMATI: The end which he foretold, it seems?

SIMON LAQUEDEEM: Such premonitions are not rare. He foretold it,
exactly. . . .

SODOMATI: Weren't the physicians forbidden to come near him?

SIMON LAQUEDEEM: He refused their aid, thrust them aside, and
treated them as jackals. Since you are making investigations, learn
that his distrust was intense. His strength was obviously declining.
From day to day the skeleton's grin shaped itself in the mummified
flesh of his face.

SODOMATI: You describe with talent, but what disorder . . .

REAL-TREMBLOR: Hadn't he passed the seventy years mark? Long
ago. . . .

SIMON LAQUEDEEM: Since he loved the prophetic manner, he gave up
his stubborn silence to utter some phrases that can be considered
heavy with meaning, or as childish as the ramblings of comatose
old men usually are. What did he say that may be worth anything?

CARNIBOS (*raising a finger*): "The hour I am aware of is coming, fore-
stalling the one God appointed, and I accept it, since He allows it
to be forestalled. . . ." Explain that to me!

SODOMATI: That could be explained. . . . But what disorder?

SIMON LAQUEDEEM (*who pretends not to hear the question*): Yes, it
was a touching moment when I administered the last sacrament. Although overcome by a deep torpor, prefiguring the last sleep, Monsignor watched what we were doing with a half-open eye, the eye of
a scraggy old eagle. . . .

SODOMATI: Well?

SIMON LAQUEDEEM: This eye, laden with an unspeakable hatred,
missed nothing of my actions, followed my hands. And as I was
holding out the host, the eye shot a flash of steel at me, the lips
welded themselves together. But as I solemnly adjured him to receive the body and the blood of the living God, the eye grew dim
and the lips unsealed. He communicated.

(A *fairly long silence. Stillness. The rumbling of the storm is heard, greater than before.*)

SODOMATI: He communicated. . . .

SIMON LAQUEDEEM: Then? (*Speaking quickly, having become nervous.*) Suddenly erect, the dying man entered into a brief and harsh contest against invisible aggressors — angels or demons — of which we were the terrified witnesses. But the wrestler, seized around the waist and flung full length on his couch, fell broken. Death was winning! Then? The confirmation, the melted wax in the mouth, the red-hot iron on the feet — for we were still in doubt. . . . (*Pause.*) Do you know enough?

SODOMATI (*getting up*): No! I ask you a last time, what disorder. . . .

SIMON LAQUEDEEM (*bursting out*): How do I know? (*He seizes the secretary by the shoulders and speaks into his face.*) These questions! Have you an inquisitor's commission, little priest? There should have been previous notice. There is a right way of replying to such examinations. . . .

SODOMATI: Isn't it the current question I'm asking, just as all the town is asking it, all the diocese? (*He frees himself.*) Pardon the little priest. . . . He's a nasty noser, isn't he? You understand? He's amazed that his question upsets you to this extent. . . .

(SIMON LAQUEDEEM *indulges in gesticulation unaccompanied by any words. During this silence filled with gestures, a long flash of lightning makes a pale false daylight. The auxiliary finds his voice again and speaks violently.*)

SIMON LAQUEDEEM: On my conscience! I swear . . . I swear I had no part in the death of His Highness! . . . Thus I reply to the perfidious. And may a thunderbolt — if I am lying — fall in at once on our heads, may the thunder, if I am lying . . .

(*Another blinding flash of lightning. And a thunderbolt falls and strikes quite close. Everything makes a cracking sound. For a brief moment the room seems to be crackling in an outbreak of bluish fire as it is filled with a violent astral light that all at once goes out. The priests have risen at the shock and make defensive gestures. Outside, the crowd answers the thunderbolt by a tremendous outcry. A brief confusion reigns around the table. Voices are confused. Only* LAQUEDEEM *has not stirred. He dominates the uproar.*)

SIMON LAQUEDEEM: Sit down! What's the matter with you?

CARNIBOS: The thunder . . . fell on us . . . on the palace . . .

SIMON LAQUEDEEM (*roaring*): I heard nothing! (*Turning suddenly.*) What's happening to make your teeth chatter?

SODOMATI: What's happening? Why the thunder is talking, a voice from on high!

SIMON LAQUEDEEM (*roaring*): And what if I tell you that nothing is happening? (*The priests have drawn close to the auxiliary and stand around him.*) Frightened? Of what, my children? (*He does his utmost to laugh.*) A farce, a macabre farce! (*But the double door opens a little way, and one after the other the* SWISS *escape through the narrow gap. They seem incoherent and as though distracted. Without seeing anything, they make for the left. The auxiliary springs toward them and bars their exit.*) And you, vergers? Is the chamber on fire? Frightened as well? Frightened? (*The four utter inaudible words and, hustling the auxiliary, go out like madmen. The auxiliary runs to the double door.*) A farce, I say! Don't move! Frightened? Not me, ha, not me! Frightened of what?

(SIMON LAQUEDEEM *pushes the halves of the double door wide open, and the mortuary chamber is revealed, blazing with its thousand lights. Six toneless cries, the six cries of terror of the six priests, who are congregating at the left, ready to flee, and the ominous laugh of the auxiliary, rumbling above the bleatings. At the foot of the couch and turned toward the room stands* JAN EREMO, *crook in hand, made taller still by his high miter, a dark and heavy mass hieratically sculpted and as though vibrating in the light.*)

KRAKENBUS: Help! . . . An evil spell!

SODOMATI: Exorcize it!

SIMON LAQUEDEEM (*who retires backward from the chamber toward the priests*): A farce, a macabre farce! . . . Who has planted this dummy on its feet? Or what power is dwelling in this corpse? Answer, Eremo! Dead or alive. . . .

(*The bishop has stirred at his name, and takes a step forward like a block that is going to tumble down.*)

CARNIBOS: Alive!

SIMON LAQUEDEEM (*drawing farther back*): Not a genuine corpse! An impostor even in your death! What do you want? Prayers? Have you seen Hell? (*The priests are leaving. The auxiliary keeps on drawing back.*) Have you come back to disclose that you are damned? (*To the priests, who are in flight.*) Shut the doors! (*Addressing the bishop who comes forward very slowly and who has raised his right hand to his throat.*) What? Have you swallowed your tongue? What? Are toads going to shoot out of your mouth? Expect nothing from me, you automaton or ghost, nothing. . . . (*He goes out.*)

(*Noise of the door being bolted — noise of running around in the corridors, and calling. The hubbub dies away. And there is silence. A solemn silence which is aggravated by the growling of the crowd, like the rumbling of the ceaseless thunder, and on which is superimposed the deep pedal of the storm that seems vocal and growls in unison with the crowd.*

The bishop has clumsily come down the steps. With empty gaze, he comes forward in the room, his crook wielded spasmodically like a blind man's staff. At each lightning flash, his face shines like metal; the gold embroidery that covers him lights up. He bumps against the banquet table. At each lightning flash, the crystal glass and the silver plate flare up. The bishop has seized a knife with which he pokes in his mouth, flicking out the wax that was obstructing it. He spits out the pieces of wax, throws the knife down, takes hold of a goblet, and drinks with head flung back. He throws the goblet away and, like a gargoyle, spews out in a jet the wine he was trying to swallow. Then he becomes transformed. A permanent rattle, like the grating of a rusty pump, comes from his freed mouth, and nothing other than this rattle will come from it. He breathes in the air and seems to expand. He becomes animated; his empty gaze is filled with phosphorescent lights. The septuagenarian becomes a kind of jerkily moving athlete, the prey of a powerful oppression. Without respite, his right hand tries to loosen invisible bonds around his throat. From time to time he thrusts his hand in his mouth, as though he were trying to pull out some plug that was choking him. Unutterable torture! Is he an old man still in the death agony, who asks to die? Is he a deceased person come back again, thrust aside by Death, who asks to live once more? Now he is in action. His gaze has sought for exits. He walks to the right where the lightning leaps about — the balcony. He is heard shaking the windows — but the windows fly into pieces. Outside, the crowd is throwing stones and bellowing. The bishop retraces his steps and hugs the back wall. Painfully mute, he turns to the terrorized or hilarious idols, as though he were asking their help, and touches them pitiably, strokes them. Since the idols remain unchanging in their grimaces, their master turns away from them and begins to turn around on the spot where he is standing when, at the left, the bolts work and, the door opening, light marks the exit. The bishop immediately goes toward this light, while voices call him in the walls: "Monsignor! . . . Monsignor! . . ." Monsignor dashes forward and disappears. The room stays empty for a while. The noise of running around resounds in the walls. And the gang of priests rushes into the mortuary chamber from the back. The auxiliary runs nimbly around the couch, leaps the steps leading to the room, and, pursuing his course around the table, moves obliquely to the left and precipitately shuts the door through which the bishop went. Then he goes back to the center of the room where the others, breathless, have parked themselves. Only REAL-TREMBLOR *insists on locking the double door at the back, which he has closed behind him, and he returns brandishing the key.*)

REAL-TREMBLOR: He's in his cage, the evil one!

SIMON LAQUEDEEM: Locked up, eh? He won't come out of there except to the sepulcher! And if it's necessary that this dead man should die, he shall die! That's my business. You, keep cool and collected! Press your buttocks together, but do what you are told, otherwise there will be slaughter!

SODOMATI: The scandal! . . . We are lost!

SIMON LAQUEDEEM: You are, if I wish it. Pitch yourself into the water. I am staying on deck. Who will help me?

DUVELHOND: Ky — Kyrie . . .

SIMON LAQUEDEEM (*lays hold of* DUVELHOND *and pulls him away from the group*): I'll Kyrie you! Go down and fetch one of the arquebusiers of the guard. (DUVELHOND *goes out by the front left exit.*) You, Real, go and make sure the militia are still holding the approaches to the palace! And you, Carnibos, look for some lanterns! (*The archdeacon and the chaplain go out by the same exit.*) Let me know if the people's pot is still boiling. We must make haste, or we shall furnish the bones for the soup. . . .

SODOMATI: Not die . . . not like that. . . .

SIMON LAQUEDEEM: Flayed, grilled, like pigs! (*Fat laugh.*) The nuncio scented it. What a surprise, eh? Another marvel from down there! Write quickly to Rome. Can you smell the sulphur? I'm not troubled by it. . . .

(CARNIBOS *comes back carrying two lanterns which he hangs on the wall.*)

SIMON LAQUEDEEM: Light? That? then we are really in the abyss. Let the lightning illuminate my deeds. The worst has come to pass. . . .

(REAL-TREMBLOR *comes back.*)

SIMON LAQUEDEEM: What have you to say?

REAL-TREMBLOR: That the worst is to come, Monsignor. The rabble are surging forth under the lash of the storm. The militia are holding out with great difficulty. . . . But the butchers are mustering. With them, it will soon be all up. The rabble want their bishop!

SIMON LAQUEDEEM: We shall give him to them.

REAL-TREMBLOR: They will come and take him. The militia are still holding out, I said; but on the inside. And the rabble are piling up barrels of powder. We are going to be blown up. . . .

SIMON LAQUEDEEM: The ascension of the clergy. Splendid! (*Furious.*) Blow up! . . . For how are you helping me? Who is sacrificing himself?

KRAKENBUS: First, let us know is this ghost threatening us or beseeching us?

CARNIBOS: And then, his throat. . . . What does it mean?

SIMON LAQUEDEEM: The ghost is choking. The host, which he received in hate and not in love, is throttling him, this host which can neither come up again nor go down and burns the dying man whom Heaven and Hell fling back by reason of this unachieved communion. No, this living man is no longer alive, and this dead man is not so! He is suspended in Time as the host is in his body. Come, let a Christian, let a priest tear out the host — or thrust it in. . . .

SODOMATI: You are a priest and a Christian: do it!

SIMON LAQUEDEEM: He would cut through my wrist with a bite of his teeth! But you, with your woman's hands . . . (*To* REAL-TREMBLOR, *who is going toward the exit.*) Where are you going? To save your skin?

REAL-TREMBLOR (*going*): My idea. . . . Save you all!

SIMON LAQUEDEEM (*made furious by this flight*): Get out! Leave me alone. . . . Save yourselves, every one of you! . . . And your souls! . . . Get out! (*He hurls himself into the group of priests and drives them to the exit with blows from his fists.*) Up there . . . on the roof . . . and higher . . . a charge of powder in your backsides!

(*Short scuffle before the exit, through which the hustled priests are lost to sight. Alone, the auxiliary wipes his brow and comes back, listens to the crowd and the storm growling, then, catching sight of the idols, walks over to them.*)

SIMON LAQUEDEEM: And you, evil spirits, you, his faithful, are you going to help your master? Will you defend him in misfortune, you grotesque dolls? Will you escort him in the outer darkness? Have I got to struggle with you as well? You don't stir, in your immemorial ugliness? Don't expect anything more. Your master is caught in the trap. You are afraid of me? Rightly so! No living person would ever dare what I am daring. . . . (*He goes to the back and stops on the steps. Pause. Challenging.*) Eremo! (*After a pause.*) Jan Eremo! (*After a pause.*) Jan in Eremo, Bishop of Lapideopolis! (*Short pause.*) By the Archdemon who rules you . . . (*Short pause.*) Are you still wandering in this world? . . . (*A violent impact shakes the door, which makes a cracking sound and continues violently shaking for a moment. The auxiliary has taken a spring backward.*) I have my answer!

(*And* SIMON LAQUEDEEM *is making his way to the exit when* DUVELHOND *looms through it, preceding an* ARQUEBUSIER.)

DUVELHOND: The arque — que — buus — buus — buus. . . .

SIMON LAQUEDEEM: Booze? Wine for you, you villain! Set up your arquebus!

THE ARQUEBUSIER: Yes, Monsignor!

SIMON LAQUEDEEM: And hurl your grapeshot into this door, this great door. . . . (*The door is shaken again. The* ARQUEBUSIER *bustles about.*) You understand?

THE ARQUEBUSIER: No, Monsignor. . . .

SIMON LAQUEDEEM: Why?

THE ARQUEBUSIER: Is there a man behind it?

SIMON LAQUEDEEM: No.

THE ARQUEBUSIER: A beast?

SIMON LAQUEDEEM: Yes, a mad one! Go away! (*He snatches the weapon from the* ARQUEBUSIER, *who runs off. To* DUVELHOND.) And you, get out! (*He sets up the arquebus and turns its wheel lock.*)

DUVELHOND (*fleeing, his hands over his ears*): Jhesus!

SIMON LAQUEDEEM: Your Jhesus had better not be across my path. I'll . . . (*The shot fires, in a cloud of smoke. Some of door's boards are shattered. The face of* JOHN EREMO *appears, open-mouthed, in the hole, which is lit up. And the rattle resounds. The auxiliary rushes to the back, yelling.*) You, still? What do you want? Black sacraments? Gall for your thirst of the damned? I shall fill this dead mouth with lead! This mitered skull shall fly to pieces! (*He pushes the arquebus into the hole in the door. The bishop's face has disappeared, but the weapon is seized from the other side, and a struggle for possession of it begins. Panels smash; the hole grows bigger. Finally,* LAQUEDEEM *lets go of the weapon, which disappears inside. Taken aback, the auxiliary returns to the center of the room, puts his hands to his head, staggers. . . . A tremen-*

dous explosion shakes the palace and is followed by the applause and hurrahs of the crowd. LAQUEDEEM *has pulled himself together.*) Petards? Wait, my people. . . . You shall have your joint of meat. And you will commend the knacker! (*He rushes to the front left exit and disappears.*)

(*The room stands empty. But a hand, then an arm come through the hole in the door and seek the latch. Then a processional cross comes out, shaft first. This cross also feels about, digs itself under the cover molding and becomes a lever worked from inside. The double door groans under the pressure and takes the strain. The cross jerks more hurriedly and the cover molding splits away. The vanquished door gives completely. The bishop looms in the opening. He has neither crook nor miter, his gaze is mad, his neck is craned, and his hands are held forward ready for the attack. He comes down the steps and stops, as though amazed to be alone. A noise on the left. Alerted, the old man goes and stands close to the back wall, among the idols, where he remains stock-still, merged with the monstrosities. A second explosion shakes the palace and is answered by the storm, which is just now unleashed, and the crowd, crazy with lightning and gunpowder. At this juncture,* SIMON LAQUEDEEM, *carrying an ax, enters by the mortuary chamber. Having gone around the couch, he appears on the threshold of the room, ready for the attack.*)

SIMON LAQUEDEEM: Eremo! . . . (*He comes down.*) Eremo! . . . (*He goes about the room in every direction.*) Eremo! . . . (*Endlessly turning about.*) Eremo! . . . Eremo! . . . (*Having stopped, dumbfounded, in a childish voice.*) Jan! . . . (*Then, with tiny steps, he retreats toward the idols without suspecting the danger he is approaching, the bishop having held back his rattle. The auxiliary repeats a last time.*) Eremo! (*And roars.*) Murderer!

(*The idols tumble down.* LAQUEDEEM, *attacked by* EREMO, *lets his ax fall. Merciless standing struggle. The two of them rattle in their throats. The pair roll on the ground, then struggle kneeling, without letting go of each other. Hubbub and shouts in the corridors. Someone comes running. The door on the left is shaken. Voices hoot, "Monsignor! Monsignor!"* CARNIBOS *comes in through the exit, discovers the fight, shouts, "Murder," and disappears. The fight goes on, the pair struggling like stevedores. For a second they disentangle themselves, then, head down, they rush toward each other.* LAQUEDEEM *collapses under the impact but escapes on all fours.* EREMO *has picked up the ax. The door on the*

left has given, and the priests have come in. Flattened against the
walls, they stand paralyzed with terror at what they see. LAQUE-
DEEM, *who has half raised himself, bellows woefully. And the*
bishop, his rattle transformed into a kind of fiendish laugh,
comes toward him fiercely, brandishing the ax.

   But while the last stage of the fight has been going on, REAL-
TREMBLOR *has come back through the exit, violently dragging*
along VENERANDA, *the old servant. Pushing her by the shoulders,*
he catapults her into the middle of the drama. And all of a sud-
den, the drama stands still in space, just as the justiciary ax stands
still in the air. Silence has fallen in the same way the thunderbolt
fell — very fatefully. And in the silence, the emptiness rather, in
which nothing breathes — even the crowd and the storm holding
their peace — the old woman is seen hopping toward the bishop
and yelping in his face.)

VENERANDA: What are you doing? (*The bishop lowers his arm and the*
ax, which VENERANDA *snatches from him and lays down. Then.*)
Why have you come back from the dead? (*The bishop, who has*
lost his stiffness and some of his height, has bent humbly toward
the old woman, and he speaks. Nothing comes from his mouth, but
he speaks, like a dumb man swollen up with burning words. He
points to the back of his throat.) Kneel down! (*The bishop slips to*
his knees, his head thrown back. The servant thrusts her fingers into
his mouth, then takes them out.) Spit out what was tormenting
you! . . . (*The bishop has a spasm and spits out something, at*
which he gazes in amazement for a moment, on the floor. VENE-
RANDA *is already helping him to get up.*) Come along, John! . . .
(*The bishop is on his feet.*) Come and die! . . . (*And the bishop*
is no more than a tottering old man whom VENERANDA *pushes to the*
mortuary chamber. When he gets to the steps, a renewal of strength
draws the bishop up again, and he turns toward the priests and
LAQUEDEEM, *who is still on his knees as though felled. The old*
woman has anticipated this undertow of hatred and commands.)
Forgive them (*the bishop stiffens*) . . . if you want your forgiveness! . . . (*Shrunken and with his face suddenly changed, the*
bishop raises his right hand, with fist clenched, in a last pugnacious
gesture. The old woman insists, hissing.) Absolve them! . . .
(*And as the gesture persists, she slaps the bishop full in his face.*)
Your mother is ordering you to do it! . . . (*The fist opens at last,*
and becomes a hand. With his eyes closed, the bishop blesses the
bowed heads, very slowly, and as though reluctantly. His arm falls
again. And, turning his back on the assembly, supported by VENE-

RANDA, *he goes into the mortuary chamber. It seems that he hides his face before disappearing.* VENERANDA *is still heard speaking as she closes the double door again.*) Stretch yourself out, my child! And die amid your tears!

(*Silence hovers.* LAQUEDEEM *has gotten up and goes and stands calmly at the gap in the double door. He gazes on the interior. As though crushed by the blessing received, none of the priests moves, except that* SODOMATI *slips hypocritically to the place where the bishop knelt and picks up what he spat on the ground. He stands examining "it" in the hollow of his hand. The auxiliary has turned around and comes back.*)

SIMON LAQUEDEEM: The dead man is dead! (*Pause.*) Jan in Eremo, Bishop of Lapideopolis, is dead by his true and violent death, dead, twice dead, thoroughly dead! (*An immense flash of lightning, like a dawn — and there is no more thunder and lightning. The crowd has begun muttering again, but without anger, and sorrowfully. Knells comes from nearby towers.* LAQUEDEEM *has gone up to the nuncio's secretary and seizes him by the wrist.*) The host?

SODOMATI: Take it: you consecrated it. . . .

(*The other priests have begun to talk confusedly.* LAQUEDEEM *addresses them.*)

SIMON LAQUEDEEM: Who wants to take communion?

(REAL-TREMBLOR *indicates* VENERANDA, *who is slipping through the slightly open door and moving off to the left.*)

REAL-TREMBLOR: She does!

SIMON LAQUEDEEM (*who in three strides has seized the old servant, and grips her left arm*): You! Rejoin in eternity him to whom you gave birth. . . .

VENERANDA: *Och God!*

SIMON LAQUEDEEM (*who has pushed the host into the old woman's mouth. He murmurs the consecratory words, of which the only ones heard are:* — Corpus . . . custodat . . . (*And he releases* VENERANDA. *The servant takes one or two steps toward the exit, slides down the wall, and dies.*)

SODOMATI: Amen. This man will go a long way. . . .

SIMON LAQUEDEEM: To the grave, dearest! . . . Listen to that! The rabble are in the building! (*They listen. An uproar in the corridors. Shouting.*) The butchers! (*The priests fall back toward the right.* LAQUEDEEM, *in the center of the room, does not retreat.*) Rely on me, clericity!

•

(The uproar has stopped. A great blow on the door at the left. A red light floods the room. And a colossus, bald, torso bare, with sheathed cutlasses at his leather breeches, comes forward. Nine other giants enter in his wake, some of them carrying torches. They form a group on the left and wait. They are THE BUTCHERS *with their* MASTER, *who goes gravely toward the auxiliary.)*

THE MASTER OF THE BUTCHERS: *Waar ligt Jan-men-Kloote?*

*(*LAQUEDEEM *does not answer, pretending not to understand the language of the people, and looking* THE MASTER *firmly in the eye.* THE MASTER *appears to ponder, then unhurriedly lays hold of one end of the table, says, "Hop!" and turns it over, with all it bears. During the crash, several priests have cried out. Then,* THE MASTER *comes back to the auxiliary and unsheathes one of his cutlasses, passing it under his nose and repeating.)*

THE MASTER OF THE BUTCHERS: *Waar ligt Jan-men-Kloote?*

(This time, LAQUEDEEM *points his forefinger toward the mortuary chamber. At a signal from* THE MASTER, *four butchers separate from the rest and go into the chamber. The light of the candles floods the room. After a moment, the four return, carrying the couch on which lie the bishop's remains, dressed in priestly adornments. The four stop near* THE MASTER *with their burden. The auxiliary has begun to pray in a low voice.)*

SIMON LAQUEDEEM: *Chorus angelorum te suscipiat et eum Lazara quondam. . . .*

THE MASTER OF THE BUTCHERS *(interrupting him)*: *Bakkes toe!* *(And he gives another signal.)*

(The convoy goes out. THE BUTCHERS *follow the corpse, but moving backward, with their* MASTER, *who does not cease to watch the auxiliary, last.*

No one stirs when THE BUTCHERS *have gone. One guesses that the convoy is leaving the palace, for the crowd gives a final howl — of triumph — that is prolonged and becomes a kind of endless lamentation that will continue to get more distant. And the great bells, countless in number, will start ringing in the towers. Night has finally fallen. Alone in the middle of the room,* SIMON LAQUEDEEM *has put his hands on his stomach. He laughs derisively.)*

SIMON LAQUEDEEM: These obsequies. . . . Ho, ho! . . . You'll see! . . . When they invest the cathedral, they will quickly come seeking us! . . . Only the Church can bury. . . . (*Pause. Suddenly the auxiliary bends at the knees and staggers.*) Aah . . . aah!

REAL-TREMBLOR (*rushing to hold* LAQUEDEEM *up*): Monsignor! . . . Your bowels?

SIMON LAQUEDEEM (*pushing* REAL-TREMBLOR *away*): Damnation! . . . (*The priests have come forward and make a circle — the auxiliary writhes on the spot.*) Aah . . . aah! . . . (*A long shudder shakes him.*)

KRAKENBUS: Is he going to die?

SODOMATI: In that case, I believe in God!

(*But* LAQUEDEEM, *who had just lost his balance, draws himself up again to his full height.*)

SIMON LAQUEDEEM: Deliverance!

KRAKENBUS: Deliverance! The corpse is outside. . . .

CARNIBOS: The smell remains. Ugh! (*He holds his nose.*)

SIMON LAQUEDEEM: The odor of Death!

SODOMATI: Do you think so?

(CARNIBOS *disappears at the back.*)

SIMON LAQUEDEEM: True, it doesn't smell nice! . . . The odor of Death, I say! The dead stink.

REAL-TREMBLOR: The living too.

SIMON LAQUEDEEM: True, true . . . they stink! . . . (*He gives a fat laugh.*)

(CARNIBOS *comes back swinging a smoking censer.*)

SIMON LAQUEDEEM: Fine! Incense! . . . Some incense! . . . A lot of incense!

CARNIBOS (*swinging the censer majestically*): I'm censing!

SIMON LAQUEDEEM: Open the balcony! What d'you say, Pikkedoncker?

DOM PIKKEDONKER: Dung!

(*Laughter cascades. The priests sniff each other like dogs.*)

SIMON LAQUEDEEM: Dung? Who?

DOM PIKKEDONCKER: Not me! Him! . . . And you, Monsignor! . . . Dung!

(*Panic laughter breaks out, and this hilarity is accompanied by digs in the ribs and monkeylike gesticulations. Seized by frantic joy, the priests jump about comically in the clouds of incense, repeating all the time, "Dung! . . . Dung!"*)

SIMON LAQUEDEEM (*thundering*): The pigs! . . . They've filled their cassocks with dung!

(*He crouches — gown tucked up — his rabbinical face expressing demoniac bliss — while the curtain comes slowly down on these chronicles of Hell.*)

◖◗◣ IN A POETIC with beauty as norm few of Michel de Ghelderode's plays would rank high, and a more serene and more classically oriented age than ours might see in them only the idiosyncratic and ultimately abortive record of a luridly agitated vision. But in the shorter view which is the only one available to us the best of them cast a weird spell as original theatricals of sound and movement and spectacle on the old theme of man's sad and violent physicality among supernal riddles. A Catholic mystic who scorned psychology and great causes, a tireless stager of macabre medieval revels, a practising believer in a "theater of instinct" who paid small attention to close-knit verbal structures, he is not easily placed under any of the rubrics of modern drama. Yet his estrangement by circumstance and choice from any cultural community represents a plight we like to think of as peculiarly contemporary. "I wrote my plays in French," he said in an interview a few years before his death, ". . . although my blood for a thousand years has been Flemish. But I don't speak or write Flemish. My heart and mind are Flemish, but my tongue and my pen are French." Paris depressed him, he was incapable of doing creative work anywhere but in Flanders, almost all his plays have Flemish settings, and there is little evidence in them of the qualities of mind commonly thought of as characteristically French: reason, lucidity, restraint, elegance, *esprit*. He was a stranger to the twentieth century as well. He detested everything American, preferred a wooden pen and a nib to typewriter and ballpoints, and found nothing in the world's fair at Brussels — his native town — but "the necropolis of what is called the Intellect." "The present," he said, "is a fugitive which constantly escapes me. The past is more alive for me than this very day." Unchangeable, it yielded him "riches and peace." Thus, inarticulate in the language of his own culture, an alien to the culture whose language he used, aloofly self-exiled from his age, his creativity feeding on his tensions, Ghelderode seems to us an obvious exemplar of the modern artist. We discover an archetype in the ambiguities of a situation like his; his dilemma is our own. And because it is, the enduring nature of his achievement as a playwright remains to be assessed.

The past that was his refuge from the rationalism, the materialism, and the leveling of our times was Flanders of, roughly, the 16th century — half medieval, half Renaissance, at the same time sublimely spiritual and lustily violent, aristocratic and vulgar, refined and crude. He saw his nation's past not as a historian or a respectful antiquarian sees it; no one would think of calling any of his plays "histories." But no more are they anachronisms. Their characters never lived; their time is rarely more specific than the "bygone" of *Chronicles of Hell*. Rather, through the prism of temporal distance he sought in the Flanders of the late Middle Ages images that would serve his ideal: a "patrial" drama "that might be ancestral and traditionally of my home, while still being accessible to men of my time everywhere." His plays are of the kind in which the fantastic is symbolic and universal precisely because it lacks the particularity of the life-like. Hardly one of them has a single "character," in the sense in which people in Ibsen or Chekhov or Williams are three-dimensional, intimately known, psychologically complete and plausible. He escaped the urgent familiarities of the present the better to isolate eternal man. He saw him against the background of great, booming cathedral bells and the noise and filth of a medieval fair. And at least at moments, the grotesques that crowd this parochial Flemish world seem to move on a larger stage, an expansive allegorical setting for human life bounded by divinity and dirt. There is nothing ethereal about Ghelderode's otherworldliness.

He is not an intellectual playwright, and a purely verbal approach to his plays is unrewarding. His imagination is pictorial when it is not auditory; he repeatedly spoke of the strange, visionary canvases of Hieronymus Bosch and of the myriad, Rabelaisian realism of the villages, fields, and hells of the two Brueghels as inspirations for his own dramatic pageantry. He had no use for the useful drama of the post-Ibsenites — realistic, argumentative, socially concerned. Brecht, he felt, wasted his "theatrical genius" on "banal ideas." His affinities were for the Elizabethan dramatists with their sense for overstatement and the superhuman, their gusto in suffering and joy, thought and feeling, not yet dissociated, for Maeterlinck's "mysterious and supernatural" drama, for the expressionistic Strindberg. Unlike though they are in many respects, he and Yeats share a belief in a theater of poetry and passion. Art, he said, is a "quest for man," the theater a "trap" in which "this mysterious being" may be caught. He was not a sophisticated theorist or critic of drama, but he consistently and passionately defended the proposition that art transcends reality, that the artist's vision has primacy over his ideas. "The theatre," he wrote in a letter in 1957, "is lost the moment it speechifies, discusses, analyzes, preaches. It is out of danger when it dreams, digresses, laughs, cries, tells startling stupidities, and commits a thousand follies and atrocities, passing from the ecstatic to the horrible — according to Shakespeare's formula, . . . which is in some measure my own." "Art cannot be subjugated to any system of ideas." "The aim of the theatre — and of mine in particular — is not to comfort, no more is it to grieve. The theatre is a fact. . . . Morals have nothing to do with the matter." The playwright is a "dreamer" who "must live by vision and divination only." His plays bear out his theory, though Ghelderode under attack did not himself always see it so. When *Chronicles of Hell* (1929) was performed in Paris in 1949 it scandalized some people because of its "blasphemous" treatment of the Sacred Host and the "anti-Catholicism" of its depiction of the priests. Later, Ghelderode defended the orthodoxy of his play against its critics by describing its action as a conflict between "an authentic Christian . . . in a state of grace" and "shammers, fake believers, anti-Christians, . . . *so-called* priests" and claimed for it a "high moral tone." Perhaps so. But the exegesis is curiously reductive. The dead or dying bishop Jan in Eremo is not obviously in a state of grace, and his antagonist, Simon Laquedeem, whatever else he may be, is not obviously a hypocrite. Sacrilegious satire or a homily on good and evil clerics are equally inadequate labels for this miracle play about mortality and redemption in the form of an obscene pantomime of gargoyles. A more relevant retort to the charge of blasphemy is to say that to attribute a thesis to the play is to miss its point. This does not quite amount to saying that Ghelderode is an absurdist in the manner of Beckett or Genet. His imagination takes other forms than theirs, his tone is rarely either angry or sardonic, and his apparent irreverence seems like a symptom of a desperate but fervid faith in a transcendental absolute, either Christian or Satanic. His evocations of the past are varieties of a quest for insinuating images of disquietude that is not the exclusive privilege of absurdist literature. Ghelderode's play, in fact, can serve as an occasion for reminding ourselves that there are more things in modern drama than are dreamed of in an absurdist imagination.

Ghelderode subtitled *Chronicles of Hell, une tragédie bouffe,* a comic tragedy, and in the interviews he recorded for radio in Ostend in 1951 he called it an "oral symphony," "a kind of dramatic poem of epic inspiration." One may question the possibility of having tragedy, even comic tragedy, without a tragic hero or with a hero who is a dubious ghost, but a paradoxical dramatic genre, a musical term, and an epithet that comprises all the three conventional literary kinds, are useful labels for a play that relies heavily (like all of Ghelderode's plays) on non-verbal effects, that has a plot both slight and obscure, and that is theologically vague and inconclusive. It is spectacle rather than discourse; its movement is imagistic rather than dialectical. Perhaps "from funeral to carnival" best describes it. The scene throughout presents a visual contrast of ironic implications between the gloomy banqueting hall in the foreground with its "sumptuously laden" table and its walls lined with demonic shapes and the brilliantly illuminated funeral chamber in the rear where the bishop, a victim of ingestion, lies in state.

The opening movement of the play, the febrile, scurrilous dialogue among the priests who gather one by one for the vigil, never attains intellectual substance or coherence and certainly no ceremonial dignity. The second phase of the action is narrative. Simon Laquedeem, the auxiliary bishop, relates the miraculous career of Jan in Eremo, whose final obsequies he and the other priests are awaiting. But the saint's chronicle is compromised by the nature of the chronicler, who is perhaps responsible for the bishop's "disorder." The miracle that saved the plague-stricken town was the work of an "accursed being," an "anti-Christ" said to be begotten by a monk on a mermaid. True and false religion are uncertain and ambivalent values; never explicit, the play reaches the "equilibrium" that Ghelderode claimed for it in the Ostend interviews. The final movement is largely pantomimic and itself tripartite. In a hideous *danse macabre* the auxiliary seeks to exorcise the spectral bishop, a monstrous and murderous *revenant*, the sinister master of an assortment of idols and witches' masks. Next comes the regurgitation scene, a kind of anti-communion, directed by the wizened old servant Veneranda, whose name, suggestively, means "venerable woman," and who leads her "son," now a feeble old man, out to die after forcing him to bless his enemies. This mock-pietà concludes with the arrival of a band of butchers, come to carry the corpse off for funeral. The curtain scene, finally, reeks with excremental stench and is loud with the ribald laughter of grimacing priest-fiends performing their gross antics in some Dantesque inferno. By now the image of man as a creature producing dung has become so pervasive that the thunder that punctuates the action echoes with the rumblings in the troubled bowels of some indelicately corporeal deity.

The inseparability of the sacred and the scatological allusions and imagery fulfils Ghelderode's own demand for a drama that simultaneously evokes ecstasy and horror. The bishop chokes on the Host as Carnibos chokes on meat in the opening scene. The expulsion of the obstructing Host is grotesquely parodied in the final loosening of the auxiliary's constipated bowels. Both physical reliefs lead to "bliss." It has been suggested that the seven priests represent the seven deadly sins, but although the number fits (if Sodomati, the secretary of the Papal nuncius, is counted one of the seven) and though Carnibos both by name and act is obviously a glutton and Laquedeem perhaps embodies pride, it is difficult to discern specific personifications in the other five. It may be more to the point to note that the priests serve both as the bishop's collective antagonist and as a chorus reacting to and commenting upon the strange events attending his lying in state, that they belong to a vast hierarchy in which no two clerics appear to have the same title or rank or perform the same — or, indeed, any — ecclesiastical function, and that four of these presumed servants of spirituality suffer from physical defects: Krakenbus has a hump, Pikke-doncker is deaf, Duvelhond ("devil hand"?) stutters, and Real-Trem-blor is at least *said* to be a castrate.

Does all this amount to a diabolic travesty of sacred moments en-acted in Lapideopolis, "the city of the stone god," where angry, snarl-ing mobs under a tempestuous sky are precariously controlled by a totally corrupt and fallen theocracy? Should we follow Ghelderode him-self, vindicating his Catholic piety, in distinguishing between the "good, true" Christian in Jan in Eremo and his "evil, false" antago-nists, led by Simon Laquedeem, and seek to resolve the apparent am-bivalence of the former by saying that if the locale of the action is Hell it is perfectly logical — and theologically impeccable — that the Savior figure appears as a usurping enemy harrowing Hell and his antagonist as the triumphant restorer of an older, darker, chaotic or-der? Is the play demonic or sacramental or somehow both at the same time? Or do we have a feeling that to search for a consistent, unilinear, unequivocal, and specific allegorical meaning may not be the safest line of interpretation — or even that "interpretation" itself may not be the most rewarding approach? The optative "that the bishop may die" defines the theme of the play, but whose is the wish? Whose is it not? Is Jan in Eremo saint or impostor, his death miracle or murder, his enemy purger or devil, the conclusion redemption or damnation? The shifting ambiguities resist the imposition of any orthodoxy. The hellish vision of decayed religiosity remains, immediate and disturbing.)✧

Bertolt Brecht

THE CAUCASIAN
CHALK CIRCLE

Adapted by Eric Bentley

Characters

OLD MAN, *on the right*
PEASANT WOMAN, *on the right*
YOUNG PEASANT
A VERY YOUNG WORKER
OLD MAN, *on the left*
PEASANT WOMAN, *on the left*
AGRICULTURIST KATO
GIRL TRACTORIST
WOUNDED SOLDIER
THE DELEGATE, *from the capital*
THE SINGER
GEORGI ABASHWILI, *the Governor*
NATELLA, *the Governor's wife*
MICHAEL, *their son*
SHALVA, *an Adjutant*
ARSEN KAZBEKI, *a fat prince*

This adaptation, commissioned and approved by Bertolt Brecht, is based on the German MS of 1946. A German version very close to this MS was published in a supplement to *Sinn und Form*, 1949. My English text has now appeared in three versions. Maja Apelman collaborated on the first one (copyrighted 1947, 1948). The second and third were respectively copyrighted in 1961 and 1963.

— E.B., New York, 1963

443

MESSENGER, *from the Capital*
NIKO MIKADZE *and*
  MIKA LOLADZE, *Doctors*
SIMON SHASHAVA, *a soldier*
GRUSHA VASHNADZE, *a kitchen maid*
OLD PEASANT, *with the milk*
CORPORAL *and* PRIVATE
LAVRENTI VASHNADZE, *Grusha's brother*
ANIKO, *his wife*
PEASANT *and his wife*
PEASANT WOMAN, *for a while Grusha's mother-in-law*
JUSSUP, *her son*
MONK
AZDAK, *village scrivener*
SHAUWA, *a policeman*
GRAND DUKE
DOCTOR
INVALID
LIMPING MAN
BLACKMAILER
LUDOVICA
INNKEEPER, *her father-in-law*
STABLEBOY
POOR OLD PEASANT WOMAN
IRAKLI, *her brother-in-law, a bandit*
THREE WEALTHY FARMERS
ILLO SHUBOLADZE *and*
  SANDRO OBOLADZE, *lawyers*
OLD MARRIED COUPLE

SOLDIERS, SERVANTS, PEASANTS, BEGGARS, MUSICIANS, MERCHANTS, NOBLES, ARCHITECTS

PROLOGUE

(*Among the ruins of a war-ravaged Caucasian village the members of two Kolkhoz villages, mostly women and older men, are sitting in a circle, smoking and drinking wine. With them is a* DELEGATE *of the state Reconstruction Commission from Nuka, the capital.*)

PEASANT WOMAN (*left, pointing*): In those hills over there we stopped three Nazi tanks, but the apple orchard was already destroyed.

OLD MAN (*right*): Our beautiful dairy farm: a ruin.

GIRL TRACTORIST: I laid the fire, Comrade.

(*Pause.*)

DELEGATE: Now listen to the report. Delegates from the goat-breeding Kolkhoz "Rosa Luxemburg" have been to Nuka. When Hitler's armies approached, the Kolkhoz had moved its goat-herds further east on orders from the authorities. They are now thinking of returning. Their delegates have investigated the village and the land and found a lot of it destroyed.

(DELEGATES *on right nod.*)

The neighboring fruit-culture Kolkhoz (*to the left*) "Galinsk" is proposing to use the former grazing land of Kolkhoz "Rosa Luxemburg," a valley in which grass doesn't grow very well, for orchards and vineyards. As a delegate of the Reconstruction Commission, I request that the two Kolkhoz villages decide between themselves whether Kolkhoz "Rosa Luxemburg" shall return here or not.

OLD MAN (*right*): First of all, I want to protest against the time limit on discussion. We of Kolkhoz "Rosa Luxemburg" have spent three days and three nights getting here. And now discussion is limited to half a day.

WOUNDED SOLDIER (*left*): Comrade, we haven't as many villages as we used to have. We haven't as many hands. We haven't as much time.

GIRL TRACTORIST: All pleasures have to be rationed. Tobacco is rationed, and wine. Discussion should be rationed.

OLD MAN (*right, sighing*): Death to the fascists! But I will come to the point and explain why we want our valley back. There are a great many reasons, but I'll begin with one of the simplest. Makina Abakidze, unpack the goat cheese.

(A PEASANT WOMAN *from right takes from a basket an enormous cheese wrapped in a cloth. Applause and laughter.*)

Help yourselves, Comrades, start in!

OLD MAN (*left, suspiciously*): Is this a way of influencing us?

OLD MAN (*right, amid laughter*): How could it be a way of influencing you, Surab, you valley-thief? Everyone knows you will take the cheese and the valley, too. (*Laughter.*) All I expect from you is an honest answer. Do you like the cheese?

OLD MAN (*left*): The answer is: yes.

OLD MAN (*right*): Really. (*Bitterly.*) I ought to have known you know nothing about cheese.

OLD MAN (*left*): Why not? When I tell you I like it?

OLD MAN (*right*): Because you can't like it. Because it's not what it was in the old days. And why not? Because our goats don't like the new grass as they did the old. Cheese is not cheese because grass is not grass, that's the thing. Please put that in your report.

OLD MAN (*left*): But your cheese is excellent.

OLD MAN (*right*): Is isn't excellent. It's just passable. The new grazing land is no good, whatever the young people may say. One can't live there. It doesn't even smell of morning in the morning.

(*Several people laugh.*)

DELEGATE: Don't mind their laughing: they understand you. Comrades, why does one love one's country? Because the bread tastes better there, the air smells better, voices sound stronger, the sky is higher, the ground is easier to walk on. Isn't that so?

OLD MAN (*right*): The valley has belonged to us from all eternity.

SOLDIER (*left*): What does *that* mean — from all eternity? Nothing belongs to anyone from all eternity. When you were young you didn't even belong to yourself. You belonged to the Kazbeki princes.

OLD MAN (*right*): Doesn't it make a difference, though, what kind of trees stand next to the house you are born in? Or what kind of neighbors you have? Doesn't that make a difference? We want to go back just to have you as our neighbors, valley-thieves! Now you can all laugh again.

OLD MAN (*left, laughing*): Then why don't you listen to what your neighbor, Kato Wachtang, our agriculturist, has to say about the valley?

PEASANT WOMAN (*right*): We've not said all there is to be said about our valley. By no means. Not all the houses are destroyed. As for the dairy farm, at least the foundation wall is still standing.

DELEGATE: You can claim State support — here and there — you know that. I have suggestions here in my pocket.

PEASANT WOMAN (*right*): Comrade Specialist, we haven't come here to bargain. I can't take your cap and hand you another, and say "This one's better." The other one might *be* better; but you *like* yours better.

GIRL TRACTORIST: A piece of land is not a cap — not in our country, Comrade.

DELEGATE: Don't get mad. It's true we have to consider a piece of land as a tool to produce something useful, but it's also true that we must recognize love for a particular piece of land. As far as I'm concerned, I'd like to find out more exactly what you (*to those on the left*) want to do with the valley.

OTHERS: Yes, let Kato speak.

DELEGATE: Comrade Agriculturist!

KATO (*rising, she's in military uniform*): Comrades, last winter, while we were fighting in these hills here as Partisans, we discussed how, once the Germans were expelled, we could build up our fruit culture to ten times its original size. I've prepared a plan for an irrigation project. By means of a cofferdam on our mountain lake, 300 hectares of unfertile land can be irrigated. Our Kolkhoz could not only cultivate more fruit, but also have vineyards. The project, however, would pay only if the disputed valley of Kolkhoz "Galinsk" were also included. Here are the calculations. (*She hands the* DELEGATE *a briefcase.*)

OLD MAN (*right*): Write into a report that our Kolkhoz plans to start a new stud farm.

GIRL TRACTORIST: Comrades, the project was conceived during days and nights when we had to take cover in the mountains. We were often without ammunition for our half-dozen rifles. Even finding a pencil was difficult.

(*Applause from both sides.*)

OLD MAN (*right*): Our thanks to the Comrades of Kolkhoz "Galinsk" and all those who've defended our country!

(*They shake hands and embrace.*)

PEASANT WOMAN (*left*): In doing this our thought was that our soldiers — both your men and our men — should return to a still more productive homeland.

GIRL TRACTORIST: As the poet Mayakovsky said: "The home of the Soviet people shall also be the home of Reason!"

(*The* DELEGATES *including the* OLD MAN *have got up, and with the* DELEGATE *specified proceed to study the Agriculturist's drawings . . . exclamations such as:* "Why is the altitude of all 22 meters?" — "This rock must be blown up" — "Actually, all they need is cement and dynamite" — "They force the water to come down here, that's clever!")

A VERY YOUNG WORKER (*right, to* OLD MAN, *right*): They're going to irrigate all the fields between the hills, look at that, Aleko!

OLD MAN (*right*): I'm not going to look. I knew the project would be good. I won't have a pistol pointed at me.

DELEGATE: But they only want to point a pencil at you!

(*Laughter.*)

OLD MAN (*right, gets up gloomily, and walks over to look at the drawings*): These valley-thieves know only too well that we in this country are suckers for machines and projects.

PEASANT WOMAN (*right*): Aleko Bereshwili, you have a weakness for new projects. That's well known.

DELEGATE: What about my report? May I write that you will all support the cession of your old valley in the interests of this project when you get back to your Kolkhoz?

PEASANT WOMAN (*right*): I will. What about you, Aleko?

OLD MAN (*right, bent over drawings*): I suggest that you give us copies of the drawings to take along.

PEASANT WOMAN (*right*): Then we can sit down and eat. Once he has the drawings and he's ready to discuss them, the matter is settled. I know him. And it will be the same with the rest of us.

(DELEGATES *laughingly embrace again.*)

OLD MAN (*left*): Long live the Kolkhoz "Rosa Luxemburg" and much luck to your horse-breeding project!

PEASANT WOMAN (*left*): In honor of the visit of the delegates from Kolkhoz "Rosa Luxemburg" and of the Specialist, the plan is that we all hear a presentation of the Singer Arkadi Tscheidse.

(*Applause.* GIRL TRACTORIST *has gone off to bring the* SINGER.)

PEASANT WOMAN (*right*): Comrades, your entertainment had better be good. It's going to cost us a valley.

PEASANT WOMAN (*left*): Arkadi Tscheidse knows about our discussion. He's promised to perform something that has a bearing on the problem.

KATO: We wired to Tiflis three times. The whole thing nearly fell through at the last minute because his driver had a cold.

PEASANT WOMAN (*left*): Arkadi Tscheidse knows 21,000 lines of verse.

OLD MAN (*left*): He's hard to get. You and the Planning Commission should persuade him to come North more often, Comrade.

DELEGATE: We are more interested in economics, I'm afraid.

OLD MAN (*left, smiling*): You arrange the redistribution of vines and tractors, why not of songs?

(*Enter the* SINGER *Arkadi Tscheidse, led by* GIRL TRACTORIST. *He is a well-built man of simple manners, accompanied by four* MUSICIANS *with their instruments. The* ARTISTS *are greeted with applause.*)

GIRL TRACTORIST: This is the Comrade Specialist, Arkadi.

(*The* SINGER *greets them all.*)

DELEGATE: I'm honored to make your acquaintance. I heard about your songs when I was a boy at school. Will it be one of the old legends?

THE SINGER: A very old one. It's called The Chalk Circle and comes from the Chinese. But we'll do it, of course, in a changed version. Comrades, it's an honor for me to entertain you after a difficult debate. We hope you will find that the voice of the old poet also sounds well in the shadow of Soviet tractors. It may be a mistake to mix different wines, but old and new wisdom mix admirably. Now I hope we'll get something to eat before the performance begins — it would certainly help.

VOICES: Surely. Everyone into the Club House!

(*While everyone begins to move, the* DELEGATE *turns to the* GIRL TRACTORIST.)

DELEGATE: I hope it won't take long. I've got to get back tonight.

GIRL TRACTORIST: How long will it last, Arkadi? The Comrade Specialist must get back to Tiflis tonight.

THE SINGER (*casually*): It's actually two stories. An hour or two.

GIRL TRACTORIST (*confidentially*): Couldn't you make it shorter?

THE SINGER: No.

VOICE: Arkadi Tscheidse's performance will take place here in the square after the meal.

(*And they all go happily to eat.*)

1. The Noble Child

(*As the lights go up, the* SINGER *is seen sitting on the floor, a black sheepskin cloak round his shoulders, and a little well-thumbed notebook in his hand. A small group of listeners — the chorus — sits with him. The manner of his recitation makes it clear that he has told his story over and over again. He mechanically fingers the pages, seldom looking at them. With appropriate gestures, he gives the signal for each scene to begin.*)

THE SINGER: In olden times, in a bloody time,
There ruled in a Caucasian city —
Men called it City of the Damned —
A governor.
His name was Georgi Abashwili.
He was rich as Croesus
He had a beautiful wife

He had a healthy baby.
No other governor in Grusinia
Had so many horses in his stable
So many beggars in his doorstep
So many soldiers in his service
So many petitioners in his courtyard.
Georgi Abashwili — how shall I describe him to you?
He enjoyed his life.
On the morning of Easter Sunday
The governor and his family went to church.

(*At the left a large doorway, at the right an even larger gateway.* BEGGARS *and* PETITIONERS *pour from the gateway, holding up thin children, crutches, and petitions. They are followed by* IRONSHIRTS, *and then, expensively dressed, the* GOVERNOR'S FAMILY.)

BEGGARS AND PETITIONERS: Mercy! Mercy, Your Grace! The taxes are too high.
— I lost my leg in the Persian War, where can I get . . .
— My brother is innocent, Your Grace, a misunderstanding . . .
— The child is starving in my arms!
— Our petition is for our son's discharge from the army, our last remaining son!
— Please, Your Grace, the water inspector takes bribes.

(*One* SERVANT *collects the petitions, another distributes coins from a purse.* SOLDIERS *push the* CROWD *back, lashing at them with thick leather whips.*)

THE SOLDIER: Get back! Clear the church door!

(*Behind the* GOVERNOR, *his* WIFE, *and the* ADJUTANT, *the* GOVERNOR'S CHILD *is brought through the gateway in an ornate carriage.*)

THE CROWD:
— The baby!
— I can't see it, don't shove so hard!
— God bless the child, Your Grace!
THE SINGER (*while the* CROWD *is driven back with whips*): For the first time on that Easter Sunday, the people saw the Governor's heir.

Two doctors never moved from the noble child, apple of the Governor's eye.

Even the mighty Prince Kazbeki bows before him at the church door.

(A FAT PRINCE *steps forward and greets the family*.)

THE FAT PRINCE: Happy Easter, Natella Abashwili! What a day! When it was raining last night, I thought to myself, gloomy holidays! But this morning the sky was gay. I love a gay sky, a simple heart, Natella Abashwili. And little Michael is a governor from head to foot! Tititi! (*He tickles the child*.)

THE GOVERNOR'S WIFE: What do you think, Arsen, at last Georgi has decided to start building the east wing. All those wretched slums are to be torn down to make room for the garden.

THE FAT PRINCE: Good news after so much bad! What's the latest on the war, Brother Georgi?

(*The* GOVERNOR *indicates a lack of interest*.)

THE FAT PRINCE: Strategical retreat, I hear. Well, minor reverses are to be expected. Sometimes things go well, sometimes not. Such is war. Doesn't mean a thing, does it?

THE GOVERNOR'S WIFE: He's coughing. Georgi, did you hear?

(*She speaks sharply to the* DOCTORS, *two dignified men standing close to the little carriage*.)

He's coughing!

THE FIRST DOCTOR (*to the* SECOND): May I remind you, Niko Mikadze, that I was against the lukewarm bath? (*To the* GOVERNOR'S WIFE.) There's been a little error over warming the bath water, Your Grace.

THE SECOND DOCTOR (*equally polite*): Mika Loladze, I'm afraid I can't agree with you. The temperature of the bath water was exactly what our great, beloved Mishiko Oboladze prescribed. More likely a slight draft during the night, Your Grace.

THE GOVERNOR'S WIFE: But do pay more attention to him. He looks feverish, Georgi.

THE FIRST DOCTOR (*bending over the child*): No cause for alarm, Your Grace. The bath water will be warmer. It won't occur again.

THE SECOND DOCTOR (*with a venomous glance at the* FIRST): I won't forget that, my dear Mika Loladze. No cause for concern, Your Grace.

THE FAT PRINCE: Well, well, well! I always say: "A pain in my liver? Then the doctor gets fifty strokes on the soles of his feet." We live in a decadent age. In the old days one said: "Off with his head!"

THE GOVERNOR'S WIFE: Let's go into church. Very likely it's the draft here.

(*The procession of* FAMILY *and* SERVANTS *turn into the doorway. The* FAT PRINCE *follows, but the* GOVERNOR *is kept back by the* ADJUTANT, *a handsome young man. When the crowd of* PETITIONERS *has been driven off, a young dust-stained* RIDER, *his arm in a sling, remains behind.*)

THE ADJUTANT (*pointing at the* RIDER, *who steps forward*): Won't you hear the messenger from the capital, Your Excellency? He arrived this morning. With confidential papers.

THE GOVERNOR: Not before Service, Shalva. But did you hear Brother Kazbeki wish me a happy Easter? Which is all very well, but I don't believe it did rain last night.

THE ADJUTANT (*nodding*): We must investigate.

THE GOVERNOR: Yes, at once. Tomorrow.

(*They pass through the doorway. The* RIDER, *who has waited in vain for an audience, turns sharply round and, muttering a curse, goes off. Only one of the palace guards —* SIMON SHASHAVA — *remains at the door.*)

THE SINGER:
The city is still.
Pigeons strut in the church square.
A soldier of the Palace Guard
Is joking with a kitchen maid
As she comes up from the river with a bundle.

(*A girl —* GRUSHA VASHNADZE — *comes through the gateway with a bundle made of large green leaves under her arm.*)

SIMON: What, the young lady is not in church? Shirking?

GRUSHA: I was dressed to go. But they needed another goose for the banquet. And they asked me to get it. I know about geese.

SIMON: A goose? (*He feigns suspicion.*) I'd like to see that goose. (GRUSHA *does not understand.*) One has to be on one's guard with women. "I only went for a fish," they tell you, but it turns out to be something else.

GRUSHA (*walking resolutely toward him and showing him the goose*): There! If it isn't a fifteen-pound goose stuffed full of corn, I'll eat the feathers.

SIMON: A queen of a goose! The Governor himself will eat it. So the young lady has been down to the river again?

GRUSHA: Yes, at the poultry farm.

SIMON: Really? At the poultry farm, down by the river . . . not higher up maybe? Near those willows?

GRUSHA: I only go to the willows to wash the linen.

SIMON (*insinuatingly*): Exactly.

GRUSHA: Exactly what?

SIMON (*winking*): Exactly that.

GRUSHA: Why shouldn't I wash the linen by the willows?

SIMON (*with exaggerated laughter*): "Why shouldn't I wash the linen by the willows!" That's good, really good!

GRUSHA: I don't understand the soldier. What's so good about it?

SIMON (*slyly*): "If something I know someone learns, she'll grow hot and cold by turns!"

GRUSHA: I don't know what I could learn about those willows.

SIMON: Not even if there was a bush opposite? That one could see everything from? Everything that goes on there when a certain person is — "washing linen"?

GRUSHA: What does go on? Won't the soldier say what he means and have done?

SIMON: Something goes on. And something can be seen.

GRUSHA: Could the soldier mean I dip my toes in the water when it is hot? There is nothing else.

SIMON: More. Your toes. And more.

GRUSHA: More what? At most my foot?

SIMON: Your foot. And a little more. (*He laughs heartily.*)

GRUSHA (*angrily*): Simon Shashava, you ought to be ashamed of yourself! To sit in a bush on a hot day and wait till a girl comes and dips her leg in the river! And I bet you bring a friend along too! (*She runs off.*)

SIMON (*shouting after her*): I didn't bring any friend along!

(*As the* SINGER *resumes his tale, the* SOLDIER *steps into the doorway as though to listen to the service.*)

THE SINGER: The city lies still
  But why are there armed men?
  The Governor's palace is at peace
  But why is it a fortress?
  And the Governor returned to his palace
  And the fortress was a trap
  And the goose was plucked and roasted
  But the goose was not eaten this time
  And noon was no longer the hour to eat:
  Noon was the hour to die.

(*From the doorway at the left the* FAT PRINCE *quickly appears, stands still, looks around. Before the gateway at the right two* IRONSHIRTS *are squatting and playing dice. The* FAT PRINCE *sees them, walks slowly past, making a sign to them. They rise: one goes through the gateway, the other goes off at the right. Muffled voices are heard from various directions in the rear: "To your posts!" The palace is surrounded. The* FAT PRINCE *quickly goes off. Church bells in the distance. Enter, through the doorway, the* GOVERNOR'S FAMILY *and* PROCESSION, *returning from church.*)

THE GOVERNOR'S WIFE (*passing the* ADJUTANT): It's impossible to live in such a slum. But Georgi, of course, will only build for his little Michael. Never for me! Michael is all! All for Michael!

(*The* PROCESSION *turns into the gateway. Again the* ADJUTANT *lingers behind. He waits. Enter the* WOUNDED RIDER *from the doorway. Two* IRONSHIRTS *of the palace guard have taken up positions by the gateway.*)

THE ADJUTANT (*to the* RIDER): The Governor does not wish to receive military news before dinner — especially if it's depressing, as I assume. In the afternoon His Excellency will confer with prominent architects. They're coming to dinner too. And here they are!

(*Enter* THREE GENTLEMEN *through the doorway.*)

Go to the kitchen and eat, my friend.

(*As the* RIDER *goes, the* ADJUTANT *greets the* ARCHITECTS.)

Gentlemen, His Excellency expects you at dinner. He will devote all his time to you and your great new plans. Come!

ONE OF THE ARCHITECTS: We marvel that His Excellency intends to build. There are disquieting rumors that the war in Persia has taken a turn for the worse.

THE ADJUTANT: All the more reason to build! There's nothing to those rumors anyway. Persia is a long way off, and the garrison here would let itself be hacked to bits for its Governor.

(*Noise from the palace. The shrill scream of a woman. Someone is shouting orders. Dumbfounded, the* ADJUTANT *moves toward the gateway. An* IRONSHIRT *steps out, points his lance at him.*)

What's this? Put down that lance, you dog.

ONE OF THE ARCHITECTS: It's the Princes! Don't you know the Princes met last night in the capital? And they're against the Grand Duke and his Governors? Gentlemen, we'd better make ourselves scarce.

(*They rush off. The* ADJUTANT *remains helplessly behind.*)

THE ADJUTANT (*furiously to the* PALACE GUARD): Down with those lances! Don't you see the Governor's life is threatened?

(*The* IRONSHIRTS *of the Palace Guard refuse to obey. They stare coldly and indifferently at the* ADJUTANT *and follow the next events without interest.*)

THE SINGER: O blindness of the great!
They go their way like gods,
Great over bent backs,
Sure of hired fists,
Trusting in the power
Which has lasted so long.
But long is not forever.
O change from age to age!
Thou hope of the people!

(*Enter the* GOVERNOR, *through the gateway, between two* SOL-DIERS *fully armed. He is in chains. His face is gray.*)

Up, great sir, deign to walk upright!
From your palace, the eyes of many foes follow you!
And now you don't need an architect, a carpenter will do.
You won't be moving into a new palace
But into a little hole in the ground.
Look about you once more, blind man!

(*The arrested man looks round.*)

Does all you had please you?
Between the Easter mass and the Easter meal
You are walking to a place whence no one returns.

(*The* GOVERNOR *is led off. A horn sounds an alarm. Noise behind the gateway.*)

When the house of a great one collapses
Many little ones are slain.
Those who had no share in the *good* fortunes of the mighty
Often have a share in their *mis*fortunes.
The plunging wagon
Drags the sweating oxen down with it
Into the abyss.

(*The* SERVANTS *come rushing through the gateway in panic.*)

THE SERVANTS (*among themselves*):

— The baskets!

— Take them all into the third courtyard! Food for five days!

— The mistress has fainted! Someone must carry her down.

— She must get away.

— What about us? We'll be slaughtered like chickens, as always.

— Goodness, what'll happen? There's bloodshed already in the city, they say.

— Nonsense, the Governor has just been asked to appear at a Princes' meeting. All very correct. Everything'll be ironed out. I heard this on the best authority. . . .

(*The* TWO DOCTORS *rush into the courtyard.*)

THE FIRST DOCTOR (*trying to restrain the other*): Niko Mikadze, it is your duty as a doctor to attend Natella Abashwili.

THE SECOND DOCTOR: My duty! It's yours!

THE FIRST DOCTOR: Whose turn is it to look after the child today, Niko Mikadze, yours or mine?

THE SECOND DOCTOR: Do you really think, Mika Loladze, I'm going to stay a minute longer in this accursed house on that little brat's account?

(*They start fighting. All one hears is: "You neglect your duty!" and "Duty, my foot!" Then the* SECOND DOCTOR *knocks the* FIRST *down.*)

Oh go to hell! (*Exit.*)

(*Enter the* SOLDIER, SIMON SHASHAVA. *He searches in the crowd for* GRUSHA.)

SIMON: Grusha! There you are at last! What are you going to do?

GRUSHA: Nothing. If worst comes to worst, I've a brother in the mountains. How about you?

SIMON: Forget about me. (*Formally again.*) Grusha Vashnadze, your wish to know my plans fills me with satisfaction. I've been ordered to accompany Madam Natella Abashwili as her guard.

GRUSHA: But hasn't the Palace Guard mutinied?

SIMON (*seriously*): That's a fact.

GRUSHA: Isn't it dangerous to go with her?

SIMON: In Tiflis, they say: Isn't the stabbing dangerous for the knife?

GRUSHA: You're not a knife, you're a man, Simon Shashava, what has that woman to do with you?

SIMON: That woman has nothing to do with me. I have my orders, and I go.

GRUSHA: The soldier is pigheaded: he is getting himself into danger for nothing — nothing at all. I must get into the third courtyard, I'm in a hurry.

SIMON: Since we're both in a hurry we shouldn't quarrel. You need time for a good quarrel. May I ask if the young lady still has parents?

GRUSHA: No, just a brother.

SIMON: As time is short — my second question is this: Is the young lady as healthy as a fish in water?

GRUSHA: I may have a pain in the right shoulder once in a while. Otherwise I'm strong enough for my job. No one has complained. So far.

SIMON: That's well known. When it's Easter Sunday, and the question arises who'll run for the goose all the same, she'll be the one. My third question is this: Is the young lady impatient? Does she want apples in winter?

GRUSHA: Impatient? No. But if a man goes to war without any reason and then no message comes — that's bad.

SIMON: A message will come. And now my final question . . .

GRUSHA: Simon Shashava, I must get to the third courtyard at once. My answer is yes.

SIMON (*very embarrassed*): Haste, they say, is the wind that blows down the scaffolding. But they also say: The rich don't know what haste is. I'm from . . .

GRUSHA: Kutsk . . .

SIMON: So the young lady has been inquiring about me? I'm healthy, I have no dependents, I make ten piasters a month, as paymaster twenty piasters, and I'm asking — very sincerely — for your hand.

GRUSHA: Simon Shashava, it suits me well.

SIMON (*taking from his neck a thin chain with a little cross on it*): My mother gave me this cross, Grusha Vashnadze. The chain is silver. Please wear it.

GRUSHA: Many thanks, Simon.

SIMON (*hangs it round her neck*): It would be better to go to the third courtyard now. Or there'll be difficulties. Anyway, I must harness the horses. The young lady will understand?

GRUSHA: Yes, Simon.

(*They stand undecided.*)

SIMON: I'll just take the mistress to the troops that have stayed loyal. When the war's over, I'll be back. In two weeks. Or three. I hope my intended won't get tired, awaiting my return.

GRUSHA: Simon Shashava, I shall wait for you.
Go calmly into battle, soldier
The bloody battle, the bitter battle
From which not everyone returns:
When you return I shall be there.
I shall be waiting for you under the green elm
I shall be waiting for you under the bare elm
I shall wait until the last soldier has returned
And longer.
When you come back from the battle
No boots will stand at my door
The pillow beside mine will be empty
And my mouth will be unkissed.
When you return, when you return
You will be able to say: It is just as it was.

SIMON: I thank you, Grusha Vashnadze. And goodbye!

(*He bows low before her. She does the same before him. Then she runs quickly off without looking around. Enter the* ADJUTANT *from the gateway.*)

THE ADJUTANT (*harshly*): Harness the horses to the carriage! Don't stand there doing nothing, louse!

(SIMON SHASHAVA *stands to attention and goes off. Two* SERVANTS *crowd from the gateway, bent low under huge trunks. Behind them, supported by her* WOMEN, *stumbles* NATELLA ABASHWILI. *She is followed by a* WOMAN *carrying the* CHILD.)

THE GOVERNOR'S WIFE: I hardly know if my head's still on. Where's Michael? Don't hold him so clumsily. Pile the trunks onto the carriage. No news from the city, Shalva?

THE ADJUTANT: None. All's quiet so far, but there's not a minute to lose. No room for all these trunks in the carriage. Pick out what you need.

(*Exit quickly.*)

THE GOVERNOR'S WIFE: Only essentials! Quick, open the trunks! I'll tell you what I need. (*The trunks are lowered and opened. She points at some brocade dresses.*) The green one! And, of course, the one with the fur trimming. Where are Niko Mikadze and Mika Loladze? I've suddenly got the most terrible migraine again. It always starts in the temples.

(*Enter* GRUSHA.)

Taking your time, eh? Go and get the hot water bottles this minute!

(GRUSHA *runs off, returns later with hot water bottles; the* GOV-
ERNOR'S WIFE *orders her about by signs.*)

Don't tear the sleeves.

A YOUNG WOMAN: Pardon, madam, no harm has come to the dress.

THE GOVERNOR'S WIFE: Because I stopped you. I've been watching you
for a long time. Nothing in your head but making eyes at Shalva
Tzereteli. I'll kill you, you bitch! (*She beats the woman.*)

THE ADJUTANT (*appearing in the gateway*): Please make haste, Natella Abashwili. Firing has broken out in the city.

(*Exit.*)

THE GOVERNOR'S WIFE (*letting go of the* YOUNG WOMAN): Oh dear,
do you think they'll lay hands on us? Why should they? Why?
(*She herself begins to rummage in the trunks.*) How's Michael?
Asleep?

THE WOMAN WITH THE CHILD: Yes, madam.

THE GOVERNOR'S WIFE: Then put him down a moment and get my
little saffron-colored boots from the bedroom. I need them for the
green dress.

(*The* WOMAN *puts down the* CHILD *and goes off.*)

Just look how these things have been packed! No love! No understanding! If you don't give them every order yourself . . . At such
moments you realize what kind of servants you have! They gorge
themselves at your expense, and never a word of gratitude! I'll remember this.

THE ADJUTANT (*entering, very excited*): Natella, you must leave at
once!

THE GOVERNOR'S WIFE: Why? I've got to take this silver dress — it cost
a thousand piasters. And that one there, and where's the wine-
colored one?

THE ADJUTANT (*trying to pull her away*): Riots have broken out! We
must leave at once. Where's the baby?

THE GOVERNOR'S WIFE (*calling to the* YOUNG WOMAN *who was holding
the baby*): Maro, get the baby ready! Where on earth are you?

THE ADJUTANT (*leaving*): We'll probably have to leave the carriage
behind and go ahead on horseback.

(*The* GOVERNOR'S WIFE *rummages again among her dresses,
throws some onto the heap of chosen clothes, then takes them off
again. Noises, drums are heard. The* YOUNG WOMAN *who was
beaten creeps away. The sky begins to grow red.*)

THE GOVERNOR'S WIFE (*rummaging desperately*): I simply cannot find the wine-colored dress. Take the whole pile to the carriage. Where's Asja? And why hasn't Maro come back? Have you all gone crazy?

THE ADJUTANT (*returning*): Quick! Quick!

THE GOVERNOR'S WIFE (*to the* FIRST WOMAN): Run! Just throw them into the carriage!

THE ADJUTANT: We're not taking the carriage. And if you don't come now, I'll ride off on my own.

THE GOVERNOR'S WIFE (*as the* FIRST WOMAN *can't carry everything*): Where's that bitch Asja? (*The* ADJUTANT *pulls her away.*) Maro, bring the baby! (*To the* FIRST WOMAN.) Go and look for Masha. No, first take the dresses to the carriage. Such nonsense! I wouldn't dream of going on horseback!

(*Turning round, she sees the red sky, and starts back rigid. The fire burns. She is pulled out by the* ADJUTANT. *Shaking, the* FIRST WOMAN *follows with the dresses.*)

MARO (*from the doorway, with the boots*): Madam! (*She sees the trunks and dresses and runs toward the baby, picks it up, and holds it a moment.*) They left it behind, the beasts. (*She hands it to* GRUSHA.) Hold it a moment. (*She runs off, following the* GOVERNOR'S WIFE.)

(*Enter* SERVANTS *from the gateway.*)

THE COOK: Well, so they've actually gone. Without the food wagons, and not a minute too early. It's time for us to clear out.

A GROOM: This'll be an unhealthy neighborhood for quite a while. (*To one of the* WOMEN.) Suliko, take a few blankets and wait for me in the foal stables.

GRUSHA: What have they done with the governor?

THE GROOM (*gesturing throat cutting*): Ffffft.

A FAT WOMAN (*seeing the gesture and becoming hysterical*): Oh dear, oh dear, oh dear, oh dear! Our master Georgi Abashwili! A picture of health he was, at the Morning Mass — and now! Oh, take me away, we're all lost, we must die in sin like our master, Georgi Abashwili!

THE OTHER WOMAN (*soothing her*): Calm down, Nina! You'll be taken to safety. You've never hurt a fly.

THE FAT WOMAN (*being led out*): Oh dear, oh dear, oh dear! Quick! Let's all get out before they come, before they come!

A YOUNG WOMAN: Nina takes it more to heart than the mistress, that's a fact. They even have to have their weeping done for them.

THE COOK: We'd better get out, all of us.

ANOTHER WOMAN (*glancing back*): That must be the East Gate burning.

THE YOUNG WOMAN (*seeing the* CHILD *in* GRUSHA'S *arms*): The baby! What are you doing with it?

GRUSHA: It got left behind.

THE YOUNG WOMAN: She simply left it there. Michael, who was kept out of all the drafts!

(*The* SERVANTS *gather round the* CHILD.)

GRUSHA: He's waking up.

THE GROOM: Better put him down, I tell you. I'd rather not think what'd happen to anybody who was found with that baby.

THE COOK: That's right. Once they get started, they'll kill each other off, whole families at a time. Let's go.

(*Exeunt all but* GRUSHA, *with the* CHILD *on her arm, and two* WOMEN.)

THE TWO WOMEN: Didn't you hear? Better put him down.

GRUSHA: The nurse asked me to hold him a moment.

THE OLDER WOMAN: She's not coming back, you simpleton.

THE YOUNGER WOMAN: Keep your hands off it.

THE OLDER WOMAN (*amiably*): Grusha, you're a good soul, but you're not very bright, and you know it. I tell you, if he had the plague he couldn't be more dangerous.

GRUSHA (*stubbornly*): He hasn't got the plague. He looks at me! He's human!

THE OLDER WOMAN: Don't look at *him*. You're a fool — the kind that always get put upon. A person need only say, "Run for the salad, you have the longest legs," and you run. My husband has an ox cart — you can come with us if you hurry! Lord, by now the whole neighborhood must be in flames.

(*Both* WOMEN *leave, sighing. After some hesitation,* GRUSHA *puts the sleeping* CHILD *down, looks at it for a moment, then takes a brocade blanket from the heap of clothes and covers it. Then both* WOMEN *return, dragging bundles.* GRUSHA *starts guiltily away from the* CHILD *and walks a few steps to one side.*)

THE YOUNGER WOMAN: Haven't you packed anything yet? There isn't much time, you know. The Ironshirts will be here from the barracks.

GRUSHA: Coming.

(*She runs through the doorway. Both* WOMEN *go to the gateway and wait. The sound of horses is heard. They flee, screaming.*

Enter the FAT PRINCE *with drunken* IRONSHIRTS. *One of them carries the governor's head on a lance.*)

THE FAT PRINCE: Here! In the middle!

(*One* SOLDIER *climbs onto the other's back, takes the head, holds it tentatively over the door.*)

That's not the middle. Farther to the right. That's it. What I do, my friends, I do well.

(*While, with hammer and nail, the* SOLDIER *fastens the head to the wall by its hair.*)

This morning at the church door I said to Georgi Abashwili: "I love a clear sky." Actually, I prefer the lightning that comes out of a clear sky. Yes, indeed. It's a pity they took the brat along, though, I need him, urgently.

(*Exit with* IRONSHIRTS *through the gateway. Trampling of horses again. Enter* GRUSHA *through the doorway looking cautiously about her. Clearly she has waited for the* IRONSHIRTS *to go. Carrying a bundle, she walks toward the gateway. At the last moment, she turns to see if the* CHILD *is still there. Catching sight of the head over the doorway, she screams. Horrified, she picks up the bundle again, and is about to leave when the* SINGER *starts to speak. She stands rooted to the spot.*)

THE SINGER: As she was standing between courtyard and gate,
She heard or she thought she heard a low voice calling.
The child called to her,
Not whining, but calling quite sensibly,
Or so it seemed to her.
"Woman," it said, "help me."
And it went on, not whining, but saying quite sensibly:
"Know, woman, he who hears not a cry for help
But passes by with troubled ears will never hear
The gentle call of a lover nor the blackbird at dawn
Nor the happy sigh of the tired grape-picker as the Angelus rings."

(*She walks a few steps toward the* CHILD *and bends over it.*)

Hearing this she went back for one more look at the child:
Only to sit with him for a moment or two,
Only till someone should come,
His mother, or anyone.

(*Leaning on a trunk, she sits facing the* CHILD.)

Only till she would have to leave, for the danger was too great,
The city was full of flame and crying.

(*The light grows dimmer, as though evening and night were coming on.*)

Fearful is the seductive power of goodness!

(GRUSHA *now settles down to watch over the* CHILD *through the night. Once, she lights a small lamp to look at it. Once, she tucks it in with a coat. From time to time she listens and looks to see whether someone is coming.*)

And she sat with the child a long time,
Till evening came, till night came, till dawn came.
She sat too long, too long she saw
The soft breathing, the small clenched fists,
Till toward morning the seduction was complete
And she rose, and bent down and, sighing, took the child
And carried it away.

(*She does what the* SINGER *says as he describes it.*)

As if it was stolen goods she picked it up.
As if she was a thief she crept away.

2. The Flight into the Northern Mountains

THE SINGER: When Grusha Vashnadze left the city
  On the Grusinian highway
  On the way to the Northern Mountains
  She sang a song, she bought some milk.
THE CHORUS: How will this human child escape
  The bloodhounds, the trap-setters?
  Into the deserted mountains she journeyed
  Along the Grusinian highway she journeyed
  She sang a song, she bought some milk.

(GRUSHA VASHNADZE *walks on. On her back she carries the* CHILD *in a sack, in one hand is a large stick, in the other a bundle. She sings.*)

The Song of the Four Generals

Four generals
Set out for Iran.
With the first one, war did not agree.

The second never won a victory.
For the third the weather never was right.
For the fourth the men would never fight.
Four generals
And not a single man!

Sosso Robakidse
Went marching to Iran
With him the war did so agree
He soon had won a victory.
For him the weather was always right.
For him the men would always fight.
Sosso Robakidse,
He is our man!

(A *peasant's cottage appears.*)

GRUSHA (*to the* CHILD): Noontime is meal time. Now we'll sit hopefully in the grass, while the good Grusha goes and buys a little pitcher of milk.

(*She lays the* CHILD *down and knocks at the cottage door. An* OLD MAN *opens it.*)

Grandfather, could I have a little pitcher of milk? And a corn cake, maybe?
THE OLD MAN: Milk? We have no milk. The soldiers from the city have our goats. Go to the soldiers if you want milk.
GRUSHA: But grandfather, you must have a little pitcher of milk for a baby?
THE OLD MAN: And for a God-bless-you, eh?
GRUSHA: Who said anything about a God-bless-you? (*She shows her purse.*) We'll pay like princes. "Head in the clouds, backside in the water."

(*The* PEASANT *goes off, grumbling, for milk.*)

How much for the milk?
THE OLD MAN: Three piasters. Milk has gone up.
GRUSHA: Three piasters for this little drop?

(*Without a word the* OLD MAN *shuts the door in her face.*)

Michael, did you hear that? Three piasters! We can't afford it! (*She goes back, sits down again, and gives the* CHILD *her breast.*) Suck. Think of the three piasters. There's nothing there, but you *think* you're drinking, and that's something. (*Shaking her head,*

she sees that the CHILD *isn't sucking any more. She gets up, walks back to the door, and knocks again.*)
Open, grandfather, we'll pay. (*Softly.*) May lightning strike you!

(*When the* OLD MAN *appears.*)

I thought it would be half a piaster. But the baby must be fed. How about one piaster for that little drop?
THE OLD MAN: Two.
GRUSHA: Don't shut the door again.

(*She fishes a long time in her bag.*)

Here are two piasters. The milk better be good. I still have two days' journey ahead of me. It's a murderous business you have here — and sinful, too!
THE OLD MAN: Kill the soldiers if you want milk.
GRUSHA (*giving the* CHILD *some milk*): This is an expensive joke. Take a sip, Michael, it's a week's pay. Around here they think we earned our money just sitting around. Oh, Michael, Michael, you're a nice little load for a girl to take on!

(*Uneasy, she gets up, puts the* CHILD *on her back, and walks on. The* OLD MAN, *grumbling, picks up the pitcher and looks after her unmoved.*)

THE SINGER: As Grusha Vashnadze went northward
The Princes' Ironshirts went after her.
THE CHORUS: How will the barefoot girl escape the Ironshirts,
The bloodhounds, the trap-setters?
They hunt even by night.
Pursuers never tire.
Butchers sleep little.

(*Two* IRONSHIRTS *are trudging along the highway.*)

THE CORPORAL: You'll never amount to anything, blockhead, your heart's not in it. Your senior officer sees this in little things. Yesterday, when I made the fat gal, yes, you grabbed her husband as I commanded, and you did kick him in the stomach, at my request, but did you *enjoy* it, like a loyal Private, or were you just doing your duty? I've kept an eye on you, blockhead, you're a hollow reed and a tinkling cymbal, you won't get promoted.

(*They walk a while in silence.*)

Don't think I've forgotten how insubordinate you are, either. Stop limping! I forbid you to limp! You limp because I sold the horses, and I sold the horses because I'd never have got that price again. You limp to show me you don't like marching. I know you. It won't help. You wait. Sing?

THE TWO IRONSHIRTS (*singing*): Sadly to war I went my way
Leaving my loved one at her door.
My friends will keep her honor safe
Till from the war I'm back once more.

THE CORPORAL: Louder!

THE TWO IRONSHIRTS (*singing*): When 'neath a headstone I shall be
My love a little earth will bring:
"Here rest the feet that oft would run to me
And here the arms that oft to me would cling."

(*They begin to walk again in silence.*)

THE CORPORAL: A good soldier has his heart and soul in it. When he receives an order, he gets a hard on, and when he drives his lance into the enemy's guts, he comes. (*He shouts for joy.*) He lets himself be torn to bits for his superior officer, and as he lies dying he takes note that his corporal is nodding approval, and that is reward enough, it's his dearest wish. You won't get any nod of approval, but you'll croak all right. Christ, how'm I to get my hands on the Governor's bastard with the help of a fool like you!

(*They stay on stage behind.*)

THE SINGER: When Grusha Vashnadze came to the river Sirra
Flight grew too much for her, the helpless child too heavy.
In the cornfields the rosy dawn
Is cold to the sleepless one, only cold.
The gay clatter of the milk cans in the farmyard where the smoke rises
Is only a threat to the fugitive.
She who carries the child feels its weight and little more.

(GRUSHA *stops in front of a farm.* A FAT PEASANT WOMAN *is carrying a milk can through the door.* GRUSHA *waits until she has gone in, then approaches the house cautiously.*)

GRUSHA (*to the* CHILD): Now you've wet yourself again, and you know I've no linen. Michael, this is where we part company. It's far enough from the city. They wouldn't want you so much that they'd follow you all *this* way, little good-for-nothing. The peasant woman is kind, and can't you just smell the milk? (*She bends down to lay the* CHILD *on the threshold.*) So farewell, Michael, I'll forget how you kicked me in the back all night to make me walk faster. And you can forget the meager fare — it was meant well. I'd like to have kept you — your nose is so tiny — but it can't be. I'd have shown you your first rabbit, I'd have trained you to keep dry, but now I must turn around. My sweetheart the soldier might be back soon, and suppose he didn't find me? You can't ask that, can you?

(*She creeps up to the door and lays the* CHILD *on the threshold. Then, hiding behind a tree, she waits until the* PEASANT WOMAN *opens the door and sees the bundle.*)

THE PEASANT WOMAN: Good heavens, what's this? Husband!

THE PEASANT: What is it? Let me finish my soup.

THE PEASANT WOMAN (*to the* CHILD): Where's your mother then? Haven't you got one? It's a boy. Fine linen. He's from a good family, you can see that. And they just leave him on our doorstep. Oh, these are times!

THE PEASANT: If they think we're going to feed it, they're wrong. You can take it to the priest in the village. That's the best we can do.

THE PEASANT WOMAN: What'll the priest do with him? He needs a mother. There, he's waking up. Don't you think we could keep him, though?

THE PEASANT (*shouting*): No!

THE PEASANT WOMAN: I could lay him in the corner by the armchair. All I need is a crib. I can take him into the fields with me. See him laughing? Husband, we have a roof over our heads. We can do it. Not another word out of you!

(*She carries the* CHILD *into the house. The* PEASANT *follows protesting.* GRUSHA *steps out from behind the tree, laughs, and hurries off in the opposite direction.*)

THE SINGER: Why so cheerful, making for home?

THE CHORUS: Because the child has won new parents with a laugh,
Because I'm rid of the little one, I'm cheerful.

THE SINGER: And why so sad?

THE CHORUS: Because I'm single and free, I'm sad
Like someone who's been robbed
Someone who's newly poor.

(*She walks for a short while, then meets the* TWO IRONSHIRTS, *who point their lances at her.*)

THE CORPORAL: Lady, you are running straight into the arms of the Armed Forces. Where are you coming from? And when? Are you having illicit relations with the enemy? Where is he hiding? What movements is he making in your rear? How about the hills? How about the valleys? How are your stockings held in position?

(GRUSHA *stands there frightened.*)

Don't be scared, we always stage a retreat, if necessary . . . what, blockhead? I always stage retreats. In that respect at least, I can be relied on. Why are you staring like that at my lance? In the field no soldier drops his lance, that's a rule. Learn it by heart, blockhead. Now, lady, where are you headed?

GRUSHA: To meet my intended, one Simon Shashava, of the Palace Guard in Nuka.

THE CORPORAL: Simon Shashava? Sure, I know him. He gave me the key so I could look you up once in a while. Blockhead, we are getting to be unpopular. We must make her realize we have honorable intentions. Lady, behind apparent frivolity I conceal a serious nature, so let me tell you officially: I want a child from you.

(GRUSHA *utters a little scream.*)

Blockhead, she understood me. Uh-huh, isn't it a sweet shock? "Then first I must take the noodles out of the oven, Officer. Then first I must change my torn shirt, Colonel." But away with jokes, away with my lance! We are looking for a baby. A baby from a good family. Have you heard of such a baby, from the city, dressed in fine linen, and suddenly turning up here?

GRUSHA: No, I haven't heard a thing. (*Suddenly she turns round and runs back, panic-stricken. The* IRONSHIRTS *glance at each other, then follow her, cursing.*)

THE SINGER: Run, kind girl! The killers are coming!
Help the helpless babe, helpless girl!
And so she runs!

THE CHORUS: In the bloodiest times
There are kind people.

(As GRUSHA *rushes into the cottage, the* PEASANT WOMAN *is bending over the* CHILD'S *crib.*)

GRUSHA: Hide him. Quick! The Ironshirts are coming! I laid him on your doorstep. But he isn't mine. He's from a good family.

THE PEASANT WOMAN: Who's coming? What Ironshirts?

GRUSHA: Don't ask questions. The Ironshirts that are looking for it.

THE PEASANT WOMAN: They've no business in my house. But I must have a little talk with you, it seems.

GRUSHA: Take off the fine linen. It'll give us away.

THE PEASANT WOMAN: Linen, my foot! In this house I make the de-

cisions! "*You* can't vomit in *my* room!" Why did you abandon it?
It's a sin.

GRUSHA (*looking out of the window*): Look, they're coming out from
behind those trees! I shouldn't have run away, it made them angry.
Oh, what shall I do?

THE PEASANT WOMAN (*looking out of the window and suddenly starting with fear*): Gracious! Ironshirts!

GRUSHA: They're after the baby.

THE PEASANT WOMAN: Suppose they come in!

GRUSHA: You mustn't give him to them. Say he's yours.

THE PEASANT WOMAN: Yes.

GRUSHA: They'll run him through if you hand him over.

THE PEASANT WOMAN: But suppose they ask for it? The silver for the
harvest is in the house.

GRUSHA: If you let them have him, they'll run him through, right here
in this room! You've got to say he's yours!

THE PEASANT WOMAN: Yes. But what if they don't believe me?

GRUSHA: You must be firm.

THE PEASANT WOMAN: They'll burn the roof over our heads.

GRUSHA: That's why you must say he's yours. His name's Michael.
But I shouldn't have told you.

(*The* PEASANT WOMAN *nods.*)

Don't nod like that. And don't tremble — they'll notice.

THE PEASANT WOMAN: Yes.

GRUSHA: And stop saying yes, I can't stand it. (*She shakes the* WOMAN.)
Don't you have any children?

THE PEASANT WOMAN (*muttering*): He's in the war.

GRUSHA: Then maybe *he's* an Ironshirt? Do you want *him* to run
children through with a lance? You'd bawl him out. "No fooling
with lances in *my* house!" you'd shout, "is that what I've reared
you for? Wash your neck before you speak to your mother!"

THE PEASANT WOMAN: That's true, he couldn't get away with anything around here!

GRUSHA: So you'll say he's yours?

THE PEASANT WOMAN: Yes.

GRUSHA: Look! They're coming!

(*There is a knocking at the door. The women don't answer. Enter* IRONSHIRTS. *The* PEASANT WOMAN *bows low.*)

THE CORPORAL: Well, here she is. What did I tell you? What a nose I
have! I *smelt* her. Lady, I have a question for you. Why did you run

away? What did you think I would do to you? I'll bet it was something dirty. Confess!

GRUSHA (*while the* PEASANT WOMAN *bows again and again*): I'd left some milk on the stove, and I suddenly remembered it.

THE CORPORAL: Or maybe you imagined I looked at you in a dirty way? Like there could be something between us? A lewd sort of look, know what I mean?

GRUSHA: I didn't see it.

THE CORPORAL: But it's possible, huh? You admit that much. After all, I might be a pig. I'll be frank with you: I could think of all sorts of things if we were alone. (*To the* PEASANT WOMAN.) Shouldn't you be busy in the yard? Feeding the hens?

THE PEASANT WOMAN (*falling suddenly to her knees*): Soldier, I didn't know a thing about it. Please don't burn the roof over our heads.

THE CORPORAL: What are you talking about?

THE PEASANT WOMAN: I had nothing to do with it. She left it on my doorstep, I swear it!

THE CORPORAL (*suddenly seeing the* CHILD *and whistling*): Ah, so there's a little something in the crib! Blockhead, I smell a thousand piasters. Take the old girl outside and hold on to her. It looks like I have a little cross-examining to do.

(*The* PEASANT WOMAN *lets herself be led out by the* PRIVATE *without a word.*)

So, you've got the child I wanted from you! (*He walks toward the crib.*)

GRUSHA: Officer, he's mine. He's not the one you're after.

THE CORPORAL: I'll just take a look. (*He bends over the crib.* GRUSHA *looks around in despair.*)

GRUSHA: He's mine! He's mine!

THE CORPORAL: Fine linen!

(GRUSHA *dashes at him to pull him away. He throws her off and again bends over the crib. Again looking round in despair, she sees a log of wood, seizes it, and hits the* CORPORAL *over the head from behind. The* CORPORAL *collapses. She quickly picks up the* CHILD *and rushes off.*)

THE SINGER: And in her flight from the Ironshirts
After twenty-two days of journeying
At the foot of the Janga-Tu Glacier
Grusha Vashnadze decided to adopt the child.

THE CHORUS: The helpless girl adopted the helpless child.

(GRUSHA *squats over a half-frozen stream to get the* CHILD *water in the hollow of her hand.*)

GRUSHA: Since no one else will take you, son,
I must take you.
Since no one else will take you, son,
You must take me.
O black day in a lean, lean year,
The trip was long, the milk was dear,
My legs are tired, my feet are sore:
But I wouldn't be without you any more.
I'll throw your silken shirt away
And dress you in rags and tatters.
I'll wash you, son, and christen you in glacier water.
We'll see it through together.

(*She has taken off the* CHILD's *fine linen and wrapped it in a rag.*)

THE SINGER: When Grusha Vashnadze
Pursued by the Ironshirts
Came to the bridge on the glacier
Leading to the villages of the Eastern Slope
She sang the Song of the Rotten Bridge
And risked two lives.

(*A wind has risen. The bridge on the glacier is visible in the dark. One rope is broken and half the bridge is hanging down the abyss.* MERCHANTS, *two* MEN, *and a* WOMAN, *stand undecided before the bridge as* GRUSHA *and the* CHILD *arrive. One* MAN *is trying to catch the hanging rope with a stick.*)

THE FIRST MAN: Take your time, young woman. You won't get across here anyway.

GRUSHA: But I *have* to get the baby to the east side. To my brother's place.

THE MERCHANT WOMAN: Have to? How d'you mean, "have to"? I have to get there, too — because I have to buy carpets in Atum — carpets a woman had to sell because her husband had to die. But can *I* do what I have to? Can she? Andrei's been fishing for that rope for hours. And I ask you, how are we going to fasten it, even if he gets it up?

THE FIRST MAN (*listening*): Hush, I think I hear something.

GRUSHA: The bridge isn't quite rotted through. I think I'll try it.

THE MERCHANT WOMAN: *I* wouldn't — if the devil himself were after me. It's suicide.

THE FIRST MAN (*shouting*): Hi!

GRUSHA: Don't shout! (*To the* MERCHANT WOMAN.) Tell him not to shout.

THE FIRST MAN: But there's someone down there calling. Maybe they've lost their way.

THE MERCHANT WOMAN: Why shouldn't he shout? Is there something funny about you? Are they after you?

GRUSHA: All right, I'll tell. The Ironshirts are after me. I knocked one down.

THE SECOND MAN: Hide our merchandise!

(*The* WOMAN *hides a sack behind a rock.*)

THE FIRST MAN: Why didn't you say so right away? (*To the others.*) If they catch her they'll make mincemeat out of her!

GRUSHA: Get out of my way. I've got to cross that bridge.

THE SECOND MAN: You can't. The precipice is two thousand feet deep.

THE FIRST MAN: Even with the rope it'd be no use. We could hold it up with our hands. But then we'd have to do the same for the Iron-shirts.

GRUSHA: Go away.

(*There are calls from the distance: "Hi, up there!"*)

THE MERCHANT WOMAN: They're getting near. But you can't take the child on that bridge. It's sure to break. And look!

(GRUSHA *looks down into the abyss. The* IRONSHIRTS *are heard calling again from below.*)

THE SECOND MAN: Two thousand feet!

GRUSHA: But those men are worse.

THE FIRST MAN: You can't do it. Think of the baby. Risk your life but not a child's.

THE SECOND MAN: With the child she's that much heavier!

THE MERCHANT WOMAN: Maybe she's *really* got to get across. Give *me* the baby. I'll hide it. Cross the bridge alone!

GRUSHA: I won't. We belong together. (*To the* CHILD.) "Live together, die together" (*She sings.*)

The Song of the Rotten Bridge

Deep is the abyss, son,
I see the weak bridge sway
But it's not for us, son,
To choose the way.

The way I know
Is the one you must tread,
And all you will eat
Is my bit of bread.

Of every four pieces
You shall have three.
Would that I knew
How big they will be!

Get out of my way, I'll try it without the rope.

THE MERCHANT WOMAN: You are tempting God!

(*There are shouts from below.*)

GRUSHA: Please, throw that stick away, or they'll get the rope and follow me. (*Pressing the* CHILD *to her, she steps onto the swaying
bridge. The* MERCHANT WOMAN *screams when it looks as though
the bridge is about to collapse. But* GRUSHA *walks on and reaches
the far side.*)

THE FIRST MAN: She made it!

THE MERCHANT WOMAN (*who has fallen on her knees and begun to
pray, angrily*): I still think it was a sin.

(*The* IRONSHIRTS *appear; the* CORPORAL's *head is bandaged.*)

THE CORPORAL: Seen a woman with a child?

THE FIRST MAN (*while the* SECOND MAN *throws the stick into the
abyss*): Yes, there! But the bridge won't carry you!

THE CORPORAL: You'll pay for this, blockhead!

(GRUSHA, *from the far bank, laughs and shows the* CHILD *to the*
IRONSHIRTS. *She walks on. The wind blows.*)

GRUSHA (*turning to the* CHILD): You mustn't be afraid of the wind.
He's a poor thing too. He has to push the clouds along and he gets
quite cold doing it.

(*Snow starts falling.*)

And the snow isn't so bad, either, Michael. It covers the little fir
trees so they won't die in winter. Let me sing you a little song. (*She
sings.*)

The Song of the Child

Your father is a bandit
A harlot the mother who bore you.

Yet honorable men
Shall kneel down before you.

Food to the baby horses
The tiger's son will take.
The mothers will get milk
From the son of the snake.

3. *In the Northern Mountains*

THE SINGER: Seven day the sister, Grusha Vashnadze,
   Journeyed across the glacier
   And down the slopes she journeyed.
   "When I enter my brother's house," she thought
   "He will rise and embrace me."
   "Is that you, sister?" he will say,
   "I have long expected you.
   This is my dear wife,
   And this is my farm, come to me by marriage,
   With eleven horses and thirty-one cows. Sit down.
   Sit down with your child at our table and eat."
   The brother's house was in a lovely valley.
   When the sister came to the brother,
   She was ill from walking.
   The brother rose from the table.

   (A FAT PEASANT COUPLE *rise from the table*. LAVRENTI VASHNADZE
   still has a napkin round his neck, as GRUSHA, *pale and supported
   by a* SERVANT, *enters with the* CHILD.)

LAVRENTI: Where've *you* come from, Grusha?
GRUSHA (*feebly*): Across the Janga-Tu Pass, Lavrenti.
THE SERVANT: I found her in front of the hay barn. She has a baby
   with her.
THE SISTER-IN-LAW: Go and groom the mare.

   (*Exit the* SERVANT.)

LAVRENTI: This is my wife Aniko.
THE SISTER-IN-LAW: I thought you were in service in Nuka.
GRUSHA (*barely able to stand*): Yes, I was.
THE SISTER-IN-LAW: Wasn't it a good job? We were told it was.
GRUSHA: The Governor got killed.
LAVRENTI: Yes, we heard there were riots. Your aunt told us. Remem-
   ber, Aniko?
THE SISTER-IN-LAW: Here with us, it's very quiet. City people always

want something going on. (*She walks toward the door, calling.*) Sosso, Sosso, don't take the cake out of the oven yet, d'you hear? Where on earth are you?

(*Exit, calling.*)

LAVRENTI (*quietly, quickly*): Is there a father? (*As she shakes her head.*) I thought not. We must think up something. She's religious.

THE SISTER-IN-LAW (*returning*): Those servants! (*To* GRUSHA.) You have a child.

GRUSHA: It's mine. (*She collapses.* LAVRENTI *rushes to her assistance.*)

THE SISTER-IN-LAW: Heavens, she's ill — what are we going to do?

LAVRENTI (*escorting her to a bench near the stove*): Sit down, sit. I think it's just weakness, Aniko.

THE SISTER-IN-LAW: As long as it's not scarlet fever!

LAVRENTI: She'd have spots if it was. It's only weakness. Don't worry, Aniko. (*To* GRUSHA.) Better, sitting down?

THE SISTER-IN-LAW: Is the child hers?

GRUSHA: Yes, mine.

LAVRENTI: She's on her way to her husband.

THE SISTER-IN-LAW: I see. Your meat's getting cold.

(LAVRENTI *sits down and begins to eat.*)

Cold food's not good for you, the fat mustn't get cold, you know your stomach's your weak spot. (*To* GRUSHA.) If your husband's not in the city, where is he?

LAVRENTI: She got married on the other side of the mountain, she says.

THE SISTER-IN-LAW: On the other side of the mountain. I see. (*She also sits down to eat.*)

GRUSHA: I think I should lie down somewhere, Lavrenti.

THE SISTER-IN-LAW: If it's consumption we'll all get it. (*She goes on cross-examining her.*) Has your husband got a farm?

GRUSHA: He's a soldier.

LAVRENTI: But he's coming into a farm — a small one — from his father.

THE SISTER-IN-LAW: Isn't he in the war? Why not?

GRUSHA (*with effort*): Yes, he's in the war.

THE SISTER-IN-LAW: Then why d'you want to go to the farm?

LAVRENTI: When he comes back from the war, he'll return to his farm.

THE SISTER-IN-LAW: But you're going there now?

LAVRENTI: Yes, to wait for him.

THE SISTER-IN-LAW (*calling shrilly*): Sosso, the cake!

GRUSHA (*murmuring feverishly*): A farm — a soldier — waiting — sit down, eat.

THE SISTER-IN-LAW: It's scarlet fever.

GRUSHA (*starting up*): Yes, he's got a farm!

LAVRENTI: I think it's just weakness, Aniko. Would you look after the cake yourself, dear?

THE SISTER-IN-LAW: But when will he come back if war's broken out again as people say? (*She waddles off, shouting.*) Sosso! Where on earth are you? Sosso!

LAVRENTI (*getting up quickly and going to* GRUSHA): You'll get a bed in a minute. She has a good heart. But wait till after supper.

GRUSHA (*holding out the* CHILD *to him*): Take him.

LAVRENTI (*taking it and looking around*): But you can't stay here long with the child. She's religious, you see.

(GRUSHA *collapses.* LAVRENTI *catches her.*)

THE SINGER: The sister was so ill,
The cowardly brother had to give her shelter.
Summer departed, winter came.
The winter was long, the winter was short
People mustn't know anything,
Rats mustn't bite,
Spring mustn't come.

(GRUSHA *sits over the weaving loom in a workroom. She and the* CHILD, *who is squatting on the floor, are wrapped in blankets. She sings.*)

The Song of the Center

GRUSHA (*sings*):
And the lover started to leave
And his betrothed ran pleading after him
Pleading and weeping, weeping and teaching:
"Dearest mine, dearest mine
When you go to war as now you do
When you fight the foe as soon you will
Don't lead with the front line
And don't push with the rear line
At the front is red fire
In the rear is red smoke
Stay in the war's center
Stay near the standard bearer
The first always die
The last are also hit
Those in the center come home."

Michael, we must be clever. If we make ourselves as small as cockroaches, the sister-in-law will forget we're in the house, and then we can stay till the snow melts.

(*Enter* LAVRENTI. *He sits down beside his sister.*)

LAVRENTI: Why are you sitting there muffled up like coachmen, you two? Is it too cold in the room?

GRUSHA (*hastily removing one shawl*): It's not too cold, Lavrenti.

LAVRENTI: If it's too cold, you shouldn't be sitting here with the child. Aniko would never forgive herself! (*Pause.*) I hope our priest didn't question you about the child?

GRUSHA: He did, but I didn't tell him anything.

LAVRENTI: That's good. I wanted to speak to you about Aniko. She has a good heart but she's very, very sensitive. People need only mention our farm and she's worried. She takes everything hard, you see. One time our milkmaid went to church with a hole in her stocking. Ever since, Aniko has worn two pairs of stockings in church. It's the old family in her. (*He listens.*) Are you sure there are no rats around? If there are rats, you couldn't live here. (*There are sounds as of dripping from the roof.*) What's that dripping?

GRUSHA: It must be a barrel leaking.

LAVRENTI: Yes, it must be a barrel. You've been here six months, haven't you? Was I talking about Aniko? (*They listen again to the snow melting.*) You can't imagine how worried she gets about your soldier-husband. "Suppose he comes back and can't find her!" she says and lies awake. "He can't come before the spring," I tell her. The dear woman! (*The drops begin to fall faster.*) When d'you think he'll come? What do *you* think? (GRUSHA *is silent.*) Not before the spring, you agree? (GRUSHA *is silent.*) You don't believe he'll come at all? (GRUSHA *is silent.*) But when the spring comes and the snow melts here and on the passes, you can't stay on. They may come and look for you. There's already talk of an illegitimate child. (*The "glockenspiel" of the falling drops has grown faster and steadier.*) Grusha, the snow is melting on the roof. Spring is here.

GRUSHA: Yes.

LAVRENTI (*eagerly*): I'll tell you what we'll do. You need a place to go, and because of the child (*he sighs*), you have to have a husband, so people won't talk. Now I've made cautious inquiries to see if we can find you a husband. Grusha, I *have* one. I talked to a peasant woman who has a son. Just the other side of the mountain. A small farm. And she's willing.

GRUSHA: But I *can't* marry! I must wait for Simon Shashava.

LAVRENTI: Of course. That's all been taken care of. You don't need a man in bed — you need a man on paper. And I've found you one. The son of this peasant woman is going to die. Isn't that wonderful? He's at his last gasp. And all in line with our story — a husband from the other side of the mountain! And when you met him he was at the last gasp. So you're a widow. What do you say?

GRUSHA: It's true I could use a document with stamps on it for Michael.

LAVRENTI: Stamps make all the difference. Without something in writing the Shah couldn't prove he's a Shah. And you'll have a place to live.

GRUSHA: How much does the peasant woman want?

LAVRENTI: Four hundred piasters.

GRUSHA: Where will you find it?

LAVRENTI (*guiltily*): Aniko's milk money.

GRUSHA: No one would know us there. I'll do it.

LAVRENTI (*getting up*): I'll let the peasant woman know.

(*Quick exit.*)

GRUSHA: Michael, you cause a lot of fuss. I came to you as the pear tree comes to the sparrows. And because a Christian bends down and picks up a crust of bread so nothing will go to waste. Michael, it would have been better had I walked quickly away on that Easter Sunday in Nuka in the second courtyard. Now I *am* a fool.

THE SINGER:

The bridegroom was lying on his deathbed when the bride arrived.

The bridegroom's mother was waiting at the door, telling her to hurry.

The bride brought a child along.

The witness hid it during the wedding.

(*On one side the bed. Under the mosquito net lies a very sick* MAN. GRUSHA *is pulled in at a run by her future* MOTHER-IN-LAW. *They are followed by* LAVRENTI *and the* CHILD.)

THE MOTHER-IN-LAW: Quick Quick! Or he'll die on us before the wedding. (*To* LAVRENTI.) I was never told she had a child already.

LAVRENTI: What difference does it make? (*Pointing toward the dying man.*) It can't matter to him — in his condition.

THE MOTHER-IN-LAW: To him? But *I'll* never survive the shame! We are honest people. (*She begins to weep.*) My Jussup doesn't have to marry a girl with a child!

LAVRENTI: All right, make it another two hundred piasters. You'll have it in writing that the farm will go to you: but she'll have the right to live here for two years.

THE MOTHER-IN-LAW (*drying her tears*): It'll hardly cover the funeral expenses. I hope she'll really lend a hand with the work. And what's happened to the monk? He must have slipped out through the kitchen window. We'll have the whole village on our necks when they hear Jussup's end is come! Oh dear! I'll go get the monk. But he mustn't see the child!

LAVRENTI: I'll take care he doesn't. But why only a monk? Why not a priest?

THE MOTHER-IN-LAW: Oh, he's just as good. I only made one mistake: I paid half his fee in advance. Enough to send him to the tavern. I only hope . . . (*She runs off.*)

LAVRENTI: She saved on the priest, the wretch! Hired a cheap monk.

GRUSHA: You *will* send Simon Shashava to see me if he turns up after all?

LAVRENTI: Yes. (*Pointing at the* SICK MAN.) Won't you take a look at him? (GRUSHA, *taking* MICHAEL *to her, shakes her head.*) He's not moving an eyelid. I hope we aren't too late.

(*They listen. On the opposite side enter* NEIGHBORS *who look around and take up positions against the walls, thus forming another wall near the bed, yet leaving an opening so that the bed can be seen. They start murmuring prayers. Enter the* MOTHER-IN-LAW *with a* MONK. *Showing some annoyance and surprise, she bows to the* GUESTS.)

THE MOTHER-IN-LAW: I hope you won't mind waiting a few moments? My son's bride has just arrived from the city. An emergency wedding is about to be celebrated. (*To the* MONK *in the bedroom.*) I might have known you couldn't keep your trap shut. (*To* GRUSHA.) The wedding can take place at once. Here's the license. Me and the bride's brother

(LAVRENTI *tries to hide in the background, after having quietly taken* MICHAEL *back from* GRUSHA. *The* MOTHER-IN-LAW *waves him away.*)

are the witnesses.

(GRUSHA *has bowed to the* MONK. *They go to the bed. The* MOTHER-IN-LAW *lifts the mosquito net. The* MONK *starts reeling off the marriage ceremony in Latin. Meanwhile, the* MOTHER-IN-LAW *beckons to* LAVRENTI *to get rid of the* CHILD, *but fearing that it will cry he draws its attention to the ceremony.* GRUSHA *glances once at the* CHILD, *and* LAVRENTI *waves the* CHILD's *hand in a greeting.*)

THE MONK: Are you prepared to be a faithful, obedient, and good wife to this man, and to cleave to him until death you do part?

GRUSHA (*looking at the* CHILD): I am.

THE MONK (*to the* SICK PEASANT): And are you prepared to be a good and loving husband to your wife until death you do part? (*As the* SICK PEASANT *does not answer, the* MONK *looks inquiringly around.*)

THE MOTHER-IN-LAW: Of course he is! Didn't you hear him say yes?

THE MONK: All right. We declare the marriage contracted! How about extreme unction?

THE MOTHER-IN-LAW: Nothing doing! The wedding cost quite enough. Now I must take care of the mourners. (*To* LAVRENTI.) Did we say seven hundred?

LAVRENTI: *Six hundred.* (*He pays.*) Now I don't want to sit with the guests and get to know people. So farewell, Grusha, and if my widowed sister comes to visit me, she'll get a welcome from my wife, or I'll show my teeth. (*Nods, gives the* CHILD *to* GRUSHA, *and leaves. The* MOURNERS *glance after him without interest.*)

THE MONK: May one ask where this child comes from?

THE MOTHER-IN-LAW: Is there a child? I don't see a child. And you don't see a child either — you understand? Or it may turn out I saw all sorts of things in the tavern! Now come on.

(*After* GRUSHA *has put the* CHILD *down and told him to be quiet, they move over left;* GRUSHA *is introduced to the* NEIGHBORS.)

This is my daughter-in-law. She arrived just in time to find dear Jussup still alive.

ONE WOMAN: He's been ill now a whole year, hasn't he? When our Vassili was drafted he was there to say goodbye.

ANOTHER WOMAN: Such things are terrible for a farm. The corn all ripe and the farmer in bed! It'll really be a blessing if he doesn't suffer too long, I say.

THE FIRST WOMAN (*confidentially*): You know why we thought he'd taken to his bed? Because of the draft! And now his end is come!

THE MOTHER-IN-LAW: Sit yourselves down, please! And have some cakes!

(*She beckons to* GRUSHA *and both women go into the bedroom, where they pick up the cake pans off the floor. The* GUESTS, *among them the* MONK, *sit on the floor and begin conversing in subdued voices.*)

ONE PEASANT (*to whom the* MONK *has handed the bottle which he has taken from his soutane*): There's a child, you say! How can that have happened to Jussup?

A WOMAN: She was certainly lucky to get herself hitched, with him so sick!

THE MOTHER-IN-LAW: They're gossiping already. And gorging themselves on the funeral cakes at the same time! If he doesn't die today, I'll have to bake some more tomorrow!

GRUSHA: I'll bake them for you.

THE MOTHER-IN-LAW: Yesterday some horsemen rode by, and I went out to see who it was. When I came in again he was lying there like a corpse! So I sent for you. It can't take much longer. (*She listens.*)

THE MONK: Dear wedding and funeral guests! Deeply touched, we stand before a bed of death and marriage. The bride gets a veil; the groom, a shroud: how varied, my children, are the fates of men! Alas! One man dies and has a roof over his head, and the other is married and the flesh turns to dust from which it was made. Amen.

THE MOTHER-IN-LAW: He's getting his own back. I shouldn't have hired such a cheap one. It's what you'd expect. A more expensive monk would behave himself. In Sura there's one with a real air of sanctity about him, but of course he charges a fortune. A fifty-piaster monk like that has no dignity, and as for piety, just fifty piasters' worth and no more! When I came to get him in the tavern he'd just made a speech, and he was shouting: "The war is over, beware of the peace!" We must go in.

GRUSHA (*giving* MICHAEL *a cake*): Eat this cake, and keep nice and still, Michael.

(*The two women offer cakes to the* GUESTS. *The* DYING MAN *sits up in bed. He puts his head out from under the mosquito net, stares at the two women, then sinks back again. The* MONK *takes two bottles from his soutane and offers them to the* PEASANT *beside him. Enter three* MUSICIANS *who are greeted with a sly wink by the monk.*)

THE MOTHER-IN-LAW (*to the* MUSICIANS): What are you doing here? With instruments?

ONE MUSICIAN: Brother Anastasius here (*pointing at the* MONK) told us there was a wedding on.

THE MOTHER-IN-LAW: What? You brought them? Three more on my neck! Don't you know there's a dying man in the next room?

THE MONK: A very tempting assignment for a musician: something that could be either a subdued Wedding March or a spirited Funeral Dance.

THE MOTHER-IN-LAW: Well, you might as well play. Nobody can stop you eating in any case.

(THE MUSICIANS *play a potpourri. The women serve cakes.*)

THE MONK: The trumpet sounds like a whining baby. And you, little drum, what have you got to tell the world?

THE DRUNKEN PEASANT (*beside the* MONK, *sings*):
Miss Roundass took the old old man
And said that marriage was the thing
To everyone who met 'er.
She later withdrew from the contract because
Candles are better.

(*The* MOTHER-IN-LAW *throws the* DRUNKEN PEASANT *out. The music stops. The* GUESTS *are embarrassed.*)

THE GUESTS (*loudly*):
— Have you heard? The Grand Duke is back! But the Princes are against him.
— They say the Shah of Persia has lent him a great army to restore order in Grusinia.
— But how is that possible? The Shah of Persia is the enemy . . .
— The enemy of Grusinia, you donkey, not the enemy of the Grand Duke!
— In any case, the war's over, so our soldiers are coming back.

(GRUSHA *drops a cake pan.* GUESTS *help her pick up the cake.*)

AN OLD WOMAN (*to* GRUSHA): Are you feeling bad? It's just excitement about dear Jussup. Sit down and rest a while, my dear.

(GRUSHA *staggers.*)

THE GUESTS: Now everything'll be the way it was. Only the taxes'll go up because now we'll have to pay for the war.

GRUSHA (*weakly*): Did someone say the soldiers are back?

A MAN: I did.

GRUSHA: It can't be true.

THE FIRST MAN (*to a* WOMAN): Show her the shawl. We bought it from a soldier. It's from Persia.

GRUSHA (*looking at the shawl*): They are here. (*She gets up, takes a step, kneels down in prayer, takes the silver cross and chain out of her blouse, and kisses it.*)

THE MOTHER-IN-LAW (*while the* GUESTS *silently watch* GRUSHA): What's the matter with you? Aren't you going to look after our guests? What's all this city nonsense got to do with us?

THE GUESTS (*resuming conversation while* GRUSHA *remains in prayer*):
— You can buy Persian saddles from the soldiers too. Though many want crutches in exchange for them.
— The big shots on one side can win a war, the soldiers on both sides lose it.
— Anyway, the war's over. It's something they can't draft you any more.

(*The* DYING MAN *sits bolt upright in bed. He listens.*)

— What we need is two weeks of good weather.
— Our pear trees are hardly bearing a thing this year.
THE MOTHER-IN-LAW (*offering cakes*): Have some more cakes and welcome! There are more!

(*The* MOTHER-IN-LAW *goes to the bedroom with the empty cake pans. Unaware of the* DYING MAN, *she is bending down to pick up another tray when he begins to talk in a hoarse voice.*)

THE PEASANT: How many more cakes are you going to stuff down their throats? D'you think I can shit money?

(*The* MOTHER-IN-LAW *starts, stares at him aghast, while he climbs out from behind the mosquito net.*)

THE FIRST WOMAN (*talking kindly to* GRUSHA *in the next room*): Has the young wife got someone at the front?
A MAN: It's good news that they're on their way home, huh?
THE PEASANT: Don't stare at me like that! Where's this wife you've saddled me with?

(*Receiving no answer, he climbs out of bed and in his nightshirt staggers into the other room. Trembling, she follows him with the cake pan.*)

THE GUESTS (*seeing him and shrieking*): Good God! Jussup!

(*Everyone leaps up in alarm. The women rush to the door.* GRUSHA, *still on her knees, turns round and stares at the* MAN.)

THE PEASANT: A funeral supper! You'd enjoy that, wouldn't you? Get out before I throw you out! (*As the* GUESTS *stampede from the house, gloomily to* GRUSHA.) I've upset the apple cart, huh? (*Receiving no answer, he turns round and takes a cake from the pan which his mother is holding.*)
THE SINGER: O confusion! The wife discovers she has a husband. By day there's the child, by night there's the husband. The lover is on

his way both day and night. Husband and wife look at each other. The bedroom is small.

(*Near the bed the* PEASANT *is sitting in a high wooden bathtub, naked; the* MOTHER-IN-LAW *is pouring water from a pitcher. Opposite,* GRUSHA *cowers with* MICHAEL, *who is playing at mending straw mats.*)

THE PEASANT (*to his mother*): That's her work, not yours. Where's she hiding out now?

THE MOTHER-IN-LAW (*calling*): Grusha! The peasant wants you!

GRUSHA (*to* MICHAEL): There are still two holes to mend.

THE PEASANT (*when* GRUSHA *approaches*): Scrub my back!

GRUSHA: Can't the peasant do it himself?

THE PEASANT: "Can't the peasant do it himself?" Get the brush! To hell with you! Are you the wife here? Or are you a visitor? (*To the* MOTHER-IN-LAW.) It's too cold!

THE MOTHER-IN-LAW: I'll run for hot water.

GRUSHA: Let me go.

THE PEASANT: You stay here.

(*The* MOTHER-IN-LAW *exits.*)

Rub harder. And no shirking. You've seen a naked fellow before. That child didn't come out of thin air.

GRUSHA: The child was not conceived in joy, if that's what the peasant means.

THE PEASANT (*turning and grinning*): You don't look the type. (GRUSHA *stops scrubbing him, starts back.*)

(*Enter the* MOTHER-IN-LAW.)

THE PEASANT: A nice thing you've saddled me with! A simpleton for a wife!

THE MOTHER-IN-LAW: She just isn't co-operative.

THE PEASANT: Pour — but go easy! Ow! Go easy, I said. (*To* GRUSHA.) Maybe you did something wrong in the city . . . I wouldn't be surprised. Why else should you be here? But I won't talk about that. I've not said a word about the illegitimate object you brought into my house either. But my patience has limits! It's against nature. (*To the* MOTHER-IN-LAW.) More! (*To* GRUSHA.) And even if your soldier does come back, you're married.

GRUSHA: Yes.

THE PEASANT: But your soldier won't come back. Don't you believe it.

GRUSHA: No.

THE PEASANT: You're cheating me. You're my wife and you're not my

wife. Where you lie, nothing lies, and yet no other woman can lie
there. When I go to work in the morning I'm tired — when I lie
down at night I'm awake as the devil. God has given you sex — and
what d'you do? I don't have ten piasters to buy myself a woman in
the city. Besides, it's a long way. Woman weeds the fields and opens
up her legs, that's what our calendar says. D'you hear?

GRUSHA (*quietly*): Yes. I didn't mean to cheat you out of it.

THE PEASANT: She didn't mean to cheat me out of it! Pour some more
water! (*The* MOTHER-IN-LAW *pours.*) Ow!

THE SINGER: As she sat by the stream to wash the linen
She saw his image in the water
And his face grew dimmer with the passing moons.
As she raised herself to wring the linen
She heard his voice from the murmuring maple
And his voice grew fainter with the passing moons.
Evasions and sighs grew more numerous,
Tears and sweat flowed.
With the passing moons the child grew up.

(GRUSHA *sits by a stream, dipping linen into the water. In the
rear, a few* CHILDREN *are standing.*)

GRUSHA (*to* MICHAEL): You can play with them, Michael, but don't
let them boss you around just because you're the littlest. (MICHAEL
nods and joins the CHILDREN. *They start playing.*)

THE BIGGEST BOY: Today it's the Heads-Off Game. (*To a* FAT BOY.)
You're the Prince and you laugh. (*To* MICHAEL.) You're the Governor. (*To a* GIRL.) You're the Governor's wife and you cry when
his head's cut off. And I do the cutting. (*He shows his wooden
sword.*) With this. First, they lead the Governor into the yard. The
Prince walks in front. The Governor's wife comes last.

(*They form a procession. The* FAT BOY *is first and laughs. Then
comes* MICHAEL, *then the* BIGGEST BOY, *and then the* GIRL, *who
weeps.*)

MICHAEL (*standing still*): Me cut off head!

THE BIGGEST BOY: That's my job. You're the littlest. The Governor's
the easy part. All you do is kneel down and get your head cut off —
simple.

MICHAEL: Me want sword!

THE BIGGEST BOY: It's mine! (*He gives him a kick.*)

THE GIRL (*shouting to* GRUSHA): He won't play his part!

GRUSHA (*laughing*): Even the little duck is a swimmer, they say.

THE BIGGEST BOY: You can be the Prince if you can laugh. (MICHAEL *shakes his head.*)

THE FAT BOY: I laugh best. Let him cut off the head just once. Then you do it, then me.

(*Reluctantly, the* BIGGEST BOY *hands* MICHAEL *the wooden sword and kneels down. The* FAT BOY *sits down, slaps his thigh, and laughs with all his might. The* GIRL *weeps loudly.* MICHAEL *swings the big sword and "cuts off" the head. In doing so, he topples over.*)

THE BIGGEST BOY: Hey! I'll show you how to cut heads off!

(MICHAEL *runs away. The* CHILDREN *run after him.* GRUSHA *laughs, following them with her eyes. On looking back, she sees* SIMON SHASHAVA *standing on the opposite bank. He wears a shabby uniform.*)

GRUSHA: Simon!

SIMON: Is that Grusha Vashnadze?

GRUSHA: Simon!

SIMON (*formally*): A good morning to the young lady. I hope she is well.

GRUSHA (*getting up gaily and bowing low*): A good morning to the soldier. God be thanked he has returned in good health.

SIMON: They found better fish, so they didn't eat me, said the haddock.

GRUSHA: Courage, said the kitchen boy. Good luck, said the hero.

SIMON: How are things here? Was the winter bearable? The neighbor considerate?

GRUSHA: The winter was a trifle rough, the neighbor as usual, Simon.

SIMON: May one ask if a certain person still dips her foot in the water when rinsing the linen?

GRUSHA: The answer is no. Because of the eyes in the bushes.

SIMON: The young lady is speaking of soldiers. Here stands a paymaster.

GRUSHA: A job worth twenty piasters?

SIMON: And lodgings.

GRUSHA (*with tears in her eyes*): Behind the barracks under the date trees.

SIMON: Yes, there. A certain person has kept her eyes open.

GRUSHA: She has, Simon.

SIMON: And has not forgotten?

(GRUSHA *shakes her head.*)

So the door is still on its hinges as they say?

(GRUSHA *looks at him in silence and shakes her head again.*)

What's this? Is anything not as it should be?

GRUSHA: Simon Shashava, I can never return to Nuka. Something has happened.

SIMON: What can have happened?

GRUSHA: For one thing, I knocked an Ironshirt down.

SIMON: Grusha Vashnadze must have had her reasons for that.

GRUSHA: Simon Shashava, I am no longer called what I used to be called.

SIMON (*after a pause*): I do not understand.

GRUSHA: When do women change their names, Simon? Let me explain. Nothing stands between us. Everything is just as it was. You must believe that.

SIMON: Nothing stands between us and yet there's something?

GRUSHA: How can I explain it so fast and with the stream between us? Couldn't you cross the bridge there?

SIMON: Maybe it's no longer necessary.

GRUSHA: It is very necessary. Come over on this side, Simon. Quick!

SIMON: Does the young lady wish to say someone has come too late?

(GRUSHA *looks up at him in despair, her face streaming with tears.* SIMON *stares before him. He picks up a piece of wood and starts cutting it.*)

THE SINGER: So many words are said, so many left unsaid.

The soldier has come.

Where he comes from, he does not say.

Hear what he thought and did not say:

"The battle began, gray at dawn, grew bloody at noon.

The first man fell in front of me, the second behind me, the third at my side.

I trod on the first, left the second behind, the third was run through by the captain.

One of my brothers died by steel, the other by smoke.

My neck caught fire, my hands froze in my gloves, my toes in my socks.

I fed on aspen buds, I drank maple juice, I slept on stone, in water."

SIMON: I see a cap in the grass. Is there a little one already?

GRUSHA: There is, Simon. There's no keeping that from you. But please don't worry, it is not mine.

SIMON: When the wind once starts to blow, they say, it blows through every cranny. The wife need say no more.

(GRUSHA *looks into her lap and is silent.*)

THE SINGER: There was yearning but there was no waiting.
The oath is broken. Neither could say why.
Hear what she thought but did not say:
"While you fought in the battle, soldier,
The bloody battle, the bitter battle
I found a helpless infant
I had not the heart to destroy him
I had to care for a creature that was lost
I had to stoop for breadcrumbs on the floor
I had to break myself for that which was not mine
That which was other people's.
Someone must help!
For the little tree needs water
The lamb loses its way when the shepherd is asleep
And its cry is unheard!"
SIMON: Give me back the cross I gave you. Better still, throw it in the
stream. (*He turns to go.*)
GRUSHA (*getting up*): Simon Shashava, don't go away! He isn't mine!
He isn't mine! (*She hears the* CHILDREN *calling.*) What's the mat-
ter, children?
VOICES: Soldiers! And they're taking Michael away!

(GRUSHA *stands aghast as two* IRONSHIRTS, *with* MICHAEL *between
them, come toward her.*)

ONE OF THE IRONSHIRTS: Are you Grusha?

(*She nods.*)

Is this your child?
GRUSHA: Yes.

(SIMON *goes.*)

Simon!
THE IRONSHIRT: We have orders, in the name of the law, to take this
child, found in your custody, back to the city. It is suspected that
the child is Michael Abashwili, son and heir of the late Governor
Georgi Abashwili, and his wife, Natella Abashwili. Here is the docu-
ment and the seal. (*They lead the* CHILD *away.*)
GRUSHA (*running after them, shouting*): Leave him here. Please! He's
mine!
THE SINGER: The Ironshirts took the child, the beloved child.
The unhappy girl followed them to the city, the dreaded city.
She who had borne him demanded the child.
She who had raised him faced trial.

Who will decide the case?
To whom will the child be assigned?
Who will the judge be? A good judge? A bad?
The city was in flames.
In the judge's seat sat Azdak.*

4. The Story of the Judge

THE SINGER: Hear the story of the judge
How he turned judge, how he passed judgment, what kind of judge he was.
On that Easter Sunday of the great revolt, when the Grand Duke was overthrown
And his Governor Abashwili, father of our child, lost his head
The Village Scrivener Azdak found a fugitive in the woods and hid him in his hut.

(AZDAK, *in rags and slightly drunk, is helping an* OLD BEGGAR *into his cottage.*)

AZDAK: Stop snorting, you're not a horse. And it won't do you any good with the police, to run like a snotty nose in April. Stand still, I say. (*He catches the* OLD MAN, *who has marched into the cottage as if he'd like to go through the walls.*) Sit down. Feed. Here's a hunk of cheese. (*From under some rags, in a chest, he fishes out some cheese, and the* OLD MAN *greedily begins to eat.*) Haven't eaten in a long time, huh? (*The* OLD MAN *growls.*) Why were you running like that, asshole? The cop wouldn't even have seen you.

THE OLD MAN: Had to! Had to!

AZDAK: Blue funk? (*The* OLD MAN *stares, uncomprehending.*) Cold feet? Panic? Don't lick your chops like a Grand Duke. Or an old sow. I can't stand it. We have to accept respectable stinkers as God made them, but not you! I once heard of a senior judge who farted at a public dinner to show an independent spirit! Watching you eat like that gives me the most awful ideas. Why don't you say something? (*Sharply.*) Show me your hand. Can't you hear? (*The* OLD MAN *slowly puts out his hand.*) White! So you're not a beggar at all! A fraud, a walking swindle! And I'm hiding you from the cops like you were an honest man! Why were you running like that if you're a landowner? For that's what you are. Don't deny it! I see it in your guilty face! (*He gets up.*) Get out! (*The* OLD MAN *looks at him uncertainly.*) What are you waiting for, peasant-flogger?

* The name AZDAK should be accented on the second syllable.

THE OLD MAN: Pursued. Need undivided attention. Make proposition . . .

AZDAK: Make what? A proposition? Well, if that isn't the height of insolence. He's making me a proposition! The bitten man scratches his fingers bloody, and the leech that's biting him makes him a proposition! Get out, I tell you!

THE OLD MAN: Understand point of view! Persuasion! Pay hundred thousand piasters one night! Yes?

AZDAK: What, you think you can buy me? For a hundred thousand piasters? Let's say a hundred and fifty thousand. Where are they?

THE OLD MAN: Have not them here. Of course. Will be sent. Hope do not doubt.

AZDAK: Doubt very much. Get out!

(*The* OLD MAN *gets up, waddles to the door. A* VOICE *is heard off stage.*)

A VOICE: Azdak!

(*The* OLD MAN *turns, waddles to the opposite corner, stands still.*)

AZDAK (*calling out*): I'm not in! (*He walks to door.*) So you're sniffing around here again, Shauwa?

POLICEMAN SHAUWA (*reproachfully*): You've caught another rabbit, Azdak. And you promised me it wouldn't happen again!

AZDAK (*severely*): Shauwa, don't talk about things you don't understand. The rabbit is a dangerous and destructive beast. It feeds on plants, especially on the species of plants known as weeds. It must therefore be exterminated.

SHAUWA: Azdak, don't be so hard on me. I'll lose my job if I don't arrest you. I know you have a good heart.

AZDAK: I do not have a good heart! How often must I tell you I'm a man of intellect?

SHAUWA (*slyly*): I know, Azdak. You're a superior person. You say so yourself. I'm just a Christian and an ignoramus. So I ask you: When one of the Prince's rabbits is stolen, and I'm a policeman, what should I do with the offending party?

AZDAK: Shauwa, Shauwa, shame on you. You stand and ask me a question, than which nothing could be more seductive. It's like you were a woman — let's say that bad girl Nunowna, and you showed me your thigh — Nunowna's thigh, that would be — and asked me: "What shall I do with my thigh, it itches?" Is she as innocent as she pretends? Of course not. I catch a rabbit, but you catch a man. Man is made in God's image. Not so a rabbit, you know that. I'm a rabbit-eater, but you're a man-eater, Shauwa. And God will pass judgment on you. Shauwa, go home and repent. No, stop, there's something . . . (*He looks at the* OLD MAN *who stands trembling in the corner.*) No, it's nothing. Go home and repent. (*He slams the door behind* SHAUWA.) Now you're surprised, huh? Surprised I didn't hand you over? I couldn't hand over a bedbug to that animal. It goes against the grain. Now don't tremble because of a cop! So old and still so scared? Finish your cheese, but eat it like a·poor man, or else they'll still catch you. Must I even explain how a poor man behaves? (*He pushes him down, and then gives him back the cheese.*) That box is the table. Lay your elbows on the table. Now, encircle the cheese on the plate like it might be snatched from you at any moment — what right have you to be safe, huh? — now, hold your knife like an undersized sickle, and give your cheese a troubled look because, like all beautiful things, it's already fading away. (AZDAK *watches him.*) They're after you, which speaks in your favor, but how can we be sure they're not mistaken about you? In Tiflis one time they hanged a landowner, a Turk, who could prove he quartered his peasants instead of merely cutting them in half, as is the custom, and he squeezed twice the usual amount of taxes out of them, his zeal was above suspicion. And yet they hanged him like a common criminal — because he was a Turk — a thing he couldn't do much about. What injustice! He got onto the gallows by a sheer fluke. In short, I don't trust you.

THE SINGER: Thus Azdak gave the old beggar a bed,

And learned that old beggar was the old butcher, the Grand Duke himself,

And was ashamed.

He denounced himself and ordered the policeman to take him to Nuka, to court, to be judged.

(*In the court of justice three* IRONSHIRTS *sit drinking. From a beam hangs a man in judge's robes. Enter* AZDAK, *in chains, dragging* SHAUWA *behind him.*)

AZDAK (*shouting*): I've helped the Grand Duke, the Grand Thief, the Grand Butcher, to escape! In the name of justice I ask to be severely judged in public trial!

THE FIRST IRONSHIRT: Who's this queer bird?

SHAUWA: That's our Village Scrivener, Azdak.

AZDAK: I am contemptible! I am a traitor! A branded criminal! Tell them, flat-foot, how I insisted on being tied up and brought to the capital. Because I sheltered the Grand Duke, the Grand Swindler, by mistake. And how I found out afterwards. See the marked man denounce himself! Tell them how I forced you to walk with me half the night to clear the whole thing up.

SHAUWA: And all by threats. That wasn't nice of you, Azdak.

AZDAK: Shut your mouth, Shauwa. You don't understand. A new age is upon us! It'll go thundering over you. You're finished. The police will be wiped out — poof! Everything will be gone into, everything will be brought into the open. The guilty will give themselves up. Why? They couldn't escape the people in any case. (*To* SHAUWA.) Tell them how I shouted all along Shoemaker Street: (*With big gestures, looking at the* IRONSHIRTS.) "In my ignorance I let the Grand Swindler escape! So tear me to pieces, brothers!" I wanted to get it in first.

THE FIRST IRONSHIRT: And what did your brothers answer?

SHAUWA: They comforted him in Butcher Street, and they laughed themselves sick in Shoemaker Street. That's all.

AZDAK: But with you it's different. I can see you're men of iron. Brothers, where's the judge? I must be tried.

THE FIRST IRONSHIRT (*pointing at the hanged man*): There's the judge. And please stop "brothering" us. It's rather a sore spot this evening.

AZDAK: "There's the judge." An answer never heard in Grusinia before. Townsman, where's His Excellency the Governor? (*Pointing to the ground.*) There's His Excellency, stranger. Where's the Chief Tax Collector? Where's the official Recruiting Officer? The Patriarch? The Chief of Police? There, there, there — all there. Brothers, I expected no less of you.

THE SECOND IRONSHIRT: What? *What* was it you expected, funny man?

AZDAK: What happened in Persia, brother, what happened in Persia?

THE SECOND IRONSHIRT: What did happen in Persia?

AZDAK: Everybody was hanged. Viziers, tax collectors. Everybody. Forty years ago now. My grandfather, a remarkable man by the way, saw it all. For three whole days. Everywhere.

THE SECOND IRONSHIRT: And who ruled when the Vizier was hanged?

AZDAK: A peasant ruled when the Vizier was hanged.

THE SECOND IRONSHIRT: And who commanded the army?

AZDAK: A soldier, a soldier.

THE SECOND IRONSHIRT: And who paid the wages?

AZDAK: A dyer. A dyer paid the wages.

THE SECOND IRONSHIRT: Wasn't it a weaver, maybe?

THE FIRST IRONSHIRT: And why did all this happen, Persian?

AZDAK: Why did all this happen? Must there be a special reason? Why do you scratch yourself, brother? War! Too long a war! And no justice! My grandfather brought back a song that tells how it was. I will sing it for you. With my friend the policeman. (*To* SHAUWA.) And hold the rope tight. It's very suitable. (*He sings, with* SHAUWA *holding the rope tight around him.*)

The Song of Injustice in Persia

Why don't our sons bleed any more? Why don't our daughters weep?

Why do only the slaughter-house cattle have blood in their veins?

Why do only the willows shed tears on Lake Urmi?

The king must have a new province, the peasant must give up his savings.

That the roof of the world might be conquered, the roof of the cottage is torn down.

Our men are carried to the ends of the earth, so that great ones can eat at home.

The soldiers kill each other, the marshals salute each other.

They bite the widow's tax money to see if it's good, their swords break.

The battle was lost, the helmets were paid for.

(*Refrain*): Is it so? Is it so?

SHAUWA (*refrain*): Yes, yes, yes, yes, yes it's so.

AZDAK: Want to hear the rest of it?

(*The* FIRST IRONSHIRT *nods.*)

THE SECOND IRONSHIRT (*to* SHAUWA): Did he teach you that song?

SHAUWA: Yes, only my voice isn't very good.

THE SECOND IRONSHIRT: No. (*To* AZDAK.) Go on singing.

AZDAK: The second verse is about the peace. (*He sings.*)

The offices are packed, the streets overflow with officials.

The rivers jump their banks and ravage the fields.

Those who cannot let down their own trousers rule countries.

They can't count up to four, but they devour eight courses.

The corn farmers, looking round for buyers, see only the starving.

The weavers go home from their looms in rags.

(*Refrain*): Is it so? Is it so?

SHAUWA (*refrain*): Yes, yes, yes, yes, yes it's so.

AZDAK: That's why our sons don't bleed any more, that's why our daughters don't weep.

That's why only the slaughter-house cattle have blood in their veins,

And only the willows shed tears by Lake Urmi toward morning.

THE FIRST IRONSHIRT: Are you going to sing that song here in town?

AZDAK: Sure. What's wrong with it?

THE FIRST IRONSHIRT: Have you noticed that the sky's getting red?

(*Turning round,* AZDAK *sees the sky red with fire.*)

It's the people's quarters. On the outskirts of town. The carpet weavers have caught the "Persian Sickness," too. And they've been asking if Prince Kazbeki isn't eating too many courses. This morning they strung up the city judge. As for us we beat them to pulp. We were paid one hundred piasters per man, you understand?

AZDAK (*after a pause*): I understand. (*He glances shyly round and, creeping away, sits down in a corner, his head in his hands.*)

THE IRONSHIRTS (*to each other*): — If there ever was a trouble-maker it's him.

— He must've come to the capital to fish in the troubled waters.

SHAUWA: Oh, I don't think he's a really bad character, gentlemen. Steals a few chickens here and there. And maybe a rabbit.

THE SECOND IRONSHIRT (*approaching* AZDAK): Came to fish in the troubled waters, huh?

AZDAK (*looking up*): I don't know why I came.

THE SECOND IRONSHIRT: Are you in with the carpet weavers maybe?

(AZDAK *shakes his head.*)

How about that song?

AZDAK: From my grandfather. A silly and ignorant man.

THE SECOND IRONSHIRT: Right. And how about the dyer who paid the wages?

AZDAK (*muttering*): That was in Persia.

THE FIRST IRONSHIRT: And this denouncing of yourself? Because you didn't hang the Grand Duke with your own hands?

AZDAK: Didn't I tell you I let him run? (*He creeps farther away and sits on the floor.*)

SHAUWA: I can swear to that: he let him run.

(*The* IRONSHIRTS *burst out laughing and slap* SHAUWA *on the back.* AZDAK *laughs loudest. They slap* AZDAK *too, and unchain him. They all start drinking as the* FAT PRINCE *enters with a* YOUNG MAN.)

THE FIRST IRONSHIRT (*to* AZDAK, *pointing at the* FAT PRINCE): There's your "new age" for you!

(*More laughter.*)

THE FAT PRINCE: Well, my friends, what is there to laugh about? Permit me a serious word. Yesterday morning the Princes of Grusinia overthrew the war-mongering government of the Grand Duke and

did away with his Governors. Unfortunately the Grand Duke himself escaped. In this fateful hour our carpet weavers, those eternal
trouble-makers, had the effrontery to stir up a rebellion and hang the
universally loved city judge, our dear Illo Orbeliani. Ts — ts — ts.
My friends, we need peace, peace, peace in Grusinia! And justice!
So I've brought along my dear nephew Bizergan Kazbeki. He'll be
the new judge, hm? A very gifted fellow. What do you say? I want
your opinion. Let the people decide!

THE SECOND IRONSHIRT: Does this mean *we* elect the judge?

THE FAT PRINCE: Precisely. Let the people propose some very gifted
fellow! Confer among yourselves, my friends.

(*The* IRONSHIRTS *confer.*)

Don't worry, my little fox. The job's yours. And when we catch the
Grand Duke we won't have to kiss this rabble's ass any longer.

THE IRONSHIRTS (*among themselves*): — Very funny: they're wetting
their pants because they haven't caught the Grand Duke.
— When the outlook isn't so bright, they say: "My friends!" and
"Let the people decide!"
— Now he even wants justice for Grusinia! But fun is fun as long
as it lasts!
(*Pointing at* AZDAK.) — He knows all about justice. Hey, rascal,
would you like this nephew fellow to be the judge?

AZDAK: Are you asking me? You're not asking *me?!*

THE FIRST IRONSHIRT: Why not? Anything for a laugh!

AZDAK: You'd like to test him to the marrow, correct? Have you a
criminal on hand? An experienced one? So the candidate can show
what he knows?

THE SECOND IRONSHIRT: Let's see. We do have a couple of doctors
downstairs. Let's use them.

AZDAK: Oh, no, that's no good, we can't take real criminals till we're
sure the judge will be appointed. He may be dumb, but he must be
appointed, or the Law is violated. And the Law is a sensitive organ.
It's like the spleen, you mustn't hit it — that would be fatal. Of
course you can hang those two without violating the Law, because
there was no judge in the vicinity. But Judgment, when pronounced,
must be pronounced with absolute gravity — it's all such nonsense.
Suppose, for instance, a judge jails a woman — let's say she's stolen
a corncake to feed her child — and this judge isn't wearing his robes
— or maybe he's scratching himself while passing sentence and half
his body is uncovered — a man's thigh *will* itch once in a while —
the sentence this judge passes is a disgrace and the Law is violated.
In short it would be easier for a judge's robe and a judge's hat to

pass judgment than for a man with no robe and no hat. If you don't treat it with respect, the Law just disappears on you. Now you don't try out a bottle of wine by offering it to a dog; you'd only lose your wine.

THE FIRST IRONSHIRT: Then what do you suggest, hair-splitter?

AZDAK: I'll be the defendant.

THE FIRST IRONSHIRT: You? (*He bursts out laughing.*)

THE FAT PRINCE: What have you decided?

THE FIRST IRONSHIRT: We've decided to stage a rehearsal. Our friend here will be the defendant. Let the candidate be the judge and sit there.

THE FAT PRINCE: It isn't customary, but why not? (*To the* NEPHEW.) A mere formality, my little fox. What have I taught you? Who got there first — the slow runner or the fast?

THE NEPHEW: The silent runner, Uncle Arsen.

(*The* NEPHEW *takes the chair. The* IRONSHIRTS *and the* FAT PRINCE *sit on the steps. Enter* AZDAK, *mimicking the gait of the Grand Duke.*)

AZDAK (*in the Grand Duke's accent*). Is any here knows me? Am Grand Duke.

THE IRONSHIRTS:

— What is he?

— The Grand Duke. He knows him, too.

— Fine. So get on with the trial.

AZDAK: Listen! Am accused instigating war? Ridiculous! Am saying ridiculous! That enough? If not, have brought lawyers. Believe five hundred. (*He points behind him, pretending to be surrounded by lawyers.*) Requisition all available seats for lawyers! (*The* IRONSHIRTS *laugh, the* FAT PRINCE *joins in.*)

THE NEPHEW (*to the* IRONSHIRTS): You really wish me to try this case? I find it rather unusual. From the taste angle, I mean.

THE FIRST IRONSHIRT: Let's go!

THE FAT PRINCE (*smiling*): Let him have it, my little fox!

THE NEPHEW: All right. People of Grusinia versus Grand Duke. Defendant, what have you got to say for yourself?

AZDAK: Plenty. Naturally, have read war lost. Only started on the advice of patriots. Like Uncle Arsen Kazbeki. Call Uncle Arsen as witness.

THE FAT PRINCE (*to the* IRONSHIRTS, *delightedly*): What a screw-ball!

THE NEPHEW: Motion rejected. One cannot be arraigned for declaring a war, which every ruler has to do once in a while, but only for running a war badly.

AZDAK: Rubbish! Did not run it at all! Had it run! Had it run by Princes! Naturally, they messed it up.

THE NEPHEW: Do you by any chance deny having been commander-in-chief?

AZDAK: Not at all! Always *was* commander-in-chief. At birth shouted at wet nurse. Was trained drop turds in toilet, grew accustomed to command. Always commanded officials rob my cash box. Officers flog soldiers only on command. Landowners sleep with peasants' wives only on strictest command. Uncle Arsen here grew his belly at *my* command!

THE IRONSHIRTS (*clapping*): He's good! Long live the Grand Duke!

THE FAT PRINCE: Answer him, my little fox. I'm with you.

THE NEPHEW: I shall answer him according to the dignity of the law. Defendant, preserve the dignity of the law!

AZDAK: Agreed. Command you to proceed with the trial!

THE NEPHEW: It is not your place to command me. You claim that the Princes forced you to declare war. How can you claim, then, that they — er — "messed it up"?

AZDAK: Did not send enough people. Embezzled funds. Sent sick horses. During attack, drinking in whore house. Call Uncle Arsen as witness.

THE NEPHEW: Are you making the outrageous suggestion that the Princes of this country did not fight?

AZDAK: No. Princes fought. Fought for war contracts.

THE FAT PRINCE (*jumping up*): That's too much! This man talks like a carpet weaver!

AZDAK: Really? Told nothing but the truth.

THE FAT PRINCE: Hang him! Hang him!

THE FIRST IRONSHIRT (*pulling the* PRINCE *down*): Keep quiet! Go on, Excellency!

THE NEPHEW: Quiet! I now render a verdict: You must be hanged! By the neck! Having lost war!

AZDAK: Young man, seriously advise not fall publicly into jerky clipped speech. Cannot be watchdog if howl like wolf. Got it? If people realize Princes speak same language as Grand Duke, may hang Grand Duke *and Princes*, huh? By the way, must overrule verdict. Reason? War lost, but not for Princes. Princes won their war. Got 3,863,000 piasters for horses not delivered, 8,240,000 piasters for food supplies not produced. Are therefore victors. War lost only for Grusinia, which is not present in this court.

THE FAT PRINCE: I think that will do, my friends. (*To* AZDAK.) You can withdraw, funny man. (*To the* IRONSHIRTS.) You may now ratify the new judge's appointment, my friends.

THE FIRST IRONSHIRT: Yes, we can. Take down the judge's gown.

(*One* IRONSHIRT *climbs on the back of the other, pulls the gown off the hanged man.*)

(*To the* NEPHEW.) Now you run away so the right ass can get on the right chair. (*To* AZDAK.) Step forward! Go to the judge's seat! Now sit in it! (AZDAK *steps up, bows, and sits down.*) The judge was always a rascal! Now the rascal shall be a judge! (*The judge's gown is placed round his shoulders, the hat on his head.*) And what a judge!

THE SINGER: And there was civil war in the land.
The mighty were not safe.
And Azdak was made a judge by the Ironshirts.
And Azdak remained a judge for two years.

THE SINGER AND CHORUS: When the towns were set afire
And rivers of blood rose higher and higher,
Cockroaches crawled out of every crack.
And the court was full of schemers
And the church of foul blasphemers.
In the judge's cassock sat Azdak.

(AZDAK *sits in the judge's chair, peeling an apple.* SHAUWA *is sweeping out the hall. On one side an* INVALID *in a wheelchair. Opposite, a* YOUNG MAN *accused of blackmail. An* IRONSHIRT *stands guard, holding the* IRONSHIRT'S *banner.*)

AZDAK: In consideration of the large number of cases, the Court today will hear two cases at a time. Before I open the proceedings, a short announcement — I accept. (*He stretches out his hand. The* BLACK-MAILER *is the only one to produce any money. He hands it to* AZDAK.) I reserve the right to punish one of the parties for contempt of court. (*He glances at the* INVALID.) You (*to the* DOCTOR) are a doctor, and you (*to the* INVALID) are bringing a complaint against him. Is the doctor responsible for your condition?

THE INVALID: Yes. I had a stroke on his account.

AZDAK: That would be professional negligence.

THE INVALID: Worse than negligence. I gave this man money for his studies. So far, he hasn't paid me back a cent. It was when I heard he was treating a patient free that I had my stroke.

AZDAK: Rightly. (*To a* LIMPING MAN.) And what are *you* doing here?

THE LIMPING MAN: I'm the patient, your honor.

AZDAK: He treated your leg for nothing?

THE LIMPING MAN: The wrong leg! My rheumatism was in the left leg, and he operated on the right. That's why I limp now.

AZDAK: And you were treated free?

THE INVALID: A five-hundred-piaster operation free! For nothing! For a God-bless-you! And I paid for this man's studies! (*To the* DOCTOR.) Did they teach you to operate free?

THE DOCTOR: Your Honor, it is the custom to demand the fee before the operation, as the patient is more willing to pay before an operation than after. Which is only human. In the case in question I was convinced, when I started the operation, that my servant had already received the fee. In this I was mistaken.

THE INVALID: He was mistaken! A good doctor doesn't make mistakes! He examines before he operates!

AZDAK: That's right. (*To* SHAUWA.) Public Prosecutor, what's the other case about?

SHAUWA (*busily sweeping*): Blackmail.

THE BLACKMAILER: High Court of Justice, I'm innocent. I only wanted to find out from the landowner concerned if he really *had* raped his niece. He informed me very politely that this was not the case, and gave me the money only so I could pay for my uncle's studies.

AZDAK: Hm (*To the* DOCTOR.) You, on the other hand, can cite no extenuating circumstances for your offense, huh?

THE DOCTOR: Except that to err is human.

AZDAK: And you are aware that in money matters a good doctor is a high responsible person? I once heard of a doctor who got a thousand piasters for a sprained finger by remarking that sprains have something to do with blood circulation, which after all a less good doctor might have overlooked, and who, on another occasion made a real gold mine out of a somewhat disordered gall bladder, he treated it with such loving care. You have no excuse, Doctor. The corn merchant, Uxu, had his son study medicine to get some knowledge of trade, our medical schools are so good. (*To the* BLACK-MAILER.) What's the landowner's name?

SHAUWA: He doesn't want it mentioned.

AZDAK: In that case I will pass judgment. The Court considers the blackmail proved. And you (*to the* INVALID) are sentenced to a fine of one thousand piasters. If you have a second stroke, the doctor will have to treat you free. Even if he has to amputate. (*To the* LIMPING MAN.) As compensation, you will receive a bottle of rubbing alcohol. (*To the* BLACKMAILER.) You are sentenced to hand over half the proceeds of your deal to the Public Prosecutor to keep the landowner's name secret. You are advised, moreover, to study medicine — you seem well suited to that calling. (*To the* DOCTOR.)

You have perpetrated an unpardonable error in the practice of your profession: you are acquitted. Next cases!

THE SINGER AND CHORUS: Men won't do much for a shilling.

For a pound they may be willing.

For 20 pounds the verdict's in the sack.

As for the many, all too many,

Those who've only got a penny —

They've one single, sole recourse: Azdak.

(*Enter* AZDAK *from the caravansary on the highroad, followed by an old bearded* INNKEEPER. *The judge's chair is carried by a* STABLEMAN *and* SHAUWA. *An* IRONSHIRT, *with a banner, takes up his position.*)

AZDAK: Put me down. Then we'll get some air, maybe even a good stiff breeze from the lemon grove there. It does justice good to be done in the open: the wind blows her skirts up and you can see what she's got. Shauwa, we've been eating too much. These official journeys are exhausting. (*To the* INNKEEPER.) It's a question of your daughter-in-law?

THE INNKEEPER: Your Worship, it's a question of the family honor. I wish to bring an action on behalf of my son, who's on business on the other side of the mountain. This is the offending stableman, and here's my daughter-in-law.

(*Enter the* DAUGHTER-IN-LAW, *a voluptuous wench. She is veiled.*)

AZDAK (*sitting down*): I accept. (*Sighing, the* INNKEEPER *hands him some money.*) Good. Now the formalities are disposed of. This is a case of rape?

THE INNKEEPER: Your Honor, I caught the fellow in the act. Ludovica was in the straw on the stable floor.

AZDAK: Quite right, the stable. Lovely horses! I specially liked the little roan.

THE INNKEEPER: The first thing I did, of course, was to question Ludovica. On my son's behalf.

AZDAK (*seriously*): I said I specially liked the little roan.

THE INNKEEPER (*coldly*): Really? Ludovica confessed the stableman took her against her will.

AZDAK: Take your veil off, Ludovica.

(*She does so.*)

Ludovica, you please the Court. Tell us how it happened.

LUDOVICA (*well-schooled*): When I entered the stable to see the new foal the stableman said to me on his own accord: "It's hot today!" and laid his hand on my left breast. I said to him: "Don't do that!" But he continued to handle me indecently, which provoked my anger. Before I realized his sinful intentions, he got much closer. It was all over when my father-in-law entered and accidentally trod on me.

THE INNKEEPER (*explaining*): On my son's behalf.

AZDAK (*to the* STABLEMAN): You admit you started it?

THE STABLEMAN: Yes.

AZDAK: Ludovica, you like to eat sweet things?

LUDOVICA: Yes, sunflower seeds!

AZDAK: You like to lie a long time in the bathtub?

LUDOVICA: Half an hour or so.

AZDAK: Public Prosecutor, drop your knife — there — on the ground.

(SHAUWA *does so.*)

Ludovica, pick up that knife.

(LUDOVICA, *swaying her hips, does so.*)

See that? (*He points at her.*) The way it moves? The rape is now proven. By eating too much — sweet things, especially — by lying too long in warm water, by laziness and too soft a skin, you have raped that unfortunate man. Think you can run around with a behind like that and get away with it in court? This is a case of intentional assault with a dangerous weapon! You are sentenced to hand over to the Court the little roan which your father liked to ride "on his son's behalf." And now, come with me to the stables, so the Court may inspect the scene of the crime, Ludovica.

THE SINGER AND CHORUS: When the sharks the sharks devour
Little fishes have their hour.
For a while the load is off their back.
On Grusinia's highways faring
Fixed-up scales of justice bearing
Strode the poor man's magistrate: Azdak.

And he gave to the forsaken
All that from the rich he'd taken.
And a bodyguard of roughnecks was Azdak's.
And our good and evil man, he
Smiled upon Grusinia's Granny.
His emblem was a tear in sealing wax.

All mankind should love each other
But when visiting your brother

Take an ax along and hold it fast.
Not in theory but in practice
Miracles are wrought with axes
And the age of miracles is not past.

(AZDAK's *judge's chair is in a tavern. Three* RICH FARMERS *stand before* AZDAK. SHAUWA *brings him wine. In a corner stands an* OLD PEASANT WOMAN. *In the open doorway, and outside, stand* VILLAGERS *looking on. An* IRONSHIRT *stands guard with a banner.*)

AZDAK: The Public Prosecutor has the floor.

SHAUWA: It concerns a cow. For five weeks the defendant has had a cow in her stable, the property of the farmer Suru. She was also found to be in possession of a stolen ham, and a number of cows belonging to Shutoff were killed after he asked the defendant to pay the rent on a piece of land.

THE FARMERS:

— It's a matter of my ham, Your Honor.
— It's a matter of my cow, Your Honor.
— It's a matter of my land, Your Honor.

AZDAK: Well, Granny, what have *you* got to say to all this?

THE OLD WOMAN: Your Honor, one night toward morning, five weeks ago, there was a knock at my door, and outside stood a bearded man with a cow. "My dear woman," he said, "I am the miracle-working Saint Banditus and because your son has been killed in the war, I bring you this cow as a souvenir. Take good care of it."

THE FARMERS:

— The robber, Irakli, Your Honor!
— Her brother-in-law, Your Honor!
— The cow-thief!
— The incendiary!
— He must be beheaded!

(*Outside, a* WOMAN *screams. The* CROWD *grows restless, retreats. Enter the* BANDIT IRAKLI *with a huge ax.*)

THE BANDIT: A very good evening, dear friends! A glass of vodka!

THE FARMERS (*crossing themselves*): Irakli!

AZDAK: Public Prosecutor, a glass of vodka for our guest. And who are you?

THE BANDIT: I'm a wandering hermit, Your Honor. Thanks for the gracious gift. (*He empties the glass which* SHAUWA *has brought.*) Another!

AZDAK: I am Azdak. (*He gets up and bows. The* BANDIT *also bows.*)

The Court welcomes the foreign hermit. Go on with your story, Granny.

THE OLD WOMAN: Your Honor, that first night I didn't yet know Saint Banditus could work miracles, it was only the cow. But one night, a few days later, the farmer's servants came to take the cow away again. Then they turned round in front of my door and went off without the cow. And bumps as big as a fist sprouted on their heads. So I knew that Saint Banditus had changed their hearts and turned them into friendly people.

(*The* BANDIT *roars with laughter.*)

THE FIRST FARMER: I know what changed them.

AZDAK: That's fine. You can tell us later. Continue.

THE OLD WOMAN: Your Honor, the next one to become a good man was the farmer Shutoff — a devil, as everyone knows. But Saint Banditus arranged it so he let me off the rent on the little piece of land.

THE SECOND FARMER: Because my cows were killed in the field.

(*The* BANDIT *laughs.*)

THE OLD WOMAN (*answering* AZDAK'S *sign to continue*): Then one morning the ham came flying in at my window. It hit me in the small of the back. I'm still lame, Your Honor, look. (*She limps a few steps.*)

(*The* BANDIT *laughs.*)

Your Honor, was there ever a time when a poor old woman could get a ham *without* a miracle?

(*The* BANDIT *starts sobbing.*)

AZDAK (*rising from his chair*): Granny, that's a question that strikes straight at the Court's heart. Be so kind as to sit here.

(*The* OLD WOMAN, *hesitating, sits in the judge's chair.*)

AZDAK (*sits on the floor, glass in hand, reciting*): Granny
We could almost call you Granny Grusinia
The Woebegone
The Bereaved Mother
Whose sons have gone to war
Receiving the present of a cow
She bursts out crying.
When she is beaten
She remains hopeful.

When she's not beaten
She's surprised.
On us
Who are already damned
May you render a merciful verdict
Granny Grusinia!

(*Bellowing at the* FARMERS.) Admit you don't believe in miracles, you atheists! Each of you is sentenced to pay five hundred piasters! For godlessness! Get out!

(*The* FARMERS *slink out.*)

And you Granny, and you (*to the* BANDIT) pious man, empty a pitcher of wine with the Public Prosecutor and Azdak!

THE SINGER AND CHORUS: And he broke the rules to save them.
  Broken law like bread he gave them,
  Brought them to shore upon his crooked back.
  At long last the poor and lowly
  Had someone who was not too holy
  To be bribed by empty hands: Azdak.

  For two years it was his pleasure
  To give the beasts of prey short measure:
  He became a wolf to fight the pack.
  From All Hallows to All Hallows
  On his chair beside the gallows
  Dispensing justice in his fashion sat Azdak.

THE SINGER: But the era of disorder came to an end.
  The Grand Duke returned.
  The Governor's wife returned.
  A trial was held.
  Many died.
  The people's quarters burned anew.
  And fear seized Azdak.

(AZDAK's *judge's chair stands again in the court of justice.* AZDAK *sits on the floor, shaving and talking to* SHAUWA. *Noises outside. In the rear the* FAT PRINCE's *head is carried by on a lance.*)

AZDAK: Shauwa, the days of your slavery are numbered, maybe even the minutes. For a long time now I have held you in the iron curb of reason, and it has torn your mouth till it bleeds. I have lashed you with reasonable arguments, I have manhandled you with logic. You are by nature a weak man, and if one slyly throws an argument in your path, you *have* to snap it up, you can't resist. It is your nature to lick the hand of some superior being. But superior beings can be of very different kinds. And now, with your liberation, you will soon be able to follow your natural inclinations, which are low. You will be able to follow your infallible instinct, which teaches you to plant your fat heel on the faces of men. Gone is the era of confusion and disorder, which I find described in the Song of Chaos. Let us now sing that song together in memory of those terrible days. Sit down and don't do violence to the music. Don't be afraid. It sounds all right. And it has a fine refrain. (*He sings.*)

The Song of Chaos

Sister, hide your face! Brother, take your knife!
The times are out of joint!
Big men are full of complaint
And small men full of joy.
The city says:
"Let us drive the strong ones from our midst!"
Offices are raided. Lists of serfs are destroyed.
They have set Master's nose to the grindstone.
They who lived in the dark have seen the light.
The ebony poor box is broken.
Sesnem wood is sawed up for beds.
Who had no bread have barns full.
Who begged for alms of corn now mete it out.

SHAUWA (*refrain*): Oh, oh, oh, oh.
AZDAK (*refrain*): Where are you, General, where are you?
Please, please, please, restore order!

The nobleman's son can no longer be recognized;
The lady's child becomes the son of her slave.
The councilors meet in a shed.
Once, this man was barely allowed to sleep on the wall;
Now, he stretches his limbs in a bed.
Once, this man rowed a boat; now, he owns ships.
Their owner looks for them, but they're his no longer.
Five men are sent on a journey by their master.
"Go yourself," they say, "we have arrived."

SHAUWA (*refrain*): Oh, oh, oh, oh.
AZDAK (*refrain*): Where are you, General, where are you?
Please, please, please, restore order!

Yes, so it might have been, had order been neglected much longer.
But now the Grand Duke has returned to the capital, and the

Persians have lent him an army to restore order with. The suburbs are already aflame. Go and get me the big book I always sit on.

(SHAUWA *brings the big book from the judge's chair.* AZDAK *opens it.*)

This is the Statute Book and I've always used it, as you can testify. Now I'd better look in this book and see what they can do to me. I've let the down-and-outs get away with murder, and I'll have to pay for it. I helped poverty onto its skinny legs, so they'll hang me for drunkenness. I peeped into the rich man's pocket, which is bad taste. And I can't hide anywhere — everybody knows me because I've helped everybody.

SHAUWA: Someone's coming!

AZDAK (*in panic, he walks trembling to the chair*): It's the end. And now they'd enjoy seeing what a Great Man I am. I'll deprive them of that pleasure. I'll beg on my knees for mercy. Spittle will slobber down my chin. The fear of death is in me.

(*Enter* NATELLA ABASHWILI, *the* GOVERNOR'S WIFE, *followed by the* ADJUTANT *and an* IRONSHIRT.)

THE GOVERNOR'S WIFE: What sort of a creature is that, Shalva?

AZDAK: A willing one, Your Highness, a man ready to oblige.

THE ADJUTANT: Natella Abashwili, wife of the late Governor, has just returned. She is looking for her two-year-old son, Michael. She has been informed that the child was carried off to the mountains by a former servant.

AZDAK: The child will be brought back, Your Highness, at your service.

THE ADJUTANT: They say that the person in question is passing it off as her own.

AZDAK: She will be beheaded, Your Highness, at your service.

THE ADJUTANT: That is all.

THE GOVERNOR'S WIFE (*leaving*): I don't like that man.

AZDAK (*following her to door, bowing*): At your service, Your Highness, it will all be arranged.

5. The Chalk Circle

THE SINGER: Hear now the story of the trial
Concerning Governor Abashwili's child
And the establishing of the true mother
By the famous test of the Chalk Circle.

(*Law court in Nuka.* IRONSHIRTS *lead* MICHAEL *across stage and out at the back.* IRONSHIRTS *hold* GRUSHA *back with their lances under the gateway until the* CHILD *has been led through. Then she is admitted. She is accompanied by the former governor's* COOK. *Distant noises and a fire-red sky.*)

GRUSHA (*trying to hide*): He's brave, he can wash himself now.

THE COOK: You're lucky. It's not a real judge. It's Azdak, a drunk who doesn't know what he's doing. The biggest thieves have got by through him. Because he gets everything mixed up and the rich never offer him big enough bribes, the likes of us sometimes do pretty well.

GRUSHA: I *need* luck right now.

THE COOK: Touch wood. (*She crosses herself.*) I'd better offer up another prayer that the judge may be drunk. (*She prays with motionless lips, while* GRUSHA *looks around, in vain, for the* CHILD.) Why must you hold on to him at any price if he isn't yours? In days like these?

GRUSHA: He's mine. I brought him up.

THE COOK: Have you never thought what'd happen when she came back?

GRUSHA: At first I thought I'd give him to her. Then I thought she wouldn't come back.

THE COOK: And even a borrowed coat keeps a man warm, hm?

(GRUSHA *nods.*)

I'll swear to anything for you. You're a decent girl. (*She sees the soldier* SIMON SHASHAVA *approaching.*) You've done wrong by Simon, though. I've been talking with him. He just can't understand.

GRUSHA (*unaware of* SIMON's *presence*): Right now I can't be bothered whether he understands or not!

THE COOK: He knows the child isn't yours, but you married and not free "til death you do part" — he can't understand *that*.

(GRUSHA *sees* SIMON *and greets him.*)

SIMON (*gloomily*): I wish the lady to know I will swear I am the father of the child.

GRUSHA (*low*): Thank you, Simon.

SIMON: At the same time I wish the lady to know my hands are not tied — nor are hers.

THE COOK: You needn't have said that. You know she's married.

SIMON: And it needs no rubbing in.

(*Enter an* IRONSHIRT.)

THE IRONSHIRT: Where's the judge? Has anyone seen the judge?
ANOTHER IRONSHIRT (*stepping forward*): The judge isn't here yet. Nothing but a bed and a pitcher in the whole house!

(*Exeunt* IRONSHIRTS.)

THE COOK: I hope nothing has happened to him. With any other judge you'd have about as much chance as a chicken has teeth.
GRUSHA (*who has turned away and covered her face*): Stand in front of me. I shouldn't have come to Nuka. If I run into the Ironshirt, the one I hit over the head . . .

(*She screams. An* IRONSHIRT *had stopped and, turning his back, had been listening to her. He now wheels around. It is the* CORPORAL, *and he has a huge scar across his face.*)

THE IRONSHIRT (*in the gateway*): What's the matter, Shotta? Do you know her?
THE CORPORAL (*after staring for some time*): No.
THE IRONSHIRT: She's the one who stole the Abashwili child, or so they say. If you know anything about it you can make some money, Shotta.

(*Exit the* CORPORAL, *cursing.*)

THE COOK: Was it him? (GRUSHA *nods.*) I think he'll keep his mouth shut, or he'd be admitting he was after the child.
GRUSHA: I'd almost forgotten him.

(*Enter the* GOVERNOR'S WIFE, *followed by the* ADJUTANT *and two* LAWYERS.)

THE GOVERNOR'S WIFE: At least there are no common people here, thank God. I can't stand their smell. It always gives me migraine.
THE FIRST LAWYER: Madam, I must ask you to be careful what you say until we have another judge.
THE GOVERNOR'S WIFE: But I didn't say anything, Illo Shuboladze. I love the people with their simple straightforward minds. It's only that their smell brings on my migraine.
THE SECOND LAWYER: There won't be many spectators. The whole population is sitting at home behind locked doors because of the riots on the outskirts of town.
THE GOVERNOR'S WIFE (*looking at* GRUSHA): Is that the creature?
THE FIRST LAWYER: Please, most gracious Natella Abashwili, abstain from invective until it is certain the Grand Duke has appointed a new judge and we're rid of the present one, who's about the

lowest fellow ever seen in judge's gown. Things are all set to move, you see.

(*Enter* IRONSHIRTS *from the courtyard.*)

THE COOK: Her Grace would pull your hair out on the spot if she didn't know Azdak is for the poor. He goes by the face.

(IRONSHIRTS *begin fastening a rope to a beam.* AZDAK, *in chains, is led in, followed by* SHAUWA, *also in chains. The three* FARMERS *bring up the rear.*)

AN IRONSHIRT: Trying to run away, were you? (*He strikes* AZDAK.)
ONE FARMER: Off with his judge's gown before we string him up!

(IRONSHIRTS *and* FARMERS *tear off* AZDAK'S *gown. His torn underwear is visible. Then someone kicks him.*)

AN IRONSHIRT (*pushing him into someone else*): If you want a load of justice, here it is!

(*Accompanied by shouts of "You take it!" and "Let me have him, Brother!" they throw* AZDAK *back and forth until he collapses. Then he is lifted up and dragged under the noose.*)

THE GOVERNOR'S WIFE (*who, during this "Ball-game," has clapped her hands hysterically*): I disliked that man from the moment I first saw him.
AZDAK (*covered with blood, panting*): I can't see. Give me a rag.
AN IRONSHIRT: What is it you want to see?
AZDAK: You, you dogs! (*He wipes the blood out of his eyes with his shirt.*) Good morning, dogs! How goes it, dogs! How's the dog world? Does it smell good? Got another boot for me to lick? Are you back at each other's throats, dogs?

(*Accompanied by a* CORPORAL, *a dust-covered* RIDER *enters. He takes some documents from a leather case, looks at them, then interrupts.*)

THE RIDER: Stop! I bring a dispatch from the Grand Duke, containing the latest appointments.
THE CORPORAL (*bellowing*): Atten-shun!
THE RIDER: Of the new judge it says: "We appoint a man whom we have to thank for saving a life indispensable to the country's welfare — a certain Azdak of Nuka." Which is he?
SHAUWA (*pointing*): That's him, Your Excellency.
THE CORPORAL (*bellowing*): What's going on here?

AN IRONSHIRT: I beg to report that His Honor Azdak was already His Honor Azdak, but on these farmers' denunciation was pronounced the Grand Duke's enemy.

THE CORPORAL (*pointing at the* FARMERS): March them off! (*They are marched off. They bow all the time.*) See to it that His Honor Azdak is exposed to no more violence.

(*Exeunt* RIDER *and* CORPORAL.)

THE COOK (*to* SHAUWA): She clapped her hands! I hope he saw it!

THE FIRST LAWYER: It's a catastrophe.

(AZDAK *has fainted. Coming to, he is dressed again in judge's robes. He walks, swaying, toward the* IRONSHIRTS.)

AN IRONSHIRT: What does Your Honor desire?

AZDAK: Nothing, fellow dogs, or just an occasional boot to lick. (*To* SHAUWA.) I pardon you. (*He is unchained.*) Get me some red wine, the sweet kind. (SHAUWA *stumbles off.*) Get out of here, I've got to judge a case.

(*Exeunt* IRONSHIRTS. SHAUWA *returns with a pitcher of wine.* AZDAK *gulps it down.*)

Something for my backside. (SHAUWA *brings the Statute Book, puts it on the judge's chair.* AZDAK *sits on it.*) I accept.

(*The* PROSECUTORS, *among whom a worried council has been held, smile with relief. They whisper.*)

THE COOK: Oh dear!

SIMON: A well can't be filled with dew, they say.

THE LAWYERS (*approaching* AZDAK, *who stands up, expectantly*): A quite ridiculous case, Your Honor. The accused has abducted a child and refuses to hand it over.

AZDAK (*stretching out his hand, glancing at* GRUSHA): A most attractive person. (*He fingers the money, then sits down, satisfied.*) I declare the proceedings open and demand the whole truth. (*To* GRUSHA.) Especially from you.

THE FIRST LAWYER: High Court of Justice! Blood, as the popular saying goes, is thicker than water. This old adage . . .

AZDAK (*interrupting*): The Court wants to know the lawyers' fee.

THE FIRST LAWYER (*surprised*): I beg your pardon?

(AZDAK, *smiling, rubs his thumb and index finger.*)

Oh, I see. Five hundred piasters, Your Honor, to answer the Court's somewhat unusual question.

AZDAK: Did you hear? The question is unusual. I ask it because I listen in quite a different way when I know you're good.

THE FIRST LAWYER (*bowing*): Thank you, Your Honor. High Court of Justice, of all ties the ties of blood are strongest. Mother and child — is there a more intimate relationship? Can one tear a child from its mother? High Court of Justice, she has conceived it in the holy ecstasies of love. She has carried it in her womb. She has fed it with her blood. She has borne it with pain. High Court of Justice, it has been observed that even the wild tigress, robbed of her young, roams restless through the mountains, shrunk to a shadow. Nature herself . . .

AZDAK (*interrupting, to* GRUSHA): What's your answer to all this and anything else that lawyer might have to say?

GRUSHA: He's mine.

AZDAK: Is that all? I hope you can prove it. Why should I assign the child to you in any case?

GRUSHA: I brought him up like the priest says "according to my best knowledge and conscience." I always found him something to eat. Most of the time he had a roof over his head. And I went to such trouble for him. I had expenses too. I didn't look out for my own comfort. I brought the child up to be friendly with everyone, and from the beginning taught him to work. As well as he could, that is. He's still very little.

THE FIRST LAWYER: Your Honor, it is significant that the girl herself doesn't claim any tie of blood between her and the child.

AZDAK: The Court takes note of that.

THE FIRST LAWYER: Thank you, Your Honor. And now permit a woman bowed in sorrow — who has already lost her husband and now has also to fear the loss of her child — to address a few words to you. The gracious Natella Abashwili is . . .

THE GOVERNOR'S WIFE (*quietly*): A most cruel fate, Sir, forces me to describe to you the tortures of a bereaved mother's soul, the anxiety, the sleepless nights, the . . .

THE SECOND LAWYER (*bursting out*): It's outrageous the way this woman is being treated! Her husband's palace is closed to her! The revenue of her estates is blocked, and she is cold-bloodedly told that it's tied to the heir. She can't do a thing without that child. She can't even pay her lawyers! (*To the* FIRST LAWYER, *who, desperate about this outburst, makes frantic gestures to keep him from speaking.*) Dear Illo Shuboladze, surely it can be divulged now that the Abashwili estates are at stake?

THE FIRST LAWYER: Please, Honored Sandro Oboladze! We agreed . . . (*To* AZDAK.) Of course it is correct that the trial will also decide if our noble client can dispose of the Abashwili estates, which are rather extensive. I say "also" advisedly, for in the foreground stands the human tragedy of a mother, as Natella Abashwili very properly explained in the first words of her moving statement. Even if Michael Abashwili were not heir to the estates, he would still be the dearly beloved child of my client.

AZDAK: Stop! The Court is touched by the mention of estates. It's a proof of human feeling.

THE SECOND LAWYER: Thanks, Your Honor. Dear Illo Shuboladze, we can prove in any case that the woman who took the child is not the child's mother. Permit me to lay before the Court the bare facts. High Court of Justice, by an unfortunate chain of circumstances, Michael Abashwili was left behind on that Easter Sunday while his mother was making her escape. Grusha, a palace kitchen maid, was seen with the baby . . .

THE COOK: All her mistress was thinking of was what dresses she'd take along!

THE SECOND LAWYER (*unmoved*): Nearly a year later Grusha turned up in a mountain village with a baby and there entered into the state of matrimony with . . .

AZDAK: How did you get to that mountain village?

GRUSHA: On foot, Your Honor, And he was mine.

SIMON: I am the father, Your Honor.

THE COOK: I used to look after it for them, Your Honor. For five piasters.

THE SECOND LAWYER: This man is engaged to Grusha, High Court of Justice: his testimony is suspect.

AZDAK: Are you the man she married in the mountain village?

SIMON: No, Your Honor, she married a peasant.

AZDAK (*to* GRUSHA): Why? (*Pointing at* SIMON.) Is he no good in bed? Tell the truth.

GRUSHA: We didn't get that far. I married because of the baby. So it'd have a roof over his head. (*Pointing at* SIMON.) He was in the war, Your Honor.

AZDAK: And now he wants you back again, huh?

SIMON: I wish to state in evidence . . .

GRUSHA (*angrily*): I am no longer free, Your Honor.

AZDAK: And the child, you claim, comes from whoring?

(GRUSHA *doesn't answer.*)

I'm going to ask you a question: What kind of child is it? Is it a ragged little bastard or from a good family?

GRUSHA (*angrily*): He's just an ordinary child.

AZDAK: I mean — did he have refined features from the beginning?

GRUSHA: He had a nose on his face.

AZDAK: A very significant comment! It has been said of me that I went out one time and sniffed at a rosebush before rendering a verdict — tricks like that are needed nowadays. Well, I'll make it short, and not listen to any more lies. (*To* GRUSHA.) Especially not yours. (*To all the accused.*) I can imagine what you've cooked up to cheat me! I know you people. You're swindlers.

GRUSHA (*suddenly*): I can understand your wanting to cut it short, now I've seen what you accepted!

AZDAK: Shut up! Did I accept anything from you?

GRUSHA (*while the* COOK *tries to restrain her*): I haven't got anything.

AZDAK: True. Quite true. From starvelings I never get a thing. I might just as well starve, myself. You want justice, but do you want to pay for it, hm? When you go to a butcher you know you have to pay, but you people go to a judge as if you were going to a funeral supper.

SIMON (*loudly*): When the horse was shod, the horse-fly held out its leg, as the saying is.

AZDAK (*eagerly accepting the challenge*): Better a treasure in manure than a stone in a mountain stream.

SIMON: A fine day. Let's go fishing, said the angler to the worm.

AZDAK: I'm my own master, said the servant, and cut off his foot.

SIMON: I love you as a father, said the Czar to the peasants, and had the Czarevitch's head chopped off.

AZDAK: A fool's worst enemy is himself.

SIMON: However, a fart has no nose.

AZDAK: Fined ten piasters for indecent language in court! That'll teach you what justice is.

GRUSHA (*furiously*): A fine kind of justice! You play fast and loose with us because we don't talk as refined as that crowd with their lawyers!

AZDAK: That's true. You people are too dumb. It's only right you should get it in the neck.

GRUSHA: You want to hand the child over to her, and she wouldn't even know how to keep it dry, she's so "refined"! You know about as much about justice as I do!

AZDAK: There's something in that. I'm an ignorant man. Haven't even a decent pair of pants on under this gown. Look! With me, everything goes for food and drink — I was educated at a convent. Incidentally, I'll fine you ten piasters for contempt of court. And you're a very silly girl, to turn me against you, instead of making eyes at me and wiggling your backside a little to keep me in a good temper. Twenty piasters!

GRUSHA: Even if it was thirty, I'd tell you what I think of your justice, you drunken onion! (*Incoherently.*) How dare you talk to me like the cracked Isaiah on the church window? As if you were somebody? For you weren't born to this. You weren't born to rap your own mother on the knuckles if she swipes a little bowl of salt someplace. Aren't you ashamed of yourself when you see how I tremble before you? You've made yourself their servant so no one will take their houses from them — houses they had stolen! Since when have houses belonged to the bedbugs? But you're on the watch, or they couldn't drag our men into their wars! You bribe-taker!

(AZDAK *half gets up, starts beaming. With his little hammer he half-heartedly knocks on the table as if to get silence. As* GRUSHA'S *scolding continues, he only beats time with his hammer.*)

I've no respect for you. No more than for a thief or a bandit with a knife! You can do what you want. You can take the child away from me, a hundred against one, but I tell you one thing: only extortioners should be chosen for a profession like yours, and men who rape children! As punishment! Yes, let *them* sit in judgment on their fellow creatures. It is worse than to hang from the gallows.

AZDAK (*sitting down*): Now it'll be thirty! And I won't go on squabbling with you — we're not in a tavern. What'd happen to my dignity as a judge? Anyway, I've lost interest in your case. Where's the couple who wanted a divorce? (*To* SHAUWA.) Bring 'em in. This case is adjourned for fifteen minutes.

THE FIRST LAWYER (*to the* GOVERNOR'S WIFE): Even without using the rest of the evidence, Madam, we have the verdict in the bag.

THE COOK (*to* GRUSHA): You've gone and spoiled your chances with him. You won't get the child now.

THE GOVERNOR'S WIFE: Shalva, my smelling salts!

(*Enter a* VERY OLD COUPLE.)

AZDAK: I accept.

(*The* OLD COUPLE *don't understand.*)

I hear you want to be divorced. How long have you been together?

THE OLD WOMAN: Forty years, Your Honor.

AZDAK: And why do you want a divorce?

THE OLD MAN: We don't like each other, Your Honor.

AZDAK: Since when?

THE OLD WOMAN: Oh, from the very beginning, Your Honor.

AZDAK: I'll think about your request and render my verdict when I'm through with the other case.

(SHAUWA *leads them back.*)

I need the child. (*He beckons* GRUSHA *to and bends not unkindly toward her.*) I've noticed you have a soft spot for justice. I don't believe he's your child, but if he *were* yours, woman, wouldn't you want him to be rich? You'd only have to say he wasn't yours, and he'd have a palace and many horses in his stable and many beggars on his doorstep and many soldiers in his service and many petitioners in his courtyard, wouldn't he? What do you say — don't you want him to be rich?

(GRUSHA *is silent.*)

THE SINGER: Hear now what the angry girl thought but did not say:

Had he golden shoes to wear
He'd be cruel as a bear.
Evil would his life disgrace.
He'd laugh in my face.

Carrying a heart of flint
Is too troublesome a stint.
Being powerful and bad
Is hard on a lad.

Then let hunger be his foe!
Hungry men and women, no.
Let him fear the darksome night
But not daylight!

AZDAK: I think I understand you, woman.

GRUSHA (*suddenly and loudly*): I won't give him up. I've raised him, and he knows me.

(*Enter* SHAUWA *with the* CHILD.)

THE GOVERNOR'S WIFE: He's in rags!

GRUSHA: That's not true. But I wasn't given time to put his good shirt on.

THE GOVERNOR'S WIFE: He must have been in a pigsty.

GRUSHA (*furiously*): I'm not a pig, but there are some who are! Where did you leave your baby?

THE GOVERNOR'S WIFE: I'll show you, you vulgar creature! (*She is about to throw herself on* GRUSHA, *but is restrained by her* LAWYERS.) She's a criminal, she must be whipped. Immediately!

THE SECOND LAWYER (*holding his hand over her mouth*): Natella Abashwili, you promised . . . Your Honor, the plaintiff's nerves. . . .

AZDAK: Plaintiff and defendant! The Court has listened to your case, and has come to no decision as to who the real mother is, therefore, I, the judge, am obliged to *choose* a mother for the child. I'll make a test. Shauwa, get a piece of chalk and draw a circle on the floor.

(SHAUWA *does so.*)

Now place the child in the center.

(SHAUWA *puts* MICHAEL, *who smiles at* GRUSHA, *in the center of the circle.*)

Stand near the circle, both of you

(*The* GOVERNOR'S WIFE *and* GRUSHA *step up to the circle.*)

Now each of you take the child by one hand.

(*They do so.*)

The true mother is she who can pull the child out of the circle.

THE SECOND LAWYER (*quickly*): High Court of Justice, I object! The fate of the great Abashwili estates, which are tied to the child, as the heir, should not be made dependent on such a doubtful duel. In addition, my client does not command the strength of this person, who is accustomed to physical work.

AZDAK: She looks pretty well fed to me. Pull!

(*The* GOVERNOR'S WIFE *pulls the* CHILD *out of the circle on her side;* GRUSHA *has let go and stands aghast.*)

What's the matter with you? You didn't pull!

GRUSHA: I didn't hold on to him.

THE FIRST LAWYER (*congratulating the* GOVERNOR'S WIFE): What did I say! The ties of blood!

GRUSHA (*running to* AZDAK): Your Honor, I take back everything I said against you. I ask your forgiveness. But could I keep him till he can speak all the words? He knows a few.

AZDAK: Don't influence the Court. I bet you only know about twenty words yourself. All right, I'll make the test once more, just to be certain.

(*The two women take up their positions again.*)

Pull!

(*Again* GRUSHA *lets go of the* CHILD.)

GRUSHA (*in despair*): I brought him up! Shall I also tear him to bits? I can't!

AZDAK (*rising*): And in this manner the Court has established the true mother. (*To* GRUSHA.) Take your child and be off. I advise you not to stay in the city with him. (*To the* GOVERNOR'S WIFE.) And you disappear before I fine you for fraud. Your estates fall to the city. They'll be converted into a playground for the children. They need one, and I've decided it shall be called after me: Azdak's Garden.

(*The* GOVERNOR'S WIFE *has fainted and is carried out by the* LAWYERS *and the* ADJUTANT. GRUSHA *stands motionless.* SHAUWA *leads the* CHILD *toward her.*)

Now I'll take off this judge's gown — it's got too hot for me. I'm not cut out for a hero. In token of farewell I invite you all to a little dance in the meadow outside. Oh, I'd almost forgotten something in my excitement . . . to sign the divorce decree.

(*Using the judge's chair as a table, he writes something on a piece of paper, and prepares to leave. Dance music has started.*)

SHAUWA (*having read what is on the paper*): But that's not right. You've not divorced the old people. You've divorced Grusha!

AZDAK: Divorced the wrong couple? What a pity! And I never retract! If I did, how could we keep order in the land? (*To the* OLD COUPLE.) I'll invite you to my party instead. You don't mind dancing with each other, do you? (*To* GRUSHA *and* SIMON.) I've got forty piasters coming from you.

SIMON (*pulling out his purse*): Cheap at the price, Your Honor. And many thanks.

AZDAK (*pocketing the cash*): I'll be needing this.

GRUSHA (*to* MICHAEL): So we'd better leave the city tonight, Michael? (*To* SIMON.) You like him?

SIMON: With my respects, I like him.

GRUSHA: Now I can tell you: I took him because on that Easter Sunday I got engaged to you. So he's a child of love. Michael, let's dance.

(*She dances with* MICHAEL, SIMON *dances with the* COOK, *the* OLD COUPLE *with each other.* AZDAK *stands lost in thought. The dancers soon hide him from view. Occasionally he is seen, but less and less as more couples join the dance.*)

THE SINGER: And after that evening Azdak vanished and was never
    seen again.
The people of Grusinia did not forget him but long remembered
The period of his judging as a brief golden age,
Almost an age of justice.

(*All the couples dance off.* AZDAK *has disappeared.*)

But you, you who have listened to the Story of the Chalk Circle,
Take note what men of old concluded:
That what there is shall go to those who are good for it,
Children to the motherly, that they prosper,
Carts to good drivers, that they be driven well,
The valley to the waterers, that it yield fruit.

SIMPLICITY in art, says Eric Bentley in his Introduction to
Seven Plays by Bertolt Brecht, may be an achievement on the far side
of complexity. It is an apt comment. In Brecht, we sense the design
not as something innocent of or defiant of disorder but as immanent
in it and the artistic process as revelatory rather than creative. The
parable — the term is Brecht's own — emerges from the crowded
bustle on the stage with the clarity and strength of a folk tale. His art
is at the opposite end from classical realism. Whereas Ibsen's stage
has the stability of a room, Brecht's is open and like Shakespeare's mo-
mently capable of becoming any place the imagination calls for. The
inclusive dramatic form, fluid rather than unrealistic, embeds the moral
scheme of the fable in the promiscuous flux of actuality, but the scheme
disciplines the flux to directed movement. Parable, almost but never
quite becoming abstract scheme, balanced against stage activity, almost
but never quite becoming chaos, provides inner tension. The surface
naïveté masks a technique that orders a vast and subtle content.

If Brecht is a difficult playwright, he has been made even more
difficult by the labels of "Marxism" and "epic theater" (also his own
term) with which his plays are commonly tagged. The tags would do
less harm if they were simply wrong; then they could be removed.
They are not wrong, however, but intrusive and misleading. They
stop thought and trigger stock responses. We react, not to drama, but
to political system and esthetic theory. Like all fables, Brecht's are
concentrates of large and various experience. But the narrative that
embodies the general pattern is not abstract. "Marxist" points to certain consistent value orientations evident in the plays and "epic" to
certain distinctive ways of using the theater. But the labels say nothing
about the particulars of plot and scenic reality which the Marxist out-

look and the epic form shape into the pattern of fable. The journey motif in Grusha's story is a version of epic, but it is the particulars of the human and physical obstacles she encounters and the rhythm and direction of her progress, rather than the mere fact of narrative, that turn her journey into a superb theatrical demonstration of the "terribleness" of "the seductive power of goodness." The Azdak figure, the proletarian scamp-judge, whose moral superiority is that of the rabbit-eater over the man-eater, challenges propertied stuffiness and arrogance, legalism and feudal tyranny. There is revolutionary sentiment in the muted anger of his "Song of Injustice in Persia" and in the triumphant sarcasm of his "Song of Chaos." The old legend could be called proto-Marxist. But as a general concept Marxism is more of a hindrance than a help in a critical account of Azdak. His cowardice, vulgarity, and greed, his old cheese, bloody rags, and dirty, drunken jokes, the tragicomical implications of his futile self-condemnation for helping the Grand Duke to escape, the ironic fickleness of fortune by which he becomes first a mock, then a real, judge, then almost loses his neck, and then is reinstated as judge — are these, as scenic facts, "Marxist"?

The point, of course, is that a literary work does not contain ideology the way a pudding contains plums or even the way a cake contains butter. As a theoretical materialist Brecht wanted a more equitable distribution of economic goods and potential, and he believed in man's duty to try to improve his physical environment, and hence his conditioning, to the limit of his ability and control. Having tried Hollywood, he settled in East Berlin. But the problem of Marxism-in-Brecht is not solved by biography or by anxious search for pellets of subversive doctrine. Is property good or evil in *The Caucasian Chalk Circle* (1944-45)? Almost everyone in the play who owns anything is hardhearted, not just the feudal masters, but the peasants as well: the farmer who sells Grusha milk, Lavrenti's wife, the mother-in-law, the Invalid, the three farmers charging the old woman with theft. But then we come upon Azdak taking bribes as a matter of course and Simon Shashava being able to marry Grusha because he has been promoted to paymaster at double his earlier pay and with a house of his own. Does the play say that riches corrupt? It is less presumptuous. It says that Grusha thinks that little Michael would be corrupted if he were brought up by Natella Abashwili — a much smaller and dramatically more serviceable proposition. Is there political dynamite in Azdak's epigram, "That the roof of the world may be conquered, the roof of the cottage is torn down"? A cold-war attitude? If Azdak's awarding the child to Grusha is taken to imply an attack on property rights, doesn't "Capitalism" come to seem incompatible with kindness and

common sense? Brecht gives a new twist to the old story of the
Solomonic test of mother's love. The comfortable assumption used to
be that none but the child's real mother would sooner give up her right
to the child than cause it pain. But here the natural mother is unnatural, the foster mother truly motherly. The new version (a verse
Prologue Bentley has written for the play says) naggingly involves the
larger question of who owns anything, "and by what right"? Is this
Marxism? — or political disillusionment? The whole inquiry breaks
down.

We are aware, rather, of what Brecht perhaps had in mind when
he once referred to Azdak's "tragic side." There is in the crude farce
of his magistracy the truth that all even *his* shrewd folk wisdom
achieved was "*almost* an age of justice." Does the fault lie with his
justice or with the "dog's world" in which he is a judge? Isn't he a
bit of a brute himself? And even if we assume that the lesson which
the two kolkhozes learn from the story of Azdak is an absolute, the
modern valley setting, with evidence of Nazi ravage all around, is on-
stage proof that events rarely follow the rule "That what there is shall
go to those who are good for it." The legend of the good judge is, after
all, only an old legend.

The fact that "epic theater," unlike "Marxism," raises *literary* issues
only increases the risk of hiding the play behind a label. "Epic" is
misleading if it is taken to imply that Brecht's plays are undramatic
("epic" denoting a genre distinct from "drama" and "lyric"). Their
solidly dimensional world can be staged in its entirety, unlike the
world of novels, and by the same token is not an introspected world,
like that of lyrics. "Epic" is misleading also if it suggests the slow and
stately pace, the richness of reference, the elevated diction, the for-
mulas of image and rhetoric, the mythological machinery, and the
magnitude of theme, of classical or Miltonic epics.

What the term *should* denote is a drama that breaks the old five- or
three-act structure and proceeds by something resembling the "sta-
tions" of the guild performances of medieval mystery and miracle
plays: staged episodes in discontinuous but progressive narrative sequence. The filmic elements of large and changing cast, variety of
setting, brevity of scene, and use of flashback (in the early Azdak
scenes) also give a kind of epic effect.

But the main reason for calling Brecht's drama epic is that it is
narrated. Like the kolkhoz farmers we are in the hands of Arkadi
Tscheidse, the professional "singer" of stories from Tiflis. What we
see of Grusha's and Azdak's stories are episodes selected for dramatization from a larger entertainment-with-a-purpose, which also includes
choric comment and the narrator's linking synopses. The episodes are,

literally, *shown*. The audience understands that it does not see the characters of the legend themselves, but their twentieth-century impersonators.

Clearly, we are dealing here with a play convention quite different from that of the realist theater. By realist convention, we are unobserved observers of real life in the process of being lived — peepers and eavesdroppers. We are invited to believe, or to pretend to believe, that the actors are not actors but businessmen and housewives, that their talk is not rehearsed but spontaneous, that they are not on a stage but in an apartment. The realist convention paradoxically denies the fact of theater. As audience we get our money's worth only if we are willing to share the denial. A realist play production, we say, is successful in direct ratio to the success with which it entices us into the make-believe and keeps us there till the curtain comes down, the lights go on, and the illusion ends.

Brecht openly violates the realist convention. So does Pirandello in *Six Characters*, but what is a crucial metaphor for probing the reality of reality in Pirandello — the subject of his play — is in Brecht a casual premise for having theater at all. The devices he employs to prevent illusionism ensure theatricality.

In *The Caucasian Chalk Circle* both the most obvious and the most important of these devices is the framing of the main action in a play-within-a-play form. The device is not new. Shakespeare (for example) used it in *The Taming of the Shrew* and Beaumont in *The Knight of the Burning Pestle*. Again, *Six Characters* is the most famous example in the modern theater. However dissimilar such plays may be, they all have in common the effect they give of the theater being conscious of itself — an effect (as we already found in Pirandello) ambiguous, paradoxical, and elusive. Does the spectacle of art mocking art *as* art hint at a reaffirmation of the seriousness of art as true to life? Theatricalism, at any rate, produces a much subtler stage-audience relationship than does dramatic realism. In *The Chalk Circle* an audience in the theater watches an audience on stage, and both then watch — not a play of present life but a dramatization-narration of past legend.* The familiar but profound pun on the two meanings of the verb "to act" comes alive as the characters in the play-within "live" their theatrical existence.

Verfremdung (literally, "alienation," but most often rendered as "distancing" or "esthetic distancing") is Brecht's own term for the effect on the audience of this insistent theatricality. Its function is to

---

* In Bentley's 1961 version of his adaptation of the play, members of the fruit-growing "Galinsk" kolkhoz participate in the performance, thus further blurring the stage-audience distinction.

keep the spectator's rational faculties alert during the performance. Brecht seeks from his audience not a spellbinding imaginative projection into the life illusion on stage, but thoughtful attention to a meaningful dramatization of fable. He wants to reach minds, not to submerge them in a wash of stage-generated empathy. "I am not," he said, "greatly interested in anyone making an emotional investment in my plays." This does not mean that he fails whenever an audience gives Grusha and Azdak its sympathies or finds the play charming. It means that he uses emotional appeal as a strategy of persuasion — as a means to a rational end, not as an end in itself.

And yet, the ultimate effect of *Verfremdung* is perhaps more complex than Brecht's deliberate aim would indicate. The ambivalent status of the stage audience tends to obscure the distinction between stage and audience. From the viewpoint of the theater audience the stage audience are characters in the outer (framing) action. From the viewpoint of the performers in the inner (framed) action they are audience. Because the theater audience recognizes its own status in one of the two functions of the stage audience, it tends to identify with it in its other function as well. At the end, outer and inner action (and present and past, theater actuality and theater imagination) merge, as the dancing couples of actors and stage audience* gradually hide Azdak from view. Then the dancers, too, disappear, and the Singer is left alone on the stage to address the epilogue-moral directly to the audience in the theater. To what extent, by now, has the latter become implicated? *Verfremdung* eliminates the possibility of mistaking the theater for reality, but it does not, like the realist theater of illusion, draw a safe line of division between them.

Sets and the use of time also add to the theatricalist effect. The outdoor scene in the distant, war-torn valley plausibly limits the Singer's use of props and scenery. The sets are crude and improvised, suggestive-symbolic rather than lifelike. In the opening scene of the inner play, a doorway marks the palace side of the stage, a gateway the town side. Place is evoked rather than represented. The whole production is stylized. The "voice" of the play shifts freely back and forth between drama, narrative, and choric comment and would only be impeded by elaborate verisimilitude.

There are shifts in time as well:

THE CROWD: — The baby! — I can't see it, don't shove so hard! — God bless the child, Your Grace!

---

* It has not been made explicitly clear whether or not members of the kolkhoz audience join in the final dance, but that seems to be the implication of the stage directions of the last scene. It would, at any rate, be a scenically effective conclusion, in keeping with the play-within-the-play decorum.

THE SINGER (*while the* CROWD *is driven back with whips*): For the first time on that Easter Sunday, the people saw the Governor's heir.

The Singer's comment cuts off the gathering immediacy of the crowd scene. His viewpoint is the retrospective, generalizing one of a historian. His "saw" pulls us back sharply from the crowd's "I can't see." No sooner have we begun to suspend disbelief, accepting what we see as happening *here* and *nôw*, than the Singer steps in to remind us that the present tense applies only to the theater situation. He is presenting a show, but it is a show of what *happened — then* and *there*. Time is not always rendered realistically even within the single episode. When Lavrenti tells Grusha that she and the child must leave his farm as soon as spring comes, the accelerating drip-drip from the roof marks the passing of winter and the coming of spring even as brother and sister talk. On-stage action and dialogue proceed at normal speed, while the simultaneous off-stage sound of snow melting compresses days or weeks into the span of a few minutes.

The theatricalist fable subordinates character, too, to meaningful pattern. As the kolkhoz Prologue and the Singer's Epilogue frame the legend of Grusha and Azdak, so Grusha's scenes with Simon give a framework of romance to the hardships of her journey. We get a Chinese box effect, frame within frame. The mock-formal restraint of language in the lovers' dialogues suggests the blend of passion, liking, respect, and sheer sense of fun in their feelings for one another. But the point is their attractiveness as moral types rather than, simply, delightful romance or psychological complexity.

The most striking fact of structure in the play is the two-part division. The answer to the question whose play it is, Grusha's or Azdak's, is that it belongs to both, that the two stories are complementary halves in a dramatic whole, premises in a kind of syllogism. Parallelism prepares for their final fusion. Both Grusha and Azdak perform impulsive deeds of imprudent kindness: Grusha saves Michael, Azdak the Grand Duke. Both are rewarded for their kindness (though the reward is ironic in Azdak's case, as he regrets his kindness when he learns the old man's identity). The syllogism concludes in Grusha's and Azdak's confrontation in the chalk-circle scene. The conclusion represents a multiple climax.

It releases the suspense concerning Grusha's fate, which has been accumulating while Azdak's manner of justice has been illustrated in racy anecdote. It achieves the overt meaning of the fable. Without Azdak, Grusha's story would only have proved that in violent social upheaval there are other bitter battles fought than those on the battlefield. Without Grusha, Azdak's natural justice would have lacked a morally significant context and emotive force. Only together do the two stories have what a character in the dramatic prologue calls "a bearing on the problem" of what to do with the valley. By the test of Azdak's criterion of superior yield, as applicable to use of land as to motherliness, the settlement in favor of the fruit-growing irrigators is validated.

Finally, the chalk-circle scene completes the dramatic structure. This might have been described as two converging lines, if only Grusha's movement had not been over before Azdak's even begins, and if the flashback story of Azdak ("flashback" relative to Grusha's poignant situation at the end of Section 3 of the play) had moved at all after he becomes judge. Dramatically speaking, the near-hanging is an abortive episode, and the preceding collection of law-case anecdotes, though establishing Azdak's quality as an administrator of justice, is shapeless and static. A more accurate definition of the structural function of the chalk-circle scene is that it brings the dynamics of the brave and resourceful virgin mother's odyssey to rest in the stasis of Azdak's verdict and Simon Shashava's love, concluding the legend of how goodness once received justice in a Caucasian valley.

Tennessee Williams

THE GLASS MENAGERIE

Nobody, not even the rain, has such small hands.

E. E. CUMMINGS

Characters

> AMANDA WINGFIELD, *the mother*
> LAURA WINGFIELD, *her daughter*
> TOM WINGFIELD, *her son*
> JIM O'CONNOR, *the gentleman caller*

SCENE: *An alley in St. Louis*

PART I. *Preparation for a Gentleman Caller.*
PART II. *The Gentleman Calls.*

TIME: *Now and the Past.*

SCENE ONE

(The Wingfield apartment is in the rear of the building, one of those vast hive-like conglomerations of cellular living-units that flower as warty growths in overcrowded urban centers of lower middle-class population and are symptomatic of the impulse of this largest and fundamentally enslaved section of American society to avoid fluidity and differentiation and to exist and function as one interfused mass of automatism.

The apartment faces an alley and is entered by a fire-escape, a structure whose name is a touch of accidental poetic truth, for all of these huge buildings are always burning with the slow and implacable fires of human desperation. The fire-escape is included in the set — that is, the landing of it and steps descending from it.

The scene is memory and is therefore nonrealistic. Memory takes a lot of poetic license. It omits some details; others are exaggerated, according to the emotional value of the articles it touches, for memory is seated predominantly in the heart. The interior is therefore rather dim and poetic.

At the rise of the curtain, the audience is faced with the dark, grim rear wall of the Wingfield tenement. This building, which runs parallel to the footlights, is flanked on both sides by dark, narrow alleys which run into murky canyons of tangled clotheslines, garbage cans and the sinister latticework of neighboring fire-escapes. It is up and down these side alleys that exterior entrances and exits are made, during the play. At the end of TOM's *opening commentary, the dark tenement wall slowly reveals (by means of a transparency) the interior of the ground floor Wingfield apartment.*

Downstage is the living room, which also serves as a sleeping room for LAURA, *the sofa unfolding to make her bed. Upstage, center, and divided by a wide arch or second proscenium with transparent faded portieres (or second curtain), is the dining room. In an old-fashioned what-not in the living room are seen scores of transparent glass animals. A blown-up photograph of the father hangs on the wall of the living room, facing the audience, to the left of the archway. It is the face of a very handsome young man in a doughboy's First World War cap. He is gallantly smiling, ineluctably smiling, as if to say, "I will be smiling forever."*

The audience hears and sees the opening scene in the dining room through both the transparent fourth wall of the building and the transparent gauze portieres of the dining-room arch. It is during this revealing scene that the fourth wall slowly ascends, out of sight. This transparent exterior wall is not brought down again until the very end of the play, during TOM's *final speech.*

The narrator is an undisguised convention of the play. He takes whatever license with dramatic convention as is convenient to his purposes.

TOM *enters dressed as a merchant sailor from alley, stage left, and strolls across the front of the stage to the fire-escape. There he stops and lights a cigarette. He addresses the audience.)*

TOM: Yes, I have tricks in my pocket, I have things up my sleeve. But I am the opposite of a stage magician. He gives you illusion that has the appearance of truth. I give you truth in the pleasant disguise of illusion. To begin with, I turn back time. I reverse it to that quaint period, the thirties, when the huge middle class of America was matriculating in a school for the blind. Their eyes had failed them, or they had failed their eyes, and so they were having their fingers pressed forcibly down on the fiery Braille alphabet of a dissolving economy. In Spain there was revolution. Here there was only shouting and confusion. In Spain there was Guernica. Here there were disturbances of labor, sometimes pretty violent, in otherwise peaceful cities such as Chicago, Cleveland, Saint Louis. . . . This is the social background of the play.

(MUSIC.)

The play is memory. Being a memory play, it is dimly lighted, it is sentimental, it is not realistic. In memory everything seems to happen to music. That explains the fiddle in the wings. I am the narrator of the play, and also a character in it. The other characters are my mother, Amanda, my sister, Laura, and a gentleman caller who appears in the final scenes. He is the most realistic character in the play, being an emissary from a world of reality that we were somehow set apart from. But since I have a poet's weakness for symbols, I am using this character also as a symbol; he is the long delayed but always expected something that we live for. There is a fifth character in the play who doesn't appear except in this larger-than-life photograph over the mantel. This is our father who left us a long time ago. He was a telephone man who fell in love with long distances; he gave up his job with the telephone company and skipped the light fantastic out of town . . . The last we heard of him was a picture post-card from Mazatlan, on the Pacific coast of Mexico, containing a message of two words — "Hello — Goodbye!" and no address. I think the rest of the play will explain itself. . . .

(AMANDA'S *voice becomes audible through the portieres.*)

(LEGEND ON SCREEN: "OÙ SONT LES NEIGES.")

(*He divides the portieres and enters the upstage area.*)

(AMANDA *and* LAURA *are seated at a drop-leaf table. Eating is indicated by gestures without food or utensils.* AMANDA *faces the audience.* TOM *and* LAURA *are seated in profile.*)

(*The interior has lit up softly and through the scrim we see* AMANDA *and* LAURA *seated at the table in the upstage area.*)

AMANDA (*calling*): Tom?

TOM: Yes, Mother.

AMANDA: We can't say grace until you come to the table!

TOM: Coming, Mother. (*He bows slightly and withdraws, reappearing a few moments later in his place at the table.*)

AMANDA (*to her son*): Honey, don't *push* with your *fingers*. If you have to push with something, the thing to push with is a crust of bread. And chew — chew! Animals have sections in their stomachs which enable them to digest food without mastication, but human beings are supposed to chew their food before they swallow it down. Eat food leisurely, son, and really enjoy it. A well-cooked meal has lots of delicate flavors that have to be held in the mouth for appreciation. So chew your food and give your salivary glands a chance to function!

(TOM *deliberately lays his imaginary fork down and pushes his chair back from the table.*)

TOM: I haven't enjoyed one bite of this dinner because of your constant directions on how to eat it. It's you that makes me rush through meals with your hawk-like attention to every bite I take. Sickening — spoils my appetite — all this discussion of animals' secretion — salivary glands — mastication!

AMANDA (*lightly*): Temperament like a Metropolitan star! (*He rises and crosses downstage.*) You're not excused from the table.

TOM: I'm getting a cigarette.

AMANDA: You smoke too much.

(LAURA *rises.*)

LAURA: I'll bring in the blanc mange.

(*He remains standing with his cigarette by the portieres during the following.*)

AMANDA (*rising*): No, sister, no, sister — you be the lady this time and I'll be the darky.

LAURA: I'm already up.

AMANDA: Resume your seat, little sister — I want you to stay fresh and pretty — for gentlemen callers!

LAURA: I'm not expecting any gentlemen callers.

AMANDA (*crossing out to kitchenette. Airily*): Sometimes they come

when they are least expected! Why, I remember one Sunday afternoon in Blue Mountain — (*Enters kitchenette.*)

TOM: I know what's coming!

LAURA: Yes. But let her tell it.

TOM: Again?

LAURA: She loves to tell it.

(AMANDA *returns with bowl of dessert.*)

AMANDA: One Sunday afternoon in Blue Mountain — your mother
received — *seventeen!* — gentlemen callers! Why, sometimes there
weren't chairs enough to accommodate them all. We had to send
the nigger over to bring in folding chairs from the parish house.

TOM (*remaining at portieres*): How did you entertain those gentlemen
callers?

AMANDA: I understood the art of conversation!

TOM: I bet you could talk.

AMANDA: Girls in those days *knew* how to talk, I can tell you.

TOM: Yes?

(IMAGE: AMANDA AS A GIRL ON A PORCH, GREETING CALLERS.)

AMANDA: They knew how to entertain their gentlemen callers. It wasn't
enough for a girl to be possessed of a pretty face and a graceful
figure — although I wasn't slighted in either respect. She also
needed to have a nimble wit and a tongue to meet all occasions.

TOM: What did you talk about?

AMANDA: Things of importance going on in the world! Never anything
coarse or common or vulgar. (*She addresses* TOM *as though he
were seated in the vacant chair at the table though he remains by
portieres. He plays this scene as though he held the book.*) My
callers were gentlemen — all! Among my callers were some of the
most prominent young planters of the Mississippi Delta — planters
and sons of planters!

(TOM *motions for music and a spot of light on* AMANDA.)

(*Her eyes lift, her face glows, her voice becomes rich and elegiac.*)

(SCREEN LEGEND: "OÙ SONT LES NEIGES.")

There was young Champ Laughlin who later became vice-president
of the Delta Planters Bank. Hadley Stevenson who was drowned in
Moon Lake and left his widow one hundred and fifty thousand in
Government bonds. There were the Cutrere brothers, Wesley and
Bates. Bates was one of my bright particular beaux! He got in a

quarrel with that wild Wainright boy. They shot it out on the floor of Moon Lake Casino. Bates was shot through the stomach. Died in the ambulance on his way to Memphis. His widow was also well-provided for, came into eight or ten thousand acres, that's all. She married him on the rebound — never loved her — carried my picture on him the night he died! And there was that boy that every girl in the Delta had set her cap for! That beautiful, brilliant young Fitzhugh boy from Greene County!

TOM: What did he leave his widow?

AMANDA: He never married! Gracious, you talk as though all of my old admirers had turned up their toes to the daisies!

TOM: Isn't this the first you've mentioned that still survives?

AMANDA: That Fitzhugh boy went North and made a fortune — came to be known as the Wolf of Wall Street! He had the Midas touch, whatever he touched turned to gold! And I could have been Mrs. Duncan J. Fitzhugh, mind you! But — I picked your *father!*

LAURA (*rising*): Mother, let me clear the table.

AMANDA: No, dear, you go in front and study your typewriter chart. Or practice your shorthand a little. Stay fresh and pretty! — It's almost time for our gentlemen callers to start arriving. (*She flounces girlishly toward the kitchenette.*) How many do you suppose we're going to entertain this afternoon?

(TOM *throws down the paper and jumps up with a groan.*)

LAURA (*alone in the dining room*): I don't believe we're going to receive any, Mother.

AMANDA (*reappearing, airily*): What? No one — not one? You must be joking! (LAURA *nervously echoes her laugh. She slips in a fugitive manner through the half-open portieres and draws them gently behind her. A shaft of very clear light is thrown on her face against the faded tapestry of the curtains.* MUSIC: "THE GLASS MENAGERIE" UNDER FAINTLY. *Lightly.*) Not one gentlement caller? It can't be true! There must be a flood, there must have been a tornado!

LAURA: It isn't a flood, it's not a tornado, Mother. I'm just not popular like you were in Blue Mountain. . . . (TOM *utters another groan.* LAURA *glances at him with a faint, apologetic smile. Her voice catching a little.*) Mother's afraid I'm going to be an old maid.

THE SCENE DIMS OUT WITH "GLASS MENAGERIE" MUSIC.

SCENE TWO

(*"Laura, Haven't You Ever Liked Some Boy?"*
On the dark stage the screen is lighted with the image of blue roses.
Gradually LAURA'S *figure becomes apparent and the screen goes out.*
The music subsides.
LAURA *is seated in the delicate ivory chair at the small claw-foot table.*
She wears a dress of soft violet material for a kimono — her hair tied back from her forehead with a ribbon.
She is washing and polishing her collection of glass.
AMANDA *appears on the fire-escape steps. At the sound of her ascent,* LAURA *catches her breath, thrusts the bowl of ornaments away and seats herself stiffly before the diagram of the typewriter keyboard as though it held her spellbound. Something has happened to* AMANDA. *It is written in her face as she climbs to the landing: a look that is grim and hopeless and a little absurd.*
She has on one of those cheap or imitation velvety-looking cloth coats with imitation fur collar. Her hat is five or six years old, one of those dreadful cloche hats that were worn in the late twenties and she is clasping an enormous black patent-leather pocketbook with nickel clasp and initials. This is her full-dress outfit, the one she usually wears to the D.A.R.
Before entering she looks through the door.
She purses her lips, opens her eyes wide, rolls them upward and shakes her head.
Then she slowly lets herself in the door. Seeing her mother's expression LAURA *touches her lips with a nervous gesture.*)

LAURA: Hello, Mother, I was — (*She makes a nervous gesture toward the chart on the wall.* AMANDA *leans against the shut door and stares at* LAURA *with a martyred look.*)
AMANDA: Deception? Deception? (*She slowly removes her hat and gloves, continuing the swift suffering stare. She lets the hat and gloves fall on the floor — a bit of acting.*)
LAURA (*shakily*): How was the D.A.R. meeting? (AMANDA *slowly opens her purse and removes a dainty white handkerchief which she shakes out delicately and delicately touches to her lips and nostrils.*) Didn't you go to the D.A.R. meeting, Mother?
AMANDA (*faintly, almost inaudibly*): — No. — No. (*Then more forc-*

ibly. I did not have the strength — to go to the D.A.R. In fact, I did not have the courage! I wanted to find a hole in the ground and hide myself in it forever! (*She crosses slowly to the wall and removes the diagram of the typewriter keyboard. She holds it in front of her for a second, staring at it sweetly and sorrowfully — then bites her lips and tears it in two pieces.*)

LAURA (*faintly*): Why did you do that, Mother? (AMANDA *repeats the same procedure with the chart of the Gregg Alphabet.*) Why are you —

AMANDA: Why? Why? How old are you, Laura?

LAURA: Mother, you know my age.

AMANDA: I thought that you were an adult; it seems that I was mistaken. (*She crosses slowly to the sofa and sinks down and stares at* LAURA.)

LAURA: Please don't stare at me, Mother.

(AMANDA *closes her eyes and lowers her head. Count ten.*)

AMANDA: What are we going to do, what is going to become of us, what is the future?

(*Count ten.*)

LAURA: Has something happened, Mother? (AMANDA *draws a long breath and takes out the handkerchief again. Dabbing process.*) Mother, has — something happened?

AMANDA: I'll be all right in a minute. I'm just bewildered — (*Count five.*) — by life. . . .

LAURA: Mother, I wish that you would tell me what's happened!

AMANDA: As you know, I was supposed to be inducted into my office at the D.A.R. this afternoon. (IMAGE: A SWARM OF TYPEWRITERS.) But I stopped off at Rubicam's Business College to speak to your teachers about your having a cold and ask them what progress they thought you were making down there.

LAURA: Oh. . . .

AMANDA: I went to the typing instructor and introduced myself as your mother. She didn't know who you were. Wingfield, she said. We don't have any such student enrolled at the school! I assured her she did, that you had been going to classes since early in January. "I wonder," she said, "if you could be talking about that terribly shy little girl who dropped out of school after only a few days' attendance?" "No," I said, "Laura, my daughter, has been going to school every day for the past six weeks!" "Excuse me," she said. She took the attendance book out and there was your name, unmistakably printed, and all the dates you were absent until they decided that you had dropped out of school. I still said, "No, there must have been some mistake! There must have been some mix-up in the records!" And she said, "No — I remember her perfectly now. Her hands shook so that she couldn't hit the right keys! The first time we gave a speed-test, she broke down completely — was sick at the stomach and almost had to be carried into the wash-room! After that morning she never showed up any more. We phoned the house but never got any answer — while I was working at Famous and Barr, I suppose, demonstrating those — Oh!" I felt so weak I could barely keep on my feet! I had to sit down while they got me a glass of water! Fifty dollars' tuition, all of our plans — my hopes and ambitions for you — just gone up the spout, just gone up the spout like that. (LAURA *draws a long breath and gets awkwardly to her feet. She crosses to the victrola and winds it up.*) What are you doing?

LAURA: Oh! (*She releases the handle and returns to her seat.*)

AMANDA: Laura, where have you been going when you've gone out pretending that you were going to business college?

LAURA: I've just been going out walking.

AMANDA: That's not true.

LAURA: It is. I just went walking.

AMANDA: Walking? Walking? In winter? Deliberately courting pneumonia in that light coat? Where did you walk to, Laura?

LAURA: All sorts of places — mostly in the park.

AMANDA: Even after you'd started catching that cold?

LAURA: It was the lesser of two evils, Mother. (IMAGE: WINTER SCENE IN PARK.) I couldn't go back up. I — threw up — on the floor!

AMANDA: From half past seven till after five every day you mean to tell me you walked around in the park, because you wanted to make me think that you were still going to Rubicam's Business College?

LAURA: It wasn't as bad as it sounds. I went inside places to get warmed up.

AMANDA: Inside where?

LAURA: I went in the art museum and the bird-houses at the Zoo. I visited the penguins every day! Sometimes I did without lunch and went to the movies. Lately I've been spending most of my afternoons in the Jewel-box, that big glass house where they raise the tropical flowers.

AMANDA: You did all this to deceive me, just for the deception? (LAURA *looks down.*) Why?

LAURA: Mother, when you're disappointed, you get that awful suffering look on your face, like the picture of Jesus' mother in the museum!

AMANDA: Hush!

LAURA: I couldn't face it.

(*Pause. A whisper of strings.*)

(LEGEND: "THE CRUST OF HUMILITY.")

AMANDA (*hopelessly fingering the huge pocketbook*): So what are we going to do the rest of our lives? Stay home and watch the parades go by? Amuse ourselves with the glass menagerie, darling? Eternally play those worn-out phonograph records your father left as a painful reminder of him? We won't have a business career — we've given that up because it gave us nervous indigestion! (*Laughs wearily.*) What is there left but dependency all our lives? I know so well what becomes of unmarried women who aren't prepared to occupy a position. I've seen such pitiful cases in the South — barely tolerated spinsters living upon the grudging patronage of sister's husband or brother's wife! — stuck away in some little mouse-trap of a room — encouraged by one in-law to visit another — little birdlike women without any nest — eating the crust of humility all their life! Is that the future that we've mapped out for ourselves? I swear it's the only alternative I can think of! It isn't a very pleasant alternative, is it? Of course — some girls *do* marry. (LAURA *twists her hands nervously.*) Haven't you ever liked some boy?

LAURA: Yes. I liked one once. (*Rises.*) I came across his picture a while ago.

AMANDA (*with some interest*): He gave you his picture?

LAURA: No, it's in the year-book.

AMANDA (*disappointed*): Oh — a high-school boy.

(SCREEN IMAGE: JIM AS HIGH-SCHOOL HERO BEARING A SILVER CUP.)

LAURA: Yes. His name was Jim. (LAURA *lifts the heavy annual from the claw-foot table.*) Here he is in *The Pirates of Penzance*.

AMANDA (*absently*): The what?

LAURA: The operetta the senior class put on. He had a wonderful voice and we sat across the aisle from each other Mondays, Wednesdays and Fridays in the Aud. Here he is with the silver cup for debating! See his grin?

AMANDA (*absently*): He must have had a jolly disposition.

LAURA: He used to call me — Blue Roses.

(IMAGE: BLUE ROSES.)

AMANDA: Why did he call you such a name as that?

LAURA: When I had that attack of pleurosis — he asked me what was the matter when I came back. I said pleurosis — he thought that I said Blue Roses! So that's what he always called me after that. Whenever he saw me, he'd holler, "Hello, Blue Roses!" I didn't care for the girl that he went out with. Emily Meisenbach. Emily was the best-dressed girl at Soldan. She never struck me, though, as being sincere . . . It says in the Personal Section — they're engaged. That's — six years ago! They must be married by now.

AMANDA: Girls that aren't cut out for business careers usually wind up married to some nice man. (*Gets up with a spark of revival.*) Sister, that's what you'll do!

(LAURA *utters a startled, doubtful laugh. She reaches quickly for a piece of glass.*)

LAURA: But, Mother —

AMANDA: Yes? (*Crossing to photograph.*)

LAURA (*in a tone of frightened apology*): I'm — crippled!

(IMAGE: SCREEN.)

AMANDA: Nonsense! Laura, I've told you never, never to use that word. Why, you're not crippled, you just have a little defect — hardly noticeable, even! When people have some slight disadvantage like that, they cultivate other things to make up for it — develop charm — and vivacity — and — *charm!* That's all you have to do! (*She turns again to the photograph.*) One thing your father had *plenty of* — was *charm!*

(TOM *motions to the fiddle in the wings.*)

THE SCENE FADES OUT WITH MUSIC

SCENE THREE

LEGEND ON SCREEN: "AFTER THE FIASCO —"

(TOM *speaks from the fire-escape landing.*)

TOM: After the fiasco at Rubicam's Business College, the idea of getting a gentleman caller for Laura began to play a more important part in

Mother's calculations. It became an obsession. Like some archetype of the universal unconscious, the image of the gentleman caller haunted our small apartment. . . . (IMAGE: YOUNG MAN AT DOOR WITH FLOWERS.) An evening at home rarely passed without some allusion to this image, this spectre, this hope. . . . Even when he wasn't mentioned, his presence hung in Mother's preoccupied look and in my sister's frightened, apologetic manner — hung like a sentence passed upon the Wingfields! Mother was a woman of action as well as words. She began to take logical steps in the planned direction. Late that winter and in the early spring — realizing that extra money would be needed to properly feather the nest and plume the bird — she conducted a vigorous campaign on the telephone, roping in subscribers to one of those magazines for matrons called *The Home-maker's Companion*, the type of journal that features the serialized sublimations of ladies of letters who think in terms of delicate cup-like breasts, slim, tapering waists, rich, creamy thighs, eyes like wood-smoke in autumn, fingers that soothe and caress like strains of music, bodies as powerful as Etruscan sculpture.

(SCREEN IMAGE: GLAMOR MAGAZINE COVER.)

(AMANDA *enters with phone on long extension cord. She is spotted in the dim stage.*)

AMANDA: Ida Scott? This is Amanda Wingfield! We *missed* you at the D.A.R. last Monday! I said to myself: She's probably suffering with that sinus condition! How is that sinus condition? Horrors! Heaven have mercy! — You're a Christian martyr, yes, that's what you are, a Christian martyr! Well, I just now happened to notice that your subscription to the *Companion's* about to expire! Yes, it expires with the next issue, honey! — just when that wonderful new serial by Bessie Mae Hopper is getting off to such an exciting start. Oh, honey, it's something that you can't miss! You remember how *Gone With the Wind* took everybody by storm? You simply couldn't go out if you hadn't read it. All everybody *talked* was Scarlett O'Hara. Well, this is a book that critics already compare to *Gone With the Wind*. It's the *Gone With the Wind* of the post-World War generation! — What? — Burning? — Oh, honey, don't let them burn, go take a look in the oven and I'll hold the wire! Heavens — I think she's hung up!

DIM OUT

(LEGEND ON SCREEN: "YOU THINK I'M IN LOVE WITH CONTINENTAL SHOEMAKERS?")

(*Before the stage is lighted, the violent voices of* TOM *and* AMANDA *are heard.*)

(*They are quarreling behind the portieres. In front of them stands* LAURA *with clenched hands and panicky expression.*)

(*A clear pool of light on her figure throughout this scene.*)

TOM: What in Christ's name am I —

AMANDA (*shrilly*): Don't you use that —

TOM: Supposed to do!

AMANDA: Expression! Not in my —

TOM: Ohhh!

AMANDA: Presence! Have you gone out of your senses?

TOM: I have, that's true, *driven* out!

AMANDA: What is the matter with you, you — big — big — IDIOT!

TOM: Look — I've got *no thing*, no single thing —

AMANDA: Lower your voice!

TOM: In my life here that I can call my OWN! Everything is —

AMANDA: Stop that shouting!

TOM: Yesterday you confiscated my books! You had the nerve to —

AMANDA: I took that horrible novel back to the library — yes! That hideous book by that insane Mr. Lawrence. (TOM *laughs wildly.*) I cannot control the output of diseased minds or people who cater to them — (TOM *laughs still more wildly.*) BUT I WON'T ALLOW SUCH FILTH BROUGHT INTO MY HOUSE! No, no, no, no, no!

TOM: House, house! Who pays rent on it, who makes a slave of himself to —

AMANDA (*fairly screeching*): Don't you DARE to —

TOM: No, no, I mustn't say things! *I've* got to just —

AMANDA: Let me tell you —

TOM: I don't want to hear any more! (*He tears the portieres open. The upstage area is lit with a turgid smoky red glow.*)

(AMANDA's *hair is in metal curlers and she wears a very old bathrobe, much too large for her slight figure, a relic of the faithless Mr. Wingfield.*)

(*An upright typewriter and a wild disarray of manuscripts is on the drop-leaf table. The quarrel was probably precipitated by* AMANDA's *interruption of his creative labor. A chair lying overthrown on the floor.*)

(*Their gesticulating shadows are cast on the ceiling by the fiery glow.*)

AMANDA: You *will* hear more, you —

TOM: No, I won't hear more, I'm going out!

AMANDA: You come right back in —

TOM: Out, out out! Because I'm —

AMANDA: Come back here, Tom Wingfield! I'm not through talking to you!

TOM: Oh, go —

LAURA (*desperately*): — Tom!

AMANDA: You're going to listen, and no more insolence from you! I'm at the end of my patience! (*He comes back toward her.*)

TOM: What do you think I'm at? Aren't I supposed to have any patience to reach the end of, Mother? I know, I know. It seems unimportant to you, what I'm *doing* — what I *want* to do — having a little *difference* between them! You don't think that —

AMANDA: I think you've been doing things that you're ashamed of. That's why you act like this. I don't believe that you go every night to the movies. Nobody goes to the movies night after night. Nobody in their right minds goes to the movies as often as you pretend to. People don't go to the movies at nearly midnight, and movies don't let out at two A.M. Come in stumbling. Muttering to yourself like a maniac! You get three hours sleep and then go to work. Oh, I can picture the way you're doing down there. Moping, doping, because you're in no condition.

TOM (*wildly*): No, I'm in no condition!

AMANDA: What right have you got to jeopardize your job? Jeopardize the security of us all? How do you think we'd manage if you were —

TOM: Listen! You think I'm crazy *about* the *warehouse*? (*He bends fiercely toward her slight figure.*) You think I'm in love with the Continental Shoemakers? You think I want to spend fifty-five *years* down there in that — *celotex interior!* with — *fluorescent* — *tubes!* Look! I'd rather somebody picked up a crowbar and battered out my brains — than go back mornings! I *go!* Every time you come in yelling that God damn *"Rise and Shine!" "Rise and Shine!" I* say to myself, "How *lucky dead* people are!" But I get up. I *go!* For sixty-five dollars a month I give up all that I dream of doing and being *ever!* And you say self — *self's* all I ever think of. Why, listen, if self is what I thought of, Mother, I'd be where he is — GONE! (*Pointing to father's picture.*) As far as the system of transportation reaches! (*He starts past her. She grabs his arm.*) Don't grab at me, Mother!

AMANDA: Where are you going?

TOM: I'm going to the *movies!*

AMANDA: I don't believe that lie!

TOM (*crouching toward her, overtowering her tiny figure. She backs away, gasping*): I'm going to opium dens! Yes, opium dens, dens of vice and criminals' hang-outs, Mother. I've joined the Hogan gang, I'm a hired assassin, I carry a tommy-gun in a violin case! I run a string of cat-houses in the Valley! They call me Killer, Killer Wingfield, I'm leading a double-life, a simple, honest warehouse worker by day, by night, a dynamic *czar* of the *underworld, Mother.* I go to gambling casinos, I spin away fortunes on the roulette table! I wear a patch over one eye and a false mustache, sometimes I put on green whiskers. On those occasions they call me — *El Diablo!* Oh, I could tell you things to make you sleepless! My enemies plan to dynamite this place. They're going to blow us all sky-high some night! I'll be glad, very happy, and so will you! You'll go up, up on a broomstick, over Blue Mountain with seventeen gentlemen callers! You ugly — babbling old — *witch.* . . . (*He goes through a series of violent, clumsy movements, seizing his overcoat, lunging to the door, pulling it fiercely open. The women watch him, aghast. His arm catches in the sleeve of the coat as he struggles to pull it on. For a moment he is pinioned by the bulky garment. With an outraged groan he tears the coat off again, splitting the shoulder of it, and hurls it across the room. It strikes against the shelf of* LAURA'S *glass collection, there is a tinkle of shattering glass.* LAURA *cries out as if wounded.*)

(MUSIC LEGEND: "THE GLASS MENAGERIE.")

LAURA (*shrilly*): My glass! — menagerie. . . . (*She covers her face and turns away.*)

(*But* AMANDA *is still stunned and stupefied by the "ugly witch" so that she barely notices this occurrence. Now she recovers her speech.*)

AMANDA (*in an awful voice*): I won't speak to you — until you apologize! (*She crosses through portieres and draws them together behind her.* TOM *is left with* LAURA. LAURA *clings weakly to the mantel with her face averted.* TOM *stares at her stupidly for a moment. Then he crosses to shelf. Drops awkwardly to his knees to collect the fallen glass, glancing at* LAURA *as if he would speak but couldn't.*)

"The Glass Menagerie" steals in as

THE SCENE DIMS OUT

SCENE FOUR

(*The interior is dark. Faint light in the alley.*

A deep-voiced bell in a church is tolling the hour of five as the scene commences.

TOM *appears at the top of the alley. After each solemn boom of the bell in the tower, he shakes a little noise-maker or rattle as if to express the tiny spasm of man in contrast to the sustained power and dignity of the Almighty. This and the unsteadiness of his advance make it evident that he has been drinking.*

As he climbs the few steps to the fire-escape landing light steals up inside. LAURA *appears in night-dress, observing* TOM'S *empty bed in the front room.*

TOM *fishes in his pockets for the door-key, removing a motley assortment of articles in the search, including a perfect shower of movie-ticket stubs and an empty bottle. At last he finds the key, but just as he is about to insert it, it slips from his fingers. He strikes a match and crouches below the door.*)

TOM (*bitterly*): One crack — and it falls through!

(LAURA *opens the door.*)

LAURA: Tom! Tom, what are you doing?

TOM: Looking for a door-key.

LAURA: Where have you been all this time?

TOM: I have been to the movies.

LAURA: All this time at the movies?

TOM: There was a very long program. There was a Garbo picture and a Mickey Mouse and a travelogue and a newsreel and a preview of coming attractions. And there was an organ solo and a collection for the milk-fund — simultaneously — which ended up in a terrible fight between a fat lady and an usher!

LAURA (*innocently*): Did you have to stay through everything?

TOM: Of course! And, oh, I forgot! There was a big stage show! The headliner on this stage show was Malvolio the Magician. He performed wonderful tricks, many of them, such as pouring water back and forth between pitchers. First it turned to wine and then it turned to beer and then it turned to whiskey. I know it was whiskey it finally turned into because he needed somebody to come up out of the audience to help him, and I came up — both shows! It was Kentucky Straight Bourbon. A very generous fellow, he gave souvenirs. (*He pulls from his back pocket a shimmering rain-*

bow-colored scarf.) He gave me this. This is his magic scarf. You can have it, Laura. You wave it over a canary cage and you get a bowl of gold-fish. You wave it over the gold-fish bowl and they fly away canaries. . . . But the wonderfullest trick of all was the coffin trick. We nailed him into a coffin and he got out of the coffin without removing one nail. (*He has come inside.*) There is a trick that would come in handy for me — get me out of this 2 by 4 situation! (*Flops onto bed and starts removing shoes.*)

LAURA: Tom — Shhh!

TOM: What you shushing me for?

LAURA: You'll wake up Mother.

TOM: Goody, goody! Pay 'er back for all those "Rise an' Shines." (*Lies down, groaning.*) You know it don't take much intelligence to get yourself into a nailed-up coffin, Laura. But who in hell ever got himself out of one without removing one nail?

(*As if in answer, the father's grinning photograph lights up.*)

SCENE DIMS OUT

(*Immediately following: The church bell is heard striking six. At the sixth stroke the alarm clock goes off in* AMANDA'S *room, and after a few moments we hear her calling: "Rise and Shine! Rise and Shine! Laura, go tell your brother to rise and shine!"*)

TOM (*Sitting up slowly*): I'll rise — but I won't shine.

(*The light increases.*)

AMANDA: Laura, tell your brother his coffee is ready.

(LAURA *slips into front room.*)

LAURA: Tom! it's nearly seven. Don't make Mother nervous. (*He stares at her stupidly. Beseechingly.*) Tom, speak to Mother this morning. Make up with her, apologize, speak to her!

TOM: She won't to me. It's her that started not speaking.

LAURA: If you just say you're sorry she'll start speaking.

TOM: Her not speaking — is that such a tragedy?

LAURA: Please — please!

AMANDA (*calling from kitchenette*): Laura, are you going to do what I asked you to do, or do I have to get dressed and go out myself?

LAURA: Going, going — soon as I get on my coat! (*She pulls on a shapeless felt hat with nervous, jerky movement, pleadingly glancing at* TOM. *Rushes awkwardly for coat. The coat is one of* AMANDA'S, *inaccurately made-over, the sleeves too short for* LAURA.) Butter and what else?

AMANDA (*entering upstage*): Just butter. Tell them to charge it.

LAURA: Mother, they make such faces when I do that.

AMANDA: Stick and stones may break our bones, but the expression on Mr. Garfinkel's face won't harm us! Tell your brother his coffee is getting cold.

LAURA (*at door*): Do what I asked you, will you, will you, Tom?

(*He looks sullenly away.*)

AMANDA: Laura, go now or just don't go at all!

LAURA (*rushing out*): Going — going! (*A second later she cries out. TOM springs up and crosses to the door. AMANDA rushes anxiously in. TOM opens the door.*)

TOM: Laura?

LAURA: I'm all right. I slipped, but I'm all right.

AMANDA (*peering anxiously after her*): If anyone breaks a leg on those fire-escape steps, the landlord ought to be sued for every cent he possesses! (*She shuts door. Remembers she isn't speaking and returns to other room.*)

(*As TOM enters listlessly for his coffee, she turns her back to him and stands rigidly facing the window on the gloomy gray vault of the areaway. Its light on her face with its aged but childish features is cruelly sharp, satirical as a Daumier print.*)

(MUSIC UNDER: "AVE MARIA.")

(*TOM glances sheepishly but sullenly at her averted figure and slumps at the table. The coffee is scalding hot; he sips it and gasps and spits it back in the cup. At his gasp, AMANDA catches her breath and half turns. Then catches herself and turns back to window.*)

(*TOM blows on his coffee, glancing sidewise at his mother. She clears her throat. TOM clears his. He starts to rise. Sinks back down again, scratches his head, clears his throat again. AMANDA coughs. TOM raises his cup in both hands to blow on it, his eyes staring over the rim of it at his mother for several moments. Then he slowly sets the cup down and awkwardly and hesitantly rises from the chair.*)

TOM (*hoarsely*): Mother. I — I apologize. Mother. (AMANDA *draws a quick, shuddering breath. Her face works grotesquely. She breaks into childlike tears.*) I'm sorry for what I said, for everything that I said, I didn't mean it.

AMANDA (*sobbingly*): My devotion has made me a witch and so I make myself hateful to my children!

TOM: *No,* you *don't.*

AMANDA: I worry so much, don't sleep, it makes me nervous!

TOM (*gently*): I understand that.

AMANDA: I've had to put up a solitary battle all these years. But you're my right-hand bower! Don't fall down, don't fail!

TOM (*gently*): I try, Mother.

AMANDA (*with great enthusiasm*): Try and you will SUCCEED! (*The notion makes her breathless.*) Why, you — you're just *full* of natural endowments! Both of my children — they're *unusual* children! Don't you think I know it? I'm so — *proud!* Happy and — feel I've — so much to be thankful for but — Promise me one thing, son!

TOM: What, Mother?

AMANDA: Promise, son, you'll — never be a drunkard!

TOM (*turns to her grinning*): I will never be a drunkard, Mother.

AMANDA: That's what frightened me so, that you'd be drinking! Eat a bowl of Purina!

TOM: Just coffee, Mother.

AMANDA: Shredded wheat biscuit?

TOM: No. No, Mother, just coffee.

AMANDA: You can't put in a day's work on an empty stomach. You've got ten minutes — don't gulp! Drinking too-hot liquids makes cancer of the stomach. . . . Put cream in.

TOM: No, thank you.

AMANDA: To cool it.

TOM: No! No, thank you, I want it black.

AMANDA: I know, but it's not good for you. We have to do all that we can to build ourselves up. In these trying times we live in, all that we have to cling to is — each other. . . . That's why it's so important to — Tom, I — I sent out your sister so I could discuss something with you. If you hadn't spoken I would have spoken to you. (*Sits down.*)

TOM (*gently*): What is it, Mother, that you want to discuss?

AMANDA: *Laura!*

(TOM *puts his cup down slowly.*)

(LEGEND ON SCREEN: "LAURA.")

(MUSIC: "THE GLASS MENAGERIE.")

TOM: — Oh. — Laura . . .

AMANDA (*touching his sleeve*): You know how Laura is. So quiet but — still water runs deep! She notices things and I think she

— broods about them. (TOM *looks up*). A few days ago I came in and she was crying.

TOM: What about?

AMANDA: You.

TOM: Me?

AMANDA: She has an idea that you're not happy here.

TOM: What gave her that idea?

AMANDA: What gives her any idea? However, you do act strangely. I — I'm not criticizing, understand *that!* I know your ambitions do not lie in the warehouse, that like everybody in the whole wide world — you've had to — make sacrifices, but — Tom — Tom — life's not easy, it calls for — Spartan endurance! There's so many things in my heart that I cannot describe to you! I've never told you but I — *loved* your father. . . .

TOM (*gently*): I know that, Mother.

AMANDA: And you — when I see you taking after his ways! Staying out late — and — well, you *had* been drinking the night you were in that — terrifying condition! Laura says that you hate the apartment and that you go out nights to get away from it! Is that true, Tom?

TOM: No. You say there's so much in your heart that you can't describe to me. That's true of me, too. There' so much in my heart that I can't describe to *you!* So let's respect each other's —

AMANDA: But, why — *why*, Tom — are you always so *restless?* Where do you go to, nights?

TOM: I — go to the movies.

AMANDA: Why do you go to the movies so much, Tom?

TOM: I go to the movies because — I like adventure. Adventure is something I don't have much of at work, so I go to the movies.

AMANDA: But, Tom, you go to the movies *entirely* too *much!*

TOM: I like a lot of adventure.

(AMANDA *looks baffled, then hurt. As the familiar inquisition resumes he becomes hard and impatient again.* AMANDA *slips back into her querulous attitude toward him.*)

(IMAGE ON SCREEN: SAILING VESSEL WITH JOLLY ROGER.)

AMANDA: Most young men find adventure in their careers.

TOM: Then most young men are not employed in a warehouse.

AMANDA: The world is full of young men employed in warehouses and offices and factories.

TOM: Do all of them find adventure in their careers?

AMANDA: They do or they do without it! Not everybody has a craze for adventure.

TOM: Man is by instinct a lover, a hunter, a fighter, and none of those instincts are given much play at the warehouse!

AMANDA: Man is by instinct! Don't quote instinct to me! Instinct is something that people have got away from! It belongs to animals! Christian adults don't want it!

TOM: What do Christian adults want, then, Mother?

AMANDA: Superior things! Things of the mind and the spirit! Only animals have to satisfy instincts! Surely your aims are somewhat higher than theirs! Than monkeys — pigs —

TOM: I reckon they're not.

AMANDA: You're joking. However, that isn't what I wanted to discuss.

TOM (*rising*): I haven't much time.

AMANDA (*pushing his shoulders*): Sit down.

TOM: You want me to punch in red at the warehouse, Mother?

AMANDA: You have five minutes. I want to talk about Laura.

(LEGEND: "PLANS AND PROVISIONS.")

TOM: All right! What about Laura?

AMANDA: We have to be making plans and provisions for her. She's older than you, two years, and nothing has happened. She just drifts along doing nothing. It frightens me terribly how she just drifts along.

TOM: I guess she's the type that people call home girls.

AMANDA: There's no such type, and if there is, it's a pity! That is unless the home is hers, with a husband!

TOM: What?

AMANDA: Oh, I can see the handwriting on the wall as plain as I see the nose in front of my face! It's terrifying! More and more you remind me of your father! He was out all hours without explanation — Then *left*! *Good-bye*! And me with a bag to hold. I saw that letter you got from the Merchant Marine. I know what you're dreaming of. I'm not standing here blindfolded. Very well, then. Then *do* it! But not till there's somebody to take your place.

TOM: What do you mean?

AMANDA: I mean that as soon as Laura has got somebody to take care of her, married, a home of her own, independent — why, then you'll be free to go wherever you please, on land, on sea, whichever way the wind blows you! But until that time you've got to look out for your sister. I don't say me because I'm old and don't matter! I say for your sister because she's young and dependent. I put her in business college — a dismal failure! Frightened her so it made her sick to her stomach. I took her over to the Young People's League at the church. Another fiasco. She spoke to nobody, nobody spoke to her. Now all she does is fool with those pieces of glass and play those worn-out records. What kind of a life is that for a girl to lead?

TOM: What can I do about it?

AMANDA: Overcome selfishness! Self, self, self is all that you ever think of! (TOM *springs up and crosses to get his coat. It is ugly and bulky. He pulls on a cap with earmuffs.*) Where is your muffler? Put your wool muffler on! (*He snatches it angrily from the closet and tosses it around his neck and pulls both ends tight.*) Tom! I haven't said what I had in mind to ask you.

TOM: I'm too late to —

AMANDA (*catching his arm — very importunately. Then shyly*): Down at the warehouse, aren't there some — nice young men?

TOM: No!

AMANDA: There *must* be — *some* . . .

TOM: Mother —

(*Gesture.*)

AMANDA: Find out one that's clean-living — doesn't drink and — ask him out for sister!

TOM: What?

AMANDA: For *sister!* To *meet!* Get *acquainted!*

TOM (*stamping to door*): Oh, my go-osh!

AMANDA: Will you? (*He opens door. Imploringly.*) Will you? (*He starts down.*) Will you? *Will* you, dear?

TOM (*calling back*): YES!

(AMANDA *closes the door hesitantly and with a troubled but faintly hopeful expression.*)

(SCREEN IMAGE: GLAMOR MAGAZINE COVER.)

(*Spot* AMANDA *at phone.*)

AMANDA: Ella Cartwright? This is Amanda Wingfield! How are you, honey? How is that kidney condition? (*Count five.*) Horrors! (*Count five.*) You're a Christian martyr, yes, honey, that's what you are, a Christian martyr! Well, I just happened to notice in my little red book that your subscription to the *Companion* has just run out! I knew that you wouldn't want to miss out on the wonderful serial starting in this new issue. It's by Bessie Mae Hopper, the first thing she's written since *Honeymoon for Three.*

Wasn't that a strange and interesting story? Well, this one is even lovelier, I believe. It has a sophisticated society background. It's all about the horsey set on Long Island!

FADE OUT

SCENE FIVE

LEGEND ON SCREEN: "ANNUNCIATION." *Fade with music.*

(*It is early dusk of a spring evening. Supper has just been finished in the Wingfield apartment.* AMANDA *and* LAURA *in light colored dresses are removing dishes from the table, in the upstage area, which is shadowy, their movements formalized almost as a dance or ritual, their moving forms as pale and silent as moths.*

TOM, *in white shirt and trousers, rises from the table and crosses toward the fire-escape.*)

AMANDA (*as he passes her*): Son, will you do me a favor?

TOM: What?

AMANDA: Comb your hair! You look so pretty when your hair is combed! (TOM *slouches on sofa with evening paper. Enormous caption "Franco Triumphs".*) There is only one respect in which I would like you to emulate your father.

TOM: What respect is that?

AMANDA: The care he always took of his appearance. He never allowed himself to look untidy. (*He throws down the paper and crosses to fire-escape.*) Where are you going?

TOM: I'm going out to smoke.

AMANDA: You smoke too much. A pack a day at fifteen cents a pack. How much would that amount to in a month? Thirty times fifteen is how much, Tom? Figure it out and you will be astounded at what you could save. Enough to give you a night-school course in accounting at Washington U! Just think what a wonderful thing that would be for you, son!

(TOM *is unmoved by the thought.*)

TOM: I'd rather smoke. (*He steps out on landing, letting the screen door slam.*)

AMANDA (*sharply*): I know! That's the tragedy of it. . . . (*Alone, she turns to look at her husband's picture.*)

(DANCE MUSIC: "ALL THE WORLD IS WAITING FOR THE SUNRISE!")

TOM (*to the audience*): Across the alley from us was the Paradise Dance Hall. On evenings in spring the windows and doors were open and the music came outdoors. Sometimes the lights were turned out except for a large glass sphere that hung from the ceiling. It would turn slowly about and filter the dusk with delicate rainbow colors. Then the orchestra played a waltz or a tango, something that had a slow and sensuous rhythm. Couples would come outside, to the relative privacy of the alley. You could see them kissing behind ash-pits and telephone poles. This was the compensation for lives that passed like mine, without any change or adventure. Adventure and change were imminent in this year. They were waiting around the corner for all these kids. Suspended in the mist over Berchtesgaden, caught in the folds of Chamberlain's umbrella — In Spain there was Guernica! But here there was only hot swing music and liquor, dance halls, bars, and movies, and sex that hung in the gloom like a chandelier and flooded the world with brief, deceptive rainbows. . . . All the world was waiting for bombardments!

(AMANDA *turns from the picture and comes outside*.)

AMANDA (*Sighing*). A fire-escape landing's a poor excuse for a porch. (*She spreads a newspaper on a step and sits down, gracefully and demurely as if she were settling into a swing on a Mississippi veranda*.) What are you looking at?

TOM: The moon.

AMANDA: Is there a moon this evening?

TOM: It's rising over Garfinkel's Delicatessen.

AMANDA: So it is! A little silver slipper of a moon. Have you made a wish on it yet?

TOM: Um-hum.

AMANDA: What did you wish for?

TOM: That's a secret.

AMANDA: A secret, huh? Well, I won't tell mine either. I will be just as mysterious as you.

TOM: I bet I can guess what yours is.

AMANDA: Is my head so transparent?

TOM: You're not a sphinx.

AMANDA: No, I don't have secrets. I'll tell you what I wished for on the moon. Success and happiness for my precious children! I wish for that whenever there's a moon, and when there isn't a moon, I wish for it, too.

TOM: I thought perhaps you wished for a gentleman caller.

AMANDA: Why do you say that?

TOM: Don't you remember asking me to fetch one?

AMANDA: I remember suggesting that it would be nice for your sister if you brought home some nice young man from the warehouse. I think I've made that suggestion more than once.

TOM: Yes, you have made it repeatedly.

AMANDA: Well?

TOM: We are going to have one.

AMANDA: *What?*

TOM: A gentleman caller!

(THE ANNUNCIATION IS CELEBRATED WITH MUSIC.)

(AMANDA *rises.*)

(IMAGE ON SCREEN: CALLER WITH BOUQUET.)

AMANDA: You mean you have asked some nice young man to come over?

TOM: Yep. I've asked him to dinner.

AMANDA: You really did?

TOM: I did!

AMANDA: You did, and did he — *accept?*

TOM: He did!

AMANDA: Well, well — well, well! That's — lovely!

TOM: I thought that you would be pleased.

AMANDA: It's definite, then?

TOM: Very definite.

AMANDA: Soon?

TOM: Very soon.

AMANDA: For heaven's sake, stop putting on and tell me some things, will you?

TOM: What things do you want me to tell you?

AMANDA: *Naturally* I would like to know when he's *coming!*

TOM: He's coming tomorrow.

AMANDA: *Tomorrow?*

TOM: Yep. Tomorrow.

AMANDA: But, Tom!

TOM: Yes, Mother?

AMANDA: Tomorrow gives me no time!

TOM: Time for what?

AMANDA: Preparations! Why didn't you phone me at once, as soon as you asked him, the minute that he accepted? Then, don't you see, I could have been getting ready!

TOM: You don't have to make any fuss.

AMANDA: Oh, Tom, Tom, Tom, of course I have to make a fuss! I want things nice, not sloppy! Not thrown together. I'll certainly have to do some fast thinking, won't I?

TOM: I don't see why you have to think at all.

AMANDA: You just don't know. We can't have a gentleman caller in a pig-sty! All my wedding silver has to be polished, the monogrammed table linen ought to be laundered! The windows have to be washed and fresh curtains put up. And how about clothes? We have to *wear* something, don't we?

TOM: Mother, this boy is no one to make a fuss over!

AMANDA: Do you realize he's the first young man we've introduced to your sister? It's terrible, dreadful, disgraceful that poor little sister has never received a single gentleman caller! Tom, come inside! [*She opens the screen door.*]

TOM: What for?

AMANDA: I want to ask you some things.

TOM: If you're going to make such a fuss, I'll call it off, I'll tell him not to come.

AMANDA: You certainly won't do anything of the kind. Nothing offends people worse than broken engagements. It simply means I'll have to work like a Turk! We won't be brilliant, but we'll pass inspection. Come on inside. (TOM *follows, groaning.*) Sit down.

TOM: Any particular place you would like me to sit?

AMANDA: Thank heavens I've got that new sofa! I'm also making payments on a floor lamp I'll have sent out! And put the chintz covers on, they'll brighten things up! Of course I'd hoped to have these walls re-papered. . . . What is the young man's name?

TOM: His name is O'Connor.

AMANDA: That, of course, means fish —tomorrow is Friday! I'll have that salmon loaf — with Durkee's dressing! What does he do? He works at the warehouse?

TOM: Of course! How else would I —

AMANDA: Tom, he — doesn't drink?

TOM: Why do you ask me that?

AMANDA: Your father *did!*

TOM: Don't get started on that!

AMANDA: He *does* drink, then?

TOM: Not that I know of!

AMANDA: Make sure, be certain! The last thing I want for my daughter's a boy who drinks!

TOM: Aren't you being a little premature? Mr. O'Connor has not yet appeared on the scene!

AMANDA: But will tomorrow. To meet your sister, and what do I know about his character? Nothing! Old maids are better off than wives of drunkards!

TOM: Oh, my God!

AMANDA: Be still!

TOM (*leaning forward to whisper*): Lots of fellows meet girls whom they don't marry!

AMANDA: Oh, talk sensibly, Tom — and don't be sarcastic! (*She has gotten a hairbrush.*)

TOM: What are you doing?

AMANDA: I'm brushing that cow-lick down! What is this young man's position at the warehouse?

TOM (*submitting grimly to the brush and the interrogation*): This young man's position is that of a shipping clerk, Mother.

AMANDA: Sounds to me like a fairly responsible job, the sort of a job *you* would be in if you just had more *get-up*. What is his salary? Have you got any idea?

TOM: I would judge it to be approximately eighty-five dollars a month.

AMANDA: Well — not princely, but —

TOM: Twenty more than I make.

AMANDA: Yes, how well I know! But for a family man, eighty-five dollars a month is not much more than you can just get by on. . . .

TOM: Yes, but Mr. O'Connor is not a family man.

AMANDA: He might be, mightn't he? Some time in the future?

TOM: I see. Plans and provisions.

AMANDA: You are the only young man that I know of who ignores the fact that the future becomes the present, the present the past, and the past turns into everlasting regret if you don't plan for it!

TOM: I will think that over and see what I can make of it.

AMANDA: Don't be supercilious with your mother! Tell me some more about this — what do you call him?

TOM: James D. O'Connor. The D. is for Delaney.

AMANDA: Irish on *both* sides! *Gracious!* And doesn't drink?

TOM: Shall I call him up and ask him right this minute?

AMANDA: The only way to find out about those things is to make discreet inquiries at the proper moment. When I was a girl in Blue Mountain and it was suspected that a young man drank, the girl whose attentions he had been receiving, if any girl *was*, would sometimes speak to the minister of his church, or rather her father would if her father was living, and sort of feel him out on the young man's character. That is the way such things are discreetly handled to keep a young woman from making a tragic mistake!

TOM: Then how did you happen to make a tragic mistake?

AMANDA: That innocent look of your father's had everyone fooled! He *smiled* — the world was *enchanted!* No girl can do worse than put herself at the mercy of a handsome appearance! I hope that Mr. O'Connor is not too good-looking.

TOM: No, he's not too good-looking. He's covered with freckles and hasn't too much of a nose.

AMANDA: He's not right-down homely, though?

TOM: Not right-down homely. Just medium homely, I'd say.

AMANDA: Character's what to look for in a man.

TOM: That's what I've always said, Mother.

AMANDA: You've never said anything of the kind and I suspect you would never give it a thought.

TOM: Don't be suspicious of me.

AMANDA: At least I hope he's the type that's up and coming.

TOM: I think he really goes in for self-improvement.

AMANDA: What reason have you to think so?

TOM: He goes to night school.

AMANDA (*beaming*): Splendid! What does he do, I mean study?

TOM: Radio engineering and public speaking!

AMANDA: Then he has visions of being advanced in the world! Any young man who studies public speaking is aiming to have an executive job some day! And radio engineering? A thing for the future! Both of these facts are very illuminating. Those are the sort of things that a mother should know concerning any young man who comes to call on her daughter. Seriously or — not.

TOM: One little warning. He doesn't know about Laura. I didn't let on that we had dark ulterior motives. I just said, why don't you come have dinner with us? He said okay and that was the whole conversation.

AMANDA: I bet it was! You're eloquent as an oyster. However, he'll know about Laura when he gets here. When he sees how lovely and sweet and pretty she is, he'll thank his lucky stars he was asked to dinner.

TOM: Mother, you mustn't expect too much of Laura.

AMANDA: What do you mean?

TOM: Laura seems all those things to you and me because she's ours and we love her. We don't even notice she's crippled any more.

AMANDA: Don't say crippled! You know that I never allow that word to be used!

TOM: But face facts, Mother. She is and — that's not all —

AMANDA: What do you mean "not all"?

TOM: Laura is very different from other girls.

AMANDA: I think the difference is all to her advantage.

TOM: Not quite all — in the eyes of others — strangers — she's terribly shy and lives in a world of her own and those things make her seem a little peculiar to people outside the house.

AMANDA: Don't say peculiar.

TOM: Face the facts. She is.

(THE DANCE-HALL MUSIC CHANGES TO A TANGO THAT HAS A MINOR AND SOMEWHAT OMINOUS TONE.)

AMANDA: In what way is she peculiar — may I ask?

TOM (*gently*): She lives in a world of her own — a world of — little glass ornaments, Mother. . . . (*Gets up.* AMANDA *remains holding brush, looking at him, troubled.*) She plays old phonograph records and — that's about all — (*He glances at himself in the mirror and crosses to door.*)

AMANDA (*sharply*): Where are you going?

TOM: I'm going to the movies. (*Out screen door.*)

AMANDA: Not to the movies, every night to the movies! (*Follows quickly to screen door.*) I don't believe you always go to the movies! (*He is gone.* AMANDA *looks worriedly after him for a moment. Then vitality and optimism return and she turns from the door. Crossing to portieres.*) Laura! Laura! (LAURA *answers from kitchenette.*)

LAURA: Yes, Mother.

AMANDA: Let those dishes go and come in front! (LAURA *appears with dish towel. Gaily.*) Laura, come here and make a wish on the moon!

LAURA (*entering*): Moon — moon?

AMANDA: A little silver slipper of a moon. Look over your left shoulder, Laura, and make a wish! (LAURA *looks faintly puzzled as if called out of sleep.* AMANDA *seizes her shoulders and turns her at an angle by the door.*) No! Now, darling, *wish!*

LAURA: What shall I wish for, Mother?

AMANDA (*her voice trembling and her eyes suddenly filling with tears*): Happiness! Good Fortune!

(*The violin rises and the stage dims out.*)

SCENE SIX

(IMAGE: HIGH SCHOOL HERO.)

TOM: And so the following evening I brought Jim home to dinner. I had known Jim slightly in high school. In high school Jim was a hero. He had tremendous Irish good nature and vitality with the scrubbed and polished look of white chinaware. He seemed to move in a continual spotlight. He was a star in basketball, captain of the debating club, president of the senior class and the glee club and he sang the male lead in the annual light operas. He was always running or bounding, never just walking. He seemed always at the point of defeating the law of gravity. He was shooting with such velocity through his adolescence that you would logically expect him to arrive at nothing short of the White House by the time he was thirty. But Jim apparently ran into more interference after his graduation from Soldan. His speed had definitely slowed. Six years after he left high school he was holding a job that wasn't much better than mine.

(IMAGE: CLERK.)

He was the only one at the warehouse with whom I was on friendly terms. I was valuable to him as someone who could remember his former glory, who had seen him win basketball games and the silver cup in debating. He knew of my secret practice of retiring to a cabinet of the washroom to work on poems when business was slack in the warehouse. He called me Shakespeare. And while the other boys in the warehouse regarded me with suspicious hostility, Jim took a humorous attitude toward me. Gradually his attitude affected the others, their hostility wore off and they also began to smile at me as people smile at an oddly fashioned dog who trots across their path at some distance.

I knew that Jim and Laura had known each other at Soldan, and I had heard Laura speak admiringly of his voice. I didn't know if Jim remembered her or not. In high school Laura had been as unobtrusive as Jim had been astonishing. If he did remember Laura, it was not as my sister, for when I asked him to dinner, he grinned and said, "You know, Shakespeare, I never thought of you as having folks!"

He was about to discover that I did. . . .

(LIGHT UP STAGE.)

(LEGEND ON SCREEN: "THE ACCENT OF A COMING FOOT.")

(*Friday evening. It is about five o'clock of a late spring evening which comes "scattering poems in the sky."*)

(*A delicate lemony light is in the Wingfield apartment.*)

(AMANDA *has worked like a Turk in preparation for the gentleman caller. The results are astonishing. The new floor lamp with its rose-silk shade is in place, a colored paper lantern conceals the*

*broken light fixture in the ceiling, new billowing white curtains
are at the windows, chintz covers are on chairs and sofa, a pair of
new sofa pillows make their initial appearance.*)

(*Open boxes and tissue paper are scattered on the floor.*)

(LAURA *stands in the middle with lifted arms while* AMANDA
*crouches before her, adjusting the hem of the new dress, devout
and ritualistic. The dress is colored and designed by memory. The
arrangement of* LAURA'S *hair is changed; it is softer and more becoming. A fragile, unearthly prettiness has come out in* LAURA:
*she is like a piece of translucent glass touched by light, given a
momentary radiance, not actual, not lasting.*)

AMANDA (*impatiently*): Why are you trembling?
LAURA: Mother, you've made me so nervous!
AMANDA: How have I made you nervous?
LAURA: By all this fuss! You make it seem so important!
AMANDA: I don't understand you, Laura. You couldn't be satisfied with
    just sitting home, and yet whenever I try to arrange something for
    you, you seem to resist it. (*She gets up.*) Now take a look at your-
    self. No, wait! Wait just a moment — I have an idea!
LAURA: What is it now?

(AMANDA *produces two powder puffs which she wraps in handker-
chiefs and stuffs in* LAURA'S *bosom.*)

LAURA: Mother, what are you doing?
AMANDA: They call them "Gay Deceivers"!
LAURA: I won't wear them!
AMANDA: You will!
LAURA: Why should I?
AMANDA: Because, to be painfully honest, your chest is flat.
LAURA: You make it seem like we were setting a trap.
AMANDA: All pretty girls are a trap, a pretty trap, and men expect them
    to be. (LEGEND: "A PRETTY TRAP.") Now look at yourself, young
    lady. This is the prettiest you will ever be! I've got to fix myself now!
    You're going to be surprised by your mother's appearance! (*She
    crosses through portieres, humming gaily.*)

(LAURA *moves slowly to the long mirror and stares solemnly at
herself.*)

(*A wind blows the white curtains inward in a slow, graceful motion and with a faint, sorrowful sighing.*)

AMANDA (*off stage*): It isn't dark enough yet. (*She turns slowly before the mirror with a troubled look.*)

(LEGEND ON SCREENS "THIS IS MY SISTER: CELEBRATE HER WITH STRINGS!" MUSIC.)

AMANDA (*laughing, off*): I'm going to show you something. I'm going to make a spectacular appearance!

LAURA: What is it, Mother?

AMANDA: Possess your soul in patience — you will see! Something I've resurrected from that old trunk! Styles haven't changed so terribly much after all. . . . (*She parts the portieres.*) Now just look at your mother! (*She wears a girlish frock of yellowed voile with a blue silk sash. She carries a bunch of jonquils — the legend of her youth is nearly revived. Feverishly*) This is the dress in which I led the cotillion. Won the cakewalk twice at Sunset Hill, wore one spring to the Governor's ball in Jackson! See how I sashayed around the ballroom, Laura? (*She raises her skirt and does a mincing step around the room.*) I wore it on Sundays for my gentlemen callers! I had it on the day I met your father — I had malaria fever all that spring. The change of climate from East Tennessee to the Delta — weakened resistance — I had a little temperature all the time — not enough to be serious — just enough to make me restless and giddy! Invitations poured in — parties all over the Delta! — "Stay in bed," said Mother, "you have fever!" — but I just wouldn't. — I took quinine but kept on going, going! — Evenings, dances! — Afternoons, long, long rides! Picnics — lovely! — So lovely, that country in May. — All lacy with dogwood, literally flooded with jonquils! — That was the spring I had the craze for jonquils. Jonquils became an absolute obsession. Mother said, "Honey, there's no more room for jonquils." And still I kept on bringing in more jonquils. Whenever, wherever I saw them, I'd say, "Stop! Stop! I see jonquils!" I made the young men help me gather the jonquils! It was a joke, Amanda and her jonquils! Finally there were no more vases to hold them, every available space was filled with jonquils. No vases to hold them? All right, I'll hold them myself! And then I — (*She stops in front of the picture. MUSIC.*) met your father! Malaria fever and jonquils and then — this — boy. . . . (*She switches on the rose-colored lamp.*) I hope they get here before it starts to rain. (*She crosses upstage and places the jonquils in bowl on table.*) I gave your brother a little extra change so he and Mr. O'Connor could take the service car home.

LAURA (*with altered look*): What did you say his name was?

AMANDA: O'Connor.

LAURA: What is his first name?
AMANDA: I don't remember. Oh, yes, I do. It was — Jim!

(LAURA *sways slightly and catches hold of a chair.*)

(LEGEND ON SCREEN: "NOT JIM!")

LAURA (*faintly*): Not — Jim!
AMANDA: Yes, that was it, it was Jim! I've never known a Jim that wasn't nice!

(MUSIC: OMINOUS.)

LAURA: Are you sure his name is Jim O'Connor?
AMANDA: Yes. Why?
LAURA: Is he the one that Tom used to know in high school?
AMANDA: He didn't say so. I think he just got to know him at the warehouse.
LAURA: There was a Jim O'Connor we both knew in high school — (*Then, with effort.*) If that is the one that Tom is bringing to dinner — you'll have to excuse me, I won't come to the table.
AMANDA: What sort of nonsense is this?
LAURA: You asked me once if I'd ever liked a boy. Don't you remember I showed you this boy's picture?
AMANDA: You mean the boy you showed me in the year book?
LAURA: Yes, that boy.
AMANDA: Laura, Laura, were you in love with that boy?
LAURA: I don't know, Mother. All I know is I couldn't sit at the table if it was him!
AMANDA: It won't be him! It isn't the least bit likely. But whether it is or not, you will come to the table. You will not be excused.
LAURA: I'll have to be, Mother.
AMANDA: I don't intend to humor your silliness, Laura. I've had too much from you and your brother, both! So just sit down and compose yourself till they come. Tom has forgotten his key so you'll have to let them in, when they arrive.
LAURA (*panicky*): Oh, Mother — *you* answer the door!
AMANDA (*lightly*): I'll be in the kitchen — busy!
LAURA: Oh, Mother, please answer the door, don't make me do it!
AMANDA (*crossing into kitchenette*): I've got to fix the dressing for the salmon. Fuss, fuss — silliness! — over a gentleman caller!

(*Door swings shut.* LAURA *is left alone.*)

(LEGEND: "TERROR!")

(*She utters a low moan and turns off the lamp — sits stiffly on the edge of the sofa, knotting her fingers together.*)

(LEGEND ON SCREEN: "THE OPENING OF A DOOR!")

(TOM *and* JIM *appear on the fire-escape steps and climb to landing. Hearing their approach,* LAURA *rises with a panicky gesture. She retreats to the portieres.*)

(*The doorbell.* LAURA *catches her breath and touches her throat. Low drums.*)

AMANDA (*calling*): Laura, sweetheart! The door!

(LAURA *stares at it without moving.*)

JIM: I think we just beat the rain.

TOM: Uh-huh. (*He rings again, nervously.* JIM *whistles and fishes for a cigarette.*)

AMANDA (*very, very gaily*): Laura, that is your brother and Mr. O'Connor! Will you let them in, darling?

(LAURA *crosses toward kitchenette door.*)

LAURA (*breathlessly*): Mother — you go to the door!

(AMANDA *steps out of kitchenette and stares furiously at* LAURA. *She points imperiously at the door.*)

LAURA: Please, please!

AMANDA (*in a fierce whisper*): What is the matter with you, you silly thing?

LAURA (*desperately*): Please, you answer it, *please!*

AMANDA: I told you I wasn't going to humor you, Laura. Why have you chosen this moment to lose your mind?

LAURA: Please, please, please, you go!

AMANDA: You'll have to go to the door because I can't!

LAURA (*despairingly*): I can't either!

AMANDA: Why?

LAURA: I'm *sick!*

AMANDA: I'm sick, too — of your nonsense! Why can't you and your brother be normal people? Fantastic whims and behavior! (TOM *gives a long ring.*) Preposterous goings on! Can you give me one reason — (*Calls out lyrically.*) COMING? JUST ONE SECOND! — why should you be afraid to open a door? Now you answer it, Laura!

LAURA: Oh, oh, oh . . . (*She returns through the portieres. Darts to the victrola and winds it frantically and turns it on.*)

AMANDA: Laura Wingfield, you march right to that door!

LAURA: Yes — yes, Mother!

(*A faraway, scratchy rendition of "Dardanella" softens the air and gives her strength to move through it. She slips to the door and draws it cautiously open.*)

(TOM *enters with the caller,* JIM O'CONNOR.)

TOM: Laura, this is Jim. Jim, this is my sister, Laura.

JIM (*stepping inside*): I didn't know that Shakespeare had a sister!

LAURA (*retreating stiff and trembling from the door*): How — how do you do?

JIM (*heartily extending his hand*): Okay!

(LAURA *touches it hesitantly with hers.*)

JIM: Your hand's *cold*, Laura!

LAURA: Yes, well — I've been playing the victrola. . . .

JIM: Must have been playing classical music on it! You ought to play a little hot swing music to warm you up!

LAURA: Excuse me — I haven't finished playing the victrola. . . .

(*She turns awkwardly and hurries into the front room. She pauses a second by the victrola. Then catches her breath and darts through the portieres like a frightened deer.*)

JIM (*grinning*): What was the matter?

TOM: Oh — with Laura? Laura is — terribly shy.

JIM: Shy, huh? It's unusual to meet a shy girl nowadays. I don't believe you ever mentioned you had a sister.

TOM: Well, now you know. I have one. Here is the *Post Dispatch*. You want a piece of it?

JIM: Uh-huh.

TOM: What piece? The comics?

JIM: Sports! (*Glances at it.*) Ole Dizzy Dean is on his bad behavior.

TOM (*disinterest*): Yeah? (*Lights cigarette and crosses back to fire-escape door.*)

JIM: Where are *you* going?

TOM: I'm going out on the terrace.

JIM (*goes after him*): You know, Shakespeare — I'm going to sell you a bill of goods!

TOM: What goods?

JIM: A course I'm taking.

TOM: Huh?

JIM: In public speaking! You and me, we're not the warehouse type.

TOM: Thanks — that's good news. But what has public speaking got to do with it?

JIM: It fits you for — executive positions!

TOM: Awww.

JIM: I tell you it's done a helluva lot for me.

(IMAGE: EXECUTIVE AT DESK.)

TOM: In what respect?

JIM: In every! Ask yourself what is the difference between you an' me and men in the office down front? Brains? — No! — Ability? — No! Then what? Just one little thing —

TOM: What is that one little thing?

JIM: Primarily it amounts to — social poise! Being able to square up to people and hold your own on any social level!

AMANDA (*off stage*): Tom?

TOM: Yes, Mother?

AMANDA: Is that you and Mr. O'Connor?

TOM: Yes, Mother.

AMANDA: Well, you just make yourselves comfortable in there.

TOM: Yes, Mother.

AMANDA: Ask Mr. O'Connor if he would like to wash his hands.

JIM: Aw, no — no — thank you — I took care of that at the warehouse. Tom —

TOM: Yes?

JIM: Mr. Mendoza was speaking to me about you.

TOM: Favorably?

JIM: What do you think?

TOM: Well —

JIM: You're going to be out of a job if you don't wake up.

TOM: I am waking up —

JIM: You show no signs.

TOM: The signs are interior.

(IMAGE ON SCREEN: THE SAILING VESSEL WITH JOLLY ROGER AGAIN.)

TOM: I'm planning to change. (*He leans over the rail speaking with quiet exhilaration. The incandescent marquees and signs of the first-run movie houses light his face from across the alley. He looks like a voyager.*) I'm right at the point of committing myself to a future that doesn't include the warehouse and Mr. Mendoza or even a night-school course in public speaking.

JIM: What are you gassing about?

TOM: I'm tired of the movies.

JIM: Movies!

TOM: Yes, movies! Look at them — (A *wave toward the marvels of Grand Avenue*.) All of those glamorous people — having adventures — hogging it all, gobbling the whole thing up! You know what happens? People go to the *movies* instead of *moving!* Hollywood characters are supposed to have all the adventures for everybody in America, while everybody in America sits in a dark room and watches them have them! Yes, until there's a war. That's when adventure becomes available to the masses! *Everyone's* dish, not only Gable's! Then the people in the dark room come out of the dark room to have some adventures themselves — Goody, goody! — It's our turn now, to go to the South Sea Island — to make a safari — to be exotic, far-off! — But I'm not patient. I don't want to wait till then. I'm tried of the *movies* and I am *about* to *move!*

JIM (*incredulously*): Move?

TOM: Yes.

JIM: When?

TOM: Soon!

JIM: Where? Where?

(THEME THREE MUSIC SEEMS TO ANSWER THE QUESTION, WHILE TOM THINKS IT OVER. HE SEARCHES AMONG HIS POCKETS.)

TOM: I'm starting to boil inside. I know I seem dreamy, but inside — well, I'm boiling! Whenever I pick up a shoe, I shudder a little thinking how short life is and what I am doing! — Whatever that means. I know it doesn't mean shoes — except as something to wear on a traveler's feet! (*Finds paper*.) Look —

JIM: What?

TOM: I'm a member.

JIM (*reading*): The Union of Merchant Seamen.

TOM: I paid my dues this month, instead of the light bill.

JIM: You will regret it when they turn the lights off.

TOM: I won't be here.

JIM: How about your mother?

TOM: I'm like my father. The bastard son of a bastard! See how he grins? And he's been absent going on sixteen years!

JIM: You're just talking, you drip. How does your mother feel about it?

TOM: Shhh! — Here comes Mother! Mother is not acquainted with my plans!

AMANDA (*enters portieres*): Where are you all?

TOM: On the terrace, Mother.

(*They start inside. She advances to them.* TOM *is distinctly shocked at her appearance. Even* JIM *blinks a little. He is making his first contact with girlish Southern vivacity and in spite of the night-school course in public speaking is somewhat thrown off the beam by the unexpected outlay of social charm.*)

(*Certain responses are attempted by* JIM *but are swept aside by* AMANDA's *gay laughter and chatter.* TOM *is embarrassed but after the first shock* JIM *reacts very warmly. Grins and chuckles, is altogether won over.*)

(IMAGE: AMANDA AS A GIRL.)

AMANDA   (*coyly smiling, shaking her girlish ringlets*): Well, well, well, so this is Mr. O'Connor. Introductions entirely unnecessary. I've heard so much about you from my boy. I finally said to him, Tom — good gracious! — why don't you bring this paragon to supper? I'd like to meet this nice young man at the warehouse! — Instead of just hearing him sing your praises so much! I don't know why my son is so stand-offish — that's not Southern behavior! Let's sit down and — I think we could stand a little more air in here! Tom, leave the door open. I felt a nice fresh breeze a moment ago. Where has it gone to? Mmm, so warm already! And not quite summer, even. We're going to burn up when summer really gets started. However, we're having — we're having a very light supper. I think light things are better fo' this time of year. The same as light clothes are. Light clothes an' light food are what warm weather calls fo'. You know our blood gets so thick during th' winter — it takes a while fo' us to *adjust* ou'selves! — when the season changes . . . It's come so quick this year. I wasn't prepared. All of a sudden — heavens! Already summer! — I ran to the trunk an' pulled out this light dress — Terribly old! Historical almost! But feels so good — so good an' co-ol, y'know. . . .

TOM: Mother —

AMANDA: Yes, honey?

TOM: How about — supper?

AMANDA: Honey, you go ask Sister if supper is ready! You know that Sister is in full charge of supper! Tell her you hungry boys are waiting for it. (*To* JIM.) Have you met Laura?

JIM: She —

AMANDA: Let you in? Oh, good, you've met already! It's rare for a girl as sweet an' pretty as Laura to be domestic! But Laura is, thank heavens, not only pretty but also very domestic. I'm not at all. I

The Glass Menagerie

never was a bit. I never could make a thing but angel-food cake. Well, in the South we had so many servants. Gone, gone, gone. All vestige of gracious living! Gone completely! I wasn't prepared for what the future brought me. All of my gentlemen callers were sons of planters and so of course I assumed that I would be married to one and raise my family on a large piece of land with plenty of servants. But man proposes — and woman accepts the proposal! — To vary that old, old saying a little bit — I married no planter! I married a man who worked for the telephone company! — That gallantly smiling gentleman over there! (*Points to the picture.*) A telephone man who — fell in love with long-distance! — Now he travels and I don't even know where! — But what am I going on for about my — tribulations? Tell me yours — I hope you don't have any! Tom?

TOM (*returning*): Yes, Mother?

AMANDA: Is supper nearly ready?

TOM: It looks to me like supper is on the table.

AMANDA: Let me look — (*She rises prettily and looks through portieres.*) Oh, lovely! — But where is Sister?

TOM: Laura is not feeling well and she says that she thinks she'd better not come to the table.

AMANDA: What? — Nonsense! — Laura? Oh, Laura!

LAURA (*Off stage, faintly*): Yes, Mother.

AMANDA: You really must come to the table. We won't be seated until you come to the table! Come in, Mr. O'Connor. You sit over there, and I'll — Laura? Laura Wingfield! You're keeping us waiting, honey! We can't say grace until you come to the table!

(*The back door is pushed weakly open and* LAURA *comes in. She is obviously quite faint, her lips trembling, her eyes wide and staring. She moves unsteadily toward the table.*)

(LEGEND: "TERROR!")

(*Outside a summer storm is coming abruptly. The white curtains billow inward at the windows and there is a sorrowful murmur and deep blue dusk.*)

(LAURA *suddenly stumbles — she catches at a chair with a faint moan.*)

TOM: Laura!

AMANDA: Laura! (*There is a clap of thunder.*) (LEGEND: "AH!") (*Despairingly*). Why, Laura, you *are* sick, darling! Tom, help your sister into the living room, dear! Sit in the living room, Laura —

rest on the sofa. Well! (*To the gentleman caller.*) Standing over the hot stove made her ill! — I told her that it was just too warm this evening, but — (TOM *comes back in.* LAURA *is on the sofa.*) Is Laura all right now?

TOM: Yes.

AMANDA: What *is* that? Rain? A nice cool rain has come up! (*She gives the gentleman caller a frightened look.*) I think we may — have grace — now . . . (TOM *looks at her stupidly.*) Tom, honey — you say grace!

TOM: Oh . . . "For these and all thy mercies —" (*They bow their heads,* AMANDA *stealing a nervous glance at* JIM. *In the living room* LAURA, *stretched on the sofa, clenches her hand to her lips, to hold back a shuddering sob.*) God's Holy Name be praised —

THE SCENE DIMS OUT

SCENE SEVEN

(A Souvenir.)

(*Half an hour later. Dinner is just being finished in the upstage area which is concealed by the drawn portieres.*

As the curtain rises LAURA *is still huddled upon the sofa, her feet drawn under her, her head resting on a pale blue pillow, her eyes wide and mysteriously watchful. The new floor lamp with its shade of rose-colored silk gives a soft, becoming light to her face, bringing out the fragile, unearthly prettiness which usually escapes attention. There is a steady murmur of rain, but it is slackening and stops soon after the scene begins; the air outside becomes pale and luminous as the moon breaks out.*

A moment after the curtain rises, the lights in both rooms flicker and go out.)

JIM: Hey, there, Mr. Light Bulb!

(AMANDA *laughs nervously.*)

(LEGEND: "SUSPENSION OF A PUBLIC SERVICE.")

AMANDA: Where was Moses when the lights went out? Ha-ha. Do you know the answer to that one, Mr. O'Connor?

JIM: No, Ma'am, what's the answer?

AMANDA: In the dark! (JIM *laughs appreciably.*) Everybody sit still. I'll light the candles. Isn't it lucky we have them on the table? Where's a match? Which of you gentlemen can provide a match?

JIM: Here.

AMANDA: Thank you, sir.

JIM: Not at all, Ma'am!

AMANDA: I guess the fuse has burnt out. Mr. O'Connor, can you tell a burnt-out fuse? I know I can't and Tom is a total loss when it comes to mechanics. (SOUND: GETTING UP: VOICES RECEDE A LITTLE TO KITCHENETTE.) Oh, be careful you don't bump into something. We don't want our gentleman caller to break his neck. Now wouldn't that be a fine howdy-do?

JIM: Ha-ha! Where is the fuse-box?

AMANDA: Right here next to the stove. Can you see anything?

JIM: Just a minute.

AMANDA: Isn't electricity a mysterious thing? Wasn't it Benjamin Franklin who tied a key to a kite? We live in such a mysterious universe, don't we? Some people say that science clears up all the mysteries for us. In my opinion it only creates more! Have you found it yet?

JIM: No, Ma'am. All these fuses look okay to me.

AMANDA: Tom!

TOM: Yes, Mother?

AMANDA: That light bill I gave you several days ago. The one I told you we got the notices about?

TOM: Oh. — Yeah.

(LEGEND: "HA!")

AMANDA: You didn't neglect to pay it by any chance?

TOM: Why, I —

AMANDA: Didn't! I might have known it!

JIM: Shakespeare probably wrote a poem on that light bill, Mrs. Wingfield.

AMANDA: I might have known better than to trust him with it! There's such a high price for negligence in this world!

JIM: Maybe the poem will win a ten-dollar prize.

AMANDA: We'll just have to spend the remainder of the evening in the nineteenth century, before Mr. Edison made the Mazda lamp!

JIM: Candlelight is my favorite kind of light.

AMANDA: That shows you're romantic! But that's no excuse for Tom. Well, we got through dinner. Very considerate of them to let us get through dinner before they plunged us into everlasting darkness, wasn't it, Mr. O'Connor?

JIM: Ha-ha!

AMANDA: Tom, as a penalty for your carelessness you can help me with the dishes.

JIM: Let me give you a hand.

AMANDA: Indeed you will not!

JIM: I ought to be good for something.

AMANDA: Good for something? (*Her tone is rhapsodic.*) You? Why, Mr. O'Connor, nobody, *nobody's* given me this much entertainment in years — as you have!

JIM: Aw, now, Mrs. Wingfield!

AMANDA: I'm not exaggerating, not one bit! But Sister is all by her lonesome. You go keep her company in the parlor! I'll give you this lovely old candelabrum that used to be on the altar at the church of the Heavenly Rest. It was melted a little out of shape when the church burnt down. Lightning struck it one spring. Gypsy Jones was holding a revival at the time and he intimated that the church was destroyed because the Episcopalians gave card parties.

JIM: Ha-ha.

AMANDA: And how about coaxing Sister to drink a little wine? I think it would be good for her! Can you carry both at once?

JIM: Sure. I'm Superman!

AMANDA: Now, Thomas, get into this apron!

(*The door of kitchenette swings closed on* AMANDA's *gay laughter; the flickering light approaches the portieres.*)

(LAURA *sits up nervously as he enters. Her speech at first is low and breathless from the almost intolerable strain of being alone with a stranger.*)

(THE LEGEND. "I DON'T SUPPOSE YOU REMEMBER ME AT ALL!")

(*In her first speeches in this scene, before* JIM's *warmth overcomes her paralyzing shyness,* LAURA's *voice is thin and breathless as though she has just run up a steep flight of stairs.*)

(JIM's *attitude is gently humorous. In playing this scene it should be stressed that while the incident is apparently unimportant, it is to* LAURA *the climax of her secret life.*)

JIM: Hello, there, Laura.

LAURA (*faintly*): Hello. (*She clears her throat.*)

JIM: How are you feeling now? Better?

LAURA: Yes. Yes, thank you.

JIM: This is for you. A little dandelion wine. (*He extends it toward her with extravagant gallantry.*)

LAURA: Thank you.

JIM: Drink it — but don't get drunk! (*He laughs heartily.* LAURA *takes the glass uncertainly; laughs shyly.*) Where shall I set the candles?

LAURA: Oh — oh, anywhere . . .

JIM: How about here on the floor? Any objections?

LAURA: No.

JIM: I'll spread a newspaper under to catch the drippings. I like to sit on the floor. Mind if I do?

LAURA: Oh, no.

JIM: Give me a pillow?

LAURA: What?

JIM: A pillow!

LAURA: Oh . . . (*Hands him one quickly.*)

JIM: How about you? Don't you like to sit on the floor?

LAURA: Oh — yes.

JIM: Why don't you, then?

LAURA: I — will.

JIM: Take a pillow! (LAURA *does. Sits on the other side of the candelabrum.* JIM *crosses his legs and smiles engagingly at her.*) I can't hardly see you sitting way over there.

LAURA: I can — see you.

JIM: I know, but that's not fair, I'm in the limelight. (LAURA *moves her pillow closer.*) Good! Now I can see you! Comfortable?

LAURA: Yes.

JIM: So am I. Comfortable as a cow. Will you have some gum?

LAURA: No, thank you.

JIM: I think that I will indulge, with your permission. (*Musingly unwraps it and holds it up.*) Think of the fortune made by the guy that invented the first piece of chewing gum. Amazing, huh? The Wrigley Building is one of the sights of Chicago. — I saw it summer before last when I went up to the Century of Progress. Did you take in the Century of Progress?

LAURA: No, I didn't.

JIM: Well, it was quite a wonderful exposition. What impressed me most was the Hall of Science. Gives you an idea of what the future will be in America, even more wonderful than the present time is! (*Pause. Smiling at her.*) Your brother tells me you're shy. Is that right, Laura?

LAURA: I — don't know.

JIM: I judge you to be an old-fashioned type of girl. Well, I think that's a pretty good type to be. Hope you don't think I'm being too personal — do you?

LAURA (*hastily, out of embarrassment*): I believe I *will* take a piece of gum, if you — don't mind. (*Clearing her throat.*) Mr. O'Connor, have you — kept up with your singing?

JIM: Singing? Me?

LAURA: Yes. I remember what a beautiful voice you had.

JIM: When did you hear me sing?

(VOICE OFF STAGE IN THE PAUSE.)

VOICE (*off stage*):

> O blow, ye winds, heigh-ho,
> A-roving I will go!
>   I'm off to my love
>   With a boxing glove —
> Ten thousand miles away!

JIM: You say you've heard me sing?

LAURA: Oh, yes! Yes, very often . . . I — don't suppose you remember me — at all?

JIM (*smiling doubtfully*): You know I have an idea I've seen you before. I had that idea soon as you opened the door. It seemed almost like I was about to remember your name. But the name that I started to call you — wasn't a name! And so I stopped myself before I said it.

LAURA: Wasn't it — Blue Roses?

JIM: (*springs up. Grinning*): Blue Roses! My gosh, yes — Blue Roses! That's what I had on my tongue when you opened the door! Isn't it funny what tricks your memory plays? I didn't connect you with the high school somehow or other. But that's where it was; it was high school. I didn't even know you were Shakespeare's sister! Gosh, I'm sorry.

LAURA: I didn't expect you to. You — barely knew me!

JIM: But we did have a speaking acquaintance, huh?

LAURA: Yes, we — spoke to each other.

JIM: When did you recognize me?

LAURA: Oh, right away!

JIM: Soon as I came in the door?

LAURA: When I heard your name I thought it was probably you. I knew that Tom used to know you a little in high school. So when you came in the door — Well, then I was — sure.

JIM: Why didn't you *say* something, then?

LAURA (*breathlessly*): I didn't know what to say, I was — too surprised!

JIM: For goodness' sakes! You know, this sure is funny!

LAURA: Yes! Yes, isn't it, though . . .

JIM: Didn't we have a class in something together?

LAURA: Yes, we did.

JIM: What class was that?

LAURA: It was — singing — Chorus!

JIM: Aw!

LAURA: I sat across the aisle from you in the Aud.

JIM: Aw.

LAURA: Mondays, Wednesdays and Fridays.

JIM: Now I remember — you always came in late.

LAURA: Yes, it was so hard for me, getting upstairs. I had that brace on my leg — it clumped so loud!

JIM: I never heard any clumping.

LAURA (*wincing at the recollection*): To me it sounded like — thunder!

JIM: Well, well, well, I never even noticed.

LAURA: And everybody was seated before I came in. I had to walk in front of all those people. My seat was in the back row. I had to go clumping all the way up the aisle with everyone watching!

JIM: You shouldn't have been self-conscious.

LAURA: I know, but I was. It was always such a relief when the singing started.

JIM: Aw, yes, I've placed you now! I used to call you Blue Roses. How was it that I got started calling you that?

LAURA: I was out of school a little while with pleurosis. When I came back you asked me what was the matter. I said I had pleurosis — you thought I said Blue Roses. That's what you always called me after that!

JIM: I hope you didn't mind.

LAURA: Oh, no — I liked it. You see, I wasn't acquainted with **many** — people. . . .

JIM: As I remember you sort of stuck by yourself.

LAURA: I — I — never had much luck at — making friends.

JIM: I don't see why you wouldn't.

LAURA: Well, I — started out badly.

JIM: You mean being —

LAURA: Yes, it sort of — stood between me —

JIM: You shouldn't have let it!

LAURA: I know, but it did, and —

JIM: You were shy with people!

LAURA: I tried not to be but never could —

JIM: Overcome it?

LAURA: No, I — I never could!

JIM: I guess being shy is something you have to work out of kind of gradually.

LAURA: (*sorrowfully*): Yes — I guess it —

JIM: Takes time!

LAURA: Yes —

JIM: People are not so dreadful when you know them. That's what you have to remember! And everybody has problems, not just you, but practically everybody has got some problems. You think of yourself as having the only problems, as being the only one who is disappointed. But just look around you and you will see lots of people as disappointed as you are. For instance, I hoped when I was going to high school that I would be further along at this time, six years later, than I am now — You remember that wonderful write-up I had in *The Torch?*

LAURA: Yes! (*She rises and crosses to table.*)

JIM: It said I was bound to succeed in anything I went into! (LAURA *returns with the annual.*) Holy Jeez! *The Torch!* (*He accepts it reverently. They smile across it with mutual wonder.* LAURA *crouches beside him and they begin to turn through it.* LAURA's *shyness is dissolving in his warmth.*)

LAURA: Here you are in *Pirates of Penzance!*

JIM (*wistfully*): I sang the baritone lead in that operetta.

LAURA (*rapidly*): So — *beautifully!*

JIM (*protesting*): Aw —

LAURA: Yes, yes — beautifully — beautifully!

JIM: You heard me?

LAURA: All three times!

JIM: No!

LAURA: Yes!

JIM: All three performances?

LAURA (*Looking down*): Yes.

JIM: Why?

LAURA: I — wanted to ask you to — autograph my program.

JIM: Why didn't you ask me to?

LAURA: You were always surrounded by your own friends so much that I never had a chance to.

JIM: You should have just —

LAURA: Well, I — thought you might think I was —

JIM: Thought I might think you was — what?

LAURA: Oh —

JIM (*with reflective relish*): I was beleaguered by females in those days.

LAURA: You were terribly popular!

JIM: Yeah —

LAURA: You had such a — friendly way —

JIM: I was spoiled in high school.

LAURA: Everybody — liked you!

JIM: Including you?

LAURA: I — yes, I — I did, too — (*She gently closes the book in her lap.*)

JIM: Well, well, well! — Give me that program, Laura. (*She hands it to him. He signs it with a flourish.*) There you are — better late than never!

LAURA: Oh, I — what a — surprise!

JIM: My signature isn't worth very much right now. But some day — maybe — it will increase in value! Being disappointed is one thing and being discouraged is something else. I am disappointed but I am not discouraged. I'm twenty-three years old. How old are you?

LAURA: I'll be twenty-four in June.

JIM: That's not old age!

LAURA: No, but —

JIM: You finished high school?

LAURA (*with difficulty*): I didn't go back.

JIM: You mean you dropped out?

LAURA: I made bad grades in my final examinations. (*She rises and replaces the book and the program. Her voice strained.*) How is — Emily Meisenbach getting along?

JIM: Oh, that kraut-head!

LAURA: Why do you call her that?

JIM: That's what she was.

LAURA: You're not still — going with her?

JIM: I never see her.

LAURA: It said in the Personal Section that you were — engaged!

JIM: I know, but I wasn't impressed by that — propaganda!

LAURA: It wasn't — the truth?

JIM: Only in Emily's optimistic opinion!

LAURA: Oh —

(LEGEND: "WHAT HAVE YOU DONE SINCE HIGH SCHOOL?")

(JIM *lights a cigarette and leans indolently back on his elbows smiling at* LAURA *with a warmth and charm which lights her inwardly with altar candles. She remains by the table and turns in her hands a piece of glass to cover her tumult.*)

JIM (*after several reflective puffs on a cigarette*): What have you done since high school? (*She seems not to hear him.*) Huh? (LAURA *looks up.*) I said what have you done since high school, Laura?

LAURA: Nothing much.

JIM: You must have been doing something these six long years.

LAURA: Yes.

JIM: Well, then, such as what?

LAURA: I took a business course at business college —

JIM: How did that work out?

LAURA: Well, not very — well — I had to drop out, it gave me — indigestion —

(JIM *laughs gently.*)

JIM: What are you doing now?

LAURA: I don't do anything — much. Oh, please don't think I sit around doing nothing! My glass collection takes up a good deal of my time. Glass is something you have to take good care of.

JIM: What did you say — about glass?

LAURA: Collection I said — I have one — (*She clears her throat and turns away again, acutely shy.*)

JIM: (*abruptly*): You know what I judge to be the trouble with you? Inferiority complex! Know what that is? That's what they call it when someone low-rates himself! I understand it because I had it, too. Although my case was not so aggravated as yours seems to be. I had it until I took up public speaking, developed my voice, and learned that I had an aptitude for science. Before that time I never thought of myself as being outstanding in any way whatsoever! Now I've never made a regular study of it, but I have a friend who says I can analyze people better than doctors that make a profession of it. I don't claim that to be necessarily true, but I can sure guess a person's psychology, Laura! (*Takes out his gum.*) Excuse me, Laura. I always take it out when the flavor is gone. I'll use this scrap of paper to wrap it in. I know how it is to get it stuck on a shoe. Yep — that's what I judge to be your principal trouble. A lack of confidence in yourself as a person. You don't have the proper amount of faith in yourself. I'm basing that fact on a number of your remarks and also on certain observations I've made. For instance that clumping you thought was so awful in high school. You say that you even dreaded to walk into class. You see what you did? You dropped out of school, you gave up an education because of a clump, which as far as I know was practically non-existent! A little physical defect is what you have. Hardly noticeable even! Magnified thousands of times by imagination! You know what my strong advice to you is? Think of yourself as *superior* in some way!

LAURA: In what way would I think?

JIM: Why, man alive, Laura! Just look about you a little. What do you see? A world full of common people! All of 'em born and all of 'em going to die! Which of them has one-tenth of your good points! Or mine! Or anyone else's, as far as that goes — Gosh! Everybody excels in some one thing. Some in many! (*Unconsciously glances at himself in the mirror.*) All you've got to do is discover in *what!* Take me, for instance. (*He adjusts his tie at the mirror.*) My interest happens to lie in electro-dynamics. I'm taking a course in radio engineering at night school, Laura, on top of a fairly responsible job at the warehouse. I'm taking that course and studying public speaking.

LAURA: Ohhhh.

JIM: Because I believe in the future of television! (*Turning back to her.*) I wish to be ready to go up right along with it. Therefore I'm planning to get in on the ground floor. In fact, I've already made the right connections and all that remains is for the industry itself to get under way! Full steam — (*His eyes are starry.*) Knowledge — Zzzzzp! Money — Zzzzzzp! — Power! That's the cycle democracy is built on! (*His attitude is convincingly dynamic. LAURA stares at him, even her shyness eclipsed in her absolute wonder. He suddenly grins.*) I guess you think I think a lot of myself!

LAURA: No — o-o-o, I —

JIM: Now how about you? Isn't there something you take more interest in than anything else?

LAURA: Well, I do — as I said — have my — glass collection —

(*A peal of girlish laughter from the kitchen.*)

JIM: I'm not right sure I know what you're talking about. What kind of glass is it?

LAURA: Little articles of it, they're ornaments mostly! Most of them are little animals made out of glass, the tiniest little animals in the world. Mother calls them a glass menagerie! Here's an example of one, if you'd like to see it! This one is one of the oldest. It's nearly thirteen. (*He stretches out his hand.*) (MUSIC: "THE GLASS MENAGERIE.") Oh, be careful — if you breathe, it breaks!

JIM: I'd better not take it. I'm pretty clumsy with things.

LAURA: Go on, I trust you with him! (*Places it in his palm.*) There now — you're holding him gently! Hold him over the light, he loves the light! You see how the light shines through him?

JIM: It sure does shine!

LAURA: I shouldn't be partial, but he is my favorite one.

JIM: What kind of a thing is this one supposed to be?

LAURA: Haven't you noticed the single horn on his forehead?

JIM: A unicorn, huh?

LAURA: Mmm-hmmm!

JIM: Unicorns, aren't they extinct in the modern world?

LAURA: I know!

JIM: Poor little fellow, he must feel sort of lonesome.

LAURA (*smiling*): Well, if he does he doesn't complain about it. He stays on a shelf with some horses that don't have horns and all of them seem to get along nicely together.

JIM: How do you know?

LAURA (*lightly*): I haven't heard any arguments among them!

JIM (*grinning*): No arguments, huh? Well, that's a pretty good sign! Where shall I set him?

LAURA: Put him on the table. They all like a change of scenery once in a while!

JIM (*stretching*): Well, well, well, well — Look how big my shadow is when I stretch!

LAURA: Oh, oh, yes — it stretches across the ceiling!

JIM (*crossing to door*): I think it's stopped raining. (*Opens fire-escape door.*) Where does the music come from?

LAURA: From the Paradise Dance Hall across the alley.

JIM: How about cutting the rug a little, Miss Wingfield?

LAURA: Oh, I —

JIM: Or is your program filled up? Let me have a look at it. (*Grasps imaginary card.*) Why, every dance is taken! I'll just have to scratch some out. (WALTZ MUSIC: "LA GOLONDRINA") Ahhh, a waltz! (*He executes some sweeping turns by himself then holds his arms toward* LAURA.)

LAURA (*breathlessly*): I — can't dance!

JIM: There you go, that inferiority stuff!

LAURA: I've never danced in my life!

JIM: Come on, try!

LAURA: Oh, but I'd step on you!

JIM: I'm not made out of glass.

LAURA: How — how — how do we start?

JIM: Just leave it to me. You hold your arms out a little.

LAURA: Like this?

JIM: A little bit higher. Right. Now don't tighten up, that's the main thing about it — relax.

LAURA (*laughing breathlessly*): It's hard not to.

JIM: Okay.

LAURA: I'm afraid you can't budge me.

JIM: What do you bet I can't? (*He swings her into motion.*)

LAURA: Goodness, yes, you can!

JIM: Let yourself go, now, Laura, just let yourself go.

LAURA: I'm —

JIM: Come on!

LAURA: Trying!

JIM: Not so stiff — Easy does it!

LAURA: I know but I'm —

JIM: Loosen th' backbone! There now, that's a lot better.

LAURA: Am I?

JIM: Lots, lots better! (*He moves her about the room in a clumsy waltz.*)

LAURA: Oh, my!

JIM: Ha-ha!

LAURA: Oh, my goodness!

JIM: Ha-ha-ha! (*They suddenly bump into the table.* JIM *stops.*) What did we hit on?

LAURA: Table.

JIM: Did something fall off it? I think —

LAURA: Yes.

JIM: I hope that it wasn't the little glass horse with the horn!

LAURA: Yes.

JIM: Aw, aw, aw. Is it broken?

LAURA: Now it is just like all the other horses.

JIM: It's lost its —

LAURA: Horn! It doesn't matter. Maybe it's a blessing in disguise.

JIM: You'll never forgive me. I bet that that was your favorite piece of glass.

LAURA: I don't have favorites much. It's no tragedy, Freckles. Glass breaks so easily. No matter how careful you are. The traffic jars the shelves and things fall off them.

JIM: Still I'm awfully sorry that I was the cause.

LAURA (*smiling*): I'll just imagine he had an operation. The horn was removed to make him feel less — freakish! (*They both laugh.*) Now he will feel more at home with the other horses, the ones that don't have horns . . .

JIM: Ha-ha, that's very funny! (*Suddenly serious.*) I'm glad to see that you have a sense of humor. You know — you're — well — very different! Surprisingly different from anyone else I know! (*His voice becomes soft and hesitant with a genuine feeling.*) Do you mind me telling you that? (LAURA *is abashed beyond speech.*) I mean it in a nice way . . . (LAURA *nods shyly, looking away.*) You make me feel sort of — I don't know how to put it! I'm usually pretty good at expressing things, but — This is something that I don't know how to say! (LAURA *touches her throat and clears it — turns the broken uni-*

corn in her hands.) (*Even softer.*) Has anyone ever told you that you were pretty? (PAUSE: MUSIC.) (LAURA *looks up slowly, with wonder, and shakes her head.*) Well, you are! In a very different way from anyone else. And all the nicer because of the difference, too. (*His voice becomes low and husky.* LAURA *turns away, nearly faint with the novelty of her emotions.*) I wish that you were my sister. I'd teach you to have some confidence in yourself. The different people are not like other people, but being different is nothing to be ashamed of. Because other people are not such wonderful people. They're one hundred times one thousand. You're one times one! They walk all over the earth. You just stay here. They're common as — weeds, but — you — well, you're — *Blue Roses!*

(IMAGE ON SCREEN: BLUE ROSES.)

(MUSIC CHANGES.)

LAURA: But blue is wrong for — roses . . .
JIM: It's right for you — You're — pretty!
LAURA: In what respect am I pretty?
JIM: In all respects — believe me! Your eyes — your hair — are pretty! Your hands are pretty! (*He catches hold of her hand.*) You think I'm making this up because I'm invited to dinner and have to be nice. Oh, I could do that! I could put on an act for you, Laura, and say lots of things without being very sincere. But this time I am. I'm talking to you sincerely. I happened to notice you had this inferiority complex that keeps you from feeling comfortable with people. Somebody needs to build your confidence up and make you proud instead of shy and turning away and — blushing — Somebody ought to — Ought to — *kiss* you, Laura! (*His hand slips slowly up her arm to her shoulder.*) (MUSIC SWELLS TUMULTUOUSLY.) (*He suddenly turns her about and kisses her on the lips. When he releases her* LAURA *sinks on the sofa with a bright, dazed look.* JIM *backs away and fishes in his pocket for a cigarette.*) (LEGEND ON SCREEN: "SOUVENIR.") Stumble-john! (*He lights the cigarette, avoiding her look. There is a peal of girlish laughter from* AMANDA *in the kitchen.* LAURA *slowly raises and opens her hand. It still contains the little broken glass animal. She looks at it with a tender, bewildered expression.*) Stumble-john! I shouldn't have done that — That was way off the beam. You don't smoke, do you? (*She looks up, smiling, not hearing the question. He sits beside her a little gingerly. She looks at him speechlessly — waiting. He coughs decorously and moves a little farther aside as he considers the situation and senses her feelings, dimly, with perturbation. Gently.*) Would you —

care for a — mint? (*She doesn't seem to hear him but her look grows brighter even.*) Peppermint — Life Saver? My pocket's a regular drug store — wherever I go . . . (*He pops a mint in his mouth. Then gulps and decides to make a clean breast of it. He speaks slowly and gingerly.*) Laura, you know, if I had a sister like you, I'd do the same thing as Tom. I'd bring out fellows and — introduce her to them. The right type of boys of a type to — appreciate her. Only — well — he made a mistake about me. Maybe I've got no call to be saying this. That may not have been the idea in having me over. But what if it was? There's nothing wrong about that. The only trouble is that in my case — I'm not in a situation to — do the right thing. I can't take down your number and say I'll phone. I can't call up next week and — ask for a date. I thought I had better explain the situation in case you misunderstood it and — hurt your feelings. . . . (*Pause. Slowly, very slowly,* LAURA'S *look changes, her eyes returning slowly from his to the ornament in her palm.*)

(AMANDA *utters another gay laugh in the kitchen.*)

LAURA (*faintly*): You — won't — call again?
JIM: No, Laura, I can't. (*He rises from the sofa.*) As I was just explaining, I've — got strings on me, Laura, I've — been going steady! I go out all the time with a girl named Betty. She's a home-girl like you, and Catholic, and Irish, and in a great many ways we — get along fine. I met her last summer on a moonlight boat trip up the river to Alton, on the *Majestic*. Well — right away from the start it was — love! (LEGEND: LOVE!) (LAURA *sways slightly forward and grips the arm of the sofa. He fails to notice, now enrapt in his own comfortable being.*) Being in love has made a new man of me! (*Leaning stiffly forward, clutching the arm of the sofa,* LAURA *struggles visibly with her storm. But* JIM *is oblivious, she is a long way off.*) The power of love is really pretty tremendous! Love is something that — changes the whole world, Laura! (*The storm abates a little and* LAURA *leans back. He notices her again.*) It happened that Betty's aunt took sick, she got a wire and had to go to Centralia. So Tom — when he asked me to dinner — I naturally just accepted the invitation, not knowing that you — that he — that I — (*He stops awkwardly.*) Huh — I'm a stumble-john! (*He flops back on the sofa. The holy candles in the altar of* LAURA'S *face have been snuffed out. There is a look of almost infinite desolation.* JIM *glances at her uneasily.*) I wish that you would — say something. (*She bites her lip which was trembling and then bravely smiles. She opens her hand again on the broken glass ornament. Then she gently takes his hand and raises it level with her own. She carefully places*

the unicorn in the palm of his hand, then pushes his fingers closed upon it.) What are you — doing that for? You want me to have him? — Laura? (*She nods.*) What for?

LAURA: A — souvenir . . .

(*She rises unsteadily and crouches beside the victrola to wind it up.*)

(LEGEND ON SCREEN: "THINGS HAVE A WAY OF TURNING OUT SO BADLY!")

(OR IMAGE: "GENTLEMAN CALLER WAVING GOODBYE! — GAILY.")

(*At this moment* AMANDA *rushes brightly back in the front room. She bears a pitcher of fruit punch in an old-fashioned cut-glass pitcher and a plate of macaroons. The plate has a gold border and poppies painted on it.*)

AMANDA: Well, well, well! Isn't the air delightful after the shower? I've made you children a little liquid refreshment. (*Turns gaily to the gentleman caller.*) Jim, do you know that song about lemonade?
"Lemonade, lemonade
    Made in the shade and stirred with a spade —
    Good enough for any old maid!"

JIM (*uneasily*): Ha-ha! No — I never heard it.

AMANDA: Why, Laura! You look so serious!

JIM: We were having a serious conversation.

AMANDA: Good! Now you're better acquainted!

JIM (*uncertainly*): Ha-ha! Yes.

AMANDA: You modern young people are much more serious-minded than my generation. I was so gay as a girl!

JIM: You haven't changed, Mrs. Wingfield.

AMANDA: Tonight I'm rejuvenated! The gaiety of the occasion, Mr. O'Connor! (*She tosses her head with a peal of laughter. Spills lemonade.*) Oooo! I'm baptizing myself!

JIM: Here — let me —

AMANDA (*setting the pitcher down*): There now. I discovered we had some maraschino cherries. I dumped them in, juice and all!

JIM: You shouldn't have gone to that trouble, Mrs. Wingfield.

AMANDA: Trouble, trouble? Why it was loads of fun! Didn't you hear me cutting up in the kitchen? I bet your ears were burning! I told Tom how outdone with him I was for keeping you to himself so long a time! He should have brought you over much, much sooner! Well, now that you've found your way, I want you to be a very frequent caller! Not just occasional but all the time. Oh, we're going to have a lot of gay times together! I see them coming! Mmm, just breathe that air! So fresh, and the moon's so pretty! I'll skip back out — I know where my place is when young folks are having a — serious conversation!

JIM: Oh, don't go out, Mrs. Wingfield. The fact of the matter is I've got to be going.

AMANDA: Going, now? You're joking! Why, it's only the shank of the evening, Mr. O'Connor!

JIM: Well, you know how it is.

AMANDA: You mean you're a young workingman and have to keep workingmen's hours. We'll let you off early tonight. But only on the condition that next time you stay later. What's the best night for you? Isn't Saturday night the best night for you workingmen?

JIM: I have a couple of time-clocks to punch, Mrs. Wingfield. One at morning, another one at night!

AMANDA: My, but you *are* ambitious! You work at night, too?

JIM: No, Ma'am, not work but — Betty! (*He crosses deliberately to pick up his hat. The band at the Paradise Dance Hall goes into a tender waltz.*)

AMANDA: Betty? Betty? Who's — Betty! (*There is an ominous cracking sound in the sky.*)

JIM: Oh, just a girl. The girl I go steady with! (*He smiles charmingly. The sky falls.*)

(LEGEND: "THE SKY FALLS.")

AMANDA (*a long-drawn exhalation*): Ohhhh . . . Is it a serious romance, Mr. O'Connor?

JIM: We're going to be married the second Sunday in June.

AMANDA: Ohhhh — how nice! Tom didn't mention that you were engaged to be married.

JIM: The cat's not out of the bag at the warehouse yet. You know how they are. They call you Romeo and stuff like that. (*He stops at the oval mirror to put on his hat. He carefully shapes the brim and the crown to give a discreetly dashing effect.*) It's been a wonderful evening, Mrs. Wingfield. I guess this is what they mean by Southern hospitality.

AMANDA: It really wasn't anything at all.

JIM: I hope it don't seem like I'm rushing off. But I promised Betty I'd pick her up at the Wabash depot, an' by the time I get my jalopy down there her train'll be in. Some women are pretty upset if you keep 'em waiting.

AMANDA: Yes, I know — The tyranny of women! (*Extends her hand.*) Good-bye, Mr. O'Connor. I wish you luck — and happiness — and success! All three of them, and so does Laura! — Don't you, Laura?

LAURA: Yes!

JIM (*taking her hand*): Good-bye, Laura. I'm certainly going to treasure that souvenir. And don't you forget the good advice I gave you. (*Rises his voice to a cheery shout.*) So long, Shakespeare! Thanks again, ladies — Good night!

(*He grins and ducks jauntily out.*)

(*Still bravely grimacing,* AMANDA *closes the door on the gentleman caller. Then she turns back to the room with a puzzled expression. She and* LAURA *don't dare to face each other.* LAURA *crouches beside the victrola to wind it.*)

AMANDA (*faintly*): Things have a way of turning out so badly. I don't believe that I would play the victrola. Well, well — well — Our gentleman caller was engaged to be married! Tom!

TOM (*from back*): Yes, Mother?

AMANDA: Come in here a minute. I want to tell you something awfully funny.

TOM (*enters with macaroon and a glass of the lemonade*): Has the gentleman caller gotten away already?

AMANDA: The gentleman caller has made an early departure. What a wonderful joke you played on us!

TOM: How do you mean?

AMANDA: You didn't mention that he was engaged to be married.

TOM: Jim? Engaged?

AMANDA: That's what he just informed us.

TOM: I'll be jiggered! I didn't know about that.

AMANDA: That seems very peculiar.

TOM: What's peculiar about it?

AMANDA: Didn't you call him your best friend down at the warehouse?

TOM: He is, but how did I know?

AMANDA: It seems extremely peculiar that you wouldn't know your best friend was going to be married!

TOM: The warehouse is where I work, not where I know things about people!

AMANDA: You don't know things anywhere! You live in a dream; you manufacture illusions! (*He crosses to door.*) Where are you going?

TOM: I'm going to the movies.

AMANDA: That's right, now that you've had us make such fools of ourselves. The effort, the preparations, all the expense! The new floor lamp, the rug, the clothes for Laura! All for what? To entertain some other girl's fiancé! Go to the movies, go! Don't think about us, a mother deserted, an unmarried sister who's crippled and has no job! Don't let anything interfere with your selfish pleasure! Just go, go, go — to the movies!

TOM: All right, I will! The more you shout about my selfishness to me the quicker I'll go, and I won't go to the movies!

AMANDA: Go, then! Then go to the moon — you selfish dreamer!

(TOM *smashes his glass on the floor. He plunges out on the fire-escape, slamming the door.* LAURA *screams — cut by door.*)

(*Dance-hall music up.* TOM *goes to the rail and grips it desperately, lifting his face in the chill white moonlight penetrating the narrow abyss of the alley.*)

(LEGEND ON SCREEN: "AND SO GOOD-BYE . . .")

(TOM's *closing speech is timed with the interior pantomime. The interior scene is played as though viewed through soundproof glass.* AMANDA *appears to be making a comforting speech to* LAURA *who is huddled upon the sofa. Now that we cannot hear the mother's speech, her silliness is gone and she has dignity and tragic beauty.* LAURA's *dark hair hides her face until at the end of the speech she lifts it to smile at her mother.* AMANDA's *gestures are slow and graceful, almost dancelike, as she comforts the daughter. At the end of her speech she glances a moment at the father's picture — then withdraws through the portieres. At close of* TOM's *speech,* LAURA *blows out the candles, ending the play.*)

TOM: I didn't go to the moon, I went much further — for time is the longest distance between two places — Not long after that I was fired for writing a poem on the lid of a shoe-box. I left Saint Louis. I descended the steps of this fire-escape for a last time and followed, from then on, in my father's footsteps, attempting to find in motion what was lost in space — I traveled around a great deal. The cities swept about me like dead leaves, leaves that were brightly colored but torn away from the branches. I would have stopped, but I was pursued by something. It always came upon me unawares, taking me altogether by surprise. Perhaps it was a familiar bit of music. Perhaps it was only a piece of transparent glass — Perhaps I am walking along a street at night, in some strange city, before I have found companions. I pass the lighted window of a shop where perfume is sold. The window is filled with pieces of colored glass, tiny transparent bottles in delicate colors, like bits of a shattered rainbow. Then all at once my sister touches my shoulder. I turn around and look into her eyes . . . Oh, Laura, Laura, I tried to leave you behind me, but I am more faithful than I intended to be! I reach for a cigarette, I cross the street, I run into the movies or a bar, I buy a drink, I speak to the nearest stranger — anything that can blow your candles out! (LAURA *bends over the candles.*) — for nowadays the world is lit by lightning! Blow out your candles, Laura — and so good-bye. . . .

(*She blows the candles out.*)

THE SCENE DISSOLVES

PRODUCTION NOTES

Being a "memory play," *The Glass Menagerie* can be presented with unusual freedom of convention. Because of its considerably delicate or tenuous material, atmospheric touches and subtleties of direction play a particularly important part. Expressionism and all other unconventional techniques in drama have only one valid aim, and that is a closer approach to truth. When a play employs unconventional techniques, it is not, or certainly shouldn't be, trying to escape its responsibility of dealing with reality, or interpreting experience, but is actually or should be attempting to find a closer approach, a more penetrating and vivid expression of things as they are. The straight realistic play with its genuine frigidaire and authentic ice-cubes, its characters that speak exactly as its audience speaks, corresponds to the academic landscape and has the same virtue of a photographic likeness. Everyone should know nowadays the unimportance of the photographic in art: that truth, life, or reality is an organic thing which the poetic imagination can represent or suggest, in essence, only through transformation, through changing into other forms than those which were merely present in appearance.

These remarks are not meant as comments only on this particular play. They have to do with a conception of a new, plastic theater which must take the place of the exhausted theater of realistic conventions if the theater is to resume vitality as a part of our culture.

THE SCREEN DEVICE

There is *only one important difference between the original and acting version of the play* and that is the *omission* in the latter of the device which I tentatively included in my *original* script. This device was the use of a screen on which were projected magic-lantern slides bearing images or titles. I do not regret the omission of this device from the . . . Broadway production. The extraordinary power of Miss Taylor's performance made it suitable to have the utmost simplicity in the physical production. But I think it may be interesting to some readers to see how this device was conceived. So I am putting it into the published manuscript. These images and legends, projected from behind, were cast on a section of wall between the front-room and dining-room areas, which should be indistinguishable from the rest when not in use.

The purpose of this will probably be apparent. It is to give accent to certain values in each scene. Each scene contains a particular point (or several) which is structurally the most important. In an episodic play, such as this, the basic structure or narrative line may be obscured from the audience; the effect may seem fragmentary rather than architectural. This may not be the fault of the play so much as a lack of attention in the audience. The legend or image upon the screen will strengthen the effect of what is merely allusion in the writing and allow the primary point to be made more simply and lightly than if the entire responsibility were on the spoken lines. Aside from this structural value, I think the screen will have a definite emotional appeal, less definable but just as important. An imaginative producer or director may invent many other uses for this device than those indicated in the present script. In fact the possibilities of the device seem much larger to me than the instance of this play can possibly utilize.

THE MUSIC

Another extra-literary accent in this play is provided by the use of music. A single recurring tune, "The Glass Menagerie," is used to give emotional emphasis to suitable passages. This tune is like circus music, not when you are on the grounds or in the immediate vicinity of the parade, but when you are at some distance and very likely thinking of something else. It seems under those circumstances to continue almost interminably and it weaves in and out of your preoccupied consciousness; then it is the lightest, most delicate music in the world and perhaps the saddest. It expresses the surface vivacity of life with the underlying strain of immutable and inexpressible sorrow. When you look at a piece of delicately spun glass you think of two things: how beautiful it is and how easily it can be broken. Both of those ideas should be woven into the recurring tune, which dips in and out of the play as if it were carried on a wind that changes. It serves as a thread of connection and allusion between the narrator with his separate point in time and space and the subject of his story. Between each episode it returns as reference to the emotion, nostalgia, which is the first condition of the play. It is primarily Laura's music and therefore comes out most clearly when the play focuses upon her and the lovely fragility of glass which is her image.

THE LIGHTING

The lighting in the play is not realistic. In keeping with the atmosphere of memory, the stage is dim. Shafts of light are focused on selected areas or actors, sometimes in contradistinction to what is the apparent center. For instance, in the quarrel scene between Tom and Amanda, in which Laura has no active part, the clearest pool of light is on her figure. This is also true of the supper scene, when her silent figure on the sofa should remain the visual center. The light upon Laura should be distinct from the others, having a peculiar pristine clarity such as light used in early religious portraits of female saints or madonnas. A certain correspondence to light in religious paintings, such as El Greco's, where the figures are radiant in atmosphere that is relatively dusky, could be effectively used throughout the play. (It will also permit a more effective use of the screen.) A free, imaginative use of light can be of enormous value in giving a mobile, plastic quality to plays of a more or less static nature.

T.W.

IN RETROSPECT one sees that the appearance of *The Glass Menagerie* in 1945 marked the beginning (at any rate, the public beginning) of the most exciting dramatic career in post-war America. Williams' later plays, all dealing with love's failure in a world brutalized and perverse to the extent to which it betrays love, have not fulfilled the promise of quiet loveliness that *The Glass Menagerie* gave, but his imaginative use of the stage and the poetry of his realistic dialogue have hardly diminished in power. He argues no themes, is not a master of suspense, but he makes of the theater significant space for living characters. A dimension of meaning — wistfulness, tragicomedy — is (to take an example) added to the bittersweet drama of the Wingfields by the smiling face of the footloose father, the happy doughboy, that presides over the heartbreaks of his deserted family. The aliveness is harder to analyze. The effect of Amanda's speech, "Sticks and stones may break our bones, but the expression on Mr. Garfinkel's face won't harm us!" has something to do with the way the associations of the first half clash with the prosaism of rhythm and reference of the second. The child's jingle of studied unconcern at being spiritually hurt becomes a brittle defense against poverty and humiliation and does not quite cover the cruelty that poverty and humiliation entail: Laura's having to face Mr. Garfinkel. The speech is a sad, soft woman's effort to be gay and hard. Williams' plays are full of such speeches. They ring true; people seem to talk like that. The very idiosyncrasies of image, diction, and cadence amount to lifelikeness.

Williams' success as the realist of frustration and despair may at first seem to contradict the artistic theory he propounds in the "Production Notes" to *The Glass Menagerie*. Actually, the theory explains the success. "Everyone" (he says in the notes) "should know nowadays the unimportance of the photographic in art: that truth, life, or reality is an organic thing which the poetic imagination can represent or suggest, in essence, only through transformation, through changing into other forms than those which were merely present in appearance." The crucial words here are "in essence." Williams' characters get their faintly fantastic inner glow from being "essences." They are convincingly real *because* they are more than life-like prototypes. They are defined, assume shape and three dimensions, in terms of their obsessions, their mannerisms, their associations with certain objects. Amanda is fluttering gentility, forlorn Southern belle of vivacious humor long frayed by wear, puzzled and panicked because of her daughter's failure to attract a single specimen of the breed of males by which, in Amanda's set of values, a woman's success and happiness are measured. Laura is defined by her glass menagerie. The animals both symbolize her fragility and her quaint beauty and represent the world of lovely imagination into which she escapes from typing charts and speed tests. Tom writes poems on the lids of shoe boxes, and his emblems are the movies and the pirate ship, escapist symbols of glamorous adventure. Jim O'Connor chews gum and believes in Dale Carnegie and the future of television. These are portraits not in depth but in sharp focus. The method may represent Williams' limitation; he is neither a profound nor a versatile writer. But it makes his plays.

Williams' vignettes of the frustrations of ordinary people suggest Chekhov in their reliance on mood and atmosphere and in their near-plotlessness. No one who reads Chekhov right will find anything paradoxical in the fact that Williams also scorns dramatic photography. His attitude, of course, is quite orthodox among contemporary playwrights, who all have read their Strindberg and Pirandello. But in *The Glass Menagerie* Williams is not just following fashion; the break with realism can be justified on the intrinsic grounds that the play is a "memory play." Its premise is the subjectivity of modern relativism: reality, it implies, is not what happened but how you feel about what happened. Clearly, the solidities of naturalistic staging would have crushed Tom's delicate memories of mother and sister. The transparent apartment, the easy transitions from one point of time to another, the use of light and music to throw characters, objects, and events into relief — all this is a kind of poetry of the theater and psychologically true to the play's status as a record of inner experience. At the same time, the inner experience has been objectified by the theater medium. When Tom gulps his breakfast and quarrels with his mother he is simply another character, though the stage is his own mind. His double function in the play insures esthetic distance. The play is enclosed by the narrator-director-character's memory, the Shakespeare of the shipping room.

But the memory device has not made the play rigid nor us uncomfortable. Only the literal-minded would object to Tom's staging a scene at which he was not himself present — the climactic one between Laura and Jim. By the strict logic of Tom's being the rememberer, the scene is construction by inference or, possibly, by report by either one or both of the two principals. But merely to begin speculating and explaining along these lines shows up the irrelevance of the whole issue. The play works by a higher logic than mere consistency of decorum, just as it is also too subtle to need the projection of theme-focusing "legends" and "images" on a screen wall that Williams had planned originally. It makes its meaning without such obvious and heavy-handed new stagecraft devices.

In keeping with the memory-play premise the plot is slight. Much of the play is little more than a tenuously coherent sequence of scenes of people getting on each other's nerves when their dreams and longings clash and wound. What story there is begins late: Tom, giving in to his mother's nagging, provides a gentleman caller for his sister, and for a few moments there is a promise of happy ending as the princess almost comes out of the spell that shyness and lameness have cast upon her. But the prince of the magic kiss turns out to be very much engaged, and the music from the old victrola again takes over from the Paradise Dance Hall band. In these elusive, fleeting, pastel reminiscences of moods, the only element of intrigue — the coincidence that Tom's friend turns out to be Laura's secret high-school ideal — seems almost to belong to another, more mechanical, kind of playwriting.

Whose play is *The Glass Menagerie*? Not Tom's; he is not himself the main character of his memories. And Jim is even more than Tom primarily a means to an end: a nice young man caught in an awkward situation, decent enough to sense its pathos and half-educated enough to try to remedy it with newspaper column psychology, socially deft enough to get out without too much embarrassment. The end both he and Tom serve is one they share with most of Tennessee Williams' male characters: to reveal female lovelornness and broken illusions. The play is Laura's and Amanda's, mother's and daughter's both, not the one's more than the other's, although Amanda mainly exists in terms of Laura's situation. Laura's unfitness for social life — her scene

with Jim is an almost tender parody of a home date — is her distinction. She is exquisite because she is different and rare — blue roses
among red, unique as a unicorn. Like her unicorn, she is fragile. She
would be less precious were she more robust. The unicorn loses its horn
during the dance, and Laura — dancing, kissed — becomes for a moment like other girls. But as her mother's laughter tinkles in the
kitchen the gentleman caller announces his unavailability, and her and
her mother's dream shatters — not on human cruelty, for Jim is not
cruel, but on the blind, casual cruelty of life itself: "Things have a way
of turning out so badly." There is hardly the stuff of tragedy in middle-
aged girlishness and pathetic shyness due to a physical defect, in frustration by coincidence. The play is squarely in the modern democratic
tradition that assumes that serious drama can be made of the sufferings
of small people and which proceeds to write such plays, foregoing
claims to traditional tragic magnitude of destiny and language. But
The Glass Menagerie is something more as well. In Tom's final memory
image Amanda passes from exasperating silliness to a kind of tragic
dignity as the eternal mother sorrowing for her sorrowing child. The
child becomes the girl of candles in a world "lit by lightning."

The Glass Menagerie fittingly introduces the sequence of Williams'
plays, for it anticipates important themes and motifs and images of
his later, more violent critiques of the spiritual desolation of the modern world. The notion that the weakest, the most vulnerable, are the
best because their weakness and vulnerability signify sensitivity and
imagination has become almost a hallmark with Williams. Fragile objects have continued to be important symbols in his plays. And the
moon rising over Garfinkel's delicatessen suggests the blend of romantic
daydream and sordidness, of sentimentality and comic realism, that
defines his dramatic world.

Edward Albee

THE ZOO STORY

For William Flanagan

The Players

> PETER, *a man in his early forties, neither fat nor gaunt, neither handsome nor homely. He wears tweeds, smokes a pipe, carries horn-rimmed glasses. Although he is moving into middle age, his dress and his manner would suggest a man younger.*

> JERRY, *a man in in his late thirties, not poorly dressed, but carelessly. What was once a trim and lightly muscled body has begun to go to fat; and while he is no longer handsome, it is evident that he once was. His fall from physical grace should not suggest debauchery; he has, to come closest to it, a great weariness.*

THE SCENE: *It is Central Park; a Sunday afternoon in summer; the present. There are two park benches, one toward either side of the stage; they both face the audience. Behind them: foliage, trees, sky. At the beginning,* PETER *is seated on one of the benches.*

STAGE DIRECTIONS: *As the curtain rises,* PETER *is seated on the bench stage-right. He is reading a book. He stops reading, cleans his glasses, goes back to reading.* JERRY *enters.*

JERRY: I've been to the zoo. (PETER *doesn't notice.*) I said, I've been to the zoo. MISTER, I'VE BEEN TO THE ZOO!

PETER: Hm? . . . What? . . . I'm sorry, were you talking to me?

JERRY: I went to the zoo, and then I walked until I came here. Have I been walking north?

PETER (*puzzled*): North? Why . . . I . . . I think so. Let me see.

JERRY (*pointing past the audience*): Is that Fifth Avenue?

PETER: Why yes; yes, it is.

JERRY: And what is that cross street there; that one, to the right?

PETER: That? Oh, that's Seventy-fourth Street.

JERRY: And the zoo is around Sixty-fifth Street; so, I've been walking north.

PETER (*anxious to get back to his reading*): Yes; it would seem so.

JERRY: Good old north.

PETER (*lightly, by reflex*): Ha, ha.

JERRY (*after a slight pause*): But not due north.

PETER: I . . . well, no, not due north; but, we . . . call it north. It's northerly.

JERRY (*watches as* PETER, *anxious to dismiss him, prepares his pipe*): Well, boy; *you're* not going to get lung cancer, are you?

PETER (*looks up, a little annoyed, then smiles*): No, sir. Not from this.

JERRY: No, sir. What you'll probably get is cancer of the mouth, and then you'll have to wear one of those things Freud wore after they took one whole side of his jaw away. What do they call those things?

PETER (*uncomfortable*): A prosthesis?

JERRY: The very thing! A prosthesis. You're an educated man, aren't you? Are you a doctor?

PETER: Oh, no; no. I read about it somewhere; *Time* magazine, I think. (*He turns to his book.*)

JERRY: Well, *Time* magazine isn't for blockheads.

PETER: No, I suppose not.

JERRY (*after a pause*): Boy, I'm glad that's Fifth Avenue there.

PETER (*vaguely*): Yes.

JERRY: I don't like the west side of the park much.

PETER: Oh? (*Then, slightly wary, but interested.*) Why?

JERRY (*offhand*): I don't know.

PETER: Oh. (*He returns to his book.*)

JERRY (*He stands for a few seconds, looking at* PETER, *who finally looks up again, puzzled.*): Do you mind if we talk?

PETER (*obviously minding*): Why . . . no, no.

JERRY: Yes you do; you do.

PETER (*puts his book down, his pipe out and away, smiling*): No, really; I don't mind.

JERRY: Yes you do.

PETER (*finally decided*): No; I don't mind at all, really.

JERRY: It's . . . it's a nice day.

PETER (*stares unnecessarily at the sky*): Yes. Yes, it is; lovely.

JERRY: I've been to the zoo.

PETER: Yes, I think you said so . . . didn't you?

JERRY: You'll read about it in the papers tomorrow, if you don't see it on your TV tonight. You have TV, haven't you?

PETER: Why yes, we have two; one for the children.

JERRY: You're married!

PETER (*with pleased emphasis*): Why, certainly.

JERRY: It isn't a law, for God's sake.

PETER: No . . . no, of course not.

JERRY: And you have a wife.

PETER (*bewildered by the seeming lack of communication*): Yes!

JERRY: And you have children.

PETER: Yes; two.

JERRY: Boys?

PETER: No, girls . . . both girls.

JERRY: But you wanted boys.

PETER: Well . . . naturally, every man wants a son, but . . .

JERRY (*lightly mocking*): But that's the way the cookie crumbles?

PETER (*annoyed*): I wasn't going to say that.

JERRY: And you're not going to have any more kids, are you?

PETER (*a bit distantly*): No. No more. (*then back, and irksome*) Why did you say that? How would you know about that?

JERRY: The way you cross your legs, perhaps; something in the voice. Or maybe I'm just guessing. Is it your wife?

PETER (*furious*): That's none of your business! (*a silence*) Do you understand? (JERRY *nods.* PETER *is quiet now.*) Well, you're right. We'll have no more children.

JERRY (*softly*): That *is* the way the cookie crumbles.

PETER (*forgiving*): Yes . . . I guess so.

JERRY: Well, now; what else?

PETER: What were you saying about the zoo . . . that I'd read about it, or see . . . ?

JERRY: I'll tell you about it, soon. Do you mind if I ask you questions?

PETER: Oh, not really.

JERRY: I'll tell you why I do it; I don't talk to many people — except to say like: give me a beer, or where's the john, or what time does the feature go on, or keep your hands to yourself, buddy. You know — things like that.

PETER: I must say I don't . . .

JERRY: But every once in a while I like to talk to somebody, really *talk*; like to get to know somebody, know all about him.

PETER (*lightly laughing, still a little uncomfortable*): And am I the guinea pig for today?

JERRY: On a sun-drenched Sunday afternoon like this? Who better than a nice married man with two daughters and . . . uh . . . a dog? (PETER *shakes his head.*) No? Two dogs. (PETER *shakes his head again.*) Hm. No dogs? (PETER *shakes his head sadly.*) Oh, that's a shame. But you look like an animal man. CATS? (PETER *nods his head, ruefully.*) Cats! But, that can't be your idea. No, sir. Your wife and daughters? (PETER *nods his head.*) Is there anything else I should know?

PETER (*He has to clear his throat.*): There are . . . there are two parakeets. One . . . uh . . . one for each of my daughters.

JERRY: Birds.

PETER: My daughters keep them in a cage in their bedroom.

JERRY: Do they carry disease? The birds.

PETER: I don't believe so.

JERRY: That's too bad. If they did you could set them loose in the house and the cats could eat them and die, maybe. (PETER *looks blank for a moment, then laughs.*) And what else? What do you do to support your enormous household?

PETER: I . . . uh . . . I have an executive position with a . . . a small publishing house. We . . . uh . . . we publish textbooks.

JERRY: That sounds nice; very nice. What do you make?

PETER (*still cheerful*): Now look here!

JERRY: Oh, come on.

PETER: Well, I make around eighteen thousand a year, but I don't carry more than forty dollars at any one time . . . in case you're a . . . a holdup man . . . ha, ha, ha.

JERRY (*ignoring the above*): Where do you live? (PETER *is reluctant.*) Oh, look; I'm not going to rob you, and I'm not going to kidnap your parakeets, your cats, or your daughters.

PETER (*too loud*): I live between Lexington and Third Avenue, on Seventy-fourth Street.

JERRY: That wasn't so hard, was it?

PETER: I didn't mean to seem . . . ah . . . it's that you don't really carry on a conversation; you just ask questions. and I'm . . . I'm normally . . . uh . . . reticent. Why do you just stand there?

JERRY: I'll start walking around in a little while, and eventually I'll sit down. (*recalling*) Wait until you see the expression on his face.

PETER: What? Whose face? Look here; is this something about the zoo?

JERRY (*distantly*): The what?

PETER: The zoo; the zoo. Something about the zoo.

JERRY: The zoo?

PETER: You've mentioned it several times.

JERRY (*still distant, but returning abruptly*): The zoo? Oh, yes; the zoo. I was there before I came here. I told you that. Say, what's the dividing line between upper-middle-middle-class and lower-upper-middle-class?

PETER: My dear fellow, I . . .

JERRY: Don't my dear fellow me.

PETER (*unhappily*): Was I patronizing? I believe I was; I'm sorry. But, you see, your question about the classes bewildered me.

JERRY: And when you're bewildered you become patronizing?

PETER: I . . . I don't express myself too well, sometimes. (*He attempts a joke on himself.*) I'm in publishing, not writing.

JERRY (*amused, but not at the humor*): So be it. The truth *is: I* was being patronizing.

PETER: Oh, now; you needn't say that.

(*It is at this point that* JERRY *may begin to move about the stage with slowly increasing determination and authority, but pacing himself, so that the long speech about the dog comes at the high point of the arc.*)

JERRY: All right. Who are your favorite writers? Baudelaire and J. P. Marquand?

PETER (*wary*): Well, I like a great many writers; I have a considerable . . . catholicity of taste, if I may say so. Those two men are fine, each in his way. (*warming up*) Baudelaire, of course . . . uh . . . is by far the finer of the two, but Marquand has a place . . . in our . . . uh . . . national . . .

JERRY: Skip it.

PETER: I . . . sorry.

JERRY: Do you know what I did before I went to the zoo today? I walked all the way up Fifth Avenue from Washington Square; all the way.

PETER: Oh; you live in the Village! (*This seems to enlighten* PETER.)

JERRY: No, I don't. I took the subway down to the Village so I could walk all the way up Fifth Avenue to the zoo. It's one of those things a person has to do; sometimes a person has to go a very long distance out of his way to come back a short distance correctly.

PETER (*almost pouting*): Oh, I thought you lived in the Village.

JERRY: What were you trying to do? Make sense out of things? Bring order? The old pigeonhole bit? Well, that's easy; I'll tell you. I live in a four-story brownstone roominghouse on the upper West Side between Columbus Avenue and Central Park West. I live on the top floor; rear; west. It's a laughably small room, and one of my walls is made of beaverboard; this beaverboard separates my room from another laughably small room, so I assume that the two rooms were once one room, a small room, but not necessarily laughable. The room beyond my beaverboard wall is occupied by a colored queen who always keeps his door open; well, not always, but *always* when he's plucking his eyebrows, which he does with Buddhist concentration. This colored queen has rotten teeth, which is rare, and he has a Japanese kimono, which is also pretty rare; and he wears this kimono to and from the john in the hall, which is pretty frequent. I mean, he goes to the john a lot. He never bothers me, and he never brings anyone up to his room. All he does is pluck his eyebrows, wear his kimono and go to the john. Now, the two front rooms on my floor are a little larger, I guess; but they're pretty small, too. There's a Puerto Rican family in one of them, a husband, a wife, and some kids; I don't know how many. These people entertain a lot. And in the other front room, there's somebody living there, but I don't know who it is. I've never seen who it is. Never. Never ever.

PETER (*embarrassed*): Why . . . why do you live there?

JERRY (*from a distance again*): I don't know.

PETER: It doesn't sound like a very nice place . . . where you live.

JERRY: Well, no; it isn't an apartment in the East Seventies. But, then again, I don't have one wife, two daughters, two cats and two parakeets. What I do have, I have toilet articles, a few clothes, a hot plate that I'm not supposed to have, a can opener, one that works with a key, you know; a knife, two forks, and two spoons, one small, one large; three plates, a cup, a saucer, a drinking glass, two picture frames, both empty, eight or nine books, a pack of pornographic playing cards, regular deck, an old Western Union typewriter that prints nothing but capital letters, and a small strongbox without a lock which has in it . . . what? Rocks! Some rocks . . . sea-rounded rocks I picked up on the beach when I was a kid. Under which . . . weighed down . . . are some letters . . . please letters . . . please why don't you do this, and please when will you do that letters. And when letters, too. When will you write? When will you come? When? These letters are from more recent years.

PETER (*stares glumly at his shoes, then*): About those two empty picture frames . . . ?

JERRY: I don't see why they need any explanation at all. Isn't it clear? I don't have pictures of anyone to put in them.

PETER: Your parents . . . perhaps . . . a girl friend . . .

JERRY: You're a very sweet man, and you're possessed of a truly enviable innocence. But good old Mom and good old Pop are dead . . . you know? . . . I'm broken up about it, too . . . I mean really. BUT. That particular vaudeville act is playing the cloud circuit now, so I don't see how I can look at them, all neat and framed. Besides, or, rather, to be pointed about it, good old Mom walked out on good old Pop when I was ten and a half years old; she embarked on an adulterous turn of our southern states . . . a journey of a year's duration . . . and her most constant companion . . . among others, among many others . . . was a Mr. Barleycorn. At least, that's what good old Pop told me after he went down . . . came back . . . brought her body north. We'd received the news between Christmas and New Year's, you see, that good old Mom had parted with the ghost in some dump in Alabama. And, without the ghost . . . she was less welcome. I mean, what was she? A stiff . . . a northern stiff. At any rate, good old Pop celebrated the New Year for an even two weeks and then slapped into the front of a somewhat moving city omnibus, which sort of cleaned things out family-wise. Well no; then there was Mom's sister, who was given neither to sin nor the consolations of the bottle. I moved in on her, and my memory of her is slight excepting I remember still that she did all things dourly: sleeping, eating, working, praying. She dropped dead on the stairs to her apartment, my apartment then, too, on the afternoon of my high school graduation. A terribly middle-European joke, if you ask me.

PETER: Oh, my; oh, my.

JERRY: Oh, your what? But that was a long time ago, and I have no feeling about any of it that I care to admit to myself. Perhaps you can see, though, why good old Mom and good old Pop are frameless. What's your name? Your first name?

PETER: I'm Peter.

JERRY: I'd forgotten to ask you. I'm Jerry.

PETER (*with a slight, nervous laugh*): Hello, Jerry.

JERRY (*nods his hello*): And let's see now; what's the point of having a girl's picture, especially in two frames? I have two picture frames, you remember. I never see the pretty little ladies more than once, and most of them wouldn't be caught in the same room with a camera. It's odd, and I wonder if it's sad.

PETER: The girls?

JERRY: No. I wonder if it's sad that I never see the little ladies more than once. I've never been able to have sex with, or, how is it put? . . . make love to anybody more than once. Once; that's it. . . . Oh, wait; for a week and a half, when I was fifteen . . . and I hang my head in shame that puberty was late . . . I was a h-o-m-o-s-e-x-u-a-l. I mean, I was queer . . . (*very fast*) . . . queer, queer, queer . . . with bells ringing, banners snapping in the wind. And for those eleven days, I met at least twice a day with the park superintendent's son . . . a Greek boy, whose birthday was the same as mine, except he was a year older. I think I was very much in love . . . maybe just with sex. But that was the jazz of a very special hotel, wasn't it? And now; oh, do I love the little ladies; really, I love them. For about an hour.

PETER: Well, it seems perfectly simple to me. . . .

JERRY (*angry*): Look! Are you going to tell me to get married and have parakeets?

PETER (*angry himself*): Forget the parakeets! And stay single if you want to. It's no business of mine. I didn't start this conversation in the . . .

JERRY: All right, all right. I'm sorry. All right? You're not angry?

PETER (*laughing*): No, I'm not angry.

JERRY (*relieved*): Good. (*now back to his previous tone*) Interesting that you asked me about the picture frames. I would have thought that you would have asked me about the pornographic playing cards.

PETER (*with a knowing smile*): Oh, I've seen those cards.

JERRY: That's not the point. (*laughs*) I suppose when you were a kid you and your pals passed them around, or you had a pack of your own.

PETER: Well, I guess a lot of us did.

JERRY: And you threw them away just before you got married.

PETER: Oh, now; look here. I didn't *need* anything like that when I got older.

JERRY: No?

PETER (*embarrassed*): I'd rather not talk about these things.

JERRY: So? Don't. Besides, I wasn't trying to plumb your post-adolescent sexual life and hard times; what I wanted to get at is the value difference between pornographic playing cards when you're a kid, and pornographic playing cards when you're older. It's that when you're a kid you use the cards as a substitute for a real experience, and when you're older you use real experience as a substitute for the fantasy. But I imagine you'd rather hear about what happened at the zoo.

PETER (*enthusiastic*): Oh, yes; the zoo. (*then, awkward*) That is . . . if you . . .

JERRY: Let me tell you about why I went . . . well, let me tell you some things. I've told you about the fourth floor of the rooming-house where I live. I think the rooms are better as you go down, floor by floor. I guess they are; I don't know. I don't know any of the people on the third and second floors. Oh, wait! I do know that there's a lady living on the third floor, in the front. I know because she cries all the time. Whenever I go out or come back in, when-ever I pass her door, I always hear her crying, muffled, but . . . very determined. Very determined indeed. But the one I'm getting to, and all about the dog, is the landlady. I don't like to use words that are too harsh in describing people. I don't like to. But the landlady is a fat, ugly, mean, stupid, unwashed, misanthropic, cheap, drunken bag of garbage. And you may have noticed that I very seldom use profanity, so I can't describe her as well as I might.

PETER: You describe her . . . vividly.

JERRY: Well, thanks. Anyway, she has a dog, and I will tell you about the dog, and she and her dog are the gatekeepers of my dwelling. The woman is bad enough; she leans around in the entrance hall, spying to see that I don't bring in things or people, and when she's had her midafternoon pint of lemon-flavored gin she always stops me in the hall, and grabs ahold of my coat or my arm, and she presses her disgusting body up against me to keep me in a corner so she can talk to me. The smell of her body and her breath . . . you can't imagine it . . . and somewhere, somewhere in the back of that pea-sized brain of hers, an organ developed just enough to let her eat, drink, and emit, she has some foul parody of sexual desire. And I, Peter, I am the object of her sweaty lust.

PETER: That's disgusting. That's . . . horrible.

JERRY: But I have found a way to keep her off. When she talks to me, when she presses herself to my body and mumbles about her room and how I should come there, I merely say: but, Love; wasn't yester-day enough for you, and the day before? Then she puzzles, she makes slits of her tiny eyes, she sways a little, and then, Peter . . . and it is at this moment that I think I might be doing some good in that tormented house . . . a simple-minded smile begins to form on her unthinkable face, and she giggles and groans as she thinks about yesterday and the day before; as she believes and re-lives what never happened. Then, she motions to that black monster of a dog she has, and she goes back to her room. And I am safe until our next meeting.

PETER: It's so . . . unthinkable. I find it hard to believe that people such as that really *are*.

JERRY (*lightly mocking*): It's for reading about, isn't it?

PETER (*seriously*): Yes.

JERRY: And fact is better left to fiction. You're right, Peter. Well, what I have been meaning to tell you about is the dog; I shall, now.

PETER (*nervously*): Oh, yes; the dog.

JERRY: Don't go. You're not thinking of going, are you?

PETER: Well . . . no, I don't think so.

JERRY (*as if to a child*): Because after I tell you about the dog, do you know what then? Then . . . then I'll tell you about what happened at the zoo.

PETER (*laughing faintly*): You're . . . you're full of stories, aren't you?

JERRY: You don't *have* to listen. Nobody is holding you here; remember that. Keep that in your mind.

PETER (*irritably*): I know that.

JERRY: You do? Good.

(*The following long speech, it seems to me, should be done with a great deal of action, to achieve a hypnotic effect on* PETER, *and on the audience, too. Some specific actions have been suggested, but the director and the actor playing* JERRY *might best work it out for themselves.*)

ALL RIGHT. (*as if reading from a huge billboard*) THE STORY OF JERRY AND THE DOG! (*natural again*) What I am going to tell you has something to do with how sometimes it's necessary to go a long distance out of the way in order to come back a short distance correctly; or, maybe I only think that it has something to do with that. But, it's why I went to the zoo today, and why I walked north . . . northerly, rather . . . until I came here. All right. The dog, I think I told you, is a black monster of a beast: an oversized head, tiny, tiny ears, and eyes . . . bloodshot, infected, maybe; and a body you can see the ribs through the skin. The dog is black, all black; all black except for the bloodshot eyes, and . . . yes . . . and an open sore on its . . . *right* forepaw; that is red, too. And, oh yes; the poor monster, and I do believe it's an old dog . . . it's certainly a misused one . . . almost always has an erection . . . of sorts. That's red, too. And . . . what else? . . . oh, yes; there's a gray-yellow-white color, too, when he bares his fangs. Like this: Grrrrrr! Which is what he did when he saw me for the first time . . . the day I moved in. I worried about that animal the very first minute I met him. Now, animals don't take to me like Saint Francis had birds hanging off him all the time. What I mean is: animals are indifferent to me . . . like people (*he smiles slightly*) . . . most of the time. But this dog wasn't indifferent. From the very beginning he'd snarl and then go for me, to get one of my legs. Not like he was rabid, you know; he was sort of a stumbly dog, but he wasn't half-assed, either. It was a good, stumbly run; but I always got away. He got a piece of my trouser leg, look, you can see right here, where it's mended; he got that the second day I lived there; but, I kicked free and got upstairs fast, so that was that. (*puzzles*) I still don't know to this day how the other roomers manage it, but you know what I *think*: I think it had to do only with me. Cozy. So. Anyway, this went on for over a week, whenever I came in; but never when I went out. That's funny. Or, it *was* funny. I could pack up and live in the street for all the dog cared. Well, I thought about it up in my room one day, one of the times after I'd bolted upstairs, and I made up my mind. I decided: First, I'll kill the dog with kindness, and if that doesn't work . . . I'll just kill him. (PETER *winces*.) Don't react, Peter; just listen. So, the next day I went out and bought a bag of hamburgers, medium rare, no catsup, no onion; and on the way home I threw away all the rolls and kept just the meat.

(*action for the following, perhaps*)

When I got back to the roominghouse the dog was waiting for me. I half opened the door that led into the entrance hall, and there he was; waiting for me. It figured. I went in, very cautiously, and I had the hamburgers, you remember; I opened the bag, and I set the meat down about twelve feet from where the dog was snarling at me. Like so! He snarled; stopped snarling; sniffed; moved slowly; then faster; then faster toward the meat. Well, when he got to it he stopped, and he looked at me. I smiled; but tentatively, you understand. He turned his face back to the hamburgers, smelled, sniffed some more, and then . . . RRRAAAAGGGGGHHHH, like that . . . he tore into them. It was as if he had never eaten anything in his life before, except like garbage. Which might very well have been the truth. I don't think the landlady ever eats anything but garbage. But. He ate all the hamburgers, almost all at once, making sounds in his throat like a woman. *Then*, when he'd finished the meat, the hamburger, and tried to eat the paper, too, he sat down

and smiled. I think he smiled; I know cats do. It was a very gratify-
ing few moments. Then, BAM, he snarled and made for me again.
He didn't get me this time, either. So, I got upstairs, and I lay down
on my bed and started to think about the dog again. To be truthful,
I was offended, and I was damn mad, too. It was six perfectly good
hamburgers with not enough pork in them to make it disgusting. I
was offended. But, after a while, I decided to try it for a few more
days. If you think about it, this dog had what amounted to an antipathy toward me; really. And, I wondered if I mightn't overcome this
antipathy. So, I tried it for five more days, but it was always the
same: snarl, sniff; move; faster; stare; gobble; RAAGGGHHH;
smile; snarl; BAM. Well, now by this time Columbus Avenue was
strewn with hamburger rolls and I was less offended than disgusted.
So, I decided to kill the dog.

(PETER *raises a hand in protest.*)

Oh, don't be so alarmed, Peter; I didn't succeed. The day I tried
to kill the dog I bought only one hamburger and what I thought
was a murderous portion of rat poison. When I bought the hamburger I asked the man not to bother with the roll, all I wanted
was the meat. I expected some reaction from him, like: we don't
sell no hamburgers without rolls; or, wha' d'ya wanna do, eat it
out'a ya han's? But no; he smiled benignly, wrapped up the hamburger in waxed paper, and said: A bite for ya pussy-cat? I wanted
to say: No, not really; it's part of a plan to poison a dog I know.
But, you can't say "a dog I know" without sounding funny; so I
said, a little too loud, I'm afraid, and too formally: YES, A BITE
FOR MY PUSSY-CAT. People looked up. It always happens when
I try to simplify things; people look up. But that's neither hither
nor thither. So. On my way back to the roominghouse, I kneaded
the hamburger and the rat poison together between my hands, at
that point feeling as much sadness as disgust. I opened the door to
the entrance hall, and there the monster was, waiting to take the
offering and then jump me. Poor bastard; he never learned that the
moment he took to smile before he went for me gave me time
enough to get out of range. BUT, there he was; malevolence with
an erection, waiting. I put the poison patty down, moved toward
the stairs and watched. The poor animal gobbled the food down as
usual, smiled, which made me almost sick, and then, BAM. But, as
I sprinted up the stairs, as usual, and the dog didn't get me, as
usual. AND IT CAME TO PASS THAT THE BEAST WAS
DEATHLY ILL. I knew this because he no longer attended me,
and because the landlady sobered up. She stopped me in the hall

the same evening of the attempted murder and confided the information that God had struck her puppy-dog a surely fatal blow. She had forgotten her bewildered lust, and her eyes were wide open for the first time. They looked like the dog's eyes. She sniveled and implored me to pray for the animal. I wanted to say to her: Madam, I have myself to pray for, the colored queen, the Puerto Rican family, the person in the front room whom I've never seen, the woman who cries deliberately behind her closed door, and the rest of the people in all roominghouses, everywhere; besides, Madam, I don't understand how to pray. But . . . to simplify things . . . I told her I would pray. She looked up. She said that I was a liar, and that I probably wanted the dog to die. I told her, and there was so much truth here, that I didn't want the dog to die. I didn't, and not just because I'd poisoned him. I'm afraid that I must tell you I wanted the dog to live so that I could see what our new relationship might come to.

(PETER *indicates his increasing displeasure and slowly growing antagonism.*)

Please understand, Peter; that sort of thing is important. You must believe me; it *is* important. We have to know the effect of our actions. (*another deep sigh*) Well, anyway; the dog recovered. I have no idea why, unless he was a descendant of the puppy that guarded the gates of hell or some such resort. I'm not up on my mythology. (*He pronounces the word myth-o-*logy.) Are you?

(PETER *sets to thinking, but* JERRY *goes on.*)

At any rate, and you've missed the eight-thousand-dollar question, Peter; at any rate, the dog recovered his health and the landlady recovered her thirst, in no way altered by the bow-wow's deliverance. When I came home from a movie that was playing on Forty-second Street, a movie I'd seen, or one that was very much like one or several I'd seen, after the landlady told me puppykins was better, I was so hoping for the dog to be waiting for me. I was . . . well, how would you put it . . . enticed? . . . fascinated? . . . no, I don't think so . . . heart-shatteringly anxious, that's it; I was heart-shatteringly anxious to confront my friend again.

(PETER *reacts scoffingly.*)

Yes, Peter; friend. That's the only word for it. I was heart-shatteringly et cetera to confront my doggy friend again. I came in the door and advanced, unafraid, to the center of the entrance hall.

The beast was there . . . looking at me. And, you know, he looked better for his scrape with the nevermind. I stopped; I looked at him; he looked at me. I think . . . I think we stayed a long time that way . . . still, stone-statue . . . just looking at one another. I looked more into his face than he looked into mine. I mean, I can concentrate longer at looking into a dog's face than a dog can concentrate at looking into mine, or into anybody else's face, for that matter. But during that twenty seconds or two hours that we looked into each other's face, we made contact. Now, here is what I had wanted to happen: I loved the dog now, and I wanted him to love me. I had tried to love, and I had tried to kill, and both had been unsuccessful by themselves. I hoped . . . and I don't really know why I expected the dog to understand anything, much less my motivations . . . I hoped that the dog would understand.

(PETER *seems to be hypnotized.*)

It's just . . . it's just that . . . (JERRY *is abnormally tense, now*) . . . it's just that if you can't deal with people, you have to make a start somewhere. WITH ANIMALS! (*much faster now, and like a conspirator*) Don't you see? A person has to have some way of dealing with SOMETHING. If not with people . . . if not with people . . . SOMETHING. With a bed, with a cockroach, with a mirror . . . no, that's too hard, that's one of the last steps. With a cockroach, with a . . . with a . . . with a carpet, a roll of toilet paper . . . no, not that, either . . . that's a mirror, too; always check bleeding. You see how hard it is to find things? With a street corner, and too many lights, all colors reflecting on the oily-wet streets . . . with a wisp of smoke, a wisp . . . of smoke . . . with . . . with pornographic playing cards, with a strongbox . . . WITHOUT A LOCK . . . with love, with vomiting, with crying, with fury because the pretty little ladies aren't pretty little ladies, with making money with your body which is an act of love and I could prove it, with howling because you're alive; with God. How about that? WITH GOD WHO IS A COLORED QUEEN WHO WEARS A KIMONO AND PLUCKS HIS EYEBROWS, WHO IS A WOMAN WHO CRIES WITH DETERMINATION BEHIND HER CLOSED DOOR . . . with God who, I'm told, turned his back on the whole thing some time ago . . . with . . . some day, with people. (JERRY *sighs the next word heavily.*) People. With an idea; a concept. And where better, where ever better in this humiliating excuse for a jail, where better to communicate one single, simple-minded idea than in an entrance hall? Where? It would be A START! Where better to make a beginning . . . to understand and just possibly be understood . . . a beginning of an understanding, than with . . .

(*Here* JERRY *seems to fall into almost grotesque fatigue.*)

. . . than with A DOG. Just that; a dog.

(*Here there is a silence that might be prolonged for a moment or so; then* JERRY *wearily finishes his story.*)

A dog. It seemed like a perfectly sensible idea. Man is a dog's best friend, remember. So: the dog and I looked at each other. I longer than the dog. And what I saw then has been the same ever since. Whenever the dog and I see each other we both stop where we are. We regard each other with a mixture of sadness and suspicion, and then we feign indifference. We walk past each other safely; we have an understanding. It's very sad, but you'll have to admit that it is an understanding. We had made many attempts at contact, and we had failed. The dog has returned to garbage, and I to solitary but free passage. I have not returned. I mean to say, I have *gained* solitary free passage, if that much further loss can be said to be gain. I have learned that neither kindness nor cruelty by themselves, independent of each other, creates any effect beyond themselves; and I have learned that the two combined, together, at the same time, are the teaching emotion. And what is gained is loss. And what has been the result: the dog and I have attained a compromise; more of a bargain, really. We neither love nor hurt because we do not try to reach each other. And, *was* trying to feed the dog an act of love? And, perhaps, was the dog's attempt to bite me *not* an act of love? If we can so misunderstand, well then, why have we invented the word love in the first place?

(*There is silence.* JERRY *moves to* PETER's *bench and sits down beside him. This is the first time* JERRY *has sat down during the play.*)

The Story of Jerry and the Dog: the end.

(PETER *is silent.*)

Well, Peter? (JERRY *is suddenly cheerful.*) Well, Peter? Do you think I could sell that story to the *Reader's Digest* and make a couple of hundred bucks for *The Most Unforgettable Character I've Ever Met?* Huh?

(JERRY *is animated, but* PETER *is disturbed.*)

Oh, come on now, Peter; tell me what you think.

PETER (*numb*): I . . . I don't understand what . . . I don't think I . . . (*now, almost tearfully*) Why did you tell me all of this?

JERRY: Why not?

PETER: I DON'T UNDERSTAND!

JERRY (*furious, but whispering*): That's a lie.

PETER: No. No, it's not.

JERRY (*quietly*): I tried to explain it to you as I went along. I went slowly; it all has to do with . . .

PETER: I DON'T WANT TO HEAR ANY MORE. I don't understand you, or your landlady, or her dog. . . .

JERRY: *Her* dog! I thought it was my . . . No. No, you're right. It *is* her dog. (*looks at* PETER *intently, shaking his head*) I don't know what I was thinking about; of course you don't understand. (*in a monotone, wearily*) I don't live in your block; I'm not married to two parakeets, or whatever your setup is. I am a *permanent transient*, and my home is the sickening roominghouses on the West Side of New York City, which is the greatest city in the world. Amen.

PETER: I'm . . . I'm sorry; I didn't mean to . . .

JERRY: Forget it. I suppose you don't quite know what to make of me, eh?

PETER (*a joke*): We get all kinds in publishing. (*chuckles*)

JERRY: You're a funny man. (*He forces a laugh.*) You know that? You're a very . . . a richly comic person.

PETER (*modestly, but amused*): Oh, now, not really. (*still chuckling*)

JERRY: Peter, do I annoy you, or confuse you?

PETER (*lightly*): Well, I must confess that this wasn't the kind of afternoon I'd anticipated.

JERRY: You mean, I'm not the gentleman you were expecting.

PETER: I wasn't expecting anybody.

JERRY: No, I don't imagine you were. But I'm here, and I'm not leaving.

PETER (*consulting his watch*): Well, you may not be, but I must be getting home soon.

JERRY: Oh, come on; stay a while longer.

PETER: I really should get home; you see . . .

JERRY (*tickles* PETER's *ribs with his fingers*): Oh, come on.

PETER (*He is very ticklish; as* JERRY *continues to tickle him his voice becomes falsetto.*): No, I . . . OHHHHH! Don't do that. Stop, Stop. Ohhh, no, no.

JERRY: Oh, come on.

PETER (*as* JERRY *tickles*): Oh, hee, hee, hee. I must go. I . . . hee, hee, hee. After all, stop, stop, hee, hee, hee, after all, the parakeets will be getting dinner ready soon. Hee, hee. And the cats are setting the table. Stop, stop, and, and . . . (PETER *is beside himself now*) . . . and we're having . . . hee, hee . . . uh . . . ho, ho, ho.

(JERRY *stops tickling* PETER, *but the combination of the tickling and his own mad whimsy has* PETER *laughing almost hysterically. As his laughter continues, then subsides,* JERRY *watches him, with a curious fixed smile.*)

JERRY: Peter?

PETER: Oh, ha, ha, ha, ha, ha. What? What?

JERRY: Listen, now.

PETER: Oh, ho, ho. What . . . what is it, Jerry? Oh, my.

JERRY (*mysteriously*): Peter, do you want to know what happened at the zoo?

PETER: Ah, ha, ha. The what? Oh, yes; the zoo. Oh, ho, ho. Well, I had my own zoo there for a moment with . . . hee, hee, the parakeets getting dinner ready, and the . . . ha, ha, whatever it was, the . . .

JERRY (*calmly*): Yes, that was very funny, Peter. I wouldn't have expected it. But do you want to hear about what happened at the zoo, or not?

PETER: Yes. Yes, by all means; tell me what happened at the zoo. Oh, my. I don't know what happened to me.

JERRY: Now I'll let you in on what happened at the zoo; but first, I should tell you why I went to the zoo. I went to the zoo to find out more about the way people exist with animals, and the way animals exist with each other, and with people too. It probably wasn't a fair test, what with everyone separated by bars from everyone else, the animals for the most part from each other, and always the people from the animals. But, if it's a zoo, that's the way it is. (*He pokes* PETER *on the arm.*) Move over.

PETER (*friendly*): I'm sorry, haven't you enough room? (*He shifts a little.*)

JERRY (*smiling slightly*): Well, all the animals are there, and all the people are there, and it's Sunday and all the children are there. (*He pokes* PETER *again.*) Move over.

PETER (*patiently, still friendly*): All right.

(*He moves some more, and* JERRY *has all the room he might need.*)

JERRY: And it's a hot day, so all the stench is there, too, and all the balloon sellers, and all the ice cream sellers, and all the seals are

barking, and all the birds are screaming. (*pokes* PETER *harder*) Move over!

PETER (*beginning to be annoyed*): Look here, you have more than enough room! (*But he moves more, and is now fairly cramped at one end of the bench.*)

JERRY: And I am there, and it's feeding time at the lions' house, and the lion keeper comes into the lion cage, one of the lion cages, to feed one of the lions. (*punches* PETER *on the arm, hard*) MOVE OVER!

PETER (*very annoyed*): I can't move over any more, and stop hitting me. What's the matter with you?

JERRY: Do you want to hear the story? (*punches* PETER'S *arm again*)

PETER (*flabbergasted*): I'm not so sure! I certainly don't want to be punched in the arm.

JERRY (*punches* PETER'S *arm again*): Like that?

PETER: Stop it! What's the matter with you?

JERRY: I'm crazy, you bastard.

PETER: That isn't funny.

JERRY: Listen to me, Peter. I want this bench. You go sit on the bench over there, and if you're good I'll tell you the rest of the story.

PETER (*flustered*): But . . . whatever for? What *is* the matter with you? Besides, I see no reason why I should give up this bench. I sit on this bench almost every Sunday afternoon, in good weather. It's secluded here; there's never anyone sitting here, so I have it all to myself.

JERRY (*softly*): Get off this bench, Peter; I want it.

PETER (*almost whining*): No.

JERRY: I said I want this bench, and I'm going to have it. Now get over there.

PETER: People can't have everything they want. You should know that; it's a rule; people can have some of the things they want, but they can't have everything.

JERRY (*laughs*): Imbecile! You're slow-witted!

PETER: Stop that!

JERRY: You're a vegetable! Go lie down on the ground.

PETER (*intense*): Now you listen to me. I've put up with you all afternoon.

JERRY: Not really.

PETER: LONG ENOUGH. I've put up with you long enough. I've listened to you because you seemed . . . well, because I thought you wanted to talk to somebody.

JERRY: You put things well; economically, and, yet . . . oh, what is the word I want to put justice to your . . . JESUS, you make me sick . . . get off here and give me my bench.

PETER: MY BENCH!

JERRY (*pushes* PETER *almost, but not quite, off the bench*): Get out of my sight.

PETER (*regaining his position*): God da . . . mn you. That's enough! I've had enough of you. I will not give up this bench; you can't have it, and that's that. Now, go away.

(JERRY *snorts but does not move.*)

Go away, I said.

(JERRY *does not move.*)

Get away from here. If you don't move on . . . you're a bum . . . that's what you are. . . . If you don't move on, I'll get a policeman here and make you go.

(JERRY *laughs, stays.*)

I warn you, I'll call a policeman.

JERRY (*softly*): You won't find a policeman around here; they're all over on the west side of the park chasing fairies down from trees or out of the bushes. That's all they do. That's their function. So scream your head off; it won't do you any good.

PETER: POLICE! I warn you, I'll have you arrested. POLICE! (*pause*) I said POLICE! (*pause*) I feel ridiculous.

JERRY: You *look* ridiculous: a grown man screaming for the police on a bright Sunday afternoon in the park with nobody harming you. If a policeman *did* fill his quota and come sludging over this way he'd probably take *you* in as a nut.

PETER (*with disgust and impotence*): Great God, I just came here to read, and now you want me to give up the bench. You're mad.

JERRY: Hey, I got news for you, as they say. I'm on your precious bench, and you're never going to have it for yourself again.

PETER (*furious*): Look, you; get off my bench. I don't care if it makes any sense or not. I want this bench to myself; I want you OFF IT!

JERRY (*mocking*): Aw . . . look who's mad.

PETER: GET OUT!

JERRY: No.

PETER: I WARN YOU!

JERRY: Do you know how ridiculous you look *now*?

PETER (*his fury and self-consciousness have possessed him*): It doesn't matter. (*He is almost crying.*) GET AWAY FROM MY BENCH!

JERRY: Why? You have everything in the world you want; you've told me about your home, and your family, and *your own* little zoo. You have everything, and now you want this bench. Are these the things men fight for? Tell me, Peter, is this bench, this iron and this wood, is this your honor? Is this the thing in the world you'd fight for? Can you think of anything more absurd?

PETER: Absurd? Look, I'm not going to talk to you about honor, or even try to explain it to you. Besides, it isn't a question of honor; but even if it were, you wouldn't understand.

JERRY (*contemptuously*): You don't even know what you're saying, do you? This is probably the first time in your life you've had anything more trying to face than changing your cats' toilet box. Stupid! Don't you have any idea, not even the slightest, what other people *need*?

PETER: Oh, boy, listen to you; well, you don't need this bench. That's for sure.

JERRY: Yes; yes, I do.

PETER (*quivering*): I've come here for years; I have hours of great pleasure, great satisfaction, right here. And that's important to a man. I'm a responsible person, and I'm a GROWNUP. This is my bench, and you have no right to take it away from me.

JERRY: Fight for it, then. Defend yourself; defend your bench.

PETER: You've *pushed* me to it. Get up and fight.

JERRY: Like a man?

PETER (*still angry*): Yes, like a man, if you insist on mocking me even further.

JERRY: I'll have to give you credit for one thing: you *are* a vegetable, and a slightly nearsighted one, I think . . .

PETER: THAT'S ENOUGH. . . .

JERRY: . . . but, you know, as they say on TV all the time — you know — and I mean this, Peter, you have a certain dignity; it surprises me. . . .

PETER: STOP!

JERRY (*rises lazily*): Very well, Peter, we'll battle for the bench, but we're not evenly matched.

(*He takes out and clicks open an ugly-looking knife.*)

PETER (*suddenly awakening to the reality of the situation*): You *are* mad! You're stark raving mad! YOU'RE GOING TO KILL ME!

(*But before* PETER *has time to think what to do,* JERRY *tosses the knife at* PETER's *feet.*)

JERRY: There you go. Pick it up. You have the knife and we'll be more evenly matched.

PETER (*horrified*): No!

JERRY (*rushes over to* PETER, *grabs him by the collar;* PETER *rises; their faces almost touch*): Now you pick up that knife and you fight with me. You fight for your self-respect; you fight for that goddamned bench.

PETER (*struggling*): No! Let . . . let go of me! He . . . Help!

JERRY (*slaps* PETER *on each "fight"*): You fight, you miserable bastard; fight for that bench; fight for your parakeets; fight for your cats, fight for your two daughters; fight for your wife; fight for your manhood, you pathetic little vegetable. (*spits in* PETER'S *face*) You couldn't even get your wife with a male child.

PETER (*breaks away, enraged*): It's a matter of genetics, not manhood, you . . . you monster.

(*He darts down, picks up the knife and backs off a little; he is breathing heavily.*)

I'll give you one last chance; get out of here and leave me alone!

(*He holds the knife with a firm arm, but far in front of him, not to attack, but to defend.*)

JERRY (*sighs heavily*): So be it!

(*With a rush he charges* PETER *and impales himself on the knife. Tableau: For just a moment, complete silence,* JERRY *impaled on the knife at the end of* PETER'S *still firm arm. Then* PETER *screams, pulls away, leaving the knife in* JERRY. JERRY *is motionless, on point. Then he, too, screams, and it must be the sound of an infuriated and fatally wounded animal. With the knife in him, he stumbles back to the bench that* PETER *had vacated. He crumbles there, sitting, facing* PETER, *his eyes wide in agony, his mouth open.*)

PETER (*whispering*): Oh my God, oh my God, oh my God. . . .

(*He repeats these words many times, very rapidly.*)

JERRY (JERRY *is dying; but now his expression seems to change. His features relax, and while his voice varies, sometimes wrenched with pain, for the most part he seems removed from his dying. He smiles*): Thank you, Peter. I mean that, now; thank you very much.

(PETER'S *mouth drops open. He cannot move; he is transfixed.*)

Oh, Peter, I was so afraid I'd drive you away. (*He laughs as best he can.*) You don't know how afraid I was you'd go away and leave

tine's question, a Peter's kind of irritated impatience with whatever bewilders or provokes or disgusts or generally stirs and probes the sluggish lees of the conformist soul. That Jerry is *not* a beatnik from Greenwich Village upsets the Peters of our culture, obsessed with what Jerry calls "the old pigeonhole bit." There is, of course, a certain logic to the artist's position. In an age in which the dominant, recurrent image for man is that of a homeless wanderer in a vast void among painful, grotesque, mis-shapen forms, a being paradoxically both rigidly circumscribed and frighteningly free, it follows that the arts can only *show* his existence or evoke its quality in symbolic images and not presume to explain it or protest against it. Who is there to lodge the protest with? And who is sufficiently removed from the scene to understand an explanation of it? At the heart of absurdism is the conviction that life makes no sense and a consequent disengagement too absolute for any ideology to violate. *Angst* — undirected fear and irrational guilt — is man's condition, and none of us can do more than hope that his expression of his private anxieties will set another soul ringing in responsive concord. No rational system can validate absurdism. And certainly the most prudent and quite possibly the wisest critical procedure with a play which, like *The Zoo Story*, combines hardness of extraordinary and grotesque surface with a rich and haunting but elusive suggestiveness of inner substance is not to ask specific questions of it, let alone try to answer them, but to adopt the playwright's own objective, discreetly insinuating method and call attention to some of the play's exhibits of patterns of image and action. Approached in this manner, it may come to seem less like a perverse avant-garde shocker than a work of desperate human concern. Its shock may be therapy for blunted sensibilities — and thus imply a kind of thesis, after all.

There is, obviously, an element of anti-bourgeois satire in the comical encounter of smug decency with radical alienation. Peter is the involuntary straight man in Jerry's terrible comic act. When he runs away at the end in horror and panic because of the consequences of his defense of his honor, the "human vegetable" has become, at least, a "wounded animal." The radical act of violence unites society's insider and outsider in a common animality. Choreographically, the stage shows Jerry in restless motion — walking, standing, gesturing, sitting, hitting, rising, lunging — always actively seeking to elicit a genuine response. Peter sits, passive and inert, till the final moments of violence.

But as the terms that come to mind in an attempt to define this contrast suggest, social satire alone does not fully describe the play. Accumulating realistic detail fitfully hints at larger issues. The miserable perverts, aliens, and unseen weepers who inhabit the squalid rooming-house are all, somehow, God, for an empty universe can exist only in the mind of suffering man. The inventory of Jerry's possessions suggests a withdrawal that ends in isolation: an empty picture frame, unanswered letters of "please!" and "when?", and pornographic playing cards (in youth, a substitute for experience; later, the fantasy for which experience is a substitute). Jerry gradually elicits a picture of Peter's comfortable domestic zoo, complete with wife, daughters, cats, and parakeets. And "The Story of Jerry and the Dog" is a parable about a man deprived of every human relationship seeking communion with a beast that is both Cerberus guarding the entrance to a big-city Hades and a disgusting embodiment of the rapacious lust — "malevolence with an erection" — that in this dark underworld drives man on his devious quest for fellowship, traveling "a very long distance out of his way to come a short distance correctly." Like a visitation from another region Jerry imposes his westside story on Peter's eastside contentment. The frustrated dog lover becomes a reluctant listener to a story about a dog. The "teaching emotion" of the story, its moral, is that neither love nor hate alone can serve to establish a viable relationship. And all they achieve "combined, together, at the same time" is a balance of wary indifference, a gain that is really a loss and which accounts for Jerry's "great weariness" with life. He has walked "north" or "northerly, rather" (towards frozen wastes?), as if in search of a point between West and East at which to confront someone — anyone — with his failure to either kill or love a beast. There is, perhaps, a hint of homosexuality in the climactic tableau in which Jerry is impaled on the knife that Peter holds before him, and the hint is strengthened by the double fact that Jerry's one satisfying sexual relationship was with the park superintendent's son and that the stabbing takes place in a part of the park to which Peter has established a kind of proprietary claim. The ambivalence of the murder-suicide suggests that Jerry is a scapegoat figure, immolating himself in order to arouse the human vegetable to animal consciousness. There is a sense in which the play can be read as allegory on a divided self — one part alienated and incapacitated by an excess of insight, the other adjusted and socially efficient through an excess of blindness. One is aware, the other unaware; one is eloquently articulate; the other speaks either brokenly or in platitudes and clichés.

The almost painful explicitness of "The Story of Jerry and the Dog" intrudes upon the developing dramatic form in a fashion analogous to the way in which Jerry's underground existence intrudes upon the sunny peacefulness of Peter's. There is also a contrast between the story of the dog and the story of what happened at the Zoo; the latter, though often referred to in the course of the play, remains untold at the end or at least told only fragmentarily and very obscurely. If all that happened was that Jerry after watching the caged beasts at the Zoo decided to find someone to whom to communicate his discovery that man like beast alternates between hunger for love and lust to kill — that he leads, literally, "a dog's life" — how can Peter expect to see what happened to Jerry at the Zoo on TV? Are we to infer that Jerry's walk northwards followed an earlier act of violence at the Zoo? And is the TV screen to be taken as a mirror in which Peter can observe his own domestic menagerie? The questions pose themselves, and that, conceivably, could be the whole extent of their "meaning."

A final note on matters of more certainty. *The Zoo Story* was written in 1958. According to Albee's preface it was "refused by a number of New York producers" and first produced in the Schiller Theater Werkstatt in Berlin in September, 1959 — a circumstance that to Albee seems like an example of "the Unusual, the Unlikely, the Unexpected, which, with the exception of the fare the commercial theatre setup spills out on its dogged audience each season, is the nature of the theatre." The play was Albee's first and the first to be given performance. His later plays have not reduced it to the status of apprentice work.)

APPENDIX

Biographical Notes and Suggested Reading

HENRIK IBSEN (1828-1906) was born in Skien, a small town in southern Norway. His father, a merchant, went bankrupt when the boy was eight. At sixteen he was apprenticed to a druggist. Two years later a maid in the household gave birth to his illegitimate child. These early events may have conditioned his later reticence and excessive outer propriety. Both financial ruin and bastardy are recurrent motifs in his plays. He wrote his first play in 1848, under the influence of the liberalism of the February revolution of that year. In the 1850's and early 1860's he held positions as salaried playwright and director at theaters in Bergen and Christiania (Oslo). Norway's failure to help Denmark in her war against Prussia in 1864 disillusioned him deeply (though he did not himself volunteer), and he and his wife and son left Norway for twenty-seven years of self-imposed exile in Italy and Germany. He died in Christiania after several years' illness.

Ibsen's iconoclasm, naturalistic symbolism, and novel and influential dramaturgy have earned him the label "father of modern drama." His early plays dealt with saga and peasant subject matter. His first popular success was the philosophical dramatic poem *Brand* (1866), followed by the complementary, antithetical *Peer Gynt* (1867). His third period comprises the so-called social thesis plays on which his world fame largely rests. The main ones are: *A Doll's House* (1879), *Ghosts* (1881), *An Enemy of the People* (1882), *Rosmersholm* (1886), and *Hedda Gabler* (1890), though the last two are only incidentally thesis plays at all. His last plays are heavily symbolic and internalized and partly of autobiographical import, such as *The Master Builder* (1892) and *When We Dead Awaken* (1899).

Suggested Reading

Bradbrook, M. C., *Ibsen the Norwegian*. London: Chatto & Windus, 1948.

615

Downs, Brian W., *A Study of Six Plays by Ibsen.* Cambridge: Cambridge University Press, 1950.

Lucas, Frank L., *The Drama of Ibsen and Strindberg.* London: Cassell, 1962.

McFarlane, James W., ed., *Discussion of Henrik Ibsen.* Boston: D. C. Heath and Co., 1962.

McFarlane, James W., *Ibsen and the Temper of Norwegian Literature.* London: Oxford University Press, 1960.

Northam, John, *Ibsen's Dramatic Method.* London: Faber and Faber, 1953.

Sprinchorn, Evert, ed., *Ibsen: Letters and Speeches.* New York: Hill and Wang, 1964 (Dramabook).

Tennant, P., *Ibsen's Dramatic Technique.* Cambridge: Bowes & Bowes, 1948.

Weigand, Hermann, *The Modern Ibsen.* New York: E. P. Dutton & Co., 1960 (first published in 1925).

August Strindberg (1849-1912) was born in Stockholm, the son of a stolid, middle-class father and a working-class mother. The couple had children together before their marriage, but the future playwright was born in wedlock. Strindberg unsuccessfully tried for an advanced university degree and a career in acting. The eight years of his young manhood when he worked as a librarian, became a scholar of some note, and wrote his earliest plays and tales, may have been the happiest in his restless, tragic life. In 1877 he married for the first time. Two years later he made a name for himself with the satiric, realistic novel *The Red Room* and left Sweden to live by his pen abroad. In 1884 he was acquitted of a charge of blasphemy, but the affair strained his hypersensitive nerves. There followed a period of frenetic literary activity, partly in Sweden, partly on the Continent. His autobiographical writing from the 1880's and the naturalistic plays *The Father* (1887), *Miss Julie* (1888), and *Creditors* (1888) reflect the growth of the misogyny which contributed to the dissolution of his marriage in 1891. Through most of the 1890's Strindberg suffered from a persecution complex attended by hallucinations, though authorities disagree as to whether he ever actually became what should be called insane. Between voluntary stays at mental hospitals he studied and wrote on botany and chemistry — but also alchemy, occultism, and demonology. A second marriage failed in 1894. The autobiographical narrative *Inferno* (1897) records the critical years of his psychopathy. From 1902 till his death Strindberg lived in Stockholm, indubitably sane though hardly serene. His third marriage ended in divorce in 1904, but his amazing literary creativity never again left him: novels, tales, short stories, historical writings, philological, anthropological, and political essays, and plays, poured from his pen. Among the last were religious dramas: *To Damascus* (1898); *Dance of Death* (1902), another play about married horrors; *The Dream Play* (1901), an early example of expressionism; a long series of plays with subjects from Swedish history; and, finally, a group of esoteric, often fantastic "chamber plays," performed at the Intimate Theater, Strindberg's own stage, managed by a younger friend. *The Ghost Sonata, The Storm,* and *The Pelican* (all 1907) are the most important of these last plays.

Suggested Reading

Dahlström, C. E. W. L., *Strindberg's Dramatic Expressionism.* Ann Arbor: University of Michigan Press, 1930.

Klaf, Franklin S., *Strindberg: the Origin of Psychology in Modern Drama.* New York: Citadel Press, 1963.

Madsen, Borge Gedso, *Strindberg's Naturalistic Theatre.* Seattle: University of Washington Press, 1962.

Mortensen, Brita M. E., and Brian W. Downs, *Strindberg: An Introduction to His Life and Work.* Cambridge: Cambridge University Press, 1949.

Sprigge, Elizabeth, *The Strange Life of August Strindberg.* London: Hamish Hamilton, 1949.

(GEORGE) BERNARD SHAW (1856-1950) was born in Dublin of impoverished English parents. His formal education ended when he was fifteen. In 1876 he arrived in London, entered journalism, wrote five unsuccessful novels, and joined the Fabian Society, a group of radical socialist intellectuals. His political views, however, never became the orthodoxy of any ideological camp. Between 1886 and 1898 he wrote art, music, and drama criticism for leading periodicals. *The Quintessence of Ibsenism,* which he published in 1891, is enthusiastic propaganda for Ibsen as a playwright of liberal ideas, but it says perhaps more about Shaw himself than about Ibsen. The long series of his plays began in 1891 with *Widowers' Houses,* a play of social criticism, and ended only in 1947. Shaw's prefaces to his plays, in impeccably lucid, incisive prose, are often as good clues to his thought as the plays themselves. In 1905 he bought the house at Ayot St. Lawrence in Hertfordshire in which he lived till his death. He received the Nobel Prize in 1925. He was a life-long vegetarian and teetotaller, was against vivisection and vaccination, and willed the bulk of his fortune to a project for reforming English spelling.

Shaw's plays are drama of dialectics rather than of character — brilliant and caustic exposures of sham and nonsense, more serious than their flamboyant wit immediately suggests. The following are among his best and most representative: *Candida* (1894), *Cæsar and Cleopatra* (1898), *Man and Superman* (1903), *Major Barbara* (1905), *The Doctor's Dilemma* (1906), *Pygmalion* (1912), *Heartbreak House* (1916), *Back to Methuselah* (1921), *Saint Joan* (1923).

Suggested Reading

Abbott, Anthony, *Shaw and Christianity*. New York: Seabury Press, 1965.

Bentley, Eric, *Bernard Shaw*, rev. ed. New York:·New Directions, 1957.

Henderson, Archibald, *George Bernard Shaw: Man of the Century*. New York: Appleton-Century-Crofts, 1956.

Kronenberger, Louis, ed., *George Bernard Shaw: A Critical Survey*. Cleveland: World Publishing Company, 1953.

Meisel, Martin, *Shaw and the Nineteenth-Century Theater*. Princeton, N.J.: Princeton University Press, 1963.

Nethercot, Arthur H., *Men and Supermen*. Cambridge, Mass.: Harvard University Press, 1954.

Purdom, Charles B., *A Guide to the Plays of Bernard Shaw*. London: Methuen, 1963.

Shaw, Bernard, *Shaw on Theatre*, ed. E. J. West. New York: Hill and Wang, 1958.

Williamson, Audrey, *Bernard Shaw: Man and Writer*. New York: Cromwell-Collier Press, 1963.

ANTON PAVLOVICH CHEKHOV (1860-1904) was born in Taganrog on the Sea of Azov in southern Russia, the grandson of a serf. A harsh boyhood was followed by medical studies in Moscow. He received his degree in 1884, but he rarely practiced medicine regularly and during his last years hardly at all. While he was still a student he began to write — and to get published — small, comical sketches. In 1886 a successful collection of short stories, somewhat in the manner of de Maupassant, brought him acceptance in leading literary circles. His early plays failed on the stage, but in 1898 *The Seagull*, which had been a humiliating fiasco in St. Petersburg two years earlier, was a brilliant success in the newly opened Moscow Art Theater, under the direction of Konstantin Stanislavsky. *The Seagull* established Chekhov's reputation as playwright, the success of the "Stanislavsky method" of naturalistic acting, and the finances of the new theater. During the few remaining years of his life, Chekhov, already desperately ill with tuberculosis, spent his winters in Yalta on the Crimea. He wrote three additional plays for the Moscow Art Theater: *Uncle Vanya* (1899), *Three Sisters* (1901), and his greatest success, *The Cherry Orchard* (1904). In 1901 he married one of the Theater's leading actresses. He died at a sanatorium in southern Germany.

Suggested Reading

Hingley, Ronald, *Chekhov; a Biographical and Critical Study.* London: Allen & Unwin, 1950.

Magarshack, David, *Chekhov the Dramatist.* New York: Hill and Wang, 1960.

Shestov, Lev, A. *Tschekhov and Other Essays.* Dublin and London: Maunsel and Co., 1916.

Simmons, Ernest J., *Chekhov.* Boston: Little, Brown and Company, 1962.

Toumanova, Princess Nina Andronikova, *Anton Chekhov: The Voice of Twilight Russia.* New York: Columbia University Press, 1960.

JOHN MILLINGTON SYNGE (1871-1909) was of Protestant Irish landowner stock. He grew up in a Dublin suburb. His mother, widowed a year after the playwright's birth, was deeply religious in a somewhat dour and puritanical way. Synge graduated B.A. from Trinity College, Dublin, in 1892, went to Germany to prepare himself for a career in music, but moved to Paris in 1895, trying to make his way as a writer. For several years he divided his time between Ireland and Paris. The decisive event in his literary career was his meeting with W. B. Yeats in Paris in 1896. Yeats, poet, playwright, the founder of the Irish Literary Society (1892), and a dynamic leader of an Irish literary revival on native grounds, urged Synge to go to the Aran islands for material — three bleak and windswept rocks at the mouth of Galway Bay, off the west coast of Ireland. Synge spent the next five summers in the Arans. The meeting with the hardy peasant environment sparked his genius. The first literary fruits of his visits were a nonfictional description of the islands and the two plays, *The Shadow of the Glen* and *Riders to the Sea* (both 1902). The latter, a classic of the modern theater, is a taut, stark, one-act tragedy of man against the sea, not at all in the mood of the Celtic twilight which the young Yeats cultivated. Synge was one of the three directors (with Yeats and Lady Gregory) of the Abbey Theatre when it opened in 1904. His early plays had begun to win for him a European reputation even before the controversial fame of *The Playboy of the Western World*, and the success of *Playboy* on the London stage secured it. But at the time of his triumph Synge was already incurably ill with a malignant growth in the neck. When he died (at the age of 36) he was at work on *Deirdre of the Sorrows*, a lyrical tragedy based on old Irish legend.

Suggested Reading

Ellis-Fermor, Una M., *The Irish Dramatic Movement*, second ed. London: Methuen & Co., 1954.

Gerstenberger, Donna, *J. M. Synge*. New York: Twayne Publishers, 1964.

Greene, David H. and Edward M. Stephens, *J. M. Synge, 1871-1909*. New York: The Macmillan Company, 1959.

Persse, Augusta (Lady Gregory), *Our Irish Theatre*. London, 1913.

Price, Alan, *Synge and Anglo-Irish Drama*. London: Methuen & Co., 1961.

Yeats, W. B., "The Death of Synge," *Dramatis Personae*. London: Macmillan, 1936.

———, "The Irish Dramatic Movement," *Explorations*. London: Macmillan, 1962.

WILLIAM BUTLER YEATS (1865-1939) was the son of a distinguished Dublin portrait painter, and he, too, for a time practiced painting. His childhood was divided between London and his mother's home in Sligo county in western Ireland, a country that influenced motif and imagery in his poetry. His early verse was in the contemporary manner of the pre-Raphaelites and their successors — sensuously romantic, rich, a little soft and vague. In 1899 he was one of the founders of the Irish Literary Theater and was for many years its leader. He dreamed of making it a center for the revival of a mystical, poetic theater, but though several of his own plays were performed there and he brought to the theater John Millington Synge, perhaps the greatest dramatic talent of the Irish literary renaissance, and though the Abbey Theater (as it came to be known) became one of modern Europe's great stages,

Yeats never realized his dream of a poetic Irish theater. In the 1920's and '30's Yeats's poems gained in depth and in taut, sparse strength, but his growing reliance on a semi-private stock of metaphors and symbols derived from his reading in mysticism and occultism often made them difficult. For some years after 1922 he was a member of the Senate of the newly independent Irish republic, though many aspects of politics in a modern democracy were distasteful to his aristocratic, tradition-oriented, non-pragmatic loyalties. In 1923 he received the Nobel Prize.

Yeats's early, most popular plays are based on themes from Irish folklore: *The Countess Kathleen* (1889-1892), *The Land of Heart's Desire* (1894), *Cathleen ni Houlihan* (1902), *The Hour-Glass* (1902, 1913). *At the Hawk's Well* (1914) and *The Death of Cuchulain* (1938-1939) are early and late examples of his later, terse and emblematic manner.

Suggested Reading

Ellis-Fermor, Una, *The Irish Dramatic Movement*. London: Methuen & Co., 1954.

Ellmann, Richard, *Yeats, the Man and the Masks*. New York: The Macmillan Co., 1948.

Popkins, Henry, "Yeats as Dramatist," *Tulane Drama Review*, III, iii (1959), 73-82.

Saul, George Brandon, *Prolegomena to the Study of Yeats's Plays*. Philadelphia: University of Pennsylvania Press, 1958.

Ure, Peter, *Yeats the Playwright*. New York: Barnes & Noble, 1963.

Wilson, F. A. C., *Yeats's Iconography*. New York: Macmillan, 1960.

Wilson, F. A. C., *W. B. Yeats and Tradition*. London: Victor Gollancz, 1958.

LUIGI PIRANDELLO (1867-1936) was the son of a rich owner of sulphur mines in the town of Agrigento on the south coast of Sicily. After studies at the University of Rome he went on to take his doctorate at the University of Bonn, Germany, on a philological study of his home dialect. His early literary production — composed for pleasure, not to make a living — included poems and prose fiction, mostly short stories. By family arrangement he married the daughter of his father's partner. Both families lost their money when the mines were flooded in 1904, and Pirandello was forced to make a living as instructor at a woman's teacher's college in Rome. Soon after, his wife's mind gave way. Too poor to put her in a private institution and too conscientious to put her in a public one, Pirandello endured life with a lunatic till her death in 1918. By then he had attained fame as playwright and could give up teaching. By the early twenties he was an international celebrity. In 1925 he founded his own art theater, which successfully toured some of the world's great stages. Pirandello's brooding, restless, cerebral inquiries into the nature of reality seem quite alien to the muscular aggressiveness of Mussolini's Italy, but Pirandello himself was not hostile to Fascism. "I am a Fascist because I am an Italian," he said once in an interview in New York. His acceptance of the Nobel Prize in Literature in 1934 was officially approved.

It does not seem unreasonable to assume a connection between his domestic tragedy and the philosophical relativism of his plays. To the unhappy, the belief that all experience is illusory is not a remote solace. The titles of several of his best known plays suggest his paradoxical scepticism: *It Is So! (If You Think So)* (1917), *Each In His Own Way* (1924), *As You Desire Me* and *Tonight We Improvise* (both 1930). Another famous and characteristic play is *Henry IV* (1922), along with *Six Characters* generally considered his best work.

Suggested Reading

Bishop, Thomas, *Pirandello and the French Theater*. New York: New York University Press, 1960.

MacClintock, Lander, *The Age of Pirandello*. Bloomington: Indiana University Press, 1951.

Nelson, Robert J., *Play within a Play*. New Haven, Conn.: Yale University Press, 1958.

Starkie, Walter, *Luigi Pirandello: 1867-1936*, 3rd ed., rev. Berkeley: University of California Press, 1965.

Vittorini, Domenico, *The Drama of Luigi Pirandello*. Philadelphia: University of Pennsylvania Press, 1935.

MICHEL DE GHELDERODE (1882-1962) was nominated for the Nobel Prize in literature in 1961, but he is not listed in recent editions of the *International Who's Who, Current Biography*, or *Contemporary Authors*. It seems somehow in keeping with the character and life of this playwright who wrote his first play during World War I and his last in 1952 that his fame should be largely posthumous. His life was lacking in external events. He was partially made an invalid from asthma and lived obscurely in an 18th-century house, regulating his daily routine by the Church calendar, working in a room filled with Ensor masks, crucifixes, department store mannequins (some of them dressed in costumes for his plays), posters, dolls, shells, and stuffed fish. For a number of years he was associated with the Flemish Popular Theater. During the last twenty-five years of his life he made only one public appearance. An international festival was held in his honor in Ostend in July, 1961.

Of his many plays, the following have attracted particular attention: *Christopher Columbus* (1927), *The Women at the Tomb* (1928), *Barabbas* (1928), *Pantagleize* (1929), *Chronicles of Hell* (1929), *Red Magic* (1931), *The Blind Men* (1933), *Lord Halewyn* (1934).

Suggested Reading

Abel, Lionel, "Our Man in the Sixteenth Century: Michel de Ghelderode," *Tulane Drama Review*, VIII, i (1963), 62-71.

Draper, Samuel, "An Interview with Michel de Ghelderode," *Tulane Drama Review*, VIII, i (1963), 39-50.

Hauger, George, "Dispatches from the Prince of Ostrelande," *Tulane Drama Review*, VIII, i (1963), 24-32.

———, ed. and tr., *Ghelderode: 7 Plays*. I-II. New York: Hill and Wang, 1964.

Herz, Micheline, "Tragedy, Poetry, and the Burlesque in Ghelderode's Theatre," *Yale French Studies*, no. 29 (1962), 92-101.

Wellwarth, George E., "Ghelderode's Theatre of the Grotesque," *Tulane Drama Review*, VIII, i (1963), 11-23.

BERTOLT BRECHT (1898-1956) was born in the south German town of Augsburg in Bavaria. He studied medicine, served in World War I, began writing plays and in the 1920's was part of a group of avant-garde and leftist poets, playwrights, actors, and artists in Berlin. He fled Germany when Hitler came to power, lived in Denmark during the late '30's and in California from 1941 to 1947. For a while he worked in Hollywood. For two years after his return to Europe after the war he wrote and produced plays for the National Theater in Zürich, Switzerland. He moved to East Berlin in 1949, where he worked with his own ensemble till his death, staunchly supporting the Communist régime. Some of his anti-war poems are modern classics in Germany, but abroad he is most famous for his dramas: *The Three-Penny Opera* (1928) with music by Kurt Weill (a modern version of the early eighteenth century *Beggar's Opera* by John Gay); *The Private Life of the Master Race* (1937), an anti-Nazi play; *The Good Woman of Setzuan* (1941); *Mother Courage* (1941); *Galileo* (1943, 1947); *The Cau-*

casian Chalk Circle (1944-45). Brecht has been influential not only as a playwright and director but also as theorist of the theater. Today, the school of his "epic theater" represents, perhaps, the major, non-expressionistic alternative to dramatic naturalism.

Suggested Reading

Brecht, Bertolt, "On the Experimental Theatre," *Tulane Drama Review*, VI (1961), i, 3-17.

————, *Seven Plays by Bertolt Brecht*, ed. and with an introduction by Eric Bentley. New York: Grove Press, Inc., 1961.

Demetz, Peter, ed., *Brecht* (Twentieth Century Views series). Englewood Cliffs, N.J.: Prentice-Hall, Inc., 1962.

Esslin, Martin, *Brecht, the Man and His Work*. Garden City, N.Y.: Doubleday & Company, 1960.

Gray, Ronald, *Bertolt Brecht*. New York: Grove Press, Inc., 1961.

Weideli, Walter, *The Art of Bertolt Brecht*. New York University Press, 1963.

Willett, John, ed. and tr., *Brecht on Theatre*. New York: Hill and Wang, 1964.

Willett, John, *The Theatre of Bertolt Brecht*. London: Methuen & Co., 1959.

TENNESSEE WILLIAMS (1914-   ) was born in Columbus, Ohio. Of his family he has said that "there was a combination of Puritan and Cavalier strains in my blood which may be accountable for the conflicting impulses I often represent in the people I write about." The family's move to St. Louis in 1926 brought the boy a sense of loss of social class; it is the "feel" of his own home milieu (though not many of its particulars) that he sketches in *The Glass Menagerie*. His college career during the depression was interrupted by a job as clerk in the shoe company for which his father was a salesman. He received his B.A. degree from Iowa in 1938. After a succession of odd jobs (including Hollywood scriptwriting) he won recognition as playwright with *The Glass Menagerie* in 1945. Early in his career he substituted "Tennessee" (in honor of the state of his pioneer forefathers) for his given name, Thomas Lanier. His early works include poetry and fiction. He has written one novel, *The Roman Spring of Mrs. Stone* (1950).

Noteworthy in a long series of plays are A *Streetcar Named Desire* (1947, awarded the Pulitzer Prize), *Summer and Smoke* (1948), *The Rose Tattoo* (1951), the expressionistic *Camino Real* (1953), *Cat on a Hot Tin Roof* (1955, awarded the Pulitzer Prize), *Sweet Bird of Youth* (1959), *The Night of the Iguana* (1961). Several of his plays have been made into successful motion pictures, most of them representative of Hollywood's "new trend" in the treatment of sex. Among them are *Twenty-Seven Wagons Full of Cotton* (1946, filmed as *Baby Doll*) and *Suddenly Last Summer* (1957). Many critics have found his recent plays "decadent" denials of all human values. In an autobiographical sketch some years ago he called his "politics" "humanitarian."

Suggested Reading

Downer, Alan S., *Fifty Years of American Drama*. Chicago: Henry Regnery, 1951.

Falk, Signi Lenea, *Tennessee Williams*. New York: Twayne Publishers, 1962.

Jackson, Esther Merle, *The Broken World of Tennessee Williams*. Madison: University of Wisconsin Press, 1965.

Jones, Robert E., "Tennessee Williams' Early Heroines," *Modern Drama*, II (1959), 211-219.

Nelson, Benjamin, *Tennessee Williams*. New York: Ivan Obelensky, 1961.

Popkin, Henry, "The Plays of Tennessee Williams," *Tulane Drama Review*, IV (Spring, 1960), 45-64.

Tischler, Nancy M., *Tennessee Williams*. New York: The Citadel Press, 1961.

Vowles, Richard B., "Tennessee Williams: The World of His Imagery," *Tulane Drama Review*, III (Dec., 1958), 51-56.

Williams, Edwina [the playwright's mother], *Remember Me to Tom* (as told to Lucy Freeman). New York: Putnam, 1963.

EDWARD FRANKLIN ALBEE (1928-   ), today the chief American practitioner of the absurd drama, is the adopted son of a well-to-do New York family. He does not know his real parents. He wrote his first play at the age of 12. He went through the dismissals from school (he left Trinity College without a degree) and the sequence of odd jobs (one as a Western Union messenger boy) which have become almost obligatory experience, in the mind of the public, for a successful American writer. In 1958 what Albee himself calls an "explosion" led to the writing of *The Zoo Story*. It was first produced in Germany in 1959. *The American Dream* was begun in 1959 but laid aside, completed in

1960, and produced on Broadway early in 1961. In the meantime he wrote two other short plays, *The Sand Box* and *The Death of Bessie Smith*. His first full-length play, *Who's Afraid of Virginia Woolf?* opened on Broadway in 1962. Production of the play on the major stages of Europe in 1963-64 elicited enthusiasm, controversy, and enraged charges of "obscenity." In the spring of 1963 two members of the Pulitzer Prize drama jury resigned in protest against the refusal of the advisory board to make public their nomination of *Who's Afraid of Virginia Woolf?* for the 1962 drama award. In 1963 he dramatized Carson McCullers's novella, *Ballad of the Sad Café*. His most recent play is *Tiny Alice* (1964), a religious allegory variously judged and interpreted.

Suggested Reading

Albee, Edward F., "Which Theatre Is the Absurd One?" *The New York Times Magazine*, Feb. 25, 1962.

Harris, Wendell V., "Morality, Absurdity, and Albee," *Southwest Review*, XLIX (1964), 249-256.

Zimbardo, Rose A., "Symbolism and Naturalism in Edward Albee's *The Zoo Story*," *Twentieth Century Literature*, VIII (1962), 10-17.

SUGGESTED GENERAL READING

Theory

Abel, Lionel, *Metatheatre*. New York: Hill and Wang, 1963.

Barnet, Sylvan, *et al.*, eds., *Aspects of the Drama: A Handbook*. Boston: Little, Brown and Company, 1962.

Bentley, Eric, *The Life of the Drama*. New York: Atheneum, 1964.

Brooks, Cleanth, and Robert B. Heilman, *Understanding Drama: Twelve Plays*. New York: Henry Holt and Company, 1948.

Butcher, S. H., *Aristotle's Theory of Poetry and Fine Art*. New York: Dover Publications, 1951.

Clark, Barrett H., ed., *European Theories of Drama, with a Supplement on the American Drama*. New York: Crown Publishers, 1947

Cole, Toby, ed., *Playwrights on Playwriting: The Meaning and Making of Modern Drama from Ibsen to Ionesco*. New York: Hill and Wang, 1960.

Corrigan, Robert W., ed., *Comedy: Meaning and Form*. San Francisco: Chandler Publishing Company, 1965.

————, ed., *Tragedy: Vision and Form*. San Francisco: Chandler Publishing Company, 1965.

Corrigan, Robert W. and James L. Rosenberg, eds., *The Context and Craft of Drama*. San Francisco: Chandler Publishing Co., 1964.

Downer, Alan S., *The Art of the Play: An Anthology of Nine Plays*. New York: Henry Holt and Company, 1955.

Drew, Elizabeth, *Discovering Drama*. New York: W. W. Norton & Co., 1937.

Eliot, T. S., *Poetry and Drama*. Cambridge, Mass.: Harvard University Press, 1951.

Ellmann, Richard and Charles Feidelson, Jr., eds., *The Modern Tradition: Backgrounds of Modern Literature*. New York: Oxford University Press, 1965.

Enck, John J., Elizabeth T. Forter, Alvin Whitley, eds., *The Comic in Theory and Practice*. New York: Appleton-Century-Crofts, 1960.

Felheim, Marvin, ed., *Comedy, Plays, Theory, and Criticism*. New York: Harcourt, Brace and World, Inc., 1962.

Fergusson, Francis, *The Human Image in Dramatic Literature*. Garden City, N.Y.: Doubleday & Company (Anchor), 1957.

————, *The Idea of a Theater*. Garden City, N.Y.: Doubleday & Company (Anchor), 1949.

Frye, Northrop, *Anatomy of Criticism*. Princeton, N.J.: Princeton University Press, 1957.

Levin, Richard, ed., *Tragedy: Plays, Theory, and Criticism*. New York: Harcourt, Brace & World, Inc., 1960.

Lauter, Paul, ed., *Theories of Comedy*. Garden City, N.Y.: Doubleday & Company (Anchor), 1964.

Mandel, Oscar, *A Definition of Tragedy*. New York University Press, 1961.

Nicoll, Allardyce, *The Theatre and Dramatic Theory*. New York: Barnes & Noble, Inc., 1962.

————, *The Theory of Drama*. London: G. G. Harrap & Company, 1937.

Nietzsche, Friedrich, *The Birth of Tragedy* and *The Genealogy of Morals*. Tr. Francis Golffing. Garden City, N.Y.: Doubleday & Company (Anchor), 1956.

Peacock, Ronald, *The Art of Drama*. London: Routledge & Kegan Paul, 1957.

Raphael, D. D., *The Paradox of Tragedy*. Bloomington: Indiana University Press, 1960.

Sewall, Richard B., *The Vision of Tragedy*. New Haven, Conn.: Yale University Press, 1959.

————, and Lawrence Michel, eds., *Tragedy: Modern Essays in Criticism*. Englewood Cliffs, N.J.: Prentice-Hall, Inc., 1963.

Styan, J. L., *The Elements of Drama*. Cambridge: Cambridge University Press, 1960.

Thompson, Alan R., *The Anatomy of Drama*, 2nd ed. Berkeley: University of California Press, 1946.

History and Criticism

Bentley, Eric, *In Search of Theater*. New York: Alfred A. Knopf, 1953.

————, *The Playwright as Thinker*. New York: Meridian Books, 1957.

Bogard, Travis and William I. Oliver, eds., *Modern Drama: Essays in Criticism*. New York: Oxford University Press, 1965.

Brustein, Robert, *The Theatre of Revolt*. Boston: Atlantic-Little, Brown, 1962.

Clark, Barrett H. and George Freedley, eds., *A History of Modern Drama*. New York: D. Appleton-Century Co., 1947.

Corrigan, Robert W., ed., *Theatre in the Twentieth Century*. New York: Grove Press, Inc., 1963.

Downer, Alan S., *Fifty Years of American Drama*. Chicago: Henry Regnery, 1951.

Esslin, Martin, *The Theatre of the Absurd*. Garden City, N.Y.: Doubleday & Company (Anchor), 1961.

Freedman, Morris, ed., *Essays in the Modern Drama*. Boston: D. C. Heath and Co., 1964.

Gassner, John, *Form and Idea in Modern Theatre*. New York: Dryden Press, 1956.

————, *Masters of the Drama*, 3rd rev. ed. New York: Dover Publications, 1954.

————, *The Theatre in Our Times*. New York: Crown Publishers, 1954.

Grossvogel, David I., *Four Playwrights and a Postscript: Brecht, Ionesco, Beckett, Genet*. Ithaca, N.Y.: Cornell University Press, 1962.

————, *The Self-Conscious Stage in Modern French Drama*. New York: Columbia University Press, 1958.

Knight, G. Wilson, *The Golden Labyrinth*. New York: W. W. Norton & Company, 1962.

Krutch, Joseph Wood, *"Modernism" in Modern Drama*. Ithaca, N.Y.: Cornell University Press, 1953.

Lucas, Frank L., *The Drama of Chekhov, Synge, Yeats, and Pirandello*. London: Cassell, 1963.

Lumley, Frederick, *Trends in Twentieth Century Drama*. New York: Oxford University Press (Essential Books), 1960.

Nicoll, Allardyce, *World Drama from Aeschylus to Anouilh*. London: G. G. Harrap & Company, 1949.

Steiner, George, *The Death of Tragedy*. New York: Alfred A. Knopf, 1961.

Valency, Maurice, *The Flower and the Castle: An Introduction to Modern Drama*. New York: Macmillan, 1963.

Wellwarth, George E., *The Theater of Protest and Paradox*. New York: New York University Press, 1964.

Williams, Raymond, *Drama from Ibsen to Eliot*. London: Chatto & Windus, 1952.

Theater Arts

Cole, Toby, and Helen Krich Chinoy, eds., *Actors on Acting*. New York: Crown Publishers, 1949.

Goodman, Randolph, *Drama on Stage*. New York: Holt, Rinehart and Winston, 1961.

Gorelik, Mordecai, *New Theatres for Old*. New York: S. French, 1940.

Macgowan, Kenneth, and William Melnitz, *The Living Stage: A History of the World Theater*. New York: Prentice-Hall, Inc., 1955. (A shorter version is *The Golden Ages of the Theater*, 1959.)

Stanislavsky, Constantin, *An Actor Prepares*, tr. Elizabeth Reynolds Hapgood. New York: Theatre Arts Books, 1936.

Reference

Bowman, Walter P., and Robert Hamilton Ball, *Theatre Language: A Dictionary of Terms in English of the Drama and Stage from Medieval to Modern Times*. New York: Theatre Arts Books, 1961.

Hartnoll, Phyllis, ed., *The Oxford Companion to the Theatre*, 2nd ed.

Some Useful Collections of Plays

Bentley, Eric, ed., *The Play: A Critical Anthology*. New York: Prentice-Hall, Inc., 1951.

————, *The Modern Theatre*, I-VI. Garden City, N.Y.: Doubleday & Company (Anchor), 1955-1960.

Block, Haskell, and Robert Shedd, eds., *Masters of Modern Drama*. New York: Random House, 1961.

Clayes, Stanley, David Spencer, E. Bradlee Watson, Benfield Pressey, *Contemporary Drama Series* [five collections]. New York: Charles Scribner's Sons, 1941-1962.

Gassner, John, ed., *Treasury of the Theatre*, I-II. New York: Simon and Schuster, 1950-1951.

Grene, David, and Richmond Lattimore, eds., *The Complete Greek Tragedies*, I-IV. University of Chicago Press, 1959.

Kernan, Alvin, *Character and Conflict: An Introduction to Drama*. New York: Harcourt, Brace and World, Inc., 1963.

Kernan, Alvin B., *Classics of the Modern Theater. Realism and After*. New York: Harcourt, Brace & World, 1965.

Ulanov, Barry, ed., *Makers of the Modern Theater*. New York: McGraw-Hill Book Co., Inc., 1961.